THE GREAT ESCAPE

A SOURCE BOOK
OF
DELIGHTS & PLEASURES
FOR THE
MIND & BODY

BANTAM BOOKS

TORONTO/NEW YORK/LONDON

THE GREATE ESCAPE

Acknowledgments

"Overcoming Our Metagrumbles" adapted from "The Whole
Soul Catalog," *Psychology Today* magazine, April 1972, © 1972
by Ziff-Davis Publishing Company. "The Underground Crash
Pad Directory," by David Saltman. From *The New York Times*,
© 1972 by The New York Times Company. Reprinted by
permission. "I Swim the Hellespont" excerpt from *The Glorious
Adventure*, by Richard Halliburton, © 1927 by The Bobbs-Merrill
Company, Inc., renewed 1955, reprinted by permission of the
publisher. "Cheap Thrills" by Scot Morris, "The Waterbed: How
to do it," by Amie Hill, © 1971 by Straight Arrow Publishers
Inc.; "Spacewar!" by Stewart Brand, © 1972 by Straight Arrow
Publishers Inc.; "Running into a Gig" and portions of "To
Africa by Freighter in Nine Days," by David Saltman, © 1973
by Straight Arrow Publishers, Inc. All rights reserved. Reprinted
by permission. "The Underground Kingdom of IRT and IND,"
by Carolyn Jabs, © 1973 by *Wisdom's Child*. Reprinted by
permission. "Story-telling: Learning to be a Bodymind"
excerpted from *Telling Your Story: A Guide to Who You Are and
Who You Can Be*, by Sam Keen and Anne Valley Fox, © 1973
by Sam Keen and Anne Bartlett. Reprinted by permission of
Doubleday & Company, Inc. "Optimistic Voices," from the
MGM film, *The Wizard of Oz*, Lyrics by E. Y. Harburg, music
by Harold Arlen and Herbert Stothart, copyright © 1939, renewed
1967 by Metro-Goldwyn-Mayer, Inc. Rights throughout the
world controlled by Leo Feist, Inc., New York, N.Y. Used by
permission.

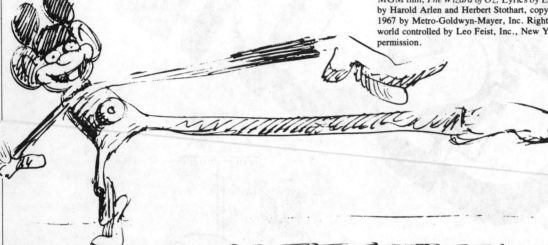

Illustration by Karl Nicholason

STAFF

Library of Congress Cataloging in Publication Data
Main entry under title:

The Great escape.

1. Handbooks, vade-mecums, etc.
[AG105.G668]   031'.02   74–5365

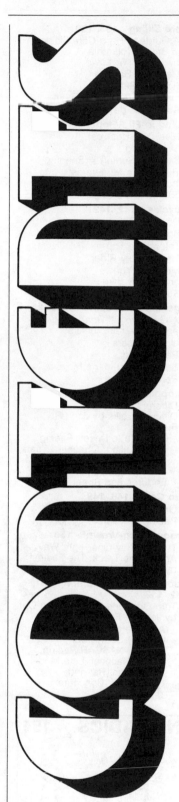

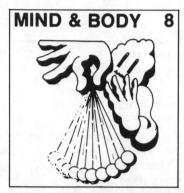

MIND & BODY 8

WATER 56

Address all editorial inquiries to:
THE GREAT ESCAPE
150 Shoreline Highway
Mill Valley, Calif. 94941
Tel. (415) 332-3211, 332-2233

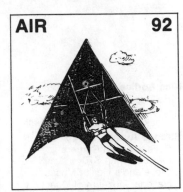

AIR 92

LAND 116

NOMADICS 154

PLACES 188

GAMES 220

Cohorts, Contributors and Friends of Friends

Any publication is a tremendous, frantic conglomeration of stuff. Ideas are freely stolen, then mangled beyond repair. People get sweet-talked and roughed up, sassed back at and frazzled. If we could see an impartial computer print-out of the energy flow, it would look like one of those Arabic designs: seemingly aimless wandering lines that somehow suddenly converge to make a coherent and meaningful whole. Just to give you some idea of how it all happens, here are a few capsule biographies of some of our contributors. There are hundreds more we don't have room to list, but to them we give our sincere and heartfelt gratitude.

Bill Allen is a native Texan and a graduate of the Iowa Writers' Workshop; he now teaches creative writing at Ohio State. His interests range from setting world records to watching meteor showers to sending messages by balloon. **Trudy Bell** has been turned on to astronomy since she was 13, when she built a planetarium projector out of a tin can, a light bulb and some aluminum foil with holes punched in it. She's an editor at *Scientific American*. **Roy Bongartz's** articles appear regularly in the *New York Times* Sunday Travel section. He lives on a Rhode Island rock farm and loves shooting pool, clearing brush with a grass whip and machete, and keeping old cars running past 100,000 miles. **Bill Cook's** lawyer wife says he can't talk about anything but hang gliding, something he latched onto while covering the new sport for *Newsweek*. **Alan Copeland** is an expatriate Canadian who has taken a lot of good photographs for various magazines, like *Newsweek, Time, Playboy* (not to mention the *Berkeley Tribe*) and now points his camera for the AP. A Virginian who lives in California, **Dr. Eleanor Criswell** teaches psychologies which are preceded by words like physiological, yoga, developmental, humanistic, transpersonal and parapsychological. Her research interests are bio-feedback and optokinetic training. She's the director of the Humanistic Psychology Institute. **David Cudhea**, former director of publications at Harvard and a former managing editor of *Saturday Review of Education*, lives in San Francisco where he is a media consultant. He works between volleyball matches.

Sam Daijogo is a free-lance graphic artist living in San Francisco. He worked in Japan for a year for a graphics firm and in San Diego for General Dynamics. He digs woodcarving and fishing. **James Egan** is a travel free-lancer who has logged some 200,000 miles in the past few years while writing for the *Atlantic Monthly, Holiday, Harper's Bazaar* and the *New York Times*. He says he's living in Connecticut with his "original wife." **Lee Foster**, author and ghostwriter, has published four

Mary Alice Kellogg

Dirk Kortz

Barbara Sleeper

Joel Vance

Mike Miller

John Fuchs

Trudy Bell

Scot Morris

Bill Allen

Anne Valley Fox

Mike Michaelson

books; he also writes poetry and takes photographs, both of which have been published in various journals. In a recent poem, **Anne Valley Fox** described her death: "how easy it was / feigning sleep in the middle of the world." In 1951, she "discovered Elvis, sex and art on the Ed Sullivan show." In 1973, she says, she started waking up again, going for embellishment, exaggeration of the ugly and beautiful twists. **John Fuchs**, engineering editor of *Motor Trend* magazine, travels far and wide, tight and close in a variety of fast two-

wheel and four-wheel machines. (He has also been known to ride threewheelers.) *Newsweek* correspondent **Peter Greenberg** can only write to rock and soul music. He requires quiet only for bumper pool. **Peter Janssen**, editorial consultant to *Saturday Review/World*, got married some months after he wrote our gold spread and a number of short articles.

Mary Alice Kellogg climbs mountains for *Newsweek* articles, but for us she rubbed some gravestones. She describes herself as "25, blonde, nubile, etc." **Marion Knox**, who is a pilot, wrote some of our flying articles. She's a senior staff reporter at *Time*. **Dirk Kortz**, who has not been published elsewhere, passed most of his well-spent youth wandering around the United States, Mexico, Europe and North Africa. He is currently editing a poetry anthology.

Sam Daijogo

Bill Cook

Peter Greenberg

Nicholason

Roy Bongartz

Susan Sands

David Popoff

Howard Saunders

McGinnis

Eleanor Criswell

Ron Kriss

Charles Kuralt

earning a Ph.D. in clinical psychology with a *Playboy* Editorial Award for their best satire in 1973. Not unexpectedly, he's working on two books, one on the evolution of human behavior and one which he describes as a "collection of useless but fascinating information." Some of that information is between our covers. Although he's listed on his own masthead as photography consultant at *Psychology Today*, **John Oldenkamp** writes, designs, edits, builds —and does them all well. The model airplane he designed and built for one of our articles won for *The Great Escape* and Bantam Books an editorial art award. **Karl Nicholason** describes himself as a Pisces who is secretly in love with Buffy St. Marie. He finished his wonderful drawings for this book despite a hangover and an impossible deadline. Then, he cleaned his house.

Ken Pierce, who brainstormed with us on story-ideas, is managing editor of the *Columbia Journalism Review*. **Dick Pietschmann**'s life, in his words, has been one of aimless wandering "from newsreels to PR to hapless free-lancing." Right now, he's writing two books, a sports book and a pornographic novel. **David Popoff**, who is sort of our games editor, works regularly in New York City where he is on the editorial board at *Scientific American*. A Canadian by birth, Popoff had been firmly rejected by all the major hockey teams by the time he reached the age of 18. He recently spent three months trekking across the Arctic tundra and claims to be the first white man to have acquired a natural tan north of the Arctic Circle. One of the guys who helped us develop our concept is **John Poppy**, who is now writing a book but was an editor of *Look* and managing editor of *Saturday Review of the Arts*.

Prior to life as a free-lancer, **Susan Sands** was editor of *Rags*, a fashion magazine, and associate editor of *Saturday Review of Education*. **Howard Saunders** is currently billing himself as a multiphrenic. That's a schizophrenic artist who cannot hold himself to drawing in two styles only. **Brooke Shearer**, who wrote about Eastern Europe, hangs out there and writes for *The Washington Post* and *Parade* magazine. **Barbara Sleeper** grew up with a pocketful of frogs, and when she's not writing for Educational Expeditions International, she travels all over the place. **Carol Tavris**—Dr. Tavris, that is—has been trying to teach us how to dance the hora and the miserlou. When she's not doing that or helping us on story conferences she works at *Psychology Today*, where she is assistant managing editor. **Brian Vachon**, who took us to the ultimate supermarket, a country auction, is editor of *Vermont Life*. **Joel Vance** plays banjo and dulcimer, writes for the Missouri Department of Conservation and contributes regularly to a variety of outdoor magazines. He claims to be "average in all activities." **Lynn Young**, who wrote about such things as historic "living farms" and orienteering, is an editor at *Newsweek*.

Ron Kriss, senior editor at *Time*, has been responsible for that magazine's international coverage and has written and edited more than 70 cover stories. In TGE, he writes freely about what he and his family enjoy in life, from aerial trams to cog railways, from ghost towns to international gambling tables. **Charles Kuralt** became a CBS News correspondent in 1959 and began a long and brilliant career reporting the "old, the unusual and the enduring," spinning a few stories and sending postcards to Walter Cronkite. When

he's not on the road, he's in New York with his wife Susan. His great escape is a can of cold beer, the Sunday *New York Times* and a football game.

Bill McGinnis has spent nine years on whitewater rivers and has written the book on the subject, *Whitewater Rafting*—it'll be published by Quadrangle Books in the fall of 1974.

He's 26 and says he avoided the Army by teaching chess as a conscientious objector. **Mike Michaelson**, who has won five journalism writing awards, is editor of *Canoe* magazine. He writes columns on sports and outdoor cooking for a slew of newspapers and recently co-authored a book on bicycling. Three months a year, **Mike Miller** is a member of the Alaska House of Representatives. The rest of the time he travels and writes about the United States and Europe. **Scot Morris** is the kind of guy who can combine

MIND & BODY

Illustration by Karl Nicholason

I absolutely flatly deny that I am a soul,
or a body, or a mind, or an intelligence,
or a brain, or a nervous system,
or a bunch of glands,
or any of the rest of these bits of me.
The whole is greater than the part.
And therefore, I, who am man alive,
am greater than my soul,
or spirit, or body, or mind,
or consciousness, or anything else
that is merely a part of me.
I am a man, and alive.

—D. H. LAWRENCE

The longest journey
is the journey inwards
Of him who has chosen his destiny,
who has started upon his quest
for the Source of his being.

—DAG HAMMARSKJOLD

To see a world in a Grain of Sand
And a Heaven in a Wild flower,
Hold Infinity in the palm of your hand,
And Eternity in an hour.

—WILLIAM BLAKE

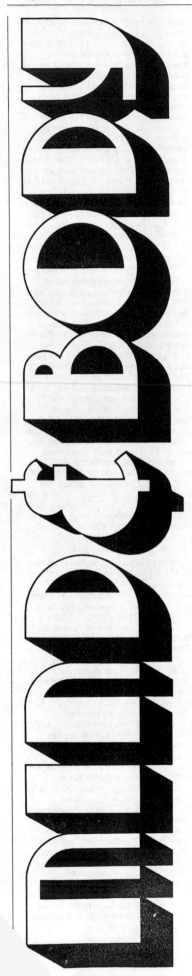

Overcoming Our Metagrumbles

By Eleanor Criswell

The Human Potential Movement is a call to full humanity. It senses the immanent poetry within us and resonates to the beauty in others. It seeks to know love and the capacity to give it.

For more than a decade, in a protest against self-limited living, the Human Potential Movement has been growing and flourishing in the subcultures of the United States, Western Europe, the Soviet Union and Japan. More revolutionary than bombs, bullets or slogans, the movement deals with nonverbal experience, altered states of consciousness and various techniques whereby people can find new ways to identify themselves and live their lives more fully.

The richness of the Human Potential Movement ranges from A to Y and Z, from aikido, ashrams, autogenic training and ASCID (for Altered States of Consciousness Induction Device) to yoga and zen. There is a coherence in such a scattered movement, however, and to understand it better you need to know more about its founding father, the late Abraham Maslow.

Abe's agile mind absorbed and engulfed all the scientific definitions of man and found them too small and too limiting to hold the subject. Our whole soul, Abe argued, is more, much more than the sum of our responses to stimuli or the interplay of id and ego and superego. He hated the artificial splitting of mind from body, of psyche from soma, of soma from soul.

Abe believed that once men and women get beyond fear of hunger and cold, maybe lose their obsession with status, they move on toward a distinctly human need for self-actualization. But even here our human nature does not allow us to wallow in a slough of contentment. Each experience of fulfillment just leads to the next need in an endless series that Maslow, too serious to fall

into jargon, called higher grumbles or metagrumbles.

In the strictest sense, Maslow was an elitist. His own definition of higher grumbles did not include the neuroses of the effete: higher grumbles were the benign discontents that call the strong to full humanity, to know love and know the capacity to give it, to sense the immanent poetry of the self as it resonates to the beauty in others.

As the Sixties came to a close, such a vision began to dazzle hundreds of people into peculiar activities. In fact, much had already begun outside of Maslow's influence. People were swapping their modernist superstitions for older, richer ones—sensory awareness, bio-feedback, encounter, meditation, parapsychology (ESP), the *I Ching* and the Tarot. The encounter movement was infecting big business, churches, schools, the media, even police departments. Like people at old-fashioned Baptist revivals, groupers rejoiced in confessing the worst about themselves —and others—in situations ruled by unconditional acceptance of each person (unless that person sinned by getting uptight or, worse, by holding back).

Maslow's thought offered coherence and direction to those touched by the soaring excitement of such experiences. He invited them to greater daring. He encouraged places like the Esalen Institute in Big Sur, where California's tolerance for peculiar life styles gave the Human Potential Movement its first experimental laboratory. Other "growth centers," as they came to be called, spread across North America and into Europe.

The humanists seemed to infect everything they touched. At each successive year's American Psychological Association convention, the buttoned down academics found that more and more their colleagues were bearded or braless, that such colleagues even enrolled in the touchie-feelie seminars run by that wild bunch, the Association for Humanistic Psychology. (AHP members created culture shock in convention hotels —they tended to lie around lobby floors communicating by hugs. And they kept forgetting to wear swimsuits in hotel pools. The battle to maintain the balance between the theoretical and experiential still rages.)

The joyous movement is now threatened by death-by-victory. It is dying into the general culture, pouring its nourishment (some say poison) into entire institutions. What looked nutty a few years ago now seems Rotarian. ESP and the alpha waves of transcendental meditators are now in the laboratories of hard-nosed experimentalists. A full range of states of consciousness is now accepted in psychological research. Once a simple enthusiasm, the transpersonal (religious, mystical) side of man is now a matter of serious concern. The boldest of Human Potential folk are saying that their mind-body work is leading to a true science of somatology.

Indeed, the American Psychological Association has opened its doors and soma to the movement, making "Humanistic Psychology" Division 32 in its flavorful array of sciences. This means, of course, that the Human Potential Movement may well become a discipline, which is what Maslow meant it to be. The movement is swapping some of its freaky audacity, its readiness to try anything that stretches the self, for a systematic study of higher grumbles and metagrumbles.

At this moment in the movement's life we should catalog its unique activities and list its wild array of technology. It would be dishonest to pretend that this is a consumer's guide. At best, it is a report of the partisan claims of believers. What you're hearing are the pitches of the advocates. Let the buyer beware.

36 Ways to Make Your Life Your Hobby

ASCID, The When government blocked most psychedelic-drug research with normal subjects, researchers R. E. L. Masters and Jean Houston, at the Foundation for Mind Research, led the movement into testing non-chemicals. Masters chanced upon a description of a swing reputedly used by medieval witches to fly

to their Sabbats. He devised a similar cradle that immobilizes a person's body as it rocks him through space. Experimental subjects who use the ASCID (Altered States of Consciousness Induction Device) report deep trips; artists unlock blocked creativity, and almost everyone sees visions. Available from: Cambridge

Cyborgs Research Division, Faulkner St., North Villerica, Mass. 01862; phone (617) 667-3826.

Ashrams Now you don't have to fly to India to drop out into a community in which you both meditate and play basketball, in which you work on head and body together. The underdeveloped West, centuries behind the Orient, is closing the ashram gap, opening centers across the United States. Eight years ago the Yoga Society of New York founded Amanda Ashram 50 miles outside of the city. Contact: Yoga Society of New York, Inc., 100 W. 72nd St., New York, N.Y. 10023.

Astrology Newspapers have turned astrology into a cliché, a foolish

magic with which to whammy the outside world. But the grandmother of science, once the language for man's understanding of himself, still lets you relate to strangers without going through the "what-do-you-do?" turnoff. Dane Rudhyar's book, *The Astrology of Personality* (Llewellyn, $8; Doubleday, paper, $2.45) uses Jungian analysis to build a bridge between the zodiac and humanistic psychology.

Autogenic training Ever wonder how those venerable Indian fakirs appeared to control heartbeat, body temperature, even gravitation? Tricks, right? Wrong. [...] sic powers anyone can [...]

(continued on

(continued from previous page)
the proper training. Menninger Foundation's Alyce and Elmer Green have refined a system first introduced by Johannes Schultz, professor of neuropsychiatry at the University of Berlin. It teaches awareness and control of bodily functions once thought to be involuntary. Autogenic training makes *you* the boss.

Bio-energetics When you're hung up in the head, your body's in bad shape too. Most of us are emotionally muscle-bound—our feelings are frozen into rigid muscles. Break these blocks and repressed emotions boil into consciousness, says Alexander Lowen, founder of bio-energetics. With a Lowen therapist, weak muscles toughen but there's a scary dive to emotional depths before you bounce to the heights. Read Lowen's *Pleasure* (Lancer Books, 95 cents) before you write for the name and address of the nearest practitioner —Institute for Bio-energetic Analysis, 114 E. 36th St., New York, N.Y. 10016; phone (212) 532-7742.

Bio-feedback devices Zen masters lost in the heights of meditation produce unusual quantities of alpha waves. By hooking electrodes to your skull, you can monitor your own brain waves and control them. Hailed as short-cuts to meditation, the electrode devices show you how to get into the relaxed, diffused alpha consciousness. In Texas, the Silva mind-control cult preaches about alpha waves without ever measuring them. Cautionary note: alpha-wave

training is a little-explored area —some experimenters fear unsupervised trips. Also, scores of monitoring devices are flooding the market, and quality varies. Better consult *Altered States of Consciousness: A Book of Readings*, edited by Charles T. Tart (Wiley, $9.95), before you consider any electrode trips, and find a competent researcher. If you still want to know about devices now on the market, here are the names of some manufacturers:

Autogenics Systems Inc., 809 Allston Way, Berkeley, Calif. 94929.

Bio-Feedback Systems, Inc., P.O. Box 1827, Boulder, Colo. 80302— EMG and alpha-theta brain-wave feedback devices ($450-$2,000).

Bio-Feedback Technology, Inc., 3520 Long Beach Blvd., Suite 215, Long Beach, Calif. 90807—EMG and brain-wave feedback devices ($590-$1,990).

Cambridge Cyborgs Corp., Faulkner St., North Villerica, Mass. 01862— temperature and brain-wave feedback devices ($129-$1,375).

Books Literally thousands of books now feed and push the movement. Here are a few:

A Catalog of the Ways People Grow by Severin Peterson. Peterson spent seven years creating the definitive encyclopedia of growth techniques (Ballantine, paper, $1.65).

Here Comes Everybody by William C. Schutz, author of *Joy, More Joy*, and *Firo*. Psychologist Schutz, who is in residence at Esalen in Big Sur, provides the crusading manifesto of humanistic experimentalism (Harper, $6.95).

Bodies in Revolt by Thomas Hanna, Director, Humanistic Psychology Institute, San Francisco, Calif. The evolution-revolution fostered by our technological environment is creating a new kind of man, a cultural mutant, and a somatic culture, argues the founder of Somatology as a field of study (Holt, $6.95; Delta, paper, $2.65).

The Frontiers of Being by Duncan Blewett, Canadian psychologist. We're on the way to becoming the gods of our ancestors, he argues from a psycho-religious perspective, and heaven is coming here on earth (Award Books, 95 cents).

The Master Game by biochemist Robert S. De Ropp, secret guru. He describes little-known techniques from East and West, charts mind-body psychology, and tells where nirvana is (Delacorte, $5.95; Dell, paper, $1.95).

Golf in the Kingdom by Michael Murphy, Esalen founder and nonguiding spirit. With a child's innocence, Murphy uses the business-suit metaphor of golf to explore possibilities for expanding serenity in ordinary life (Viking Press, Esalen Series, $6.95).

Chanting It's probably the oldest way in the world to blow your mind. Pick a sound (mantra), chant it. Concentrate your whole being on the sound, feel it resonate inside your being. Soon your intellect—the ceaseless wandering of the mind—shuts down, and mystical experience may come. Listen to Gregorian chants by the Choir of the Monks of the Abbey of Saint-Pierre de Solesmes (London Record Albums: *Holy Thursday, Good Friday* and *Septuagesima Mass*, list price, $5.98 each).

Dreams The original altered state of consciousness. Carl Jung built his therapy on dreams. Our nightly visions, he believed, are the unconscious mind's effort to inform the conscious. *Man and His Symbols* is the best layman's introduction to the dream world available in hard and softbound editions (Doubleday, $6.95; Dell,

paper, $1.25). For a list of Jungian analysts, write the C. G. Jung Foundation for Analytical Psychology— 815 Second Ave., Room 501, New York, N.Y. 10017; phone (212) 228-4900.

Fasting Here's the Ultimate Diet, the one that *really* works, not only for losing weight but for achieving a beautiful high and for getting a peek into your cosmic consciousness. Try fasting! Eat nothing—for three days,

or a week, or more. It's the latest trip, and the cheapest. Warning: some have overdone food deprivation to death.

Feldenkrais exercises Sometimes accused of being functional integration, the more than 1,400 gentle exercises created by the incomparable Moshe Feldenkrais, Israeli body therapist, move you toward increased awareness through movement. New movement possibilities help perfect normal movements and lead to a new sense of body liberation. Guided exercises are available on tape (Big Sur Recordings, 117 Mitchell Blvd., San Rafael, Calif.) or in his book, *Movement Through Awareness* (Esalen Book Store, 1793 Union St., San Francisco, Calif. 94123).

Gestalt therapy To join the eternal Now and blast free of your former ways of seeing, try the Gestalt group. Read *Gestalt Therapy Verbatim* (Real People, $5; paper, $3.50), and other movement scriptures by the late Fritz Perls. Go sit upon the hot seat while the leader and 14 fellow sufferers make you act out who you are. The agony is temporary, the freedom lasting. To find the nearest of many institutes, check your phone book or write Gestalt Therapy Institute of Los Angeles, 337 S. Beverly Drive, Beverly Hills, Calif. 90212; phone (213) 277-2918.

Illustrations by Howard Saunders

Hare Krishna You are nothing. You are less than the dirt of the earth. Hare Krishna. Hare Krishna Krishna Krishna Hare Hare Hare Rama Hare Rama Rama Rama Hare Hare. The International Society for Krishna Consciousness, 439 Henry St., Brooklyn, N.Y. 11231, or 3764 Watseka Ave., Los Angeles, Calif. 90034. Festivals, including a 10-course Indian meal, every Sunday at 5 p.m.

Humanistic Psychology, The Association for Departing from traditional behaviorism and psychoanalysis, the AHP says that *all* human beings are basically creative and that *all* human action is determined by values and intentions. Anyone can join the AHP and get its *Journal of Humanistic Psychology* and its monthly newsletter, which lists growth centers spreading like little Esalens all over the United States and Europe. There are two membership requirements: you have to pay a $29 membership fee ($19 for students, retired people, residents outside the United States), and, most important, you must be a card-carrying member of the human race. John Levy, AHP, 325 Ninth St., San Francisco, Calif. 94103.

I Ching For 3,000 years this Chinese classic has guided man in his attempts to govern, to run businesses, to deal with others, to act under difficult conditions, and to contemplate the future. The *I Ching*'s 64 situations help one in his search for success and tranquility. *I Ching* is a set of casting sticks, instructions and interpretations. Confucius, a wise man, knew he needed help; he consulted his *I Ching* so often that he wore out its leather binding thongs three times. You can make your own sticks (or use coins, if you want a faster reading). Of the several translations, the best is Richard Wilhelm's, put out by Princeton University Press (Bollingen Series, $8.50). A new key to the *I Ching* is R. G. H. Siu's *The Portable Dragon* (MIT Press, paper, $1.95).

International Transcendental Meditation Society At last, a group of learned men have found a meditation discipline ideally suited for the American way of life. Maharishi Mahesh Yogi's way requires no effort at all. All the meditator has to do is utter a sacred syllable—a mantra designed especially for him—over and over. No concentration required; no physical or mental control. The mind will eventually arrive at the *source* of all thought. Transcend now. Or consult an experienced meditator or an ex-Beatle. (John, Paul, Ringo, and George all did it.) International Meditation Society, 1015 Gayley Ave., Los Angeles, Calif. 90024.

Massage The Swedish art, pacing old paths in new parlors, has been debased into a senseless indulgence of the idle and the obese. But now it

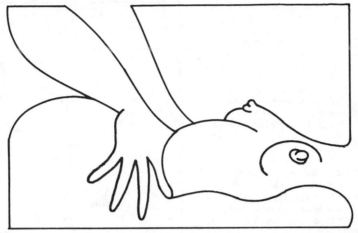

is being regenerated and refined. The new massage strokes the mind, soothes the spirit, and can actually be a way for two people to communicate, to exchange energy. It's Please Touch at the Please Touchiest. Ask a growth-center friend to introduce you to this postgraduate stage of learning.

Natural foods So MSG, BHA, BHT are not your favorite chemicals. Those are just a few of some 3,000 additives poured into commercially prepared foods. Try the organic route; get back to foods that taste the way they used to grow. Some information sources if you want to grow organic: Rodale Press and its monthly magazine, *Organic Gardening and Farming* ($5.85 per year), 33 E.

Minor, Emmaus, Pa. 18049; Health Science, 329 S. San Fernando Blvd., Burbank, Calif. 91502; Ehret Literature Publishing Co., P.O. Box 337, Beaumont, Calif. 92223; London Vegetable Society, 53 Marlses Road, London W8, England; Nature's Herb Co., 281 Ellis St., San Francisco, Calif. 94102; The Ecological Food Society, 114 E. 40th St., New York, N.Y. 10017.

Nude research The human body. Everybody has one. But for some reason we spend boundless energy devising new means to cover it up, hide it, "enhance" it. The nude encounter, once only a tenuous speculation, then the experimental power play of ill-trained leaders, is now being given careful, quiet, serious research. Paul Bindrim, a Los Angeles psychotherapist, has made a considerable splash with therapy-in-the-buff and produced experimental data to suggest that it has its place. It's spreading to the growth centers.

Open encounter The last word in honesty, the open encounter doesn't

just let it all hang out—it pushes it all out. Rules for couples: "Tell your mate the three things that could most jeopardize your marriage." Developed by William C. Schutz, former research psychologist at the University of California at Berkeley. Open encounter is based on the premise that absolute honesty opens the door to richer and fuller relationships. Not for the timid or the restrained. It's the group with guts! William Schutz, Esalen Institute, Big Sur, Calif. 93920.

Optokinetic Perceptual Learning Device The OPLD is child's play to build and use (all you need is a 33⅓ rpm record player and a light bulb), but the OPLD can quicken motor reflexes and induce altered states of consciousness. It's a revolving drum-shaped light box developed by physiological psychologist Eleanor Criswell, whose data show that it increases reading speed, enhances learning, improves visual perception and hastens motor responses. One football coach is using it to try to speed up his backfield. Center for the Distribution of Everything Good, P.O. Box 2510, San Francisco, Calif. 94126.

Paranormal research Out of the pages of the farthest-out science fiction come some documented findings by Lawrence LeShan, psychologist and psychic healer. He and others have been exploring astral travel, psychic reading and the ultimate head

trip, ESP. You don't go alone. Parapsychology Foundation, Inc., 29 W. 57th St., New York, N.Y. 10019.

Parapsychology (ESP) Many researchers are now checking out ESP, telepathy and other forms of parapsychology. It's all a joy to Joseph Banks Rhine, Duke University's grand old man of psychic research: "Behavioral psychologists often don't like us because, if we're right, man is something more than a conditioned organism—he's an immortal being." Clearinghouse for ESP research is Rhine's Foundation for Research on the Nature of Man—Box 6847, College Station, Durham, N.C. 27708.

Progressive relaxation Physician Edmund Jacobson has perfected a 150-hour training course that enables you to put each muscle group to rest, then call it to vibrant wakefulness. Don't leave anything uptight—read Jacobson's *Anxiety and Tension Control: A Physiologic Approach* (Lippincott, $10), and *Progressive Relaxation* (University of Chicago, second edition, $25).

Psychodrama There are no plots. No heroes or villains. No props or lines or stage directions. Psychodrama takes up where the cathartic Greek tragedies left off, and goes as far as you can take it. First used therapeutically by J. L. Moreno, psychodrama trains performers to give spontaneous portrayals of themselves and the persons they love or hate. Participants re-enact the past to find out what happened. Spiro Agnew hates it. To find the qualified psychodramatist near you, write Moreno Institute, 259 Wolcott Ave., Beacon, N.Y. 12508.

Psychosynthesis Italian Roberto Assagioli has deve series of techniques—from b
(continued on nex

(continued from previous page)
movements to visual imagery experiences—that help harmonize intellect, strengthen will, and expand emotion. If what Assagioli's disciples say is true, psychosynthesis may prove to be the ultimate weapon system in the armament of psychotechnology. Psychosynthesis Research Foundation, 40 E. 49th St., Room 1902, New York, N.Y. 10017.

Sensory awakening Put yourself back together by eliminating the tyranny of the head. Sensory-awareness methods developed by Esalen poet Bernard Gunther include relaxation, verbal and nonverbal communication, sensory encounter, meditation, massage, and a dash of Yoga and Zen. Explore his bag of tricks in two books, *Sense Relaxation: Below Your Mind* (Macmillan, $6.95; paper, $3.50), and *What To Do Until the Messiah Comes* (Macmillan, $7.95).

Sensory deprivation Struggle into a wet suit, suspend yourself in a tank of body-temperature water, breathe through a mouthpiece. Your eyes are covered and no light can touch them. Your ears are covered and no sound reaches you. Your senses have nothing to sense, so they let loose the energy of incredible psychedelic ecstasy.

It's not a toy. To find out what happened to one man—John Lilly, famous for his efforts to communicate with dolphins—get his newest mind blower, *The Center of the Cyclone* (Julian Press, $6.95; Bantam, paper, $1.95).

Structural Integration (Rolfing) Tears flood; outraged muscles scream in protest against terrible pressure; the past comes flickering in painful images—you're being rolfed. Rolfing is a body-manipulation technique developed by biochemist Ida P. Rolf. She argues that traumas—physical as well as psychological—twist the body during early development and throw it off balance. The pains of the past are built into one's posture. So Ms. Rolf and her rolfers, now turning up everywhere, dig right into the muscle bindings to knead the very soul. For names of rolfers in your area, write the Guild for Structural Integra-

tion, c/o Esalen Institute, 1793 Union St., San Francisco, Calif. 94123.

Tai-chi chuan We know all about massaging the outside of the body, but there's also the inside. Perhaps the internal organs need stimulation as badly as skin and muscles. Tai-chi chuan, an ancient Chinese movement, turns your body on from the inside. Gia-Fu Feng, venerable tai-chi sage who lives in Colorado, provides an introduction in *Tai-chi—A Way of Centering* (Macmillan, Collier, paper, $2.95). Alan Watts was and Laura Huxley is a tai-chi adept. For information—Tai-chi Society of New York, 1947 Broadway, New York, N.Y. 10023.

Tibetan Buddhism Just over a decade ago, when Chinese troops invaded their mountains, more than 4,000 lamas fled Tibet. They took their eclectic religion (it incorporates all forms of Buddhism) around the world. Tibetan Nyingmapa Meditation Center, 2425 Hillside Ave., Berkeley, Calif. 94704; Karma Dzong, Salina Star Route, Boulder, Colo. 80302; or Tail of the Tiger Buddhist Community, Star Route, Barnet, Vt. 05821.

Transpersonal Association When the tools of psychotechnology have done their job, when man is stripped of his hangups, freed from the agony of self-doubt—then where do we go? It's the ultimate mystical quest, the search for the elusive entelechy. And it's what the Association for Transpersonal Psychology is all about. If the Association for Humanistic Psychology is the focus of what's happening now, the Transpersonals are about eight beats ahead. ATP seeks the states that transcend indi-

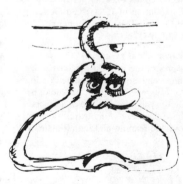

vidual differences and free unlimited potentials that are enshrouded in the Social mummification process. Telepathy, psychokinesis, astral projection—all are innate human abilities. God is within. We can set ourselves free. It's human lib. *Journal of Transpersonal Psychology* ($7.50 a year, two issues), P.O. Box 3049, Stanford, Calif. 94305.

Witchcraft Out of the Black Forest and down from the Scottish Highlands—make way for one of man's oldest religions, now back in

business in public. Witchcraft is surfacing in universities and suburbs, communes and cities across the country. Anyone can be a witch or a warlock and use universal energy for man's betterment. Be the first on your block to start a coven. Witches come in two varieties: black or white. For information about the black art, contact the Church of Satan. Address unlisted, but you can phone (415) 752-3583. And read High-Priest Anton S. LaVey's *Compleat Witch or What To Do When Virtue Fails* (Dodd, $6.95). White Witch Sybil Leek has written two pertinent books: *Cast Your Own Spell* (Pinnacle, paper, 95 cents), and *The Complete Art of Witchcraft* (World, $6.95). Also read Paul Huson's *Mastering Witchcraft* (Putnam, $6.95; Berkley, paper, $1.25).

Women's liberation The initial impassioned protest and rhetoric—which reminded women that discrimination was not personal hallucination—have turned into politics and action. The National Organization for Women (NOW), 1957 E. 73rd St., Chicago, Ill. 60649; the National Women's Political Caucus, 707 Warner Bldg., 13th and E Sts. NW, Washington, D.C. 20004; and the Women's Action Alliance, 200 Park Ave., New York, N.Y. 10017, among other groups, have settled in for the long haul of fighting for legal and economic reforms. Discussion or "consciousness-raising" groups help women deal with their conflicts, provide strategies for coping with daily discrimination, and explore ways to combine men, marriage and work.

Yoga The gateway to higher self-realization and unification is cosmic consciousness—and it comes in many colors: Hatha, Raja, Bhakti and Juana. The fun comes with picking the one that suits you best. Don't be thrown by the spooky words. The oldest tool kit in psychotechnology lets you turn on both psyche and soma. For a new understanding of what the techniques do, read Mircea Eliade's *Yoga, Immortality and Freedom* (Princeton University Press, Bollingen Series, $10; paper, $3.95), or Sachindra Kumar Majundar's *Introduction to Yoga Principles and Practice* (University Books, $7.50). Consult your phone book for yoga teachers near you.

Zen The classic meditative practice. Zen. Doorway to the superconscious. Zen. State of no mind. Zen. Self without image. Zen. Suspend thoughts, concentrate on your living, breathing self. Do it sitting or walking. Zen uses Koans, vexing little phrases that seem to make no sense; they paralyze the internal computer and open up the void within. What is the sound of one hand clapping? Warning: Sohaku Kobori of Kyoto Temple, Japan, fears that Western Zen, a head trip without rigorous discipline, may be a poison mushroom, so you cannot just taste it. Zen Studies Society Inc., 223 E. 67th St., New York, N.Y. 10021, or Cimarron Zen Center, 2505 Cimarron St., Los Angeles, Calif. 90018.

For further information about these and other growth trips write to Eleanor Criswell, *The Great Escape*, 150 Shoreline Highway, Mill Valley, Calif. 94941. ☐

How to Choose a Guru

Let's say you're really serious about it. You realize there are Bengali dental students, Chinese headwaiters, millionaires and toothless desert maniacs all claiming to be able to lead you to . . . well, you know . . . nirvana, or salvation, or super-powers, or peace, or happiness, or the poorhouse.

How can you choose among them? Who can you trust? Who is so far advanced that you'll let him take your personal aura and jimmy around with it?

It's a serious question. I've been at it for years now, searching for something—*higher*. My experiences may be able to help you.

The basic question, it seems to me, is rarely asked. It is: "What do I want?" Do I want to be a better person? Do I want to be more flexible? Do I want to "grow"? Do I want some kind of "power"? What do all these concepts mean to me, in a *real* sense? Why do I want a guru at all? What's the matter with letting things go along as they are? Isn't life pretty-all-right anyway?

Every person who is thinking about gurus has to answer this for himself, in a simple, serious and sincere way. There's no room for wiseacring.

When this basic question is answered to your satisfaction, the search can go on. Now there's something fundamental to work with. It's now a question of finding someone, some teaching or some practice that will lead you to your goal.

Of course, everyone knows there are all sorts of spiritual practices. It is fashionable nowadays to say that "all paths are the same, they all lead to the same place." In *my* experience, this is *not* true. Each path, each religion, has its own particular emotional content, makes its own particular demands and develops its own particular faculties in the student. There are "arcane schools" that concentrate on developing thought power and mental knowledge; there are occultists, theosophists, "schools of the natural order," Rosicrucians, meditation societies, magical fraternities, witch covens, bio-energetic groups, "Maitreyan Yoga" ashrams, "Omniversal Families," Subud, Arica, Gurdjieff, Ouspensky, Sufis and God knows what-all else.

The only realistic way to choose among them is to go back to your original aim. What do you want? Do you want certain kinds of mental dexterity? Do you want to become psychically sensitive? Do you want your body to develop in a certain way? Do you want magical powers? Do you simply want to be "fully human"? The decision is crucial, and it has to be based on a fundamental life aim, what you realistically want for yourself as a certain kind of being living on earth under certain conditions. Does the teaching seem like it will give you what you want, with no compromises and no fancy dancing?

The next step is the big plunge. You have to take stock of the guru himself. The great Hasidic Rabbi, Israel Baal Shem Tov, once was asked how to tell a true guru. He said, "Ask him how you can permanently rid yourself of the temptation to Evil." If he can tell you, says Baal Shem Tov, he is not worth much. For "a man must struggle with the urge to Evil until his last moment. . . ."

From this point on, the only criterion is results. Are you getting them? Are they definite? Are they what you want? If you're not getting them, is there any reason to stick it out? The fact is that some teachings and practices are just not right for some people. As the Sufis say: "A cloak is no longer a cloak if it doesn't keep you warm."

My advice, for what it's worth, is—carry on! Some practices have hidden charges that don't become apparent until you've invested a year or two. But don't be afraid to give it up if you gradually feel it's just not right. There's no sense throwing good karma after bad.

—David Saltman

Worm Grunting, or, Fishing Worms Cost a Dollar a Dozen at the Bait Store, But You Can Make Them Come to You

What you do is, you cut yourself a length of hickory or sweet gum about four feet long and sharpen one end with an ax. Then you find yourself a length of flat iron—a leaf spring from a car or truck is ideal. Drive your stake into the ground. Rub the top of it *hard* with the flat of the iron. This will create a vibration you can feel in your feet, and an ugly sound. Every earthworm for about 20 feet around will find the vibration

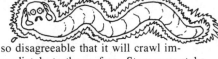

so disagreeable that it will crawl immediately to the surface. Stow your stake and your iron, fill your bait can and go fishing.

If you feel you need lessons, these are available free any morning outside Mr. M. B. Hodge's bait store in Sopchoppy, Fla. Mr. Hodge buys worms from dozens of people who make their living this way. In Sopchoppy, it is called "worm grunting." In neighboring counties of the Florida panhandle, it is also called "twiddling" or "fiddling" or "scrubbing" for worms, and it is thought that square stobs or triangular ones work best. People in Sopchoppy are contemptuous of these deviations from the common round stake and truck spring. More than 30 million earthworms a year are grunted around Sopchoppy, so Sopchoppy people know what they are talking about.

One word of caution, which sounds like a lie but is the truth: if you want to grunt worms for pay in a National Forest, you need a U.S. Worm Gathering License.

—Charles Kuralt

Scaring Yourself Makes You Feel Good

If you ever find yourself down in the mouth, try walking over Niagara Falls on a tightrope. Or hunting Siberian tigers with a bow and arrow. Or jumping out of an airplane or walking under a burning building or taking a hammer in your right hand and bringing it down smartly on your left.

That'll cure you. It introduces the Risk Factor.

There's a Risk Scholar, a man named Dr. Sol Roy Rosenthal, in San Diego. He used to teach preventive medicine at the University of Illinois, and he studied hundreds of amateur and professional athletes in all sports, from polo to rock climbing to roller derby to parasailing.

The essence of his findings is contained in this remark made by a bullfighter: "I am happiest when I am physically threatened."

There's a definite elation that comes when you walk "tightrope" on that railroad trestle over the bay, even if you're just *pretending* it's Niagara Falls. The fog in your nodes is dispelled, you discover new territory: tightrope walking is more a matter of *speed* than anything else.

A man who was once on a runaway horse said: "After I survived that one, I knew I could survive anything."

Ranking the Risks

The harder the task and the riskier, the greater the benefits to you, according to Dr. Rosenthal. Just don't take any foolhardy dares. Here are some Risk Quotients for you to keep in mind:

High R.Q. Skiing, surfing, mountain climbing, fox hunting, auto racing, bobsledding, sky diving, ski jumping, playing polo.

Very high R.Q. Gang warring, building atomic bombs, flipping the bird to voodoo priests, French-kissing with cobras.

R.Q. squared and cubed Driving an automobile, crossing the street, going out at night in the city, eating TV dinners.

—David W. Cudhea

Sexy Yoga

"The world is a wedding. In every act of every day, you are either the bridegroom or the bride. You are the strong or the weak, the electric or the magnetic, the lover or the beloved."

—Omar Garrison, in
Tantra: The Yoga of Sex

Tantrism is maverick yoga. It's sex yoga; it's art yoga; it's literary yoga. It uses ritualized erotic contact to bring people in touch with something higher. In its pure, non-Westernized form, Tantrism permits only a special kind of orgasm. The Westernized version, where Tantric practices prolong intercourse and heighten sexual enjoyment, bears the intriguing name "Tantric sex."

It is impossible to put the essence of Tantra into words. But a highly simplified description of the *Panchatattva,* the "secret ritual," of Tantrism will make clear the possibilities—and the strangeness—of Tantric practices. First, both partners bathe completely, from head to toe. The woman puts on a silk negligee (red is best), the man a robe (of any color). Red stimulates the male sexual organs, according to the Tantric esoteric color code.

For those who have not mastered the complicated preliminary disciplines, the next step is for the man to enter the room alone, light candles and meditate in prescribed ways (controlled breathing is involved). The woman then enters the room, and together they ceremonially drink wine and eat small amounts of fish, biscuit and cardamom.

Then the couple go to a couch or bed for the *maithuna,* the actual sexual union. The woman undresses and sits on the edge of the bed. The man stands before her, admires her, and while reciting a mantra, touches her near the heart, head, eyes, throat, ears, breasts, upper arms, navel, thighs, knees, feet and vagina.

The man then undresses and joins the woman in the bed. She lies on her back, he on his left side, facing her. They assume the *maithuna* position this way: she raises her legs. He moves his upper body away from her, bringing his penis close to her vagina. She lowers her legs and he places his right leg between hers. The man then inserts his penis, but only part way. Tantric discipline makes the hard requirement that the couple lie motionless and relaxed in this position for exactly 32 minutes, during which time they are asked to concentrate on the flow of energy between them. As one might imagine, it is likely to be considerable. One guru (ideally, Tantric practices, like all yoga, should be learned only from a guru), says that a nirvanic peak of sensation occurs between the 28th and 32nd minute. According to Omar Garrison, "Tantriks believe that the partners become for the time being a divine couple. Through them flows the cosmic, creative energy of the universe. The *mudra* is no longer a woman—she is Parashakti herself. The man, likewise, is no longer merely a man, but incarnates Shiva."

If the goal of the couple is less spiritual and more sexual, the partners are of course free to be less stringent in their observance of the ritual. But anyone who believes sex is sacred will find Tantrism a challenging way to put the belief into practice.

—*R. C. Smith*

MANTRAS FOR TANTRAS

If you're serious about Tantric sex, here are some of the mantras which go with it:

ANG. Salutation to the circle of the Sun, with His 12 parts.

UNG. Salutation to the mandala of the Moon, with its 16 digits.

O KULA-RUPINI! Infuse into the essence of this excellent wine that which produces full and unbroken bliss and its trembling thrill of joy!

YANG to the yogin. To Shiva I bow!

HUNG. Let us bring to mind the bonds of the life of a beast. Let us meditate upon the Creator of the Universe!

DEVAYAY NAMAH. This head with the light upon it I offer to the Devi!

RANG. Salutation to the Seat of Fire!

ONG. Salutation to the Seat of Fire!!

HUNG PHAT. To the eaters of raw flesh!!!

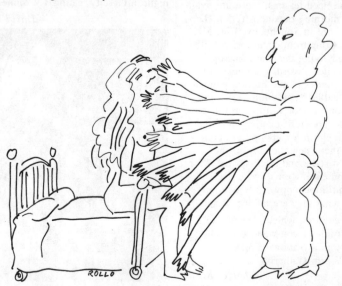

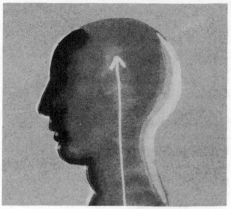

Zen + Yoga + Sufism + Cabala + Martial Arts = ARICA!

For those interested in the new religious awakening, but who are bewildered by all the possibilities, there is the Arica Institute, which has sought to gather into one highly eclectic philosophy and course of training insights from many of the spiritual disciplines now claiming Western converts: Zen, cabala, Sufism, yoga, the martial arts and others.

The institute was founded in 1971 by a group of pilgrims from the Esalen Foundation in California who were the first Americans to study under Oscar Ichazo, a Bolivian-born mystic who first formulated the basic precepts of Arica. (Arica was the city in Chile where Ichazo was then living. The word means "open door" in Quechua, according to Arica literature.) The institute has graduated more than 2,000 students and now offers courses in 18 teaching centers in the United States, Canada, England and Chile.

The basic premise of Arica's teachings is that man, in essence, is quite different from what Western man has become. The goal of Arica training is to destroy the socially-determined ego and to replace it with pre-existing, cosmically-created essence. "In essence," Ichazo says, "every person is perfect, fearless, and in a loving unity with the entire cosmos; there is no conflict within the person between head, heart and stomach or between the person and others." The goal of Arica training is to help students recapture this lost wholeness.

Courses of various lengths, intensity and expense are available—from a weekend to three months, from $40 to $650. The courses take up analysis of energy centers and systems, levels of consciousness, meditation, mantra (chants or short songs), mudras ("the study of the objective positions of the human body") and psychocalisthenics.

If you're interested in Arica, and there isn't a teaching center where you live, you can write to Arica Institute, 24 W. 57th St., New York, N.Y. 10019. There are introductory sessions at all Arica teaching centers each Wednesday evening at 7:30.

—*The Editors*

If You Can't Ask God Direct, Ask the *I Ching*

The Chinese believe that when God doesn't want to sign his real name, he signs "Chance."

There is a power in chance, a meaningfulness more than just heedless hap. But the Western mind has always been made uneasy by chance. Rather than dealing with it, or accepting it, we have generally tried to get rid of it by assuming that truth lies in finding causes, not in learning about chance without trying to explain it away.

One of the great works of world literature is organized—if that's the word—around the idea that wisdom can come out of close attention to what chance tells us. It's the *I Ching*, or *Book of Changes*, a work of oracular philosophy that is thousands of years old and was a source of inspiration to Confucius and other Chinese philosophers for centuries.

The premise of the *I Ching* is that the constant change in the universe can be divined, can even be consulted and asked questions. That this change, in short, has meaning and relevance, however shadowy and mysterious. The *Book of Changes* has evolved over the centuries as a means of communication between man and the universe of change, as a way of "plugging in" to the meaning of things.

Traditionally, one does this by throwing 49 yarrow stalks and interpreting the random patterns of their fall by means of the 64 hexagrams that make up the *I Ching*. A simplified method is possible using three coins that are thrown six times to form the hexagram. The coins are thrown after asking a question—a serious question with a complex, rather than simple, answer; the coins are thrown to find the hexagram that forms the answer to the question at that moment in time.

The *Book of Changes* can also be read as a book of wisdom. Indeed, many authorities believe this to be the proper function of the book, and regard using it as an oracular, or fortune-telling, device as a trivialization of its content.

However, many people who were entirely skeptical about the value of throwing the *I Ching* have been astonished by the results—assuming that asking the question and consulting the oracle have been done in good faith and with a reasonably open mind. At the very least, the *I Ching* is one of the best means of self-examination or self-analysis ever developed. At best, according to Jung and others, consulting or studying the *I Ching* is a way to penetrate the unconscious.

(There are several translations and editions of the *I Ching* in English, but by far the best and most authoritative is the Richard Wilhelm translation, available from Princeton University Press, hardbound only, for $8.50.)

—*R. C. Smith*

Overhaul Your Mind For $35–$75

By meditating for 20 minutes twice a day you may be able to change completely your attitude toward life. You could be more energetic, more creative, generally more able to cope with stress. And you can learn to do it after only a few days of training.

If it all sounds too good to be true, consider that for many thousands of Americans, it works. We're talking about transcendental meditation (TM), a technique developed and introduced into this country in 1959 by the Maharishi Mahesh Yogi. Since then more than 300,000 Americans have been trained according to the Seven Steps: two introductory lectures, a personal interview, an initiation, and three small-group meetings. The cost: $35 for high school students, $45 for college students, $75 for adults.

Hundreds of articles about TM have appeared in scientific and professional journals, including *Scientific American* and *Science*. Scientists have found, for example, that measurable physiological changes take place during meditation, lending some credence to the claim that TM represents a fourth state of consciousness (in addition to waking, sleeping and dreaming).

TM is being taught by 3,600 qualified instructors in 205 locations in the United States. Check the phone book under "Students International Meditation Society" or "International Meditation Society." Or write the SIMS-IMS National Center, 1015 Gayley Ave., Los Angeles, Calif. 90024 for the address of the closest teaching center.

"Clam sandwich" asana, or posture, which eventually develops a pearl in the navel of the yogin or yogini.

HOW TO CONSULT I CHING WITH THREE COINS

RESULTS OF TOSSING THREE COINS	SYMBOL USED IN BUILDING HEXAGRAM	NUMBER DESIGNATION	DESCRIPTION
3 HEADS	—O—	9	"OLD YANG" (positive, moving)
2 HEADS, 1 TAIL	— —	8	"YOUNG YIN" (negative, static)
2 TAILS, 1 HEAD	———	7	"YOUNG YANG" (positive, static)
3 TAILS	—X—	6	"OLD YIN" (negative, moving)

1. Ask your question.
2. Throw the coins six times, and using the symbols given above, build the hexagram from the bottom line up.
3. Consult the table of hexagrams in the back of the Wilhelm/Baynes *I Ching* (Princeton University Press, $8.50) to identify, by number, which of the 64 possible hexagrams you have thrown.
4. Turn to the hexagram in the text and interpret the answer to your question. Be sure to read the last section, "The Lines," for the so-called "moving numbers," which are 6 or 9 (three heads [0] or three tails [

Beyond Kung Fu

By R. C. Smith

Kung fu, as we understand it, is a slow-motion orgy of striking, throwing and maiming—all done con brio *for a television camera—but always followed by much heaviness of spirit at having had to resort to violence. But there is another way of self-defense that makes hostility irrelevant and goes far beyond kung fu . . .*

The martial arts have been turned into successful show business. In both movies and TV, oriental mysticism mixed with crippling blows offer Hollywood script-writers still another profitable way to show us their violence and deplore it too. The hero of the TV show "Kung Fu," for example, wants only the peace made possible by a spirit that is wholly at one with the Universe. But both the ratings and the world are impure and cry out for lethal self-defense techniques. When our hero is pushed beyond endurance, after a sufficient number of brutalized innocents have assembled to watch, he satisfies us with a slow-motion orgy of striking, throwing and maiming, all done *con brio* for the camera, but followed always by much heaviness of spirit at the tragedy of once again having had to resort to violence.

If this cheap version of one of the martial arts panders to the instinct in all of us to act out our hostility, it might be good to consider another way of self-defense that makes hostility irrelevant and goes far beyond kung fu. It is aikido, the nonviolent Japanese martial art. It just may be the sport whose time has come.

Aikido is the newest martial art, developed in the 1920s by Morihei Uyeshiba after he had mastered the others and was dissatisfied with what he found in them, an emphasis on what could only be temporary and transitory: winning. But today's victors are on their way to being tomorrow's losers, and in this struggle to stay on the right side he felt the spiritual possibilities of sport were lost entirely. Professor Uyeshiba sought to develop a martial art that would focus not on determining the superiority of one combatant —a self-limiting and finally self-defeating

approach to sport—but on the task of self-mastery and on the spiritual attitudes that help or hinder self-mastery.

The best way to be introduced to aikido, and to see the difference between it and Western sports, is to attend a session at a *dojo*, or place of practice. (Practice sessions are about all there is to aikido: there are no matches or games, although an expert may give a "performance," or demonstration, of aikido techniques.) The beginner can begin whenever he wishes; there is no set sequence of lessons, no beginning and no end. A typical session (depending on the habits of the group and the preferences of the instructor) may begin with aikido exercises, first done individually, then as a group, following the lead of the instructor. Most members of the group wear the *gi*, the quilted practice uniform familiar to anyone who has seen a judo or jujitsu demonstration.

The *gi* is worn with the belt appropriate to the wearer's level of accomplishment. Aikido does recognize grades like those of the other martial arts, although the number used varies in different parts of the country: in Japan and in most of the United States, there are only white belts for beginners and black belts for experts. In West Coast *dojos*, however, four belts are awarded: white, blue, brown and black. The black belt has ten degrees, leading up to Tenth Dan, of which there is only one. The first aikido Tenth Dan was Professor Uyeshiba himself; his successor is Koichi Tohei, who is now the chief instructor at the General Headquarters Arena in Tokyo.

After the exercises, the group practices techniques selected and demonstrated by the instructor. Then the students choose partners and practice the techniques themselves. They alternate as the thrower and the thrown, the attacked and the attacker. Aikido, in fact, is nothing but self-defense: the one attacked is called the *nage*, which means "the one who throws"; the attacker is called the *uke*, "the one who falls." Each technique is practiced from the right and the left; then the partners change roles, practice right and left again, then change roles once more—this continues until the instructor calls a halt and demonstrates another technique. (There are more than 10,000 of them.)

The most striking feature of aikido in practice sessions is its similarity to dance. There is none of the grappling and panting, none of the struggle and conflict we associate with wrestling or other hand-to-hand sports. Probably the most important principle of aikido, in fact, is *not* to pit your force directly against your attacker's. What happens if your attacker is stronger than you are? You will be overwhelmed. But what if you use his force, by leading him where he wants to go, blending your force with his? Aikido trains one to sense the direction of your opponent's force so that it can be used to throw him while the defender effortlessly retains his own physical and mental repose.

In practice, then, the role of the attacker is to accept the throw and to learn from what his partner is doing. Much of the teaching is done from partner to partner. Members of a group are very helpful to beginners, and are careful to keep two beginners from pairing up. The speed with which techniques are practiced varies with the talent of the partners—the more experienced are able to do them faster, and more gracefully. And logically enough, the techniques tend to get more strenuous as the session goes on.

If the observer watches two skilled partners on the mat, he will see in action moves that even the ignorant eye can tell are very different from the throw-'em-down-and-rack-'em-up techniques that

In aikido, the nonviolent martial art, it's always the attacker who is thrown. This demonstration took place at the first New Games Tournament in California.

Photography by Alan Copeland

are found in some of the *macho*-oriented Westernized karate parlors and judo joints (although aikido students are instructed not to criticize the other martial arts—ever). The differences all come from the implied assumption that the two persons are partners, not enemies—again, the similarity to dancing. As one watches practice, the easy distinctions between fighting and blending begin to disappear: one person is being thrown, but there seems to be almost no force involved, no struggle. There is no sense, however, that the attacker—the one being thrown—is in any way really cooperating or pretending to be thrown, as professional wrestlers (whose athletic skills are a tawdry combination of mimicry and endurance) do.

In aikido, the partners simply merge; the question of who is active and who is passive does not apply. What happens happens, and it seems right and necessary that it does. In fact, watching a practice session can be treacherously seductive, because you are liable to find yourself feeling that it looks easy, that anyone can do it. That's the time for you to plan to get on the mat for the first time.

The first try at aikido is bound to be a humbling experience. Even the ceremonious beginnings of the session may be embarrassing to an American. The Japanese custom of kneeling and bowing to the instructor at the beginning and end of the session; bowing from the waist to your partner as you end your practice time with him, and to the instructor after he coaches you—all this takes some getting used to.

But the techniques themselves are even more of a shock to the beginner. It turns out, of course, that they're not easy at all. As you watch the instructor demonstrate them two or three times you realize that you're just not taking it all in well enough to repeat what he is doing. In a good group, you'll be recognized as new and someone skilled at both practice and teaching will lead you gently through your first clumsy attempts to imitate what

you saw the instructor do a few seconds before.

What the partner is obliged to point out to the novice, as kindly as possible, is that he is working against himself and against his partner. If he is using some variety of arm- or wristlock, say, to lead his partner to the floor, chances are he will be pulling on the wrist and pushing on the arm at the same time. And instead of sensing where the partner is heading—where his own force is leading him—the beginner will develop a fixed notion of what to do and try to force his opponent (his enemy!) to bend to his will by heaving and hauling, pushing and pulling, twisting and tugging. The result, of course, is that you succeed if you're physically stronger—at a considerable expense of energy—and that if you're smaller or weaker, you fail.

The term used in aikido for the energy, the life-force that flows through all of nature, is *ki*. When you struggle against your partner, you are matching your *ki* against his. The result may be that you cancel each other out: the energy is expended to no purpose. But if you blend your *ki* with his, you double the force of what is happening: you lead him with your own power and with his. It's the easier way, the natural way, the way without struggle. The emphasis with aikido is on grace and naturalness. *Ki*, then, is not just an obscure Japanese word meant to arouse in the credulous visions of the mystical powers of the Orient, but a useful metaphor for the flow of life, movement, vitality through all living things.

This concrete expression of grace and harmony joined with strength and competence, of self-defense joined with nonviolence, has led many people in the direction described by Robert Frager, an instructor of aikido and a black belt, who is a psychologist at the University of California at Santa Cruz. "Many of my students have found a philosophical home in aikido," he says. "They are no longer tempted to associate nonviolence with passivity or weakness."

Those who have practiced aikido for any length of time are likely to stress how much it has changed their lives. They say they have greater energy, greater powers

of concentration and a generally more positive and competent attitude toward life. "I pay twenty-five dollars a month for sixteen hours of aikido instruction," a brown belt from San Francisco told me. "Hell, a therapist costs forty bucks an hour."

According to the teachings of aikido the way to self-mastery is through learning to sense the *ki* in yourself and in others. Practically speaking, this translates into the common advice from instructors, when they're explaining how to parry a particular kind of attack: "If he wants to do that, *let him do it*." You never stop a blow, you step aside or deflect it. The satisfaction of the sport lies in the harmony it creates—harmony between the mind and body, between you and your partner, perhaps even between you and your perceptions of the world. Aikido is a sport that doesn't require enemies or losers. The object is never victory, only self-mastery. □

How To Get Started

The best books on aikido are those by Koichi Tohei who, as Professor Morihei Uyeshiba's successor, is the only Tenth Dan (the highest degree of black belt) in the world. Some of his books are in paperback, some are only in hardbound editions. Probably the best of the paperbacks are *Aikido* and *What Is Aikido?*, both published by the Rikugei Publishing House in Tokyo, and distributed in the U.S. by the Japan Publications Trading Company, 1255 Howard St., San Francisco, Calif. 94103. For information about aikido classes in the United States, contact one of these three regional centers of aikido instruction:

New York Aikido Club
142 W. 18th St.
New York, N.Y. 10011
(212) 675-9606

Midwest Aikido Federation
1103 W. Bryn Mawr Ave.
Chicago, Ill. 60660
(312) 784-5821

Western States Aikido Federation
P.O. Box 25425
Los Angeles, Calif. 90025
(213) 733-5347

Even in attacks from behind, the nage *(the one attacked) is able to throw by moving with the force of the* uke *(the attacker).*

A Guide to the Deadly Arts

Could Muhammad Ali take Kao Fang-Hsien? It depends. Are they fighting on a gym floor or in a back alley in Taipei? Is Kao allowed to use his "Ting" punch? Would Ali shuffle himself right into an "Iron Claw"?

Every part of the world has its own fighting art, and each one is probably invincible on its own turf. Ali's fancy stepping wouldn't last long in the mucky jungles of Malaya.

For some reason we have a great fascination with secret ways of self-defense. We love to theorize about whether Marciano could duke it out with a sumo wrestler, or about how that two-finger jab to the breadbasket could fend off the midnight muggers. So next time somebody kicks sand in your face, just flash him this guide to the martial arts of Asia —and run like hell!

Ninjitsu   Japanese all-round armed and un-armed combat, with elements of disguise, woodlore, camouflage, espionage and poison. Those men in black in the James Bond movie *Thunderball* were supposed to be ninjitsu.

It is said the ninja can hide himself completely in an open field, or curl up to look like a rock, or wedge himself into the rafters of a room. He can catch a sword with his hands, breathe under water and walk sideways so you can't tell where his footsteps point. He carries an ingenious body-pack something like Batman's utility belt, complete with nine throwing blades (like spiked jacks) and Jesus feet. He can run 100 miles without stopping, and cover 300 miles in three days without resting.

Tai-Chi Chuan   Chinese yin-yang shadow boxing. An exercise, a sport, a meditation, a philosophy, a deadly fighting art. The soft and graceful movements have names like "White Stork Spreads Wings," "Snake Creeps Down," "Monkey Retreats," "Owl at the Bottom of the Sea," "Opening the Fan" and "Grasping the Bird's Tail." There are also esoteric exercises like "Walking Inside the Mountain," and medical exercises

like "Shooting Arrows at an Eagle."

There are a great number of excellent tai-chi teachers in Chinese communities throughout the world.

Bersilat   The Malay unarmed fighting art. It is based on the movements of snakes and tigers. It is said bersilat came to a famous Malay prince in a dream.

The fighters approach each other warily, low to the ground, nearly crawling, until they are within striking distance. What happens then is far too swift for the eye to follow—a mercury blur, a red power tinged with black, the screaming lunge of a crafty tiger and the evasive sway of a murderous cobra.

There is a sport form of bersilat called silat gayong that puts the unique fighting movements into a long and sensual dance. It is sometimes seen at Malay weddings.

The only teachers of bersilat are found in the Malay archipelago.

Plum Blossom Sword   A Chinese method of swordfighting, mainly practiced by women. It uses two short swords and small, swift movements.

Her swinging sword flashes
  Like the nine falling suns
Shot by Yi, the archer of legend;

She moves with the force
  Of a team of dragons
Driven by the gods through the sky;

Her strokes and attacks
  Are like those of terrible thunder;

And when she stops, all is still
  As water reflecting clear moonlight.

—Tu Fu

Tae Kwon Do   A Korean fighting art which literally means "To-smash-with-the-feet-to-destroy-with-the-hands."

Illustrations by Sam Daijogo

It is strictly a "hard" unarmed fighting art (there's no dance version), and it involves blows, kicks, dodges, parries, evasive spins, stuns and killing strikes. There is a series of blows to be used while on horseback.

As in samurai training, there is great emphasis on building the moral character of the student, thank God.

Tae kwon do is taught in many large cities in this country and, of course, all over Korea.

Philippine Arnis   This is a deadly combination of black magic and stick-fighting. The student learns to concentrate his gaze on a certain vital spot on his opponent's body while feinting and whirling one or two hardwood sticks. It is very difficult, very arcane and very dangerous.

The unique thing about arnis is that it concentrates on first disarming the opponent, rather than injuring him. Of course, once he's disarmed. . . .

It is taught exclusively in the Philippines.

Bando   Bando is unlike any of the other martial arts. It has been kept in relative secrecy in Burma for many centuries, and would probably leave practitioners of the other fighting arts gaping—and flat on their backs.

A basic bando technique has the expert actually climbing up his attacker, "like an eagle climbing a ladder." The expert rushes like a boar, strikes like a bull, weaves like a cobra. He is alert as a deer, confident as a monkey. He tears like a panther, pinches like a scorpion, strangles like a python and escapes like a high-flying paddy bird.

Aikido A modern method developed by M. Uyeshiba in the 1920s. He had studied Japanese sword and spear fighting, as well as jujitsu, and created his own personal form for his own personal physical and spiritual development.

Aikido is unusual in that there is no definite and rigorous format. The movements depend on what the opponent does, and are made according to definite principles of circular flow and rhythm. Since Uyeshiba was a religious man, there is a strong philosophical and spiritual content throughout.

As with many of the martial arts, aikido has spawned a number of sub-styles: the Yoshin, which stresses actual combat; the Tomiki, which is more sport and self-defense; and the original aiki-jutsu form, which emphasizes vital weak spots and resuscitation.

Kenjitsu This is the swordsmanship you see in the samurai movies. Musashi the Invincible uses a wooden club to defeat Kojiro, the Emperor's sword-fighting teacher. Since it's the fight of the century, it takes place on a deserted island at sunrise. Kojiro maneuvers Musashi into the water and you think it's curtains for our calm hero. But Musashi is no dupe—he gets the rising sun at his back, and at the crucial moment it blazes right into Kojiro's eyes. A flash of the wooden stave . . . and honor is kept.

Kenjitsu is an extremely complex arsenal of combat moves—some 1,700 movements are known. It was the chief armed art used by the samurai (the *bushi*), but as Japan got more peaceful it developed into an aesthetic sport called kendo.

The swords themselves are critical in kenjitsu. In Japan today, there is still living a man who makes swords as they were made in Musashi's day. The government has declared him to be a "Living National Treasure."

Karate Karate is very well-known, and very overrated. It is primarily a sport and not a "true" martial art at all. It can be used for self-defense, but the main systems taught in the United States and Japan are sport forms.

The original karate came from Okinawa, and was called karate-jutsu. It was for physical training and self-defense, although originally its combat role was dominant. It is a melange of indigenous Okinawan empty-hand combat, Chinese boxing and Japanese *jutsu.*

Jujitsu and Judo Jujitsu was originally part of the samurai's arsenal, and was intended to be used as a complement to swordsmanship.

The forms of jujitsu taught in the West are all sport forms, and will usually be of no help in combat situations. Combat jujitsu is based on fighting opponents who have weapons, and emphasizes striking certain weak points.

As Japan grew more peaceful, jujitsu (like kenjitsu) became more aesthetic and less bellicose; as it fell into decay, judo became more popular. But judo, again, is primarily a sport and a method of physical training, and has little relation to the realities of actual combat.

Kung Fu This is a big hoax. Kung fu is not a system of fighting. It is a generic term for exercise. (In Chinese, the martial arts are called "wu-shu.") If you say someone is practicing kung fu, you are not referring to a specific style of boxing, but to anything from doing push-ups to punching a bag.

Shaolin Shaolin is two things: it is a specific style of Chinese boxing, and it is a temple on the northern side of Shao-shih Mountain in Honan Province.

The Shaolin Temple once was a center for the study of martial arts and other kinds of disciplines (it is said Bodidharma stayed here before he brought Zen to Japan). But, in fact, very little is known about the training that went on at Shaolin temple. It is said that the originator of tai-chi chuan learned his boxing here; it is also said the temple was impervious to fire.

Shaolin boxing has spawned some 400 forms of fighting, ranging from White Crane to Praying Mantis to Monkey to Buddha to Legendary Hero, Deity, Dragon and Snake.

The current master of Shaolin boxing, in its pure form, is said to be Kao Fang-Hsien, of Taiwan. —*David Saltman*

Living With Zen

The color of mountains is Buddha's pure body; the sound of running water is his great speech.

—Dogen Zenji, 13th-Century Zen Master

Zen Mountain Center. usually called Tassajara, has two faces. For hundreds of guests who visit it deep in the national forest near Big Sur, Calif. during the summer months, it is a resort, a health spa. For the 50 or so students who live there, it is a monastery, a place to practice Zen Buddhism. Fortunately, Tassajara is happy to show either face, or both, to the interested visitor.

Before it was bought by Zen Center in 1966, Tassajara Hot Springs was the area's oldest resort; people traveled there from miles around to "take a cure." Parts of it were built by Chinese immigrants at the end of the last century; before that the springs were used by the Indians. Today, you can immerse yourself entirely in the hot (108°) sulfur water of the Giant Plunge, take individual baths in private rooms or wade in hot or cold sulfur springs outside. Tassajara also offers a large (non-sulfur) swimming pool and, at the end of a 15-minute hike, a deep, clear, rock-bound swimming hole. Many visitors also hike the lovely mountain trails near the center, some of which wind all the way to the ocean.

There's little other "recreation"—except meals, which are gourmet-vegetarian and unforgettable. Non-vegetarians will undoubtedly be surprised at how rich, substantial and tasty this food is. At the urging of the public, Tassajara has already published a bread book and a general cookbook.

Otherwise, what Tassajara-the-resort offers is peace and quiet—the most adamant peace and quiet you've ever heard with so many people around. Because there is no electricity, there are no humming or buzzing machines, no TVs, radios, appliances, stereos or electric lights (kerosene lamps give the camp a magic quality at night). Cars are left outside the gate. Practically the only sounds are of people speaking softly or chanting or using handtools, and of the gongs and woodblocks that announce the students' meditation, services, meals and working hours.

Most people who make their way over the precarious 20-mile dirt road to Tassajara, however, come for more than swimming, eating and quiet. They come to see the first Soto Zen monastery built outside Asia; they come to learn about Buddhism; and they come to see how Americans like themselves adjust to such reclusive and ascetic practice.

In fact, Tassajara is perfectly happy to let outsiders attend all activities except meals with the students. Your day could go something like this: arise to the sound of a clanging bell at 4:40 a.m., walk to the *zenda* (meditation hall) at the sound of the *han* (woodblock), sit *zazen* (meditating in the

(continued on next page)

(continued from previous page)

"lotus" or comparable position) for 40 minutes, do *kinhin* (walking meditation) for 10 minutes, sit *zazen* for another 40 minutes, then attend a service of sutra chanting and bowing. Guests may also participate in the same meditation series in the evening and attend services before meals and special lectures. *Zazen* instruction for visitors is offered every afternoon; you'll learn how to place your hands in various *mudras* (positions), how to *gassho* (bow), how to position yourself on your *zafu* (pillow), how to count your breaths during meditation.

But one learns most about Zen by simply being at Tassajara. Students of Zen are striving for pure awareness ("Big Mind") of mind, emotions, body. ("To express enlightenment in each moment is to live each moment afresh without ideas or attachment anywhere.") Hence everything the students do—cooking, cleaning up, gardening, bathing—they try to do with their fullest attention. The visitor cannot help but notice. There is a different feel to activities done in a careful, "one-pointed" Zen way.

Unlike Transcendental Meditation and the Divine Light Mission, Buddhism has been around for 2,500 years, Zen Buddhism for 1,400; and Zen Buddhism has had a serious following in this country since the 1930s. In this time of eclectic searching, there's something comfortingly "proven" about Zen.

Tassajara is just one arm of the San Francisco Zen Center, founded a decade ago. There are five other *zendos* (meditation halls) attached to this Zen Center, as well as the Greengulch farm, a 70-acre site half an hour north of San Francisco where advanced students live and practice Zen.

—Susan Sands

WHERE TO BEGIN
If you are interested in becoming a student of Zen or learning more about it, you might contact one of the following Zen Centers:

San Francisco Zen Center
300 Page St.
San Francisco, Calif. 94102

California Bosatsukai Flower Sangha
5632 Green Oak Drive
Los Angeles, Calif. 90028

New York Zendo
The Zen Studies Society, Inc.
223 E. 67th St.
New York, N.Y. 10021

These Zen Centers will be able to steer you to a *zendo* in your part of the country.

here the bee sucks,
there suck I,
In a cowslip's bell I lie,
There I couch when owls do cry,
On the bat's back I do fly
After summer merrily.
Merrily, merrily, shall I live now
Under the blossom
that hangs on the bough.

—WILLIAM SHAKESPEARE

Rolfing: Body Therapy Your Dog Can Pronounce

Rolfing is sort of a mugging that you sit still for—and it's hard to deny the masochistic overtones of this "structural integration." It does hurt, and it is sometimes mystifying that an estimated 30,000 people have paid $30-plus a session to have their deep muscle tissue prodded and probed like a slab of Kobe beef. After all, if pain is the goal, a customer can hire a good flogging quicker and cheaper down in the local Tenderloin district. No, there must be some other benefit.

Rolfers tend to refer to physical dividends: better posture due to realignment of the muscle structure, removal of lower back pain, reduced tension. But the discipline of rolfing (named after its chief practitioner, Dr. Ida Rolf) is also unquestionably part of the last decade's wave of efforts to explore inner space, part of what has been labeled, badly, the consciousness expansion movement. (Actually, in rolfing, just as much effort has gone into consciousness contraction, into the focusing disciplines, into binding and shaping one's own consciousness to one's own purposes.) The rolfer's specialty is developing body consciousness.

Rolfers have adapted and elaborated Wilhelm Reich's theory of "character armor." Most people, according to the theory, are uncomfortable with certain of their emotions, and try to lock them out of consciousness. Doing so not only establishes mental stress, but creates physical tension as well—fear of sexual feelings leads to an actual clenching of the pelvic muscles, for example. When this tension is chronic, it eventually passes under the control of the autonomic nervous system, beyond conscious recall, and the pattern of rigidity is "built in"—we experience tension and distortion as normal. The immobilized muscle sheaths actually develop fibrous connections that keep the muscles from a-slippin' and a-slidin' over one another.

The rolfer, using fingertips, knuckles, even elbows, goes into the rigidified muscles and breaks down these connections and realigns the muscles. This "deep massage" can be quite painful physically, but the real doozer, according to the rolfees I've met—and in my own experience—is the rush as the locked-out feelings and remembrances come surging back into consciousness.

Sure, sure, but what does it *do* for you? Well, it makes you feel better, it tempers the body. Muscle groups that have been flaccid tone up; points where you've been constricted and uptight become loose and supple. But the real benefits are emotional: when the old familiar feeling of tightness in the chest and shortness of breath comes around, you accept those fear messages from your body and go with them, rather than denying them and locking them out. You experience not the concept of fear but rather your own unique concoction of panic, terror,

anguish, trembling and streaming sensations. And you find that, once experienced, those feelings are gone, your body is loose, balanced, poised for the next encounter with the now. You've learned to shift your consciousness to the appropriate parts of your body, to go with the energy flow.

Try renting *that* from your local massage parlor.

If you're interested in learning more, write:
Guild for Structural Integration
P.O. Box 1868
Boulder, Colo. 80302.

—Ned Riley

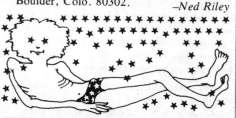

Organizing a Body Day

A quiet change in body consciousness has been taking place in the United States. It is reflected in the growing numbers of joggers, meditators, dancers, natural food eaters, the growing support for healing practices like acupuncture, the growing interest in the oriental martial arts and physical-mental disciplines, the growing belief in keeping the body healthy and high through natural means.

We are what we eat, breathe, think and feel. Body consciousness is the awareness that health is not just the absence of disease, but the enjoyment of your peak physical and psychic potentialities.

For years there has been growth in the seemingly unconnected fields of women's consciousness, ecology, yoga, biofeedback, psychic healing. Isn't it time to acknowledge the essential unity of these various movements? Isn't it time to organize a Body Day?

Body Day should be organized as a festival, a workshop, a moving catalog of body and health activities. It really should run for at least two days, and should be held outside—obtain permission to use an area of a county fairground or large park. Then try to get as many people as you can who have knowledge of a body discipline to come to Body Day, to demonstrate and talk about their disciplines to other people. (See the accompanying list for an idea of what might go on at a Body Day.) People who come to your Body Day should have a chance to hear about, see and try out new things—sufi dancing, football without scores, meditation. Perhaps you will want to have someone on hand to give out information about abortions, community health programs, preventive dental care.

Remember to keep it loose and fun. Body Day should be a day for the family, with belly dancing for children, physical activities for senior citizens, shouting contests for everybody.

—Stella Resnick and Jerry Rubin

Blocking One Sense at a Time

The senses may be able to tell us a whole lot more about our physical environment than we suspect. By altering the relation of the senses to physical stimuli, we can experience them in a new and refreshing way. Obviously, if you block one sense completely, the other four will become proportionately more important because they will have to handle as much of the information formerly handled by the blocked sense as they possibly can. Perhaps each sense is capable of a whole range of perceptions that we had not realized it could handle. Here are some suggestions for exploring those capabilities.

Sight   Wear a blindfold for 24 hours. Put two wads of cotton or dough over your eyes beneath the blindfold to block out all light. Have a friend take care of you during this

What Goes on at a Body Day

The more demonstrations and activities you can get together for your Body Day, the bigger a success it will be. See if you can get at least one person to participate who has knowledge of:

acupuncture	juggling
aikido	massage
Arica	meditation
belly dancing	mime
bicycling	natural childbirth
bio-energetics	natural foods
bio-feedback	play therapy
breathing techniques	psychic healing
	psychic research
chanting	rolfing
chiropractic	sensory awareness
dancing (folk and other)	sensory deprivation
extra-sensory perception (ESP)	sex education and therapy
	softball
football	tai-chi chuan
gestalt therapy	vitamins and nutrition
herbal medicine	
hiking	volleyball
jogging	yoga

Add your own ideas to the list—the number of disciplines that could be represented at a Body Day is almost infinite.

time. (Put the blindfold on at night before going to bed—or if you're the type who wakes up before you open your eyes, have the blindfold put on in the morning before you get up.)

Go for a walk. If you live in the city, notice the *distance* of a city block and how it differs from your normal/visual perception of it now that the only measure of distance that you have is your own footstep.

Go to the beach if you're near one. Notice the feeling of space around you; notice the sound of the waves, gulls, bathers, etc. and the textures of the sand and the shells.

Go to a supermarket and wander down the aisles. Listen to the activity around you. Feel the meat and poultry if you can get your hands on it. Go to the spice rack and have your friend open several containers and give you a whiff. (Try Vietnamese cinnamon and orange peel together. Great!)

At home, have your friend put a variety of objects into your hand and *don't* try to guess what they are. Have him feed you different foods that you might not know without trying to guess what they are. Just discover what they are for you.

Go for a ride in a car or bus and notice the motion, the stops, the sounds of the vehicle, the traffic outside, etc. Have your friend take you to some specific point that you have often ridden to before and notice how the time/space reality is different when you cannot see the usual landmarks along the way.

Go to an amusement park and have your friend take you on some of the rides (skip the shooting gallery).

Another fine, very tactile experience is to have yourself carried when you're blindfolded. If you can get five or six friends to do this, have them carry you around the house from room to room. Then have them throw you up in the air several times and catch you. Obviously, you'll have to have five or six friends that you can trust for this one.

Hearing   For blocking the ears use rubber plugs (obtainable at almost any pharmacy) or the old wax-type plugs—they're better in ways and cheaper too. Cotton wads won't work—they don't block out enough sound. (Even the wax plugs won't block out all the sound, but enough of the high frequencies will be gone to get the effect.)

I found having my ears stuffed with wax a particularly uncomfortable feeling for the first hour, but then I got used to it and settled back.

As long as you're alone you won't notice the loss of hearing too much, so it's a good idea to get outside. Go for a walk or a drive and feel yourself moving through the silence of the environment. If possible, go somewhere where you would normally interact socially—a party, classroom, political rally or just a gathering of friends. Your lack of hearing will be especially noticeable here

(and probably confusing or annoying at first). You're likely to become withdrawn, maybe even lose your balance—you won't know just how much you depend on your hearing for orientation until you lose it for awhile, because most of our conscious attention goes into our eyes.

Another thing you are likely to notice is that time is altered. It may slow down quite a lot or even seem to stop. I felt very comfortable when this happened—no anxiety, no hurry, no need to get any place at all.

Smell   Like taste, the sense of smell is not stimulated much during the normal course of the day. It is also blocked during the common cold. The nose is responsible for much of what we call taste—actually, a cold does not affect our taste buds, but it does affect the nose and consequently there is the lack of "taste." Try eating a meal with your nose plugged and you will see that this is true. (Personally, I like the "taste" of food too much to do this just to prove a point.)

Touch   It is practically impossible to block the sense of touch with anything short of the sensory deprivation tank. One way to do this with limited effect is to lie down on the floor on your back and remain that way without moving *anything* until all bodily sensations fade away and you have a feeling of floating. Have a friend give you things to smell and taste. Listen to music or just enjoy the airy feeling of everything being asleep except your mind.

At first you may be so busy noticing the deprivation of one kind of experience that you don't notice the new experience you're having, so give yourself time. Blocking one sense is, in effect, something like taking a drug: altering the senses alters the consciousness. However, in all these situations it is necessary to *pay attention*. Just because you are getting new stimuli does not mean that you will perceive them. The new stimuli are, for the most part, stimuli that the brain is used to ignoring and therefore it takes a special effort to bring the new sensations into the realm of conscious experience. I'd say it's worth the effort—and once things start to happen, paying attention takes no effort at all.

—Dirk Kortz

Build a Kirlian Camera for Less Than $10

Life, Russian scientists are now saying, constantly radiates and absorbs an energy we cannot see. They call this energy the "bio-plasma" and they claim it can reveal the health, vigor and even the emotional state of living things.

Two prominent scientists, Semyon and Valentina Kirlian, have developed a simple way to make the bio-plasma visible. Their device radiates high frequency electrical energy (sometimes loosely called static electricity). The effect of the energy on an object is immediately recorded on film, with rather startling results. Inanimate objects (such as coins) show a simple corona existing around the periphery. Living objects, however, show a remarkable characteristic glow quite different from that given off by non-living things. This strange glow is the so-called "aura."

Aura is actually a loose word for a whole series of very complex phenomena. We are only now beginning to understand its operation and potential. While most researchers in the United States are still attempting to understand the physical mechanisms responsible for the Kirlian effect, Russian scientists claim they can already tell things about a person's health by watching the bio-plasma as it leaves acupuncture points. In the United States, Dr. Thelma Moss and Dr. Kendall Johnson of the UCLA Neuro-Psychiatric Institute are studying the process of psychic healing with a low-frequency adaptation of a Kirlian device. And NASA is investigating using Kirlian photography as a way to detect microscopic fissures in metals. At Stanford University in California work is being done by William Tiller, a materials scientist, to quantify the effect of various electrodes on the image.

If all this excites you, here is a plan for building your own Kirlian camera. It uses easy-to-find parts and your camera should cost less than $10 to build. With it you can photograph the aura of almost anything.

In operation the camera consists of a controlled source of high-voltage electricity (harmless because of the low current levels), electrodes or condensor plates and film. The diagram and the photograph provide all the information you'll need to build the camera. Most of the materials can be found in any automobile junk yard and in hardware stores (or you might try electronic surplus stores).

Exposing an aura depends on the physical make-up of the object you're dealing with. First get set up to photograph in a dark room (with a safelight). Lay a piece of film, emulsion side up, on the mylar insulator covering the bottom electrode plate of your camera. To photograph fingertips, place your thumb on the ground plate and your fingertip(s) on the film. Make your exposure by pressing the "start" button for about one second. You can try having a friend place

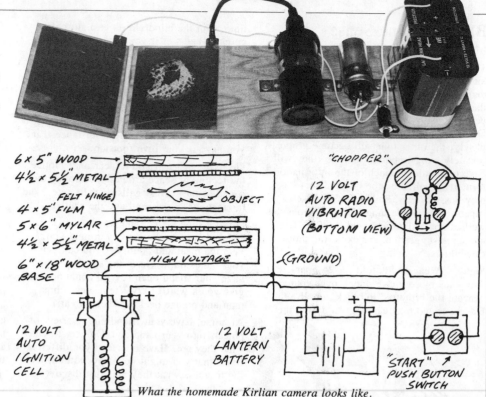

What the homemade Kirlian camera looks like.

his fingertips near yours on the film.

For coins: repeat above, but use a piece of wire to connect the coin to the ground plate (small objects need a better ground than large objects). For leaves: proceed as for fingertips, but ground the leaf by folding the ground plate onto it. Apply a light pressure and expose for one to two seconds.

Developing the photographs is simple if you use a good photographic paper such as Kodabromide, F2-RC instead of film. Though not as sensitive as film, photographic paper is easy to use, economical and can be handled in safelight. The developer to use is Kodak "Dektol." (For complete details on developing see the instructions packaged with the paper—but don't open the package in room light!) Note that your process will produce a negative print. To make a positive print, simply place your print face to face with another piece of the same paper, place this under a sheet of glass and expose to light. This is a contact print.

Plans for building more sophisticated Kirlian devices, as well as other exotic electronic machines, can be found in *Unusual Electronic Circuits* by Mitchell Waite, published by Howard W. Sams.

Auras, acupuncture, parapsychology and other extraordinary subjects under scientific investigation are discussed in enthusiastic and non-scientific language in *Supernature* by Lyall Watson, published by Doubleday.

A detailed and technical account of the physics of the Kirlian process is described by W. A. Tiller in *Some Energy Field Observations of Man and Nature*. (Write to The Materials Science Department at Stanford University, Palo Alto, Calif. 94305, for a full list of Tiller's publications.)

For an interesting account of Kirlian photography along with beautiful color photographs see an article in *Popular Photography*, February 1973—"Kirlian Imagery—Photographing the Glow of Life."

–Mitchell Waite and Bruce Brower

These are Kirlian pictures of the electromagnetic auras surrounding the authors' fingertips and the authors' bank balance. Pictures taken with above apparatus.

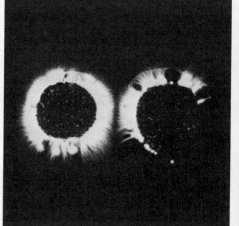

Cleveland's Museum of Your Health

At Cleveland's unique Health Museum and Education Center—the only one of its kind in the world—you can find out how to stay healthy and live longer. And you'll probably learn some things about yourself and health that you never knew before.

The Cleveland Health Museum combines the best of Disneyland and the movie *The Fantastic Voyage*. Unlike most museums, this one has no hawk-eyed guards, roped-off exhibits or "Hands Off" signs. Instead, you are invited to push buttons, pull levers, twirl knobs and turn cranks on about 5,000 electrical and mechanical exhibits that are designed to show you how you tick from birth right up through old age.

You can push a button to hear your own heart beat, listen to the nation's first transparent human model (a woman) speak, shake hands with a real skeleton and ride a unique bicycle designed to show how much energy you use at various speeds.

Museum directors are aware that the average American knows more about his automobile than about his own body, and that countless deaths and diseases are the result solely of ignorance. So the museum uses dramatic de-

vices, advertising techniques and even gimmicks to get across its health message.

You are urged to test your heart, eyes, lungs, hands and even feet (this last thanks to a local mailman's suggestion). You can also visit special health exhibits for the handicapped and the blind, a king-sized (three-foot) tooth that impresses upon you the importance of brushing your teeth and the Gallery of Nutrition and Diet—where it is definitively proved that young visitors cannot live by hamburgers and french fries alone.

The Cleveland Health Museum is located at 89th St. and Euclid Ave. in Cleveland (it's housed in a 52-room former mansion). It's open daily from 9 a.m. to 5 p.m. and Sunday from 1 p.m. to 5 p.m. Admission is 25 cents for children, 50 cents for adults.

The National Museum of Quackery

A favorite attraction at the National Museum of Quackery in St. Louis, Mo. is Dr. Wilhelm Reich's zinc-lined, telephone-booth-sized "orgone box," which Reich claimed would "draw into it a form of cosmic energy." Reich called this mysterious energy orgone, and alleged that it would cure sexual impotency, cancer and practically anything else. Reich sold orgone blankets, orgone funnels to clamp onto your head and orgone "shooter boxes" for applying the invisible stuff to any particular area of the body. Reich was finally jailed in 1954 for violating a court injunction that ordered him to quit selling the orgone machines, and he died a prisoner three years later.

Among some 165 displays in the museum are all sorts of worthless medicines, gadgets and miracle-working devices. Medical chicanery runs rampant in such areas of suffering as arthritis, cancer, rheumatism, weight control, alcoholism, baldness, skin disease and sex troubles, and "cures" for all are in the museum. The ills of the aging are a target beloved of medical charlatans, who have come up with every variation on the Fountain of Youth and other rejuvenators. One quack's machine was the Ellis Micro-Dynameter, supposed to diagnose any ailment. All it had inside its big fancy cabinet was a tiny device for measuring electric current, but over 5,000 of them were sold for $875 apiece, mainly to chiropractors. A court banned it as unsafe in 1962.

Hollister S. Smith, executive secretary of the St. Louis Medical Society, which runs the exhibition, says his group established the museum in order to help with the education of the public on the dangers of being duped by medical quacks. Most of the materials were acquired from the Food and Drug Administration; they are on view daily from 11 a.m. to 4 p.m. on the premises of the Medical Society, 3839 Lindell Blvd., St. Louis, Mo.; phone (314) 371-5225.

—*Roy Bongartz*

How to Plot Your Biorhythms

I once kept a record of my dreams, and I was astounded to discover I had certain periods where I'd constantly dream of eight-sided figures. Later in the year, I'd dream of three-sided figures, or exclusively of French salads.

There are various cycles clocking around in there, in the old bod, that we don't know anything about. It's not astrology, I don't think, and it's a lot more than conventional dream analysis.

It seems some people knew it all the time, and they first "discovered" it in 1890. It was a guy in Vienna named Hermann Swoboda, and he experimentally verified a 23-day "period" for a person's physical body. For 11½ days, the body is strong and full of stamina; for the next 11½ days, it is weaker and more susceptible to disease, Swoboda found.

Swoboda and his sidekick Wilhelm Fliess also found a distinct, independent rhythm for a person's emotional life. This one appeared to have a span of 28 days—14 days of affection and affability, followed by a fortnight of gloom, irritability and depression.

In the Twenties, an Austrian professor named Teltscher came up with a 33-day cycle for one's intellectual life as well. On the upswing, a person could grasp new ideas more easily; on the skid, you might as well talk to the wall.

Enough theoretical chitchat. You can plot out your own biorhythms and find out for yourself. If the theories are right, you should be able to tell what days are good for you to go out and punch the income tax inspector. (On second thought, you'd better get *his* chart, beforehand.)

Here's how you do it. First, make a graph that shows each day you've been alive. (So it's a little work, these biorhythms—but think of the stock market! Think of the racetrack!) Then, in smooth and sinuous curves, beginning at zero on your birthdate, plot out a different-colored serpentine wave for each of the three cycles: the 23-day phys-

ical, the 28-day emotional and the 33-day intellectual. You'll find, naturally, that on some days all three are high, and sometimes all three are low.

According to biorhythm researchers, the important thing to look for is not so much the highs and lows. It's the time when the lines hit the "zero point" that's important. That seems to be the time the personality is at low ebb, most blah, least able to cope with shocks from the outside.

A case study in Zurich showed that out of 1,400 accidental death victims, 65 percent of them kicked off exactly as their cycles went to the zero point physically or emotionally or both. On the other hand, Franco Harris, the football star, made his fabulous "play of the century" exactly as all three of his curves reached a simultaneous peak.

Good luck, and I think I'll go back to dreaming about those delicious French salads.

—*Jane Torch*

Have You Seen These Global Grafitti?

It may come from any part of the world—maybe it's a bird's-eye view of the Moscow subway system, or maybe it's a closeup of the ear of the Sphinx.

We've put 9 of these tantalizing sketches throughout the book. See how many you can identify, or how many you can make good guesses about.

The correct answers are on page 250.

GLOBAL GRAFFITI

Psychic Exercises: Moral, Legal and Mind-Expanding

There are trips and there are . . . trips. Forget about drugs. There's another way to travel that's not only more dependable—it's legal. It combines an occidental extension of the oriental way with many of the attributes of drug trips and just plain "letting it happen." A few simple exercises, tapping what goes on inside you, can expand your awareness of what goes on *around* you.

Prepare yourself for these exercises with this basic set-up: first, close your eyes. You now have a whole world at your disposal. Instead of wasting it on some old daydream, put some energy into it. With any method at your disposal, experience these inner spaces. The main idea is to start something going and then get out of the way.

Then, with your eyes still closed, take three deep breaths and let them fill your whole body; then exhale fully. Now continue to breathe normally and notice your breathing. As you do this, notice the relaxation that seeps through you. When you feel it, you're ready to get into yourself. Then try one of these exercises:

Want to solve a problem? Do the basic set-up and imagine yourself standing before a door with a metal-rimmed card holder on it. Beside the door is a table with blank cards just the size of the holder. By the cards are pens. Write on the cards whatever you want, as long as it is positive—"the answer to . . ." or "how I will . . ." or "when I will . . ."—followed by your problem. Put the card in the holder. You have now purchased a tour of the solution.

Prepare yourself for the unexpected. Open the door and go through to experience whatever is behind it. When you feel ready to return, reach behind you and the door will be there, no matter how far you have traveled; go back through it and take the card out of the holder. You'll find, when you open your eyes, that you're on your way to solving your problem, if you haven't actually found *the* solution.

The door can also be the entryway to many other experiences. Want to experience a past life you feel you lived in Egypt? Just write it on a card and walk through the door to a trip.

Set a goal Is there something you'd like to have happen? Do the basic set-up and then visualize the ending just as you'd like it to happen. Then trust that in time—in two hours to two years (or more)—you will experience that happy ending in real life.

Why not climb a mountain today? In fact, why not let an old wise man be up there with a secret he's been saving just for you? Do the basic set-up and then discover yourself in a field just at the foot of a mountain. Everything you need to get up the mountain safely is right there. Start right out; when you get to the top and find the old man, ask him for the secret he has for you,

get it, say thank you and come back down the mountain. Write down your secret as soon as you open your eyes again, or you might forget it.

What has all this got to do with the psychic? Everything. The psychic is sometimes called the sixth sense; too often we think that amazing feats of clairvoyance, astral travel, seeing auras and telepathy are all that "psychic" is, but they are just a small portion of it. The psychic really follows from allowing, and expanding. It is a bridge to wider, enhanced experiencing of your life.

"Going-inside" trips enhance your life. Another way to get more living into life is to *ritualize* what you're doing—that's a fancy way of saying "slow down."

Here are two ways to ritualize—and enhance—your external life', and you can think up lots of other ways for yourself.

Body enhancing Want to look fantastic for somebody? Set aside 15 to 30 minutes just before you put the final touches on your outfit, and lie down on your back. Close your eyes, do the basic set-up and then go over your body from toe to head and feel each part being *gorgeous*. (Gorgeous works whether you're aiming to be more handsome or more beautiful.) Feel your hair, eyes, mouth, clothes, makeup . . . after all your body and your attire feel gorgeous, expand the feeling into the air around you. Just let yourself know you're emitting marvelous energy and you can continue to as long as you wish. Then watch those magnetic happenings: people approaching you from out of nowhere to converse, stares of appreciation and flirtation, compliments. . . .

Hand games For this one you need a partner. Sit comfortably with him or her. Close your eyes and do the basic set-up. Keep your eyes closed or open them just

enough to see the hands as if they were entities unto themselves. Now allow your hands to explore your partner's. Be both a receiver and an explorer as you go. Learn what fingers feel like, how the skin of the palm differs from the skin on the back of the hand. Look closely and carefully at the lines on the palm; then see if you can feel the lines without looking. Let the hands rub each other very slowly and gently. Outside the palm at the little finger edge of the hand is a very sensitive place; gently rub yours with your partner's and *experience* what you feel. Allow yourself to get really involved.

And here are two basic exercises in further stretching of the vision and the mind. It's easier to try them after you've become really adept at getting inside your own head and at becoming beautiful at will, and when you're really high on noticing your own physical sensations.

Seeing auras Auras, in this day of scientific probing into the psychic, are usually identified as electromagnetic fields. For everyday purposes, auras are the colors that some of us automatically, others of us sporadically, and some of us never see around each other. They are clues to personality and event.

Set up a mirror with a chair directly in front of it, and place a small candle in a corner of the room away from the mirror and in back of the chair. With the dim glimmer of the candle the only illumination in the room, sit down on the chair in front of the mirror— make sure the candle is not reflected in it. Spend about 10 minutes at each session in this dark room just looking toward your reflection in the mirror. (You should not be able to see your body's reflection well.) As you allow your eyes to do what they want to, you may see flashes of color.

Once you know what to look for, check for similar flashes of color (in different shades) around other people at other times. Notice the feeling in your eyes and your body when you get those flashes. Re-create that feeling when you look for colors around others. Practice and patience are what make this exercise work. A word of warning: excitement with success often makes the flash of color disappear as the energy you were using is sidetracked into feeding your delight. Stay calm and focused as you look.

You might keep a record of which colors you see around whom; although there are many books on aura color, remember that we each have our own light filters, so that where one sees blue another may see green.

Telepathy Telepathy is cheaper than telephone, but it's not as reliable at this point. With a little work, though, who knows? Maybe you can cut your phone bill.

Any place will work to practice telepathy once you have a willing partner. (Some of the best sendings and receivings have been from a bathroom.) The most important elements of success are time and sharing.

Decide with a partner or a group that you're

Illustrations by Howard Saunders

going to work on telepathy. Then with one person chosen as the sender and the others as receivers, pick a date and time for transmission.

Let's say you're the sender. You decide that Tuesday at high noon you will send a message. As sender, choose anything you wish: a nature scene, a scent, a taste, a feeling, a symbol —anything. Picture the receivers in your mind's eye and imagine them receiving you clearly. Then focus on your choice of material; work to let nothing interfere with you as you focus on it for the agreed-on time, anywhere from five to 15 minutes. (If you do drift, keep a record of any drift thoughts or pictures, since they may be what your receivers pick up.)

Receivers begin by picturing you sending, then work on being receptive to whatever they get mentally, emotionally, physically, perceptively. Receivers need to make careful notes of what they get.

When you meet later, receivers tell what they got, one by one, before you tell what you sent. Compare what was happening and then make a date to do it again. Do not expect immediate or continual success at first. Even the best ESP people are not "on" all the time. Let it be a game; having fun will open the way for you to work more fully and quickly than if you're deadly serious about it.

–Billie Hobart

Get Back Away From That Pool, Narcissus!

"Americans have fallen into the deep hole of self and they like it there," says Dr. Irma Klombull, founder and director of the Klombull Institute, a nonprofit foundation dedicated to the task of "consciousness lowering." It is Dr. Klombull's opinion that thousands upon thousands of Americans are getting so infatuated by their own thoughts and emotions that they are finding it hard to pay attention to anything else.

She points—persuasively—to these alarming case histories from the Institute's files:

● A New Jersey stockbroker attended a month of sexual awareness-heightening sessions—and two months later had lost 40 pounds and was a male prostitute on Seventh Avenue. "I didn't mind a little honey and peanut butter spread here and there, but when he came at me in the shower with a can of whipped cream, I kicked him out," said his wife, who is filing for divorce.

● A brilliant sociology graduate student in Los Angeles abandoned her studies and went to live in a lean-to in the San Gabriel Mountains because, she said, "Anyone else is such a drag compared to what I've become to myself. I mean, I'm so much more fascinating than anyone else—wow! Learning about myself is a really profound experience—it's like, you know, a natural high."

● A second-grade teacher in Kansas at-

tended an encounter group during summer school and in the fall returned to her job with an itch for full and frank disclosure of her inner life. She was fired by the school board two months later after she invaded the men's room to share with the superintendent of schools her latest feelings about teaching.

"We've got to learn all over again how not to take ourselves seriously in an indiscriminate way," Dr. Klombull insists. Paraphrasing theologian Paul Tillich's famous definition of grace, Dr. Klombull suggests that *psychological* grace may be "accepting that sometimes you are *not* accepted, simply because you *shouldn't* be."

She offers these specific guidelines for those who wonder whether they've gone off the deep end:

● If your sexual activities are legal, you probably shouldn't worry about them.

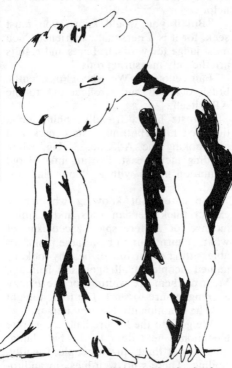

● If you find yourself speaking in dead earnest, in absolute seriousness, more than once a day—you're overdoing it. No one can be earnest any more than once a day, Dr. Klombull believes, without being tiresome to others and a danger to himself.

● If you live around San Francisco, watch out. "People in the San Francisco Bay Area take themselves far more seriously than people anywhere else in the country," she says, "with the possible exception of the U.S. Senate."

Dr. Klombull is fond of quoting the advice the Greek seer Tiresias had for antiquity's most famous self-absorbed youth: "Narcissus will live to a ripe old age—provided that he never knows himself."

"Let's face it," she concludes, "very few people have any ideas or feelings worth mucking about in. Most of us would be much better off just getting on with it."

–R. C. Smith

Intellectual Jogging

When you've been a long-distance runner all your life, there comes the day when you begin to wonder what it's all been about.

I could feel myself becoming an automaton, calculating my physical condition, figuring intermediate and final goals—each improvement I made was a necessary stepping stone. My weekends were usually filled with hard training or competitive racing. Racing is a largely solitary undertaking that made me very nervous; there is little camaraderie except in the moment of relief that follows pushing the body to its limits.

I was totally preoccupied with winning. No wonder that hiking through the woods with a group of friends on a balmy spring day seemed to me quite frivolous.

But then some friends, more intellectual than athletic, began showing some interest in running, and I started jogging with them. From the outset, our running together was a pleasant ritual. In fact, the sensation of another person's presence and energy, after so many months of lonely running, prompted me—and some of the others—to write poems about it.

I began to try to understand what passed through people's minds when they were running. My main interest was in the impressions of people who had been jogging only a short time. I even tried an experiment once during a teaching session about running and creativity. When members of the group arrived, I asked them not to say anything to each other, and I suggested that each person jog one lap around the track, allowing their thoughts free rein. After this run each was to write down his thoughts during the run —haphazard though they might be.

A long line of joggers made their way around the oval track, and when we had each written down our personal impressions, we read what we had written to the group. And then we all ran together for 10 minutes, enjoying each other more because we shared a certain special pool of thought.

I think our cities and towns would be better places to live if people made a point of getting together to jog—which would be good for their bodies—and to share the thoughts they had while running with the others —which would bring them closer to the group. There is something of the tense, striving long-distance runner in every city dweller who works long and sometimes boring hours at his job. There is nothing like jogging with others to liberate you.

–Mike Spino

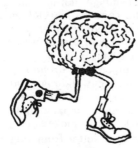

Miracles at Virginia Beach

By Dean Riddlewell

A hotbed of psychic activity in the United States? Naaaaw! On a Balinese mountaintop, maybe, but in Virginia Beach, Va.? Afraid so: that's the home of the Cayce Institute, where they say enlightenment is rampant.

You hear about seekers laboring up mountains to bring forth a mouse, simmering in dark deserts aching to glimpse a ragged sage, wandering in dank woods risking flesh and wit for a pry at the crack between the worlds.

As yet there's no occult Dun and Bradstreet (hot tip?) and we naturally rely on our prejudices. No one is skeptical any more about believing bizarre stories of spiritual enlightenment in Burma or Mexico, but when it comes to the good ol' U.S.A.—well, come on, use your common sense!

And that brings us, sharp-eyed, hands on our billfolds, to Virginia Beach, the vortex of one of America's biggest psychic research operations.

We deplane at Norfolk in the late afternoon, keeping a steady lookout for glassy stares and three-card monte men. Mainly, we see sailors. We go outside to the taxis to ride to the beach, a few miles east.

"Goin' out to the Cayce Institute, eh?" asks the friendly cab driver. Indeed we are. The Cayce Institute is more formally the Association for Research and Enlightenment (ARE), a multidimensional psychic development organization whose "guru" was a "psychic" named Edgar Cayce (pronounced "Casey").

"Yep. You know anything about it up there?"

"Oh, yeah, sure. Bunch of weirdies up there. Hell, I must take two, three people a day over. Why, I even took Jeannie Dixon up there a couple of times!" he announces proudly, naming the clairvoyant who predicted President Kennedy's assassination.

"What do they do up there, anyway?"

"Oh, I guess they do all sorts of way-out things. They're always talkin' about their former lives and such. Enough to make the hair rise all up your back!"

We arrive and walk into The Marshalls, a seemingly normal enough motel across the road from ARE headquarters. To get to our room we have to skirt the swimming pool, and as we do, a lilting female voice calls out:

"Be sure you walk *around* the water— not everyone can walk *on* it, you know!"

A little dazed, we find our room. We unclog our ears, unpack and open an ARE booklet we've picked up.

It contains a letter from Edgar Cayce to all "tourists" at the ARE.

"Neither I, nor the Association . . . has anything to sell, or any instant answers," it reads.

"What we do have is a body of information. Of this information I can only say that in my life and in the lives of many of those who have come in contact with the readings there seems to be much that is a help.

"But if you would know, you must seek, for it is a personal experience. You must judge for yourself. Facts and results are the only measuring rods."

Fair enough. We shoot our cuffs, brush our hair and stroll across to the ARE itself.

It rests like a friendly sphinx on a flowered hill, abutting a state park and overlooking the Atlantic. A big, white building facing east, like an inflated old plantation house with a jillion windows. Solid.

We enter, not knowing whether to expect thick Persian rugs and jasmine incense, or austere spare asceticism, or what. It turns out to be a large, comfortable sitting room full of healthy-looking, tanned people of all ages and haircuts. Most of them are waiting for the Friday evening lecture to start. The topic tonight is "The Emotionally Healthy Person."

We go into the lecture hall, a concrete blockhouse next door to the big plantation. About three dozen people, friendly, smiling. There's no weirdness in auditoriums. Have to pay 50 cents each, student rate, or $1.50 for adults. If you sign up for a weekly deal the whole shebang of 27 lectures costs $25, or $35 for a couple. Each week, the general theme of the lectures changes. This week it is "The Golden Age." (Other themes: "Contemporary Issues," "Psychic Research and Psychic Development," "Living the Joyous Life," "A Personal Program for Soul Development," and so on.)

I meet a very nice couple. The wife is heavily into it, come to find her God. The husband is a retired lawyer, logical, good-natured and used to all manner of human weirdness. He's just along for the ride, and maybe to take a few baths in the ARE saunas.

"Oh, my, I just bubble over down here," the wife bubbles. "Why, it's amazing—we came down South to escape the snow upstate and accidentally fell into the ARE! We've been here three weeks now. It's simply amazing!"

During the weekend we loll on the deserted, clean sand beach. It is late April, right before the season, so both the beach and the motel are relatively unpopulated.

When we tired of the beach we would browse in the very well-stocked ARE library, or hit one of the many excellent seafood restaurants in town. Virginia Beach is all-out for tourists, crammed with fine restaurants, motels and curio shops. There's also a special herbalist who stocks the Edgar Cayce remedies.

On Monday a new bunch of tourists arrive wanting their heads unfolded. Most of them sign up for a week of "classes" and I join them. We go into the lecture hall to listen to "The Trustworthiness of the Edgar Cayce Readings." It's very interesting; the classic clairvoyant legend with a modern twist: the young boy who shows psychic ability, the townsfolk who get hip to him as a local wise man and healer, the newspaper stories, the visiting doctor. Then, 43 years of intensive service work—going into trances to heal sick people by mail—ending with Cayce's death in 1945. Over 14,000 readings, most of them medical, all of them literally "incredibly" full of information on healing and psychic phenomena. A truly phenomenal number of cures.

All the readings were taken down verbatim. Along with follow-up research, they have been put out for public perusal in the ARE library. Numerous doctors who come to the beach to debunk have ended up sweating far into the night and finally joining the ARE staff.

And of course, there are the predictions: Cayce predicted the finding of an Essene colony on the north shore of the Dead Sea years before the discovery of the Dead Sea Scrolls—which confirmed his forecast. He would often read off all 52 cards of an ordinary shuffled deck. He predicted the 1929 stockmarket crash six months in advance, and in 1926 was predicting California earthquakes in the 1960s and 1970s.

As for skepticism, I'd say almost anyone who makes the trip here is at least willing to accept it all as a working hypothesis.

Why? A redhaired lady told us: "I'm so sick of living someone else's life! All my life I was actually living my *husband's* life—not my own. Now *I* want to take control over my life, and do what *I* really want to do!"

What really leads people to encounter groups, or to Esalen, or Arabs to Mecca? That old eternal search for something higher. The search for one's self. A search for an unchanging truth beyond one's body, emotions or mind. Isn't this the essence of tourism, to seek out far places and then bring it all back home? □

A Subjective Drug Report From

STONED MOUNTAIN

	MARIJUANA	MESCALINE	ACID	COCAINE
Origin	Cannabis plant	Cactus	Synthetic	Coca leaves
Average Amount Taken	Varies	350 milligrams	150-200 micrograms	Varies
How Taken	Inhaled/swallowed	Swallowed	Swallowed/injected	Sniffed/injected
Duration	3 - 4 hours	12 - 14 hours	10 - 12 hours	4 hours
Effects of Average Amount	Relaxation, breakdown inhibitions, alteration of perceptions, euphoria, increased appetite	Perceptual changes—especially visual; increased energy, hallucinations, panic		Feelings of self-confidence and power; intense exhilaration
Effects of Overdose	Panic, stupor	Anxiety, hallucinations, psychosis, exhaustion, tremors, vomiting, panic		Irritability, depression, psychosis
Effects of Continued Excessive Use	Fatigue, psychosis	Increased delusions and panic, psychosis		Damage to nasal septum and blood vessels; psychosis
Alice	Everything slows down. I'm thinking fiendishly. Out of synch with people. They seem funnier, more dramatically sinister when I'm high. Often I feel like laughing and talking elaborately but if that doesn't happen, I tend to turn inside and stay there. Sex can be powerful, tangential, unconscious or else cross-currents keep it from happening at all.	Lifts me gently into a sensational world of color and cartoon and fluidity. Reds, blues, greens, yellows, melting like rainbows. It urges me to the desert and the sea, or under it. Once a wave smashed me against a rock because it was so lacy and intricate I didn't realize it was actually approaching. Things generally playful and benign.	Acid I love. Pushes me out on extensive journeys. Comes in stages: (1) adjust to queasiness, time and space displacement; (2) loving some aspect of objective world, water, a cat, Beethoven, a friend, my hands; (3) outerspace, visions, fantastic horrors, revelations on revelations on revelations, astounding; (4) coming down slowly very relaxed, tasting food maybe, readjusting. On acid, the world is always dazzling, tricky, often horrifying, but I always choose it and agree to die or whatever is necessary.	Feel clear, open, hollowed out, none of the muddling as in grass. Words come easily because thoughts fall into clean geometric shapes. Funny taste in the back of my throat, numbness. Sex can be fun. I think of cocaine and wish I was rich.
Michael	Tremendous variations according to quantity, quality. Three responses for me: (1) the mind unravels like the inside of a golf ball and thoughts become four-dimensional; (2) I become a quietly raving sex maniac; (3) I go to sleep.	My favorite. The highs without the distortions of acid and no roller-coaster lows. Cerebral and sensual at once. Exciting and relaxing. Feelings of well-being and compassion for friends, enemies, all planetary beings and any other beings too.	Right into the belly of the monster and out the butt-end of an angel. Savage, celestial vignettes of myself racing by like a film off its sprockets, senses become mirrors, mind like a Jackson Pollock painting. Paranoia—euphoria; the two sides of a coin flipping through the air. One minute a god pinned beneath a speck of dust, the next a maniac about to fly across Puget Sound. Thirty hours of pituitary gymnastics, and never a dull moment!	Jet fuel in a go-cart. I rap for hours and lose at least five pounds. The mind is a dervish on a tight-rope and never misses a beat of the cellular music. No sexual desire, no desire at all—just a runny nose and my brain clogged with sparks. Great!
Elaine	I used to smoke a lot but I don't use it much anymore, mostly for the reasons and fears I mentioned about acid. It's fun and pleasant and sometimes exciting but I seem to be very far away from the people I'm with. We may all be laughing but we're laughing at different things. Sometimes my hearing is very weak when I'm stoned. Still, I would not put it down—I've had some very fine times on it.	Some mescaline trips I've had have been as intense and religious as the acid trips. Generally, mescaline is a much more benevolent and less jarring drug than acid. It gives me a very pleasant sense of peace and warmth. Time seems to stand still and colors and sounds are exquisite. Very nice for sexual experiences too.	Very often, when I'm on acid, I have a strong feeling that even though it may be beautiful and exciting, it may not be real. This tends to bring me down and I have had several very bad trips because of it. I see brilliant colors, hear lots of sounds and have an extremely heightened sense of awareness. But these things don't seem to mean too much to me. Several times I have had what I considered truly religious experiences on acid but as the days passed, the effects have always faded.	I was pretty inarticulate when I tried to talk yet my thoughts were sometimes crystal clear and the inside of my nose felt like an ice cave. Everything and everyone seems rather friendly. You can have a good time in bed.
David	Grass does very little for me these days. Maybe I've grown immune since I've been smoking 10 or 15 joints a day. Maybe the quality just ain't what it used to be. It's nice for relaxing and slowing down. Also, it enhances the senses nicely.	[No comments submitted.]	On my first acid trip, I thought I was God. On my second acid trip I thought I was Jesus. On my third trip I thought I was Napoleon and on my fourth trip I thought I was a toadstool. It's been going down that way, trip after trip, until my last acid trip when I thought I was Richard M. Nixon and I'm not going to take any more acid.	If you can imagine somebody from another planet watching the "Dating Game" on television and reporting back to their planet what Earth was about, then you can understand the kind of information my brain gets from my senses when I'm on coke.

ALL THESE DRUGS ARE ILLEGAL. The maximum Federal penalty for the possession of illegal drugs is one year in prison and $5,000 fine for the first offense and two years in jail and a $10,000 fine for subsequent offenses. Of course, much harsher penalties apply to the sale of these drugs. However, most drug convictions are made under state laws, which vary widely and arbitrarily and are often stricter than the Federal laws.

An Introduction to the Occult

Here's some basic information about Tarot, witchcraft, magic, alchemy, palmistry, crystal balls, spiritualism, ESP and Don Juan.

Tarot The Tarot is a picture book of wisdom, disguised as a deck of cards. It can be used for instruction or divination. No one knows how it works, but if used correctly it definitely *does* work. It is recommended that you consult it only for serious problems —otherwise, it will tell you more than you care to know.

To learn to read the cards, you should get someone to teach you. Failing that, there are several books available. The best beginning guide is *The Tarot* by Paul Foster Case. The most comprehensive is probably *The Book of Thoth* by Aleister Crowley, but it is extremely arcane.

You also need a deck. There are many types available. The most popular is called the "Rider" deck, designed by Arthur Edward Waite; the most ornate is called the "OTO" deck, designed by Aleister Crowley.

Witchcraft Someone once defined witchcraft as "magic without science." It is a kind of craft, like woodworking, and it must likewise be learned from someone who practices it. Books won't really help much here.

Witches cast spells, they really do, and the spells often really work, but not always. Witches can also locate lost objects, exorcise ghosts and generally read minds and events. They gather into covens, or societies, and are not particularly secretive these days.

It is still not definitely decided whether a male witch is a warlock.

Magic This is a science. There are definite experiments and records of them, which can be duplicated by anyone who follows the correct procedure. The procedure involves a long period of self-training and meditation, covering branches of knowledge from ancient languages to celestial mechanics.

Magic is generally self-taught, but you must have some kind of guide or idea of where to start. There are many books. Aleister Crowley wrote *Magick in Theory and Practice*, which pretends to be simple but is very difficult and full of snares. There is also a book called *A Treatise on White Magic* that some people find very useful and informative. It's by Alice Bailey. An excellent guide to cabalistic magic is *The Sacred Magic of Abra-Melin the Mage*, by Abraham the Jew, edited by S.L. Macgregor-Mathers.

Alchemy This is more than trying to turn lead into gold, and more than just the ancestor of modern chemistry. According to Carl Jung, the ancient alchemical writings are disguised guidebooks to discovery of the soul. (Alchemists had to disguise them to evade charges of witchcraft.)

A serious study of alchemy will take you into symbols, linguistics and general psychology. So studying Jung's works, mainly *Alchemical Studies* and *Psychology and Alchemy*, is probably the best place to begin. These books will provide plenty of food for thought and give an idea of where to go for seconds.

The practice of alchemy is strictly unorganized, and is carried on in secret laboratories. Alchemists wear high conical hats and robes decorated with crescent moons.

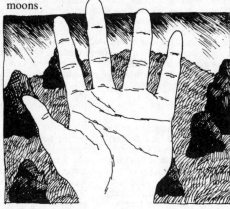

Palmistry The art of divination through the lines in the hand. Actually, a good palm reader studies the shape of the hand and fingers as well.

A topflight palmist can tell you exactly what year which events will happen to you: "In your 27th year you will learn to speak Malay. In your 28th year you'll forget it entirely, until you meet a dark woman with almond eyes. . . ."

Palmists can be very accurate.

There are scores of books on palmistry—you can peruse them at any occult bookstore. There are also scores of palmists, who charge what their market will bear. But to give an example, an excellent reader in Los Angeles charges $25 for a reading that takes you through your whole life and lasts about two hours.

Crystal balls The art of divining with them is called scrying. The only way to learn it is to get a crystal ball and look into it.

The size of the ball does not matter—you should pick one that feels right for you. They come in all kinds of sizes. It should be

kept—traditionally, anyway—in a silk coverlet inside an amber box.

A good crystal gazer is more of a psychic than a diviner. It's not so scientific a method as Tarot cards, but scrying can be very accurate, and the crystal can accumulate tremendous power.

Spiritualism The practice of communicating with discarnate spirits. It's still an open question how much of this is authentic and how much is fraud. Houdini spent his whole life exposing spiritualists. But he also allowed that they might be real—he didn't know. There's an interesting story about him: he left a message, known only to his wife, and instructed her to try to contact him after his death. His wife did this, using the famous medium Arthur Ford. The first reports said they got in contact and that he gave her the correct message. There was a great hubbub.

But then, for some reason, she recanted the whole thing. She said it never happened and that she didn't really get the message at all. So it's still an open question.

There are many spiritualist societies, in all cities, and several spiritualist churches.

ESP The general term for any kind of extraordinary, or "extra-sensory," perception. There is now an immense literature of a more-or-less scientific nature on this phenomenon. Everyone claims to know something about it; no one really does.

The granddaddy of modern ESP is Joseph Banks Rhine, a guy with a Ph.D. who used to be at Duke University. He wrote a book called *Parapsychology: Frontier Science of the Mind*. It's one of the basic books in the field.

To cultivate your own ESP can be very difficult, in spite of what some gurus claim. It is said that ESP is a natural by-product of a correctly conducted program of "soul development." What I always wonder is this: what happens when you read someone else's mind? What do you do with the information?

Don Juan Whether *he* really exists or not, there are a great many *brujos* in Mexico. There's even a whole town of them: Tateposco, near Guadalajara. But if you visit—beware. A *brujo* told me the last foreigners who went to visit found nothing, but on the way back they were attacked by an army of three-foot-tall clay men!

–*David Saltman*

Illustrations by Sandra Forrest

Talking to Ghosts

This happened in England. We lived in this perfectly ordinary flat behind the railroad yard. Airline stewardesses lived upstairs. Nothing could be more plain, less esoteric.

One night we came home from someplace or other with two friends of ours and their dog. Let's see—their names were Francine and Robert, and the dog's name was Simba. My name is Dave, and my wife is Barbara.

You know how it is when you come into your own house. You mill around for a few minutes, hanging up the coats, going to the john and doing things like that. So there was a little milling around. I was in the bathroom, and when I came out I saw Robert standing in the corner in the most peculiar manner. He was like a dunce, with his back curved and his head right in the corner. I said, "What the hell . . . !"

Robert said to me, "Come here. See if you feel anything."

I didn't get it, but I went over to the corner and got the shock of my life. It was like walking into a huge magnetic field. My hair actually stood on end. It was as if I had walked into a rubber wall or something. I was completely stonkered.

Suddenly, "it" was gone. The corner felt perfectly ordinary again.

"What the hell's going on?" I exclaimed to Robert.

"I don't know."

We all held a conference. Simba was not included, but she was absolutely freaking out, running around like . . . well, like a mad dog. Usually she was obedient and well trained.

At the conference, hastily assembled around a card table in the living room, we decided we had a poltergeist. None of us exactly knew what they were, although Robert and Francine had had neighbors in Greece who had said they had one too. Anyway, we figured that's what it was, and we had to decide how to handle it. After all, this was our house.

We decided to reason with it.

Maybe we got the idea from the Ouija board or something, but we took a drinking glass and turned it upside down. All four of us touched it very lightly with our fingertips.

Then we nervously and a little foolishly called out, "OK, poltergeist! If you want to communicate with us, we're ready!"

We sat a minute while nothing happened. There was a little discussion about how to handle the powwow: should one person speak for all of us, or should we take turns asking questions, or what? No one knew the correct procedure, and there wasn't time to call up the library.

Suddenly, we all felt it. The ghost had come in to see what was happening. It was like a cold wind, sort of, and I began to get the shakes a little bit.

We hastily improvised that a "yes" answer would be indicated by the glass moving over to the right; "no" would be to the left.

Finally, one of us called out: "Do you want to communicate with us?"

We waited. Nothing. And then, slowly, the glass began to move over to the right.

Each one of us knows *we* didn't move it.

By bits and pieces, by yeses and nos, we gradually built up a picture of this strange presence, Mr. Ghost. (I felt it was a Mister.) It seemed that he didn't mean us any harm. He was just interested in the *site* of our flat, it turned out, but he wouldn't elaborate. Hidden treasure? A coveted object lost? Who knew what poltergeists wanted? When we tried to probe more deeply, a very strange thing happened: the glass would start moving in circles, bigger and bigger and faster and faster, and it wouldn't stop until we changed the subject.

This went on for hours.

Eventually, something dawned on me. *A ghost can be dumb.* And *a ghost can lie.* I started to get the feeling that this Mr. Ghost character was just playing with us. That gave the thing a different slant, and suddenly I was very tired.

We made an appointment to communicate again the next night, same time, same station. But Barbara and I stayed out late that night, and missed the date. When we finally came home, Robert and Francine were asleep. We went to bed, and nothing strange happened except that at three in the morning we both woke up with a start. There was something out there wailing like a banshee.

We left England the next day and never went back.

—David Saltman

L am half inclined to think we are all ghosts. . . . They are not actually alive in us; but there they are dormant, all the same, and we can never be rid of them. Whenever I take up a newspaper and read it, I fancy I see ghosts creeping between the lines. There must be ghosts all over the world. They must be as countless as grains of sand, it seems to me. And we are so miserably afraid of the light, all of us.

—HENRIK IBSEN

GET YOUR DEGREE IN ESP

The following institutions have courses of study in ESP and parapsychology. Some of them grant accredited degrees.

Andhra University, Department of Psychology and Parapsychology, Waltair, Visakhapatam 3, India. Grants Ph.D. in parapsychology.

University of Virginia, Medical Center, Division of Parapsychology, Department of Psychiatry, Charlottesville, Va. 22901. Offers several fellowships and one professorship in parapsychology.

Institut für Grenzgebiete der Psychologie, 78 Freiburg in Breisgau, Eichhalde 12, West Germany. Grants graduate degrees in psychology for work in parapsychology.

Manchester College, Oxford University, Religious Experience Research Unit, Oxford OX2 6JU, England.

Rajasthan University, Jaipur, India. Has Faculty of Parapsychology, offers graduate degrees. *—The Editors*

ESP in Holland

Holland is famous for its wooden shoes, windmills, cheese, tulips and canals. One of its *least*-known national institutions is the extraordinary Parapsychology Institute at the 338-year-old University of Utrecht. It is the world's leading research center for the study of extra-sensory perception (ESP) and nothing in America, including the former Parapsychology Laboratory at Duke University in North Carolina, can compare with it.

The Dutch institute, housed in an unpretentious remodeled 16th-century building on a winding cobblestone street in the sleepy university town of Utrecht, has on hand more documented case histories on ESP than any school in the world. The institute conducts experiments with "paragnosts" (vulgarly called "clairvoyants" or "psychics" in this country) who help the police solve crimes, locate missing children and find lost documents, and who identify ancient historical objects for scholars. (The best-known and most gifted paragnost is Gerard Croiset, who, helping American police officials, has shed light upon crimes in California, Illinois, New York, Ohio and elsewhere—and has done it from the other side of the Atlantic.)

The director of the Parapsychology Institute is Professor W.H.C. Tenhaeff, who probably knows more about paranormal phenomena than any living investigator. A bearded, pipe-smoking 79-year-old scholar who speaks six languages fluently, Professor Tenhaeff was named to the world's first university chair in parapsychology in 1953. Today he still works seven days a week in his simple, book-lined study. The professor welcomes visits from serious students of parapsychology from America and elsewhere. But write him first at the Parapsychology Institute, Springweg 5, Utrecht, The Netherlands.

Story-Telling: Learning to Be a Bodymind

Man is a story-telling animal. As our primitive ancestors sat around the fire carving spearheads and eating blackberries they told stories that in time were woven into a tapestry of myth and legend. These tales were the first encyclopedia of human knowledge. They explained where the world came from, why there were people, why snakes have no legs, why conch shells are sacred, why coyotes howl at night and why the gods put fire and death on earth.

Story-telling is more than merely a way to explain away the inexplicable, and it's more than just fun. Story-telling is also a wonderfully simple and useful way to get to know yourself better.

Find a friend or lover to listen, and tell your multiple stories: stories of your childhood, your family, your visions, your roots, your dreams. *Be* all those characters who wander around in your head. Start to really *appreciate* yourself, in every sense of the word.

The Present

If we were fully integrated persons we might refer to ourselves as *being* bodyminds rather than as *having* bodies. You are a body in a given time and place. The way you experience your body reflects your sense of existence.

Try this: take a large sheet of paper and an assortment of colored pencils and draw a picture of yourself in any way you want. It might be symbolic or literal, clothed or nude, a portrait or a full figure.

Now assume that the paper on which you just drew yourself is the world. What does your body-image tell you about your world? For instance: do you fill all or part of your space? How realistic or symbolic is your representation? Is your outline sharp, fuzzy, disconnected, flowing? Is your figure open or closed? What parts of your body are missing? out of proportion? hidden? What colors predominate? Are you clothed or nude? Is your body designed to be seen? touched?

Secrets come in all sizes and shapes, from adultery to xenophobia, but they tend to cluster around the emotional centers of shame and elation. Many of the things we feel, desire or do seem too shameful to be shared. We hide from public view fear, guilt, despair, impotence, cruelty, self-hatred, ugliness and coldness of heart. But we also conceal our tender ideals, grandiose visions and ecstasies.

Sometimes you can dispel shame or expand pleasure by sharing your secrets. What are the secrets that you never (or only on airplanes) share with anyone? Which secrets would you be relieved to share? With whom? What will become of them, once told?

In fantasy, allow yourself to be as weak, passive and ineffectual as you have ever feared yourself to be. Remember the times when you felt most small and helpless.

Create a story in which you become the fulfillment of your ideal self: you are strong, loving, beautiful, brilliant, etc. What do you do with your power? What gives you the most pleasure?

The Past

There are always good guys and bad guys. Stories and personalities would be dull without them. It helps to exaggerate good and evil and to create clear targets, because in real life the best and the worst are so entwined that we usually can't tell which is which. Exaggeration pulls apart what life joins together.

Trace the history of the heroes and heroines you have admired and imitated as personality models. Begin with your earliest heroes and bring the tale up to date. Whom did you admire when you were five, 15, 21? What heroes and heroines did you find in books? in the movies? in life around you? Whose costumes did you wear? Whose speech did you imitate?

Do the same with the villains (dark, sinful, unforgettable) in your life. Have your heroes and villains switched places over the years? If they could speak to you now, what would they say to you?

Our inner time sense records intensity and importance rather than duration: an October afternoon of love among the dunes may be written larger in memory than months surrounding it. When you put together the story of your life you face the central question of how to punctuate time. What moments will you isolate and give symbolic importance, single out for dramatic effect?

Choose 10 scenes from your past that were important, pivotal events in your life and describe them. Detail the circumstances, characters and backgrounds of each scene.

How are the scenes you have chosen representative of your present life? How did they change or affect you? How has your view of them altered over the years?

Make an outline of your autobiography. What are the major divisions? chapter titles and subsections? the title? What stages does your life seem naturally to fall into? When did you cease to be a child? When did you become old? What personal, family and social rituals or celebrations were involved in changing stages?

After you've outlined your autobiography, put it aside and do another that uses entirely different organizing principles, chapter titles, pivotal events, key persons and time scales. Turn your story inside out; try a new way of punctuating time. If your life story has the feel of a tragedy flip it over and make it a comedy; if it sounds like a romance change the tone slightly so that it is ironic; if it has a pathetic ring turn it into a heroic tale.

The Future

Fantasies put us in touch with our repressed or unrealized desires. Imagine that you have a fatal disease and have one month left to live. What do you still want to do? How will you spend the month of life that remains to you? Give yourself full energy, plenty of money and freedom from pain to the end. What will be the epitaph on your tombstone?

Good news! You've been granted a reprieve. You have a long time to live—10, 20, 70 years. What will you do with your time now?

Draw a floor plan of a house (or space) you would like to be living in 10 years hence. Who lives with you? What are the physical surroundings like? What is the mood of the place? How do you spend your time inside and outside of this house? with whom? What is your work? What feelings do you experience that were strange to you 10 years ago?

When you have done this fantasy put it aside and do it another way. Give yourself a variety of alternative futures to move around in. You'll begin to see where you've come from, where you're at, where you're going.

—Anne Valley Fox

Mind Games

With the help of a new book of mental exercises, you'll be able to die and look back on your own life, relive experiences you had as a small child or transform yourself into a mythical animal.

Mind Games (Delta, $2.65) may be the most systematic and practical system for achieving altered states of consciousness (ASCs) to come out of this era of spiritual tripping. It's not a game book in the sense that it's light entertainment; the authors expect you to play with deadly seriousness, preparation and rigorous attention to procedure.

The mind games' creators are Robert Masters and Jean Houston (*Varieties of Psychedelic Experience*) who together direct New York's Foundation for Mind Research and who for years have been trying out these games on research subjects and friends.

To play, you first assemble a group of five to 11 people who get along well together. One, who should be a good "practical psychologist," serves as guide. By reading the exercises, written in purposely hypnotic language, the guide induces trance and then, by suggesting settings and sensations, helps you to move into non-ordinary realities. All exercises, the authors insist, are safe and effective for the "average person."

Playing the mind games, they promise, should make you more imaginative, more creative and more able to "gain access to your capacities" until "we one day look back astounded at the impoverished world of consciousness we once shared, and supposed to be the real world, our officially defined and defended 'reality.' "

–Susan Sands

Psychological Exercises From the Guru's Den

Here are a few exercises they do in certain wiggy esoteric schools:

Say the Gettysburg address while counting backwards from 100 . . . by threes. Recite the address out loud, but do the counting in your head.

Break your habits by exaggerating them. If you eat too much candy, eat twice as much the next day. Then abstain the third day. The fourth day, eat half a piece, then abstain from the second one. Eat half the third piece and abstain from the fourth. On the fifth piece, eat two. Skip the sixth, seventh and eighth. Then get on a "J" bus and have the driver open the doors at 19th Street. You will be contacted.

Rub your stomach and pat your head, noticing your breathing at the same time. Don't try to change your breathing—just notice the way it is naturally. Then, while still doing all that, with your feet go heel-toe, heel-toe, alternating right and left feet. Continue for five minutes, then shift: rub your head, pat your stomach, notice your heartbeat and continue with the feet.

How to Become a Hypnotist

Part of being a good hypnotist is picking good subjects. My first subject was my mother. She's a fairly suggestible type of person, and also would do anything to have her son be a success. She was also the only person available.

I had learned the technique by getting hypnotized myself. I had Mother relax in a reclining chair. For "focusing," I used a piece of paper with a dark dot in the middle, which I taped to a wall five feet in front of her. I hung the paper high enough on the wall so she'd have to look up a bit. (This causes relaxation for the eyes.) Next, I set the stage by clearing away any distracting objects. And then I got her psyched up by telling her what to expect.

The rap went something like this: "This is going to be a very relaxing but extraordinary experience, if you cooperate. The best hypnotist in the world can't hypnotize a person against her will. In a sense, you must hypnotize yourself; I'm only a catalyst here to help. I can tell you the instructions, but unless you repeat them to yourself and *want* to be hypnotized, nothing will happen and we'll only be wasting our time." What mother could resist that?

"There is nothing to be afraid of, and I won't let you do anything crazy or embarrassing. I won't go into anything personal about your past or present life, but instead just give you a taste of what hypnosis is by doing sensory exercises and interesting feats. You will be in control at all times. You can get up and leave, if you want to.

"You will be aware of what is happening the whole time. Yet you will be so relaxed that when we're through you'll feel fresh and alert, like you've just awakened from a good night's sleep. Just concentrate on the dot and my voice, nothing else. Are there any questions?

"All right. We're ready to begin."

During "induction" a good hypnotist pays close attention to the subject's body cues and feeds this information right back. For example, you say to the subject: "Your eyes are wet and burning," or, "Your eyelids feel heavy, like there were weights on them, and it will feel soo-o good to close them and relax."

The hypnotist should speak slowly and with frequent pauses. If you see that the subject's eyes are still open, feed back: "That's right, keep your eyes open until you feel like closing them." Make the situation work for you—if there's a disturbing noise, say: "Any noise you hear will make you more hypnotized and relaxed."

When my mother's eyes closed, I suggested: "I am going to count to ten. With each number I say, you will slip deeper and deeper into hypnosis. When I get to ten, you will be completely hypnotized."

This is the technique that worked on my mother, and I've used it successfully ever

since. The important thing is not to mimic the exact words, but to get the general flavor across, molding the technique to suit the individual.

To bring a subject *out* of hypnosis, simply reverse the induction technique. (There is a myth about the stubborn subject who refuses to come out of hypnosis. This is rare, and even the most reluctant can be coaxed by hinting you're going to splash some water on him.)

Hypnotizing your friends (or your mother) can be a lot of fun—for example, try this on somebody:

"Now . . . you are going back in time . . . way back to the fifth grade. You are sitting in class . . . and it's a beautiful day. The teacher is talking . . . and passes out papers and pencil. [You hand them to the subject.] Your teacher tells you to write down your name . . . and age."

Usually, the subject scrawls out his name and writes his age as 10 or 11. If you keep regressing down to third grade and first, you end up with a steadily deteriorating handwriting that totally blows your subject's mind when he sees it after the session.

Or tell the subject he won't be able to smell, and then place a bottle of alcohol or perfume or wintergreen or turpentine under his nose briefly. Wow! It really works!

Then, you reverse it: "OK, now you can smell." The subject usually responds with a wave of the hand and a grimace: "Whew! Get that junk away!"

But clinical "digging up" of a person's past should *only* be done by a trained psychotherapist. The sensory stuff is fun, but if you get too heavy the results will be more than you bargained for.

Not everyone can be hypnotized successfully. People are different, and even someone who's a good subject at one time might be totally intransigent later on. It's one of those things where sometimes it works, and sometimes it doesn't.

–Ron De Stefano

EXIT

. . . from Debtor's Prison

We're all debtors. They say there are no more debtors' prisons, but anyone who's gotten in over his head knows that's a lie.

Here's how to get out, gracefully. It's called Chapter XIII of the Bankruptcy Act, and it's one of those rare laws that can be used to the advantage of the average person.

Essentially, when you file a "Chapter XIII," you turn your case over to the courts. You figure out exactly how much of your pay you want to go for your expenses—including entertainment and miscellaneous—and the court uses the rest to pay off your debts a little at a time. The creditors can't make any more trouble for you, your credit rating ends up A-1, you don't need a lawyer, it's cheaper than filing bankruptcy and it can be kept secret from your employer.

You get the forms from the U.S. District Court, and you can get lots of information on filing a "Chapter XIII" from a book called *The Layman's Guide to Bankruptcy*, by Robert E. Burger and Jan J. Slavicek (Van Nos Reinhold, $4.95)—or, if you're bankrupt, get it free from the library.

Letter Writing: the Return Winds Will Keep You Flying

Most people are delighted—some are overjoyed—to open their mailboxes and find something unexpected and personal there; some poor souls even scan junk mail in hopes of finding some vague reference to themselves. Doctor bills and magazine subscription renewal notices are "personal," of course, but they're really about as much like a *personal letter* as a grapefruit is like a grape.

So you're pining away for a personal letter or two, to brighten your existence just a little. Well, the first thing you've got to remember is that you've got to write them to get them.

A good letter, like a declaration of war, will elicit a quick, warm response. Try writing long-but-lost friends sad letters about the horrible black attraction of The Abyss and see how fast your mailbox fills with heartwarming assurances that you are still loved. Or send someone an ordinary what-I-did-today letter by special delivery (be sure to write SPECIAL DELIVERY in large red letters all over the envelope). Your friend will skim it, check the postmark, read it again carefully, discover some kind of hidden significance in all this and write you back immediately.

Picture postcards don't leave you much room for writing, but if you make a point of selecting the funkiest (or the most pretentious) postcard you can find and writing a message to match, you'll get a much more interesting response than if you send the average old postcard with the average old "Wish you were here" scribbled on it.

A truelove, and a lot of miles between you and same, are not requisites for exciting correspondence. It may be more thrilling to get that little lavender envelope scented with cologne (or that big beige envelope with the dynamic handwriting on it) than to get a letter from your mother, but if your mother is so glad she heard from you that she sends you a $50 check—well!

One of the fun things about letter-writing is that it gives you a chance to really get into the different sides of your personality—to really *become* the dutiful child as you write your parents, the greatest lover of the century when you write your truelove, the noblest and most generous of beings when you write your ex-truelove, etc.

Of course there will be times, after you launch into all this correspondence, when your own mailbox will remain sadly empty. Those times will be Sundays and holidays, when there's no mail delivery.

–Ruby Rich

Choosing Your Indian Name

Little Bear. Running White Moons. Fawn Who Writes on Paper. Thundermouth. Bright Pine. Swift Pale Moon.

Colorful, descriptive names that call to us out of our past, names that get close to the heart of what a person is, names that aren't chosen merely because they sound good, names that weren't plucked from the middle of an uncle's moniker.

But those names I mentioned aren't from any book of Indian lore—they aren't from the past at all. They're names of people I know.

Yes, they have "regular" names as well —Greg, Chris, Eric, Betsy, Paula—and they use those most of the time. But recently they decided they wanted to "find" Indian names for themselves. The process is an interesting one, whether you want to take it seriously or just have fun with it.

Here's an idea of the way to go about finding your Indian name. Gather together at least two or three people whom you know and who know you, and begin by searching yourself for accurate descriptions of yourself in terms that are somehow close to nature and tell something about your appearance, your prevailing mood or moods, the way you move through life—or something that happened to you that you consider important. You search, saying some of the words that come to mind out loud, testing their sound and getting feedback from others.

Colors come to mind. Animals. Features of the land. The wind. Water. Day. Night. The heavens. The idea is to get as close to yourself as possible and find a name that you have affection for and that carries a great deal of meaning for you.

Others help by reacting negatively to some ideas, encouraging others and suggesting their own. Each person should spend as much time as he needs, in turn, until each has an Indian name.

If you get into this it might take the good part of a day, and it can be a very rewarding experience for each person involved. Don't settle on a name until you feel comfortable with it; you are the final judge.

A natural setting is ideal for this. Take a long walk in the woods, or spend an evening around the campfire, with your friends. Long periods of silence may help.

May your new name speak from your heart.

–Bear Who Looks in the Woods
(John Wood)

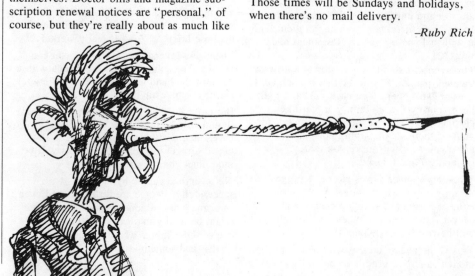

If You Leave Your Diary Lying Around Sooner or Later Someone Will Read It Greedily

"Melancholy diminishes as I write. Why then don't I write it down oftener?"
–Virginia Woolf,
A Writer's Diary

There was a time when almost everyone who was literate kept a diary. Sadly, the practice has fallen out of fashion now (except among 13-year-old girls). Keeping a diary is a very rewarding pastime, and it's not hard at all. Here are some pointers on how to become a diarist in the best old tradition.

How to Keep a Diary

Get yourself a notebook, journal, little black book or anything else with blank pages between two covers.

Take it with you when you go places (to the kitchen, to bed, to Nebraska by bus, to Small Claims Court).

Date what you write and make at least two entries.

Consider yourself a diarist.

Why Keep a Diary?

Vanity: the pages reflect you like a mirror.

Revelation: the notebooks and diaries of Che Guevara, Baudelaire, Nijinsky, Kafka, da Vinci, John Cage, Anne Frank, Anaïs Nin, Cotton Mather, Sherwood Anderson, and Kierkegaard (to name just a few) reveal much that encyclopedias don't.

Therapy: the recording process can undo knots.

Sheer pleasure.

Historical commemoration: "Dear Diary, At last! He finally kissed me! The cat has fleas again. Sleeping in tomorrow. Good night!"

Confession: "I'm an incurable cur, and despicable too. Today once again I . . ."

Source material for art, philosophy, alibis and fiction, e.g., *Diary of a Mad Housewife, One Day in the Life of Ivan Denisovitch, A Diary of Love* (Maude Hutchins), *Diary of a Country Priest, Diary of an Idle Woman in Spain.*

What to Put in a Diary

Your feelings and perceptions about your mate, wars of the world, sex, books, the Persian Shah, etc.

What you did today: "We walked only a little due to the bad road, abandoned many years ago. On the advice of Aurelio, we killed one of the mayor's cows, eating sumptuously. My asthma is better. Barrientos announced the Operation Cintia to wipe us out in a few hours." (From *The Diary of Che Guevara*, Bolivia, July 15, 1967.)

What you plan for tomorrow:
    Wash clothes and sheets
    Eat carrots only
    Be nice (?)
    Don't watch TV
    Cancel magazine subscriptions.

Last night's dreams.

Anecdotes not to be missed (though easily forgotten): "Today in front of the American Indian Exhibit at the Museum of History a little girl said to her father, 'If *I* was an Indian I wouldn't leave *my* beautiful things here!' "

Weather reports: "A day of sunshine and clouds. The cold spangled with yellow. I ought to keep a diary of each day's weather. The fine, transparent sunshine yesterday. The bay trembling with light like a moist lip. . . ." (From Albert Camus' *Notebooks*, March 1936.)

Dialogue.

How your Big Project progresses: "This will be one of the most closly read papers since the Scrolls in those caves. And I couldn't find a pen for 40 seconds & went mad. My fuse is about bernt. There's gona be an explosion soon. I had it. I want something to happen. I was sopposed to be dead a week & a day ago. Or at least infamous." (From the notebooks of Arthur Bremer, April 24, 1972—three weeks before he shot George Wallace.)

Instant drawings, word doodles, recipes, songs, maps and the like.

Locks of hair, flattened flowers and other dead things.

Letters you didn't send.

Guarantees

Inside your diary you will be supreme.

Secrets and private perceptions will increase when they are encouraged.

Your motivations and gratifications as a diarist will change along with your life. "The diary was a disease. I do not take it up for the same reasons now. Before it was because I was lonely, or because I did not know how to communicate with others. I needed the communion. Now it is to write not for solace but for the pleasure of describing others, out of abundance." (From Anaïs Nin's diaries, summer 1937.)

If you leave your diary lying around sooner or later someone will read it greedily.
    –Anne Valley Fox

Thus, great with child to speak, and helpless in my throes,

Biting my tongue and pen, beating myself for spite:

"Fool!" said my muse to me, "look in thy heart, and write."

—SIR PHILIP SIDNEY

Sunday Dancer

I have no illusions. I know I will never be a Martha Graham soaring through space, or even the last girl in the last row in a Las Vegas chorus line. I will probably never be able to wrap one leg around my neck or touch my toe to my nose or spread my legs out at a 180° angle. These things I have accepted, but I'm still addicted to dancing and to modern dance classes. If I don't dance for awhile all the tiny special muscles in my feet and calves go to sleep. At parties I last 15 minutes on the dance floor. But when I'm taking lessons I dance on into the night, muscles awake and spirit humming.

So once a week, to insure my sense of physical well-being and to put to use whatever modicum of physical grace I possess, I put on my leotard and head for a drafty studio or gymnasium. For anyone who doesn't have the time, equipment or guts for mountain climbing, river rafting or esoteric martial arts, I suggest that a dance class may be just the right form of physical exertion and psychological release for you. The payoff is high and the risks are low: no humiliation, no danger, little expense. But you must find the right teacher and the right class.

First, and most important, you must talk to a teacher before going to her class. I like to find teachers who are relaxed and affable (if they're poker-faced, they remind me of unpleasant high school gym teachers); beyond that, the first question you ask should be, "Is this really a *basic* class?" I remember one teacher who, with a class of all beginners (and I am a perpetual beginner), expected us to do the impossible: stand on our heads, stretch into various double-jointed positions, go for several minutes without breathing. She seemed oblivious to the moaning and refused to give us a chance to rest between tortures. I left in the middle of the lesson and did not return, vowing never to take "basic" on faith again.

It is also important to find out if everyone in the class is roughly at the same dance level you are. It is depressing to be surrounded by well-trained and limber dancers when you're just starting—while you struggle to untangle

(continued on next page)

(continued from previous page)
your feet someone beside you will be blithely leaping 10 feet into the air. Of course everyone in your class is going to be different from you in some ways and if some are better, fine—just remember you don't have to prove yourself to anyone. But neither do you want to be left behind completely before you even start.

Make absolutely sure that the teacher you choose does a warm-up before getting into the hard stuff. "Warm-up" means doing some very basic stretching exercises. Without this you can strain your muscles and hurt yourself seriously. The most dedicated professional dancers always warm up—but I once ran into a teacher who had us leaping and swinging with no preparation. My body was hung over for days.

Avoid any class that requires equipment other than your own body—toe shoes, tutus, bloomers and grass skirts are accessories you don't need. A studio lined with full-length mirrors can be a dream come true or incredibly intimidating, depending on your degree of self-esteem. I like co-ed classes, especially when the men are just starting to relate to their bodies in a graceful and unself-conscious way. And music—canned or live—can help you relax and glow.

I want a class to exhaust me but not finish me off. After a good workout I can face the rest of the week with high energy. I run up steps, leap across streets, stand tall. My teachers may move away, change class times or quit teaching, but I find new classes and dance on. Even though I have no illusions, and no ambition other than to let go and move my body, occasionally in the middle of a very soulful sway I remember a nice phrase from Bucky Fuller and I too seem to be a verb.
            —Deborah Berson

CBS News Goes Square Dancing

Dancing is older than civilization. American feet have danced their way through several crazes, from long-lived ones such as the Charleston, the jitterbug and the twist, to less influential gyrations such as the funky chicken and something called the penguin. But for hundreds of years square dancing has survived in varying degrees of popularity. And it's been enjoying such a revival lately that some folks now take their entire holidays, as Joan Snyder found out, to work on their do-si-dos.

Snyder: They came to spend their vacations square dancing, for hours—in the morning, afternoon and night. That's one measure of the kind of ardent, single-minded enthusiasm that this kind of dancing has aroused all around the country.

The basic pattern is centuries old: four couples in each set or square, and the variations they can swing and shuffle into. It's estimated there are more than a million square dancers in this country—from the casual to the committed—and so many are committed that the dance has its own subculture. A dress code: full-skirted dresses and bouffant petticoats, long-sleeved shirts for the men so their partners never touch a damp arm. Dozens of square dance magazines. And lots of records, which generally have replaced the old-time fiddler.

At Kirkwood Lodge, as at other hotels that specialize in square dancing, people come to absorb the intricacies of the dance. This is a workshop—lessons in new movements.

The star attractions are the top callers

The great equalizer: square dancing. "Chicken in the bread pan, bacon on the stove. . . ."

like Marshall Flippo, a master of the sight call, which means he can watch the dancers and improvise the movements he'll call, forming new patterns every time.

Flippo: [Calling] . . . pretty little girls; take a little walk, go around the world. All around the left-hand ladies. Zip up to the . . .

Snyder: Why spend all that time and energy?

Flippo: The fellowship. You can be in a square with a millionaire and not have a penny and you'll never know the difference. And you might even become real friends with each other. It's a great equalizer.

Snyder: The democratic square dance evolved from elitist ancestors: the elaborate quadrille and cotillion of 18th-century French salons. The American version started in rural New England and traveled across the country, shaking the rafters of barns and beer halls. The calls were relatively few and simple. Square dancing was fading away early in this century, but had a big revival in the Thirties and has been steadily increasing in popularity ever since. Today's prevalent style is called "contemporary Western": balls of feet on the floor, and shuffle smoothly; many stylized movements.

Caller: [Fiddle music] Hey, everybody up and going around! All the way around, all the way around! Turn her around, and let's go right. . . .

Snyder: But there are still some places where square dancing is free-form and come-as-you-are. The old hoe-down style.

Caller: [Fiddle music] . . . all the way around! Hurry, hurry, hurry, don't get lost! Chicken in the bread pan, bacon on the stove . . .

Snyder: At Bald Mountain Park in Hiawassee, Ga., people from the Blue Ridge Mountains get together Saturday night for the kind of dancing they and their forebears grew up with. [Fiddling, calling] Ross Brown, a left-handed fiddler, has played at square dances for more than 50 years now, and he doesn't know anybody who ever took dancing lessons.

Brown: Up here in these mountains, you know, it gets so darned cold you got to dance to keep warm most of the time. It—it just comes natural, you know. And most of these children around here, well, they—they can all dance when they leave the cradle.

Snyder: There's a move currently underway to get Congress to declare the square dance the official national dance. But whether it's official or not, all styles of square dancing—stomping or shuffling, down-home or fancy—have in common a sense of 300 years of an American dance that has always meant good times to be shared with friends and neighbors.

Caller: Is everybody happy?

Dancers: Yeah!
            —Joan Snyder, CBS News, Hiawassee, Ga.

Belly Dancing

The hootchy-kootchy belly dance popularized by Little Egypt around the turn of the century was a relaxed, stylized form of the "oriental dance" Middle Eastern women have been performing for a couple of thousand years. The belly dance is a mixture of erotic, rhythmic contractions and sedate, flowing motion. The result is a gorgeous, powerful, expressive dance. You've got to see it to believe it, and do it to know it.

No one seems to know exactly when and where belly dancing originated. Egyptian cultural authorities, who are now insisting that belly dancing did *not* originate in Egypt, say that belly dancing was the dance of the slaves under Turkish and Mameluke rule, and that once it left the palace and went into the streets it was hopelessly degraded. In the early 1960s Egyptian belly dancers were ordered to cover themselves from shoulder to ankle when performing. It was hoped that tourists would be attracted to the finer arts, like local folk dancing and ballet. . . .

Regardless of who's responsible for the creation and/or degradation of this ancient art, Americans are in possession of it now. For at least a decade, thousands of American women (and a few men) have been studying belly dancing in colleges, dance academies, free universities and with private teachers in burgs and cities across the nation.

If you've never seen it you probably think of oriental dancing as some sort of bare-footed, bare-bellied burlesque. If you haven't tried it you probably assume that the movement is a simple pelvic gyration that any loose-hipped woman can execute easily.

But the chiffoned and sequined grinding that's passed off as belly dancing in Las Vegas nightclubs and on table tops at the Western Dentists' Convention is likely to have about as much in common with sophisticated belly dancing as a case of stomach cramps. The actual dance form involves the rotation of many separate pelvic, hip, chest, neck, arm and shoulder muscles; intricate footwork; continuous cymbal playing ("zils" are worn on the thumb and middle fingers of both hands) and the manipulation of a long veil.

The trained belly dancer improvises each dance from a basic repertoire of movements, according to the rhythms of the accompanying music (which may be Greek, Russian, Persian, Asian—or anything with strong rhythms). At first her face and shoulders are draped in a veil, which she uses to frame specific parts of her body as she unwraps it. Once the veil is discarded she dances on for 30 minutes or so, employing various knee bends, head movements, walks and abdominal rolls and flutters. All the while her arms and hands (floating like serpents out of her shoulders) beat the rhythms with her finger cymbals. She wails out the eerie *zahreet.*

The exquisite beauty of the belly dance has

Belly dancing is a perfect art for the housewife, student or streetwalker who wants to leap beyond her ordinary means of expression. Above, Masha Archer and students dance at the Las Pulgas Water Temple in San Mateo, Calif.

to do with throwing the torso into graceful, exotic angles. Mastery of this requires daily practice. Belly dancing classes usually begin with exercises to oil the joints, isolate muscle groups and build up strength. Belly contractions and deep breathing (such as you might see a toad doing on her lunch hour) are also essential to the finished movement.

The belly dancing classes that I've taken have always involved an intense, provocative aura. Both teachers and students are literally dressed to the teeth in flowing veils, colorful floor length skirts or pantaloons (cut low to lengthen the torso), halter tops (*choli*) or sheer blouses over bare breasts—and they adorn themselves with rings and armbands, heavy gold and silver coin jewelry draped over hips and chest (the added weight aids the flutters and shimmies) and finely detailed headgear. The costuming and the insistent rhythms help to ease the dancers into semi-hypnotic states, thus inducing more beautifully sinuous, elliptical movements. (In the old days in the old countries, it is said, belly dancing was performed in harems and among gypsies to entrance and relax a woman in labor.)

Belly dancing is a perfect art for the housewife or student or streetwalker who wants to leap beyond her ordinary means of expression. (The dance itself is extremely tough, though, so that unsuspecting beginners often drop out after the first exotic rush.) Unfortunately, it's almost impossible to make a living from belly dancing in this country unless you're willing to play up the writhing-bare-skin angle of it—and even if you slit your skirts up to the hip and roll your eyes as expertly as your belly there's not much money in it.

Many American belly dancers live by other means and dance mainly for pleasure. Opportunities to perform publicly are numerous—there are art and music festivals, Middle Eastern shop and craft exhibits, gallery openings, benefits for hospitals and other public institutions and, of course, the parties of friends and society. After the two or three years of disciplined study that it takes to learn the belly dance, and the money and handwork invested in jewelry and costume, most dancers who love their art are delighted to perform for an audience.

—Anne Valley Fox

Blue Bear Waltzes School of Rock and Roll

Time was when rock and roll was considered a brief and passing fad among teenagers, about as likely to be around next year as the Davy Crockett T-shirt. Rock was anathema to persons of musical taste, and certainly was not something to be given serious attention, much less studied in schools.

But, 20 years later, there is finally a college where you can "major" in the serious study and pursuit of that good ol' rock and roll music.

It's the College of Rock and Roll in San Francisco, operated by a group calling itself the Blue Bear Waltzes School of Music. The entrance requirements are simple: the student must possess an interest in the theory and history of rock and roll and either some ability or the desire to play or sing rock music.

In its first 30 months, the college has attracted more than 200 students. (Because the college has only two buildings, enrollment is limited to 115 students per 12-week term.) While most of the students are under 30—many are students at other colleges, as well—some are older, professional people.

The halls echo with "good vibrations" from early in the morning until late at night. In one studio, a six-piece combo plays "A Little Help From My Friends," while two vocal students upstairs force their voices into a high-pitched harmony. Next door, seminar students huddle together to make themselves heard as they discuss the classical roots of rock.

Students pay $50 tuition a month to enroll in three seminar courses, four workshops, and four privately tutored music lessons. They may also use the school's studio facilities to practice their music at any time.

"This is a serious school," says Steve Strauss, one of the college's founders.

"We're involved in our music as much as classical musicians are involved in theirs."

While the only degree the college offers is a certificate of achievement, the student body and the 16 faculty members spend from 18 to 55 hours a week at the campus studying, discussing and practicing music, either alone or in small groups.

The college offers classes—both workshops and seminars—that range well beyond what most people would consider the boundaries of rock. Workshops in classical and blues theory are offered, as is a new course in "Dancing as Seen in Jazz." Ragtime, country, and acoustical folk guitar are taught, as well as rock. The faculty is made up of professional musicians and a voice teacher.

The college's business manager is Ed Denson, who has managed such successful artists as guitarist John Fahey and rock stars Country Joe MacDonald and the Fish. Denson and other faculty members offer advanced seminars in business, in which students learn how to manage their own rock groups, how to get their music published, how to find jobs performing and how to win a recording contract.

Although the College of Rock and Roll has not yet produced any stars, a few of its former students are playing professionally. Others have taken positions as teachers and administrators at the college. But most of the students do not give the impression that they are particularly interested in stardom.

"I'm here because I love the music," explains one student, as he strums his guitar between seminars. "I love to learn about it, listen to it, play it—and to get feedback on my playing from other musicians. I never thought *college* could be so beautiful."

(For further information, write The College of Rock and Roll, 2403 Ocean Ave., San Francisco, Calif. 94127.)

–Bill Sievert

Wolf Howling by Car Light

On four or five August nights each year in southern Ontario's Algonquin Provincial Park, more than a thousand people in up to 300 cars follow park rangers to a remote spot where they stop, turn off engines and lights and stand quietly beside their cars, waiting. They wait hoping to hear a pack of timber wolves howl in answer to two rangers who call the wolves by imitating their howls. First, one ranger howls alone, three times. If there is no response, the two of them howl together twice. Then, if the wolves still don't answer, they repeat the process after 10 minutes.

The spot for the howl has been carefully chosen after scouting trips by park rangers, but there is no guarantee that the wolves will be there when the crowds arrive. (Roughly three of four howls are successful.)

Rangers at Algonquin have been conducting the wolf howls since 1963, and the event is so popular that at times hundreds of cars are turned away. The howls are on Thursday evenings, but exact scheduling depends on the unpredictable movements of the wolves themselves. Ranger Dan Strickland says there is no point in contacting the park about exact times before Aug. 1, but after that interested people should call the Park Museum, (705) 633-5592. Even if no wolves are heard, Strickland says, the visitors still are thrilled by the eerie North Woods experience. "If they don't hear wolves, they leave the woods about one foot off the ground—if they do hear them, it's three feet."

–The Editors

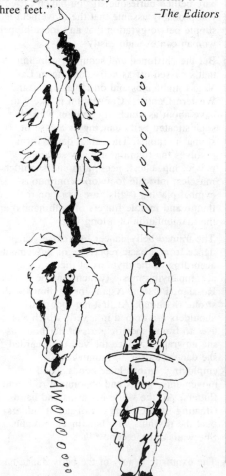

Meet Queen Mallard

If you can attune your ears to the finer music hidden in a cacophony of squawks, wails, trills, squeaks, screeches, hoots, honks and croaks, you may be a good prospect for a trip to Stuttgart, Ark. For in Stuttgart, during the first weekend of December, you can attend the 39th annual World's Championship Duck Calling Contest. Folks in divisions including statewide, women's, junior and world's champ will compete in the Grand Prairie War Memorial Auditorium. Queen Mallard, who will have been crowned earlier in the week (she's a pretty Arkansas girl, not a duck) will hand out the prizes: a shotgun, a trophy with a duck on it, an archery set and savings bonds in denominations up to $1,000 (this last for the world's champion).

You might wonder what the wife of a

duck-calling champion does while her husband bleats away in faraway duck blinds, or practices his quacking in the privacy of an insulated cellar. Well, Eddie Holt of Little Rock, a three-time world's champ who also won the quinquennial Champion of Champions Duck Calling Contest here in 1970, is married to a lady named Dixie who toots and pipes right alongside him, and she has twice won the women's title for herself. The family that calls ducks together stays together, apparently.

Stuttgart, Ark. also prides itself on being the Rice and Duck Capital of the World, and offers tours of rice and soybean mills, but duck callers like hunting better. A 50-day duck season opens in November.

Information from Gene Ramsey, Chamber of Commerce, Stuttgart, Ark. 72160; phone (501) 922-6989.

–Roy Bongartz

How to Write Music

Music is everywhere, and it is for us to bring it through ourselves and out into the air. If we aren't satisfied with what is available, why shouldn't we make up our own?

If, when you think of composing, you have visions of Beethoven slaving through the night over his scores, or of the child genius Mozart composing symphonies in a matter of hours—don't. Knowledge and skills give you the freedom to develop compositions, but all that is *really* necessary is to hear sounds, sounds worth saving. As for rhythm, if you feel you're lacking, put your hand over your heart.

If you begin to listen closely to the sounds of your life, the music, speech, animals, wind and machines, you'll probably find some you want to keep. The idea of composition is to bring those sounds through your experience and out into a form you can use. When you've created a piece of music, you have made something that you have not only put energy into, but something that gives off its own energy, something that contains feelings and ideas—and can change the air when it's played.

Before our electronic age, almost the only way a composer could preserve his best sounds so that others could play them was on paper. And music could be heard only when played, or by the well-trained musical mind that could hear a written score (Beethoven, of course, composed his later works—including the famous Ninth Symphony—while he was nearly deaf). There were no electric recorders or recordings.

Today, though, there are plenty of composers who do not read or write music. Their tape recorders are their pencils, and their tape recordings are their scores. Pencil and paper are still reliable; a system of notation is needed, and Western notation is the most widespread in the world today, but there is increasing use of personal notation systems devised by individual composers. The important thing is to preserve the sounds so that they can be reheard.

There are countless ways to approach composing and no reason why you should choose just one method. You might find a more deliberate approach works best —setting a certain time for composing, a place, a state of mind. You can have an idea in mind, an impression of an event or a familiar experience as the basis for a work.

But for some, the best sounds come spontaneously, unpredictably. If you haven't tried it, you might think getting down the real goods whenever they come (on a walk, before breakfast) would be extremely difficult. But you'll find you'll be more successful the more you try this approach. The notes you write down or record will more and more be those you *hear*. And for spontaneous composition, the small cassette recorders are a most useful tool.

At times, ideas come all at once, and a composition can be completed in one sitting. But more often a composition is the result of various ideas, and after listening and notating or recording for awhile, you might very well find yourself with bits of pieces. In putting ideas together, the temporal aspect of music becomes important. The question is "What goes with what and when?" and the answer is not always easy to find. Oftentimes phrases must be repeated with others, and repeated again, perhaps in different order, to hear the ways the ideas sound together—and what they convey.

Developing the composition can often involve the search for a particular form. It can be dangerous—ideas can be changed for the worse or even lost. This problem can teach you the "economical gathering of ideas." Too many ideas can get in the way of good compositional flow.

Finally, incorporating your ideas of action, narration and mood can be the most challenging and satisfying task in the whole process.

"LYNX"

copyright 1973 by David Berson

Your compositions will, hopefully, be pieces you'll want to share with listeners. For performance, notation can be a necessity, and if you're short on the basics, you might want to absorb the principles involved in actually writing music. Elementary music books are widely available (a particular favorite of mine is *The Road to Music* by Nicholas Slonimsky). There are also people who specialize in producing lead sheets from recordings, and this service is usually available at a reasonable rate.

If you feel your composition has commercial possibilities, it is a very good idea to copyright it as soon as you have it in a good written form (there is, at present, no way to gain copyright protection for recorded music). The basic information on copyrighting is available free—write:

Registrar of Copyrights
Library of Congress
Washington, D.C. 20540.

—David Berson

GLOBAL GRAFFITI

Compose on Your Telephone

Several years ago, when they first came out with touch-tone telephones, I was amazed to find out that the last note of "Dixie," whistled in the right key, will instantly cut off any long distance call!

I learned it from a guy who can only be described as an electronic pirate. His whole mission in life was fiddling around with technology, and he happened to have perfect pitch. He could whistle a 2,600-cycle tone on demand, and that's the tone the phone company happens to use on its long-distance lines.

All of which leads to the discovery that for an extra $1.60 a month you can have your own electronic musical instrument—the push-button telephone.

It boils down to this: on the standard push-button phone, you've got three *columns* and four *rows*. Columns stand straight up and down; rows go across. If you push *two* buttons in the same column, or two buttons in the same row, you will get a single, pure note.

Altogether, there are seven notes: F, F sharp, G sharp, A sharp, high D, high E and high F sharp. It's a little bit of a peculiar scale, but you can play all kinds of songs with it.

We'll start off by playing the rows, designated R1, R2, R3 and R4, and punch out "Old MacDonald Had a Farm":

    R3 R3 R3 R1 R2 R2 R1
    R3 R3 R2 R2 R1

Playing the columns, C1, C2 and C3, you can knock out "Mary Had a Little Lamb":

    C3 C2 C1 C2 C3 C3 C3
    C2 C2 C2
    C3 C3 C3
    C3 C2 C1 C2 C3 C3 C3
    C2 C2 C3 C2 C1 C3

Toronto's Do-It-To-Yourself Science Museum

Try your hand at guiding a lunar vehicle to a simulated landing on the moon, beat the energy crisis by generating electricity on a bicycle, test your reactions as a driver and challenge a computer to a game of tic-tac-toe and see if you can't bully *it* for a change. There's a push-button world awaiting you at the Ontario Science Centre in Toronto, Canada that interprets science and technology and, in doing so, makes it fun.

One of the exhibits actually makes your hair stand on end—it's a demonstration of a Van der Graaf generator, showing the power of static electricity. You'll also see (safely out of reach) a 250,000-volt spark jump between two poles.

Spaceship Earth demonstrates the delicate balance of life in its many forms, tracing, for example, the predator-prey pattern of the ocean food chain. You'll also see exhibits showing where oil and gas are found and some of the ingenious techniques required to harness these supplies.

With a zap and a puff the French laser mercilessly decimates objects put before it—glass, asbestos (but no hands, please). Fifteen-minute films you watch in mini-theaters and start with buttons explore such subjects as space, cities, Continental drift and animal behavior. There are many live animals, too—white rats, radioactive ants, eels and three generations of guinea pigs to provide an introduction to genetics.

The center's designers also created a child's garden of scientific toys called the Science Arcade. Since there is a little child in each of us, this exhibit with its captivating gizmos and gadgetry is one of the most universally popular. Ontario Science Centre, 770 Don Mills Road, Don Mills (Toronto), Ont., Canada; phone (416) 429-4100.

—Mike Michaelson

But, of course, you don't want to play nursery rhyme tunes all your life. For the serious composer, here are the chords made by the different numbers when pressed alone:

    1—B-flat major, D minor
    2 and 3—dissonant chords
    4—D major, B minor
    5—A minor 6th
    6—F-sharp octave
    7—G-sharp diminished 7th
    8—E major, C-sharp diminished 7th, C
      augmented
    9—B minor 6th
    10—E diminished 7th

Using the chords, here's the telephone version of "My Old Kentucky Home":

    45664 5696996
    45664 5645 . . .

This should give the general idea. It's cheaper than a Moog Synthesizer, anyway.

—David Saltman

"Terrible-Tempered Barnes's" Museum

A little-known, cream-colored, French limestone building housing some of the world's greatest art treasures—which was autocratically closed to the public for decades—now admits 200 eager visitors every Friday and Saturday, thanks to a Pennsylvania judge's ruling. After a nine-year court battle, the once exclusive Barnes Foundation in Merion, Pa. (outside Philadelphia), for years an oyster closed to art lovers, was finally pried open.

Its pearl, an amazing collection of masterpieces—estimated to be worth more than $250 million—was collected by the late Dr. Albert C. Barnes, an eccentric, controversial, fiercely individualistic art collector who made millions through his manufacture of the drug Argyrol. The "Terrible-Tempered Dr. Barnes" infuriated art connoisseurs by barring them from his famous foundation.

The collection includes 200 Renoirs, 100 Cézannes, 65 Matisses, 30 Picassos of the rare Blue and Rose periods; other masterpieces by Corot, Daumier, Manet, Van Gogh, Gauguin, Seurat, Degas, Soutine and Modigliani; works by such Old Masters as El Greco, Titian, Tintoretto, Rubens; and priceless Greek, Egyptian, Persian, Chinese and African art and sculpture.

When he was alive, Barnes permitted only a handful of special guests and selected students to view his treasures. Countless other art experts from all over the world, whom Barnes deemed dilettantes, ignorant, or artistic enemies, were denied admittance. Barnes thought that most of the would-be visitors to his foundation would be better off bowling or watching grade-B movies.

Barnes's "public-be-damned" philosophy kept almost everyone away from his treasures for decades (he created the foundation in 1924)—it was only a few years ago that a Pennsylvania court ordered that the foundation be opened to the public.

Since the Barnes Foundation admits only 200 persons each Friday and Saturday, you should write or phone ahead to make sure you'll be able to get in on the day you want to go. Write to the Barnes Foundation, Merion, Pa. 19066; phone (215) 667-0290.

Layer upon layer, past times preserve themselves in the city until life itself is finally threatened with suffocation; then, in sheer defense, modern man invents the museum.

—LEWIS MUMFORD

San Francisco's Museum of Love

A granite building in downtown San Francisco that was originally the home of the Elks Club now houses the first and so far the only Museum of Erotic Art in the world. It's three floors of earthly delights celebrating humanity's favorite pastime East and West, a collection of nine centuries of erotica. The bulk of the exhibition is composed of some 2,000 selections from the famed collection of Drs. Phyllis and Eberhard Kronhausen, pioneers in sexual psychology.

The museum boasts that it has the world's largest assemblage of uncompromising artistic expressions of mankind's sexual feelings and fantasies in its portfolio of paintings, lithographs, engravings, sculpture, cartoons and sex devices ranging from the frank to the lyrical, from the satirical to the whimsical. The spectrum covers works by Picasso, Dali, Hans Belmer, Leonor Fini, Betty Dodson, John Lennon, Tomi Ungerer, George Grosz, Larry Rivers and Loren Michel.

On the main floor is a free public gallery featuring exhibits of individual artists or group shows such as women's or gay erotica. On the same floor is a bookstore offering the museum catalog, postcards, reproductions, gifts and a wide selection of sex literature. The cost of proceeding upstairs to the Kronhausen Collection is $2.50 (admission for senior citizens and students is $1.75, with reduced rates for tour groups). An alphabet on the walls of the stairway, composed of figures coupling—"enjoy your initials," the staff advises—leads to the first gallery, a collection of erotic art by women, who in the last decade or so have begun to express their own sexual fantasies in art. This gallery section even has an entry by a 10-year-old Swedish girl, Stella Svedberg.

In an adjoining gallery is a delightful display of temple sculptures and miniatures from India, most dating from 1600 to 1900.

There was a young man named Kent . . .

There was a young woman from France . .

A jaded old lady from Phlox . . .

A G.I. in a smoker in Thule . . .

A hygienic young miss from out West . . .

There was an old lady from Cork . . .

He stood with his legs spread apart . . .

A gay Irish priest in New Delhi . . .

There was a young man from New York .

A Galapagos lizard, the gecko . . .

There was a grand dame of Regina . . .

There was a young lady named Alice . . .

There was a young man from East Anglia

I dined with the Duchess of Dee . . .

Prominent here are several so-called trick paintings, watercolors from the British colonial period in which groupings of coital couples assume the shape of, say, a horse when considered in toto. The temples that originally housed many of these works were places where one learned the "valuable lessons of physical pleasure . . . to attain spiritual enlightenment."

The core of the collection is in a restored, gilded ballroom. Here is a rare and comprehensive exhibit of Japanese *shunga* scrolls, or pillow books, which generally were presented to brides by their mothers for purposes of sex education and sex arousal. Emphasized in these *shungas* are vibrant colors and sensually textured garments, and there is a manifest tendency in them to depict the male phallus in startlingly oversized proportions.

Unlike Western artists, most of the great Japanese painters whose work is known "dedicated a normal proportion of their total output to erotic subject matter," the catalog declares. Japanese tourists are visiting the museum in increasing numbers, according to the staff, since such material is relatively inaccessible in Japan today because of censorship.

Down the hall from the Japanese exhibit is a sampling of Chinese erotica and scrolls dating to the Han Dynasty (206 B.C.-221 A.D.) that place emphasis on sexual adequacy and skill, viewing sexual intercourse as life's greatest pleasure and blessing.

Western art begins in the ballroom and spills over into a third floor hallway, and here are Dali, Picasso, Belmer, Grosz, et al. (One Picasso etching has Pablo peeking through a curtain at a young artist who opted for cunnilingus with his model.) In the basement is an exhibit of Western pop art, an incredible feast of humor, fantasy and socio-political commentary, including two self-portraits by John Lennon showing the artist performing orally on wife Yoko Ono. Gadgetry and sculpture abound in the pop art grouping.

While the Kronhausen Collection is the museum's mainstay, more works have been added on loan by artists from around the world since the night 6,000 guests sipped champagne with grand-opening hostess Shirley MacLaine in March 1973.

The museum is open from 11 a.m. to 9 p.m. daily (no one under 18 admitted), and is an educational activity of the National Sex Forum, which, in turn, is an educational service of San Francisco's Genesis Church and Ecumenical Center, a nonprofit corporation "dedicated to the furtherance of human potential and dignity through sexual enlightenment." The museum stresses that all income from entrance fees, donations and sale of articles is used for direct upkeep, new acquisitions, sex education and other religious and charitable purposes of Genesis.

—Bill Cardoso

To Walk, Perchance to Learn Ay, There's the Rub

By Mary Alice Kellogg

Visiting graveyards for rubbings gives you something to hang on the wall, a good reason to travel and a sense of history besides.

There are two ways to look at grave rubbings as a leisure activity. The first is to admit that there is a touch of the necrophiliac in all of us. The second—and the one I prefer—is to look upon gravestone rubbings as the cheapest and most instructive way to own American folk art of the 18th and 19th centuries.

To walk through a pre-Revolution graveyard in New England is to walk through history. That's what I was doing four years ago on the Boston Common when I saw three people intently bent over a tilting gravestone. The stone, beautifully carved with a delicate weeping willow and scalloped border, was covered with white rice paper, and the people were using purple rubbing wax to get the carving on the paper. The result of 20 minutes' work was a relief of the stonecutters' lost art—and it was free. I was hooked.

Gravestone carvings of this era are probably the most representative works of American art the 18th century gave us, and they have gone largely unnoticed. Gilbert Stuart portraits notwithstanding, the crudely carved death's-head, the misspelled names and total bluntness of the inscriptions reveal a rough and creative people, who knew what the term "up front" meant before it was invented. It's like owning a piece of history, and depending on your inclination, your pieces can be elaborately carved, excruciatingly human or just plain funny.

I spent one whole summer stopping off at tiny country graveyards and large municipal ones dating back 200 years. From region to region, the stones changed: there were the carved hex signs of the Pennsylvania Dutch; the rising suns and elaborately carved trees of Vermont and New Hampshire; the mournful cherubic faces of Massachusetts death's-heads; an occasional skull and crossbones in Rhode Island; and the flowers and urns of 18th-century Connecticut.

As the Puritan influence began to wane (and with it the stern skull-and-crossbones school of grave carving), cherubs became fashionable, some of their faces supposedly strongly resembling the deceased. After cherubs came the last stage of the truly indigenous grave carvings—urns, graceful trees and medallions. The men who carved these stones were the practitioners of a unique

art, one handed down from generation to generation.

The plunge into gravestone art is a cheap one. All the novice needs is some white rice paper, some masking tape and a ball or crayon of rubbing wax (you choose the color). Pick out a stone which suits you, scrape off the moss (if there is any), tape the rice paper snugly to the stone and begin to rub with the wax. It should be noted here that slate stones are the best for rubbing purposes—slate is relatively smooth, has worn well through the centuries and was the most common stone used for the common folk. Ironically, marble—used for the wealthy—wears badly and many marble stones from this period have been completely worn away.

There is a wealth of art to be had for the rubbing (no expeditions on nights of the full moon, please), but be careful that you have permission in the case of a churchyard which is still functioning. Trinity Church in Manhattan's Wall Street district is known for a fine collection of blunt sayings about deceased Dutch settlers, but you must call for permission to take rubbings. The city graveyard at Providence, R.I. (just off the freeway) contains a wealth of early tombstone lore, and this is my favorite place for sheer variety. Here we find a stone which is "sacred to the memory of Capt. JEREMIAH BROWN, who was born December 28, 1746, o.s. and after many trying misfortunes and vicissitudes in life, which he sustained with fortitude and resignation, calmly exchanged this in full

IN MEMORY OF Enſign David Elliot, who died Auguſt the 4th 1793, in the 49th Year of his Age

hope of a happier state of existence, Jan. 4, 1817, n.s." We find slaves, Rhode Island society, settlers, educators and hookers all together—and remembered with stones which in many cases bluntly tell what happened to them and how they were received by their peers.

For sea captains lost at sea and exciting retellings of the early settlers' run-ins with Indians, Massachusetts (especially the Cape Cod area) has the best selection. For a vivid description of New Englanders that could never come alive in history books, try walking around some of the larger Vermont graveyards.

The one important thing I received from this whole thing was the realization that people haven't changed much. The same sorrows, joys and peeves which afflict us now afflicted people then. And the same tragedies. In East Woodstock, Conn., I came across the "Remains of the Respectable Elisha Lyon . . . His Death is mournfully memorable on account of the manner and occasion. For as He was Decently going thro the military manual Exercise, in the Company under Comand of Capt. Elisha Child, the Capt Giving the words of Command. He was Wounded by the discharge of Firearms used by one of the Company, his arms having been Loaded Intirely unknown to him, the wound was Instantaneous DEATH." Even in 1767 the family of the deceased managed to get a dig in.

Then in Canterbury, Conn. we have the Rev. Mr. Solomon Paine, whose tombstone was a victim of a stonecutter who didn't plan ahead. The cutter just started carving and when he got to the end of a line just continued the word on the next line, regardless of spelling. Thus we have:

"In Memory of the Rev.
 Mr. Solomon Pain
 e, Pastor of a Congre
 gational Church of
 Christ in Canterbur
 y, Who Departed Th
 is Life October 25 ..."

But the fun of it all is discovering your own, finding those personages who were memorialized 200 years ago in carved stones that provoke a laugh or a tear. If anything, walking through a churchyard full of people who died when struck by lightning, when a tree fell on them, when the plague hit or when the "ruthless savages captivated them" should make you feel a lot better about your troubles. □

"Dragon Crazy!"—Learning Tibetan Rug Weaving From a Master

From the beginning of my stay in Nepal, I was strongly attracted to the Tibetan rugs; I liked the dragons, the colors, the medallions, the borders. The rhythm of the knotting had something infinite and ageless about it. I began to wonder if there was a way I could learn to weave them myself.

I spoke no Tibetan—I had to relate to those Tibetans who knew a few words of English. By the grapevine, I heard of a woman master weaver who lived outside of Kathmandu.

She and her old husband lived in two small rooms, one for entertaining and the other for cooking and weaving.

The woman spoke only a few words of English. After long explanations, requests, jokes and countless cups of tea, it was agreed that I would be allowed to learn: the warping and knotting from her, and the shearing from her husband. For a small fee, I could come and work with them daily.

The next day I began to learn the Tibetan way. I sat by the teacher, who was weaving her own rug. She gave me a piece of cotton string to learn the knot. My teacher was very concerned that I should do it exactly right, and it took many days before she was satisfied.

From then on, instead of unraveling what I had done, she left it, and it became part of her rug. The design was difficult—four dragons holding balls of fire and flying through fluffy clouds.

The shearing, which I learned from the husband, is very difficult and delicate. You have to make the rug surface as smooth as possible, and my hands would ache from prolonged cutting.

For the next month, I studied the traditions of design. Each time I wove, I penetrated a little deeper into the evolving shape of the dragon. I copied many of the traditional designs onto paper, and it seemed as if I was totally immersed in the universe of Tibetan patterns and lore.

After three months, I had learned the basic techniques. I was ready to start on my own rug. Every day, for a few hours, my house was filled with the rhythm of the knots, the beating of the hammer on the wool. The rug grew a few inches at a time.

My third rug was a red dragon on a dark blue background, with a border of rocks and clouds. It took two months to make it, and I was overjoyed when I finally took it off the loom. I took it to my teachers and proudly unrolled it.

They both looked very pleased. But then, inexplicably, they began to howl with laughter. They laughed and laughed for fully five minutes. When they saw that I was totally bewildered, the husband, choking on his guffaws, pointed to the head of the dragon: "Dragon crazy! Dragon one horn having!"

I had never learned about the horns of dragons. But it turned out that for a Tibetan, a dragon with only one horn is like a yak with three legs. As we sheared that rug together, the husband would look at the dragon's head and chuckle—but it *was* a chuckle with a touch of pride in it.

–Jacques Bessin

Drawing Together

One way my children and I use lazy weekend afternoons and, at the same time, step towards new ways of looking at the world, is to create pictures together.

It's not a case of drawing one picture while they draw another—that's fun, but the way we've been drawing since they were four or five stretches our mind's eye a little further.

One of us starts by drawing an abstract line, a wavy line, a zig-zag, a straight line with a curve on the top—anything, as long as we don't lift the pencil from the paper. We just let our hands go where they want to. We might make our lines starkly simple and leave the drawing open to almost any interpretation, or draw something crazy and complex that will drive our partners up the wall trying to find something realistic in it.

The idea is that your drawing partner takes your drawing and, turning it round and round, looks for shapes and lines that seem familiar, and then proceeds to finish the animal, face, flower or whatever you unknowingly started.

If you're working (playing) with more than one person, you could designate a drawing partner ahead of time, or leave that open and let the first person who sees something finish your drawing.

This is a very good way to free children—and others—from the idea that their drawings have to be true to "real" life or they're "not very good"; the finished products often turn out to be distorted caricatures of the real thing. The value is in the seeing more than in the execution. Above all, it's fun.

–John Wood

National Dump Week Is Beautiful

Thousands of dump addicts will be crowding into the pretty, old-fashioned beach resort of Kennebunkport, Maine this summer to take part in the exciting festivities of National Dump Week and to savor the crowning moment, the march to America's Number One Dump. Ed Mayo, a local watercolor artist who started Dump Week a decade ago, says, "In many communities, incinerators are being built, replacing the trash piles, which are becoming a disappearing segment of Americana. Dump viewing has become a lost art, except at homey and cluttered dumps such as ours."

Hundreds of sculptors and collagists will show their work in a Dump Art show, and Miss Dumpy will be crowned at the Hotel Nonantum (last year she was dressed in garbage-can lids, beer cans and old newspapers). A lucky tourist may be named millionth visitor, and receive lifetime dump-picking privileges at the famous Kennebunkport dump. Dump Week has inspired a Boston TV station to run a contest for best entry completing in 25 words or less the phrase,

"I like to go to the dump because. . . ." Mayo is terribly proud of an article about the dump that appeared in *Solid Waste Management Magazine*, but when asked what has been done to improve the dump, he says, "Not much—we like to keep it slightly cluttered, to keep that homely appearance."

Some 30 floats will parade dumpward —one last year had a live goat on it with the legend, "Litter Gets Our Goat." Mayo has designed an insignia for his Kennebunkport Dump Association: Rickey Rat on a yellow background, with the words "Dump Wildlife." Mayo admits that "some strangers seem to think that to celebrate our dump makes a poor way of publicizing our town, but nothing else ever brought nearly so many visitors." (No matter that last year, when a carload of New York tourists trailed the parade right into the dump, with its smoking garbage and mewling gulls, one of them was heard to shout, "What the hell—this is nothing but a God-damned *dump*!") Dump Week begins July 1, with main events July 5 and 6.

–Roy Bongartz

Where the Gay Blades Go to Take the Edge Off

Every major city throughout the country —and most minor ones—contain one or more "baths." These can usually be found in the Yellow Pages under "baths" or "health clubs." In some rare cases— especially in the case of health clubs— they are legitimate, but generally they are meeting places for gay men. A few have a "ladies' night," but this hasn't caught on yet, and women should opt out of this experience.

For a fee (as low as $3 in the Midwest and as high as $15 for a room in New York City's fabulous Continental Baths) the client is entitled to a locker and a towel. Some baths check everyone in for a flat rate and, as rooms become available, they are assigned on a first-come, first-served basis, whereas some others allow clients to select lockers of various sizes (gym, walk-in, etc.) or rooms, and fees are scaled accordingly. Most fees cover a 12- to 24-hour stay, so that often the baths are the cheapest hotel in town.

The facilities generally contain showers, sauna, steam rooms, exercise equipment, sun lamps, dormitory-style beds, private rooms, TV rooms, reading rooms—and in some cases, pools. Often there are lounges with food bars and large Jacuzzi pools, and usually there is at least one totally dark "orgy" room. The point is to get it on as realistically or as fantastically as you desire.

One bath has a black-painted chapel-like room. High overhead, suspended in a sort of dome, is a gigantic (12-foot) penis and testicles made of styrofoam and illuminated in black light. On floor level there are countless pillows, and men in groups of two or more. Another bath has a room in which a mirrored revolving ball with a light trained on it is the only source of illumination —there are snowflakes of light.

Going to the baths is intended as an experience in total sensuality without the usual problems you encounter when you get involved with another "personality." It's body time.

An important thing to remember is that nobody forces anyone to do anything and rejecting advances is hardly a problem. If a hand is placed on your thigh in the steam room, a simple movement can indicate that you're not interested, and the hand will disappear. (A simple movement can also indicate that you *are* interested.)

A special trip at the baths is the fact that someone else who cares what you are doing and enjoys watching can just watch, and that

Sun-Buffing on the Adriatic Riviera

What's nude in European vacations? Most of Yugoslavia's Adriatic Riviera. But few American newspapers or magazines will let the Yugoslav government advertise the *au naturel* lifestyle that's taken over at 20 excellent resorts between the Italian border near Trieste and the Albanian border some 300 miles south.

The closest of these nude resorts for Americans dot the Istrian peninsula; Koversada on the island of Vrsar, near ancient Porec, is the biggest. Well-patronized by European sun-buffs for years, it now has more than 3,000 beds for May-September occupancy. A happier destination, according to a personable young lady named Felicitas Stehlo who arranges bookings for all of these bikini-less beach complexes, is the island of Hvar opposite the interesting city of Split. Other resorts at Zadar and Ulcinj are so over-booked (on exclusive contracts with German naturist clubs) that Ms. Stehlo can only obtain a half-dozen rooms at a time for Americans.

Rates (covering all meals and a room with twin beds and bath) in first-class hotels run about $150 a week in May and September; about $200 a week the rest of the summer. Bookings can be made only through Travel Itinerary Planners, 6 E. 39th St., New York, N.Y. 10016. Their free brochure is the most sought-after booklet on the travel scene: it is totally unexpurgated.

–Paul Andrews

someone who's simply not interested in your sexual encounters nevertheless may be lying on the next pillow. Since you are doing nothing "wrong," the presence of other people is a resource to use, and not something to threaten you.

Baths generally have an aura of camaraderie, and there is an unspoken code of honor —seeing your boss or your brother-in-law is not a devastating experience for either of you. It is the simplest, most uncluttered, most physically satisfying way of getting it on in times of sexual need. It really beats playing the bar games.

After the initial contact many people feel satisfied enough to get up and leave. This is silly. Stay a while. Have a cup of coffee and watch some TV or listen to some music. Another adventure will present itself, eliminating the "satisfaction" of the previous one. Stay a while! Enjoy!

Most gay bars have free newspapers sitting on top of the cigarette machines; these indicate the locations of all gay places in the area, including the baths. If no newspaper is available, look in the Yellow Pages, telephone a place and ask openly if they have a gay clientele. (Anything "subtle" may be interpreted as possible police activity.) The safest way of all to find a bath is to contact the local gay organization switchboard.

–Richard Piro

Making It on Mass Transit

America's sensual awakening unhappily comes at a time when we are being driven out of our automobiles, in the cramped interiors of which two generations of American contortionists let it all hang out for the first time. If people are without cars, where is a body to go? Bedrooms are a popular and sensible solution, of course, but there is another alternative: do it on the bus.

Anyone genuinely alive to the throbbing beauty of the human body and its endless yearnings can see the possibilities. But for those not yet awakened, the San Francisco Municipal Railway (Muni), which runs the city's streetcars and buses, has commissioned two psychologists to suggest ways in which buses can be useful in teaching people how to be more versatile and open sexually. The psychologists' report, according to a source close to the project, bears the provocative title "The New Mellow Muni: Find Me, Touch Me, Explore Me All Over." And it makes these recommendations:

● Specially designed buses—called Waterbuses in the report—should be purchased. The Waterbuses would be windowless, except in front, with subdued lighting, a built-in stereo system and a dozen "compartments," each with a small water bed.

● To be eligible to ride a Waterbus, a potential passenger (minimum age 21) would have to attend sensitivity sessions, which would qualify him to carry a special "Mellow Muni" pass. (The psychologists even went so far as to script training films for the sessions, with titles such as *Muni Love, Good Vibes from the Back of the Bus* and *Let's All Move to the Rear*.)

● Special Mellow Muni training schools for drivers, who would be selected for their tolerance and even temperaments, should be set up. "We couldn't have drivers getting so turned on they had accidents," said a Muni spokesman, who asked not to be identified.

● Also, drivers would have to learn how to drive so that they wouldn't cause Mellow Muni passengers to injure themselves. "A panic stop or fast turn in a Waterbus could toss people right off those little beds," the spokesman said.

What does Muni management think of the proposals? "I don't know why they didn't pick on the suburban bus lines," the spokesman said. "That's where all those touchie-feelie freaks are anyway. There and in the colleges. City buses are for ordinary people, and your average guy just isn't ready for purple bordellos rolling around the streets."

The psychologists, on the other hand, think their approach is humane and sensible. "Sex is the body's way to meet people," they say.

Nevertheless, at least for now the future of the new Mellow Muni looks as dim as the interior of a Waterbus.

–R. C. Smith

Sexuality Workshops

When it comes to sex, we learn by trial and error. We've all made a lot of "errors," so talking seriously about our sexual feelings and preferences is something not many of us feel comfortable doing.

The aim of "human sexuality" seminars is to get you to reassess your attitudes about sex, to loosen you up and encourage you to do your own thing as an expression of your uniqueness.

Usually the workshops begin with some kind of heavy endorsement of sex. (In the workshop, everything's OK, whether you get turned on or not.) Next, there might be a talk about the sex research of Masters and Johnson, and then a glance at what's on the agenda for the rest of the seminar. Topics might include: heterosexuality—what people actually do and how they feel about it; masturbation—sexual responses and fantasies, and myths surrounding masturbation; lesbianism and homosexuality; sexual enrichment—broadening your range of fantasies, responses, and behaviors; and finally cultural expressions of sexuality—how sexuality permeates our culture in the arts, music and media.

Featured at the workshops are films of sexual activity: heterosexual and homosexual relations, masturbation and massage. Some of the films are old stag movies like *Big Tits*. Others, like *Unfolding*, *Holding* and *Brief Interlude* are produced by the National Sex Forum especially for sex education purposes. Together, they depict every fantasy.

A "sensual lunch" is part of the fare that one workshop offers. You close your eyes while a partner feeds you a variety of foods with different textures, consistencies and smells. You might hear the sound of celery breaking near your ear, then feel peanut butter being spread on your lips, over your teeth and under your tongue. A peach tickles your cheek; you get a whiff of orange and then drops of its cool juice slowly fall into your mouth. Sensual, you're told, is between the ears, sexual between the legs.

Who should take the course? Not surprisingly, workshop leaders recommend the course for everyone. They claim that with all the sexual taboos society has laid on us, it is essentially impossible to be "perfectly adjusted" sexually. We have strengths and weaknesses, and it helps to be aware of them.

Single and married people, experienced and inexperienced people can grow and learn in the context of the workshops. A good rule of thumb might be that if you feel you want to expand your sexual horizons and explore why you feel the way you do about your sexual behavior (and the way others feel about their sexual behavior), then you are ready to take the course.

Of course, if you are in the helping professions—if you're a doctor, clergyman, counselor or social worker—you probably need to update your training with additional information now available on human sexuality. It is not easy to provide a comfortable climate in which sexual problems can be discussed freely without some special training.

A workshop course is not therapy geared for those with sexual problems such as premature ejaculation, frigidity and inability to reach orgasm. The workshops *are* for people who might like to feel more comfortable with their sexual fantasies, or more appreciative of the erotic stimuli which routinely confront us, or more understanding of their heterosexual and homosexual desires.

The price of the workshops almost immediately limits the enrollment to the middle class. With the exception of the scholarships, it takes a significant amount of money to attend.

If you see an advertisement for a human sexuality workshop, how do you find out whether it's legitimate or just some fly-by-night establishment? John Holland, who coordinates the human sexuality program at the University of California in San Francisco, advises: "If someone loudly proclaims his expertise, beware. The key words in a good program are 'exploration, sharing, group ventures.' " He also suggests that if you have a question about the program, you should come right out and ask, "Does your group engage in sexual relations?" (If they answer, "Do you want to?" you may want to start looking for another workshop.) You can also ask whether nudity is involved in the group's activities. Then you know where you stand. Don't go if the group will be doing things you don't want to do.

–*Enid Rubin*

WHERE TO GET STARTED

Sexuality workshops are held in large cities around the country. Some of the organizations that sponsor or conduct them are:

EAST

Marriage Council of Philadelphia
4025 Chestnut St.
Philadelphia, Pa. 19104
(215) 222-7574

Quest
4933 Allverne Ave.
Bethesda, Md.
(301) 652-0697
Sexuality is dealt with in context of massage, gestalt and bioenergetic workshops. Costs $65 per person.

Pre Term Workshops
1726 I St. NW
Washington, D.C. 20026
(202) 298-7300
Couples groups, groups exploring sexuality, women's group. Short sessions which deal with sexual mythology, parents and teenagers, women and masturbation. Costs $25 for one-day workshops, $100-$200 for six evening sessions.

Anthos
24 E. 22nd St.
New York, N.Y. 10010
(212) 673-9067

SOUTH

Frances Nagata
35-82 Columbia Parkway
Decatur, Ga. 30034
(404) 289-4012
Workshops in Human Sexuality and Intimacy emphasize getting in touch with one's attitudes, feelings and values about sexuality in order to develop intimacy and closeness with others. Communication.

MIDWEST

Program in Human Sexuality
Medical School
2630 University Ave. SE
Minneapolis, Minn. 55414
(612) 376-7520

National Institute of Human Relations
180 N. Michigan Ave., Room 1040
Chicago, Ill. 60601
(312) 236-7368

Midwest Association for the
Study of Human Sexuality
100 E. Ohio St.
Chicago, Ill. 60611
(312) 467-1290
They offer beginning and advanced courses—new perspectives on human sexuality, sensual and sexual enrichment for couples, workshops on female sexuality and homosexual men, and workshop for physically handicapped. Costs $50 per person, $75 per couple.

Akron Forum, Inc.
111 Cascade Plaza, Suite 514
Akron, Ohio 44308
(216) 253-4684
Sexual Attitude Reassessment Workshop. An important part of the program involves discussion with individuals leading a variety of sexual life styles. Costs $75 per person, $125 per couple.

Institute for Sex Research
416 Morrison
Indiana University
Bloomington, Ind. 47401
Designed for professionals—attitude-reassessment program, informal workshops. Tuition—$250 for two week seminar; housing—$66.

WEST COAST

VIDA (Ventures in Developing Awareness)
1934 E. Charleston
Las Vegas, Nev. 89104
(702) 384-4844

National Center for the Exploration
of Human Potential
8080 El Paseo Grande
La Jolla, Calif. 92037
(714) 459-4469

Center for Marital and Sexual Studies
5199 E. Pacific Coast Highway
Long Beach, Calif. 90804
Mainly for professionals.

Elysium Institute
5436 Fernwood
Los Angeles, Calif. 90027
(213) 465-7121

Esalen Institute
1793 Union St.
San Francisco, Calif. 94123
(415) 771-1710
The new women's studies program is oriented toward getting in touch with the buried parts of oneself and coming out, thereby trading skills: female sexuality, orgasm, lesbianism, bisexuality, child sexuality. Costs $0-$35 on a sliding scale.

National Sex Forum
540 Powell St.
San Francisco, Calif. 94108
(415) 989-6176
They offer an introductory course in human sexuality twice a month. You are urged to bring your "significant other" when attending. Costs $50 per person, $75 per couple.

Human Sexuality Program
School of Medicine
University of California, San Francisco
727 Parnassus Ave.
San Francisco, Calif. 94122
(415) 666-4787
Program is specifically designed to help individuals become aware of their present sexual attitudes and develop positive sexual attitudes. Costs $50 per person, $75 per couple.

Warm Wallows in a Cold World

By Susan Sands

Here's how to renew yourself by returning from whence you came, to the warm waters and the primal slime.

Human beings, thrust at birth out of secure, watery sacs into a hostile, dry world, have spent a good deal of their collective history trying to get back. Since the beginning, we have been immersing ourselves in one fluid medium or another hoping to make our bodies or our spirits feel better.

Water, of course, has been the major medium, and watering places have been regarded throughout time as holy, even magical, domains. The earliest men gave each lake, creek or pond its own guardian spirit, or naiad. The Nile, the Jordan, the Euphrates were revered as the Ganges is today.

Society's attitude toward water has also tended to mirror its feelings about sensuality. The Romans glorified bathing (and eventually promiscuity) with their ornate *balnae publicae*, the largest of which could accommodate 2,000 bathers. But during the Middle Ages, bathing was tolerated grudgingly and, among ascetics, dirtiness was next to godliness; St. Agnes is said to have died unwashed at the age of 13. In colonial America, Puritans condemned soap and water as paving stones in the road to nudity and promiscuity. A Philadelphian who took more than one bath a month went to jail.

It is not surprising, then, that in our own era of increased body awareness, health consciousness and "touchie-feelie" Esalenish sensibilities, communal immersion in hot springs, mud, huge tubs, etc. is seeping back into vogue.

Because such activities are still rather esoteric, however, information on them is scattered. I offer here only a few suggestions on directions you might move in during your own search for interesting immersions.

HOT MINERAL SPRINGS
Spas

The Romans erected spas all across Europe at mineral springs like Baden-Baden, which, despite centuries of neglect in the Middle Ages, reached a pinnacle of popularity in the 18th century and survive today. Settlers carried the idea to the New World and erected their own spas at hot springs that the Indians had regarded for centuries as holy places. American spas were in their heyday during the last century; their popularity declined after World War I and they are just now enjoying a new vogue.

Inspired by reports of miraculous cures, people throughout the ages have gone to spas hoping to cure everything from nerves to arthritis. Why mineral water "works"—if it does—is still debated by the experts. While there is evidence that trace elements can be absorbed through the skin, most spa operators avoid the issue, explaining (as one did to me) that hot mineral water, mud and steam "create deep-heat penetration to painful areas of the body, stimulate the circulatory system and produce sweating to rid the body of toxic wastes."

Single bath/massage treatments at spas usually cost under $10. A personalized regimen of baths, massage, diet and exercise at one of the poshest beauty spas may run $1,000 a week. Spas range from rustic mountain retreats to The Greenbriar Hotel at White Sulphur Springs, W. Va., which has hosted the Duke and Duchess of Windsor and 18 presidents. The world's largest hot mineral spring swimming pool—over two city blocks long—is claimed by Glenwood Springs, 40 miles northwest of Aspen, Colo.

The United States is one of the few spa-pocked countries whose government does not print a directory of its health resorts. For the closest thing I could find, see a Pan Am book called *Pleasures of the Spa*, by John Duguid (Macmillan, 1968), which lists over 50 spas in 18 states.

"Wild" Hot Springs and Hideouts

The real fun, it seems to me, is to go a-hunting for your own personal naiad at a "wild" spring or funky resort hidden deep in a verdant forest or a blazing desert.

Information about these places is entirely underground, save for a scientific booklet called *Thermal Springs of the U.S. and*

Other Countries of the World, published by the Government Printing Office in 1965. It lists and pinpoints on maps all the thermal springs (any spring whose average temperature is naturally above the average air temperature) in the country, along with their locations, temperatures and major minerals. Sadly, the document is out of print; if you can't find it at a library, you'll find most of it reprinted in *Place* magazine, Vol. 1, Number 2. For a copy send $2 to *Place*, P.O. Box 515, Walnut Grove, Calif. 95690.

Northern California, southern Oregon, central Idaho, Wyoming, Colorado, Utah, Montana, New Mexico and the Virginias are richest in thermal springs.

All the hunting gear you'll need to find hot springs is this guide, a map and a compass. And if you do find an old resort (most are privately owned) you might just want to purchase it—the Sadhana Foundation of Los Altos Hills, Calif., for example, is buying up hot springs on the West Coast and turning them into spiritual communities.

Getting someone to let you publish the location of his favorite hot spring is like getting a transcendental meditator to divulge his mantra, but here are a few I've been to myself or have heard good things about:

California

The Geysers is 10 miles northwest of Cloverdale—follow signs. Park for $1 on private property. Pool in an old bathhouse, but, better, a hot sulphur creek with tiny pools wending its way down a wooded hill.

Tassajara Hot Springs is 40 miles south of Carmel Valley in deep mountain forest on the property of Zen Mountain Center. Costs $2 a day. Large communal bath, hot and cold sulphur springs outside.

Grover's Hot Springs State Park is east of

A satisfied wallower floats on her back.

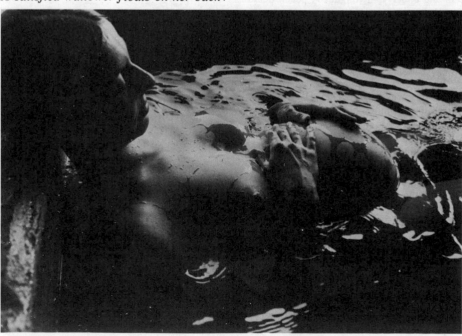

Markleeville, south of South Lake Tahoe. Two outdoor pools, one warm, one hot. In the High Sierra—great after cross-country skiing.

Colorado

Routt Hot Springs is seven miles from Steamboat Springs on a dirt road through the valley, past cabins and campsites to natural pools of varying size and dressing rooms; nestled in national forest.

Idaho

Murphy's Hot Springs (formerly Kitty's Hot Hole) is in a canyon 50 miles west of Rogerson. Campsites, trailersites, cabins.

Baumgarten is 10 miles east of Featherville at public campgrounds in the lovely Boise National Forest. Pool. Free.

Challis Hot Springs is five miles south of Challis. Funky, old, family-owned resort with hot indoor pool in raftered room and outdoor pool. Costs $1.

Nevada

Gerlach Hot Springs is two hours northeast of Reno, out U.S. 80 to Wadsworth, north through Nixon on Nevada 34, through Gerlach to the springs. Large hot or warm pools, steam cabin, diving platforms.

New Mexico

Rancho de Taos is three miles outside Taos; take a right on a dirt road and you'll find ruins of an old resort with a huge outdoor hot pool and little pools.

Oregon

Lehmann Hot Springs is 25 miles west of La Grande on beautiful Camas Creek. An old resort with large and smaller pools. Costs $1.25.

Ritter Hot Springs is 10 miles from Route 395 on the Middle Fork of John Day River. Family-owned resort. Fun, funky buildings. Pool, individual concrete tubs and cold creek.

Antelope Springs is in the Hart Mountain National Antelope Refuge near Rock Creek, at the only campground. Roofless, pinkish concrete bath house.

Wyoming

Yellowstone National Park, Madison Junction Campground. Past last numbered campsite, parallel to Yellowstone River. Inspiring neck-deep hot creek; its temperature varies.

MUD

For the less fastidious, mud is a stimulating immersion medium. Volcanic mud (usually with mineral water circulating through it) is used at many resorts around the world. Here are three in the United States:

Camas Hot Springs on the Flathead Indian Reservation, north of Missoula, Mont.

Pacheteau's Original Calistoga Hot Springs is a resort in Calistoga, Calif.

Riggins Hot Springs is a resort on the Big Salmon River, 130 miles north of Boise, Idaho.

The Duchess of Denver (left) *and Lord Muggles* (below). *The ruling class has a little fun.*

Again, the real enjoyment comes from finding your own "wild" mud wallows, often near hot sulphur springs, where getting *that* filthy can't help but bring a new sort of lascivious pleasure. One such renowned mud wallow:

Skaggs, between Healdsburg and Cloverdale, Calif. Ten miles in on Skaggs Point Road in a grove of old eucalyptus trees. Warning: folks have been arrested there.

IMMERSIONS AT HOME

Other immersion-media? Do what turns *you* on—use your imagination. Here are some homemade bath formulae from *The Bath Book,* by Gregory and Beverly Frazier (Troubador Press, San Francisco, 1973).

Chocolate Milk

2   cups fresh milk
2   tablespoons sesame oil
10   drops chocolate oil

Shake all ingredients well and pour under full force of running water.

Summer Wine

1   cup white wine
1   teaspoon ground ginger
1   tablespoon rosemary
10   drops jasmine oil

Mix all ingredients, cover container, and let stand in refrigerator for 24 hours. Strain before adding to bath.

Oatmeal

½   cup powdered oatmeal
1   tablespoon borax
1   tablespoon grated mild soap
10   drops musk oil

Mix ingredients in a bowl and place in bath bag (easily made out of muslin, doubled cheesecloth, old nylon stockings or superfine net.) Squeeze bag several times to release ingredients and rub it over your body.

Finally, for those who want to share their home-immersions with others, there's another new book out called *Hot Tubs,* by Leon Elder (Capra Press, 1973), that will show you how to make your own communal bathtub. □

The Waterbed and How to Do It

By Amie Hill

What you need to know about buying and installing them to keep your bedroom from becoming a reflecting pool

OK, so you've decided to buy a waterbed. Because you're an insomniac, because you've heard it'll improve your sex life, because you read about it in *Playboy, Time, Mechanix Illustrated* or elsewhere. Unfortunately for you, the waterbed market is as filled with get-rich-quick schemers as the dope market and it's just as easy to get burned.

No matter how much anybody hypes you to the contrary, a water *bag* is not a waterbed. Merely laying a water bag on the floor and filling it with water makes for an entirely different and rather less desirable sleeping surface. Without a frame, you are not supported, as you should be, by the water—taking advantage of Archimedes' Law: a floating body is buoyed up by a force equal to the weight of the water displaced. Instead, you will be supported by a tightly stretched skin, held taut by the water as an air mattress is held taut by air, which is far from the real waterbed thing.

Wear is also a factor with an unsupported bladder. The pressure and stretch on the material is much greater, especially at the seams, and the bag is more likely to age and develop weak spots.

Frames come in a number of sizes and descriptions, as do bags, usually single, double, king- and queen-size. The rub is that there's no real standardization yet, so you can't expect to buy your mattress from one dealer, pick up a bargain liner from another and a frame from a third.

One pleasant thing, however, is that a frame need not be fancy to do the job—which is essentially to form four sides of a rectangle containing the water bag—and anyone who can put up a shelf can cage a waterbed. Many waterbed dealers carry ready-to-assemble frames presized to fit the beds they sell. These usually consist of four finished and pre-measured two- by eight-inch boards and some means of joining them together—lag bolts, round or panhead wood screws, L brackets, glue—as well as some sort of cap molding or strips for fastening the liner securely to the frame. (More about liners forthcoming.) You can also, more cheaply, have a lumberyard cut appropriate lengths of clear, dry two-by-eight boards (cost: around $15, depending on wood), sand them free of protrusions, rough edges and splinters, and start from scratch; dealers *should* hand out free frame instructions to those who buy bags.

Charles Hall, one of the several people who independently invented the waterbed, says it is eminently desirable to have some way of heating your bed. While his project was in its experimental stages, Hall slept on it using various forms of insulation, and reached the conclusion that with almost any amount of insulation under which the bed still feels and supports like a waterbed, the heavier parts of the body get chilled. No matter what temperature the water is when it goes in (warm, *not* hot, water is recommended for filling) it will eventually settle to room temperature, usually about 70° F. The body's normal temperature is, of course, around 98.6°, with skin around 90°. Your sleeping pocket in a normal bed, which retains heat, can be warmed and maintained by your body at its own temperature. Trying to heat up a waterbed with your body is like trying to raise the temperature of a swimming pool by floating in it.

An unheated waterbed drains body heat, making your system work to manufacture energy to replace lost warmth instead of resting and renewing energies. Foam insulating pads are, according to Hall, better than nothing, but detract from the floating sensation, and in general reduce the ideal support qualities of the whole enterprise. He describes it as like floating on a foam pad in the water, rather than on the water itself, much less on a waterbed.

The ideal temperature has been found to be from 85° to 95°, and to maintain it, the ideal hookup includes a sensitive thermostat. The most elaborate heating devices, those sealed into fiberglass or other insulated frames, are naturally the safest at this point, but such outfits sell at prices from $300 to $400. More accessible and in greater demand are insulated heating pads placed on the floor beneath the mattress and liner.

As of this writing there is no heating pad completely UL-approved, but a number are pending approval, and in some cases have had all separate components approved but are awaiting their approval in combination.

You will need a guarantee with the bed you buy, since about 3 percent of all water bags sold turn out to be defective, but be leery of dealers who offer an unconditional lifetime guarantee. The bag should be made of material that is at least 0.02 inch thick, ideally enough to stand up under heavy use, but even Union Carbide, maker of the material used in most bags, refuses to guarantee it for a lifetime. The material is much the same as that used for pool liners and covers, which have been found to deteriorate over a number of years, especially if placed in direct sunlight.

Ideally a waterbed only has to be filled once. The whole thing hasn't been in existence long enough for anyone to know any different. When filling the bag, turn the water on slowly until the *raised* hose is filled with water, then connecting it with the adapter.

You will, of course, have to empty the bed out to move it from one room to another or from house to house. A filled water bag weighs from a ton to a ton and a half. For the same reason you should check to see whether the floor in your house is capable of supporting the extra strain of your bed—and make sure the waterbed is *exactly where you want it* before filling. Once even an inch of water is in it, with water at 62.3 pounds per cubic foot, the bag is there to stay.

Once you get the bed placed inside the frame and liner, with the heater, if you use one, between the liner and the floor, fill the mattress up to the edge of the frame or slightly higher; it should be fitted squarely in the frame before filling to prevent uneven stress, and after the bag is filled, there should be a few wrinkles visible to insure that the surface isn't too taut for proper water support. Make the bed with a cotton bed pad if your bed is heated—it's necessary to allow the skin to breathe—with unfitted sheets and your own choice of further bedding (quilt, fur throw, whatever).

OK, now you've done it right. Relax.□

Babbington's Breakfast: Stay in That Bed!

There's this outfit in New York named Babbington and Friend, see, and for a measly $35 they'll fix you a gourmet breakfast in bed *and* throw in the Sunday paper.

"They're even doing it at bar mitzvahs," says Joseph Babbington, the big cheese. "Richard Avedon is one of my best customers, and Liza Minnelli lives right across the street."

Babbington's special breakfast ($35 for two people—such a deal) is:

Poached oysters on a bed of spinach with green sauce
Fine ratatouille
Strawberries in Beaujolais
French chocolate cake with crème chantilly
Champagne orange juice
Apricot brandy

Babbington's "friend," Harold Arent, will trot right over to your place with his tools and whomp up this meal right on the premises. The problem, according to Babbington, is that the customers refuse to stay in bed.

"Yeah, they blow the whole thing—they want to eat at a table! I mean, we make our living doing wacky things, and there's nothing wacky about eating at a table."

For the regular breakfasts, Babbington also specializes in smoked trout pâté and a special omelet with Danish ham, eggplant, chicken livers and leeks.

Personally, Babbington can't stomach a thing on Sunday mornings, not even the *New York Times*. You can contact him at Babbington and Friend, (212) 850-1170. There are other breakfast-in-bed places in New York and in other cities. But Babbington's is . . . well, it's the wackiest.

—The Editors

Superbrunch

Your best bet for brunch may be in Las Vegas. Versions of the big, late breakfast have turned brunch into big business in cities and vacation centers around the world. But none seem to inspire the praise and envy heaped upon the spread laid out at Caesar's Palace in Las Vegas.

Every weekend eager customers queue up to pay $2.95 for the opportunity to attack mounds of chopped chicken livers and to quaff prodigious quantities of champagne. The popularity of the Caesar's Palace brunch is documented by the 3,500 people who normally show up on Saturday and Sunday. Even jaded Las Vegas residents—that heavy-lidded crew of off-duty croupiers and entertainers—are there every weekend.

840 DOZ. EGGS

Such massive popularity means a provisions list that reads like a decade's worth of Truman Capote soirees. Caesar's Palace says the average weekend horde downs 840 dozen scrambled eggs, 600 pounds of sausage and 440 pounds of bacon, and 600 pounds of chicken livers. Around 500 dozen bagels are served, along with 240 pounds of Nova Scotia lox. The hotel pastry shop turns out 14,000 pieces just for brunch.

But champagne is what fuels brunch. Unlike many tight-fisted champagne brunches, this one serves up all you can drink from draught-beer-style 4.9-gallon kegs. Fifty kegs are cheerfully consumed each and every weekend—that's nearly 250 gallons.

The management makes only one request: please don't pyramid the glasses.

—Richard John Pietschmann

Eating Dirty

For those who occasionally weary of civilities and amenities, there is a cheap and simple way to partake of the harmlessly primitive: eat a meal without any plates, silverware or serving dishes. For the proper mind-cleansing effect, you should of course choose foods that normally require implements. There's no therapeutic effect in hamburgers and French fries served this way, or pizza.

Spaghetti and meat balls are just right for this kind of meal. Or, if you prefer the middle ground of mess, serve just a conventional meal of meat, salad and vegetables, all dumped on the table (no separate servings). A communal bowl of wine, beer or whatever should be served with the meal. Wear old clothes, swimsuits or no clothes. When you're finished, instead of delicately patting your mouth with a linen napkin—take a shower.

We guarantee that if this rude feast is eaten in the proper spirit of absurd abandon, you will leave the table messy but refreshed and at least temporarily liberated. You have nothing to lose but your manners.

Poor Man's Lobster

Other people may have their limpets, their periwinkles, their scallops and their whelk, but in the Louisiana delta they have *crawfish*.

They've actually got crawfish *festivals*, for sportsmen, gourmets and gourmands.

For sportsmen there are the crawdad races and the pirogue races. (The pirogue is a boat, hewn out of a cypress log, that crawdad fishermen use.) For gourmets and gourmands there are shelling and eating records just begging to be assaulted: 33 pounds in 15 minutes, 2½ pounds in one month. . . .

Every year, people there consume some 10 tons of "anklebone"—just plain, bisque or—as Hank Williams sang it—"jambalaya, crawfish pie and filet gumbo."

The festival in Breaux Bridge is held every two years. The Pierre Part-Belle River celebration is annual. It's held on the edge of the Atchafalaya Spillway.

Both festivals are in late April or early May. You can write to the Chamber of Commerce in either place for the exact dates.

Grow Your Own . . . Sandwich

Like jellied eels and jam pudding, it's a popular English food seldom found outside England. Yet there's an important difference. It's available right here with a minimum of trouble and a maximum of fun.

What is it? Cress—the garden, not water, variety.

Although not available—as it is in England—at the local supermarket, cress can be bought in seed form and is remarkably easy to raise. It grows indoors, year round. It's ready to eat in two weeks. And it adds a piquant touch to salads, makes an attractive garnish for cold cuts and is just about perfect in sandwiches.

Known also as "curled cress" or "pepper cress;" this savory little plant will grow in very shallow pans, no more than ½ to ¾ inch deep. Most garden-supply centers carry suitable metal trays, but a shallow baking pan will serve as well.

Cover the bottom of the pan with about ¼ inch of fine soil and then spread a

(continued on next page)

(continued from previous page)
piece of muslin over the top. Sow the seed thickly and evenly on the muslin and sprinkle on enough water to moisten all of the cloth.

Next, put the tray in a dark place so the seeds can germinate—an infrequently used cupboard or some little nook in the basement will do (or even under the bed!). Water liberally each day.

The quick-sprouting nature of cress seed is proverbial. You almost can see it grow. Within 48 hours the seed will split and tiny roots bite into the cloth. By one week, your crop will have grown one-quarter of an inch high and, at this point, the tray should be moved to a sunny, inside window.

Cress is ready for harvest when it is close to two inches tall, a height it usually attains in about two weeks. Cut the stalks close to the cloth so as to get as much of the tender young shoots as possible.

For a continual supply, make successive plantings. Use two (or more) trays and sow a fresh batch every week.

To add extra pungence to this tasty little salad green, when you plant the cress sprinkle in a handful of fine, white mustard seed. Don't, however, expect the same growth ratio from mustard seed as you get from cress (practically every cress seed seems to flourish). Mustard grows just as fast, but you will only get about 25-percent productivity from the seed. This is enough, though, to add extra zip to your crop.

Serve cress sandwiches with the cress heaped on generously for full flavor and seasoned with salt and pepper. Or try it in a sandwich combination with ham or cheese. With a cold drink on a warm day it beats the devil out of jam pudding.

—*Mike Michaelson*

Porron in Juárez

Since the dawn of civilization, men have searched tirelessly for new and better ways to attain that blissful state we call drunkenness. One of the most artful, and least known, of these pursuits is the custom of pouring *porron*.

There is no exact translation for the Spanish word *porron*. By simple description, it is a glass flask. Sticking out of one side is a long, curved tube through which the vessel is filled; on the other side is a conical spout which, when tipped downward, ejects sweet red wine into the mouth of the drinker.

Any visitor to Juárez on the Mexican border may observe the practice of *porron* at a hokey little bar called the Alcazar.

Rafael Sampedro, the Alcazar's manager, will first explain that this mirthful method of wine-drinking is a centuries-old custom in his native province of Galicia, in northern Spain. His partner, Miguel Bilbao, will then present a series of *porron* demonstrations designed to leave his audience bewitched, bedazzled and bumfuddled. Finally, clutching a fat cigar between his teeth, Miguel will grasp a *porron* in each hand, elevate both of them high above his head, and simultaneously catch the flow from each in the corners of his mouth, without removing the cigar or spilling a single drop.

At this point, the uninitiated viewer is so overcome with desire to imitate Bilbao's wonderful feats that he completely forgets his lack of experience and dexterity in the use of the *porron*, and proceeds, with utter abandon, to drench his face, neck and shoulders with wine.

The pouring of *porron* may not be the simplest, most efficient way to fill yourself with wine, but it is artful and, after all, there's the joyous end result to look forward to.

—*Patrick Lowe*

In New Braunfels Ist das Leben Schön

There are 10 days every autumn when you can fling yourself into a vast moving shoving pushing dancing singing and drinking human mass, lose yourself and become one with a collective existence greater than any individual—or at least noiser—and you don't have to go all the way to Munich to do it, either. This is the annual Wurstfest in New Braunfels, Tex., a sausage-making town between Austin and San Antonio that has not quite had its Germanness rubbed out by all the Texas around it.

On the two weekends of this fest you'll find 20,000 polkaing, arm-linking, stomping, temporary Germans—along with a few real ones—practically pushing out the sides of a festival hall that was once a great cotton warehouse. Real Germans founded the town in 1845, but a couple of world wars gave townsfolk a complex about talking, singing, thinking or acting German, though they did keep making sausages. Finally in 1961 Ed Girt broke them out of it by organizing a Wurstfest sponsored by the town's 19 sausage makers. It started out as a modest display of sausage, but now nearly 150,000 visitors swarm into town each year to devour 40 tons of meats and 40,000 gallons of beer during the event.

Bumper stickers proudly proclaim the liberated Germanic euphoria at fest time: "*In New Braunfels Ist Das Leben Schön*" ("In New Braunfels, life is beautiful"). A Wurst Band plays concerts outside the waltz area, Miss Loverwurst is crowned and a melodrama is given by the local repertory company: "Wilhelm Wonka and the Sausage Factory, or, Do Your Wurst, Evil Sydney!" A rock group, the Sauer Krauts, draws the younger set into a circus tent, and there is a dachshund show, but the fest's origins are not forgotten, and the big attraction remains the scores of stands selling wurstburgers, sausage burgers, leberwurst, bratwurst, blutwurst, mettwurst, wurstkebobs, potato pancakes, sauerkraut, apple strudel and such crossbreeds as wurst nachos, wurst tacos and sausage and bean tacos.

The Wurstfest will run from Nov. 1 to 10, in 1974. Information: Wurstfest Association, P.O. Box 180, New Braunfels, Texas 78130.

—*Roy Bongartz*

Juanita's: the Most Outrageous Restaurant?

In the gigantic dining room, a prim, permanented, older woman is belting out bawdy songs ("Roll me over in the clover do it again . . .") accompanied by an autoharp, while dozens of drunken dinner guests stomp and clap. In a room off the front lobby, a 50-year-old woman lying on a brass bed shouts invitations to guests to dine in her boudoir. Upstairs, a hundred guests in Renaissance dress are celebrating a wedding. On the sleeping porch, four monkeys are screeching to be let out. It's a typical weekend night at Juanita's.

Juanita's is a restaurant in Fetters Hot Springs, near Sonoma in Northern California, and the brash woman on the brass bed is Juanita herself. That her restaurant has become enough of a conversation piece to be written up in the *New York Times* and *Playboy* and every local travel book is no accident. Juanita, a veteran restaurateur (and, rumor has it, an ex-madam), works at it. Since buying the abandoned old resort

hotel in 1969 (her other nearby restaurant had burned down), she has filled it with an astounding quantity of antiques and funk —bird cages, brass spittoons, cash registers, roll-top desks. Christmas tree lights festoon the palm trees around the circular driveway. The ladies' restroom is decorated with old crinolines! Sadly enough, the health department has put an end to Juanita's endearing habit of carrying a chicken called "Chicken Shit" under her arm, and the monkeys are no longer allowed to swing from the chandeliers.

By the way, the food at Juanita's is something else, too. The gorgeous buffet costs $3 before 5 p.m. and $4 after; steak plus salad is $7. But the pièce de résistance is the prime rib; an entire rib—enough for two, sometimes weighing three pounds—goes for $8.50. To take care of leftovers, there's a roll of aluminum foil at the door—just wrap up what you want to take home.

Juanita's is open seven days a week, from 10 a.m. to 11 p.m. The address is 17300 Sonoma Highway, Sonoma, Calif.; phone (707) 996-7010.

—*Susan Sands*

1520 A.D. Restaurants

This is one restaurant you won't go to because of the food—although it's fine. 1520 A.D. represents life as it really was in 16th-century England. What you go for is entertainment, the show and the great chance to make a perfect ass out of yourself.

When you enter 1520 A.D. you step back in time about 400 years. Women, you are informed, are second-class citizens. A knight in armor stands guard over the desk. Master Horiatio doesn't run to the bar to fetch you drinks; instead he performs somersaults. But liberated women needn't worry—it's all in an evening's fun.

You are escorted (men first) into the large eating room. Your "tables and chair" are wooden affairs with benches. One of the first things you'll notice is no salt on your table. (Since it was a precious commodity in those times, it had to be watched carefully. If you find you need some, just send over a female companion to kiss the Keeper of the Salt.) And don't be upset if you don't get a glass of ice water. Ice was unheard of, and no one drank water because it was contaminated. Pepper you'll just have to forget about for one night.

Your serving wench (as the waitresses are called) comes over to introduce herself and teach you the Drinking Toast. When the King arrives, he'll lift his glass and announce, "Drink Hale!" To which you reply (and you'd better if you don't want to end up in the stocks) "Wassail!"

While you wait for King Henry the Eighth, his Fool, Master Summers, delights you with songs. Messrs. Bates and Horiatio add to the show. A Keeper of the Salt and Knight of the Tavern are selected from among the guests.

Dinner consists of four courses: soup, salad (try the Stilton cheese dressing, made just the way Queens Anne, Jane, etc. used to make it), choice of barbecued ribs or Cornish game hens and dessert. Be sure to save your soup spoon—it serves as a "table banger."

All this royal treatment costs $9.95. If you go during the astrological time of your birth, your dinner will only cost $1—provided you bring along a paying customer.

Some guests prefer to come in costume. But whatever century you wish to represent, 1520 A.D. is a *great* escape. There are 1520 A.D. restaurants at: 333 S. La Cienega (Los Angeles); 201 Broadway (Oakland, Calif.); 875 S. Brookhurst (Anaheim, Calif.); 2633 El Cajon Blvd. (San Diego); 2727 W. Sixth St. (Denver) and St. Martin's Lane (London). Reservations are required. —*Jody Long*

Have we not grovel'd here long enough, eating and drinking like mere brutes?

—WALT WHITMAN

GOOD FOOD AGES WELL

By David Saltman

At the end of his monumental work on the Chinese people, Lin Yutang says: ". . . but if there is anything we are serious about, it is neither religion nor learning, but food."

So are we all, to a greater or lesser extent. Here's a little survey of great meals through the ages.

Belshazzar Feasts as the Persians Creep In

This is the meal the King of Babylon ate when the handwriting appeared on the wall:

Fig wine
Salted river perch garnished with locusts
Roast ducks
Geese in mint and mustard sauce
Salad of turnips, leeks, carrots, onions, cress, lettuce and endive
Honeyed barley cakes
"Unguent of the Heart" spiced wine

You Stuffed Too, Brutus?

That Pompeia could really whomp up some grits for her husband, Julius Caesar:

Oysters
Game pie
Filet of wild boar
Sow's udders
Pig's head
Ragout of hare
Satura (barley mash, dried raisins, pine kernels and pomegranate seeds, laced with condiments and honeyed wine)

When the 19th Dynasty Burps, the Whole World Gets Hungry

Our remote ancestors, the Egyptians, made it mandatory that each man drink two jugs of spiced bread beer every day. A typical Egyptian breakfast:

Bread
Meat
Beer

And for lunch, the well-to-do Egyptian ate:

Cakes and figs
Onions, okra and lotus root
Roasted goose
Honey and grapes
Wine

Supper With the Pope, 1566

This was consumed by one of the fattest Popes on record, the infallible Pius V:

Sausages cooked in wine
Ravioli Fiorentina
Capon aspic
Turnip Duck
Brain Fritters with orange sauce
Lamb with rosemary
Stuffed artichoke hearts
Tender peas with bacon
Skewered golden pork
Veal pie
Salad
Torta di Sparagi
Nun's Cake
Custard pastry
Pears in wine
Sweet fennel stalks

JOE'S PIZZA

Sabbath Dinner in Pren, Lithuania, 1886

This is a traditional meal that can still be eaten, at any time, at certain grandmothers' houses:

Challah
Chopped liver
Chopped herring
Gefilte fish with horseradish
Dill pickles
Radishes
Matzo ball soup
Pot roast
Cholent
Tzimmus
Strudel
Fruit compote
Wine
Cherry cider

What They Ate When the Earthquake Stopped

From May to October 1906, after the San Francisco Earthquake, you got your food from a "Hot Food Station." The stations served almost 1,500,000 meals during that six-month period. Most of them were free; if you could scrounge the money, you paid 15 cents. Here's a typical menu:

Breakfast
Hash, or mush, and milk
Bread or hot biscuit
Coffee and sugar

Lunch
Soup
Hash
Vegetable
Bread
Coffee and sugar

Supper
Soup
Bread or hot biscuits
Tea and sugar

What George V Ate After His Coronation, 1911

Enough to make you abdicate:

Caviar
Canteloupe
Clear turtle soup
Cold veloute of chicken soup
Roast chicken George V
Saddle of Welsh lamb
Peas a l'Anglaise
Duckling breasts in port wine aspic
Quail with grapes
Salade Orientale
Hearts of Artichokes Grand Duc
Peaches Queen Mary
Petits fours
Fruits

The Church of England Strikes Back

Not to be bested by a mere Pope, Sir Roger North served this feast to Queen Elizabeth I at his Country Dinner in 1578:

Smoked sturgeon
Mussels with sweet herbs
Pease potage
Roasted cygnet, quail and snipe
Oysters, bacon and pullets
Mutton with cucumbers
Neat's tongue roasted with Rhenish wine
Venison pasty
Boiled beef with Sauce Robert
French puffs with green herbs
Salad
Apple cream
Maids of Honour
Mince pie
Pears in syrup
Clouted cream
Syllabub
Mulled cider
Mead

The British Sure Know How to Pack It In

Breakfast with Samuel Johnson, Scotland, 1726:

Oatmeal with cream
Smoked herring
Sardines with mustard
Broiled trout
Cold meat pie
Braised kidneys
Woodcock
Sausage with mashed potatoes
Tongue with hot horseradish
Singing Hinnies
Bannocks
Barmbrack
Coffee with honey

What They Eat With Oil Money

This is the menu for the 2,500th anniversary of the Persian Empire. It was served at Persepolis in October 1971, and was wolfed down in five and a half hours:

Quail eggs stuffed with Persian caviar
Mousse of crayfish tails in Nantua sauce
Stuffed rack of roast lamb
Roast peacock stuffed with *foie gras*
Fig rings
Raspberry champagne sherbet

The wines included innumerable bottles of Chateau Lafite Rothschild 1945, at $150 per.

Chateau Lafite Roth 1945

Escape Through the Alimentary Canal

Roast Stuffed Camel

This is served occasionally at Bedouin wedding feasts. It is the largest single dish in the world. To prepare it, you need:

200	hard-boiled eggs
100	gutted Mediterranean trout
50	cooked chickens
1	roasted sheep
1	camel

Stuff the eggs into the fish. Stuff the fish into the chickens. Stuff the chickens into the sheep carcass. Stuff the sheep into the camel. Roast over a spit until done. (Serves 100-300.)

Hunter's Game Bird Cassoulet

This dish should be served as an early Saturday dinner in the fall to guests who deserve it and who have been warned to eat no lunch before coming. A green salad and French bread and, later, some cheese and fruit are all that need go with it. The recipe is Angus Cameron's.

2	pounds marrowfat beans or Great Northern beans
1	pound pig skins
½	pound salt pork
½	pound ham butt
1½	cups chopped onions
1	bouquet garni (made up of 6 cloves garlic, 6 sprigs parsley, 4 cloves, 3 bay leaves, ½ teaspoon thyme)
2	pounds pork loin
1	wild duck, or breast of wild goose
1	pheasant
1	grouse
2-4	quail or woodcock butter, oil
3	cups white wine
1	6-ounce can tomato paste
4	crushed cloves garlic
½	teaspoon thyme
2	bay leaves
1	quart beef broth
1½	pounds Italian sausage
2	cups chopped onions
½	cup flavored bread crumbs chopped parsley

Soak the beans overnight in a six- to eight-quart kettle.

Take half of the pig skins, bring to boil, rinse, change water, bring to boil again and simmer for 30 minutes. Cut them into ½-inch strips and then ½-inch squares.

Bring remaining skins to boil, rinse and dry, and set the skins aside separately, ready for the morrow's continuation.

Drain the beans in the morning, replace in kettle, cover with boiling water, and add the pig-skin squares, the ½ pound salt pork (in one piece) and the ½ pound ham butt, 1½ cups chopped onions and the bouquet garni. Bring to a boil and skim once or twice, then boil over low flame until the beans are just tender (about one hour). When the beans are just chewable set them aside with other ingredients in their liquor.

While the beans are cooking put the pork loin and the duck, uncovered, in the oven, set at 400°. When duck has browned, reduce heat to 350° and roast covered until done (40 minutes for the duck, 40 minutes to the pound for the pork). Set aside with juices.

Cut the pheasant into pieces (as you would a frying chicken), quarter the grouse and leave the woodcock and/or quail whole. Brown the birds in butter and oil in a heavy skillet. Remove and keep warm.

Add three cups white wine to the skillet and scrape loose the brown goodies. Pour this wine and drippings liquor into a large container and add the tomato paste, crushed garlic, ½ teaspoon thyme, the bay leaves and the quart of beef broth.

Drain the beans (reserving the liquid) and add them to the container. If need be, cover beans with part of the bean-cooking liquid, then simmer for five minutes, and let stand in this herbed liquor.

Brown the 1½ pounds sausage in a little oil, set aside the meat and sauté the two cups chopped onions in the sausage fat. Then stir into the skillet the reserved juices and pan scrapings from the roasted pork and duck. Reserve.

Assembling the cassoulet: line the bottom of an eight-quart cassoulet with the pig skins. Slice the pork loin, the duck, the salt pork and the ham butt. Put in cassoulet a layer of beans, then some of the meats (the ham butt, pigskin squares, pork loin, sausages) and game birds (duck, pheasant pieces, grouse quarters and quail and/or woodcock), and alternate the layers until you finish with a layer of beans and sliced salt pork.

Then add the herbed liquor the beans stood in and the onions with their meat juices until the beans are just covered. Sprinkle with the bread crumbs and chopped parsley, and bring the cassoulet to a simmer on top of the stove.

Put the cassoulet into a 350° oven, covered, and after about 20 minutes check to see if a crust has formed. When it has formed, break through with a spoon and baste the crust with the juices. Repeat this two or three times while the cassoulet bakes (for about one hour altogether). When the cassoulet has been in the oven for one hour, remove the lid and let the crust brown.

If during baking it is necessary to add some liquid, use the reserved bean-cooking liquid.

Platina di Pera Romana

This dish comes from Charles Perry, who spends his life digging for such things. He says it's from Imperial Rome.

8	Bosq pears
3	tablespoons clover honey
¾	bottle Blanc de Blancs
¼	teaspoon cumin
⅛	teaspoon lovage or celery seed
⅛	teaspoon salt
2	tablespoons honey
1	pint heavy cream
3	eggs (separated)

Peel the pears, leaving the stems on. Poach them *slowly* in the wine, clover honey and spices, basting often and pricking with a fork when soft. Take them out and arrange in a dish.

Reduce the juices in the pan to one cup or less and put them into a double boiler. Mix with the cream and the second batch of honey; add the salt and the egg yolks. Stir on heat until the liquid forms a sauce.

Pour the sauce over the pears.

Leung-Yee Kuo-tieh

Among China scholars, Sinophiles and the Chinese themselves, the meat dumplings known as *kuo-tieh* or *jao-tze* are considered to be among the most exquisite of all northern Chinese dishes.

There are three ways to cook these dumplings: fried they are known as *kuo-tieh* (which loosely translates as pot or pan stickers); boiled or steamed, they are smaller and are known as *jao-tze* (which translates as meat dumplings).

The following recipe was developed by Yuk-mai Leung Thayer and Min S. Yee.

The filling

½ pound minced pork
½ pound Chinese celery cabbage
    (bok toy can be substituted)
1 or 2 stalks minced green onion
2 teaspoons light soy sauce
2 teaspoons sherry or rice wine
¼ teaspoon salt
¼ teaspoon sugar
1 teaspoon sesame oil

Steam or boil the celery cabbage until crisp but tender and drain well. Run cabbage immediately under cold water, and squeeze to extract as much excess water as possible. Mince the cabbage and squeeze again.

Put the minced pork into a mixing bowl and add all the other ingredients except the cabbage. Mix well.

Add the cabbage. Mix well again. (If you plan to cook the *kuo-tieh* immediately, place the filling mix in the freezer for about five minutes. This will facilitate later handling of the filling. Do not freeze. Or, the filling can be placed in the refrigerator overnight.)

The dumpling dough

2 cups flour
½ cup cold water
½ cup boiling water

In one bowl, gradually mix one cup of flour and the cold water, stirring with chopsticks until blended and dough is smooth.

In another bowl, mix one cup of flour with the hot water, stirring and blending until the dough becomes soft, but not sticky.

Mix the two dough parts together until they are both soft.

Cover and let the dough rise for about 15 minutes.

Lightly flour a working surface and pour out the dough. Knead it for about five minutes, creating some elasticity, then stretch it into one or more long sausage shapes.

With floured fingers, pull off or cut off about 20 equal pieces. Roll each into a ball, then flatten each into a biscuit shape. Roll each biscuit into a circle about three inches in diameter. Keep circles covered with a wet cloth to prevent them from drying out while you work.

Filling the dumpling

Place about 1½ level teaspoons of the filling in the center of a circle of dough in a slightly oval shape, as shown:

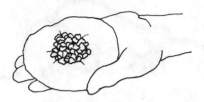

Slightly moisten the top half of the circle, then bring the edges of the dough together and pinch together firmly in the center, forming a filled crescent. Leave the two ends open. Make one pleat with your fingers on the side facing you:

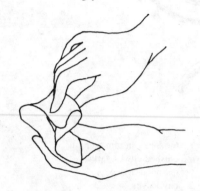

Gathering up the balance of the dough on the other side, pleat toward the center in three or four pleats. Then pleat the other end toward the center. This sealing method should give the dumpling a broad bottom.

As you finish each dumpling, place it on a lightly floured board or plate. Again, keep them all covered with a damp cloth to prevent them from drying out. With an invisible cover, they should look like this:

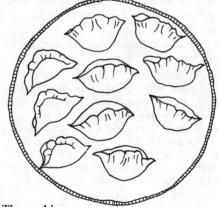

The cooking

Arrange the dumplings neatly, bottom side down, in a cold iron skillet. Pour in cold water to half cover the dumplings. Cover the pan.

Using medium heat, cook for about five to seven minutes, until the dumplings are half done. Drain the water from the pan, and neatly rearrange the dumplings.

Pour in four tablespoons of peanut, vegetable or corn oil. Cover the pan and cook for about another seven minutes. The dumplings are done when they no longer stick to the pan. You may turn the heat to high at the end of the cooking time to darken the bottoms of the dumplings, but be careful not to burn them. Serve bottom side up. (Makes 20 dumplings.)

Kuo-tieh are generally served with a combination of light Chinese sauces. Most Chinese combine vinegar with soy sauce and add shredded ginger. Others also add red pepper oil. It is entirely possible for a *kuo-tieh* lover to eat this entire recipe. However, if you're serving other dishes, this should serve as an appetizer—but please don't serve anyone less than four dumplings, even as appetizers.

If you have your own personal escape through the alimentary canal and would like to share it, please send the full recipe to
    The Great Escape (Burp)
    150 Shoreline Highway
    Mill Valley, Calif. 94941.

America's Greatest Hot Dog Stand

The hot dog has fallen on hard times. Between Ralph Nader's complaints about its quality (often justified) and Ronald McDonald's ubiquitous competition (who knows *how* many billion of those things have been served so far?), the hot dog seems in danger of losing its status as the favorite food of America at play. Yet the frankfurter is a durable old dog; even today, all we have to do is think of a baseball field in the warm sun, or a backyard barbecue, or a picnic in a grassy meadow, and we can practically smell the mustard.

Finding a superior hot dog stand, though, poses a special problem. You can buy a frank just about anywhere—the man with a pushcart just outside your office building sells them, and so do tiny diners on lonely roads in the Western desert. What you get may be as soggy as the sauerkraut in which it is drowning, or so over-grilled that it has the consistency of old bark; its innards can range from pure beef, subtly seasoned, to things unspeakable and over-spiced; its casing may have just the right snap or it may be tough enough to sheathe a howitzer shell. Some franks, in short, can be real dogs.

Perhaps the *best* hot dog stand anywhere is the one that has long been, and is still, the best-known: Nathan's Famous in the heart of Brooklyn's Coney Island amusement center. The area has been going downhill for a decade, but the chances are that if you see a throng gathered on Surf Avenue of a summer's day (or night), it's not an incipient riot—it's just the usual waiting line at Nathan's. The price has gone from five cents when Nathan Handwerker opened his stand in 1916 to 50 cents today, but any *aficionado* of the hot dog will tell you it's well worth it: the casing is a delight to bite into; the beef is lean and deliciously spiced with garlic and

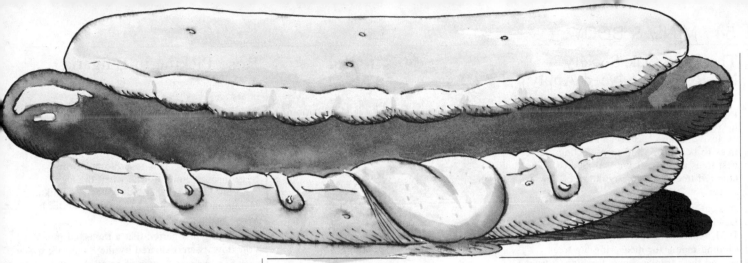

paprika according to a recipe devised by Nathan's wife Ida; and the nimble-fingered countermen almost never fail to whisk your frank off the grill at precisely the right moment.

Soon after Nathan's first opened, in the days when Eddie Cantor and Jimmy Durante were singing waiters in nearby establishments, the 24-hour hot dog stand became a favorite late-hours spot for café society and an obligatory whistle-stop for campaigning politicos. Practically everybody from Woodrow Wilson to the brothers Kennedy has sampled a Nathan's dog, and Nelson Rockefeller once said: "No one can hope to be elected in this state without being photographed eating a hot dog at Nathan's Famous." When the King and Queen of England visited Hyde Park in 1940, President Franklin D. Roosevelt asked Nathan to send up a batch from Coney Island.

With his block-long stand dispensing eight million hot dogs a year and showing a comfortable profit, Nathan Handwerker long resisted the pressures to expand or go into franchising. In 1958, however, he reluctantly began to yield, and now there are more than a dozen Nathan's scattered throughout the metropolitan New York area—in Times Square, Yonkers, Oceanside and Long Island, and in the cafeteria at the Brooklyn Museum.

Nathan's has just announced plans to begin operating on the West Coast in a big way; Nathan's will hit Los Angeles first and eventually move into at least 18 other locations. After that, a major expansion is scheduled for Florida, where Nathan's already has one unit. In addition to hot dogs, the new outlets (like the existing ones) will offer hamburgers (!), corned beef, roast beef, pastrami, salami, fried shrimps, soft shell crabs, clams and even frog's legs. There is, of course, a danger that such expansion will bring a dilution of quality. For that reason, Nathan Handwerker once vowed: "I won't have my name over the door unless I can be there myself to keep an eye on the grill."

Well, Nathan may not be there in person, but a visit to one of his establishments —particularly the gaudy green-and-white stand on Surf Avenue—is well worth it for anyone who fancies a crackling good hot dog. And that, of course, means just about everyone.

—Ronald P. Kriss

How to Grow Things in Your Car

You can make a vegetable garden out of your car in one morning—or you can stretch it out for months if you prefer. All you need is a hacksaw—or a neighbor with one—some busted-up concrete, 40 pounds of local earth and about 10 pounds of peat. First, you cut off the top of your car with the saw. This may take some work if you're not used to this type of activity. If you can't get into it, or if you're just impatient and want to get to the guts of your garden fast, cave in the roof with a good sledge hammer.

After you've got the top off, carefully rip out the seats. Experts say they pop right out if you pull, then push. But experts always say things like that and it might be wise not to put away the sledge hammer after the top part. You may have to pound them out.

Anyway, after the seats are out, it's time to throw a lot of broken bricks and rocks or concrete in the bottom of the car. Then, take out the bricks and rocks or concrete and poke about 50 holes in the bottom of the car for drainage. Then, put the rocks and bricks or concrete back in the car. Or, if you want to take a short cut, put the holes in the bottom of the car *first*.

Now, you're ready for the soil. Spread it around gently, mixing in a handful of peat every two minutes or so, except for the top foot which should be a full 28 percent peat. (This allows for 1 percent drainage of peat.)

You're ready now to choose the vegetables that you want in your car. I think you'll find

that nothing climbs a steering wheel more beautifully than zucchini—the legume that in Greek mythology was called "Dionysus' second favorite vegetable." The 500-pound Calabrian poet-gourmet, Dario Grazzo, once said, "When I tasted zucchini, I knew there was a God." And Pino Fiacco, a Roman bureaucrat, used to always tell his mistress, "Taste my mother's zucchini and die." (Actually, she did. The mother got two years.)

Anyway, if you plant zucchini on the dashboard, tomatoes on the rear deck, and corn in the middle, your garden will grow in a nice pyramid shape, which will save you money on shaving supplies if you elect to sleep under the car. (People who sleep under pyramid-shaped gardens do not grow beards. This experiment has been verified by experts.)

The great thing about a mobile garden is the fact that you can push your garden around to where the sun is, instead of waiting for it to come to you. This takes the help of a few people, but will surely pay off when they get the chance to eat the delicious fruits of their labor.

For more information see:

Hair, the Second Greatest Fertilizer Known to Man, by Harold Moore.

He Makes Me Eat It First, by Maureen Gibbons.

Beardless Gardeners of Pharos, by Hans Schultz.

—Don Novello

The Live Oak Society— No Red Oaks Need Apply

Everybody in the South loves trees, but the people of Lafayette, La. love trees so much they have honored them by making an exclusive, high-class organization for the trees to belong to, and then electing the very best trees to it: the Live Oak Society. The honored trees have to pay dues of 25 acorns a year.

A local college president named Edwin Lewis Stephens founded the Society back in 1931 as a sort of inevitable result of his lifelong mania for measuring big trees around their trunks. Since the biggest trees are the live oaks, he eventually restricted his measuring to these, which then became the only ones eligible for membership in his fancy tree club. "To my mind the live oak is the noblest of all our trees, the most to be admired for its beauty, most to be praised for its strength, most to be respected for its majesty, dignity and grandeur, most to be cherished and venerated for its age and character and most to be loved with gratitude for its beneficence of shade for all the generations of man dwelling within its vicinity," wrote Stephens.

Many of the 284 members of the Live Oak Society can be admired on the campus of the late Dr. Stephens' college, the University of Southwestern Louisiana, in Lafayette. To be admitted a tree must be presented for membership by a human attorney, with proof of a girth of 17 feet or more. The President of the Society is 35 feet in circumference; the four vice presidents range from 33 to 27 feet around. Rules are strict; the famous St. Denis oak of Natchitoches was expelled when it was discovered to be an impostor, actually a red oak. A tree may be banned for permitting itself to be whitewashed or—far worse—to carry advertising.

—*Roy Bongartz*

L*ike trees because they seem
more resigned to the way
they have to live
than other things do.*

—WILLA CATHER

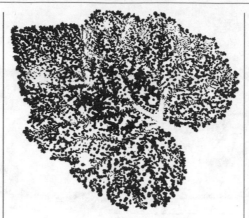

Following Fall Through the Northeast

From Labrador down through Nova Scotia, from New Brunswick through Vermont and New Hampshire, from the rocks of Maine through Massachusetts, Connecticut, New York, Pennsylvania and Ohio, fall sweeps like a firestorm. Autumn in the Northeast is a wonder, something not equaled anywhere in the world. Only in the Northeast do you find the exact combination of dry cold, stony soil and bitter sap full of auxin that causes the trees to explode into color every October. Leaves die quietly in other places; in the Northeast they go out with a bang.

The autumn is God's guarantee against defects in parts or workmanship. Even the rankest atheist, the staunchest Republican, the shrewdest horse trader has to take off his hat to fall in the Northeast. The people who live up there take it more or less in stride: "Shore nice colors this year." But there are tens of thousands who trek up the Appalachian Trail every fall to become "leafers"—tourists there just to take in the magnificent Northeastern fall.

The leafers are such an intent and significant bunch that the natives have gone into the leafer business. They now offer you:

Flaming Leaves Cruises on Lake Champlain. From Charlotte, Vt. to Essex, N.Y.; from Burlington, Vt. to Port Kent, N.Y.; from Grand Isle, Vt. to Cumberland Head, N.Y.—and vice-versa. Operated by the Lake Champlain Transportation Co.

Scenic Line Cruises also on Lake Champlain ("America's inland sea"). Three-hour round trip cruises up and down the lake, with the Adirondacks on one side and the Green Mountains on the other.

Autumn in New England motorcoach tours, run by Continental Trailways.

Green Carpet Tours through the Northeast and the Gaspé Peninsula of French Canada by motorcoach.

"Fall Foliage Tour" train trip through the Canadian Rockies and the Northeast, run by American Rail Tours.

(Your travel agent can arrange any of these leafer tours for you.)

—*David Saltman*

Rose Picking in Bulgaria

A rose is a rose is a rose, but in Bulgaria it is also a sacred essence, an attar of roses which visitors and tourists can help create.

Historically, Bulgaria's Queen of Roses traces its origins to the Persian palaces of Isfahan, the mosques of Damascus and the vale of Kashmir. This rose blooms from May through June, a time when the air of the Valley of Roses, nestled between the Balkan Range and Sredna Gora Mountain, is kissed by sweet drifting rose scents.

It is during this period that a thousand million flowers are gathered by the local folk to make an expensive attar of roses. Legend has it that the attar was discovered when an Indian princess bathed in water strewn with rose petals.

The blossoms are plucked in the early morning, before the high sun can dry up the essential oils. For the past several seasons, visitors and tourists have been allowed to join in the harvest. Arrangements for accommodations can be made in any of the official camping sites or in the towns of Plovdiv (on Stoletov Peak), Kalofer or Hissar.

—*The Editors*

Discovering Wildflowers

Spring wildflowers abound in every state of the union, especially after a winter of heavy rains. Some species, such as the blue lupin, are found almost everywhere. By contrast, the Golden Blazing Star is a yellow flower of great beauty that only a knowledgeable eye will recognize.

Wildflower hikes in the spring can be delightful outings if you know where to go and how to identify the flowers.

Usually your state's Parks and Recreation Department, c/o your state capital, can suggest some of the better local ranges. The national Sierra Club chapter nearest you can be helpful and may be sponsoring wildflower outings. In Northern California some of the most abundant wildflower ranges are the north face of Mt. Tamalpais for iris, the narrow road through the San Antonio valley between Mt. Hamilton and Livermore for all species, Pescadero Beach south of San Francisco for beach flowers, the Carmel Valley road for all species and the Hunter Liggett military reservation roads for all species.

You will want a good guide to identifying the flowers if you plan to proceed beyond ecstatic comments about their color. *Spring Wildflowers* by Helen Sharsmith (University of California Press, $2.25) is a good book for beginners. It focuses on Northern California, but the instruction in identifying flowers by sexual parts, seeds and leaves, "keying into families" as the botanists put it, is universally useful. Supplement this book with the local guide to flowers in your area that Parks and Recreation departments or the Sierra Club may suggest.

—*Lee Foster*

Working the French Grape Harvest

If you're in Europe in October, make sure you head for the southwestern part of France. This is the time each year for the *vendanges*, or grape harvest. For the most part, France's grapes still come from small privately-owned vineyards where the owner hires workers just for the harvest. Go to any village, ask around to find out who is hiring, and you're sure to find a job. In the past, France was invaded each year by pickers from Spain, but pay is as good in Spain now as it is in France, so not as many pickers come over, and the French need new sources of cheap labor.

When you are hired, this is what you can expect: a place to sleep, food, about $12 pay a day, all the wine you can drink and some of the hardest work you have ever done in your life.

I worked on a small farm outside of Toulouse; we were a group of 12 from the United States, Canada, Australia, Spain and France. We were given two old farm houses to live in and treat as our own. Our *patron* gave us fresh eggs, milk, vegetables and occasional chickens and we made our own meals. (Some farms serve meals as part of the wage and you are sure to get delicious French cuisine. But we enjoyed taking turns making our own meals every day.)

You begin cutting the grapes at 8 a.m. and work till noon. Then you have two hours for lunch and enough time to give each other back rubs. Then it's back to the vines until 6 p.m. As I said before, it's extremely hard work, but it's also a good chance to get to know your body again. For the most part, the festival spirit prevails—lots of singing, laughing and great grape fights. No need to speak French; you'll learn some before you've been on the job very long. When all the grapes are picked at one farm, you can move on to another. I talked to a lot of people who had worked on other farms and they had had pretty much the same experience.

You will be working in one of the loveliest regions of France, and the fall season is unbelievably colorful. The grape leaves turn from a green to a yellow to a rust and then to a beautiful maroon shade; you're surrounded by fields of other crops and small hills covered with forests. And wine will never taste so good as after you've spent a day toiling in the vineyards.

–Sondi Field

ON THE ROAD

Walter Meisenheimer's Garden

In Surry County, Virginia, there's a place just off the road where travelers can rest. It's a special place because of its loveliness and because of the man who spends his days keeping it that way.

Charles Kuralt: It happens almost every day. A tourist, driving along Route 10 here in Surry County, Virginia, sees the picnic table signs and drives in, expecting to find another wayside park. That's when he gets his big surprise. That tourist quickly finds out this isn't exactly like other wayside parks he's visited before.

For one thing, there are flowers on the tables, and fresh tomatoes in season, put there for the use of whoever passes by. Beyond the tables, there is a paradise, a rare and beautiful garden of 13 acres, alive with the blooms of thousands of azaleas, bordered by dogwood blossoms and laced by a mile of pleasant walks in the dappled shade of tall pines. In all our travels, it is the loveliest garden we've ever seen. The startled traveler must speculate how large a battery of state-employed gardeners it takes to keep this place pristine. The answer is: one old man, and he's nobody's employee.

Walter Meisenheimer, a former nurseryman, created all this in the woods next to his house, created it alone, after he retired at the age of 70. He's 82 now, and he spends every day tending his garden for the pleasure of strangers who happen to stop here.

Walter Meisenheimer: I like people, and this is my way of following some of the teaching of my parents. When I was a youngster, one of the things they said was: "If you don't try to make the world just a little bit nicer when you leave here, what is the reason for a man's existence in the first place?"

Kuralt: Have you ever speculated, if one man can do all this, and keep it so clean and beautiful, why the states don't have places like this?

Meisenheimer: Now, I offered to give this to the state without any cost. I've talked to a number of [state people]. I was told by the Highway Department it was too large. I was told that it was too small for the Parks Service. And both of them told me, with the strings that I put on—that it be maintained and kept open to the public—that the costs would be prohibitive.

Kuralt: What's going to happen to this place after you're gone?

Meisenheimer: Well, I imagine that within a very few years, this will be undergrowth or nature will take it over again.

Kuralt: You mean it's not going to survive?

Meisenheimer: Well, I doubt it.

Kuralt: That's a terribly discouraging thing, isn't it?

Meisenheimer: Well, that's the way I see it now.

Kuralt: Others stopped at Walter Meisenheimer's garden the same day we did. There were school kids and old folks, and the daily quota of surprised and delighted tourists. We stood for a while in the peace of the garden before it was time to move on, and watched the sun appear from behind a cloud to light a branch of dogwood which Walter Meisenheimer planted here. The words of a corny turn-of-the-century poem suddenly didn't seem so corny any more. Something about living in a house by the side of the road and being a friend to man.

–Charles Kuralt, CBS News, On The Road, Surry County, Virginia

A Home Full of Orchids in San Miguel

Probably the foremost collector of orchids in Mexico is Stirling Dickenson, director of the Instituto Allende in San Miguel de Allende, a tourist center and art colony 175 miles north of Mexico City. At his home, Los Pocitos (Little Springs), Dickenson has gathered together a fantastic display of orchids. His gardens and orchid houses cover several acres, and they are open to the public—free.

Dickenson started collecting orchids in 1946, and has since traveled to Nepal and other exotic lands for rare specimens. "I don't know how many thousands of plants I have now," he says. "Orchid collecting is a progressive disease—you can't stop it."

A visit to Los Pocitos is an adventure in forms and colors. There are always orchids blooming. You may encounter anything from a Burro's Ear orchid with tiny yellow-and-green sprays (shaped, naturally, like a burro's ear) to a showy San Miguel variety with six-inch purple-and-white blooms.

The address of Los Pocitos is Santo Domingo 38, San Miguel, Mexico. Visiting hours are 9 a.m. to 1 p.m. and 3 p.m. to 6 p.m. daily. (The two hours from 1 p.m. to 3 p.m. are for siesta time.)

–James Egan

WATER

If there is magic on this planet, it is contained in water. . . .

Once in a lifetime, perhaps, one escapes the actual confines of the flesh.
Once in a lifetime, if one is lucky, one so merges
with sunlight and air and running water that whole eons, the eons that mountains
and deserts know, might pass in a single afternoon without discomfort. . . .
One can never quite define this secret;
but it has something to do, I am sure, with common water. Its substance reaches everywhere;
it touches the past and prepares the future;
it moves under the poles and wanders thinly in the heights of air.
It can assume forms of exquisite perfection in a snowflake,
or strip the living to a single shining bone cast up by the sea.

—LOREN EISELEY

Dowsers Are the Wizards of Water

Take care not to get zapped by the weird electricity flowing in all directions on the handsome common in Danville, Vt. during the three-day dowsers' convention held there in the fall. Diviners of all sizes, shapes and ages move along as if they were sleepwalking in crisscrossing trajectories, led by their dowsing rods, which are made of wood, wire, car aerials, whalebone, iron bars or coat hangers. One man gets news of underground water or metals simply through the soles of his bare feet. Pendulums made of such things as phonograph-needle containers and automobile transmission gears swing obediently at the ends of strings for their masters.

A Minnesota dowser who came to a recent convention claims he has so much electricity in him that he's had to have his wristwatch encased in plastic to prevent his magnetism from causing the hairspring to attach itself to the inside of the case. An annual treasure hunt is child's play for the dowsers, who simply ask their forked sticks where the loot is hidden and then follow them to it. One old-timer can dowse with his neck and back. In what he calls a "rigid spine" demonstration he vibrates on a stage, his body stiff as a board. "I activate over water," he explains.

Farthest-out dowsing is called map dowsing, which consists of letting a pendulum point out, on a map, where real water will be found on the land indicated. Some dowsers have a sense of humor; one of them answers the phone: "Water you want to know?" A sailing dowser says he has found his way safely to port through fog by following his divining rod, and another diviner, who had to move away to a new state, found a house to buy in the new location by asking his pendulum how to find it.

Although one skeptic claims that "dowsing is by far the most widespread example of mass self-delusion in the history of civilization," most of the diviners who attend the convention in Danville get all the work they can handle finding places to dig wells for people. Visitors to this year's convention, which will be held Oct. 4-6, are entirely welcome. Write for information to the American Society of Dowsers, Inc., Danville, Vt. 05828.

—Roy Bongartz

*The stream I love unbounded goes
Through flood and sea
and firmament;
Through light, through life,
it forward flows. . . .
Through years, through men,
through Nature fleet,
Through love and thought,
through power and dream.*

—RALPH WALDO EMERSON

Jugging for Cats

Way down around the levee towns of the Mississippi, folks used to have a sport called "jugging for cats." Of course, that was maybe a hundred years ago and you don't see many people out jugging these days. It's almost a lost art, but it's worth recapturing.

The time to start jugging is when the catfish are jumping. The tackle required is very simple: five or six empty jugs tightly corked with corn cobs and as many stout lines, each about five feet long with a sinker and large hook at the end. Tie each line to the handle of a jug.

Old-timers say fresh liver, angleworms and balls made of corn meal and cotton make good bait, and a bit of cheese, tied up in some mosquito netting, is also considered a tempting morsel.

Once the hooks are baited, the fisherman rows out on the river and drops the earthenware floats about 10 feet apart in a line across the middle of the stream. The jugs will be carried with the current so they'll have to be followed and watched. Whenever one starts behaving strangely, bobbing about, turning upside down, darting upstream and down, the fisherman knows he's hooked something, and the chase begins.

It sometimes requires hard rowing to catch a jug. Many times when you think you've got it in your outstretched hands, the jug darts off anew, frequently disappearing beneath the water only to come up again yards away.

Of course, you'd think the pursuit of just one jug would be exciting enough, but imagine the discombobulation when four or five jugs start bobbing frantically at the same time. It's at such times that the skills, patience and steady hands of the jugger are really put to the test. Most novices hurry the hauling—instead of carefully pulling in each of his jug lines, the inexperienced jugger works so hastily he loses his fish.

To be a successful jugger, you've got to be careful and deliberate in taking out the fish, no matter how many other lines may be vying for your attention with their frenetic signals. Jugging for cats is no mere sport—it's an art.

—Min S. Yee

Rent a Canoe Trip

It's a park, yes. But it also is a 3,000-square mile wilderness the size of Delaware and Rhode Island. It has more than 2,100 lakes, and the only way to see it is by canoe. And all you need bring along to enjoy a wilderness adventure into Ontario's Algonquin Provincial Park is yourself.

For under $10 a day, outfitters will provide everything you need, including food, tent, canoe, sleeping bag, air mattress, cooking and eating utensils and such incidentals as soap, matches and pot cleaners. They'll even provide a reflector oven.

Make a single, short portage, and civilization can seem as remote as the dark side of the moon. Pitch your tent at a campsite that is little more than a rough clearing in the bush with a few boulders to cradle a fire and go to sleep in a solitude that may be disturbed only by a bark of a prowling fox or the weird, startling cry of a loon.

Encountering a deer in the forest can become a common occurrence and chances are good of spotting a moose or gliding a canoe within a paddle length of a beaver. The canoeing camper is sure to meet many of the park's smaller denizens, such as raccoons, chipmunks and such furbearers as marten, fisher, otter and mink. The visitor also will see many of the 116 species of birds known to nest in Algonquin—perhaps a ruffed grouse, osprey or woodpecker.

Perhaps the most knowledgeable outfitter in the park—organized by a former Deputy Chief Ranger—is Algonquin Outfitters, RR 1, Dwight, Ont., Canada. Phone (705) 635-2243.

Snake River Raft Trips: Wet and Wild

The traveler who vacations in the Grand Teton–Yellowstone region of Wyoming should spend a half day on the Snake River south of the city of Jackson. No less than 18 river-running outfits offer U.S. Forest Service-approved excursions which feature safe but sensational runs through white-water rapids. Nobody, but nobody stays dry as their flexing rubber boat dips, plunges, drops and leaps through waves and spray. One of the outfits (Parklands Expeditions) even offers a trip with a gourmet luncheon stop—complete with hearty rich burgundy wine, marvelous Swiss cheese, French bread (unsliced . . . you tear off hunks), and native buffalo salami. The trip runs 12 miles, lasts four hours. Price without lunch stop is $15, with meal $30—the lunch trip is likely to be much less crowded.

—Mike Miller

Down the Boiling River on a Twelve-by-Six Island

By William McGinnis

A whitewater raft is a little ship. Stable, tough, riverworthy, it glides through the wilderness, slipping across calms, bucking through thunderous rapids. It carries an intimate society of four or maybe five people past sandy beaches, lush forests and sheer rock cliffs. For days or weeks on end the boat sweeps along, dodging waterfalls, sneaking up on goats, bears, donkeys and elk sipping the river's water; each night the crew makes camp beside deep salmon pools perfect for swimming and diving.

Life in the little boat alters with the mood of the river, growing lazy when the river is quiet and alert when the river explodes into tumultuous foam. Sometimes life on the raft seems too intimate, and the people feel trapped: nerves chafe, tempers flare, anger divides the crew—but open talk usually clears the air. Most of the time the mood is high and feelings are good. Journeying through dangerous, isolated canyons, members of the group come to trust and depend upon one another—at times, especially when running violent rapids, the group functions as a single being. Life in the boat is always intense, always utterly absorbing, and at times members of the crew may feel that the voyage is the richest experience of their lives.

Begin whitewater rafting by going on a trip either with an experienced friend or with a group from one of the many fine whitewater schools all across the United States. Bear in mind that whitewater expeditioning is dangerous unless it is approached with the thorough understanding of rivers and rafting technique that only experienced people have. Once you've been initiated by a friend or school, you can start putting together your own expeditions and rafting down beautiful wilderness rivers on your own.

WHITEWATER RAFTING SCHOOLS

In the East

Mountain Streams & Trails Outfitters, 2420 Saunders Station Road, Monroeville, Pa. 15146. One-day paddle trips in rafts and inflatable kayaks on the Cheat and Youghiogheny rivers.

Smokey Mountain River Expeditions, P.O. Box 252, Hot Springs, N.C. 28743. One-day paddle raft trips on the French Broad River of western North Carolina.

Wilderness Voyageurs, Inc., P.O. Box 97, Ohiopyle, Pa. 15470. One-day paddle raft trips on the Youghiogheny River.

Wildwater Expeditions Unlimited, Inc., P.O. Box 55, Thurmond, W. Va. 25936. Two-day paddle raft voyages on the New and Gauley rivers of West Virginia.

A primer on whitewater rafting, with information on the gear you'll need, the schools that will teach you rafting skills and a couple of rivers you might want to run after you've got the skills. You'll soon see that while this is one of the most exciting of all sports, it's not for the casual or the unprepared.

In the West

American Whitewater School, American River Touring Association, 1016 Jackson St., Oakland, Calif. 94607. Month-long whitewater course covering oar and paddle raft, plus kayak. Also paddle option on trips in the West.

Grand Canyon Youth Expeditions, Inc., RR 2, Box 755, Flagstaff, Ariz. 86001. Three-week rowing expeditions through the Grand Canyon.

Hatch River Expeditions, 411 E. Second N., Vernal, Utah 84078. Will arrange paddle trips on request.

Orange Torpedo Trips, P.O. Box 1111, Grants Pass, Ore. 97526. Paddle trips in inflatable kayaks.

Parklands Whitewater School, P.O. Box 371, Jackson Hole, Wyo. 83001. Ten-day course in "Sport Yaks" (little one-man whitewater boats) and rafts on rivers in Jackson Hole area.

Travel Institute, 714 Ninth Ave., Salt Lake City, Utah 84103. Paddle option on trips in Utah area.

Wilderness World, 1342 Jewell Ave., Pacific Grove, Calif. 93950. Boatman's training.

Whitewater Expeditions—River Exploration, P.O. Box 2, Dillon Beach, Calif. 94929. Oar and paddle expeditions on the rivers of British Columbia, Alaska, Mexico and the West. Small groups.

Whitewater Guide Trips, 12120 SW Douglas, Portland, Ore. 97225. Whitewater youth camp for boys aged 12 to 17.

What You Need to Go Whitewater Rafting

Raft

Oars and rowing frame or paddles (plus full set of spare oars or paddles)

Life jackets (should be Class I, Coast Guard-approved, full-jacket type)

Patch, tool and spare parts kit

Bailing buckets

400 feet of strong line

Watertight bags

Air pump

Shovel

Crash helmets for rocky rivers

Cooking gear

Sturdy bags for all unburnable garbage

Camping gear: sleeping bags, tent, etc.

Clothes & personal stuff: sun cream, insect repellent, sun hat, tennis shoes, windbreaker, sweater, etc.

Books

First aid kit

Maps

Emergency & survival gear: flares, signal mirror, dextrose, extra food, winch, etc.

Author William McGinnis on the Green River with passengers and a full load of gear for a week in the wilderness

BUYING A WHITEWATER RAFT

When you get ready to buy your own raft, ease your mind and prolong your life by getting a raft you can depend on. Rugged, inflatable boats designed for whitewater cost anywhere from $400 to $1,000 (or more). Made of thick, tough material and usually weighing more than 85 pounds, good rafts can withstand the punishment dealt out by rocky streambeds and, if punctured, they are kept afloat by their multiple air chambers.

For stability and maneuverability, optimum sizes are the "seven-man" raft, which measures approximately 12 feet long by six feet wide and actually carries three to four people; and the "10-man" raft, which is about 16 feet long by eight feet wide and carries five people. Not only can both of these boats dodge down the smallest of raftable streams, they can also go bravely, at moderate water levels, on even the largest rivers.

Some rafts can be purchased for as little as $50. They are cheap suicide. Generally yellow, imported and lightweight (less than 60 pounds), "Kamakazi" rafts are so thin that with their first brush against a rock they literally pop.

At present, only a few companies make high quality inflatable boats suitable for whitewater. They are:

Seagull Marine
1851 McGaw Ave.
Irvine, Calif. 92705
Handles Avon rafts, the best boats available.

Inflatable Boats Unlimited
P.O. Box O
Kanab, Utah 84741
Handles the most complete line of fine rafts, from pontoons to "six-man" boats.

Campways
415 Molino St.
Los Angeles, Calif. 90013
Handles a less expensive raft that is less durable than some, but adequate.

American Safety Equipment Corp.
7652 Burnet Ave.
Van Nuys, Calif. 91405
Handles a new raft called the "Rivermaster."

Oars or Paddles?

The novice rafter putting together his own outfit must make a basic choice between oars and paddles. The difference may seem insignificant, but your decision will have drastic impact on the type of experience you and your companions will have on the river.

Paddles unite a raft's crew into a pack of uncomfortable, fatuously happy slaves. Everyone in a paddle raft must pull like a wild demon to guide the raft through rapids. Sitting astride the buoyancy tubes cowboy fashion, paddlers meet the river head on, taking waves in the teeth and often getting washed overboard. In paddle rafts the people are drawn close by their shared exertion, forming a tight bond of trust and good feeling that is rare in modern life. It is paddlers who experience the most intense adventure; there they are, with nothing but inefficient paddles between them and disaster.

Oars are a different story. One man with a frame and oars can easily do what four men with paddles break their backs to accomplish. Because someone wielding long oars can maneuver a boat with a speed and certainty that paddlers cannot duplicate, the crews of oar boats feel safer, further from the edge. But the confrontation is largely between the oarsman and the river—and the group is not drawn together by common effort.

An incidental factor to consider is the increased carrying capacity afforded by a rowing frame. If your raft is 12 feet long or smaller, the extra baggage space the frame gives you is essential for extended trips.

Understanding Whitewater Terminology

To comprehend "standard" descriptions of whitewater rivers and rapids, you need to know something about the difficulty rating scale and river gradients and volumes.

Whitewater rafters rate rapids and rivers on a one-to-10 scale of difficulty—one is easy and 10 is almost unrunnable. Respect this scale. Even a number two rapids requires some skill, and a number three rapids on the Middle Fork of the Salmon River in Idaho once flipped an entire party of rafts, so terrorizing the group that rather than continue down the river they packed their gear miles back to the nearest road.

Because rapid and river ratings are determined by experts who slip with ease down difficult rivers, many ratings are lower than they should be. What an expert considers "medium difficulty," may be extremely tough indeed for an intermediate or novice boater. So be careful. Do not attempt a river or rapids you are not ready to handle.

Rapid and River Rating System*

American Scale Used by Rafters		European Scale Used by Kayakers
1, 2	Easy. Waves small; passages clear; no serious obstacles.	I
3, 4	Medium. Rapids of moderate difficulty with passages clear. Requires experience plus fair outfit and boat.	II
5, 6	Difficult. Waves numerous, high, irregular; rocks; eddies; rapids with passages that are clear though narrow, requiring expertise in maneuver; inspection usually needed. Requires good operator and boat.	III
7, 8	Very difficult. Long rapids; waves powerful, irregular; dangerous rocks; boiling eddies; passages difficult to scout; scouting mandatory first time; powerful and precise maneuvering required. Demands expert boatman and excellent boat and outfit.	IV
9	Exceedingly difficult. Extremely difficult, long and violent rapids, following each other almost without interruption; riverbed extremely obstructed; big drops; violent current; very steep gradient; scouting essential but difficult. Requires best man, boat, and outfit suited to the situation.	V
10	Utmost difficulty. All previously mentioned difficulties carried to the very limit of navigability. Cannot be attempted without risk of life. For teams of experts only, at favorable water levels, and after close study. All possible precautions must be taken.	VI
U	Unrunnable.	U

*Based in part on a similar chart by Leslie Jones and in part on the American Whitewater Association River Classification System.

Rafting through the Moonshine Rapids, on the Green River, in the Dinosaur National Monument, Utah

A river's gradient is measured in foot drop per mile (fpm), and it provides a rough indication of the river's speed and level of difficulty. Rivers with gradients less than 10

(continued on next page)

A GUIDE TO TWO RIVERS

(continued from previous page)

fpm are usually slow and easy, while rivers with gradients of more than 20 fpm are usually fast, difficult and dangerous. However, this is not always true; in the Grand Canyon the Colorado has a gradient of less than 10 fpm, yet this is one of the most challenging stretches of water on earth.

Water volume is the crucial variable in the rafter's life—too little volume creates a long, narrow rock patch, too much a rampaging monster. To measure volume, river people use a volume/time unit—cubic feet per second (cfs). Casually referred to as "second feet," cfs indicates the amount of water flowing past any given point along a river in one second. Most of the better rafting rivers have between 1,000 and 10,000 cfs. Some rivers are runnable when they're as low as 500 cfs and others when they're as high as 400,000 cfs, but these are freak extremes.

Volume largely determines power. A small river of, say, 1,000 cfs simply does not have the speed or force of the large river of 4,000 cfs or more. Although it may have rock-strewn channels and other difficulties, the small, weak river tends to be easier because it allows for greater maneuvering and is more forgiving of mistakes.

Because spring floods can transform even mild rivers into raging torrents, it is imperative that all rivers be approached with great caution during the spring. (This also goes for smaller rivers. Even though a creek suddenly seems large enough to run, do not attempt it without thoroughly scouting it first. Creeks in flood often spell red, muddy death; many seasoned river people have drowned in their local, flood-swollen creeks.) There are, of course, those rivers which become runnable only during the spring melt; the safest way to locate these is through reliable river guidebooks.

Good flows and weather for rafting are found anywhere from April to October, depending on the river and climate.

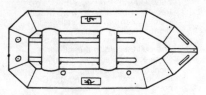

Directions: To reach the put in at the base of Summersville Dam, drive south from Summersville on Highway 19, then west on Highway 129. To shuttle to the take out near Swiss, go northwest on Highway 129, then west on Highway 39. The take out is one mile upriver from Swiss along Road 19/25. After paralleling a railroad siding for several hundred yards, this road turns up Laurel Creek. Stop just before the turn. The sandy peninsula across the tracks is the take-out beach.

Two of the most beautiful whitewater rivers in America are the Gauley in West Virginia and the East Fork of the Carson in California and Nevada. If you plan to run one of these rivers, you should not only obtain maps—you should also inquire of park rangers and local residents about conditions on the river just before you make your raft trip.

By no means should anyone attempt to raft the Gauley without first perfecting his whitewater skills on less treacherous streams. But when you are ready for this river, it will give you endless pleasure. The East Carson is not as difficult a stream; less experienced rafters can run this river.

Gauley River

Deep in the Appalachians of West Virginia a rugged defile reverberates with a thunderous roar. The mighty Gauley gnaws at the foundations of thousand-foot cliffs and awesome wooded inclines. The relentless flow shifts great boulders and snaps logs like twigs. Man ventures into the Gauley Canyon at some risk; meeting the challenge of that risk provides an intense experience of permanent, personal value. The Gauley is without doubt one of America's finest whitewater rivers. Run it while you can: the Army Corps of Engineers, always busy as beavers, want to build a dam across it.

Location: Appalachian Mountains of West Virginia. About 40 miles east of Charleston.

Put in and take out: Summersville Dam to Swiss

Difficulty rating: nine—exceedingly difficult

Gradient: 27 fpm

Volume: 500-10,000 cfs (raftable between 2,000 and 3,000)

Wilderness quality: excellent

Time: two days

Distance: 24 river miles

Best time to run: fall; after Oct. 1 an adequate water level is assured by the release schedule of Summersville Dam. The flow at the put in can be obtained from the dam-keeper's office, and the flow for the lower 18 miles of the run (often a bit higher than at the put in) is obtainable from the Weather Service as the "Belva Gauge." Flow information for rivers in the Kanawha Basin (the Gauley is part of the Kanawha System) can be obtained by calling (304) 529-2318, extension 604.

Weather: variable

Type of raft: use boat 11 to 18 feet long

Fishing: smallmouth bass, largemouth bass, catfish, northern pike and walleye

Maps: U.S. Geological Survey topographic maps. Run covered by two quadrangles of the 15' series: Winona and Fayetteville. Send 50 cents per map to: Distribution Section, U.S. Geological Survey, 1200 S. Eads St., Arlington, Va. 22202. Be sure to specify map name, series and state.

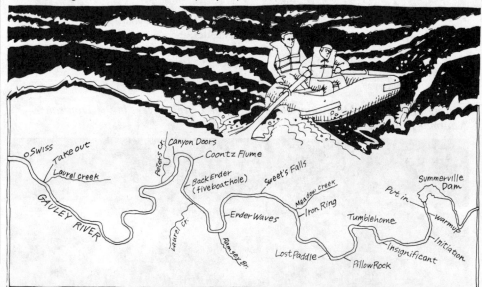

Hazards: With over 60 rapids rated seven or higher, including at least two of class 10, the Gauley is considered by many to be the most difficult stretch of foam in West Virginia. It is powerful, treacherous and intoxicating. Long, intricate rapids follow one upon another in wonderful, terrible procession. Ledges, stopper waves, house boulders, souse holes and undercut rock join forces with devastating effect, often causing even veteran rafters to falter.

An ultimate challenge, this fascinating, perilous voyage should be attempted only by expert boaters in the company of others who have previously made the run. One such individual, who guides expeditions through the canyon, is Jon Dragan, of Wildwater Expeditions Unlimited, P.O. Box 55, Thurmond, W. Va. 25936.

East Fork, Carson River

Swift yet calm, this little river glides smoothly from high mountain meadows to desert canyons. Though its steep gradient suggests otherwise, it is an easy stream with only minor rapids. Unlike most rivers, which alternately pool up in calms and crash down in rapids, the East Carson flows fast and steady with few interruptions. It sweeps along easily from bank to narrow bank.

Directions: The quaint California settlement of Markleeville is best approached from the west via Highway 50 and then Highway 89 and from the east via Highway 88. An easy put in is found one mile southeast of Markleeville at Hangman's Bridge, where Highway 89 crosses the East Carson River. Shuttle to Nevada take out up Highway 89 to Woodfords, northeast on Highway 88 to Centerville, across to Gardnerville and southeast five miles on Highway 395 to take-out turnoff. (Finding this turnoff takes attention. Keep an eye on the river as you drive south along Highway 395. Just south of where the river veers sharply westward away from the highway, a dirt road leaves the highway and follows the river's southern bank. The take out is immediately upstream from the abandoned dam, shown on the Mt. Siegel quadrangle map as "pump." As you drive in along the crude road this dam appears as a 40-foot waterfall.)

Hazards: Though this is a mild river with relatively easy rapids, the East Carson can present special problems. Fallen trees sometimes block the narrow channel, and the total absence of eddies (places where the current stops or turns to head upstream) often makes stopping difficult. Be alert.

Also be careful not to go over the old dam at the end of the run, where the river plunges 40 feet into a hypnotizing caldron of foam. You can tell you're approaching the dam by the many willows lining the banks just above it—and by the loud roar of the falls.

A rest after a day's run down the Yampa River, Utah

Location: Eastern slope of Sierra-Nevada Mountains, Northern California/Nevada. About 20 miles southwest of Lake Tahoe.

Put in and take out: Hangman's Bridge near Markleeville, Calif. to abandoned dam near Highway 395 in Nevada.

Difficulty rating: three—medium difficulty

Gradient: 27 fpm

Volume: 60-2,500 cfs (raftable above 800 cfs)

Wilderness quality: excellent

Time: allow two days

Distance: 20 river miles

Best time to run: June (too low in July)

Weather: fair and cool in June; cold nights

Type of raft: use boat nine to 16 feet long

Fishing: rainbow, cutthroat and brook trout; also the primordial Carson River cutthroats, Piute trout; license required

Maps: U.S. Geological Survey topographic maps. Run covered by three quadrangles of the 15' series: Markleeville (Calif.), Topaz Lake (Calif.) and Mt. Siegel (Calif./Nev.). Send 50 cents per map to Denver Distribution Section, U.S. Geological Survey, Denver Federal Center, Building 41, Denver, Colo. 80225. Be sure to specify map name, series and state. Also get U.S. Geological Survey "Plan and Profile: Carson River, Nev.-Calif.," sheets 2 and 3. Available from Denver Distribution Section for 75 cents per sheet.

U.S. WHITEWATER AT A GLANCE

West	East
Selway (Idaho)	Allagash (Maine)
Yellowstone (Mont.)	St. Croix (Maine)
Salmon (Idaho)	Machias (Maine)
Middle Fork, Salmon (Idaho)	St. John (Maine)
Hell's Canyon (Idaho, Ore.)	New (W. Va.)
	Gauley (W. Va.)
Upper Snake (Wyo.)	Youghiogheny (Pa.)
Green (Colo., Utah)	Cheat (W. Va.)
Yampa (Colo.)	Big Sandy Creek (Va.)
Rogue (Ore.)	Stony Creek (Va.)
McKenzie (Ore.)	Shavers Fork (W. Va.)
John Day (Ore.)	Moccasin Creek (Va.)
Grand Ronde (Ore.)	Nantahala (N.C.)
Salt (Ariz.)	Ammonoosac (N.H.)
Owyhee (Ore.)	Ashuelot (N.H.)
Clackamas (Ore.)	Ottauquechee (Vt.)
Deshutes (Ore.)	Mad (Vt.)
Klamath (Calif.)	Saco (N.H.)
Eel (Calif.)	Shepaug (Conn.)
Sacramento (Calif.)	Pine Creek (Pa.)
South Fork, American (Calif.)	Shade Creek (Pa.)
	Chattooga (Ga., S.C.)
Stanislaus (Calif.)	Potomac (Md.)
Carson (Calif.)	Smoke Hole (W. Va.)
Tuolumne (Calif.)	Cacapon (W. Va.)
Westwater Canyon (Colo., Utah)	French Broad (N.C.)
	Shenandoah (W. Va.)
Cataract Canyon (Ariz.)	Russell (Va., Ky.)
Grand Canyon (Ariz.)	Clinch (Va.)
Rio Grande (Tex.)	Maury (Va.)
	Back Creek (Va.)
	Tygart (W. Va.)
Midwest	West (Vt.)
	Millers (Mass.)
Wolf (Wis.)	White (Vt.)
Eau Claire (Wis.)	Winooski (Vt.)
Swan Creek (Mo.)	Farmington (Mass., Conn.)
Peshtigo (Wis.)	
St. Francis (Mo.)	Westfield (Mass.)

In the United States there are a large number of fine whitewater rivers. While most of the longer, more rugged streams are found in the West, the East is not without its share of superlative whitewater.

Tahiti Boats: Try Rubber on the Wild Rivers

Tahiti boats—bullet-shaped, inflated rubber vessels from France—combine the best points of the lowly inner tube and the noble kayak. And that's why you're seeing more and more of them on the wild rivers.

Like inner tubes, Tahiti boats shoot rapids in that wonderful, reckless, rollicking way— rearing up over waves, *kerplunking* down on the other side. But because your body is nestled into the cozy space between two fat, pontoon sides and because you can use a paddle to steer the boat, they're faster, safer and more manageable than inner tubes. Tahiti boats have several advantages over kayaks, too:

They're less destructible. Because they're made of inflated rubber, they bounce—off rocks, trees, other boats.

They're more practical. Just tuck your boat (neatly folded into a two-foot package) under your arm, head for a river and inflate it on the bank. At the end of the trip, deflate it and hitchhike back to your car. You can also carry an extra boat along with you in your boat in case it springs a leak.

And Tahiti boats are cheaper than kayaks. A one-person 11-footer (K-77) sells for $69.50 and a two-person 12½-footer (K-107) goes for $83 at most big department stores. Sevylor-U.S.A., the Los Angeles-based American branch of the French company, has more or less cornered the market, so I'm quoting their prices. But Pirawa, in New York, sells some slightly more expensive variations.

The biggest commercial venture using Tahiti boats is Orange Torpedo Trips, run by Jerry and Helen Bentley; they offer one- and three-day trips on the Rogue, Klamath and Deschutes Rivers in Oregon. (For more information on these, write P.O. Box 1111, Grants Pass, Ore. 97526.)

–Susan Sands

Float Down the Buffalo

Designated by Congress as a wild river to be preserved in perpetuity, the Buffalo River of northwest Arkansas winds lazily under the overhang of rock palisades and beside occasional meadows to a juncture with the White River. Trippers can put canoes and johnboats into the stream anywhere below the bridge where State Highway 7 crosses the river to Buffalo River State Park. The idea is to float silently through the wilderness of abandoned farmlands, soaking up the peace. Firearms and outboards are not considered good form. The loudest instrument accepted is a well-oiled fishing reel.

For information or to lease a boat or guide, write: Buffalo River State Park Headquarters, Yellville, Ark. 72689.

–Bern Keating

Whitewater Kayaking

Like skiing 40 years ago, whitewater and wildwater kayak racing today is virtually a way of life for the adventuresome types who catch the fever. The really gung-ho boaters practically live with their kayaks, on the water or camped by the rivers they'll be running the next day.

Kayaks and "canoes" used by racers are a far cry from the sealskin-covered frames developed as hunting vessels, dim centuries ago, by Eskimos. Modern kayaks are tough, light fiberglass craft, about 13 feet long, and Americans of all ages race in them—against each other and nature—in some of the most turbulent rivers they can find. The first requirement for any event in whitewater and wildwater kayak racing is a stretch of river with fast, challenging water, and streams in New England, Colorado and the mid-Atlantic states provide these in abundance.

In whitewater slalom, as in its skiing namesake, a racer must negotiate a course containing a series of gates that weave in an intricate criss-crossing pattern across the boiling river. But there the parallel with ski racing ends. Instead of driving skis down a steep slope in a ballet of speed, whitewater boaters must guide their arrow-like craft down surging, swirling rapids, fighting off whirlpools and rocks while making the gates (which are hung across the river from a network of overhead wires).

Just to make it more challenging, each gate is coded to tell the boater how he must go through it—downstream or upstream, bow-first or stern-first. Each racer is penalized 10 points for touching with paddle, body or boat the inside of a gate, 20 points for touching the outside of a gate and 50 points for missing a gate or going through it the wrong way. A final score in the race is time in seconds, plus accumulated penalty points. A whitewater slalom will customarily have from 12 to 30 gates on a course something under a half mile long that is full of menaces like whirlpools, haystacks, curlers, holes and, of course, rocks.

Whitewater stretches chosen for race courses can easily overturn the slender, sensitive kayaks, and racers must know how to "roll" their boats up again in fast water or how to "flush" out of their craft—or be able to fight their way to shore.

Wildwater races are longer and physically more punishing. The course is usually at least two miles long, and runs down a rapids portion of a river. There are no gates and the water usually is not as difficult as in whitewater racing; in wildwater, the emphasis is on endurance more than on boat handling skill.

Whitewater and wildwater boaters may race in either kayaks or "canoes." In a kayak, the racer sits and uses a double-bladed paddle, while in the "canoe" (which is actually more like a kayak than the canoes you used to paddle at Scout camp) the racer kneels and uses a single-bladed paddle. A meet, therefore, usually will have races for K-1 (single kayaks), K-1-W (single kayaks for women), C-1 (single canoes), C-1-W (single canoes for women), C-2 (canoe built for two) and C-2 mixed (for men-women teams).

The best times for racing are early spring, when the streams are swollen with water from melting snow, and fall, when the rains begin again. Races are held right up to November in New England, and racers must wear wetsuits to protect themselves from the frigid waters.

Equipment costs for kayaking can vary widely. A racing kayak purchased commercially costs from $300 to $400, but many of the canoe and kayak clubs have their own molds and members can "build" a kayak in three to four days for about $100.

Other equipment you need for kayaking includes: paddle, $55; life jacket especially constructed for lightness and ease of movement, $30; crash helmet, ranging in price from $7 to $27; neoprene spray skirt worn around the boater's waist and hooked over the cowling of the kayak cockpit to keep the water out, $10 to $20; flotation gear, such as a plastic air bag and foam; rubber sandals; a light wind jacket; leather gloves (ladies' golf gloves are ideal); and, finally, a car rack on which to carry your kayak.

For those of you who'd like to watch some races, some of the best places to do it are at Salida, Colo. (the Arkansas River); Hartford, Conn. (the Salmon); Wilmington, Del. (the Brandywine); and Lebanon, N.H. (the Mascoma).

–Robert B. Graham

Exploring the Channel Islands Sea Caves

In a small boat, you can explore sea caves worn by the waves into cliffs of the Channel Islands off the coast of southern California just as pirates might have done. It's a fun trip and the cost is reasonable.

The eight Channel Islands are offshore remnants of the Santa Monica Mountains that rise in downtown Los Angeles. Two, Anacapa and Santa Barbara, make up the Channel Islands National Monument; others are privately owned—one is a cattle ranch.

Putting out from Ventura (about an hour's drive north of Los Angeles), the 65-foot cruiser *Paisano* makes the trip to Anacapa in about an hour and a half. In winter you may see the great grey whales migrating by the hundreds from the Bering Sea to Baja California, where they will calve. There may be flying fish in summer, seal, big steamers.

Anacapa is really three small islands totaling about a square mile of land. The *Paisano* loafs along close to the cliffs of lava rock, which are pitted and pocked like the face of the moon. Hundreds of brown pelicans cluster along a ridge, nesting. You'll skirt a sea arch 10 stories high.

There are numerous sea caves. Aboard the *Paisano*'s skiff you explore one so big that the boat can make a turnaround deep in the island. Another cuts clear through the island to a shallow lagoon where you see abalone and other sea creatures.

There's a stop at a cove of tidal pools teeming with sea life and then a trip ashore and up a steel stairway to the high flat top of the island, where an automated lighthouse flashes and a fog horn bellows. There are marvelous views to photograph.

Stay back from the cliff edges or you may be sorry, as some dogs once were. Coast Guardsmen who used to man the lighthouse turned dogs loose on the island's rabbits, but soon there were no dogs left. The bunnies scooted for the cliff and swerved back just in time, while the dogs sailed on over.

From June 15 to Sept. 15 the *Paisano* makes regular cruises to Anacapa; fares are $9 for adults, $4.50 for children. In winter there are frequent charter trips that you can join, usually for $7. Make reservations with the Island Packers Co., P.O. Box 993, Ventura, Calif. 93001; phone (805) 642-1393.
–Alan R. McElwain

Your true pilot cares nothing about anything on earth but the river,
  and his pride in his occupation surpasses the pride of kings.
—MARK TWAIN

Thy shores are empires, changed in all save thee—
Assyria, Greece, Rome, Carthage, what are they?
Thy waters wash'd them power while they were free,
And many a tyrant since; their shores obey
The stranger, slave, or savage; their decay
Has dried up realms to deserts:—not so thou,
Unchangeable save to thy wild waves' play;
Time writes no wrinkle on thine azure brow;

Such as creation's dawn beheld, thou rollest now.
And I have loved thee, Ocean! and my joy
Of youthful sports was on thy breast to be
Borne, like thy bubbles, onward. From a boy
I wanton'd with thy breakers—they to me
Were a delight; and if the freshening sea
Made them a terror—'t was a pleasing fear,
For I was as it were a child of thee,
And trusted to thy billows far and near.
And laid my hand upon thy mane—as I do here.
—LORD BYRON

ON THE ROAD

Tubing on the Apple

Charles Kuralt's reporting assignment for CBS News is to find some of the more delightful things happening in this country. Usually, he can be found On The Road. This time, he was on a river.

Kuralt: This river may not look like much to you, but to people around here it looks like money in the bank. This is the biggest industry of Somerset, Wis. What is? This is. Tubin' on the Apple River.

People have gone inner tubing on the Apple for more than 50 years, or as long as there have been inner tubes. But in the last ten years, like everything else in America, tubing has gone big time. And now Somerset, which has only 729 people, has 15,000 inner tubes. And some summer weekends they're all rented out.

What you do is you go out to a place called River's Edge, four miles up the Apple, get yourself a tube, and head for town. You head for town by sitting down and letting the Apple River do the rest.

Youths may cavort along the way. Aging correspondents mostly cool it, enjoying the cow and corn country scenery, and the company of veteran tuber Bob Raleigh. Hey, I think I hear white water behind us. Is this dangerous anywhere along the line?

Raleigh: Well, it can be if you have an extraordinarily large bottom.

Kuralt: Then you're going to have trouble.

Raleigh: Or you don't have a big enough inner tube. From the starting point, oh, for a half a mile or so, it's relatively fast. Once you get down a little ways, the river slows down an awful lot, widens out, and becomes very tranquil, peaceful. One could almost fall asleep on the tube. You wouldn't be bothered by anyone, and you'd eventually end up down in Somerset and somebody'd wake you up. Someone didn't wake you up, the rapids would.

Kuralt: Tubing in Somerset, which started in the Twenties as a diversion, has become in the Seventies an institution, fabled in story and song, like the song Terri Lovell

sings every night at River's Edge on the banks of the Apple.

Terri Lovell [Singing]:

It's fun in the sun.
We're on cloud number one.
There's a rock up ahead in your way.
Can't wait to hear the rapids up ahead,
You know the feelin' is ever so fine.
Over and down, around and about,
In your rental tube and mine.
You know, we're just tubin' in Somerset,
Got nothin' to do all day.
With a good friend along,
You can float to the line,
And do the slow ride all the way.
It's a long way to go,
From the top to the bottom below,
Watchin' the girls on the side,
Just takin' Big Ben on a ride.

Kuralt: Floating down this river it's possible to feel sorry for presidents and kings, who've always had to content themselves with yachting on the Potomac, or punting on the Thames. Poor fellows, they never had a chance to go tubin' on the Apple.

–Charles Kuralt, CBS News
On The Road, Somerset, Wis.

"A Very Happy Event"— 10,000 Jews Splashing in the Sea of Galilee

Shortly after sunrise on a mid-September Sabbath every year about 10,000 people wade placidly, comfortably, amiably into the sweet waters of the Sea of Galilee in Israel and set forth on one of the most odd and impressive mass sporting events in the world. It is, by all counts, the largest single participatory sports event now held in the world. True, the XX Summer Olympic Games drew close to 12,000 competitors to Munich, but that was a one-time thing—the Sea of Galilee Swim passed its 20th anniversary in the autumn of 1973. It is a unique affair, actually first done back in 1929 when a half dozen hearty residents of the Kinnereth Kibbutz on the Sea of Galilee's shores leaped into the lake and paddled from Tiberias to the Ein Gev Kibbutz on the other side. It was just for fun and no one did it again until 1953 when someone decided to make the swim again—for the hell of it. About 210 people swam the Sea of Galilee that year.

Gradually, the event's fame spread through Israel. In 1966, 1,000 people turned up and, in the past couple of years, the Swim has suddenly become an event of immense proportions. The manager of the affair is one Giora Glazer, the bronzed, tough, 35-year-old physical activities director of the Kinnereth Kibbutz.

"I really do not know quite why we have become so popular," he says. "There is no competition, you know. Everyone who goes in the water and comes out the other end is given a medal and a certificate and something to eat. I suppose you could say that, in these troubled times, it is a fine peaceful display of Israeli strength, physical conditioning and good will. It is, you know, a very *happy* event. People are here to enjoy themselves. The oldest entry, I think, is seventy-four years old—an old man from Tel Aviv. The youngest—well, the age limit is supposed to be ten years old. But we are certain that a few eight-year-olds or maybe children even younger make the swim."

Each swimmer is issued a colored beanie—there are four different colors, for different cities in Israel. Each beanie is numbered and a list is kept of all the entries—and later checked against a numbered tag that each entrant must take to the finish area to show he has safely finished the swim. ("Never has there been a drowning," says Giora Glazer.)

The distance across the Sea of Galilee is six kilometers, about 2.4 miles. It is a pleasant, easy, congenial swim. The water is filled with the bobbing colored beanies, like a sea of balloons. There are many conversations across the water and snatches of song rise here and there. Every variety of stroke is used—from the grand old trudgeon to a comfortable dog paddle. The quickest swimmers finish in about two hours; the slowest may take as long as five hours with a leisurely Sabbath sidestroke. All along the route, powerboats glide among the bobbing caps, watching for swimmers in trouble. The weary are taken aboard boats if they wish. No one minds if he has to rest, for this is a serene and lovely event—everyone wins by simply finishing.

To enter, you need only to write to Giora Glazer at the Kinnereth Kibbutz near the Sea of Galilee. The lake is, of course, located just below the Golan Heights, where bunkers for Syrian guns were once located, and it is no more than a few hundred yards from the border with Jordan. Yet the Swim goes on no matter what tensions prevail.

—William Johnson

Swimming on Wake Island

A fjord in Norway, the rock-girt sea off Acapulco, the Hellespont—all are places worth a special trip for a very special swim, the kind you can dine out on for weeks. But *Wake Island*? Hardly anybody goes there voluntarily; the few people who have visited Wake at all in the last 30 years or so have been victims either of World War II or of engine trouble. But should you find yourself aboard a trans-Pacific flight that has to set down on Wake for repairs or fuel, keep in mind that it offers one of the world's really memorable swimming spots.

Wake is made up of three coral islets —Wake, Peale and Wilkes—smack astride the major shipping and air lanes in the west-central portion of the North Pacific. The triangular-shaped atoll and a curving reef enclose a shallow, gem-like lagoon. If you're stuck on Wake for awhile, beg or borrow a Jeep from the airlines people (they're usually very obliging) and head down a rutted road to the lagoon. Once

Freeze in the Devil's Punchbowl

Usually going to the devil means having a hot old time, but a plunge into the Devil's Punchbowl will freeze yo' ass. There are two Devil's Punchbowls in Aspen, Colo.—they are small rock pools at an elevation of about 10,000 feet, formed by icy torrents of melted snow. The temperature of the water in the Devil's Punchbowls never gets much above 35°. In summertime the show at the Punchbowls is spectacular—the *macho* locals do gainers, jack-knives, flips and combinations thereof through jagged cuts in the rocks into the tiny freezing pools 20 or 30 feet below.

Punchbowl Number One, the easier of the two to get to, is the narrowest—it's only 10-15 feet in diameter (depending on the time of year) and divers plunge from a height of 30 feet. To get there, go about half way up the road to Independence Pass and look for a little sign that says "The Grottoes" on the right. Park there and follow the path down about 100 feet to find the Punchbowl.

Devil's Punchbowl Number Two is more of a trek. Continue on the road to Independence Pass about two to three miles farther, and turn right on the road to Grizzly Reservoir—there's a campground and a ranger station near the turn. Follow the dirt road about four or five miles until you see a few bare bottoms bouncing around in the sunshine and you'll know you've arrived. At Punchbowl Number Two, a white waterfall creates a large deep diving pool; but the 20-foot-deep cut in the rocks the divers plunge through is only a yard wide—you can step over it at the top. If diving into the Punchbowl is not your cup of tea, lounging lizardlike on the rocks is an acceptable alternative—dress is optional.

—Susan Root

you're in the clear, pale green water, there's not much to see on shore—Wake has very scant vegetation. But look down, for at your feet is a gorgeous, miniature marine world, and you don't need even so much as a face mask to see it quite clearly. On a moonlit night, the view is almost as good as on a cloudless day; in some ways, it's even better, for the underwater vegetation takes on subtle pastel hues and casts eerie shadows.

The lagoon is a bit on the warm side; those who prefer more bracing temperatures should steer clear of Wake's Pacific beaches, though, enticing as they may look. (Only a few feet from a lounge where waiting airplane passengers can while away their time, the main beach is a fascinating sight, littered even now with the detritus of war —here a grotesquely twisted propeller stuck in the sand, there a rusted hull thrusting up from the waves just offshore.) Sharks are especially fond of the waters off Wake's beaches—but they never venture into the lagoon.

—Ronald P. Kriss

THE GRAND & GLORIOUS ADVENTURES OF
RICHARD HALLIBURTON

Swimming the Hellespont

We all have our dreams. Otherwise what a dark and stagnant world this would be. I've dreamed of swimming the most dramatic river in the world—the Hellespont. Lord Byron once wrote that he would rather have swum the Hellespont than written all his poetry. So would I!

To me the Hellespont was not just a narrow strait of cold blue water: it was a tremendous symbol—a symbol of audacity, of challenge, of epic poetry and heroic adventure.

The nature of the Hellespont's first records seem to have set an example for all the historic events that have clustered about it. Its very naming is a dramatic story. The name "Hellespont" ("Dardanelles" on the modern maps) goes back to legendary ages, receiving its title from Helle, the King of Thessaly's daughter who fell into the channel from the winged ram with the golden fleece, on whose back she was fleeing from her enemies.

Through this same Hellespont Jason, in his immortal ship, the *Argo,* sailed in quest of this same fleece. For ten years, from 1194 to 1184 B.C., the fleets of the Greeks were beached at its entrance, while their armies, led by Agamemnon, Achilles and Ulysses, thundered at the lofty walls of Troy. It was across this stream that Leander nightly swam to keep his clandestine trysts with Hero. In the very wake of Leander, in one of the most spectacular military exploits in history, King Xerxes of Persia, the mightiest ruler of his time, crossed from Asia to Europe with a colossal army for the invasion of Greece. Here in the following century Alexander the Great ferried his Macedonians from Europe to Asia to begin his conquest of the world. Back once more in the 14th century rolled the tide of invasion from east to west: this time the Turkish conquests were to turn the Hellespont from that day to this into Saracenic property. Through this strait the piratical Turkish cruisers moved for generations, making all the eastern Mediterranean a Turkish lake. Since 1600 Russia has fought periodic wars for the possession of this storied channel. And now the shores of this same Hellespont are dotted with the wrecks of sunken Allied battle fleets and strewn with the graves of a hundred thousand French and English soldiers, whose blood was squandered in rivers in the desperate attempt in 1915 to plant the Allied flags over

Richard Halliburton, daredevil and adventure writer, spent his life re-creating ancient adventures and dreaming up new ones. He was lost at sea in 1939.

the rocks where Hero joined her drowned romantic lover in dim antiquity. Indeed one's spirits surge to read the amazing record of this fateful stream and realize how repeatedly it has shaped the destiny of the world.

This, then, is the Hellespont, and the scene where my dream came true.

Nature was most capricious when she created this eccentric corner of the earth. She drives the enormous volume of the Black Sea past Constantinople through a narrow channel called the Bosporus—and then again by more reluctant, prolonged, tortuous degrees, through a winding canal-like gash in the mountains, 40 miles long, and from one to five miles broad. Down this insufficient Hellespont, with Europe on her right side and Asia on her left, the Black Sea, unleashed at last, rushes at top speed, foaming with indignation at her long imprisonment. For 10,000 years she has poured herself into the greater ocean, season in and season out. Tides she scorns. South—south—south, her waters always swirl so that one may well call the strait a river since but for its briny nature it qualifies in every respect to this term.

The sites of Sestos and Abydos were conspicuously, unmistakably, there. At the former place the acropolis ruins establish its exact location. The Mound of Xerxes, up the slopes of which Abydos climbed, and the sand peninsula, which is a spur of the mound, establish Abydos with equal certainty. The only way to "investigate" my ability to swim the intervening distance was to dive in and swim. As previous endurance tests I had swum the Nile and the Mississippi, but either of these was mere paddling compared with the Hellespont.

The first problem was to reach Sestos, the starting point, in a boat big enough to buck the savage current, and yet small enough to escort and safeguard me on my return journey.

Being by no means a swimmer of Leander's caliber I thought it wise to take the precaution Byron had taken, and continue on upstream some two miles more above Sestos in order to give myself more time to get across before the current swept me past Abydos point.

Finding a semi-sheltered cove, we anchored our craft and waded ashore for a rest. At two o'clock I removed my clothing and, my heart pounding with excitement, stood at the water's edge, praying to the water gods to deliver me safely on the other side. My body whispered: "You can not possibly swim five miles in such a current," but Inspiration shouted: "This is the *Hellespont*—what matter if it's fifty!"

I plunged.

The Asiatic shore across the channel rose hazily. I struck out straight for it, with Roderic and the boat hovering close beside.

Before I had gone half a mile, whatever "form" I may have begun with soon vanished, and I thought only of covering the greatest possible distance with the least possible exertion: backstroke, sidestroke, dog paddle, idle floating, any old thing to keep going.

By half past two I looked back toward Europe to find, to my alarm, that I was already abeam the Sestos bluffs. Before three o'clock I was in mid-stream. The wind had constantly increased, and was now churning the water with whitecaps. Every few minutes I was half drowned when the resentful waves broke unexpectedly over my head. It seemed to me I swallowed half the Black Sea. Nausea seized me so painfully that several times I was ready to give up. But the increasing cold was the worst thing of all. The water flows so rapidly, even the surface has no opportunity to be warmed by the sun. After the first hour I began to grow uncomfortably numb.

However, the Throne of Xerxes was not far off now. All along, this had been a guide-point. And yet, as I drew near to it, I realized the ricocheting current was sweeping me parallel to the shore about ten times as fast as I was approaching it. The trees and rocks began to gallop past. After two hours in the water, within 300 feet of shore I was being swept past the "last chance" of solid ground, just as and where Leander had been swept 2,500 years before . . . and should I fail to reach the beach by ever so little, the current would drag me across the Hellespont, back to the European shore whence I had started.

Never have I felt such utter despair: a five-mile swim—my Hellespont—to miss achievement by 100 yards! Never have I struggled so desperately. My eyes became blurred, seeing only the land not far from me. I ceased to know where I was or what I was doing, here in this cold, tormenting boundless ocean. Mechanically I thrashed the water with my weary arms and legs.

Then—bump!—my *knees* struck bottom. I was swimming hysterically in less than three feet of water, for the shore sloped so gradually that, even at 300 feet out, the water was not waist deep. With not one second to lose, I stood upright, and staggered ashore, with Rod, who had jumped into the surf, right beside me, and flopped on the last foot of ground at the point.

And so the Hellespont, that treacherous and briny river, was swum once more.

Adventure for Credit

Want to ride the Amazon in a dugout or search the Pacific for the breeding ground of the grey whale—and get university credit for it? Then sign up with the Overseas Natural Environment Studies Program at the University of California.

Many universities have been running extension programs for years; most tell bored housewives about the mysteries of Renaissance paintings or ambitious salesmen how to get a real estate license. The UC program, however, is designed to get students into first-hand observation of local ecology and natural history around the world. The program is expanding rapidly. In 1963 it enrolled only 200 "students" (many non-students just sign up for a specific trip); in 1974 the university expects three times as many. Some samples:

—Trace the grey whale to Scammon's Lagoon in the Pacific, where you'll also find the northern elephant seal, the harbor seal and sea lions. The fee is $400 (including room and board on ship) from San Diego.

—Take a boat and dugout through the rain forest of the Amazon, studying plants, birds, snakes, fish and people. The fee is $990 from Colombia.

—Take a ship from Ecuador to the Galapagos to learn about the geology, plants, animals, culture and status of research on evolution. The fee is $750 from Ecuador.

The university is planning other trips to East Africa, Alaska and Hawaii. Register for all trips three months in advance at Overseas Natural Environment Studies Program, Dept. SA, University Extension, 2223 Fulton St., Berkeley, Calif. 94720. Pay by check or BankAmericard.

—The Editors

Sand Trekking on South Padre Island

Drop out—for a day, at least—and sample the carefree, beachcombing life of a sand-trekker. Ride in the enclosed crew-cab of a four-wheel-drive vehicle along 26 sweeping miles of undeveloped beach at South Padre Island at the southeast tip of Texas.

There's beachcombing—find Portuguese glass floats, shells, sand dollars, rope, driftwood and maybe a sealed bottle with its inevitable message (usually sent by Gulf Coast schoolchildren). There's surf fishing—for redfish, speckled trout and mackerel.

As the vehicle wheels along the beach at the edge of the pounding surf, gulls rise to its approach, sand crabs scuttle for their holes and you see an occasional blue heron wading in a tidal pool. As you travel, your guide, an accomplished raconteur well versed in the island's colorful and sometimes violent history and in its wildlife and shells, tells of Spaniards shipwrecked off Padre in 1553 being first fed and then hounded, tortured

Thousands of Sleeping, Swimming, Screaming Seals

Far, far out in the Bering Sea, hundreds of miles from the nearest landfall, is St. Paul Island, one of the Pribilof Islands. Each year more than a million fur seals—and several hundred tourists—migrate to the islands from May through September. The seals come to breed and then return to their wintertime haunts in the ocean; the tourists come to see and photograph the really wild spectacle of literally miles and miles of ocean and ocean beach jammed with yowling, sleeping, fighting, swimming, screaming sea mammals.

At the other end of the island you find complete tranquility and a number of major rookeries where more than 180 bird species can be seen and photographed. Accommodations for humans on St. Paul are spartan but clean, warm and comfortable. The excursion from Anchorage via Reeve Aleutian Airways is not cheap ($279 for three days, two nights; $299 for four days, three nights), but when you come home you're almost guaranteed to be the only person on your block who's been there.

—Mike Miller

and cannibalized by Karankawa Indians. (A wounded priest, buried with just his head exposed, escaped when the sand helped congeal his wounds. The tale he told was so horrifying that no one ventured back to the island for years.)

Inspect the scant remains of Padre's once-prosperous King and Singer ranches—slabs of shell-reinforced concrete foundations scattered amidst stands of tasseled sea oats. The guide explains that John Singer was shipwrecked on the island in 1847, liked what he found there, and decided to build a ranch with the $150,000 return on $500 he had invested in his brother's invention—a sewing machine. The family returned after the Civil War to find the ranch in ruins and the area so changed by wind and water that they couldn't find $80,000 in gold they had buried there. Legend says it's still there.

Beach trips cost $50 for four persons for a day-long outing; efforts are made to match smaller parties. Write to Don & Judy Veach, P.O. Box 663, Port Isabel, Tex. 78578.

—Mike Michaelson

Sandcastles: Ethereal Art at Low Tide

Why would a serious artist ever want to build sandcastles? Sand is a tentative and temperamental medium, at best. You can spend hours molding an intricate tower or turret, only to have it disintegrate before your eyes after even the slightest confrontation with a frisky puppy ("Oh, I'm *terribly* sorry he did that. Were you building something?"), a wayward Frisbee or one of your own clumsy elbows.

Even if you are spared such accidental calamities, there is still the one ultimate, inexorable destroyer of all sand art: high tide. You can't save sand sculpture. You can't sell it. You can't hang it on the wall or take it home to show your mother. It's art for art's sake, as pure as you can get. Everyone's an amateur—by necessity. Whatever you create will be gone tomorrow, and unless you took your camera to the beach, all you'll have to show for your efforts will be some tantalizing but pointless stories.

No matter how clear and rational such arguments sound on paper, they do not dissuade hundreds of seaside Michelangelos from spending thousands of hours creating their magnificent but momentary edifices on any given summer's day.

There are three ways to build a sandcastle, but for the aficionado the first two don't count.

First there's the "Pat-On" method, where you keep adding handfuls of sand until you get the shape you want. Very primitive. Strictly for the shovel-and-pail set.

Then there's the "Drip-On" technique, where you scoop handfuls of sopping sand and let it drip through your fingers to form surrealistic mounds, towers and spires. Very nice, but you're pretty much limited to mounds, towers and spires.

Finally, there's true sand-sculpture, where you carve shapes out of wet, compacted sand. If you're serious about it, take a big four-sided wooden box to pile sand in. Compact the block of sand with water and bare feet until it can stand alone, then remove the frame, carefully, and start sculpting—first with shovels and trowels, finally with butter knives and nail files.

If you're a competitive sort you can have your skills certified in various annual contests held up and down the coasts. The contests are very official, involving entry fees, judges, rules, time limits and trophies. (See accompanying list.)

If you enter one of the Southern California contests, you might find you're competing against Norman Richard Kraus, a Rancho Santa Fe designer and the self-proclaimed king of the castles. When Kraus and his friends build a sandcastle they don't mess around. They bring plans and sketches of their architectural intentions, or pictures of real castles in Germany or England that they try to reproduce in sand. They have been known to bring a skiploader to the beach at seven in the morning and start piling and compacting a mountain of sand that they don't start sculpting until noon. One of their creations was seven feet tall; another used an estimated 50 tons of sand.

Kraus and his friends are serious about sandcastling. One of them, Melvin Schmatzmeyer, suspects that sand sculpture is one of the oldest forms of art known to man, and he'll tell you so after a few beers, and then give you his thoughts about those who would prostitute the art.

"Some of these contests aren't even worth entering," Schmatzmeyer says. "In some, people build frameworks out of wood or chicken wire or whatever, and then pile their sand on top of it. Or they add chemicals to the sand to change its consistency. I think that's cheating—the object is to learn how to work in natural sand, how to compact it and shape it into the figure you want.

"Some people embellish their sculptures with crepe paper or plastic cars or little cardboard cutouts. Or they'll spray paint it different colors. I think decorations should be limited to the natural props of the seashore—shells, stones, feathers, starfish or pieces of kelp. It all goes back to the sea, after all, so there's no reason to pollute it with spray paint and chicken wire."

So why not try sandcastling? Your only limits are your imagination, your endurance, the number of friends you can get to help you, and the time until high tide. Take a bucket, a shovel, a butter knife, a tube of Coppertone, an Instamatic and a tidetable, and go build a sand castle. But leave the dog and the Frisbee at home.

–Scot Morris

Sandcastle Contests

To try your hand at competitive sand sculpture, or to see how the experts do it, or just to have an enjoyable day at the beach, consider going to one of the annual contests sponsored by different cities and towns on the Pacific coast. You can build anything—a sea monster, a sphinx, a reclining nude or the more traditional castle. Entrants are given a specific time limit to complete their sculpture (usually three hours), and are judged separately by age, group size and sculpture category. For the specific times and places, watch the "coming events" sections of local papers, especially during the months and in the areas listed below:

June—Oceanside, Calif. and Moonlight Beach in Encinitas, Calif.
July—Cannon Beach, Ore.; Imperial Beach, Calif. (on July 4); Ventura, Calif.; Mission Bay in San Diego, Calif. (at Crown Point).
August—Long Beach, and Manhattan Beach, Calif.; and Santa Monica, Calif. (at the foot of Bay Street).
September—Laguna Beach, Carmel, Santa Cruz and Del Mar, Calif.; and Officer's Beach on Coronado Island, Calif.
February-March—There's an off-season contest, just to keep everyone in shape, at the Winter Festival in Laguna Beach, Calif.

he sea lies all around us. . . . The continents themselves dissolve and pass to the sea, in grain after grain of eroded land. . . . In its mysterious past it encompasses all the dim origins of life and receives in the end, after, it may be, many transmutations, the dead husks of that same life. For all at last returns to the sea—the beginning and the end.

—RACHEL CARSON

REALLY CHEAP THRILLS!

IN HAWAII

By Mike Miller

Most travelers (even, sad to say, many who have vacationed there) seem to have this feeling that to vacation in Hawaii is to spend a small fortune. Not so. Definitely not so.

Of course *if you want to* you can blow your whole life's savings in a week or a month of high living in hula land. But such spending is certainly not necessary in order to have one of the really memorable vacations of a lifetime. Fact is, a great number of Hawaii's grandest travel attractions are not only low cost, they're no cost. Here is a sampling of some the Tropic State's best bargains:

Hawaii's beaches, of course, are the biggest and probably the best of the islands' free offerings. Shorelines on all the islands of the state are public; they belong to everyone. This means that even though you may be staying at one of the more economical off-the-beach hostelries in Honolulu or elsewhere, you still have as much right to the sand and the water and the view of Diamond Head at Waikiki as the guests who pay $50 a day or more to stay in the posh hotels right on the water.

Kapiolani Park, only a couple of blocks from the heart of Waikiki, is seldom touted by travel agents, but it is unquestionably one of the great city parks and zoos in the United States. Along paths meandering through acres of banyon trees, koas, palms and other luxuriant Polynesian plantlife you can see more than 1,500 big and little creatures, including elephants, giraffes, hippos, barkless Polynesian dogs, apes and all kinds of multi-hued South Seas birds. Seaward from the zoo is the Waikiki Aquarium, complete with performing seals, thousands of tropical fish, sharks, octopuses and fanged moray eels. (Sight of the latter, incidentally, is almost guaranteed to keep you from going into the water for the rest of the day.)

On Saturdays the park fence becomes an Art Mart between the hours of 10 a.m. and 4 p.m. as hundreds of island artists display their paintings. On Sundays at Kapiolani's Waikiki Shell, the fabulous Royal Hawaiian

Band entertains in a free concert. Last song of the day is always "Aloha Oe," the sentimental going-away song written by Hawaii's last reigning monarch, Queen Liliuokalani.

Pearl Harbor can be seen and toured in either of two ways. You can pay $7 and take a commercial cruise from Honolulu to and through the harbor, or you can stand in line at Halawa gate (sometimes for a few minutes, sometimes for a couple of hours or more) and take a free U.S. Navy launch tour of the harbor. If you're interested in going aboard the remains of the battleship U.S.S. *Arizona*, which sank during the Japanese attack Dec. 7, 1941, then you should definitely opt for the Navy offering. The commercial cruises from Waikiki do not stop at the memorial, though they do cruise around it.

Iolani Palace, in the heart of Honolulu, is the hub of a fascinating walking tour, map and directions for which can be obtained from the Hawaii Visitors Bureau in downtown Waikiki. The tour covers not only the 19th-century palace, residence of

Illustrations by Sam Daijogo

Hawaiian monarchs, but also the fortress-like Iolani barracks, the 1883 coronation bandstand (where the Royal Hawaiian Band plays in free concert each Friday), the first frame house on the island, an 1823 printing shop, an adobe school, Washington Place (the Hawaiian Governor's mansion) and the spectacular new state capitol building—the $25 million pride of Hawaii and the envy of the 49 other states.

Aloha Tower, at Pier 9 at the foot of Fort Street, has been a favorite free observation and photo-taking vantage point for decades. The 10th floor observation deck is open from 8 a.m. until 9 p.m. daily.

The Falls of Clyde, a four-masted square-rigged old sailing vessel, is berthed adjacent to the Aloha Tower. The ship, built in 1878, has been restored as a state historical maritime museum. Admission is $1.25 for adults, 75 cents for kids.

Bishop Museum is probably the most famous museum in the Pacific. Located at 1355 Kalihi St., it contains one of the world's greatest collections of Polynesian culture displays. It's open all day Monday through Saturday and in the afternoon on Sundays. No charge for children; adults $2.

Byodo Temple, a $2 million replica of the 900-year-old national treasure of Japan, is located on the Kahekili Highway near Kaneohe. (Admission $1.)

A Chinatown walking tour through downtown Honolulu's oriental district is scheduled every week (no charge). For details call the Chinese Chamber of Commerce—the phone number in Honolulu is 533-3181.

Foster Botanical Gardens, 180 N. Vineyard Blvd., is a mind-boggling experience for the visitor who digs rare, exotic and brilliantly colored orchids. There are also ferns, trees and vines of Pacific origin. The 20 acres of gardens are open daily and are free, as are **Liliuokalani Gardens,** adjoining Foster Gardens off School Street. The Liliuokalani Gardens are a hideaway of which even many Hawaiians are unaware. A marvelous place to sneak away for a *mahimahi* sandwich and a can of Primo beer, the gardens contain Waikahalulu Falls, which tumble to form a swimming hole in Nuuanu stream.

The Kodak Hula Show, a performance planned especially with the photo phreak in mind, is presented free at Kapiolani Park each Tuesday and Thursday morning between 10 a.m. and 11:15 a.m.

The Royal Mausoleum, 2261 Nuuanu Ave., contains the tombs of five Hawaii kings and six queens; it's open daily, and there is no charge.

All of the attractions mentioned above are to be found on Oahu (except the free beaches, which are everywhere in the islands). Free or low-cost activities and attractions are no less available on the Neighbor Islands as well. On Maui, for instance, is Haleakala Crater, with miles of no-charge hiking trails

through eerie, desert-like lava fields. On Maui too are tours through sugar mills and coral jewelry factories, and perhaps the greatest low-cost bargain in all the islands—comfortable state-owned cabins in Waianapanapa State Park that rent completely furnished for as low as $70 a week for six persons.

Hawaii is big on travel bargains too. Low budget attractions include the nation's only "drive-in" volcano, displays and exhibits at Lyman House Museum in Hilo which trace Hawaii's culture from the Stone Age to the present, and tours through Macadamia nut processing plants, orchid nurseries, a sugar mill and America's only coffee plantations.

The Hawaiian islands also offer, free of charge, Waimea Canyon (the Grand Canyon of the Pacific) on Kaui, ancient *heiaus* (sacrificial alters) on Molokai, and Shipwreck Beach—a beachcomber's heaven on earth—on little Lanai Island.

Moncton, New Brunswick's Fabulous Bore

Moncton, New Brunswick has throughout her history tried to outdo the city of St. John and to become the cultural center of New Brunswick—but has always failed. So she's had to fall back on making extravagant claims for a fabulous natural phenomenon the likes of which no other New Brunswick city can claim: the Bore. The Bore is a great terrifying wall of water—or so it is described—that sweeps up the Petitcodiac River, right through downtown Moncton, twice a day, whipped along by the giant tides of the Bay of Fundy. The Bore can reach 53 feet in height.

Bore View Park is the vantage point for tourists, who flock here from every state and province to witness the ferocity of the onrushing, uncontrollable wave. They arrive early so as to have time to fill their cameras with film and lay out routes for quick getaways in case the Bore should come in with especially vicious force and threaten to kill everybody. Some tourists—rash fools!—station themselves right on the river's edge to get a better view. But—and this is why Moncton can never really hope to rival St. John—when the Bore finally appears, it is a huge disappointment. Unless the winds are unusually high, the Bore comes in as a muddy little wave about five inches high.

We Call It the Gulf of California; Mexicans Call It the Sea of Cortez

The Gulf of California, a kaleidoscope of tropical blues, oranges and greens, is one of the richest fishing areas in the entire world. More than 300 species of game fish make their home there, including dolphins, sailfish, enormous whales and delicious *mahimahi*. At its southern tip, armadas of fish parade in from the surging waters of the Pacific, making the Gulf a 650-mile-long warmwater aquarium. Strings of brown islands, uninhabited except for giant iguanas, fish-eating bats and sharp-beaked sea birds, dot its surface. Hundreds of miles of white, almost entirely deserted beaches line its shores.

The Gulf, known in Mexico as the Sea of Cortez, starts just 50 miles south of the U.S. border, but few Americans or other tourists go there. Now the Mexican government is spending $50 million to build roads, airstrips and marinas, to improve the water supply, and to help private investors develop modern resorts—in short, to make the Sea of Cortez the new Mediterranean.

The Gulf contains almost every variety of fish and seagoing mammal found anywhere in the Pacific—sea lions, giant sea turtles, black and striped marlin, tuna, sharks, manta rays, barracuda, dolphinfish, jack, 300-pound totoaba, half-ton jewfish, giant needlefish, sea bass, grouper, snapper,

(continued on next page)

(continued from previous page)
pompano, snook, lobsters and shrimp. Birds include cormorants, osprey and Canadian geese that winter there.

Much of the Gulf Coast along Baja California is still unexplored wilderness with only a sprinkling of isolated villages. Many remote beaches and streams have never been fished, the coastal jungle and upland forest never hunted. The road marked on maps as Mexican Highway 1 from Tijuana down Baja to La Paz is hard to find. It is paved for 150 miles south of Tijuana and less than 100 miles north of La Paz; 500 miles of desert and mountains lie in between.

The adventuresome can try to make it in four-wheel-drive vehicles or dune buggies. But it is easier to take a commercial airline to La Paz and then—to reach the southern tip of Baja—take the air taxi to a dirt strip at Cabo San Lucas. The pilot will buzz the hotel there so a taxi can meet guests. Commercial airlines serve Santa Rosalia and Loreto, the capital of all California in 1697. Private planes can fly into small airports at San Ignacio and San Jose del Cabo.

The first port on the Baja side of the Gulf is San Felipe, home of the giant totoaba. Farther down is Mulege, gateway to a tropical jungle. The river flowing past town is crowded with giant black snook; the largest run six feet and weigh 80 pounds. At La Paz and Cabo San Lucas, luxurious cruisers rent for $60 to $70 a day and go out—almost always successfully—after

marlin, sailfish, wahoo and yellowtail. Fishing is less expensive at Loreto, Mulege and Bahia de Los Angeles.

The best fishing season is late January to July for marlin, January through September for sailfish, spring to fall for cervina, dolphinfish, grouper, bass, snapper and snook, and all winter for sierra, yellowtail and roosterfish.

Tourists can water ski in La Paz harbor and in most of the Gulf's southern bays. Most hotels on Baja also have their own stables to offer rides along white sand beaches. Just watch for *vagabundos del mar*, sea gypsies who roam the Gulf in small open boats and camp on shore.

A car ferry sails across the Gulf from Mazatlán to La Paz; it leaves Mazatlán on Tuesday and Saturday night and sails from La Paz on Thursday and Sunday. The 16-hour crossing is enlivened by a swimming pool and an excellent dining room and bar. First class passage is $28 a person one way, plus $30 for a foreign compact car and $40 for the average American car.

The ferry is changing the nature of Baja California. In 1964, when the ferry started, La Paz had only 4,200 tourists a year; now it has more than 100,000. Anyone looking for an unspoiled part of the world should head for the Sea of Cortez soon; it may yet be the new Mediterranean.

—Peter Janssen

A Beach for Every *Norteamericano* on Mexico's West Coast

Ten years ago there was only Acapulco. Puerto Vallarta was a tiny village in a permanent siesta. Now the entire 1,000-mile stretch of Mexico's west coast is filling with Americans, who are filled with *hamburguesas* to go.

The problem becomes one of where to go. Most of the beach action lies in the hundreds of miles north of Acapulco (although there is some fine beach country south, notably Puerto Angel). From our list of seven arrived or soon-to-arrive beach centers, pick the one that suits you best.

Acapulco *The* place for many sybarites, but too high-rise and grasping for some. Air conditioning and uninhibited night life, but it seems the beaches sometimes are secondary. Rumors (denied) of pollution in the bay. Easy to fly to from the United States.

Barrade Navidad Tiny corner of a beach south of Puerto Vallarta. All the credentials but few of the comforts. Tiny thatched-roof village. Rural Mexico on great beaches. Road from Manzanillo or Guadalajara.

Manzanillo Small, colonial port city in the midst of the best beach country around. The Club Méditerranée believes and is building. A place to watch. Good small hotels plus Las Hadas, just opened by a tin billionaire to cater to jet set. Fishing and climate superb. Not too far from Guadalajara; air from there and Mexico City. But soon a jetport.

Mazatlán Old reliable with the thrifty set. Northernmost major beach area. Sophisticated small city more caught up in business and fishing than tourism. Bargains on good hotels on fine beaches north of town. Good restaurants. Fishing spectacular. Near the Tropic of Cancer. Direct air from the United States, 25 hours by car from the border. Trains unreliable.

Playa Azul South of Puerto Vallarta, but reachable only from the interior. Urapan, 150 miles inland, is jumping-off point. Tough to get there but the beaches are worth it. Coco plantations right down to the water. Hotels basic to simple. Bring Frisbee for entertainment.

Puerto Vallarta With all the notice, still a small village. Good beaches north and south, including a few luxury class hotels. Still quiet, not a stripling Acapulco. Good selection of hotels in all categories. A must is downtown's Oceano Bar where Burton held forth. Direct air from U.S.

Zihuatanejo Jewel of a bay and ideal beaches. You'll swear you're in the South Seas. Easy, quiet and on the verge of discovery. Where the Aztec kings came to unwind. You'll see why. Small but decent hotels. Fly piston in from Mexico City, or drive up from Acapulco in a half day—if the road hasn't been washed out.

—Richard John Pietschmann

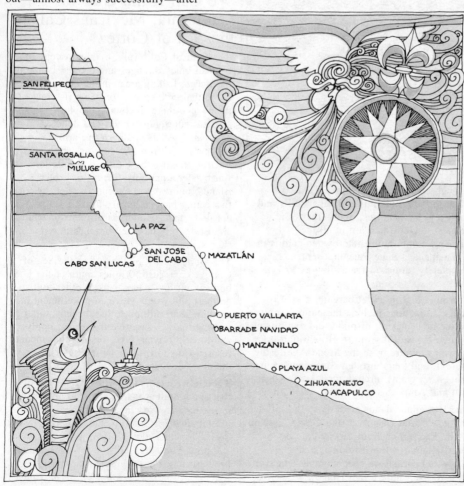

SAN FELIPE

SANTA ROSALIA
MULEGE

LA PAZ

CABO SAN LUCAS
SAN JOSE DEL CABO

MAZATLÁN

PUERTO VALLARTA
BARRADE NAVIDAD
MANZANILLO

PLAYA AZUL
ZIHUATANEJO
ACAPULCO

The Compleat Angler's Guide to the Pacific

By Mark L. Reed

Where the fish are, how big they run and when to get them while the getting is good.

Sir Izaak Walton's *Compleat Angler* was never really complete because he only fished in 17th-century England. Today's fisherman casts his lures on the waters of the world. It's not surprising, then, that some of the most exciting and least fished areas are to be found in the Pacific and Indian Oceans and in the streams of southern Asia.

In the Pacific, the angler can fight almost all of the great game fish to be found anywhere on earth: blue and black marlin, sailfish, swordfish, a variety of tuna and dolphin (known through the Pacific by its Hawaiian name, *mahimahi*), thresher and mako sharks and the Pacific barracuda.

Some species—like India's giant freshwater mahseer—are unique, while others, like the American rainbow and brook trout and the European brown trout, have been successfully transplanted.

What follows tells you where the fish are, how big they run and when the best times are to get them while the getting is good.

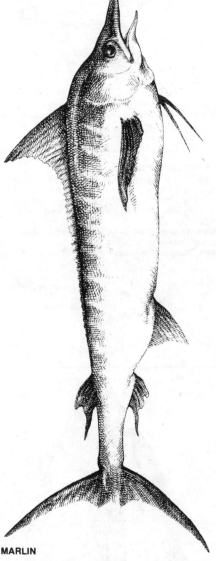

DOLPHIN (MAHIMAHI)

There are many reasons why the dolphin is considered to be one of the world's most superb and spectacular game fish. A speedy swimmer, it is often seen greyhounding along the surface, chasing flying fish. Once hooked, it may go through 11 color changes. Since it cannot be preserved, it must be eaten fresh. (This fish is not related to the mammal dolphins, which are members of the porpoise family.) Sizes run up to six feet and 82 pounds.

Papeete, Tahiti. They normally run 35 to 70 pounds in the waters off Tahiti, and usually they are caught in pairs, since the dolphins travel as couples. Year round fishing, but November to March is best.

Great Barrier Reef, Australia. Fine dolphin fishing here but it's expensive, $80 a day for three to a boat. Early spring is best.

Trincomalee, Ceylon. All manner of fish but dolphins run well. All-year action, but best results in March to October and December to January. It is cheap—17 cents to $1.70 an hour for a boat. Stay at the Ceylon Sea Anglers Club in China Bay for $2.86 per person per day. Waters also good for sailfish, sawfish, spearfish, swordfish, marlin, tuna and shark.

American Samoa Game fishing just starting in Samoa but there are plenty of dolphins.

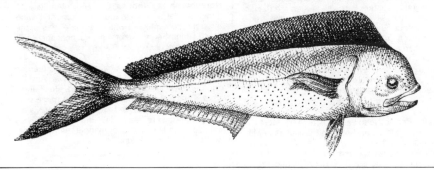

MARLIN

The thrill of hooking and playing a marlin is hard to beat. It is a furious fighter, capable of breathtaking leaps above the surface and 1,000-foot runs. The Pacific blue is the superb game fish while the black, also a fighter, is highly prized and is delicious cooked or raw.

Kona Coast, Hawaii. Blue marlin seem to make this their headquarters. The 1,100-pound record was taken off the Kona Coast, and average catches run about 200 pounds. Year-round fishing, but best is June to September. Lee anchorage unsafe between October and April.

Yanuca Island, Fiji. Black marlins run up to 400 pounds. A 16-year-old girl landed a 420-pound black marlin but was disqualified from a record because she was helped. Year-round fishing but October to April is best.

Cairns, Queensland, Australia. Located at the northern end of the Great Barrier Reef, these waters are another major marlin region. In one 12-month period, two American charter skippers landed more than 200 game fish, including three black marlin weighing more than 1,000 pounds each, and good for three world records. At least four black marlins hooked but lost were estimated to have weighed close to 2,000 pounds. February to April best.

Mazatlan, Guaymas, La Paz, Cabo San Lucas: Mexico. More than 1,000 marlin a year, to 750 pounds each, are caught off Mazatlan. Guaymas, which is only 200 miles south of the U.S. border, is second only to Mazatlan. Marlin fishing also good out of La Paz and Cabo San Lucas, but much less expensive to fish out of Loreto, Mulege and Bahia de Los Angeles.

SALMON

King salmon, also called chinook salmon, is the most sought after by sportsmen and commercial packers. They run up to 70 pounds in Alaska and the Pacific Northwest—a record 126-pounder was taken (but not by rod) off Petersburg, Alaska. The rod record is 92 pounds, from the Skeena River in British Columbia.

Petersburg, Ketchikan, Sitka and Juneau: Alaska. Biggest fish are landed from May to July but good catches from April to August. Coho or silver salmon from July to the end of September.

Discovery Passage, Courtenay, Port Alberni: Vancouver Island. Almost entirely done by rowboat with the big run of chinook ("tyee" fishing, locals call it) beginning in August. There are salmon runs all summer.

Ilwaco, Wash. Season is May to September, with July and August best. During last two weeks of August, limit catches are almost certain.

Lake Te Anau, New Zealand. If you're not in season or mind for Alaska salmon, try landing some good-sized Atlantic salmon in the Pacific. It's stocked here. Season is October to April; best is February to April.

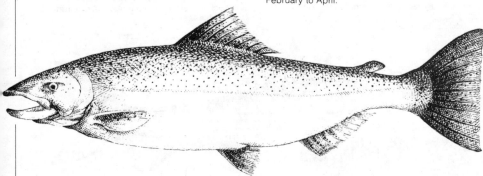

Illustrations by Laszlo Kubinyi

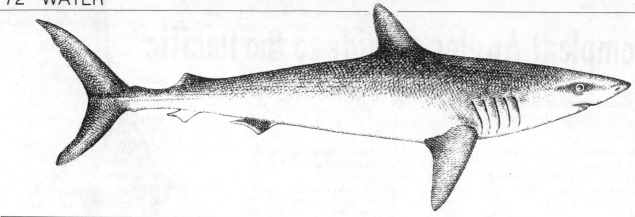

PACIFIC BARRACUDA

A fine, light tackle sport fish, the Pacific barracuda is always good for a quick, hard fight. It has become more popular as a game fish in waters between Santa Barbara and Baja because the tuna are diminishing.

Santa Barbara, Calif. to Mazatlan. Best season is April to December.

Kona Coast and Hanalei, Hawaii. Rich waters for many game fish; the barracuda is one that runs well here. Sizes run to eight feet in length.

Pulau Tioman Island, Malaysia. Since they run best in tropical and subtropical waters, the Pacific barracuda are particularly suited to the southern reaches of the South China Sea. The season is May to October, but just before the November monsoons and in early May are best. Pulau Tioman is about 30 miles off the coast of the Malay Peninsula.

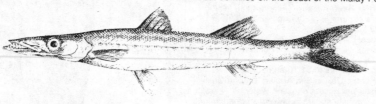

SHARK

There are at least 29 species of shark in the Pacific but big game fishermen go after only a few of them: the thresher, a scrappy fighter; the maneater, because it's so dangerous; the blue, which is also scrappy; and the mako, which is almost the equal of the marlin as a game fish. The mako is noted for its out-of-the-water leaps and is exceedingly dangerous, attacking boats at will. One captured maneater was found to contain whole sea lions, a Newfoundland dog and parts of a horse. Such finds have given legend to some mighty hairy tales.

West Coast, United States to Baja. You can search for maneaters in this range but should know that they are more abundant toward the southern end of the range. They run as long as 35 to 40 feet and weigh 600 pounds. (Eight-footers are more common.)

Mayor Island, New Zealand. The world records for both the thresher and mako sharks were taken here, at 922 and 1,000 pounds respectively. Season is Oct. 1 to April 30 but best is February to April. Decidedly not the place to go swimming.

Horseburgh Lighthouse, Singapore. Anglers understand that a three- to four-knot current flowing through shark-infested waters at the edges of the South China Sea makes for sensational shark fishing. Here, you'll be near Singapore's oldest lighthouse.

We add one final word of caution. Sharks feed on anything, especially anything that moves. And they can perceive what's edible by sound, smell and sight. They are most dangerous to the game fisherman *after* they are landed and in the boat. Even hours after they're hauled in, lying on a boat, they will "come to life" and bite, mangle, eat whoever or whatever is within reach.

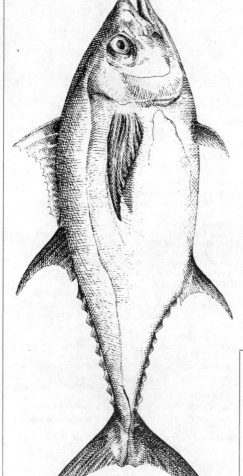

TUNA

The albacore—the "chicken of the sea" of marketing fame—migrate counter-clockwise around the Pacific rim. When young, off the U.S. West Coast, they run 15 to 35 pounds. By the time they reach Japan, they weigh as much as 200. Experienced anglers will tell you that when a school of albacore is encountered, the action is fantastic. Bluefin tuna fishing was pioneered by Zane Grey off Catalina in the early 1900s. (He also discovered and publicized Tahiti's great fishing in the 1930s.) The Pacific bonito is prized for its fighting qualities and superb flavor when baked.

Baja to the Pacific Northwest. To catch albacore, fish off Baja in March and April, off California in May and June and off the Pacific Northwest from July to October. Bluefins run the same area.

San Diego, Calif. There are overnight "albacore specials"—charters which run to Cabo San Lucas, Guadalupe Island, Cedros, Magdalene Bay and San Bonito Island.

Pacific City, Ore. One of the most exciting trips around is the run out the blue water in one of the 22-foot Cape Kiwanda dories that are launched through the surf near Pacific City. The albacore runs in as close as 10 miles. Peak time is August.

Hanalei, Hawaii. Beautiful fishing in summer. Yellowfin tuna record, 270 pounds, taken here in May.

Cabo Blanco, Peru. Late spring, early summer produce the best results. Pacific big-eye tuna record, 435 pounds, landed in mid-April.

Sydney, Australia. Allison and five other varieties of tuna are available, but we should add that most of the world's light tackle tuna records are held by Sydney anglers.

BONEFISH

A good game fish, the bonefish readily takes sport lures and live bait. Sizes run to three feet and up to 18 pounds.

Hanalei, Kauai, Hawaii. The former world record, at 18 pounds two ounces, was taken here; there is year-round good fishing. These waters also yielded the world record catch for Yellowfin (Allison) tuna. Late spring is best but expensive.

Oceanside, Calif. south to Baja, Mexico. Lively battles with bonefish from Southern California down to La Paz; many fish in backwaters. July and August best. Bonefish are more plentiful toward the south of this range.

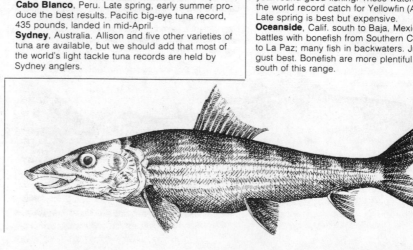

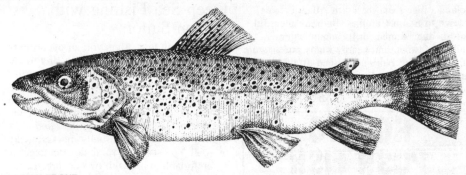

BROWN TROUT

The brown trout is probably the most wily species for fly fishermen. For example, only one brown is caught for every five rainbow. They run from Northern California to Vancouver but are not abundant. Better fishing is in Asia. Size is 3 feet; maximum recorded weight is 30 pounds, but a 10-pounder is exceptional.

Fiordland National Park, South Island, New Zealand. The Fiordland is one of the loneliest and most beautiful regions on earth. Fishing is on Lake Te Anau but *the* fishing adventure includes renting a shallow-draft jet boat to range far upstream in the turbulent Waian River.

Vancouver Island Rarer off these coastal waters. Brown trout were introduced here from Wisconsin and Montana in 1932.

Kashmir The famed Vale has so many, there's a two-rod limit. Season is April 1 to Sept. 30.

Punjab The Kulu Valley, located halfway between Lahore and the Himalayas, offers excellent trout fishing, including rainbows.

RAINBOW TROUT

A superb sport fish, the steelhead rainbow trout is a worthy equal to the Atlantic salmon in most qualities. In fact, many anglers prefer the flesh of this fish to Atlantic salmon or fresh-cooked steaks. Sizes run to 4 feet and 40 pounds.

Ketchikan, Juneau, Petersburg, Sitka: Alaska. Spring and fall.

Gold Beach, Ore. The mouth of the Rogue River is a good place to start but pick areas near any tidal river. With the fishing you get one of the world's most beautiful and spectacular coastlines. Summer.

Fuji - Hakone - Izu National Park, Japan. Just south of Mount Fuji is Lake Hakone, which is well-stocked with rainbow trout (and brook trout and black bass). A wonderful excuse to go to Japan, even climb Mt. Fuji.

Tasmania Some of the finest rainbow and brown trout fishing in whole Pacific area. Great runs of sea trout, too; it is exciting country for the dry fly folks. September to mid-December, March to April.

Madras, India. Someone sometime put some good trout stock in the streams leading into the Nilgiris in Madras. Not many people fish there.

New Zealand Rainbow and brown trout were brought to New Zealand 70 years ago. As a reward for careful management and an abundance of natural food, the trout have thrived. This probably explains why more five-pound rainbows are taken in New Zealand than anywhere else in the world. And they're generous with their limits. Season is October to April but best is February to April. (See also our comments under brown trout.)

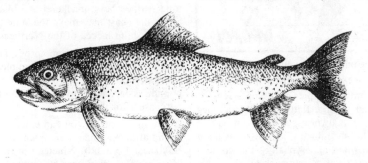

SWORDFISH

Once plentiful from California to Oregon, the swordfish is practically extinct in West Coast waters. And yet it is still highly prized as meat—even though in many cases restaurants substitute shark instead. The swordfish migrate seasonally north and south and seem to prefer cool currents. They run up to 1,000 pounds but are under 600 when caught off the California coast.

Iquique, Chile. A world record 1,182-pounder was once taken out of the waters off Iquique in May, a month when the swordfish are running but the weather's not so good. November to February.

Great Barrier Reef, Australia. Year-round fishing for swordfish but waters are also good for marlin, Spanish mackerel, wahoo, sailfish and giant grouper.

SAILFISH

Like the marlin, to which it is related, the sailfish is a hard fighter, capable of spectacular leaps and 1,000-foot runs. They run to 14 feet and about 200 pounds.

Santa Cruz Island, Galapagos. A world record was taken here. Best time is late spring, early summer.

La Paz, Cabo San Lucas, Loreto, Mulege, and Bahia de Los Angeles: Baja. January to September.

Fiji As with other game fish, sailfish run well in the Fijis, especially between October and April.

Trincomalee, Ceylon. Already recommended for dolphins, we add an amen for sailfish. March to October and latter part of December to January.

Sydney, Australia. We just have to tell you that two Melbourne men landed nine sailfish in one day from one boat just outside Sydney.

Bermagui, Australia. This beautiful little fishing village, nestled at the foot of wooded hills, is a wonderful launching point for sailfish (and marlin and shark). It is 260 miles south of Sydney.

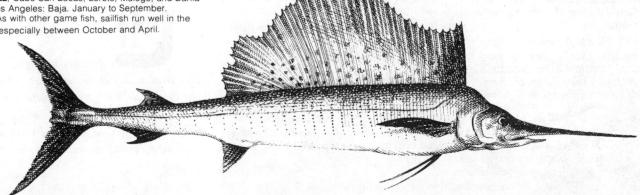

Quahogging

When kids around Shediac in the Canadian Maritimes want to raise a few clams, they do just that. Digging clams and diving for quahogs for fun and profit seems to have the plebeian paper route or supermarket checkout job completely beat. Who wouldn't want to get paid to go fishing?

Quahogs are large, thick-shelled clams so named by Indians, who cut discs from the shells and used them as the currency known as wampum (corrupted by white settlers from the Indian "wamp-unp-eeg"). Because this species of mollusk does not burrow deeply in the bays around Shediac, New Brunswick, fishermen anchor their dories and have only to prod into the water with long-handled rakes to dislodge quahogs partially buried in the eel grass.

When youngsters go quahogging they usually have infinitely more fun. Working in pairs, they row out to a quahog bed. Gunny sacks in hand, they plunge overboard into water that is waist- or shoulder-deep. They tread the seabed until they locate a quahog with their feet and then dive to retrieve it. Often they will find several in the same spot. Sometimes they'll combine quahogging with plain old clamming—digging at low tide around the telltale breathing holes that betray concealed colonies of soft-shelled clams. They sell both varieties to local restaurateurs at a price dictated by supply and demand but which can start at $2 a peck or 10 cents a pound. They don't get rich, but they do have fun.

You can find quahogs, native to the coastal waters of the Gulf of St. Lawrence, as far south as the Gulf of Mexico. Soft-shelled clams range from the north Atlantic coast down to South Carolina. Both are plentiful at Shediac, famed for its annual summer lobster festival and nearby sandy beaches on the temperate Northumberland Strait (warmest water north of Washington, D.C., it is claimed).

–Mike Michaelson

HOW TO PUSH FISH

Physical culture experts universally agree that pushing fish tones the muscles, brings a rosy hue to the complexion and gives fresh impetus and motivation to the blood, causing it to flow with renewed vigor through one's arterial network. Yet, alas, despite the enormous popularity of fish-pushing, not one person in ten knows how to push fish the right way, and authorities tell us that wrong fish-pushing is often worse than no fish-pushing at all! "All it gets you is aching muscles and a lot of scales all over your floor," states a leading Professor.

RIGHT!

WRONG!

Easy Flounder

Let the whole family flounder? Why not? Catching flatfish with a handline is an uncomplicated, relaxing sport. It requires neither special skill nor elaborate equipment—literally a hook, line and sinker obtainable from any tackle shop for less than $1.

Look for some member of the flatfish family along most American seacoasts. Winter flounder are found almost anywhere off the Atlantic shore, including the Canadian Maritimes. The fluke, or summer flounder, ranges from the Carolinas to Cape Cod. The colorful starry flounder is widely distributed along the Pacific shore. Other members of the family include the Gulf flounder and the various sand dabs, small soles and turbot of the West Coast.

You won't need a high-powered boat to catch these fish. Mostly, they are found in comparatively shallow water close to shore and can be fished from docks and piers, from bridges over channels or from small

rowboats in inlets, bays and estuaries.

For bait, pry loose a handful of mussels from the pilings of a pier or dig up a few clams. Other favorite flatfish fodder includes sandworms, bloodworms, shrimp, cut bait and live killifish (minnows). It also has been claimed—perhaps apocryphally—that these fish sometimes will accept such exotic offerings as chunks of wiener.

Lower your bait until the sinker touches the bottom and the line slackens. Keep the line taut enough so that it is sensitive to the feel of the fish taking the bait, but don't be overanxious to set the hook. Rather than snapping at bait, flatfish tend to suck it in. Give the fish a chance. Lift the line gently, and often it will hook itself.

Winter flounder average from one to three pounds, while fluke may weigh up to eight pounds with an occasional "doormat" scaling upward of 20 pounds. Whatever the size, pan-fried flounder fillets make a fast, tasty meal. West Coast sand dabs are sought by epicureans while a British cousin, the Dover sole, has a gourmet rating. Ask a French chef about *filets de soles Marguery* and he'll tell you that poaching also is good for the sole.

–Mike Michaelson

Deep-Sea Fishing with Breton Sailors

This sporting tour offers you an opportunity to participate in the real life of a Breton sailor off the coast of Brittany in the northwest corner of France. You take a four- to five-hour trip every day in a seaworthy boat, either in the morning for fishing only or in the afternoon for laying down bait *and* fishing. Your catch is usually mackerel, ray or sole. You stay in a rural stone cottage in a comfortable room with two or three beds; there's a bathroom on the same floor, a large living room with fireplace, a kitchen. Cook your own catch (a maid will help) or go out for meals.

Arrangements are by the week from the end of April to the end of September. Rental includes a self-drive Renault from Paris/Orly Airport for a week—with unlimited mileage. Rates per person per week, including fishing: for two, 690 francs (about $156); for three, 590 francs (about $133); for four, 540 francs (about $123). Singles also available. For more information, see your travel agent or write Hobby Voyage, 8 rue de Milan, 75009 Paris.

–James Egan

Maine's Main Fishing Mecca

Knowledgeable down-easters are stating very emphatically that Maine's coast has the distinction of providing the only Atlantic salmon runs in the country. That, and the regular full-scale migrations of giant bluefin tuna, striped bass, mackerel and bluefish along the coast may make the state the sports fishing mecca of the Northeast.

Some of it pays good money too. The first tuna landed last season, for example, brought an all-time record price of $1 a pound, as Japanese buyers bid with local purchasers for the catch.

If you like contests you can enter the Bailey Island all-tackle tuna tournament off Casco Bay (near Portland). Nineteen of the big bluefins, averaging over 500 pounds each, were landed in one day of the competition in 1973. The Bailey Island tournament is held annually in late July, and you can write the Maine Department of Sea and Shore Fisheries, Augusta, Maine 04330, for exact dates and/or more information.

–The Editors

e may say of angling as Dr. Boteler said of strawberries: "Doubtless God could have made a better berry, but doubtless God never did:" and so if I might be judge, God never did make a more calm, quiet, innocent recreation than angling.

—ISAAK WALTON

Ice Fishing for Rent

Seven miles out on a frozen lake is a village of wooden huts. Inside, snug and warm, are intrepid fisherpersons—for there are many women—many of whom have traveled hundreds of miles, from many parts of the United States and Canada, to fish Lake Simcoe, a 280-square-mile lake about 50 miles north of Toronto.

Many of these huts—and there are 4,000 of them on the frigid lake—are for rent and come in sizes ranging from two-fisherman models to huts accommodating parties of 14 or more. Cost is about $6 per person for a day or night of fishing, including transportation (in an enclosed snowmobile bus), stove fuel, tackle, bait and precut ice holes (accessible through trap doors cut in the hut's wooden floor).

Heated by wood, oil or propane stove, the simple wooden huts usually have a bench for sitting or sleeping, and become so drowsily warm (despite below-zero temperatures outside) that it often is necessary to open the door. Some private huts have cots, easy chairs, cooking stoves, television and, in at least one case, a telephone hookup. Fishing is done with a tip-up rig that you simply watch, so bring reading, knitting, macramé, booze or other diversion (plus food to heat on the stove).

Fish January through March for lake trout, whitefish, perch and herring. Reserve in advance. For a list of commercial ice hut operators write: Ontario Department of Tourism and Information, Parliament Buildings, Toronto, Ont., Canada.

—Mike Michaelson

I did not get hold of a 70-pound salmon, but I did get one of 56 pounds, and one of 40 pounds, besides lots of little ones under 20 pounds. My wife got three which weighed 120 pounds, viz.:—43, 40, and 37 pounds, besides about a dozen between 20 and 7 pounds. These fish were all caught on your "Murdoch" rods; and, in fact, in the week these rods killed over 300 pounds of fish—not counting several very large fish that got away. I never saw such fish in my life. The 56-pound fish I had on 47 minutes, and he took me down the coast 2 miles before we could get him killed.

—LETTER FROM BRITISH COLUMBIA, IN *HARDY BROTHERS CATALOGUE*, 1907

Bass-Busting and Hawg-Sticking in Mississippi and Louisiana

The black bass—red-eyed, thick-lipped and pot-bellied—is not exactly the aristocrat of American game fish. For one thing, its family name just doesn't make it with the tweedy followers of *Salmo salar* and *Salvelinus fontinalis*. For another, it dwells in the dammed-up rivers and reservoirs of the South and Midwest, areas that are anathema to the anglophiliacs who once ruled American angling. Despite these drawbacks, the black bass has become the most sought after fish in the United States.

The bass' prominence is largely due to the rise of a new fishing culture more attuned to the temper of the Seventies than to the Izaak Walton days of trout traditionalists, Tonkin bamboo and horsehair tippets. In the last few years, the nation's burgeoning army of six million "bass busters" has even developed its own language of "hawg sticks," "bloopers," "limpers" and "lunkerluggers." Bass busters no longer share sensitivities about lightweight rods and tiny leaders; instead, they'd just as soon blow their prey out of the water.

This hard-line attitude is accompanied by a new technology. Sleek bass boats—typically 16-foot outboards costing about $1,600—are the hottest-selling boats on the market. More than 200,000 have been sold in the last four years—most in the South.

The roots of bass busting are deep in the South, particularly in the cypress-studded lakes of Mississippi and Louisiana where fishermen in stub-nosed, flat-bottomed prams have sought bass for generations. Now these craft have been replaced by ultra-light, shallow-draft boats such as the Convincer, made by the Ouachita Marine Corp. of Little Rock, that lists for $1,516.70. Add another $1,550 for an 85-hp Evinrude and the compleat bass buster has a start. From

there he can go on to items such as a ship-to-shore radio-phone, a trailer, automatic anchor winch, electric cigarette lighter, electronic fish finder and a stalking motor for silent running and his investment can easily come to $4,000 before he's out on the water.

The exploding interest in bass fishing has led to a new organization, the Bass Anglers Sportsman's Society. With 90,000 card-carrying members, it is the fastest growing outdoor association in the country. It sponsors half a dozen annual tournaments —limited to 150 bass-busters who pay a $150 entry fee—on the hottest lakes in the country. It even holds a Bass Masters Classic in October for the 24 top scorers in the six previous tournaments. These champions meet on a chartered plane in the Atlanta airport—destination unknown. Once the flight is airborne a B.A.S.S. official opens a sealed envelope containing the name of the lake to be fished. Wherever that is, it's a long way from the lone fisherman casting flies for trout in an icy stream in the high Sierras.

—Peter Janssen

See 1940s Florida in Key Largo

Key Largo is one of the last unspoiled places in Florida. It's just a sleepy little fishing village, connected to the mainland only by a narrow two-lane highway, and apparently it hasn't changed much since *Key Largo*, the movie with Humphrey Bogart and Lauren Bacall, put it on the map in 1948. It's the place to go if you like your Florida uncluttered by condominiums and high-rise hotels and tourists in rhinestone-studded shades.

The restaurants in Key Largo are mostly funky old roadhouses with stuffed fish hung on the walls and fresh fish listed on the menus. At some places they even serve your meals on fish-shaped plates—with tartar sauce in the eye socket. Naturally, Key Lime pie is a specialty everywhere.

In Key Largo you can bake yourself in the sun, collect shells or just sleep 12 or 14 hours a day—this is the place for it. (They don't call them "sleepy" fishing villages for nothing.) If you find yourself yearning for adventure, go to the John Pennekamp State Park. Just off Key Largo, it's the "world's only underground state park." Glass-bottom boats go out several times a day (weather permitting) to give tourists a look at the coral reef and the marine life. For the more intrepid, there are scuba and snorkel trips to the reef offered by the park and by several local diving centers.

The Bay Harbor Lodge in Key Largo will rent you your very own completely furnished and equipped one-bedroom cottage overlooking the water. Rates are reasonable, even during the winter. (For current rates and reservations, write to Bay Harbor Lodge, RR 1, Box 35, Key Largo, Fla. 33037.)

I'm not quite sure why the recent Florida construction boom hasn't touched Key Largo, but I'm sure grateful it hasn't. Anyone with a soft spot for the peaceful, hokey charm of Florida in the Forties just has to love this place.

–Carol White

I have lost myself in the sea many times
with my ear full of freshly-cut flowers,
with my tongue full of love and agony.
I have lost myself in the sea many times
as I lose myself in the heart of certain
children. . . .
I have lost myself in the sea many times,
ignorant of the water I go seeking
a death full of light to consume me.

—FEDERICO GARCIA LORCA

Skin Diving for Alaska's Big, Ugly, Armor-Plated, Fast-Moving King Crabs

Skin divers on the East Coast get their kicks searching for and catching lobster; West Coast skin divers have their crayfish. In Alaska when divers take to the chill depths, they're most frequently seeking the king crab—a big, ugly, armor-plated, fast-moving crustacean known and respected not only for its giant size (they're three feet to as much as five or six feet from arm tip to arm tip) but for the shattering power of its big pincer-like claw as well.

Here's what happens on a typical dive for one of the critters.

You're at 60 feet and your visibility is about average for Alaska diving—roughly 15 feet. The bottom too is typical, with lots of rocks, boulders, rises and dips. Already you've seen some halibut, a couple of cod, one or two greenling. Then you spot the quarry you came for—a king crab meandering slowly across the bottom.

He sees or senses you too, and suddenly he's running swiftly away in that peculiar sideways gait. You kick your flippers hard and catch up with him. Now you're over and just behind him.

Quickly you grab a back leg and flip him over on his back. What you're doing is looking for the "apron" across the bottom of his belly. You see it, and the balanced, symmetrical lines which decorate it tell you he's a male. You can keep him—if you can capture him.

Already he's righted himself and, running faster than ever now, he's making a getaway. You kick hard again, and this time you swim right over him. Swiftly now, praying you don't miss, you reach down and wrap your fist around that big, lethal claw that is already waving and flailing in your direction.

The crab, of course, has two claws. One, which you grabbed, is many times bigger than the other. It's a powerhouse, used for crushing shells and splintering tough food. The other is small and relatively weak. He uses it for scooping the splintered food into his mouth.

As long as you hold onto the big claw, and hold its pincers closed, the crab can't harm you. He might scare you to death as he thrashes around, his eight horny arms and legs pushing and pulling and jerking, seeming to surround you and making you think you're wrestling a dozen monsters. But if you don't let go your grip on his big claw he can't really do you any harm.

Your next move is to ascend to the surface, you and your unwilling charge. Once there the sudden change of altitude seems to take a great deal of the fight out of him. It's relatively easy to bring him to shore; or, you can tie him to a buoy or load him aboard a waiting skiff. Then, your catch secure, you can descend to the depths again for more crabs and more chases, more sport.

It's exciting, satisfying sport, skin diving for crab. It's all the more satisfying later when, beside a beach fire or at home, you dip big, white hunks of freshly cooked crab meat in hot drawn butter and pop the morsels into your mouth. Most Alaskans will agree it's some of the tastiest eating to come out of the sea.

–Mike Miller

The Second Great Barrier Reef

The second-longest barrier reef in the world (outranked only by Australia's Great Barrier Reef) lies just a few miles off the coast of British Honduras, a little country that shares the Yucatan Peninsula with Mexico. The reef is a diver's paradise, with everything from low-lying islands to 15-foot dips. Bonefishing may be the world's best. (Probably the scrappiest of game fish, the bonefish of British Honduras are so aggressive that they will hit any lure whatsoever—as long as it's yellow.)

Stay in the capital of British Honduras, Belize, at either the Bellevue Hotel or the Fort George, a modern resort offering a swimming pool, skin diving, tours and many other amenities. The managers at both hotels can tell you about the availability of charter boats—they come and go.

Taca Airlines flies to Belize from Miami and New Orleans. Contact the airline or a travel agent for more information or reservations.

Scuba Diving Perfect

Carl Roessler is a toothy ex-Yalie who got tired of putting a computer through its paces and dropped out to skin dive his way to Inner Peace. But, Calvinist training being as powerful as it is, diving in the West Indies turned for Roessler into a full-time vice presidency of See & Sea Travel Service in San Francisco—the oldest and probably the largest packager of tours for skin divers.

See & Sea takes small groups of experienced divers to dive-perfect places like Micronesia, Australia, New Caledonia, the New Hebrides, the Cayman Islands, the Galapagos, Cozumel, Africa, the Indian Ocean, and Curaçao and Bonaire in Roessler's old splashing grounds in the Dutch West Indies.

The company takes care of everything from air tanks to accommodations for one price that includes everything but air fare. Sample rates: $1,695 for 17 days of diving at Australia's Great Barrier Reef and in the Coral Sea; $455 for eight days to Cozumel and Akumal on Mexico's Yucatan coast.

Roessler, a published underwater photographer and writer, personally leads many underwater expeditions, and also makes sure that none of *his* divers disturb the marine life they find. The only shooting done is with an underwater camera.

"One diver with a spear-gun can wipe out all the large fish in one area in a matter of hours," Roessler points out. "We want to appreciate the sea, not decimate it."

Possibly a good man to dive with, this computer dropout from Yale.

For more information on See & Sea's diving tours, write:

> See & Sea Travel Service
> 680 Beach St.
> San Francisco, Calif. 94133.
> *–Richard John Pietschmann*

Spearfishing

Spearfishing takes patient practice, but the enjoyment you'll get out of striking a fine fish is considerable.

The basic tool is a straight stick or pole seven or eight feet long. Instead of having a single point, however, as in game-hunting, the fishing spear has two points, as shown in the illustration. These points can be any hard, elastic material—split bamboo, sugar cane stalk, or even two pieces of heavy iron wire—filed to a point and notched into barbs on the inside. Hard wood also works.

After the head pieces are notched and pointed, they should be firmly bound to the spear at a point a few inches below the end of the shaft. Then drive in a couple of small wedges between the shaft and points—this firms up the tension between the points and the head of the spear shaft. Lash the points the rest of the way up—up to the head of the spear shaft.

The elastic points spread as they strike the fish's body; then they instantly contract, holding the fish a secure prisoner. The idea is that the fish should not be able to escape no matter how slippery or smooth its body may be. Once upon a time, when life wasn't so hectic, night spearfishing was considered great fun. Folks went out in rowboats, waving torches. The torch not only illuminated the water but was thought to dazzle the fish.

(One way to make a torch is to wind lampwick around a forked stick. The ball of wick is saturated with kerosene or some other flammable fluid. All torches should be prepared before use and no kerosene should be taken on the water.)

A smaller spear can be used for catching snakes or other reptiles that are not safe or pleasant to handle. Works when you go frogging, too.

–Min S. Yee

Underwater Park

It was conceived to protect the natural beauty of North America's only living coral reef, and it is the first underwater park in the United States. Today, the John Pennekamp Coral Reef State Park, at Key Largo in the Florida Keys, attracts droves of skin and scuba divers (many with underwater cameras), as well as legions of tourists who view the reef from glass-bottom boats. There's plenty of room for all, since this preserve—which protects the beautiful reef from treasure hunters and shell and coral merchandisers—covers about 75 square miles of the Atlantic Ocean.

South of the artificial glitter of Miami Beach, the park conceals its own underwater city of kaleidoscopic shapes and colors, built of more than 40 varieties of coral and home to hundreds of species of multihued tropical fish. Sheltered in the blue-green waters of Pennekamp are stands of antler-like elkhorn coral, whorled boulders of brain coral and such fish as multicolored parrot fish and angelfish, sergeant majors replete with chevrons, black and silver spadefish, neon gobies. There are also many chameleon-like species that rely on an ability to blend with the surroundings either to attack a prey or to evade a predator in their beautiful but ruthless underwater world.

Fish soon become accustomed to a diver's presence, so you can get remarkably close to many of the denizens of the reef. Snorkeling equipment may be rented at the park's land base, and scuba trips onto the reef are available by arrangement. The park's marina has a variety of boats for rent—skiffs with motors, canopied pontoons, sailboats and rowboats. Glass-bottom boats make two-hour trips daily—weather permitting. (The fares are $5 for adults, $2.50 for children.) For information phone (305) 852-5134 or (305) 248-4300.

–Mike Michaelson

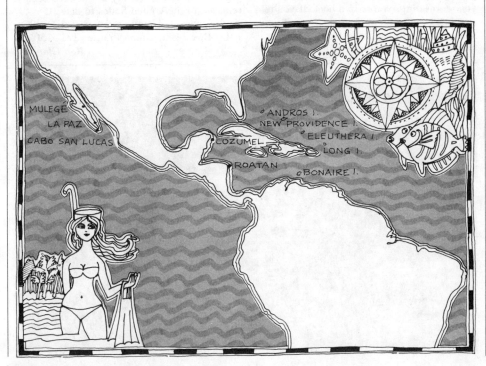

Row, Row, Row Your Floe

If the annual ice-floe marathon at Peterborough, Ontario, isn't the toughest contest in North America, it surely has to be one of the most frigid. It is held on the Trent Canal in March, when hardy competitors clad in wet suits and flippers cut rafts from the ice on the canal bank, jump aboard these improvised craft, paddle for two miles—and then dive head-first into the freezing water and swim ashore. Fastest team wins (and keeps warmest).

Sponsored by the Trident Underwater Club of Peterborough, the event last year attracted more than 200 spartan types who made up 30 teams. Most use either kicking power or paddles to travel the chilly course. In one contest, a team equipped its ice raft with a small sail; another used a parachute to harness a frosty breeze.

It all started about a dozen years ago, when Trident Club members, strolling the snow-covered banks of the canal, wondered how they possibly could survive without their favorite sport until warmer weather arrived. Then someone had the bright idea of chopping ice from the banks and floating with the current. Next, they organized the annual race for all-year swimming enthusiasts and, since then, they've been as happy as polar bears with a new iceberg.

—Mike Michaelson

A Jet-Propelled Water Ski

Want a water ski that slaloms at 35 m.p.h. —without a pull boat? Try Jet Ski, a jet-propelled water ski that doubles as a Class A inboard boat, and is among the most innovative marine products to come out in years.

Jet Ski is a small bullet of a boat with an open stern that looks like a misplaced nose cone. Nearly seven feet long but only two feet wide, Jet Ski must be ridden to be believed. You ride it by slipping through the open stern onto a foam cushioned pad. You grasp Jet Ski's swivel handlebars, turning a motorcycle-style handgrip to accelerate. A jet impeller whooshes you on your way. If you're kneeling, you're in a boat. If you're standing, you're on a water ski. And if you spill, Jet Ski automatically slows down, circling at low speed until you climb back aboard to go again.

Like a water ski, Jet Ski turns as you shift your body weight. The movable impeller nozzle serves as a rudder as well. The craft will turn inside a nine-foot radius. Also, since it's jet powered, there is no dangerous propeller—just a harmless jet of burbling water.

Jet Ski weighs 220 pounds (when dry), is powered by a 400cc, two-cycle, two-cylinder engine rated at 26 hp, is equipped with an electric starter and is priced at approximately $1,000.

But there's one catch. Jet Ski will be hard to find until 1975, when mass distribution begins in this country. Only 2,000 have been released to the United States to date. If you're interested, write to Kawasaki Jet Ski, P.O. Box 1490, Grand Prairie, Tex. 75050.

—Bob Clampett

Waterfall Walking

At Dunn's River Falls in Ocho Rios, Jamaica, you can climb a 600-foot waterfall, splashing your way to the top in refreshing, pleasingly cool 63° water. It looks scary but isn't—it's easy, even if you aren't particularly athletic. For your protection, young Jamaican Tarzans linger on the waterfall rocks to lend a helping hand. Or you can bring your own experienced guide, if you're the nervous type. The waterfall cascades over wedding-cake tiers of smooth rock directly to the beach below—where you can rest, swim or have hot dogs and soda after you've climbed the falls. Or, you can forget the hot dogs and try Jamaican food.

For further information about Ocho Rios and Dunn's River Falls, write the Jamaica Tourist Board, 200 Park Ave., New York, N.Y. 10017.

Guess When the Ice Will Break Up and Win $100,000

Why are all those people standing around watching that tripod out on the ice of the Tanana River up there in the town of Nenana, Alaska? They are waiting for the tripod to tip over when the ice under it breaks up, which is the *big moment* in the Nenana Ice Classic, in which everybody around Nenana, and from over in the Yukon Territory too, has bet a dollar. Each bettor makes one guess as to the exact date, hour and minute the ice will break up, and whoever comes closest this year will pick up over $100,000 in prize money.

The world's biggest ice pool started in 1917 "to ease the monotony of a long winter," writes a historian. By mid-April Nenanans and visitors begin loitering around the riverbank hoping not to miss the action, which some years holds off till the middle of May. Mayor Jack Coghill describes one such exciting moment: "I was present on the bank of the river. The tripod started moving, the cable released, the siren opened up, the last cable parted, stopping the clock when the tripod had traveled 100 feet, and in a matter of seconds the entire sheet of ice was moving down the river."

On weekends rubberneckers drive hundreds of miles from as far away as Fairbanks and Anchorage to stare at the fateful tripod. Watchmen guard it at night to make sure the great event has human witnesses. At last, writes a Chamber of Commerce booster, "the ice pack is cracked into huge ice floes that are twisted and crumbled by tons of surging river water. The tripod shudders, then moves. . . ." After the breakup, the tension slackens in Nenana, but life goes on; the Yutana Barge Line begins carrying freight up and down the river, and the fish wheels begin turning once again. Then will come fall and winter, and once again the Ice Classic tripod will be set out on the Tanana.

—Roy Bongartz

Nude Beaches at Group Rates

Nudity has never made it big on American beaches, although it's estimated that more than 10 million Europeans jiggle, flop and bounce on "free beaches" every summer. No, apparently we are not significantly more modest as a nation—it's just that we have so few places to shed our suits and still stay out of the slammer.

A pity, but help may have arrived. Mike Kong and VIB Tours fix to do something about the sadly repressed state of American skinnydipping. Kong is director of VIB (Vacations in the Buff), which for four years has packaged strip trips to sunny places such as Guadeloupe, Greece, France, Scandinavia, Hawaii and other bastions of nude bathing.

Surfing + Sailing = Windsurfing

Want a tiny inexpensive sailboat that can handle a stiff 40-mile-an-hour wind, is almost impossible to tip over, and only takes a few hours to master? Then try a windsurfer, one of the fastest growing types of boats in the United States and Europe.

The windsurfer looks like a surfboard with an attached sail. You sail it by standing on the middle of the board and holding onto the rear of the sail with one hand and a boom handle just aft of the mast with the other. Tilt the sail forward or to one side to catch the wind—and hang on.

There was a time, not very long ago, when a tour was a wimpy excursion for little old ladies who wanted to be herded from one musty museum to another. This image has been shattered by tour operators and customers, who now realize that group rates need not mean group activities. VIB's idea, of course, is to get people together who enjoy climbing out of their clothes. But the VIB brochure uses bold type to declare, "No wild orgies," and goes on to reassure us that "people who enjoy social nudism are neither hypersexual nor asexual." What's more, (and what's possibly disappointing to some of you out there), VIB vacations aren't for the undraped alone. You don't even have to take your clothes off.

Still, the idea is to take VIB's low group rate trips to exotic destinations where there *is* at least one beach on which you can cavort nude.

A favorite VIB destination is Guadeloupe, in the central Caribbean. The hotel is Bois Joli on Terre de Haut, and the free beach is ¼-mile-long Anse Cawan. Rates begin at $269 from New York—this includes air fare, hotel room and continental breakfast for eight days.

Other VIB nudies include a schooner cruise of the Virgin Islands for eight days from

Weighing only 60 pounds, the windsurfer moves easily in a light breeze. It's when the wind moves up to about 40 m.p.h. that the windsurfer really flies. Of course, that's when the other sailboats are safely tied up back in port.

In a strong wind, the front end of the board planes out of the water. Riders meet large waves by kneeling or sitting down. If you fall off the board, don't worry. Since the mast is mounted on a universal joint, the joint lets the mast drop into the water. Thus, the mast acts as a sea anchor and the boat stops within a few feet so you can climb on.

Windsurfers can also be sailed in surf. Some riders launch it by walking out a ways and heaving the sails and mast out as far as they can, then paddling the board out beyond the waves. Then they slip the mast into the hull and take off.

Windsurfers were first sold in the United States three years ago. There are about 2,000 around now, mostly on the East and West coasts. There are, however, small fleets of windsurfers in places like Utah.

The boats are manufactured in Holland. The hull is made of soft plastic, in case you hit a rock. It's 12 feet long, four inches thick and 26 inches wide. The 14-foot mast is a fiberglass pole-vaulting pole. Sails are made of Dacron and run about 56 square feet. Unless you make it yourself, the boat costs $365.

The American distributor is Windsurfing International, Inc., 1808 Stanford Ave., Santa Monica, Calif. 90404.

—Peter Janssen

$389, ski weekends in Canada (no clothing for the pool, sauna and other things) from $139 and a weekend in the Bahamas for $179 from New York. There's also a camping tour in Hawaii—$89 for eight days. You get yourself to Hawaii and the tour collects you, transfers you to the beach and provides you with a rustic cabin or a tent. (If you want to stay longer, it'll cost you $9 per for each additional day.)

VIB's nudie tours don't come in plain brown wrappers and a travel agent can handle all the details. VIB Tours is located at 902 Second Ave., New York, N.Y. 10017.

—Richard John Pietschmann

*To and fro we leap
    And chase the frothy bubbles,
While the world is full of troubles
    And is anxious in its sleep.
Come away, O human child!
To the waters and the wild
    With a faery, hand in hand,
For the world's more full of weeping
than you can understand.*

—W. B. YEATS

Jesus Feet

You don't have to be the Messiah to walk on water. You just need 30 bucks. Jesus feet are made out of molded polystyrene plastic, and the adult size will support up to 240 pounds. For 14-year-old Saviors, there's a children's size that supports up to 145 pounds.

You too can wow your congregation! Be the first on your block to turn loaves into fishes! Get rid of your gurus and your Bibles, folks—all you need is the Hammacher-Schlemmer catalog. It's right on the backside of the page selling Turnpike Toll Guns, which shoot quarters at those toll nets on the freeways.

For one of their catalogs write:
    Hammacher-Schlemmer
    147 E. 57th St.
    New York, N.Y. 10022.

                    —The Editors

San Francisco's Vintage Regatta

If vintage sailing craft interest you, you ought to take in the Master Mariners' Regatta, held annually on San Francisco Bay on a Sunday in the latter half of May. Between 50 and 100 vintage boats participate in this fascinating sailing event.

Before the starting gun, each boat in the handicap competition passes the St. Francis Yacht Club (this begins at noon). You can watch the boats cover their 17-mile course across the bay and back from any vantage point between Aquatic Park and the Golden Gate Bridge in San Francisco.

Appropriately, the first boat in the race is always the *Alma*, an old hay scow built in 1890 at Hunter's Point on San Francisco Bay. The *Alma*, last of a fleet of some 300 hay and lumber scows that once plied back and forth across the bay, reminds us by her historic presence that the Master Mariners' Regatta is the oldest sailing competition on the West Coast. The first race took place in 1867 when the coastal lumber fleet challenged the San Francisco Bay hay scows. The race gained in popularity and flourished until 1891. The Master Mariners' Regatta was revived in 1965.

If seeing the *Alma* and the other old boats whets your appetite for vintage craft, visit the Maritime State Park at the Hyde Street Pier in San Francisco, immediately east of Aquatic Park. There you can see three other major boats from Bay Area nautical history. The *C. A. Thayer* hauled her first load of lumber in 1895. The *Wapama*, a steam schooner, carried both lumber and passengers, beginning in 1915. The paddle wheeled *Eureka*, built in 1922, was one of the last of her kind.

The Visitor's Information Center—476 Post St., San Francisco, Calif. 94109—can tell you the date set for this year's event. The phone number is (415) 421-5074.

                    —Lee Foster

Bare Boating: a Guide to Charter Sailing in the Caribbean

A few years ago, only the very rich and beautiful people were privileged enough to take sailing vacations. Pictures of their tanned and smiling faces filled the society pages—they were always sipping cocktails aboard the *Contessa*, *Barefoot Girl* or *Restless Dreamer*. The message was clear: to enjoy the pleasures of a yacht, you had to own one.

Today, however, it is possible to charter boats of every size, from the super-spare racers to the elegantly appointed teak-paneled cruisers. It costs much less than buying your own yacht, and you avoid all the worries that go along with maintaining one.

You don't even have to be much of a sailor to appreciate the pleasure and excitement of sailing—calm seas, a great breeze flapping your shirt, your boat really skipping along the water. At your request, a crew can do the sailing and you can soak up the sunshine and take in the view.

Many brokers charter both bare boats and boats with crews. With a bare boat, you charter the boat. You are the skipper and your shipmates are the crew. On a crewed boat, you charter both the yacht and the crew. You pay a charter fee and are free to select your ports of call or follow the skipper's suggestions.

Perhaps you're all ready and wondering where to go. Both the American and British Virgin Islands are a vacationer's paradise. They offer warm sunny weather, sparkling turquoise waters, spectacular snorkeling, white sand beaches and a seemingly endless choice of safe anchorages.

Sailing is smooth in the Virgin Islands. The waters are relatively sheltered, for the islands are close together and the seas don't have a dangerous fetch. The emerald depths are so clear that you can see the fish bite the bait on your hook 30 feet down. Occasionally a squall (which generally lasts no more than 10 minutes) churns the water and brings some heavy gusts of wind. But the reefs, rocks and buoys have been meticulously charted so getting lost shouldn't be a problem. (And you can consult the *Yachtsman's Guide to the Virgin Islands* to find everything from how to get through the Narrows to the name of the best restaurant in Sea Cow Bay.)

A sailboat offers many pleasures that a hotel cannot provide. Each evening you anchor in a new place: St. Thomas, St. Croix, Jost Van Dyke, Tortola, Virgin Gorda, Water Island, St. John—and each is unique. The shapes of the beaches, the lush tropical foliage, the undersea life, the restaurants on shore and the people you meet change each time you lift your anchor.

For a dramatic shift in scenery, anchor near a reef, put on your mask and snorkel and dive in. In seconds, you will see multicolored sea fans swaying silently in the surge of ocean currents. Grunts, butterfly fish, angelfish and groupers will dance a rhythmical slow motion ballet. Perhaps a pencil fish will pass you as he weaves his way through brilliant coral, placid sponges and forbidding urchins.

The sailing time between the islands is short enough to allow you to snorkel, swim, fish or have a look around the shore before the sun goes down.

Since you want a reliable seaworthy vessel, you may be wise to charter from a broker who has a fleet of the same boats rather than one who has an extensive listing of assorted boats. With a fleet, spare parts are easier to find and, overall, the boats seem to be kept in more uniform repair. If you are partial to a special size or kind of boat, you may have to charter outside a fleet.

The cost of a bare-boat charter ranges from $240 to $1,000 per week. Some boats come fully provisioned and others you have to stock yourself. (Supermarkets in St. Thomas are fully supplied with meats, produce and canned convenience foods.) If you want to leave the sailing to the crew, the price increases dramatically to about $38 per day per person for a party of six.

And now for what to bring. One seasoned sailor warns that no matter how little you bring, you'll probably bring too much.

For the women—a few shirts, a pair of slacks (lightweight) and a summer shift for wearing ashore for sightseeing or dinner.

For the men—T-shirts, one jacket and a tie for an evening visit to Little Dix or Caneel Bay.

Temperatures range between 70° and 90° year round and rainfall measures about 45 inches a year. With the exception of late August and early September, the weather is reliably sunny and beautiful.

HOW TO GET STARTED

For reservations, you can write to any one of the following charter boat brokers:

Caribbean Sailing Yachts
P.O. Box 491
Tenafly, N.J. 07670

The Moorings
Road Harbour
Tortola, British Virgin Islands

Blue Water Cruises
P.O. Box 758
St. Thomas, Virgin Islands 00801

Avery's Boathouse
P.O. Box 1512
St. Thomas, Virgin Islands 00801

Trade Wind Charters
Cruz Bay
St. John, Virgin Islands 00830

West Indies Cruising
P.O. Box 1203
St. Thomas, Virgin Islands 00801

Yacht Management
420 Lexington Ave.
New York, N.Y. 10017

—Enid Rubin

A Painless Introduction to Sailboats

Odds are, you'd rather be sailing. And with the current boom in small boats designed mainly for nautical novices, there's never been a better time to learn. But be prepared to give your entire energy to the sport, for sailing is an engrossing world of its own —complete with its own language—from which you may never recover.

Best for beginners are the catboats, small single-masted boats with no sail before the mast. Catboats are under 14 feet long and are designed for solo sailing. These are some of the best:

Sabot This is the smallest of the small, and the tamest of the first-time boats. Only eight feet long and weighing less than 100 pounds, these single-handers are made for easy sailing. Learn the basics of beating, reaching, jibbing, tacking and running the wind on these—the same rules apply for the skipper of the largest ketch. Priced from $400 to $1,000, Sabots are an ideal first boat.

Wildfire New in 1973, Wildfire is the ultimate Sabot. Ten feet long with nearly twice the Sabot's sail area, Wildfire is a high-performance, race-ready craft for the adventurous novice. Wildfire weighs only 95 pounds and is so responsive to the wind that the manufacturers added a self-righting capability because of the chance that Wildfire could capsize. Priced at $600.

Laser In a class by itself, Laser last year was America's most popular catboat. Ideal for beginners, this one also will give experienced sailors a great ride. Nearly 14 feet long and weighing 125 pounds, the cat-rigged Laser boasts 76 square feet of sail, nearly 50 percent more than the smaller Wildfire. And it's capable of carrying two persons on a comfortable (if wet) ride. Priced at $800. And you'll never outgrow it.

Most popular sailboats are sloop-rigged, meaning they have a single mast carrying a mainsail and a jib—a small triangular sail carried forward of the mast. To sail a sloop you must handle two sails to the wind. The best sloop for beginners is the Lido.

Lidos are 14 feet long with a six-foot beam (width). They weigh 310 pounds and have open cockpits. (But for the two sails you'd think it was a catboat.) The mainsail is 76 square feet, the jib 35 square feet. This is designed as a two-man boat, providing endless hours of enjoyable sailing for two. Having mastered a Lido, you're ready for any cabin yacht, from a Santana 20 to a Yorktown 38-footer. Priced at $2,000 fully rigged and with a trailer, Lidos remain the leader in small sloop popularity, especially among beginners.

But the coming boat in sailing is the catamaran, a lightweight, twin-hulled boat with massive sail area. No other boat can match the catamaran in stability, speed and pure sailing excitement. It all started with the classic catamaran, the Hobie 14. Fourteen

feet long, weighing 225 pounds, the Hobie 14 boasts a 118-square-foot single sail. Catch the wind and your Hobie will stand on one hull, skimming over water at thrilling speeds. Yet, it's easy enough to sail for any beginner—providing you're a gutsy beginner. Hobie 14s sell for $1,300.

A few tips: buy a quality boat that is well-made—boats are as different as cars and should be studied thoroughly. When you do buy, bargain with your dealer for free instruction. Most dealers will give you up to five hours of instruction free, and you're foolish not to take it. Finally, learn safe boating techniques. Expert safe boating instruction is offered nationwide at minimal cost through the U.S. Power Squadrons, a private organization dedicated to boating safety. Instruction includes valuable navigation and boat maintenance training. Call (800) 243-6000 (toll-free) for information about USPS in your area.

—Bob Clampett

Houdini's Escape From the Spanish Maiden

The Spanish Maiden is the famous instrument of torture used during the Spanish Inquisition. It is shaped like a human body, and the front is painted to look like a maiden. It opens on hinges at the side, and both sections of the interior are lined with iron spikes. It is designed to drive you mad.

Houdini himself describes it this way: "When you enter the device, you take a position between the spikes. The front is then closed, so that the spikes completely trap you within. Padlocks are attached to staples on the outside of the Maiden to prevent you from opening the device. Nevertheless, soon after the cabinet is placed over the Spanish Maiden, you make your escape."

Nevertheless! Surely only Houdini could be so casual about it. Well, here's how to do it:

When the front of the Maiden is closed, both springs engage the ratchet, and by gripping one of the spikes at the hinge side, you can work the front upward by degrees, gradually forcing the pins out of the springs. The looseness of the padlocks permits this; when the operation is complete, the padlocks serve as hinges while you open the other side of the box. Then, to make your escape look truly "magical," replace the pins by pushing them up through the hinges from the bottom.

Swamp Buggies Are Junk Sculptures You Can Race

A quarter of a century ago in the little backwoods Florida town of Naples, some of the weirdest contraptions known to man came together to compete in a mile-of-muck race that made the Indy 500 look like a competition for pantywaists. They called it the Swamp Buggy Races, and each November and February ever since it has drawn a field of competitors from all parts of the Florida swamplands and spectators from around the globe. Swamp buggy races are held at half a dozen spots in Florida, but the races in Naples are the world championships.

The true swamp buggy, with its high frame and tall tires, resembles a cross between a Rube Goldberg invention and junk sculpture. Many builders use tractor and airplane tires, and air intake stacks, exhaust snorkels and electrical-system waterproofing are essential if the buggy is to be swamp-worthy. (Swamp buggies are always home-built creations, and they're designed not only for speed but for work as well. You'll find them being used almost any day of the year as transportation and hunting vehicles in the Everglades and the Big Cypress Swamp in south Florida.)

The sunken, swampy figure-eight track at Naples is arranged so that spectators can park just out of splashing range and watch the races from their cars or campers. Racing a swamp buggy is a dangerous business; the track is flooded and, though no driver has ever been killed in a swamp buggy race, some have had to be cut out of their buggies to keep them from drowning after their machines turn over on them.

The pot in swamp buggy races varies; at Naples, the winning driver may rake in as much as $1,500 in prize money. Since most men spend considerably more than that building their buggies, the prize money doesn't really count for much—the glory is all in being named "Swamp Buggy King."

These unlikely contraptions aren't made to be beautiful–but they work in the muck.

Many racers and their pit crews come to Naples a day or two before the races for the trials, and if you come a day or two in advance yourself and camp near the track you can meet some of the drivers and find out for yourself what goes into a swamp buggy—and into swamp buggy racing. Camping near the track is primitive; for those who like luxury, there's a KOA campground 10 minutes away on the east side of Naples, and motels within 20 minutes of the track.

If you want to take a ride in a swamp buggy, you'll have to go to the Everglades or the Big Cypress Swamp south and east of Naples. Half a dozen operators offer swamp buggy tours, and until you've ridden in one of these machines on a trip from which you realize there's no way to return except by swamp buggy, you can't really appreciate them. For a list of operators who offer swamp buggy tours, write to the Florida News Bureau, State Office Building, Tallahassee, Fla. 32304.

–Bill Thomas

Cruising the Canals of France

Continental Waterways of London operates two hotel-barges that travel the centuries-old canals of France. The *Palinurus* cruises the rivers and canals of Burgundy, visiting world-famed wine *caves* and the Gothic cathedrals of the region. The *Water Wanderer* floats under the magnificent alley of plane trees planted in the 17th century along the Atlantic-Mediterranean canal across the neck of France just north of the Pyrenees. The region is planted almost entirely in grapes, and wine is an obsession with the locals. The barge ties up for a whole day to permit a visit to Carcassonne, largest walled city left in the world and a marvel of medieval fortress architecture.

Skipper and crew on both barges are English. Breakfast and light lunch served aboard; dinner at a top-ranked restaurant each night. For information, write Continental Waterways Cruises, 22 Hans Place, London SW1, England.

–Bern Keating

Drag Boats Are a-Comin'—Fast

Just a few short years ago, drag boat racing was known only to waterspeed enthusiasts in places like Long Beach, Calif., Seattle and Detroit. But drag boats are here to stay, and few sports can match the color, excitement and speed of this waterborne version of automobile drag racing.

The idea is the same as in auto drag racing—to see how fast a boat can accelerate from a standing stop to a point ¼ mile away. Speeds are measured by time traps, and elapsed time is kept. Speeds can go as high as 200 m.p.h.; times are measured in precious few seconds.

Drag boats compete in classes. The slowest class is the ski boat class, in which drag-modified family waterski boats compete, clocking speeds above 90 m.p.h. A faster class is the flatbottom class. Extra-long ski boats powered with high-performance racing engines compete in this class, reaching 150 m.p.h. Fastest class is the blown-fuel hydro class, which is as bad as it sounds. Riding on twin-hulled sponsons, powered with supercharged engines and alcohol-nitromethane blends, the blown-fuel hydros virtually fly above the water, reaching speeds near 200 m.p.h. (Current world record in this top class is 202.46 m.p.h.)

Drag boat racing is expensive—smaller class ski boats designed for competition are priced at $8,000. Top-class hydros cost approximately $20,000. And both prices exclude vital accessories like spare engines and propellers and the necessary stock of replacement parts.

However, as interest grows in the sport, so do the rewards. Purses in drag boat events sometimes reach $50,000. And there is no doubt that reaching 200 m.p.h. on water in a quarter of a mile is exciting.

The National Drag Boat Association, at 6777 Hollywood Blvd., Los Angeles, Calif., can give you information on drag boat events.

–Bob Clampett

What Kind of Duck Carries People, Doesn't Quack, Fought in World War II and Lives in Wisconsin?

Amphibious ducks saw bitter action during World War II on the shell-pocked beaches in Europe and the Pacific. After the war, many were retired and sold off as army surplus. Thirty years later, many are still seeing action splashing in and out of the Wisconsin River loaded with sightseers, for this is one of Wisconsin Dells' most popular attractions.

Today, the ducks move in a world that is far removed from human conflict. In the waters of the Wisconsin, they glide by towering walls and oddly-balanced pillars of sandstone carved by wind and water into shapes resembling a hawk's head, a baby grand piano, a hornet's nest, a toadstool—and whatever else happens to be in the eye of the beholder. On land, they bump along trails that weave through stands of pine and hemlock and slip into cool, shaded dells lush and green with ferns. (At least 27 varieties grow in the region, including the walking fern, interrupted fern and near-extinct fragrant fern.)

The Wisconsin Dells area was first the land of prehistoric mound builders, then of the

Winnebago Indians. Later came the fur-seeking voyagers, then the rafts of the loggers and, finally, the tourist ducks.

Riding the ducks is as much breath-shaking as it is breath-taking, for they wheel around hairpin curves and negotiate the steep grades of Suicide and Roller Coaster hills. Along the way are a waterfall, bass-rearing ponds—and, incongruously, a phalanx of granite statuary lines one section of the trail. They are bas-reliefs, gargoyles and columns from the old Chicago Board of Trade Building, shipped from Chicago in the 1920s—at a cost of $10,000—to adorn the grounds of Dawn Manor. (The building itself is a lovely antebellum mansion restored under the guidance of Frank Lloyd Wright; it houses a fine collection of old masterpieces, ancient porcelain, prints and antiques.)

Dawn Manor is all that remains of Newport, planned in 1853 for a population of 10,000. Assuming that the railway would cross the river at that point, 2,000 settlers flooded into Newport almost overnight, causing a lively land boom. But Newport became a ghost town almost as suddenly when a bridge and dam were ultimately located a mile downstream, creating the legitimate boom town of Kilbourn City—later to become Wisconsin Dells, Wis.

–Mike Michaelson

Portage Your Yacht by Railroad

Boaters who would like to ride—with their craft—in a giant bathtub or on a train will find both of these waiting for them on Ontario's Trent-Severn Waterway, a 240-mile blue ribbon of water that connects Lake Ontario and Lake Huron. Those who cruise this canal, which has 43 locks and a chain of interlocking lakes, will find their vessels lifted 598 feet and lowered another 260 feet. It is, in effect, like boating up a long, sloping hill and then down a smaller one. And the waterway's geography creates the need for some curious boat-toting contrivances.

First, at Peterborough, Ontario, is a remarkable lock. Billed as the world's largest lift lock, it is capable of raising (or lowering) boats 65 feet. It has two massive, water-filled chambers, each capable of floating several vessels. As one chamber is raised, the other is lowered. Boats wishing to get to the upper canal enter and tie up in whichever of the two chambers happens to be at the lower level. This chamber is then raised hydraulically—it ascends like some giant bathtub full of so many toy boats—as its mate, weighted with extra water, is lowered. Fascinated bystanders have been known to laze away a day just watching it in operation.

Canoeists who travel the waterway avoid delays at busy locks by simply portaging around them, but whoever heard of portaging a 25-foot cabin cruiser? Yet this is precisely what's done near the Lake Huron end of the waterway, where there is an overland leg across which even the largest of cruisers must be portaged. This is accomplished by a novel marine railway which runs on a narrow-gauge track and is operated on a cable. Flat cars are used to haul vessels of all kinds over a small hill. It is an interesting and entertaining experience for those making their maiden Trent-Severn cruise.

–Mike Michaelson

Kashmiri Houseboats

Although it's possible to stay at one of the Maharajah's palaces, most visitors to Kashmir opt for a houseboat.

A Kashmiri houseboat can be anything from a commune dormitory that costs $1 a night to fancy digs at $25 and more a night. The *Gulistan*—the "Garden of Roses"—is in the "special class," replete with cooks, barefoot houseboys, and platoons of servants to cater to every need. Mohamed, our houseboy on the *Gulistan*, has served us on repeat visits with shy delight, having special-order meals prepared, supervising bed making and cleaning, setting the dining room table with Sunday-best china, serving drinks to guests.

The *Gulistan* has three bedrooms, three baths, a dining room, a living room, a separate kitchen on a tiny private island where the boat is docked, a sundeck and *shikaras*—canopied canoes—with boatmen for guests' excursions and shuttling to shore. Decor is a throwback to the 1920s, with souvenir pillows in piles, saccharine romantic art, wall-to-wall Oriental rugs and a pot-bellied stove.

At dawn, we head in our *shikara* to Srinagar to watch farmers assemble with their produce piled high in round-bottomed boats. We're paddled through lotus ponds to the wake-up calls of cuckoo birds. Kohlrabi, onions, watermelons, tomatoes and cabbages nearly capsize the produce boats with their weight. Poor women handle fodder boats while their broods of kids skinny-dip in the black waters.

When the mists have evaporated and the farmers dispersed, you can spend hours along Srinagar's canals shopping for handcrafted bargains. We're especially attracted to the houseboat shop belonging to Suffering Moses, a certain Moses Mohiudin, whose three sons are the fourth generation in his family to become designers and

merchants. Moses is tall, imposing, bearded and beturbaned, an outspoken intellectual. "Art is worth more than gold or diamonds," he says, "and the grammar of art starts young with us."

Suffering Moses has refined tastes, and the work on sale in his shop has a museum quality. He's exhibited his papier-mâché designs, woven fabrics and rugs and paintings internationally. He's traveled widely in Europe and the United States. He has two wives; one of them is an American. If you can't make a deal with Suffering Moses, you can try Cheap John or Subhana the Worst, farther down the canal.

Words cannot do justice to Kashmir, even the words of the famous Emperor Jahangir: "If there be paradise on earth, it is this, it is this, it is this." You just have to rent your own houseboat and see for yourself.

–Ralph H. Peck

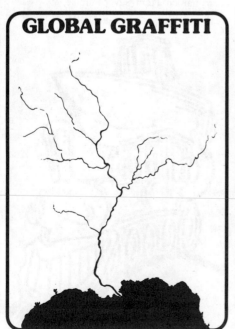

Houseboat Through France

In Burgundy or in the Midi (the South of France) you can rent yourself a houseboat and cruise idly along the canals and rivers while the world goes drifting by. Your boat will come equipped with four berths, bedding, lighting system, storage closets, sanitary facilities, kitchenette with cooking implements and gas refrigerator.

Rent by the week from late March through October (until December in the Midi). Or for the weekend, except during July and August. Weekly rates for four persons: 1,100 to 1,600 francs (about $250 to $365), depending on the season. Weekend rate is 440 francs (about $100). For more information, see your travel agent or write Nautic Voyage, 8 rue de Milan, 75009 Paris.

–James Egan

Delta Houseboats

The houseboat has emerged as a new kind of floating vacation. Basically an enclosed platform on pontoons, the houseboat has the attraction of letting you become your own skipper on a little self-contained house, roaming free on a given body of water, cruising beyond the tentacles of telephones, carrying your own food system so you are completely self-sufficient. From the houseboat platform you can fish, swim, read and simply relax. Most houseboaters comment favorably on the slow pace of life that their style of travel insures. Some houseboat vacations have been known to wind people down so far that it's advisable to allow a day for adjustment to "real life" after the vacation.

The most popular region in the country for houseboating is the Delta area of California, an area 30 miles square in northern California west of Sacramento. Over 1,000 miles of inland waterways have been created where the Sacramento and San Joaquin rivers spread out in a broad flood plain before emptying into San Francisco Bay. Between 1860 and 1930 the flood plain was gradually reclaimed by dikes that held the water to fixed channels and opened the land to pear and asparagus agriculture. Today the region's terrain resembles that of Holland.

During the summer, houseboats rent by the day or week, at $55-$75 or $320-$425. The rate drops about 25 percent during the off season.

You get a fully equipped boat that sleeps six to 10 people—you need bring only your groceries and personal effects. After you pull away from the dock you're on your own. One big houseboat rental outlet is International Houseboats, Inc., 21112 Ventura Blvd., Woodland Hills, Calif. 91364. Phone (213) 883-7350.

You can get a good map, the "Delta Region" map, to peruse in advance by sending $1.25 to Delta Marina, 100 Marina Drive, Rio Vista, Calif. 94571. The map lists all houseboat rental outlets and gives complete descriptions of waterways, small towns and waterway facilities. Best book on the area is Mike Hayden's *Guidebook to the Sacramento Delta Country* (Ward-Ritchie, $1.95).

Houseboating is not limited to the Delta, of course. From California's Lake Shasta to Minnesota's Lake of the Woods, from Florida's Everglades to Louisiana's bayous, people are lolling away their days on these restful craft. State departments of Parks and Recreation, c/o the state capital, can provide information on houseboating in their states.

–Lee Foster

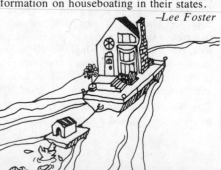

GLOBAL GRAFFITI

Island Hopping by Houseboat

A Virgin Islands cruise need not cost you and your friends or family an arm and a leg. You can spend an idyllic and inexpensive week cruising the Virgin Islands on a houseboat. The gentle motion of the boat acts as a natural tranquilizer, and you can let yourself unwind in the beauty of the islands.

One of the benefits of living on a houseboat is the chance you get to appreciate the marine life and the sea birds. Schools of small fish skim over the surface like skipping stones while gulls and sooty terns swoop down on them from above. Placid sea turtles raise their heads like submarine periscopes in Cinnamon Bay, secure in their armored shells. Brown pelicans glide on the cooling edge of the trade winds, occasionally dropping abruptly for a fish. Small groups of curious, wide-eyed squid loiter around your anchor line, their translucent bodies propelled by jets of sea water.

My family and I recently spent a week on a houseboat in the Caribbean; we had been to the Virgin Islands before, but this was the first time we had lived so intimately with the water and in such comparative luxury. Our houseboat, a Chris-Craft, was designed to sleep eight people and provided all the comforts of home, including air conditioning and a hot shower.

All the houseboat rental companies are based on St. Thomas and can be chartered for $750 per week from early May to mid-November and for $900 per week during the winter season. They come completely furnished down to the last detail. One boat manager pointed out that many people use a captain to move the houseboat from one island to another. (A full-time captain runs about $40 per day.) Details on houseboat rentals in the Virgin Islands can be obtained by writing the Director of Fishing & Water Sports, Virgin Islands Department of Commerce, P.O. Box 1692, St. Thomas, Virgin Islands.

–Carl Purcell

*Oh, give me again the rover's life—
the joy, the thrill, the whirl!
Let me feel thee again, old sea!
let me leap into thy saddle once more.
I am sick of these terrafirma toils and cares;
sick of the dust and reek of towns.
Let me hear the clatter
of hailstones on icebergs,
and not the dull tramp of these plodders,
plodding their dull way
from their cradles to their graves.
Let me snuff thee up,
sea breeze! and whinny in thy spray.*

—HERMAN MELVILLE

Slow Down on an Oregon Ferry

Before bridges were flung across its streams, Oregon had dozens of ferries. Today only five survive: two on the Columbia River and three on the Willamette.

The two ferries on the Columbia are at Westport and Arlington. Both cross to towns in Washington: the Westport ferry goes to Cathlamet and the Arlington ferry goes to Roosevelt.

Westport, 27 miles east of Astoria, is a musty, unadorned burg; it still wears the rough garb of a mill town, though the mill, down by the river, went out several years ago. The tavern here is one of the most sociable around and, as in other villages, it is as much a community center as a place to drink.

The Westport-Cathlamet ferry doesn't seem to be in a hurry to get from one side of the river to the other, and that's great if you're taking photos. The scenery begins right at the ferry landing; the river here looks a lot like the Mississippi and there is a slow, moody, catfish feel in the air. The ferry drifts around an island before it gets to the other side, where the landing is just as picturesque as at Westport.

The northernmost of the Willamette ferries is three miles east of Canby, or about 22 miles south of downtown Portland. You don't have to drive your car onto the Canby ferry to ride the boat. As a pedestrian you are welcome aboard all day, and if you're sociable, you can hear some pretty good stories from the pilot. The ferry from Canby deposits you on the west bank, near Wilsonville.

The mid-Willamette ferry, at Wheatland (about 10 miles south of Dayton on Oregon 221), crosses to the eastern bank of the river. This is the busiest of the Willamette ferries—cars are sometimes backed up half a mile waiting to get on.

The least-used of the Willamette ferries is at Buena Vista, 10 miles up a country road from U.S. 20. The town—if you can call it that—has a more dyed-in-the-history appearance than any other riverside hamlet in Oregon. The place was settled in 1847 and the first store opened in 1850. Several old buildings remain, but the only business now is a single store.

The Willamette ferries are free because they're part of Oregon's network of county highways. The Westport ferry costs $1.50 per car (regardless of the number of people in the car) and the Arlington ferry costs $1 per car.

–Ralph Friedman

To Africa by Freighter in Nine Days

By David Saltman

For $180 one way, Yugoslavian freighters offer four meals a day, peace and quiet, high-octane slivovitz and water as far as the eye can see. Besides being nice folks, the Yugoslavs don't allow tipping. They're communists, you know.

Welcome to the travel agent special: New York to Tangier on Yugoslav freighters.

It'll cost you $180 one way for a nine day trip. That includes four meals a day. No tipping allowed—communists, you know. It's just the ticket for boredom-bound Americans contemplating the occult, peace and quiet, or a piece of the action.

Far out to sea, my pal Bob and I are leaning over the poop rail, discussing pirates and such. "The earth is three-fourths water," I exclaim, squinting into the sun.

He looks peacefully at the black ocean, which flows and eddies around us as far as you can imagine. Every once in awhile we see flying fish, and the sunset is—authentic.

"Hey," he says. "Did you ever see this film about people on a freighter . . .?"

Yes, it's just like in the movies, only more so. You get hot showers. You get Yugoslavian wine with your meals—three European whoppers a day plus tea time. There's a dirt-cheap bar specializing in high-octane slivovitz. There's Yugoslav mandolin by moonlight, and you get intricately involved with your fellow travelers.

There are dope dealers, dome builders, filmmakers and sorcerers' apprentices. There are hash smokers, card players, Old Princetonians, party girls, backpackers, heiresses, UN interpreters, symphony drummers, deputy harbor masters, seventh-grade math teachers and at least two genuine enigmas. Forty-eight passengers in all, on a ship big as a city block, loaded to the Plimsoll marks with hides, sweetmeats and huge crates of little white things.

An ocean boat is a complete universe, from its teakwood walls to the crew's mess that looks like a Greek taverna. You are acutely conscious of time—how much there is of it, an infinite ocean of

The passengers may be filmmakers, dope dealers, Old Princetonians, UN interpreters—there are 48 in all, on a ship big as a city block loaded to the Plimsoll marks with hides, sweetmeats and crates of little white things.

time and black water, and a complex splatter of stars at night. The narrowish decks become racecourses and exercise yards, and coils of rope turn into sun chairs. You become an expert (or at least a talented amateur) on winds and currents and tides, on albatross and nautical talk. (There's always an albatross following you, from the seedy Brooklyn docks to the white minarets of Tangier.) Most of all you shrink as you expand—your horizon fills an ocean, but your field of contact is as tiny as a city block. Imagine—you don't see a *single other thing but water* for 10 days! And yet you see more than ever before.

You need your sea legs, of course, and your sea head. To get ours in gear we take a visit up to the bridge, that mysterious sanctum up top where they keep an old salt from Glo'ster in case the equipment fouls up. You meet a genial Yugoslav mate, who points out that sailors don't have to wear watches. He shows us the maps and gyros and compasses and that legendary old wooden wheel with the 12 knobs that the pilot gets to spin around. Basically, he says, you just point the contraption in the direction of Tangier, and steer. (There was something about a sextant, too.)

Frankly, I had anticipated having to swab the decks or polish the engine shaft or something—a freighter, after all, was not supposed to be *nice*. But it was incredible—it was actually luxurious, with paneled walls and comfortable lounges and enormous meals served by efficient Continental stewards. It was everything a cruise should be—slow and relaxing and every once in a while very stormy. I mean you wouldn't know you were on the ocean if the piano didn't slide around occasionally.

So here we are on a throbbing Yugo freighter, heading for the mysterious East, or Africa, or the Mediterranean—however you like it. The ocean breeze blows cobwebs off our brains, and a few even begin to swagger.

On the eighth day the psychic pulse goes up to maybe a million.

"Shit man, I'm gonna hitch across Algeria and Tunisia and then see them pyramids."

"I heard they got these nomads out in the Sudan, smoke this black hash. . . ."

"All I want to do is go to Persia and lose myself in the 11th century. . . ."

The last night before docking in Tangier. A party rages in the ship's lounge. The Captain is there personally, a great honor. The crew is giving the women its last and best ogle. Hot fast romances spring up like wild jungle ferns. The slivovitz is on the house. Somebody tunes in the shortwave and gets the mellow throaty crackle of Arabic.

The full impact of this dreamer's voyage hits us: this is a freighter, and we're

Illustrations by Sandra Forrest

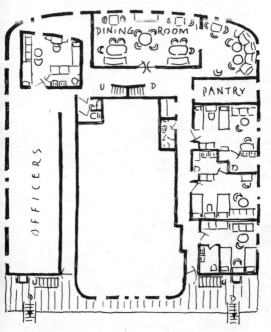

Cross section of D Deck on a typical freighter. Cabins are often quite elegant.

right off the coast of *Africa*, for God's sake! We have spinning visions of elephants, tigers and camels, and Lascars from the Levant. It is the ultimate irony of the Technological Age—the fact that the fastest jet is supremely boring, compared to this slow, groaning ocean anachronism. It's a question of giving the ocean its proper respect—that's how come Nature invented jet lag. □

The Freighter Fantasy Comes True

What is it in us that makes us long for apple trees in January, for tropical suns in the middle of a white northern winter, for a red house instead of this tiresome blue?

There's a certain fantasy nerve in all of us, I think, that is always craving something new—some experience that will *really* be meaningful, that will knock some sense into our nine-to-five. In today's grind, full of brown skies and electric typewriters and constant sitting, we need a clear breath of the days when the world was wild.

For me, at least, it means traveling to the far places. And personally, I like a means of transport that is harmonious with my aim—to "escape." So I'm talking about something like the leisurely, old-timey thrill of traveling on a freighter.

For the fact is that freighter travel is not dead, not by any means. The earth is still three-fourths water, no matter what, and cargo still has to get from port to port. The cargo is king on these boats, but there is a long and gracious tradition of letting a few lucky tourists ride along. They are gravy for the company and companionship for the captain and crew.

Since the cargo is paying the way, passenger tickets on freighters are still relatively cheap. For instance, you can travel in Old World luxury from New York to Tangier, in the wintertime, for less than $200. That includes all meals, and no tipping allowed. (See accompanying story.)

When you go by freighter you're hitching a ride on the vagaries of international commerce. This can be a delightful adventure, if you have the right spirit. For instance, your boat carrying bullhides to London may suddenly change course for Rotterdam—because the bullhide sellers have worked a complicated deal involving stock, cash and diamonds with the Dutch agents of the Kimberley minefields. For this reason, your freighter ticket might read: "Passage guaranteed from a U.S. coastal port to first European port." Vague, but interesting. You have to be flexible to take a freighter, and you need a little time.

For this same reason, of course, you find a very intriguing cut of people on board. A freighter usually takes 12 passengers, although some take up to 60 and a few will even take hundreds. But most of them are business and professional couples or artists or retirees out to do something totally new and incredibly wild, or people with a lot of reading to catch up on, or mystics who've never seen an unadulterated sunrise, or stargazers or poets or gourmets or gamblers, or people who just want a good cooling out.

It's amazing how intimate you become on a freighter, and it means you have at least a dozen close friends that you'll keep running into once you're back on dry land.

There's a thrill to freighter routes that for me far outclasses London with its proper procedures, or Paris with its poppy flour. Let these names roll off your taste buds: a Norwegian freighter sails monthly out of the Golden Gate. Twenty days away, it stops at Corregidor to load copra. Someone is taking a flyer in mahogany, so your next port is Manila, where the copra is offloaded and the precious smooth wood checked aboard. There's more mahogany in Iloilo and Cebu, on the Sulu Sea, and then you make for Hong Kong. Here it's a four-day layover, as the mahogany is traded for gold. Then south through the China Sea to Singapore, the City of the Lion, to put the metal on the stock exchange, and now a slow churn through the jungle-banked Straits of Malacca to the hilly tropical isle of Penang. Here, the dockside booms swing on huge loads of natural rubber and palm oil. Penang is the turnaround point, and these cargoes are bound for New York. At Belawan Deli and

Port Swettenham you take on bales of tin from the Klang River basin. You make a return call to Singapore, and one to Djakarta. In Bali, you pick up a load of tallow; in the Celebes, a cargo of spices. You reenter the Philippines at Zamboanga, near the Mindanao rain forest, to take on rattan headed for San Francisco. Exactly 90 days after leaving American water, your freighter again buzzes into the calm harbor of the Golden Gate.

This is a typical Far Eastern freighter run. You can travel it for less than it would cost you to fly—even on the cheapest charter! And that tosses in room and board for nothing, because on most voyages you can use the boat as a hotel while you're in port.

For some reason, passenger bookings on freighters are still virtually untapped and esoteric. There is no such thing as a freighter timetable or regular schedule, since the cargo determines everything. Nevertheless, there are a great number of more-or-less regular runs. There are also some travel agents who will handle freighter bookings. (When booking through a travel agent, you may have to make a deposit.)

In general, freighter accommodations are quite elegant, in the old tradition of long sea crossings. The reason is that, according to the informal hierarchy of the merchant marine, passengers have almost the same status as the captain. So usually the passenger cabins are large, wood-paneled, well-appointed and have private baths. Often, even the lowest-class passenger cabin is a two- or three-room suite. Cabins are usually placed amidships and slightly aft—the choicest spot, because there is the least ocean roll. To get a cabin like this on a regular ocean liner would cost more than moon dust.

In general, food and service on freighters is also first-rate. Sailors are a hungry lot, and they are not bashful about their wine; the passengers get the same consideration. Most freighters have open bars and open snack tables or refrigerators, in addition to three meals a day. Swedish ships always have a huge smorgasbord at all times, in case you get a craving for sour cream herring in the middle of the night. (If you overeat, the bigger ships have doctors.)

In short, if you have time to do a proper escape, you couldn't do better than travel by freighter. The only drawbacks are that you are subject to delays, that your itinerary might not be certain. But these days, what actually *is* certain, what *is* without risk? Tell me, and I'll devote the rest of my life to it!

THE 20 BEST FREIGHTER BUYS

TO	FROM/FREQUENCY	LINE	PORTS OF CALL	FARE	TIME	PROS	CONS	WHY GO?
1. England	Baltimore monthly	Bristol City	Avonmouth	$185	10 days	Modern	Only four passengers	Shakespeare
2. Tangier	New York twice a month	Jugolinija	Canaries (optional)	$180	9 days	Congenial, good food	Public showers	Folklore, hashish
3. Lisbon	New York every 45 days	Carregadores Acoreanos	Madeira	$200	10 days	Comfortable	Heavy bookings	Port wine
4. Genoa	San Francisco monthly	Italian	Los Angeles, Panama, Curaçao	$520	30 days	Free wine, excellent food	Book three months ahead	Old city
5. Rio	Los Angeles every two months	Mitsui OSK	Panama	$428	32 days	Luxurious, tea ceremonies	Economy class not recommended	Carnival! Copacabana!
6. Ecuador	New Orleans three times a month	Lykes	Cartagena, Santa Marta, Panama, Buenaventura	$280	5 days	Highly recommended	——	Medieval town
7. Calcutta	New York monthly	Hellenic	Capetown, Damman, Kuwait, Colombo, Coohin, Khorram-shahr, Bombay	$1,200	80 days	Friendly, library	Food not gourmet	Buy diamonds in Capetown, sell in Bombay
8. Caribbean	New York regularly	United Fruit	Tela, Belize, Guan-tanamo, P. Cortes	$180	6 days	Like a yacht	Like a banana boat yacht	Swim, paint
9. Dominican Republic	Point Comfort, Tex. three times a month	Alcoa	Cabo Rojo	$300 round trip	12 days	Luxurious	Cabo Rojo is nowhere	If you need an ocean voyage
10. Surinam	Tembladora, Trinidad four times a week	Alcoa	Cottica River to Moengo, Surinam River to Paranam	$180 round trip	6 days	Adventurous jungle cruise	Ships can roll	Wild! Headhunters!
11. Santo Domingo	New Orleans twice a month	Surinam	Port-au-Prince	$85	4 days	Cheap	Plain	Voodoo, art
12. Yokahama	Los Angeles every two months	Mitsui OSK	Honolulu	$413	18 days	Lovely hostesses; classes	Economy class not recommended	"Great Buddha" of Kamakura
13. Great Lakes	Montreal twice a month	Yugoslav	Hamilton, Cleveland, Toledo, Detroit, Mil-waukee, Chicago	$140	12 days	Excellent food, round trip discount, takes cars	——	Nice cruise
14. Canada	Boston several times a month	Columbus	Montreal, Trois Rivi-eres, Quebec, Port Alfred, New York City	$330 round trip	18 days	Hospitable	Some cabins without baths	Vieux Montreal
15. California	New York twice a month	United Philippine	Panama, Los Angeles, San Francisco	$325	14 days	Spacious	Must change in Panama	Eat *manggis*
16. Panama	Los Angeles every two months	Mitsui OSK	(Direct)	$204	8 days	Immaculate	——	Eat *langsat*
17. Inside Passage (Canada)	Vancouver, B.C. weekly	Northland	Bella Coola, Ocean Falls, Kitimat, Prince Rupert	$200 round trip	6 days	Incredible fjords	Full in summer	Indian villages
18. Round the World	Los Angeles monthly	United Yugoslav	Panama, Genoa, Beirut, Colombo, Hong Kong, Kobe	$1,650	150 days	Cheerful, good food	Singapore not included	Top value
19. Round the World	Los Angeles monthly	Orient Overseas	Acapulco, Rio, Cape-town, Mombasa, Singa-pore, Hong Kong, Yoko-hama, Seattle	$2,250	120 days	Like a liner	300 passengers	Good value
20. Australia	Los Angeles monthly	Orient Overseas	Brisbane, Sydney	$430	20 days	Chinese food, good service	Older boats, not air-conditioned	Roos, koala bears, boomerangs

Chart by David Saltman

But look! here come more crowds, pacing straight for the water, and seemingly bound for a dive. Strange! Nothing will content them but the extremest limit of the land; loitering under the shady lee of yonder warehouses will not suffice. No. They must get just as nigh the water as they possibly can without falling in. . . .

Once more. Say you are in the country; in some high land of lakes. Take almost any path you please, and ten to one it carries you down in a dale and leaves you there by a pool in the stream. There is magic in it. Let the most absent-minded of men be plunged in his deepest reveries—stand that man on his legs, set his feet a-going, and he will infallibly lead you to water, if water there be in all that region. Should you ever be athirst in the great American desert, try this experiment, if your caravan happen to be supplied with a metaphysical professor. Yes, as every one knows, meditation and water are wedded forever. . . .

Go visit the Prairies in June, when for scores on scores of miles you wade knee-deep among Tiger-lilies—what is the one charm wanting?—Water—there is not a drop of water there! Were Niagra but a cataract of sand, would you travel your thousand miles to see it? . . . Why is almost every robust healthy boy with a robust healthy soul in him, at some time or other crazy to go to sea? Why upon your first voyage as a passenger did you yourself feel such a mystical vibration, when first told that you and your ship were now out of sight of land? Why did the old Persians hold the sea holy? Why did the Greeks give it a separate deity and make him the own brother of Jove? Surely all this is not without meaning.

—HERMAN MELVILLE

Ferries Are Better Than Bridges

Ferries are better than bridges. Bridges reduce great rivers and estuaries to insignificance. Take the Golden Gate Bridge. When you cross it, all you can think of is what a great bridge it is, you don't even consider what it's crossing—*the San Francisco Bay!* The miracle is the bay, not the bridge.

When you take the ferry from Tiburon to San Francisco, and you should, you keep things in better perspective. The ferry is just for people, not cars. If you live in Tiburon, you can watch the pastel dawn wash the city skyline on your way to work, and admire the Golden Gate Bridge. From a distance.

That is one good ferry. Here are some others:

The Staten Island Ferry Takes you right past the Statue of Liberty and far enough out into New York harbor that New York City looks terrific. It only costs a nickel, but when the ride is over, you're in Staten Island. (You have to pay another nickel to get back.)

The Hatton Ferry When Thomas Jefferson left home in Charlottesville, Va. to go to Buckingham, which he did several times because he was architect of the Buckingham Court House, he was poled across the James River by the boatman. If *you* want to go from Charlottesville to Buckingham today, you can get across the same way. Drive due south from Charlottesville to Hatton. If the ferry is on the other bank when you get there, holler loudly and the man will come get you. Hardly anybody ever rides the Hatton Ferry, but when it was washed away by a hurricane a couple of years ago and the county decided not to reinstate it, the ferry lovers in Virginia set up such a howl that the county was forced to change its mind.

Everybody just likes to know it's still there.

The Roaring Bull This is a former coal-digger steamboat that crosses the Susquehanna from Crow's Landing, Pa. to Millersburg, Pa.—it's a 149-year-old route for travelers in Pennsylvania. The *Roaring Bull*'s Master, Jack Dilman, thinks he may have the last stern-wheel ferryboat going. It is certain that he has one of the coziest, complete with a wood stove and an easy chair in the cabin for chilly mornings on the river, and he offers a spot of tea to the passengers, too.

The Mississippi River ferries Take your pick. The happy fact is that from Cairo, Ill. down to Memphis, Tenn., 300 miles away, there isn't a single bridge across the Mississippi. Paradise.

The Puget Sound ferries Ocean liner-sized saltwater ferries wind through the San Juan Islands off Bellingham, Wash. down to Seattle and up to Vancouver. Their decks are lined with pairs of young men and women who have mastered the trick of wearing packs on their backs while keeping their arms around each other. Sea breezes and seascapes. If you plan carefully enough, you can ride these exhilarating ferries for a week and never get where you're going.

When you become a ferryboat fan, you begin noticing how many great ferries are left in America. But when we looked into it, nobody could tell us how many. The Department of Transportation of the federal government can tell you instantly all about containerships, turnpikes, hydrofoils, suspension bridges, turbotrains and jumbo jets, but they don't know a thing about ferries. Ferries seem to be mostly overlooked by bureaucrats and statisticians, which is probably why we still have so many of them.

—*Charles Kuralt*

Alaska's Inside Passage

Fastest growing of the cruise fleets is the flotilla plying the Inside Passage during the summer months. The 1,000 miles from Vancouver, British Columbia to Skagway, Alaska is almost entirely sheltered from Pacific storms by a belt of outer islands, so cruises are usually free from rough weather. The route runs through fjord country and wilderness as beautiful as any in Norway. Occasional shore stops are at picturesque frontier towns where Indians and tough old sourdoughs add color to the scene.

The cruises of the TSS *Fairsea* start from San Francisco, and the sharp contrast between the sophistication of that city and the wilderness beauty of the scenery along the route adds another dimension to this cruise. For information and/or reservations, contact a travel agent or Sitmar Cruises, 3303 Wilshire Blvd., Los Angeles, Calif. 90010.

—*Bern Keating*

See Russia Without a Visa

Ever toyed with the idea of a trip to Russia but given up in disgust because of the horrendously time-consuming problems involved in getting a Russian visa?

Take heart! From Helsinki, Finland, the jewel city of Scandinavia, it's possible to visit the famous Russian city of Leningrad without a visa.

How? Why, you take a cruise. Visitors to Leningrad live on the cruise ship, and so the visa requirement is waived.

Contact Bergen Lines in New York for details and a brochure. (The address is 505 Fifth Ave., New York, N.Y. 10017.) Be sure to make reservations before leaving for Helsinki, because the cruises to Leningrad usually are booked well in advance.

And don't neglect Helsinki while you're there. It's a very pleasant city, and you should plan to spend at least a couple of days seeing it.

—*Frank J. Gillespie*

Arkansas Steamboat Cruise

In January, the venerable steamboat *Delta Queen* ended her career as the sole overnight passenger boat on America's inland waterways. A 42-passenger cruise boat, the *Arkansas Explorer*, now leaves Little Rock, Ark. for two cruises a week upstream on the Arkansas River. There is an overnight stop at Morrilton, Ark., and passengers also make a wine-tasting tour of the Arkansas vineyard region.

Fares, which include berth, meals, entertainment and passage for the three-day, two-night cruises, are $135 per passenger for an "A" cabin and $125 per for a "B" cabin. For more information and/or reservations, write Capt. Gary Davis, c/o *Arkansas Explorer*, North Little Rock, Ark. 72114.

—*Bern Keating*

You Too Can Rent the SS *France*

Gurdjieff the Dervish once said, "When you go on a spree, go the whole hog including the postage." In these cybernetic days the only civilized way to go on a spree is by water, an ocean voyage. And if you're going to go the whole hog, including the postage, you'll have to charter the greatest flagship on earth—the SS *France*. The postage, in this case, is *$90,000* a day.

That'll rent you the undivided attention of 1,100 crew members, including the 180 *sous-chefs*, *potagiers*, *poissoniers*, *grilladiers*, *sauciers*, *patissiers* and *tournants* who staff one of the world's greatest restaurants: the *France*'s chef, M. Le Huédé, is proud of the fact that he has never served the same dish twice on any single cruise. That's no mean accomplishment.

When you take your spree on the *France* you are chartering an atmosphere that reeks of clipper ships, Regency dining rooms and the easy freedom of seagoing romances. The *France* is simply the best there is these days.

On a regular cruise the average stateroom runs around $10,000. People scramble to book them, and even the charter business is pretty good. The Michelin Tire Co. has twice held convention-cruises on the *France*, sailing to the West Indies. All the caviar you can eat, all the vodka you can drink.

When you charter the *France* you are chartering the traditional expertise and Continental service of stewards, waiters, barmen, gym instructors, bakers, pages, nannies, nurses, doctors and officers who have mostly grown up in the service of the French Line. They have Ph.D.s in Gallic sense, and they have miraculous stamina. (The bakers, for instance, make 5,000 *petit-pains* three times a day, all neatly incised, by hand, with a razor.) They say, with arched brows, that almost every crossing is a novel.

The *France* won't last forever. In another 10 years or so she'll be pastured and replaced by smaller cruisers with self-service bars and cafeterias. Computerized and automated and no doubt thoroughly dull.

So go on that spree while there's still a whole hog left, and damn the postage. Contact the French Line, (800) 221-2682, for more information.

–David Saltman

Cruising the Mackenzie Under the Midnight Sun

The Mackenzie River is the Mississippi of the Arctic. It's a wide, lazy river in the Northwest Territories of Canada, and during its short ice-free season dozens of barges push up and down its 1,200 miles to bring food and supplies to the small communities along its shores.

On this river you can also take one of the last great adventure cruises in the world. Every week, a 100-foot luxury houseboat casts off from either Hay River on the Great

Slave Lake or Inuvik near the Arctic Ocean with no more than 12 adventurous passengers aboard. These people will be among the few to experience the virtually unchanged wilderness of the far north. Their experience, however, will be unique: they will sail under the midnight sun in grand style, sipping champagne (or whatever they prefer from the free bar) and eating gourmet foods prepared on board by the ship's chef.

The leisurely cruise (seven days downstream to Inuvik, eight days upstream) offers unscheduled stops at points of interest on the shore. Passengers are encouraged to let Captain Don Tetrault know if they have a yen to visit any special place—say, the exact spot where the Arctic Circle crosses the river. For those who travel in June or July there is the added exhilaration of experiencing nightless days. Watching the sun dip down just to the horizon (due north) and move up again minutes later is a once-in-a-lifetime experience.

The cruises begin on June 12 and the last one is during the first week of October. In the early and late cruises you are very likely to be sharing the river with large packs of ice, and instead of a midnight sun, you'll have the fantastic, multicolored, dancing northern lights to watch at night.

For more information and reservations, contact

Arctic Cruise Lines, Ltd.
P.O. Box 63
Hay River, Northwest Territories,
Canada
(403) 874-2260.

Price for the cruise package from Edmonton, Alberta (you have to get *there* yourself) is about $1,200. This includes return flights and ground transportation, meals and booze.

–David Popoff

How to Build a Sailboat (Go Easy on the Cement)

"Understand you're building a boat. What in the hell for?"

"Oh, it's just something I've always thought about doing."

"What is it, something to fish from or what?"

"Well, no—it's going to be one we can live on, you know, we'll do some traveling and get away from things for a few years."

"Good Lord, how big is it going to be?"

"Well, about 60 feet on the deck and about 80 feet overall. It'll be a sailboat. In fact, a square-rigged sailboat, a brigantine."

"Is it going to be a wooden boat?"

"Only partly. The hull is made of cement."

"Cement! Cement doesn't float, you dummy."

At this point yet another person walks off convinced the world's full of idiots. I've gone through this routine probably 200 times in the last year and a half, since my boat-building project began.

Our boat, new, would cost between $75,000 and $100,000. Used, it could cost anywhere from $50,000 to $75,000. By building it myself with one full-time professional helper, it will cost $30,000 to $35,000. And yes, the hull really is cement.

Plans for boats of almost any material—wood, fiberglass or ferro-cement—are advertised in yachting magazines. I chose ferro-cement for three reasons: low cost of the hull, easy maintenance, and large volume of space inside (the hull thickness is only ¾ inch). I didn't buy a stock plan but hired a naval architect to work out the design with me, and I hired a professional to

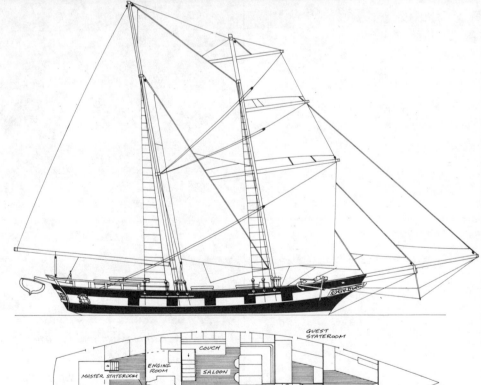

build the hull, which cost $4,200 plus $1,500 in materials and $1,500 to have the hull professionally plastered. (I simply was not interested in building the hull myself.) The hull is strong and about 10 percent less heavy than a wooden hull. I do *not* recommend cement decks or bulkheads for weight reasons.

The original schedule called for the boat to

be completed in 15 months, but by the time it's really finished it will have been about 24 months in the making. When it *is* done, we'll be able to take off and cruise, at our leisure, anywhere we damn well please. I can't think of anything you could make for $1,500 worth of cement that would give more pleasure.

–Don McQuiston

I had walked since dawn and lay down
to rest on a bare hillside
Above the ocean. I saw through half-shut
eyelids a vulture
      wheeling high up in heaven,
And presently it passed again, but lower
and nearer, its
      orbit narrowing. . . .
How beautiful he looked, gliding down
On those great sails; how beautiful he
looked, veeringaaway
      in the sea-light over the precipice.

I tell you solemnly
That I was sorry to have disappointed
him. To be eaten by that
      beak and become part of him, to
share those
      wings and those eyes—
What a sublime end of one's body, what
an enskyment;
      What a life after death.

—ROBINSON JEFFERS

Kite Racing

If you can fly a kite at all, you can go right into kite racing competition. Unlike foot racing, auto racing or sailboat racing, kite racing requires no athletic ability or technical know-how. It's more like bug or small animal racing—you just let them go.

Kites are raced over bodies of water, from the windward side. Lakes are perfect, though almost any extensive watery surface will do, outside of swamps and thick mires. It's the simplest thing in the world to do, but don't be careless about it.

First, get your kite in the air. The common two-stick paper variety works well, probably best. Avoid the sluggish box kite and the expensive plastic bat. Use enough tail to make the kite as stable as possible.

All competitors should use the same amount of string—about one ball or 250 feet. After you get the kite aloft, you must tie the end of the string to a bottle—wine bottles seem to work best. I can't tell you how best to tie the string—I've never been good at it. But if you fool around with it awhile you'll manage to get it tied. (It does help to have somebody responsible for the kite while you work.) Once the kite is securely tied to the bottle, plug the cork back in for buoyancy and you're ready to race.

All competitors should line up at the water's edge, about 15 feet apart, so that at a given signal they can easily toss in their bottles. You'll be amazed at what happens. The bottles offer just enough resistance to keep the kites aloft, yet are pulled along at a rapid clip, the bottle necks usually just breaking the surface like periscopes.

You'll have to decide for yourself how to determine the winner. You can all hustle around to the other side, or you can have judges already waiting. Some people are happy to watch through binoculars, but of course you will want to find your racer before you go home. We don't want to litter the shores and, anyway, it's too marvelous an invention not to retrieve and race again.

—William Allen

GLOBAL GRAFFITI

Ballooning Is for Romantics

I almost hate to say it, but ballooning is on the way up. After more than a century of near-oblivion, ballooning is being revived in this country. One reason for this has to be that ballooning affords a gentle pastime for people of romantic sensibilities, and such pastimes are not easy to find in these days.

Ballooning—more properly, hot-air ballooning—is a sport of beauty and serenity. The balloons themselves suggest majesty; boldly colored and rising a full 70 feet in height, these stately objects virtually defy convention. And to see them rise is awesome.

Balloons rise and fly because a propane burner directly under the air bag's neck heats the air inside until it is lighter than the atmosphere. The pilot controls the balloon's rise by adjusting the blast of heat from the burner. Only about $5 worth of propane is required for a two-hour ride.

But there's a catch. Once a balloon ascends, it's anybody's guess where it will come down. Balloons go only one way: with the wind. All the time. But of course there's a certain romance in that, too.

"Flying in a balloon is so totally irrelevant that it's beautiful," says veteran balloonist Bob Waligunda. "It's difficult to explain the feeling; unless you fly a balloon you'll never really know." Ballooning is calm; it is still. There is no sense of the wind because the balloonist is moving with it. There is only a sense of detachment from the world below.

Since hot air balloons cost between $3,000 to $10,000, it is unlikely the sport will gain instantaneous mass appeal. But more and more Americans are becoming captivated by the sport. There are approximately 250 licensed balloonists in the United States, and some 200 balloons—more than in all other countries combined. There are three major

balloon manufacturers, and numerous schools nationwide offer balloon pilot training. To become a licensed balloonist, you must log at least eight hours of flight time (one hour solo) and pass a stiff written examination and a medical exam. Once licensed, a balloonist may ride the winds wherever he chooses—or, rather, wherever they choose to take him.

Ballooning activities in this country come under the auspices of the Balloon Federation of America in Washington, D.C. Call them at (202) 737-0897 for more information.

—Bob Clampett

Learn to Boomerang in Texas

They call him Billy Boomerang, and if you want to buy a handmade boomerang and learn how to throw it, look for him on the beach at South Padre Island in southeastern Texas, usually in front of the Jetties restaurant. John McMahon, who favors an Australian bush hat although he hails from New York, figures that since 1969 he has taught the art of boomerang throwing to some 3,000 persons. He says throwing the boomerang is challenging and relaxing at the same time. He mentions that one of his greatest satisfactions as an instructor of this aborigine art came from teaching three senior citizens to throw and later seeing them having fun on the beach tossing the boomerang around.

Billy will demonstrate the difference between a boomerang, which he explains is designed for sport, and a "killer stick," which is used for hunting game and which is non-returning. Apparently this boomerang-maker-teacher *extraordinaire* speaks from some authority. For those who would seek the often fleeting fame of the *Guinness Book of World Records*, here is the challenge: Billy claims to hold 11 world records in boomerang throwing, all recorded by the Smithsonian Institution (though not, apparently, by Guinness). These include: most consecutive two-handed catches, 129; most consecutive one-handed catches, 90; longest distance in a single throw, 103 feet; and most behind-the-back catches, 37.

Boomerangs of the non-returning type were used by the ancient Egyptians, while other varieties of "killer sticks" are used by Indians in Arizona and in southern India for killing small game. Hunters also toss them into the air above flocks of game birds, who mistake the stick for a hawk and flee toward waiting nets. But at South Padre Island the boomerang is strictly another beach toy.

—Mike Michaelson

Say It With a Balloon

Balloon communication, only slightly more dependable than launching messages in a bottle, was popular back when distances seemed greater and when word from even neighboring states could cause romantic speculation about what it was like there. As a boy in Texas, there was a time when I launched balloons almost daily. I didn't get many replies but I did get some, and, if nothing else, it gave me a reason to watch for the mailman.

If you're not too jaded by Walter Cronkite and Bell Telephone, you might still enjoy trying it. The chances of anybody taking the time to answer are probably less than they were 20 years ago, but you *can* improve the chances by offering a reward—just don't, in a fit of generosity and enthusiasm, be too specific. (Who knows how much you'll want to cough up the day the answer finally arrives.)

First, get a balloon—or a dozen—that will be at least two feet in diameter when inflated. They used to be a dime at Woolworth's. Fill the balloon with a lighter-than-air gas—helium is best—then write your message. Something pseudo-scientific stands the best chance of being answered, something like: "I am studying wind currents and would like to know where this balloon comes down. There will be a reward for this information. I am enclosing a self-addressed stamped envelope for your convenience." Then put the note and envelope in another envelope, run a string through a hole in the corner, tie it onto the balloon, and launch the balloon.

If you can't locate a helium tank, you may have to settle for natural gas from the wall gas jet. This requires more work. First of all, the gas pressure probably won't be great enough to blow up your balloon. That means you'll have to stretch it by blowing it up with air. (Just keep blowing it up again and again until it's thin enough.)

Next, you will find that the lifting power of natural gas is almost zero. It can barely lift even the balloon, so the self-addressed stamped envelope is out. In fact, you can afford only the tiniest of messages on a scrap of paper secured to the balloon by a single strand of thread. Even then, your chances of getting it up into the rising wind currents are much better if you launch from the top of the house.

You can go all out, of course. You can order balloons 20 feet in diameter from the pages of magazines like *Popular Science*, and perhaps you will get an answer from China. But if I do it again, it will be the same as 20 years ago. When the balloons clear the trees, it's reminiscent of Kitty Hawk and, because most of the replies will probably come from across town, there's a real sense of triumph when word actually arrives from someplace like Ralph, Tex., or Blue Leaf, Miss.

—William Allen

Sport Parachuting

Sport parachuting continues to attract new fans, about half of whom want to jump—the other half want to watch. The largest center for parachuting activity on the West Coast is the Pope Valley Parachute Ranch, north of San Francisco and east of Napa, Calif.

The ultimate competition in parachuting is the West Coast Professional jump at Pope Valley on the first weekend of October each year. Parachutists bail out at approximately 8,000 feet, free fall until 2,000 feet and, in one event, must land on the edge of a small saucer. The winner usually hits the saucer for his several jumps or else just misses—by a distance measured in centimeters. Other events call for falling in formation, with several chutists joined together.

Weekend jumping continues year round at Pope Valley, where the weather is sufficiently benign even in winter to accommodate aerial sports. The facility includes a lodge, swimming pool, restaurant and cocktail lounge. You can live here and learn to jump. Or you can watch the jumping comfortably in the evening while having dinner outdoors by the pool. The sudden sight of a half-dozen chutes opening overhead and descending into the pasture across the airstrip is awe-inspiring.

If you decide to take up the sport, you can obtain information about parachuting around the United States by writing the United States Parachute Association, P.O. Box 109, Monterey, Calif. 93940.

—Lee Foster

For those of us with sweaty palms, an old new way to get around. Fact is, you can ride a blimp across the ocean 10 feet above the water all the way. And you don't need airports, as the picture proves.

Jumping Off Tall Buildings at a Single Bound

I first heard of the sport of jumping from high places using a rope with a slip knot in it in an advertisement for Canadian Club whiskey on the back of some adventure magazine. The ad showed a healthy young couple jumping from high mountain cliffs in Australia, and the girl was complaining about what she had to go through just to get a glass of whiskey. Not everyone will be so fortunate as to get Canadian Club for their efforts, but they are guaranteed plenty of fun and thrills.

It must have been 10 years ago that I saw that ad, and since then I've had occasion to jump out of tall trees in the very same way while working as a tree surgeon. In fact, using this method you can jump from any high place—cliff, tree, bridge, prison roof, etc., as long as you have the necessary equipment. (There is, of course, the question, *Why would you want to jump from high places?* Well, like I said, it's good for a thrill.)

What You Need

Enough ¾-inch (or ⅞-inch) Manila rope to reach from the top of whatever you're jumping from to the ground. (I'll call this the "A" rope.)

A good solid something to tie the rope to up top.

A tree surgeon's saddle. This is made of two flat nylon straps that pass around your back and under your thighs so that you are sitting in it. You need something with *at least* this much support. There is also a more elaborate saddle with three straps available. If you buy one of these saddles new, it's called

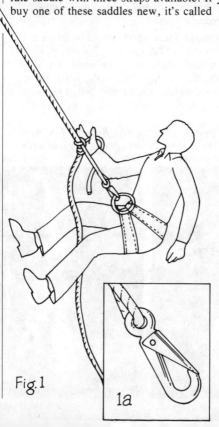

Fig. 1

1a

Model #1301. The 3-strap saddle costs about $35; it's Model #1314. They can be mail-ordered from:

Western Hardware and Tool Co.
450 Bryant St.
San Francisco, Calif.

Or check your Yellow Pages for a local dealer under Tree Service Equipment & Supplies. On the other hand, you may be able to pick up a used one or borrow one from your good friend the tree surgeon.

About five feet of ½-inch Manila rope (the "B" rope) with a heavy snap on one end. (Nylon rope is no good—the knot won't hold.) The snap is fastened to the metal ring at the front of the saddle. The snap, which costs $2, should be heavy, strong and similar to the one in the illustration.

The free end of the smaller rope ("B" rope) is tied in a special slip knot to the larger rope ("A" rope). This knot allows you to fall and to stop the fall at will.

Tying the Knot

Place the "B" rope behind the "A" rope and coil it around two and a half times, bringing it up and across the first two coils on the third time around and looping it behind the "A" rope again, finally putting it back through its own loop. Practice tying this knot until you feel very confident with it and you can get it to work every time.

How the Knot Works

This is a tubular knot that holds you up by "locking" when the stress on it (your weight) pulls at a diagonal angle from the "A" rope. When you twist the knot so that the tube is parallel with the "A" rope, the "A" rope slips through the tube and you go down. When you release the knot, your weight causes it to turn at an angle again and you stop. Because of the elasticity of the two ropes and the belt as well as the slipping action of the knot, you do not jolt to a sudden stop but come to a fairly smooth, cushioned one.

To Jump

With the knot tied there should be about two or two and a half feet of rope between the metal ring and the "A" rope. (Obviously, the knot should not be farther away from you than arm's length.)

If you're jumping from a ledge, cliff or roof, lean back against the rope and lower yourself over the side with your feet planted firmly against the wall and the knot holding you up. When you're ready to fall, push yourself back away from the wall with your feet and, at the same time, twist the knot straight so that it releases—and you're off! (Don't forget to release your grip on the knot before you reach the bottom.)

If you're jumping from the branch of a tree, lower yourself down below the branch so that you are hanging in the saddle. In this case you just drop straight down so you don't have to push off.

While falling you should remain as upright as possible. Drop only short distances at first

(until you get the "hang" of it, so to speak). Don't start higher than 20 or 25 feet and drop by degrees—say five feet at a time. Be sure to check the snap, ropes and knot after each jump.

And speaking of safety—it's not a good idea to do this alone. I would strongly advise that you find someone who has done this before to guide you for the first few jumps—try to locate a tree surgeon, steeplejack or mountain climber. Or maybe you can find a shapely young Australian cliff-jumper who'll be glad to join you in a glass of Canadian Club after your practice jumps.

—Dirk Kortz

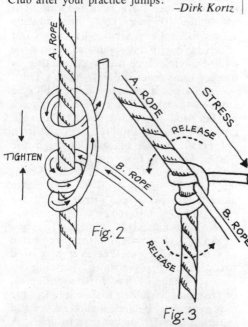

Fig. 2

Fig. 3

How to Jump Safely From a High Dudgeon

Anyone can get angry, but it takes a uniquely civilized talent to save yourself from an impending attack of rage without letting the person causing it know there is homicide in your heart. Here are two simple and proven techniques for shooing away those ulcers.

1. Send an insouciant glance his or her way and follow it with a fine old World War II zinger: "Aw, your mother wears combat boots!"

2. Chant, in a modulated scream, one of the sacred syllables of the West: "*Arrgh!*"

Frisbees: Still the Only Flying Saucers in Production

By Robert and Kate May

The world's distance Frisbee champion tells us about his sport, his passion: froupies, the overhand wrist flip, Guts, and the beloved old split-digit-14s.

People who consider themselves the old pros of Frisbee have been working at it for about 10 years, but there always seems to be a new freak who comes out of nowhere with a great distance throw or unique style. Once we were waiting in line for the movies on New York's Third Avenue when a young man on a bicycle stopped to ask why we were carrying a Frisbee and if we wanted to play. He crossed the street and proceeded to throw a fantastic round of skips through the traffic. Applause from the sidelines as we bounced a few off taxis. After a 15-minute rally he strapped on his bike lights and adjusted his beret. "Great game," we said and lost him to the city.

We never generalize about Frisbee freaks except to note that they aren't like any other athletes. Wherever you find two or more Frisbee stylists working out you will generally find Frisbee groupies, or "froupies." Male or female, the froupie may eventually become a good player and in turn attract his or her own froupies. A froupie is part of the paraphernalia of the game, like a good number 15 Moonlighter or a handmade Frisbee bag.

Frisbee traditions are eccentric and provincial. In Laguna Beach they have evolved a mellow, balletic beach game that only very vaguely resembles Plaza Frisbee as practiced in Berkeley's Sproul Plaza. Southern Californians are said to be into catching, while Northern Californians are into throwing—a distinction that tells us very little, unfortunately. In Michigan all they play is Guts, and in New York's Central Park they play Chicken, which does tell us a lot.

The Events

Any serious Frisbee tournament has most of the following events and maybe some innovations. (We went to one in Golden

Gate Park in San Francisco at which, in one event, woman players were asked to throw at a picture of Norman Mailer.)

Distance A well-run distance event has all finalists line up and throw simultaneously. This equalizes the wind-assist factor; otherwise, a freaky gust might carry a mediocre throw an extra 30 to 60 yards. The *Guinness Book of World Records* lists a throw of 95 yards over level ground as the longest in official competition. [This record is held by the author.]

Accuracy In an accuracy event the target is approximately 20 yards from the throwing line and is ideally a hoop about five feet in diameter. Part of it is free-style—everyone throws his most consistent shot, whether it's hard, soft or upside-down. A difficult contest makes you throw shots that curve around pylons or skip off the pavement before passing through the target.

Guts In a Guts match, two five-person teams line up 15 yards apart; the players on a team stand at arm's length from one another. One player at a time throws aggressively at the opposing line. Upside-down shots are not allowed, and all catches must be one-handed; no "traps" allowed, either. The receiving team scores points on wild throws; the throwing team

scores on bad catches. The game goes to 21 points, with a two-point lead required to win. A Frisbee theoretician commented that the game is essentially strategic and psychological, but you've got to give something to the muscle and speed boys. The 27-year-old perfect master of Guts, Vic Malafronte, can dazzle the opposition by a throw that begins with a faked start, proceeds into a behind-the-back shot and then drifts slowly over to the mind-blown defenders.

Maximum Time Aloft Best played on a breezy day, MTA involves finesse, power and a subtle intuition of the wind. An MTA shot is thrown directly into the wind, up to swifter air currents that may loft it higher, prolonging its glide to earth. In general,

The power shot that won Robert May the world's record for distance—95 yards over level ground.

Photography by Kate May

the steeper the shot the shorter the flight. Two to six players can compete by throwing simultaneously—the last man to catch his Frisbee wins. But MTA doesn't have to be competitive. It's great to throw solo on an empty beach where you can experience private exhilaration in the execution of a perfect, graceful flight. This kind of throwing creates a contemplative effect on players, an hypnotic empathy of object, person and elements. Aesthetically the MTA shot is a kind of kinetic air sculpture.

Ultimate Frisbee If you really want to know about UF, send for the eight-page revised pamphlet written by the originators at Columbia High School Varsity Frisbee Team, 17 Parker Ave., Maplewood, N.J. 07040 (enclose 15 cents and a self-addressed stamped envelope). You play UF roughly the way you'd play any ball passing game—no running with the Frisbee allowed. But it's not a contact sport. It takes more people to play Ultimate than can usually be rounded up for Frisbee activity.

It isn't found in most tournaments, but Frisbee Golf is a great game. The U.C. Berkeley campus may be the original course, the St. Andrews of Frisbee Golf. Not more than six players should play, for Frisbee Golf is time-consuming and confusing. You can use any reasonable site as a "hole" and specify any particular route to it. Carry spare Frisbees in case of loss, breakage or dogs.

The Throws

The basic Frisbee throw is the *backhand*. The grip is thumb on top, four fingers on the bottom. Wrist snap just before release is essential in all throws, because this produces the stabilizing spin. It's good for right and left curves and skips. It's also good for Guts, the best throw for MTA and is unbeaten in distance competition.

The sidearm or *two-finger shot* can be thrown behind the back, between the legs or while running. Keep the elbow close to the body and the forearm just a bit lower than level when throwing. The short, snappy stroke for this shot is forward and angled slightly to the left. To get it off behind the back bend the knees and arch the back slightly, using the same short, snappy stroke.

Like the two-finger shot, the *thumb throw* stroke is short, snappy and forward, with the elbow again held close to the body and the forearm close to level. A slight bow forward from the waist facilitates the throw.

The thumb-shot grip is also used for the *upside-down shot*. The stroke is like that of a ball thrown overhand; the Frisbee is close to horizontal, but upside-down, when released.

The *overhand wrist flip* is held with thumb pressed against the inner rim, index finger extended and pressed against the outer rim, middle, ring and little fingers extended on top of the Frisbee toward the center. The arm is fully extended, the elbow stiff. Start the stroke with the arm extended to the rear, wrist cocked. The swing forward is almost level with your shoulder, with a slight upward angle from back to front.

A Guide to the Best Frisbees

What does the serious player throw? While over 200 models have been put on the market, the selection of widely available, balanced, stable Frisbees is much narrower—there are really just a few. The Wham-O Professional Sports Model weighing 108 grams is one. It's a good all-around Frisbee and available everywhere across the country. It's especially good for tipping and curves, but does leave something to be desired at distances over 60 yards or so, when it becomes difficult to

keep straight. Wham-O's All-American and Moonlighter (glow-in-the-dark) models are comparable to the Pro in flight characteristics, while their Regular model is smaller and lighter (it weighs 96 grams) and good only on nearly windless days. The Master by Wham-O is much larger and heavier than the Pro (it weighs 150 grams) and feels cumbersome to most players, although its weight keeps it stable on windy days.

The other all-around excellent disc is the All-Star Saucer Tosser made by C.P.I. of Minneapolis. At 116 grams it's heavier than Wham-O's Pro, and a little less responsive at short range, but it's more stable at medium and long range. While the All-Star is hard to find outside the Midwest, it's an excellent Frisbee.

Frisbee fanatics tend to disparage Wham-O's current production models and gloat over oldies. Throwers and collectors treasure their old number one and split-digit-14 mold Frisbees (mold numbers are stamped at the center on the bottom). □

Victor Malafronte, perfect master of Guts, in his Frisbee temple.

A FRISBEE CHRONOLOGY

1948 First plastic flying disk invented. Inventor unknown, reputed to be one Fred Morrison.

1949 First "sky pie" spotted in Los Angeles.

1952 First intramural Guts game at Dartmouth College, Hanover, N.H.

1956 Dr. Julius T. Nachazel creates the first Frisbee trophy out of tomato cans.

1957 Frisbee Baking Co. goes out of business in New Haven, Conn. Namesake of pie tins thrown from Yale rooftops.

1964 First Wham-O Professional model, also known as "Olympic Ring #1," rolls off production line.

National Satellite Association formed, predecessor of today's International Frisbee Association.

1968 Frisbee thrown in Rose Bowl, Pasadena, Calif.

1969 American astronauts take first Frisbee to the moon.

The Art of Jonathan Livingston Hang Glider

By William J. Cook

The primeval urge to fly is so basic, so universal that nearly everyone has dreamed about it. And once you've done it, you're hooked. To feel what the eagles feel is an overwhelming experience.

Self-launched flight is one of man's oldest fantasies. Leonardo da Vinci dreamed of it. Aviator pioneer Otto Lilienthal actually did it, and glided to his death in Germany in the 1890s. The Wright brothers hang glided extensively before they set the course of modern flying with their powered aircraft. But now that we've flown powered vehicles to the moon and back, we're returning to the beginnings of flight, and self-launched gliding—called hang gliding or skysurfing or eco-flight—has become the newest (and some say fastest growing) adventure sport.

There are a host of reasons for the sport's fast-growing popularity. Hang gliding has beautiful, flowing movement, speed, exhilaration, all the attributes of surfing, skiing, scuba diving, with the addition of the thing man has yearned for, free flight. Hang gliding requires no license, and it is nonviolent, non-polluting, easier to learn than skiing, fairly safe, and enormous fun—while being relatively inexpensive. Hang glider kits cost as little as $200, complete models run about $600, and even the most complicated gliders cost less than $1,000. And that's the last cost, for the wind is free.

Hang gliding began catching on as a sport in 1971, largely in that cradle of new leisure activities, Southern California. The hang glider pioneers fashioned heavy craft of bamboo and plastic sheet that barely flew. In two short years the sport mushroomed as modern materials were introduced: light aluminum tubing, aircraft fittings, stabilized Dacron. Now the sport, still centered on the Pacific coast, is rapidly becoming worldwide, as more than 60 groups sell hang glider plans, kits and complete aircraft.

Hang gliding is still a highly experimental sport, with new designs and devices appearing almost daily. But the heart of the sport is the Rogallo wing, developed by NASA engineer Francis Rogallo and considered for recovering space vehicles.

The standard Rogallo wing is shaped like a large vee formed by two aluminum tubes which are the leading edges of the wing. A third tube is the center, or keel, spar. The structure is made semi-rigid by a cross-spar which connects the other three spars. The spars are covered with light polyethylene sheet or Dacron sail cloth. The length of the spars, and thus the size of the kite, is governed by the weight of the pilot. A 125-pound pilot needs a 15-foot kite while a 200-pound pilot requires an 18-footer. Complete Rogallo hang gliders weigh 28 to 40 pounds. Disassembled, they form a package about 10 inches in diameter and as long as the longest spar. The kites are easily transported atop an auto.

The sail forms two huge bellows when the air load is applied. The pilot literally hangs beneath the sail on a rope sling, suspended from the wing's center of gravity like a plumb bob. Beginning flyers sit in a child's swing seat, while advanced flyers usually lie prone, hanging in a harness.

A hang glider is controlled entirely by the pilot shifting his weight. He does this by grasping a control bar which is mounted solidly below the wing's frame. As he pushes the bar forward in flight he is actually moving himself back, shifting his weight to the rear, to push the sharp nose of the glider up. Pull the bar back, the nose is pulled down, push it to the right, the wing tips left and turns that way.

A Rogallo wing starts flying at about 15 miles per hour airspeed and can go up to 35 m.p.h. To take off, pilots climb hills and point directly into the wind. The wing is balanced overhead with the sail luffing and flapping. The pilot holds the wing up by the control bar. The nose is raised slightly to fill the sail, and the pilot begins to run, making sure he holds the control bar as high as possible to keep the rope sling taut. As soon as airspeed reaches about 15—which means running like hell in still air—the pilot pushes the control bar forward and takes off.

The hang glider lands, ideally, just like a bird. The pilot raises the nose just before he lands to stall the wing and virtually stop forward motion. Properly done, a hang glider pilot steps lightly onto the ground, drops the nose of the wing, and sets it down.

In flight, a pilot has only his senses and experience to guide him—the wind singing in the wires, the flapping of the sail, the bumps in the air. Some hang glider pilots make foolish jumps from mountains before they have flown many flights from low hills to learn what to look for, how to read the wind, what the noises mean. If the wires stop singing, the wing is stalled, a highly dangerous condition, for the glider may crash before the pilot can bring the nose down and regain flying speed. Sometimes on high-altitude flights inexperienced pilots think they are going too slowly since the ground—so far away—is moving slowly. They bring the nose down and fly too fast, inducing a dive from which it is difficult to recover.

If a pilot launches with one wingtip low, he may start immediately into a low-speed turn, with the inside wingtip stalled, which can bring the glider downwind, ultimately to crash into the hillside.

Another danger is flying in high winds. If the wind is blowing faster than the glider can fly, the glider can't "penetrate" the wind and actually can be blown backwards relative to the ground.

Rogallo wings, actually little more than controllable parachutes, are not very efficient. They sink about one foot for

The manta wing is easily carried on a microbus or even on the shoulders or a car top.

This slender package will become an airworthy glider in a few minutes.

After the stainless steel cables are attached, he's ready to unfurl the Dacron sail.

WHEEEEEEEEEEEEE

every three or four feet they fly forward. This 3-to-1 glide ratio compares poorly to the expensive, high-performance sailplanes which have 30-to-1 glide ratios, or better. Yet hang glider pilots can make their wings soar if terrain and wind conditions are exactly right. A modified Rogallo wing was kept aloft three hours and 36 minutes in 1973, riding the winds sweeping over cliffs at Torrance, Calif.

Hang gliding enthusiasts claim their sport is less dangerous than skiing, and that's true on the lower, more shallow hills. But there have been several deaths in the sport, as pilots ventured from high hills or mountains. One pilot jumped off a 1,700-foot cliff at Big Sur, glided out over the ocean, then turned back downwind. He was smashed into the ground and killed as the wind boiled over the first low cliff.

But the experts are trying higher and higher hills. One jumped from a hot-air balloon at 9,600 feet, another leaped from a 14,000-foot Colorado peak, still another made a four-mile glide into the bottom of the Grand Canyon.

Beginning pilots should made many flights from low hills which have open landing areas and a slope only slightly greater than the kite's glide ratio so they never get very high off the ground. The beginner's rule should be for many flights: "Fly no higher than you are willing to fall."

Hang gliding is in its infancy. Soon there will be competitions for time aloft, for spot landings, perhaps for aerobatics. There will be more complicated gliders, some with controls for more precision. Small biplanes and monoplanes are beginning to appear, such as the "Quicksilver" and Volmer Swingwing, which are much higher performance machines than the Rogallos, and, of course, harder to carry and launch. Some enthusiasts believe hang gliding has the potential of skiing, and they are scouting ski runs that can be converted to sky ports in the summertime.

I first tried hang gliding on the tall sand dunes facing the Pacific Ocean at Dillon Beach north of San Francisco. Just over my head a dart-shaped sail rip-

(continued on next page)

*Flight takes him
beyond the lift zone
hugging the hill.
He begins descent glide.*

*Gaining altitude and hovering
in the changing air currents like a hawk
takes skill but it can be done.*

*He feels for lift from the wind
flowing up the slope.*

*Heading directly into the wind,
the pilot begins his takeoff run.
Airborne, he corrects slightly
to gain balance,
shifting from ground reference
to air reference.
Showing good form, he passes overhead.
(Beginners do not fly prone;
they use a sling seat.)*

*Erected and ready for pre-flight inspection,
which is essential
in any mode of flying.*

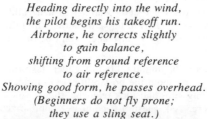

(continued from previous page)

pled in the wind on a light aluminum frame. Then I gathered my courage and ran madly down the dune into the wind, pushed the horizontal control bar forward, and I shot up like an elevator. My feet were still frantically pumping when I realized I was several feet off the sand. I was flying! Just like Icarus!

The big delta wing began to stall, I pulled the control bar back, and the wing dropped and picked up speed again. I flew for what seemed like hours on my first flight, hanging under the wing on a seat rigged like a child's swing. Only when I landed—crashed is a better word —did I realize I had covered but 25 yards or less in a flight that lasted only a few seconds. I didn't rise more than maybe five or six feet off the sandy slope, but I flew, by myself, after only a few minutes of instruction, suspended on a thin rope from a "hang glider" that weighed barely 35 pounds. It was one of the most exhilarating things I've ever done, by myself. One woman who tried it cried, "It's like an orgasm. No—" she corrected herself "—better." □

How to Get Off the Ground

Manufacturers of hang gliding equipment now operate flying schools to teach the fundamentals and allow people to try the sport without making a large investment. For as little as $15 a session, you are introduced to hang gliding by professional fliers with good equipment. The basics can be mastered in one day with proper instruction, and taking the course can save you months of trial and error.

The beginning of good technique in any sport is sound advice from those who know what they're talking about. Before you take advice from anyone, however, observe his equipment and how he handles it in the air. The sport is still too young to have an accreditation system, so look out for yourself by checking carefully before investing.

You may also be able to get help from fliers on a hill, but generally speaking you will have to coax information from them—not because they aren't helpful, but because they're more interested in flying than in talking to you. Above all, be wary of casual advice; your own safety is at stake.

One of the first things you'll find out is that there are three different kinds of hang gliders: Rogallos, monoplanes, and bi-planes. The Rogallo wing (named for its creator, Francis Rogallo, a NASA scientist), is known as the Model-T of the air, because it's doing for flying what Henry Ford's car did for motoring: taking a rich man's toy and giving it to everyone. It is the foundation of the modern hang gliding movement, and will probably always be around. It's inexpensive, light, stable, easy to fly, convenient, and versatile.

A well-made Rogallo wing weighs around 35 pounds and folds into a slim package that is easily carried on your shoulders or the top of the car. Its stability makes it a natural for beginners, and it's versatile enough to be able to fly when other types of gliders are grounded by high winds.

Monoplanes and bi-planes are capable of high performance in the hands of seasoned pilots, but are too difficult for beginners to handle. Because they're so heavy and cumbersome, they require a ground crew of at least two people who are willing to wait around patiently to assist the flier with takeoffs and carry-ups. Neither kind can be controlled by weight-shift alone, and so extra control systems are involved in flying them. They do, however, make a fine craft for the pilot who wants to broaden his flying experience.

Another word of caution: don't waste time trying to design or build your own hang glider. It takes more than a brilliant idea to end up with a practical piece of gear; it also takes a long series of painstaking minor adjustments to get a glider working well rather than half well. Anyone who tries to build his own glider is in for months of frustrating trial and error—probably without ever having a decent flight to reward him for his trouble.

It's not impossible to build an airworthy glider on your own, but the odds against it and the hidden costs make it a poor investment in time and money. Many do-it-yourselfers say afterward that they wish they had simply bought a ready-made glider or a kit instead of spending six weekends or more just chasing around for materials. (Parts for hang gliders, as you might imagine, are not easy to find.)

The best advice I can give you—if you're interested in flying instead of in fooling around—is to buy a ready-to-fly hang glider and fly it. If you want to save a little money, or if you like to make things, buy a kit, but make sure that it's a complete kit with detailed instructions. Save your ingenuity for your second glider when you'll have some experience at this type of flying. The low-speed aerodynamics of hang gliders are different from those of normal aircraft, so knowledge of airplanes won't be of much help.

Before buying any kind of glider, take time to learn about the possibilities. Go to local flying sites and look over the gliders you see there. Ask questions, compare, familiarize yourself so that you can make an informed choice. Get literature from the various manufacturers—but beware of claims that were born in the ad agency instead of in the air. While the amount you will spend on a wing is far less than for a motorcycle or dune buggy (you can get into the air for as little as $300), it is enough to sadden you considerably if you find out a week after you buy that you could have gotten much better equipment for the same money, or for even less than you spent.

—*Jack Sheridan*

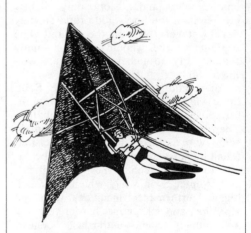

Parasailing: Aloft in the Bahamas

Parasailing, which can be briefly described as water-skiing with wings, is one of the more athletic ways to spend some time in the Bahamas. Using a nylon ribbed parachute and a harness attached by a 200-foot line to a motorboat, the parasailor zooms up as high as 150 feet and cruises at speeds up to 30 m.p.h. As the boat slows, the parachute loses altitude and the rider lands, gently, on the water.

The Sonesta Beach Hotel in Nassau is generally credited with inventing parasailing. A five-minute ride at Prudden's Watersports Center costs $10. Parachutes, for those who want their own, cost $600.

We can recommend parasailing in the Bahamas but not in Acapulco. We understand that sudden wind changes have sometimes thrown parasailors into Acapulco high-rises.

Ecstasy Through Air Power

If ever you've envied a hawk cutting lazy circles in an azure sky, his wings outstretched and motionless as he rides invisible currents of air, soaring is for you.

Soaring is done in a sailplane, also known as a glider, but there's a difference between soaring and gliding. Pull the throttle(s) back on anything from a little Cessna 150 to a giant Boeing 747 and it will glide, to a greater or lesser degree.

Because of their weight, however, power planes with engines off or idling are relatively unaffected by air currents. They're going to descend even as they glide, because unless the pilot maintains airspeed the plane will stall out.

Even though a sailplane also is heavier than air, its comparative weight is minimal and this, coupled with its tremendously large wingspan, enables it to actually ride air currents up to high altitudes and to stay aloft almost indefinitely.

Soaring is not terribly expensive to learn, either. Most soaring schools offer an introductory ride that's really a first lesson for $10 to $12.

Your first observation will be that a sailplane is, well . . . different. There's no landing gear, only a single wheel semi-recessed beneath the fuselage. The plane sits there rather forlornly, one wingtip almost on the ground.

You're in the front seat, the instructor is in the rear and ahead of you some 200 feet is the tow plane. The tow rope tightens, a line boy holding one wingtip to keep the wings level takes four or five steps until the instructor has control, the sailplane is airborne first and the tow plane rises from the runway on its way to 2,500 feet.

At altitude, and at the instructor's command, you pull the red release knob and —WHANG! It's a bit unnerving the first time you hear that mini-explosion signaling tow line away, but from then on the only noise is the gentle "whoosh" of air sliding over the wings and along the fuselage.

The tow plane banks left and dives away, your sailplane banks right and then resumes level flight. And suddenly, in one almost overpowering burst of understanding, you know what soaring is all about—a quiet, peaceful experience that gives you an almost startling feeling of sheer euphoria.

The Soaring Society of America (SSA) is the source of all information on soaring and has an up-to-date list of soaring schools and their locations. Write SSA, P. O. Box 66071, Los Angeles, Calif. 90066.

–Frank J. Gillespie

L *f God had wanted men to fly, He would have furnished them with capes.*
—SUPERMAN

Go Fly a Kite!

It always surprised me that people like Ben Franklin never got hurt playing around with kites. Kites are usually taken as toys, and are fun, but from time to time they've had some rather more serious purposes. Once, when I was a kid, I became an instant neighborhood hero by figuring out how to parachute livestock—including a frog, two young chickens and, I think, a snake—down from some horrendous altitude from the back of one of my kites. I think the key part of the device I ultimately built was an empty Wheaties box, hinged and flapped—when I gave the kite a strong tug the box turned upside down and opened, ejecting the hapless crew. (Their parachutes were made of hankies snitched from my father.) My confederate was, I think, George Miskell, and if he reads this he will probably want his frog back.

Kites have been around a long time. The Chinese are said to have got them functioning about 2000 B.C., and supposedly used them both as playthings and, occasionally, to settle territorial disputes in various crafty-kitey ways. Of course Franklin used kites in his static electricity experiments. It is said that the first rope across Niagara Falls—the one to which successively larger ropes were attached—was delivered across the virgin chasm by kite. And then there were little kids like me, risking all sorts of damnation with passenger-carrying kites. Nowadays, the kite is usually something punched out of plastic sheet or flimsy paper, and bought (along with crummy string that always seems to part) either from the supermarket or, worse, from discount "toy stores."

But *real* kites are an art form—there are elaborate and cunningly conceived animal and reptile forms in the Chinese style, graceful and stable Western devices that are more properly geometrical; there are slotted kites, articulated kites, roundtops, diamond kites, box and circle kites. And there is the Rogallo form, which was developed under the aegis of NASA as a lifting body for re-entry studies, and which, in simpler form, makes a fine kite. (In another adaptation, the Rogallo kite is a man-carrying glider wing.)

Unfortunately, information and how-to about kites is hard to come by these days. Today's materials, on the other hand, make kite building an absolute snap. The little kite in the picture was my first in many years, but it took me only about 20 minutes to do up, and it flew perfectly right off. White glue, mixed half and half with water, is a great adhesive for paper and string. Five-minute epoxy glues are valuable for their ferocious holding power and flexibility. Kite coverings can be anything from humble newspaper to bright imported tissue paper, silk, oilcloth, or colored mylar. Just remember that the weight and area of the kite ultimately determine whether it will fly or not.

For string, try fishing line. Use a tin can or flat board for a reel. Two rules: don't use anything metallic in your kite string, and don't fly near anything that looks even remotely like a power line, especially if you get caught in the rain. (Ben Franklin was just damned lucky.)

A good book on kite-making is *Kite Making and Flying*, by Harold Ridgway. It's out of print, but you can find it in most public libraries. It's illustrated and gives a very full rundown on kites and kiting. Don't be afraid to simplify Ridgway's designs or to change to lighter materials—his philosophy is a bit heavy.

You might want to join the Maryland Kite Society (7106 Campfield Road, Baltimore, Md. 21207). Membership fee is $1; the society publishes occasional newsletters, and can probably tell you about kite festivals around the country—such festivals are just starting to stage a comeback.

Better-than-average commercial kites are manufactured by
    Squadron Kites
    12821 Martha Ann Drive
    Los Alamitos, Calif. 90720.
Squadron kites are built to look very much like World War I airplanes, are rather large (around six feet long), and not cheap—they cost about $7 apiece. But they're really worth the money.

–John Oldenkamp

Freelandia: Up, Up and Far Out

By Peter Greenberg

Everything about this one-plane airline and travel club is California mellow — except the fuel, the crew and the FAA regulations.

Freelandia is, quite simply, the world's newest and freakiest airplane. It is not an airline, mind you, but a nonprofit air travel club with the cheapest rates in all the world. It flies everywhere and anywhere — truly a "people's plane," a counter-cultural phenomenon. Actually, Freelandia is the final product of a 30-year-old Syracuse University dropout and Wall Street whiz kid millionaire named Ken Moss, who in his grandest and most cosmic moment one rainy afternoon last year seized upon the plan for an airplane. The idea hatching was easy, but it was a long time in developing.

Moss's latest incarnation as a one-plane airline operator is the latest development in his wild series of careers. Six years ago, with $1,500 borrowed from his father, he turned famous as a 24-year-old puts-and-calls whiz kid for a Wall Street brokerage house. Next, he made a fortune by founding something called Bio-Medical Services and selling out his stock in it 18 months later. He netted himself $1.5 million on the deal.

Then he dropped out, all the way to Ibiza. After a year there, as a spaced-out long-haired rich man with no visible means of support, he predictably became bored and moved on — to Bombay.

"You wouldn't believe that place," he recalls. "It was beautifully insane. It was a circus." A year later he turned up in Paris with nothing but hepatitis, worms and dysentery.

It was at that point that Moss realized his destiny was California "and an avocado sandwich." He wound up first in New York, and while trying to get his by-then non-running Rolls to California he met Darcy Flynn, an aspiring actress who was more than willing to accompany him on the trek West and beyond. (He didn't tell her about his money until later.)

Moss set up housekeeping in a converted metal cowshed near a commune on the San Francisco peninsula. No one knew of his wealth even there, and it was a peaceful existence.

Nevertheless, the money in the bank made Moss restless — he's not exactly a certificate-of-deposit kind of guy — and he decided to explore ways in which it could be used. "I started to remember all the kids I met while traveling," he says, "who could hardly afford to fly. So one day, I just looked at Darcy and said, 'Let's buy our own airplane and go to Bali and we'll take all our friends along.'"

A few of Freelandia's round-trip "air shares"

In much the same way that Moss had studied the stock market, he then began to take an avid interest in the plane business. Soon, he discovered that one of the best places to find a good used plane is in Miami. Off he flew with Darcy to find the perfect aircraft.

It was to be the beginning of one of the most incredible (and expensive) short-courses on used-plane buying in history. Before finding the plane he wanted, Moss went down a number of frustrating and expensive blind alleys. There was the Lockheed Constellation that turned out to have only two drawbacks: it could be fueled in only three places in the country, and spare parts for it were almost nonexistent. There was the 747 — for $200,000 a month. Then there was a Convair 880 from a Japanese airline that turned out to have been heavily cannibalized for spare parts (Moss learned this only after he had already hired a crew, spent $80,000 working up new flight manuals in English, and signed a $58,000 contract to repaint the plane).

In June of 1973 he heard about a ready-to-fly DC-8 that National Airlines wanted to unload because of new DC-10 deliveries. Moss and Darcy sped over to the National corporate offices in Miami. When Moss first showed his face at National, the executives there were convinced the guy was either stoned or a member of the Venceremos Brigade. "Just call my banker," he would continually insist. Reluctantly, they finally did.

"Within five days," recalls Moss, "I had negotiated a DC-8, a training package, spare parts, new interiors and exteriors" — and all for $750,000.

He took his flight crews off the 880

and told them to prepare for a DC-8; however, what National had neglected to tell Moss was that this particular DC-8 was involved in a law suit. National had earlier agreed to deliver this particular plane to a private Miami-based air cargo firm. Because of delays in wide-bodied plane deliveries, National had also delayed. Because the private company had taken shipping orders and was suddenly faced without planes to carry the cargo, it went bankrupt and sued National.

While Moss's bankers and lawyers were once again setting up the deal, the National suit was settled and the plane (already painted Freelandia yellow) was, as luck would have it, part of the settlement. "Our financing was ripped off," Moss says, "and it was back to the 880 and those goddamned Japanese flight manuals. We were locked into it."

As a last resort, Moss attempted to buy the plane from the bankrupt company. But his bank balked. They would only finance the deal if he could put $150,000 in cash down on the deal — and within 24 to 36 hours after he made the proposal.

Moss came up with the money, but at the last moment the cargo company hesitated. "By that time," Moss relates, "I was totally freaked out. I had one Convair 880 all painted, I had a DC-8 all painted, and yet I didn't have anything but two flight crews and a large investment in nothing." So, Moss did the only thing he could.

He went to his astrologer. "She charted everything out," he recalls. "And at the end, she said that Darcy and I were going to go on a long air journey." With that piece of vital information in hand, Moss called the bankrupt air cargo presi-

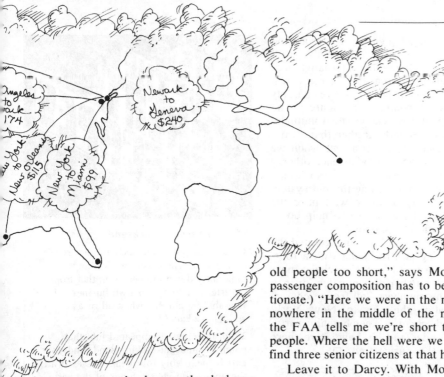

dent, to everyone's pleasure the deal was signed and, on Aug. 7, Moss had his plane—a real, live DC-8. As things turned out, he had hired the ideal crews to fly it. His chief pilot, Jim Davis, is a former McDonnell-Douglas test pilot who has taught dozens of other commercial airline pilots how to fly DC-8s. (None of Freelandia's personnel has less than 10,000 hours flight experience.)

And, to sweeten the deal, National retooled all four of the plane's engines back to "zero air time"—they are virtually new. But, sorry to say, troubles were just beginning.

Welcome the Federal Aviation Administration. By this time Moss had spent $400,000 in legal fees and in training the two crews, had invested over $750,000 for the plane and new flight manuals (new seat covers alone cost him well over $20,000)—and still didn't have much of anything to show for it.

As anyone in the airline business will tell you, a plane on the ground does not generate revenue—and a plane without an FAA certification stays on the ground.

Moss and his crew worked hard to ready the plane for the FAA inspectors. Then came the fateful night. The FAA had inspected the manuals and had found everything in order. But now the crucial test: the simulated emergency evacuation, during which, in order to pass, the fully loaded plane had to be evacuated in 90 seconds or less.

The Freelandia DC-8 was parked on an end of a deserted Miami airport runway. It was 10 on a Friday night. Moss had paid 149 people $5 apiece and had promised them a beer party if they'd help in the test. Just when they were ready to simulate a crash, the FAA abruptly halted the activity. "Fourteen FAA guys came over and told me that we were three

old people too short," says Moss. (The passenger composition has to be proportionate.) "Here we were in the middle of nowhere in the middle of the night and the FAA tells me we're short three old people. Where the hell were we going to find three senior citizens at that hour?"

Leave it to Darcy. With Moss at the airport stalling for time, she hopped into a taxicab and went to the nearest bar. Somehow, she was able to convince two traveling insurance salesmen, at 10 on a Friday night, to get back into the cab with her, drive out to the airport and jump out of a DC-8 window exit for $5 and a beer party. Still one short, she also coerced the startled cab driver to jump for glory—and the future of Freelandia.

"They all thought she was a hooker," laughs Moss.

"I would walk up to those guys at the bar," Darcy remembers, "and I'd just say, 'Excuse me, are you over sixty-five years old? . . . Yes? Well, can you leave right now?'"

Darcy and Moss hustled the three jolly geriatrics onto the plane just in the nick of time.

And, when the FAA started the simulation seconds later and window exits and escape chutes were popped open, they were hustled off just as fast by the efficient stews. The plane was evacuated in near-record time—70 seconds.

They had won their certification. But more hassles were to come. Under law, as an air travel club, they are not allowed to solicit memberships; thus, they had to hope that future Freelandians would be attracted by word of mouth.

That is exactly what has happened. Moss's Sherman Oaks, Calif. headquarters has been humming. Members (over 2,000 so far) who have paid a $50 initiation fee can fly from Honolulu to San Francisco for $69, from San Francisco to Los Angeles for $12.50, from Los Angeles to New York for $87 and from New York to Geneva for $120. And Moss has been getting some bizarre applications.

A heart surgeon offered his services free in return for membership, and even the Los Angeles Policeman's Association

has applied for group membership. Both were turned down. "It might change the atmosphere of the flight," Moss chuckles.

The fares, or "air shares," are figured on a 69-percent occupancy rate for the DC-8, and Moss has applied for landing rights in Yugoslavia, Greece, Turkey, India, Afghanistan, Australia, Tahiti, Colombia, Peru—and last, but certainly not least, Bali. (The nice thing about Freelandia is that, as membership increases, Moss can exercise his option on a second DC-8.)

"This is a great alternative way to travel," Moss explains. "It truly is a travel club for the people, by the people." As soon as Moss's loan is repaid to him, any other income will be donated to Internal Revenue Service-approved charities, such as drug rehabilitation clinics—or anything else the membership votes for. (Moss does not even draw a salary or "consultant" fee from Freelandia.)

Most of the major airlines are keeping a watchful eye on Moss's operations. While Continental's computer is used for Freelandia's Pacific flight plans and while United Airlines services Freelandia in Los Angeles, that doesn't mean they've accepted Moss as one of the boys. Far from it. And the FAA, apparently taking its cue from the airline industry, is also keeping close tabs. "We've had someone from the FAA on every flight," laughs Moss. "By now we should be the safest plane in the sky."

"We're not too worried now," one airline executive confided. "But if this kid starts adding aircraft, we're going to look seriously at his methods and try to stop him." Already, Moss has had trouble getting fuel in Hawaii. "But the problem is being handled," he says confidently.

On his inaugural flight to New York, Freelandia's passenger manifest, contrary to popular fears, represented a cross section of America. Retired schoolteachers, musicians, young mothers, two movie producers, an optometrist going through divorce—even the pilot's daughter were on board.

Everything on the plane was organic—except the fuel. Those flying Freelandia feasted on eggplant parmesan, tamales and chilis rellenos served by the flight attendants, who looked like Flash Gordon revisited and were dressed in purple. Liquor (any kind) is free. So is the music, provided by individual cassette systems in the front lounge. There's a back lounge that is usually converted into a nursery for kids and, up front, an electronic "Pong" game stands the height of the cabin. There's also backgammon, chess, cards—and a little dancing.

Perhaps the most progressive thing about the plane is the passengers' spirit. "They really feel like a club," says Pat Nelson, the chief Freelandia stew. During the inaugural New York flight, the

(continued on next page)

(continued from previous page)

divorced optometrist was walking down the aisles adjusting glasses; one girl was charting horoscopes. A guy named John just kept talking about the "good karma" at 39,000 feet. Fifty-one-year-old Howard Doolittle from Woodland Hills, Calif., a recently retired General Electric food services manager, was having the time of his life. "It's a fantastic saving, no doubt about it. A lot of my friends were apprehensive, but I was impressed by all the FAA regulations they had to subscribe to."

The only one on board who didn't seem to be enjoying himself was the FAA man. He came out of the cockpit long enough to eat, took one look at his chili relleno (served with a crunchy granola appetizer) and promptly ran back to the security of the flight deck. (The cockpit crew had requested steak and potatoes earlier, and the caterer had complied.)

Robert Chester, a 28-year-old movie producer, couldn't have been happier with the flight—and the concept. "This is the best thing to happen since the jet. Why should we have to support twenty trips a day to little-known cities in half-filled planes? I'm saving a hundred dollars on this flight (the normal one-way fare to New York: $168) and the only thing I'm not getting is a movie . . . big deal!"

Moss is convinced that Freelandia will survive and prosper. "We have created a potentially very big energy center around Freelandia," he says. "Hopefully, we'll be able to build an entire alternative economic network from this. Hotels will have to deal with us; so will restaurants and shops. By pooling our resources," he says, "I'm sure we can create a mutually cooperative network. Rather than struggle with a hostile environment when we travel, we can accommodate each other.

"We're the bridge, the transition," Moss thinks, "for trading the old system for the morality of the new. I have the insanity and the incentive to help do it. Not to mention the money."

Last November, Moss inaugurated the European leg of Freelandia with a four-day gala party to a Swiss chalet near Geneva. A number of bands flew over to play for the members—all free of charge. Earlier, after the trip to New York, Moss had given a membership party. Stevie Wonder and his band were there to provide the music—free. □

Design Your Own Jet

Jets bug us. They're too cramped, too plastic and too enclosed. The food is lousy, the movies stink and no wonder they're losing passengers. Everyone knows this.

So here's a chance to design your own. Using the space below (or a reasonable facsimile), draw in what you'd like to see on your dream commercial airliner. Send your drawing to us, at 150 Shoreline Highway, Mill Valley, Calif. 94941, and we'll forward the best ideas to the presidents of the major airlines.

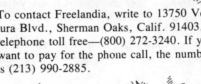

HOW TO GET ON

To contact Freelandia, write to 13750 Ventura Blvd., Sherman Oaks, Calif. 91403, or telephone toll free—(800) 272-3240. If you want to pay for the phone call, the number is (213) 990-2885.

ONE OF THE GREAT ESCAPES

How to Escape Quicksand

Getting caught in quicksand is not recommended. There you are walking pleasantly down the beach on that tropical isle, minding your own business, a law-abiding citizen, when all of a sudden—*whuck!*

Your ankle has disappeared into that patch of innocent-looking sand, and your calf is inexorably following. It's as if all the gooey and yucky things of the earth have gathered just there, for the purpose of luring moon-eyed tourists to their doom.

But do not despair! You *can* get out of quicksand, and here's how. The thing to remember is that, despite all appearances, there is no evil, sucking demon down there. There is only mud and sand mixed with water in proportions not solid enough to support your weight. Throw yourself immediately to your full length, and then crawl or swim. Do not make any sudden movements. And above all—never give up. Quicksand holes are often no bigger than an armchair, and you may be only inches from safety.

–The Editors

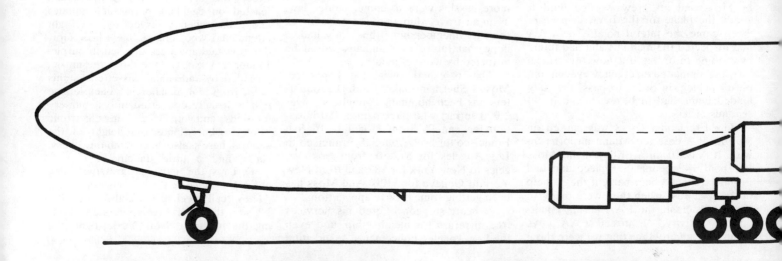

Beat Inflation— Build Your Own Airplane

Thanks to a small company in Kansas, you can now buy a new plane for the price of a Volkswagen. The catch (you knew there had to be a catch, didn't you?) is that the plane, the BD-4, comes as a kit with 4,155 parts, and it must be assembled under the supervision of an FAA inspector. But it has a base price of only $2,600, seats two, and cruises at 187 m.p.h.

If that's not good enough for you, Bede Aircraft (pronounced *beady*) has also developed a *jet* kit—for $21,400. The single-place jet cruises at 325 m.p.h. We don't know how many parts the jet kit has, but Bede Aircraft guarantees that it has absolutely no balsawood parts. Write Bede Aircraft, Newton, Kan.; phone (316) 283-8870.

SUCCESS / FOUR FLIGHTS THURSDAY MORNING / ALL AGAINST 21-MILE WIND / STARTED FROM LEVEL WITH ENGINE POWER ALONE / AVERAGE SPEED THROUGH AIR 31 MILES / LONGEST 59 SECONDS / INFORM PRESS / HOME CHRISTMAS.

—WILBUR AND ORVILLE WRIGHT

World War II Flies Again!

By Mike Michaelson

Ostensibly, it's a peaceful Sunday afternoon in 1974, but these Japanese Zeros are dive bombing this Texas airport while a squad of U.S. Navy Avengers are attacking a Japanese aircraft carrier. Meanwhile, a Messerschmitt BF-109 is strafing a limping B-17. It's almost for real and performed by the very real Confederate Air Force.

As the Texas International Airlines' DC-9 began its landing approach at Harlingen International Airport in southeastern Texas, passengers were astounded to find the airport under attack by diving Japanese Zeros. Smoke billowed from a direct hit on a building adjacent to the runway. Ground crew were scrambling for safety. And this on an ostensibly peaceful Sunday afternoon in 1974.

These startled passengers were witnessing part of a remarkable air show that included a re-enactment of the Pearl Harbor attack, a strike against a Japanese carrier by U.S. Navy TBF Avengers, the strafing of a limping B-17 by a Messerschmitt BF-109 and an air-sea rescue mission by a PBY-5A Catalina of a pilot afloat in the "Pacific." This exciting and nostalgic show was performed by colonels of the Confederate Air Force (CAF), an organization of pilots, ground crewmen and others interested in rescuing World War II aircraft—Allied and Axis—and keeping them in flying condition.

These venerable combat aircraft—and others like them—make up the Ghost Squadron of the Confederate Air Force under the command of the mythical Colonel Jethro E. Culpeper. In all, there are close to 60 aircraft representing 41 different types—a comprehensive catalog of World War II fighting machines. The remarkable part is that most of them are operational.

Almost 1,000 strong, the CAF membership is drawn from all walks of life. It includes, of course, pilots, astronauts, mechanics and technicians, but bankers and physicians—businessmen and professional men of all types—are also members. Less than 10 per cent of these men are qualified to fly the superannuated combat aircraft. They mostly are attracted to the organization by the satisfaction of restoring, maintaining and making possible the flight of the great aircraft of the 1939-1945 era.

Headquarters for the CAF is at Rebel Field, adjacent to Harlingen's commercial airport. Operations center around three large hangars and a vintage Army Air Corps office building. The latter houses an Officers' Club, Visiting Officers' Quarters and a remarkable museum of World War II aviation memorabilia.

A walk through the museum evokes memories of that era of national unity that produced jitterbug, wisecracks, gas rationing, Betty Grable and Glenn Miller. Even those not old enough to remember this nostalgic bric-a-brac are fascinated by posters urging more weapons production—"Bundles for Berlin" is the patriotic euphemism; by gun turrets, engines and war maps, by newspaper headlines screaming about European invasion and Nazi surrender.

Visitors, young and old alike, are intrigued by time-cracked leather flying jackets gaudily painted with spirited slogans and lists of completed objectives. There are flyers' pistols, gloves and map cases, navigational and radio instruments, squadron emblems and mottoes, a collection of German insignia and decorations, photographs, flags, and mannequins wearing the uniforms of the United States and Allies. Rooms are devoted to displays relating to the Army Air Corps, U.S. Navy and Marine aviation and the Confederate Air Force archives. The museum presents an absorbing chronological history of the tragedies, hardships and victories of the world-wide conflict, documenting such historic events as the Battle of Britain, Doolittle's bombing raids on Japan and the Battle of Midway.

But it is the flying museum that really entrances most visitors. When they walk out onto the apron they are likely to see such legendary adversaries as the Spitfire and Messerschmitt now sitting in peaceful company. Or they may wonder about the flight history of the P-40 Warhawk, with its Chinese Nationalist wing insignia and its nose garishly painted as eyes and mouth, trademark of General Claire Chennault's "Flying Tigers." (In a period of eight months, the American Volunteer Group flying for the Chinese was credited with shooting down 286 Japanese planes with a loss of only eight P-40s in the air.) Or visitors might peer into the nose turret of the B-17, the rugged hardworking Flying Fortress—the first view from here has shaken more than one green air-crew youngster on a landing.

"Without the B-17," declared U.S. Air Force Chief of Staff General Carl A.

Aircraft Spotted . . . Identity Unknown. Can You Name It?

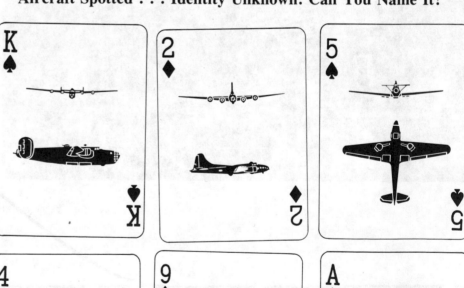

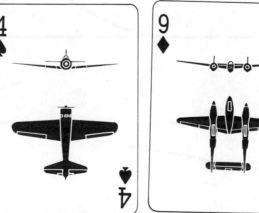

Consolidated B-24C   Boeing B-17E "Flying Fortress"   Messerschmitt Me 109F   Zero   Lockheed P-38   Curtiss P-40E

(Left to right)

Spaatz, "we might have lost the war." Yet of the 12,500 Forts produced, only 17 in flyable condition remain in the United States, while many other types of famous World War II aircraft seem to have disappeared. In fact in the mid-Fifties, when the CAF was conceived, the possibility of an airborne Ghost Squadron representing every type of World War II aircraft seemed like an impossible dream.

More than 300,000 warplanes were manufactured in the United States between 1939 and 1945, but few remained. After a few short years of glory in the skies around the world, they were being scrapped, sold abroad or simply allowed to rot in boneyards in remote parts of the American countryside. In fact, after the war the government issued a directive calling for the systematic destruction of a large part of this obsolete mothball air force. And most of the planes flown by German and Japanese pilots had been destroyed on sight at the close of the war by victorious Allied armies.

So the search began. With a dogged determination members of the fledgling Confederate Air Force began to track down aircraft in remote parts of the world. Before this quest was over, CAF officers would bring home 20 aircraft from foreign countries.

It seemed incredible that 15,684 P-47 Thunderbolts could have disappeared. Finally, one was tracked down in Nicaragua, and after months of negotiations a flyable Thunderbolt—the Jug that had the reputation of bringing home its pilots—had itself returned. Later, six more were found in Peru, and if any of those airline passengers arriving at Harlingen International Airport on that day in late January 1974 had stayed to watch the air show, they would have seen its moving climax—a sweep of five P-47 Thunderbolts, the first to fly since World War II.

From England—via Spain, the Azores and Newfoundland—the CAF puddle-jumped an MK-35 Mosquito, barely getting it across. This specimen of the all-wood Mossie, which frequently flew without guns and could outrun and outmaneuver most enemy fighters, is one of only two flyable Mosquitos in existence.

Messerschmitts were found in recent service with the Spanish Air Force; a B-29 Superfortress was tracked down in the California desert, still in military service for ballistic missile tests; a Liberator, now repainted in its wartime colors and dubbed "Diamond Lil," was found in service as an executive transport; a P-49 found scattered about a small town in New Mexico was gathered up and painstakingly put together; a P-38 Lightning was found in high grass behind an old hangar outside Yukon, Okla. The search even turned up some salty pin-ups—Sleepy-time Gal, Surprise Attack and Easy Maid—cut by some nostalgic art lover from the fuselages of destroyed B-24 and B-17 bombers. These now have been restored and are displayed in one of the hangars at Rebel Field.

The museum and static aircraft displays are open to visitors year-around. The CAF participates in about five air shows annually, and it invites support in the costly maintenance and operation of these historic combat aircraft through donations or aircraft sponsorship. For information, write: Director, Confederate Air Force, Rebel Field, Harlingen, Tex. 78550. □

Warplane Rest Home

A graveyard may not sound like much of a tourist attraction, but if the "graveyard" is the resting place for anywhere from 4,000 to 5,000 military aircraft, it qualifies.

Davis-Monthan Air Force base, on the outskirts of Tucson, Ariz., is such a place. "Graveyard" is actually a misnomer, because at least half of the aircraft here are maintained in a "ready" state and could be returned to active duty within 24 to 72 hours. Still, the place has a certain graveyard atmosphere.

A drive through the 3,000-acre storage area is truly mind-boggling. Aircraft are everywhere, arrayed in neat rows by type, and in all shapes and sizes. A few are true war-wearys dating back to World War II and, in all, more than 60 different types of aircraft are stored here.

There's an eeriness, even in broad daylight under a broiling sun. Nothing moves, save for shimmering heat waves dancing in the distance, reflections from the aluminum skins of the planes parked nose to nose and wingtip to wingtip.

Surprisingly, this aircraft "graveyard" actually makes money! Cannibalizing aircraft to retrieve parts no longer in production nets $50 for every $1 spent.

Some planes, such as transports and freighters, are actually for sale—but not to individuals, so don't bother to bring your checkbook. This is a government-to-government transaction.

Tours of the storage area (no charge) are available every Friday, but reservations must be made at least one week in advance. Write or call the Tucson Chamber of Commerce, 420 W. Congress St., Tucson, Ariz. 85701.

—Frank J. Gillespie

Airplanes Spoken Here

There are 60 or 70 real collections of antique and modern aircraft and aerospace objects scattered around the country, ranging in scope from the 1938 German Fieseler on display outside the VFW hall in Greencastle, Ind. to the completely mind-boggling exhibits at the Smithsonian in Washington, D.C.—the first aerial flight of man is memorialized there in the glider built by John J. Montgomery; there are also the Wright brothers' first power plane, *Kitty Hawk* (1903); a 1910 monoplane flown by M. H. Bleriot in the first flight across the English Channel; and Lindbergh's Ryan RYP, *Spirit of St. Louis*.

Most aircraft museums are mainly devoted to heavier-than-air machines, but many also contain aerospace *objets*—early ballistic missiles, space probes, and other futuristic goodies, as well as engines, propellers, helmets, instruments, etc. Some have very good libraries. My favorite library is the very folksy one at the San Diego Aerospace Museum; it's run by the avuncular Brewster Reynolds, whose memory bank is brimful after nearly 40 years of living, sleeping and eating airplanes.

For lovers of aircraft, here is a list of some of the most interesting museums:

Air Force Museum, Wright-Patterson Air Force Base, Dayton, Ohio. Very large collection of military and experimental or prototype aircraft. Good representation of foreign planes. Excellent library.

Air Force Space Museum, Cape Canaveral, Fla. Rockets and missiles and space vehicles galore, if that's your bag.

Experimental Aircraft Association, Hales Corner, Wis. (near Oshkosh). Incredible experimental and home-built aircraft. The EAA also sponsors many regional fly-ins around the country; they feature planes of wild design created by the nation's garage and back-yard aircraft builders. The EAA Annual Fly-In held each year in July in Oshkosh can only be described as an orgasmic experience for those who really like airplanes.

Old Rhinebeck Aerodrome, Rhinebeck, N.Y. The most complete collection of World War I and vintage "wind in the face" machinery in the country. This museum also houses Cole Palen's outstanding collection of restored, built-from-scratch fighter planes. The Old Rhinebeck Air Circus, held annually, features simulated dogfights, bomb drops and other shenanigans.

Ontario Air Museum, Ontario Airport, Ontario, Calif. Large and complete collection of U.S. military trainers and combat aircraft, mostly from World War II and the Forties.

Tallmantz Air Museum, Orange County Airport, Santa Ana, Calif. A biggie, especially as regards exotic, specialty and nostalgic airplanes types. Has most, if not all, of the machines recently featured in such Hollywood movies as *Tora, Tora, Tora!*, *Flight of the Phoenix* and *Airport*. In addition, lovely Sopwiths, Spads, Travellairs, Fokkers—you name it.

White Sands Missile Park, White Sands Missile Range, N.M. Collection of the real early birds of missilery: German V-2s, Redstones, Ajax, Nike, Zeus—and a lot of other things we needed once.

—John Oldenkamp

Building Model Airplanes

Most little boys—and, I hope, some little girls—sooner or later fall victim to the model airplane syndrome. Some well-intentioned parent or relative delivers one of those irresistibly bright and mysterious boxes marked "Airplane" that are sold in toy, hobby or department stores, and the child is hooked. The models are ingenious products, compounded of modern plastics, die-cutting and merchandising. I am told that their sales, along with sales of little motors, glues and other accessories sell on the order of $500 million worth every year. A friend of mine says that 200,000 little plastic propellers are squeezed out every week.

But I'll bet that less than the teeniest number of model plane kits ever get built. And I'll lay odds, too, that fully 99 percent of all model airplanes crash and burn, or implode and fall. I know. I've built about 200 model planes in the past 10 years, and a whole lot more before I "grew up." They all have frustrated the daylights out of me and made the hobby dealer rich. The whole idea of flying something smaller than a 747 that you've made with your own hands gets into your blood, and then you have to start coping with the gadgets and liquids and fractional mathematics involved. But when they *do* fly, the kind of bliss settles over you that you felt when you tasted your first chocolate mousse.

I'm 42 and I don't consider it foolish to stay up all night 10 days in a row just to finish off my current design for a three-hour contest.

And I haven't wrecked one in months. But the first few I built, when I was a kid laid up with a severe leg wound suffered during a plum-stealing caper, were something else. Strong kids, like strong men, do cry. My models were hopelessly cockeyed, impossibly heavy and dripped with glue globs, punctures, warps and other flaws. They flew remarkably well, for milli-seconds, from the barn, from the bedroom window ledge, from whatever was taller than I. They crashed soundly and thoroughly. By the dozens.

Somewhere along the way, I got smart. I built an extremely simple hand-launched glider. It didn't *look* like a real airplane, but did it fly! Time after time—and then, finally, into the vortex of a hefty thermal, to be seen no more. Variations, improvements, new planes followed. Spotty success, all more or less predicated on the odds that one day, another one would *have* to fly.

You can get into model airplaning on many different levels; mostly it's a matter of deciding whether you want your model to fly under control or free. (You can also build some rather decent models that are not meant to fly, but to be pondered.)

I personally like the idea of creating something from scratch that will take off under its own power, look stunningly like the real object, fly a minute or two while I chase it, and come back so I can do it again. For power, I use rubber stripping, something the

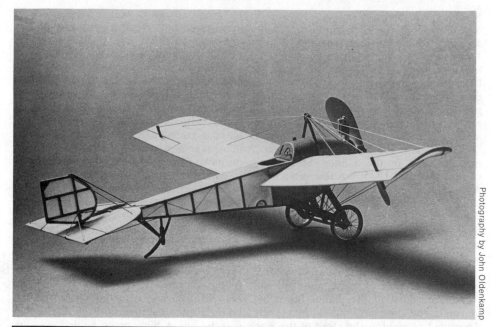

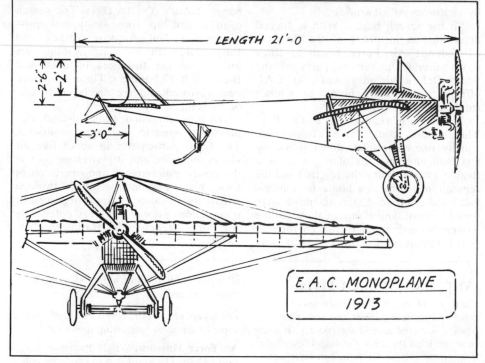

LENGTH 21'-0

2'6" 2'

3'-0"

E. A. C. MONOPLANE
1913

Photography by John Oldenkamp

earliest models (circa 1898) employed.

My propellers are sometimes commercial plastic units but if I need something bigger or more efficient, I will happily sit down and carve one. My airplanes duplicate the structure, details and color of the real airplanes. And sometimes, as in the case of the Eastbourne pictured, I'll need six months or so to track down the original drawings to begin with. The rest is pure pleasure: drawing to scale, cutting, gluing, covering. Each part gets weighed, smoothed and eyeballed to near extinction.

Comes the day of first flight, I'm a basket case. Sometimes, like the old Kentucky boresight riflemen, I'll require a little nip before proceeding. But then, winding several hundred turns into the rubber motor, it's on the line.

Most of my models are two to three feet in span, weigh an ounce or two or three, and are made principally from balsa wood, thin ply, wire and various glues, with tissue covering. My most successful models are based on real monoplanes that appeared during the Thirties. The joy involved in building them is nearly impossible to communicate verbally.

Perhaps the best way to gain an understanding of miniature airplanes is to visit a good hobby shop and ask for help. There are also a number of publications and groups that know what they're talking about and can help you. Some of the publications are *Model Airplane News*, *The Model Builder*, *American Aircraft Modeller*, *Flying Models* and *Radio Control Modeller*. All are available monthly on most newsstands.

—John Oldenkamp

Learning to Fly

Theoretically, anyone from a teenager to a grandma can learn to fly, and in fact have. Providing you can pass the Federal Aviation Agency Class III physical (and they've passed one-eyed pilots) and you have a two-way radio operator's license (just fill out a form) and a student pilot's license (ditto) you can start taking flying lessons.

Of course you've got to have money to pay for instruction—in ballpark figures anywhere from $1,000 to $1,500 these days—and a certain amount of determination. Things can be pretty frustrating at times.

Once you've made up your mind, there are people at a multitude of flying schools and "pilot centers" and even light plane owners who also hold instructor's tickets who are eager to teach you.

The FAA will license you after you've flown 40 hours of dual and solo. Twenty hours of that must be solo flying and 10 hours must be cross-country flying. Also, you're required to pass a written examination and a flight checkpoint with an FAA inspector. The former requires some concentrated study; the latter can be one of the most traumatic ordeals you'll ever go through, especially if the examiner is a real stickler, like mine was. (He had me land at five different air fields and fly "under the hood"—instruments only—much of the time. He also pulled an emergency when I least expected it, cutting off the engine and expecting me to go through the motions of making a deadstick landing.) But the feeling of elation when you get your license compensates for all that's gone before.

Having made up your mind that you're going to become a private pilot, here are a few things to keep in mind.

Don't accept the offer from a friend who happens to own a small plane but has no instructor's license, who says he'll teach you to fly "for the price of the gas."

Do research your local airport or wherever you intend to learn for the best recommended instruction.

Don't get downhearted when, after more than six hours going round and round the airfield learning to take off and land (popularly known as touch n' go's), you still don't seem to be able to do it without a series of spine-joggling bumps. It takes some longer than others.

Do avoid listening to those smart guys in the airport lounge who boast *they* soloed in eight hours. They probably didn't.

Don't turn your nose up at a woman flying instructor. According to FAA statistics women are more reliable private pilots than men and if your teacher is a woman you've probably got yourself an unusually patient, helpful instructor.

Do take advantage of every study aid there is, and if you sign on for a package course try not to miss sessions.

Don't worry if you don't pass the written exam first time around. It can take all day and you may still fail. Be comforted—many do.

Do rely on your instruments and navigational aids even when they seem to be false prophets. On early cross-country solos you can become embarrassingly lost in the shortest possible time. It's not unusual.

Don't, if you do get lost, ignore the helpful, kindly FAA personnel waiting on the ground to help you out of such an emergency. That's what they're there for.

Do, if you live in a heavy air traffic area (and even if you don't), consider taking an instrument course. This not only gives you added confidence and safety, but allows you to answer on their own level any lofty commercial airline pilots who start talking down to you.

Don't, after you've got your license, allow all your new skills to lapse. Keep up to date with flight procedures. The *Airman's Information Manual*, for example, is a splendid investment.

—Hilary Ostlere

whistling and humming of the wind as it blows against the spokes and wires that support the 430-ton contraption.

Your carriage, supported on steel arms, sways gently back and forth as you rise ever higher. As you near the top a fantastic panorama of the Prater, the Danube River, and the surrounding Viennese countryside comes into view below and before you. So engrossing is the scene that photographers have been known to forget to take pictures at this, the perfect moment.

Then, at the very top, a rather scary thing happens. All the passengers, who have been standing at the front picture windows of the carriage now move *en masse* to the back windows, in order to continue looking out from the wheel and not into its core. This mass movement of course causes the carriage to rock and sway noticeably. Your stomach, unprepared for this, will flop over at least once. But shortly the swinging slows down and the carriage begins its slow descent to earth.

Many riders, having taken the trip once, immediately purchase tickets for a second ascent. One of the best things about a second trip is that the second time around your stomach is almost guaranteed to behave, even at the peak of the turn, when the Austrian gentleman next to you murmurs "*Ach . . . mien Gott in Himmel. . . .*"

—Mike Miller

WHERE TO GET STARTED

Academy of Model Aeronautics
806 15th St. NW
Washington, D.C. 20005
Overall governing body in the United States for sport model aviation. Maintains records, sanctions contests, provides mandatory insurance for fliers. Membership: $12 annually.

National Free Flight Society
P.O. Box 322
Dallas, Ore. 97338
Dedicated to free flight design and competition, particularly international-class competition.

In addition, there are many local clubs around the country, with intriguing names like the Detroit Balsa Butchers, The Tulsa Glue Daubers, The Max Men from Fresno. The AMA, mentioned above, can direct you to the nearest local club—or ask your hobby dealer.

Das Wiener Riesenrad Is a 20-Story Ferris Wheel

If you get a special kick out of that old and all-time favorite, the Ferris wheel, at American amusement parks and carnivals, then you'll just flat out blow your mind the first time you ride Das Wiener Riesenrad.

Das Wiener Riesenrad, rather freely translated, means "The Giant Wheel of Vienna." The venerable Ferris wheel, constructed at Vienna's Prater park in 1897, rises 209 breath-sucking, eye-popping feet above the ground. It takes 15 minutes to make a full turn, and carries 10 or more passengers in each of its 15 carriages. (The carriages bear some resemblance to small railroad cars.)

The ride is like no other you'll take in your lifetime. As you rise to the heights, there is no sound except the (very discernible)

Five Aerial Tramways: Rooms With Moving Views

The gondola sways on its fragile-looking cable, inching toward the summit. Every few hundred yards, it lurches with a heart-stopping *thump* over the massive steel towers that keep the cable in place. When the car finally reaches the station at the peak, there is not only a distinct sense of relief but also a feeling of accomplishment, even though you've done nothing more than go along for the ride.

There's an indescribable thrill to being suspended above the earth that is very much a part of a ride on an aerial tramway. It no doubt belongs in the category of cheap thrill, since you're not exactly putting your life on the line as you would if you were ski-jumping or sky-diving. Still, the thrill is very definitely there.

One of the greatest and longest of the world's tramways is in a most unlikely place—Palm Springs, Calif. Most people tend to think of Palm Springs as a desert plateau, an affluent flatland of private estates, turquoise swimming pools and lovingly tended golf courses. Yet just beyond the city limits, rugged 8,500-foot Mt. San Jacinto rises from the desert floor. One of the San Bernardino Range, this mountain is part of a wilderness area that is as remote, physically and spiritually, from the manicured precincts of Palm Springs as the high Sierras are from San Francisco's financial district.

In the early 1960s, Switzerland's Von Roll, Ltd. built a 2½-mile tramway from the foothills of the mountain, 2,000 feet above sea level, to a point just below the peak of Mt. San Jacinto. Conservationists protested vigorously, but they were overridden when it was pointed out that the summit area was a difficult 10-mile climb from the nearest road and was therefore inaccessible to all but a very few, very hardy hikers. Now, 250,000 tourists a year board the 50-passenger tramcar just off California's Route 111 for the breathtaking 15-minute lift to the summit.

At first, all you see is the tawny gold of the foothills and an occasional splotch of green below. Then the gondola begins its precipitous ascent through Chino Canyon, past awesomely inhospitable outcroppings of rock, through deep gorges, over 200-foot tall towers sunk into precarious perches that could only be reached by helicopter during construction. At the top, there is a splendid three-level glass and redwood lodge where you can get a meal and enjoy a marvelous view stretching from the Coachella Valley all the way to the Salton Sea 45 miles away. (At 235 feet *below* sea level, the Salton Sea is nearly two miles below San Jacinto's summit.) Outside the lodge, 54 miles of hiking trails, many bordered by pristine pools and waterfalls, beckon to the adventurous; in the winter, there are ski-touring and sledding as well—rental equipment is available at the lodge. The cost of the ride, round trip: $3.50 per adult, $1 per child under 12, all year. For $6.95, adults can get both a meal and a round-trip ticket.

Elsewhere in the United States, aerial tramways that are primarily used to haul skiers to snowy peaks are also used off-season to carry less athletic souls to sweeping vista points. At Lake Tahoe, astride the California-Nevada border, the gondola that normally lifts skiers to the top of a challenging expert run at Heavenly Valley stays in business through the snowless months from May to early November. It rises nearly 2,000 feet to a lodge above the lake, which itself is 6,229 feet above sea level. The 10-minute ride is expensive ($3 per adult, $1 per child under 14), but it does give you a view of one of the world's most beautiful mountain lakes, ringed by the seemingly endless cloud-scraping peaks of the Sierra. A restaurant offers lunch and dinner until the last tram departs, shortly before midnight.

Some of the best summer tram rides are in New Hampshire's great granite attic, the Presidential Mountains. The longest is at Loon Mountain, just off the all-weather, always beautiful Kancamagus Highway; it's a 7,000-foot trip aboard four-passenger gondolas. At nearby Franconia Notch, the Cannon Mountain Aerial Passenger Tramway runs one mile to the summit of Cannon. At Mount Sunapee State Park, four-passenger gondolas follow a 6,800-foot route to the 2,700-foot high summit, while two-passenger, glass-enclosed gondolas at Pinkham Notch travel 6,800 feet to the summit of Wildcat Mountain. All the tramways are open from Memorial Day or mid-June at the latest until mid-October, and resume operations during the skiing season. The tabs run from $1.50 to $2.50 for adults, generally $1 for children under 12—and children under five ride free.

–Ronald P. Kriss

ail to thee, blithe Spirit!
    Bird thou never wert,
        That from Heaven, or near it,
    Pourest thy full heart
In profuse strains
        of unpremeditated art.

Higher still and higher
    From the earth thou springest
Like a cloud of fire;
    The blue deep thou wingest,
And singing still does soar,
        and soaring ever singest. . . .

What thou art we know not;
    What is most like thee?
From rainbow clouds there flow not
    Drops so bright to see
As from thy presence
        showers a rain of melody.

What objects are the fountains
    Of thy happy strain?
What fields, or waves, or mountains?
    What shapes of sky or plain?
What love of thine own kind?
    what ignorance of pain?

—PERCY BYSSHE SHELLEY

Great Roller Coasters of America

Thank God, John Allen isn't going to retire. If you've ever grabbed a friend (or anything else) at the top of a 90-foot incline and looked down into the scoop of that first roller coaster dip, if you've ever made that inevitable lurch forward with your heart in your throat and a crazy "Wheeeeeee!" on your lips, you don't want Allen to retire either.

Allen, you see, designs and builds roller coasters—he builds more of them than anyone in the world. He was going to retire because his company, Philadelphia Toboggan, was a bit queasy about putting up so many millions for giant thrill rides. The company felt safer in concentrating on smaller, continuous-production items, unexciting things like Skee-Ball.

But he called them chicken, and double-dared them, and he's still in business. His last two *oeuvres* are in Cincinnati and Atlanta. Both are unique. "You want to give people as many sensations as possible—high speed, weightlessness, compression," says Allen. "They all work on Newton's laws."

What's unique about the Cincinnati Racer at Kings Island amusement park, Cincinnati, is a double-track ride: two coasters start together and race each other through the dips, plunges and lurches to the home finish line.

In Atlanta, the Great American Scream Machine towers over the Six Flags Over Georgia park. With a 105-foot incline, the Scream Machine is the world's highest, and its 3,800-foot run is the world's longest.

Allen believes his coasters could go faster than the 50 or 60 m.p.h. they do now, but he's against superfast rides. He feels that if you go too fast, the mind just can't keep up. Folks would finish a ride and wonder what happened—they'd miss half of it.

Since roller coasters run on gravity, their speed is related to the height of the first incline. The incline at Kings Island, for example, is 85 feet—that makes it a bit smaller and slower than the 96-foot incline Allen designed for the coaster at Elitch's Garden in Denver. And nothing we've found matches the 105-foot drop Atlanta's Great American Scream Machine makes.

In the world of roller coasters, there are claims and counterclaims. There is a claim, for example, that the roller coaster in Mexico City has a 125-foot incline, which would make it the world's highest (and among the world's fastest, depending on the angle of drop)—but this claim is unverified.

Here's a list that tells you where to find the great roller coasters of America. The dates shown indicate when the coasters were built. As Hazel Hynes, an authority on roller coasters, puts it: "Roller coasters run forever."

–Min S. Yee

Where to Find Them

1909	Willow Grove Park, Willow Grove, Pa.
1910	Ocean View Park, Norfolk, Va.
1917	Paragon Park, Nantasket Beach, Mass. (reconstruction 1932)
1919	Clementon Lake Park, Clementon, N.J.
1924	Dorney Park, Allentown, Pa.
1935	Kennywood Park, Pittsburgh, Pa.
1946	Hershey Park, Hershey, Pa.
1946	Playland Park, San Antonio, Tex.
1960	Roseland Park, Canandaigua, N.Y.
1963	Miracle Strip Park, Panama City, Fla.
1965	Elitch's Garden, Denver, Colo.
1965	Fairgrounds Park, Nashville, Tenn.
1966	Grand Strand Amusement Park, Myrtle Beach, S.C.
1967	Lake Winnepeaukah, Rossville, Ga.
1968	Bells Amusement Park, Tulsa, Okla.
1968	Lakeside Park, Salem, Va.
1972	Kings Island, Cincinnati, Ohio
1973	Six Flags Over Georgia, Atlanta, Ga.
1975	Kings Dominion, Ashland, Va. (scheduled to open)
1975	Sugar Tree, Martinsville, Va. (scheduled to open)

Moon Grazing

Fireworks in Your Eyepiece

By Trudy E. Bell

Watch a star flicker off and on as it passes behind mountains and valleys at the moon's edge.

In spite of all the stuff you hear about how things take millions of years to happen in the universe, there are astronomical events that happen in minutes or seconds, and anyone can watch them. There's plenty that an amateur—or even a complete novice—can do in astronomy that is understandable and *fun*!

Take the moon, for example. Most people are unaware that it moves from west to east in the sky. Or that it is constantly blotting out the light of stars in its path, and if you're at the right place at the right time, you can watch a star flicker off and on as it passes behind mountains at the edge of the moon.

Because of its eastward movement, the moon covers up, or *occults*, stars in its path. (Please note: "occult" is a verb meaning "to eclipse" and has absolutely nothing to do with the so-called occult sciences.) These occultations of stars by the moon are extremely pretty to watch, and there are two kinds: total occultations (relatively ordinary events) and grazing occultations (the exciting events).

You'll need a telescope of some kind —even the el cheapo $25 toystore variety will suffice for most occultations of brighter stars. Unless the star is very bright and the moon is only a crescent, binoculars are not a good bet; what you need is something with a long focal length that will yield about 100 times magnification. That way most of the moon is *out* of the field of view and you won't be bothered by its brilliance making your eyes water.

You can see a total occultation of some star from any spot on the earth on any clear night. The moon will either approach the star and finally eclipse it from view (a disappearance) or it will uncover a star and you'll see a point of light that wasn't there before twinkling at the moon's limb (a reappearance).

This is tame compared to watching a graze. During a graze you can see just the very top (northern) or bottom (southern) edge of the moon approach the star—yes, you actually *see* the moon move! It gets closer and closer, then suddenly the star blinks off as it is covered by the first mountain . . . then it blinks on again in a valley . . . off . . . on . . . at irregular intervals. This may happen as many as 10 or 12 times in the space of a few minutes depending on how rough the terrain happens to be on that section of the moon. If the star happens to be a very bright one, such as Antares or Spica, it can almost

look like fireworks in your eyepiece. And if the star is double, it may blink off and on in steps instead of all at once, making the graze a very special treat indeed.

Not everyone watching the graze will see the same thing, either, because the moon is so close to the earth, only 250,-000 miles away (that's practically kissing on a cosmic scale). If you see the star disappear behind the base of a 5,000-foot mountain on the moon's southern edge, a friend of yours a mile south of you will just catch the star blinking off and then on quickly behind its peak. In fact, someone as close to you as 50 or 100 feet can see something different if the lunar terrain is rugged enough. Anyone unfortunate enough to be five miles south of you will only see the moon come very close to the star and drift away again; someone five miles north will see a total occultation lasting perhaps 10 or 15 minutes. The region on the earth's surface from which a graze can be observed is a very narrow band—only several miles wide at most (but hundreds of miles long).

The ideal way to see a graze is to round up a bunch of friends; you all take your telescopes and travel in true expedition form to some back country road of your choice within the band of visibility. You disperse to predetermined stations perhaps 500 feet apart spanning the width of this band, so each one of you will see the graze above the moon's limb.

If you want to be really scientific about the whole thing, take along a transistor tape recorder and a battery-operated shortwave radio capable of receiving time signals broadcast by the National Bureau of Standards' station WWV or Canadian station CHU. (The frequencies of WWV signals are 2.5, 5, 10, 15, 20 and

25 megacycles; of CHU 3.33, 7.335 and 14.67 megacycles.) Such radios can be purchased for as little as $35 from discount electronics outfits, and generally have AM and FM bands as well. Set up the tape recorder so it is recording both the radio time signals and your yells of "D!" (for disappearance) and "R!" (for reappearance) and "Look at the mother *go*!" You'll wind up with a precise record of the whole event.

If you're not flush enough to afford the electronics, give a stopwatch—or even a wristwatch with a sweep second hand—to an assistant, who will immortalize your timings on paper (and who will also miss seeing the graze for him- or herself).

After the graze you'll all want to congregate to compare results, curse equipment failures and gleefully discover that you saw more events than the guy just north of you. And later you can analyze your timings to get a picture of just what the edge of the moon looked like.

How do you find out where you should be to see a graze? Write the U.S. Naval Observatory in Washington, D.C. They send out computerized predictions of these events telling you exactly what to do, and will also tell you the names and addresses of the "grazers" living near you if you request them. (There are 1,000 or more avid grazers all over the United States, some of whom may travel 200 or 300 miles for a particularly spectacular event.) The address:

Peter Espenschied
c/o U.S. Naval Observatory
Washington, D.C. 20390. □

Chasing Eclipses

Do you need an excuse to go to Australia this summer? Aside from the usual contingent of kangaroos and koala bears, in western Australia there will be a total eclipse of the sun visible on June 20. Anyone who has ever seen a total solar eclipse will tell you that the exhilaration of watching one is worth any trip.

A total solar eclipse is one of those astronomical events that can be watched only from a certain defined area. The June eclipse will affect an area of the Indian Ocean more than 168 miles wide and several thousand miles long, but it will be visible from land only on the Point d'Entrecasteaux peninsula in Australia.

Those standing on this little point of land will see the landscape slowly growing darker over a period of perhaps an hour or more as the moon majestically moves in front of the sun during the partial phases. Eighty-five percent, 90 percent, 95 percent, 99 percent total . . . the blinding crescent of the sun shrinks from both ends and breaks up into brilliant little points of light known as Baily's beads, glittering in the valleys along the moon's edge. During these last few minutes, the long faint stripes of the shadow

bands run over the ground, scurrying over people and trees and telescopes, giving one the sensation of being at the bottom of a sunlit pool with shadowy ripples.

Suddenly the landscape falls into darkness. In the sky, the soft silvery corona leaps into view, surrounding the black disk of the moon. It seems to have the delicate texture and structure of a feather, poised there motionless in the cobalt blue sky. Mercury and Venus are visible, and sometimes other planets and stars as well. The countryside is dimmed, but not with the redness of sunset or the greyness of an overcast day—rather, the landscape retains its natural colors or, if anything, is slightly greenish in hue. A breeze springs up and birds go to roost. The few minutes of totality flee all too quickly, and the unearthly spectacle ends with the lovely brilliant "diamond ring" as the first bit of sunlight reappears on the trailing limb of the moon. The shadow bands reappear and then fade as the sun swells brighter, and in another hour the landscape returns to normal once again.

The marvelous thing about eclipses is that they seem to like to choose exotic places, meaning that it's possible to get to a place you might not be able to visit under ordinary circumstances. Just since 1970, for example, there have been eclipses visible from deep in old Mexico, from above the Arctic Circle and from the Sahara Desert. And don't kid yourself—hundreds of amateur astronomers and their families flocked to all of these out-of-the-way places to gaze, awestruck, at these eclipses.

One great advantage of traveling to an exotic place when an eclipse is going to happen there is that it's *cheap*. It costs about half what you'd normally pay to get there, because innumerable amateur astronomy groups and professional tourist agencies offer special charter group rates for the people clamoring to go see the eclipse.

For the upcoming Australian eclipse there are at least three professional tourist agencies scheduling trips:

Arnold Tours, Inc.
79 Newbury St.
Boston, Mass. 02116

plans to chase the eclipse in a Boeing 727 and thus lengthen time of total eclipse to about nine minutes (on the ground totality will last something over four minutes). Tours 14 to 40 days long are being planned.

Faith Tours, Inc.
265 Sunrise Highway
Rockville Centre, N.Y. 11570

is sponsoring a 22-day tour departing June 14 that will visit half a dozen major cities in Australia as well as New Zealand, Bora Bora and Honolulu.

Mackey Travel
3 W. 57th St.
New York, N.Y. 10019

is also sponsoring a 22-day tour; it will depart on June 6 from either New York or Los Angeles and will stop en route to Australia in Fiji, New Zealand and Tahiti.

Another group going is conducting an expedition, not a tour, and is ideally suited for the serious amateur astronomer. This is Educational Expeditions International (EEI), which operates as a nonprofit center for field research, channeling public contributions to scientists in all disciplines. EEI will be sponsoring a research expedition of a small team of scientists from the Harvard College Observatory and the Smithsonian Astrophysical Observatory, led by Dr. Donald H. Menzel. They will be going to the southwestern shore of Australia for June 11 through June 22. They will select some amateur astronomers to take along, and these people will be involved in assisting the research of the professional astronomers. For further information or to apply, write EEI, 68 Leonard St., Belmont, Mass. 02178; phone (617) 489-3030.

—Trudy E. Bell

Watching Meteor Showers

Watching meteor showers is not for everyone. If you're at all impatient or preoccupied, or can't stand to be away from your normal routine, it may be maddening. Also there may be some slight physical discomfort involved, such as getting a chill or a stiff neck, because what you do in order to observe falling stars is stare up at the sky for a long period of time, maybe hours. (Sedentary people and reflective types usually do well.) Some people, like amateur astronomers and members of the American Meteor Society, surround themselves with recording devices and gaze upward with a scientific eye. One Indian tribe in New Mexico has had scouts looking up all night, every night, for over a hundred years; they have a mystical concern, though, that extends beyond mere casual appreciation for meteors. Watching meteor showers can be enjoyable even for ordinary people if you approach it right—at the very least it's a pleasant break from the late night TV Creature Feature.

Meteor showers may be watched from almost anywhere, but the farther away from cities and other earthly sources of light the better. A 15-minute drive out of town can mean the difference between seeing one meteor and a hundred. According to a zealot I know, the best place in the Americas to watch meteor showers is a certain mountain top in Zacatecas, Mexico. But try it right in your backyard if you have to—just be prepared to cope with your neighbors' windows and the corner streetlight.

What you are seeing when you watch a meteor shower are collections of space debris in orbit around the sun—rocks mostly—which are pulled into the earth's atmosphere when they pass each year. Most are burned up but portions of some, called meteorites, actually hit the earth. No one's ever been killed by one, but a Mrs. Hewlett Hodges of Alabama was injured by a glancing blow in 1954. Just how many meteors you see will vary from year to year, depending on the amount of debris, atmospheric conditions and your location. Last year, sitting on a balcony in Columbus, Ohio, I saw only 10 in four hours. However, over 100,000 actually hit the earth in Poland in 1868. More typically, when I once watched the Orionids from a field in northern Texas, I saw nearly 200 in a few hours—including several that fell from the zenith to the horizon and one that left a cloud of smoke in the sky. There's never been a "Tonight" show to equal it.

Equipment you need for meteor watching: binoculars; a star map, to orient you to the constellations so you can locate the radiant of the showers; a pinlight, so you can read the star map; a reclining lawnchair; suitable clothing, and perhaps a blanket; snacks, liquor, coffee, etc. to relieve the tedium between meteors.

If you're a photographer, it's interesting to direct a mounted camera a few degrees from the radiant and open the lens for several hours; use a high-speed black-and-white film.

—William Allen

When to Look for Meteor Showers

Showers	Locations	Dates
Lyrids	Between Vega and Hercules	April 20-22
Aquarids	Southwest of the square of Pegasus	May 4-6
Perseids	Perseus	Aug. 10-13
Draconids	Draco	Oct. 8-10
Orionids	Between Orion and Gemini	Oct. 18-23
Taurids	Between Taurus, Auriga and Perseus	Nov. 8-10
Geminids	Gemini	Dec. 10-12

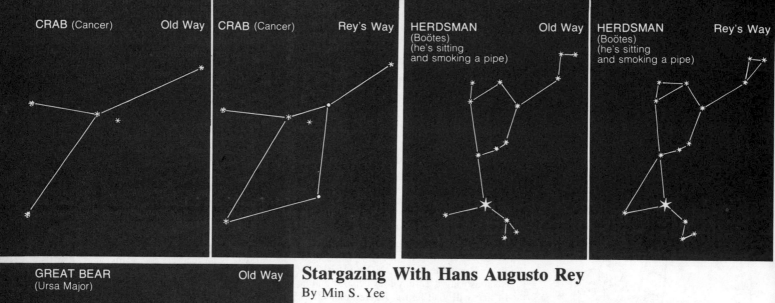

CRAB (Cancer)   Old Way

CRAB (Cancer)   Rey's Way

HERDSMAN (Boötes) (he's sitting and smoking a pipe)   Old Way

HERDSMAN (Boötes) (he's sitting and smoking a pipe)   Rey's Way

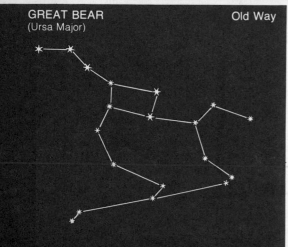

GREAT BEAR (Ursa Major)   Old Way

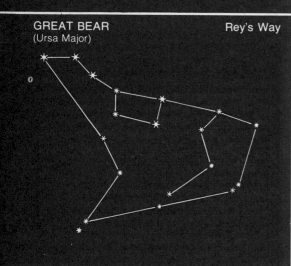

GREAT BEAR (Ursa Major)   Rey's Way

Stargazing With Hans Augusto Rey

By Min S. Yee

Hans Augusto Rey, who created the Curious George books for children, has his own unique way of graphically representing the constellations. Besides adding a warm touch to stargazing, Rey tells us how to find them and, most important, how to enjoy it all.

There have been many books written about stargazing and astronomy. Each had its own way of representing the constellations. Take, for instance, the Twins (Gemini). What you see are the stars that make up the constellation as you would see them in the sky. Some of the stars are bright. Others are faint.

The books which use allegorical drawings show the twins like this:

It's a very decorative illustration, but the drawing has very little to do with the stars. Since you can't see the drawing in the sky, it's more confusing than it is helpful.

The books which use geometrical figures represent the twins like this:

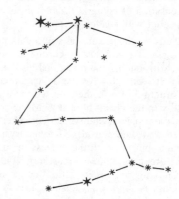

This looks a bit more rational, but it is still a hieroglyph without a meaning. Since there are no "twins," you lose track when you try to trace the constellation in the sky. Trying to remember such a shape is next to impossible.

Hans Augusto Rey, who created the Curious George books, has his own unique, graphic way of representing the

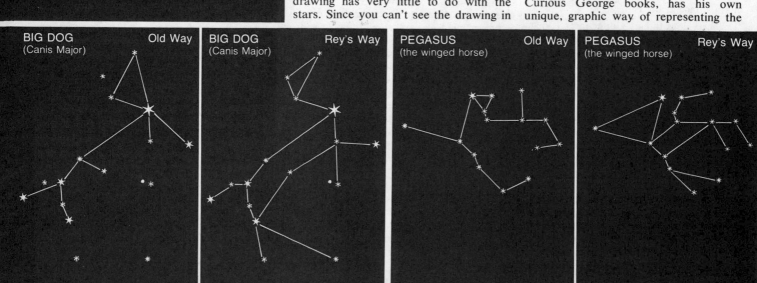

BIG DOG (Canis Major)   Old Way

BIG DOG (Canis Major)   Rey's Way

PEGASUS (the winged horse)   Old Way

PEGASUS (the winged horse)   Rey's Way

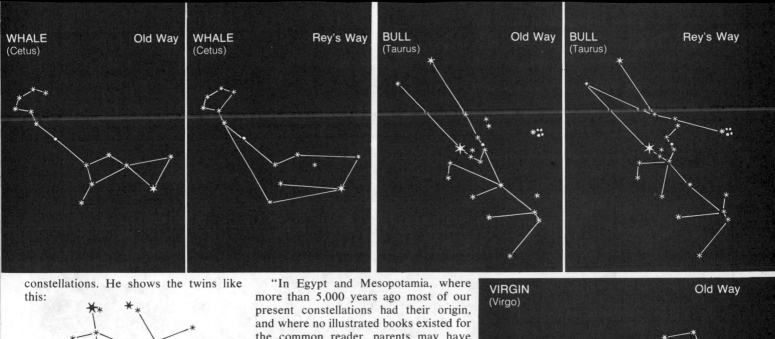

WHALE (Cetus) — Old Way   WHALE (Cetus) — Rey's Way   BULL (Taurus) — Old Way   BULL (Taurus) — Rey's Way

constellations. He shows the twins like this:

He has drawn the connecting lines between the stars with a definite shape in mind. The stars are exactly the same as the ones in the other three drawings; their positions have not been changed. But now the shape has a meaning: two matchstick men holding hands—the twins. It's much easier, with the Rey method, to trace them in the sky, first with the chart, then from memory.

"The human eye *wants* to see shapes with a meaning," writes Rey in his book, *The Stars*. "Even without intending to we see shapes of familiar things—people, animals, objects—in clouds, trees and mountains. This is more than a pastime. It is a trend deeply rooted in the human mind, and we have good reason to believe that, long before recorded history began, man first found his way among the bewildering multitude of individual stars by *seeing figures* formed by stars. Perhaps we are doing precisely what he did.

"In Egypt and Mesopotamia, where more than 5,000 years ago most of our present constellations had their origin, and where no illustrated books existed for the common reader, parents may have taught the stars to their children by drawing such figures in the sand with a stick.

"But it does not matter whether they did or didn't. In past ages, men interpreted the sky after their fashion. We today are free to do likewise. . . ."

What Rey did was to create a uniquely practical book, one intended for outdoor use. It is published by Houghton Mifflin.

The only way to really know the stars is to go out as often as you can and look at the sky. The best places are where street lights, houses or trees don't interfere with the view. In cities, the best place might be the roof of an apartment building. The countryside, especially on clear moonless nights, is ideal.

There's no need for equipment. All you have to take along is a star chart (we recommend taking Rey's book, which includes his own representations of the charts) and a flashlight so you can see the charts in the dark. Rey suggests painting the flashlight red with nail polish so the flashlight won't blind your eyes.

The important thing to leave at home is the notion that stargazing is difficult. It's not—and with Rey's book, it's grand good fun.

Star Magnitude Chart

0 and brighter   1   2   3   4   5 and fainter

VIRGIN (Virgo) — Old Way

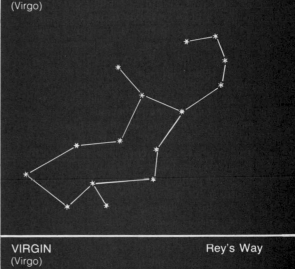

VIRGIN (Virgo) — Rey's Way

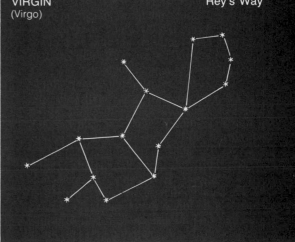

HERCULES (man with club) — Old Way

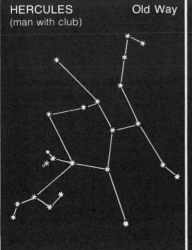

HERCULES (man with club) — Rey's Way

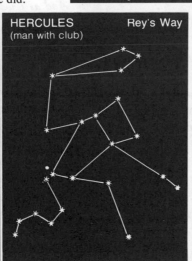

CENTAUR (Centaurus) — Old Way

CENTAUR (Centaurus) — Rey's Way

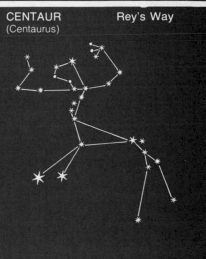

LAND

Down the blue mountain in the evening,
Moonlight was my homeward escort.
Looking back, I saw my path
Lie in levels of deep shadow . . .
I was passing the house of a friend,
When he called me from a gate of thorn
And led me twining through jade bamboos
Where green vines caught and held
        my clothes.
And I was glad of a chance to rest
And glad of a chance to drink with
        my friend. . . .
We sang to the tune of the wind in
        the pines;
And we finished our songs as the stars
        went down,
When, I being drunk and my friend
        more than happy,
Between us we forgot the world.

—LI T'AI PO

I'd like to stay in this field forever
and think of nothing but these sounds,
these smells and the tickling grasses.

—FRANK O'HARA

After rain the empty mountain
Stands autumnal in the evening
Moonlight in its groves of pine,
Stones of crystal in its brooks.
Bamboos whisper of workers bound for home,
Lotus leaves yield before a fishing boat—
And what does it matter that springtime
        has gone,
While you are here, O prince of friends?

—WANG WEI

And as I was green and carefree,
        famous among the barns
About the happy yard and singing
        as the farm was home
In the sun that is young once only,
    Time let me play and be
    Golden in the mercy of his means,
And green and golden I was
        huntsman and herdsman, the calves
Sang to my horn, the foxes on the hills
        barked clear and cold,
    And the sabbath rang slowly
In the pebbles of the holy streams.

—DYLAN THOMAS

Pack Light, Walk Slow

Here are a few suggestions about backpacking that might help you avoid the avoidable troubles.

If you have no more than a few days for walking, choose a place that's only a half day away. It's no vacation if you turn it into a frantic commute to the woods and back.

Do your homework before you go. Match your route with your own level of backpacking zeal and expertise. Be realistic. For example, if you're the kind of person who goes to the mountains for mountain scenery and you don't much care for walking for its own sake, then seek out the areas that offer something interesting (to you) on a fairly regular basis. Many first-time backpackers, expecting breathtaking views at least every hour or so, are disappointed to find themselves walking for eight or nine exhausting hours along a steeply ascending trail hemmed in by trees and generously populated with mosquitoes. Others actually seek out these routes because they discourage the crowds—and at the end of the nine hours of uninspiring walking they have not only the alpine scenery, but also solitude and the best fishing. Take your choice.

Be realistic about how athletic you are. Practically speaking, this means: how athletic have you been? People raised on sports have learned to enjoy exertion, to appreciate exhaustion as a by-product of accomplishment. Those who have never been particularly athletic find this courting of fatigue both mindless and masochistic. These two kinds of people should not go backpacking together—unless the athletic one is aware of the problem and willing to make allowances without being irritated.

Don't take too much food. If anyone tells you about the voracious appetite you develop in the wilderness, be skeptical. If you're going to the mountains and if you're not an experienced backpacker, your appetite will almost certainly be lighter than usual, at least for the first three or four days and maybe for the whole trip. A commonplace piece of advice is a good one: make your foodlist, then cut it in half. Hardly anyone heeds this advice, however, until they've trudged out of the wilderness still carrying half the food they carried in.

The best ways to prevent, or surmount, any emergency are simple to state, but require some effort and discipline to put into practice: be informed about yourself, your equipment and the country you'll be traveling in, and most important: be calm. Almost all wilderness deaths are caused by ignorance and panic, and in an emergency, nothing feeds panic like ignorance. But if you know yourself and know what you're doing, chances are you'll be able to avoid most dangerous situations in the first place.

–The Editors

On Wisconsin, Hike, Hike

Wisconsin trails are ideal for hikers. The terrain is seldom entirely flat and treeless, but trails rarely are so steep you're tempted to throw your backpack into a gorge and crawl away.

The Sparta-Elroy Trail, part of the state's bikeway system, is typical of the many fine trails in the Badger State. Located in Monroe County, just south of Interstate 80, it follows a 32-mile abandoned segment of the Chicago & Northwestern Railroad tracks. Campgrounds are spaced at intervals on gently rolling dairy farmland where the valleys are joined by a series of 32 covered trestles. Three tunnels—near Kendall, Wilton and Norwalk—add spice to the hike. Although there are no dramatic vistas, the route is scenic and Amish farms dot the area around Wilton—you'll know them by the black horse-drawn carriages parked beside barns and turning windmills.

And the natives along the trail are friendly. One farmer has a Dr. Pepper machine in his back yard (at the west end of the Norwalk tunnel), and the Wilton Lions Club offers a pancake breakfast to hikers every Sunday morning. On holidays, area civic organizations set up refreshment stands on the trail and sponsor evening barbecues and dances. Shuttles are available to get you back to your car.

If you'd rather ride than walk, you can rent bicycles in Elroy, Kendall, Wilton, Norwalk and Sparta.

Other trails are equally appealing and diverse. **The Mt. Valhalla Trail,** a 17-mile loop beginning at Mt. Valhalla, offers a view of Lake Superior and hilly, typical northern forest cover—jack pine, aspen and birch—and a chalet where the U.S. Olympic Ski Team trained.

The Flambeau Trails—11 of them in the Park Falls section of Chequamegon National Forest—were originally cut to accommodate snowmobilers, but bridges have been erected over streams and the trails can be hiked all year.

The Ahnapee Trail follows an abandoned railroad bed from Algoma to Sturgeon Bay (lots of wild apples, free for the pickin', grow along the way).

The North Country Trail, also in the Chequamegon National Forest, someday will link the Appalachian Trail in Vermont with the proposed Lewis and Clark Trail in North Dakota. It's well marked and offers something for everybody.

The 74-mile long **Park Falls-Tuscobia Trail** meanders through balsam woods, by small streams and through the wildest, most remote land in northern Wisconsin.

–Mike Michaelson

A Word About the U.S. Trail System

In 1968 Congress passed the National Trails System Act, which designated the Appalachian Trail and the Pacific Crest Trail as "National Scenic Trails." Trails to be given this designation in the future ought to have "natural, scenic or historic" qualities, Congress said. All types of trails are being considered (foot, bicycle, horse, motor, canoe or kayak), but only the Appalachian and Pacific Crest trails have so far been so designated (14 others currently are under consideration). Meanwhile, 29 trails are listed as National Recreational Trails. For more information or a complete listing write for *Proceedings of the National Symposium on Trails*, stock number 2416-0040, available for $1.25 from:

Superintendent of Documents
U.S. Government Printing Office
Washington, D.C. 20402.

Or, if you know of a trail that should be included in the National Trail System, write:

The Secretary
Bureau of Outdoor Recreation
Department of the Interior
Washington, D.C. 20402.

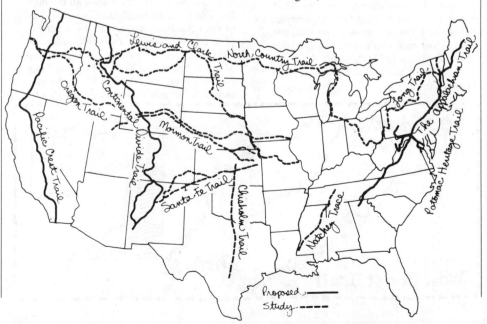

Backpacking the Coast of British Columbia

The West Coast Trail is for the backpacker who's tried everything. Your body may not be *happy* the whole time it's hiking this arduous and beautiful wilderness trail, but it certainly won't be bored.

The 35-mile trail runs along the coast of Vancouver Island (British Columbia) from the town of Port Renfrew to the fishing village of Bamfield, and why it's there at all is an interesting story. During the last century, so many hundreds of men were shipwrecked off that coast (it earned the title "Graveyard of the Pacific") that the "lifesaving trail" was built to help the men who made it to shore make it to civilization. The decaying bridges, boardwalks, ladders, telegraph wires and linemen's cabins of that original trail remain—along with the remains of 60 wrecked ships.

The trail (which should take around seven comfortable days to hike) zigzags between rain forest and beach. Muddy slides, bogs, fallen trees, tangled vegetation and rotting bridges make the forest trail varied—and grueling. But the forest's lushness, filtered green light, creeks and waterfalls atone.

When the forest becomes impassable, the trail cuts to the beach—a beautiful beach of white sands, seagulls, driftwood and tidepools squirming with life, where log-walking is the fastest means of locomotion. Hikers have put together driftwood shacks (a few quite substantial), which remain for you to inhabit as your own.

Some advice: travel light—it's no fun climbing 30-foot banks with an 80-pound pack. Be sure to bring ponchos or cagoules and gaiters for wet weather, camping stoves (you can't start a fire with wet wood), fishing rods, books on edible plants (there are lots of them) and a tide timetable. Also check to see if there have been any "red tide" reports—if not, the mussels and crabs are tasty.

You should also know that the logging roads which lead to either end of the trail are open to the public only after 6 p.m. *The West Coast Trail and Nitinat Lakes*, published by the Sierra Club of British Columbia, contains a trail map and guide. It's available from the club—1572 Monterey Ave., Victoria, B.C., Canada—as well as in some book stores.

—Susan Sands

Sleep on the Beach by the Bust of the Man Who Discovered North America

Ask almost anyone who discovered North America and the chances are that he'll say Columbus. (In fact, you're likely to get that bit of doggerel, "In Fourteen-hundred and ninety-two, Columbus sailed the ocean blue," used by children to remember the exact year.) Yet Columbus never really set foot on the mainland of North America. The actual "discovery" of North America is credited (somewhat grudgingly) to John Cabot, who in 1497 set sail from Bristol, England in a ship that was outfitted by merchants of that port after they heard of Columbus's successful voyage to the West Indies. In less than two months, Cabot crossed the Atlantic and sighted the highlands of Cape Breton Island. He came ashore at a sandy beach and under a charter granted by King Henry VII laid claim to the country. At the time, Cabot thought he was on the northeastern coast of Asia.

Today, the discoverer of North America is memorialized, after a fashion, by a highway named after him—The Cabot Trail. The trail is a 184-mile circle drive through the highlands of Cape Breton Island, which is part of the Canadian province of Nova Scotia. (The island is located about 300 miles east and 100 miles north of the easternmost tip of Maine.) The Cabot Trail is billed as "one of the most beautiful drives in North America" and each summer it attracts thousands of visitors who come to enjoy the rugged and spectacular countryside. The highlands and the coves bear a striking resemblance to the coastal regions of Scotland, and many Scots settled in Cape Breton for just that reason.

In spite of its name, at no point does the Cabot Trail touch the beach on which Cabot landed to lay claim to North America. To get to Cabot's landing, you have to leave the official trail at Cape North and drive about eight miles northeast on a secondary road. Keep a sharp lookout for a small wooden sign that points to a dirt road leading to Cabot's landing.

Unlike other historic sites, this obscure beach does not have statues, soaring phallic pillars or even an information center—there is only a solitary bust of Cabot and a plaque that modestly informs you that he landed here on June 24, 1497. A portion of the beach is a government-run park with picnic tables and fireplaces. No camping is allowed in the picnic park, but no harm is done if you take your sleeping bags and unroll them out on the beach. There also is a privately owned campsite on the shore nearby.

About half a mile south of Cabot's Landing there is a sand spit that's great for clam digging. The clams are small (about one inch long) but deliciously sweet. Dig for them at low tide.

For explorers, Sugarloaf Mountain nearby has a challenging hiking trail to its summit (1,450 feet). For the daring driver, there is a gravel road that runs over the coast mountains to Capstick and then to a small settlement called Meat Cove (presumably named by fishermen who found fresh meat and water at this cove on the northern side of the island). The road from Capstick to Meat Cove is one long series of hairpin turns, none of which are wide enough for two cars side by side. The views are thrilling, to say the least.

Information about Cape Breton can be obtained from the Department of Tourism, P.O. Box 130, Halifax, Nova Scotia, Canada, or from any Canadian Government Travel Bureau in major U.S. cities.

—David Popoff

Be a Weekend Hero

For a hobby, some of us save rare coins, stamps, comic books or old bottles. If you have the skill and the guts, however, you can join a small group of men in Southern California whose avocation is saving lives!

These are the members of the San Dimas Mountain Rescue Team, one of five such elite outfits that operates in the rugged and often treacherous terrain of the San Bernardino and San Gabriel Mountains and the Angeles National Forest.

At any time of the night or day, members of these teams can expect to be called out on a rescue mission. **HELP!!**

According to wives of team members, however, a rescue call inevitably comes either when they are just at the front door on Saturday night going out for the evening, or when the family sits down to Sunday dinner.

With the public interest in hiking, back-packing and climbing growing so rapidly, the work of these mountain rescue outfits has increased. The San Dimas team last year averaged more than a rescue a week.

Every mountain rescue team member is a volunteer. He receives only $1 a year from the county (in order to qualify for compensation or insurance payments should he be hurt while on a mission). Not only *aren't* you paid for risking your neck—you also have to put out at least $500 for personal equipment when you first join.

Each man has a belt radio page unit. When there's a report of trouble received at the Sheriff's Department, the call goes out over the page network. No matter where he is, the team member can tell from the code beep signal where he should report.

Meeting the volunteers at the rendezvous point is a truck loaded with special rescue gear—chain saw, stretchers, extra rope, spare water and fuel cans, battery lights and all the other paraphernalia they're likely to need.

Every member of the team is qualified to give first aid, and many of them have taken advanced paramedical training. Four in the San Dimas unit are certified scuba divers. (Their skills are needed when cars go "over the side" into flood-swollen rivers or into reservoirs.)

Tough and demanding as the work is, there's always a waiting list of new applicants who want to get on one of the five crack Mountain Rescue teams, and new men are on probation for the first year. Long hours of training in everything from tying knots to working with a helicopter are involved in that first year on the team, and because every team member is a reserve deputy sheriff, he must also be graduated from the Sheriff's Academy, where he takes a 56-hour course.

Mountaineering Schools

Technical rock climbing relentlessly pits the weak, uncertain human and his lonely desire against the forbidding mass and resoluteness of an isolated slab of granite. The entire episode is a lustrous experience complete with rarefied air, ungodly swinging bridges and the mad delicate ballet involved in negotiating impasses with the fingers and toes.

Rock climbing—with ropes, ice axe, pitons, nuts (metal wedges that fit into cracks), carabiners and all the other paraphernalia—is a jangling, dizzying and graceful art that gives you a profound sense of well-being and self-mastery.

Outward Bound is one organization that provides excellent "field seminars" in survival and mountaineering. Rock climbing is just one facet of the Outward Bound program—the primary emphasis is on getting to know nature, its tremendous dangers and pleasures. The usual cost for a six-week course is $500; some scholarships are available. Programs run all year and are usually booked up well in advance. The course is rough and concludes with a solo trip. The student is provided with essentials (matches, knife, rope and jacket) and must survive alone somewhere in the wilderness for three days. For more information on Outward Bound programs, write

Outward Bound, Inc.
165 W. Putnam Ave.
Greenwich, Conn. 06830.

Other schools teach the same survival and mountaineering skills but emphasize the *therapeutic* value of what they teach. A regular sensitivity workshop in alpinism (combining the technical, therapeutic and intellectual attributes of mountaineering) is offered by the excellent International Mountaineering Arts Journal School, with headquarters in a fairly unlikely spot—southern Ohio. The school offers Christmas, spring and summer sessions in the Boulder-Rocky Mountain National Park regions of Colorado. Cost is usually $250 for a six-day session—but this $250 covers the whole group (up to four people). This school provides a total mountaineering experience for the whole family at the lowest price anywhere. For more information, write:

There are similar specialized search and rescue units in almost every western state. So if you have the urge to put your outdoor skills to work to help others, contact your local county sheriff for guidance. Once you become involved with one of these rescue teams, you can expect to be challenged physically—and sometimes emotionally.

You won't receive any financial reward. You may not even get the thanks of those whose lives you save. But as Currey Robertson of the San Dimas Mountain Rescue Team says, "We're selfish, really. We have the intense satisfaction that comes of knowing you have helped, maybe even saved the life of, another human being." —*Norman Sklarewitz*

IMAJ School
c/o Eric Hoffman
Antioch Mail Room
Antioch College
Yellow Springs, Ohio 45387.

Other organizations that offer mountaineering education trips are:
Rocky Mountain Recreation Program
c/o University of Colorado
Boulder, Colo. 80302
Technical learning trips into areas of the southwestern United States.

Palisade School of Mountaineering
1398 Solano Ave.
Albany, Calif. 94706
Study trips into the Sierras in July and August.

Eastern Mountain Sports
1041 Commonwealth Ave.
Boston, Mass. 02215
Technical sessions in the East, principally in New Hampshire and the "Gunks" of northern New York State.

Recreational Equipment, Inc.
1525 11th Ave.
Seattle, Wash. 98122
Information on sessions in the Cascades and on trips into Canada.

Royal Robbins, one of the finest rock climbers in the world, usually spends his summers guiding groups on week-long trips in Yosemite; some experience is required. Robbins can be reached at his Mountain Shop, 1508 10th St., Modesto, Calif. 95354.

And for the very adventuresome, Dougal Haston offers training in the Alps. Haston is with the International School of Mountaineering in Leysin, Switzerland. For more information, write:

International School of Mountaineering
3 Lansdown Terrace Lane
Cheltenham, Gloucestershire, England.

To find out about other guide groups and mountaineering goings-on, get the two finest magazines on climbing—*Mountain* (published in London) and *Ascent* (published by the Sierra Club in California). Both are available in most backpacking and climbing equipment shops around the country.
—*Michael Charles Tobias*

To Survive...

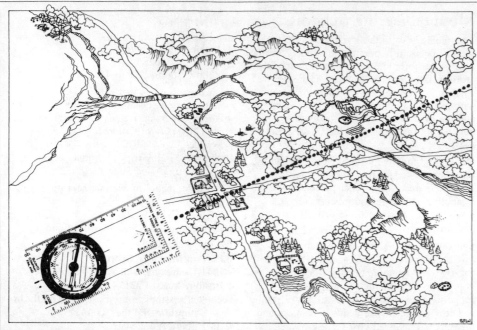

Beelining by Compass

When it comes to traversing wild country, the human species is split into two types: there are hikers, and there are walkers. Hikers are destination freaks, focusing on *getting there*; they tend to go hard and fast. For walkers, it's *being there* that's important; they want to immerse themselves in the wild rather than hustle through it.

Trails are for hikers. They follow the contours of the land, taking an efficient and elegant line-of-least-resistance across country. They shun more remote and rugged terrain.

The compass walk is for walkers, people who aren't going anyplace in particular, whose only destination is the richest possible wilderness experience. It is a way to savor a piece of landscape. It also gives you practice in basic land navigation skills that could come in handy in an emergency.

Once the map-and-compass mechanics are mastered, a compass walk is simple: you pick a random destination, find its direction on the compass, and take off in a beeline, valiantly disregarding intervening swamps, chasms, thickets and other obstacles. Once off the trail, your perceptions of the wilderness begin to change. You're no longer following another's footsteps—you're the first person in this land, picking a new route across unknown terrain. After the first painful encounters with chaparral or bottom-land undergrowth, you begin to scan for vegetation patterns, looking for slope and watershed and sunlight configurations that suggest thinned-out and open spaces for easy travel. Learn to use the network of tiny game trails that criss-crosses even the roughest land.

After awhile your pace adjusts to the texture of the country: an easy flow across mountain meadows and down the ridges, a patient plodding and weaving through the denser shrubbery. Your senses open up; you learn where to look for mushrooms, the stream bottoms where the cress is found.

It's important not to expect to get anywhere. Last time out, I had planned a brisk afternoon cattycorner walk across the Bolinas peninsula just south of the Point Reyes National Seashore. Now, this is an area I know fairly well, having walked many of the trails. I had about five hours of light and a deadline coming up. I parked the car near the beach, took a compass reading and strode off at 110°. Half an hour later, cursing and drenched with sweat, I took a break, realizing that I had made about 100 yards map distance (and maybe three times that vertically). And it was just about there that that magic of the country took over, swamping all thoughts of time and destination. A young buck broke cover off to the right, soaring in effortless bounds above the chaparral. My goofy dog tore off after him—there was no hope of his catching up, and I knew he'd get lost. I looked down, saw an unknown species of mushroom by my right foot; I smelled the rich moist crumbling loam underfoot, smelled my own sweat—and decided that it could all take care of itself and all I had to do was be there.

From then on, it was an enjoyable afternoon. I slowly wound my way to the ridge top, sat in the breeze in an oak-clump with a 50-mile view of the coast, and took another compass reading. I looked up from that compass at a piece of land that I hadn't known existed—thickly tangled, fiercely angled, absolutely impenetrable—about three square miles of raw wilderness in the midst of rolling grazing lands. One awed look, and a glance at the sinking sun, and I knew this compass walk had gone about as far as it could go. An hour later (I found a firebreak and cheated) I was sipping a beer and watching the sunset, still a little under the spell of timelessness and purposelessness that is the reward for going off-trail.

—Ned Riley

HOW TO BEELINE

First, pick out your basepoint, something easily recognizable both on the map and on the ground—a trail or stream junction, a hilltop or bridge, for example. Go to the basepoint. Now look at the map and pick any interesting-looking destination—perhaps a spring, a dam or a ruin. Draw a line between them on the map.

Get out the compass and use it to orient the map, so that the top of the sheet points north. (Do this away from the car or you'll have some crazy compass readings.) Now place the compass on the map so that the compass frame points along your line from basepoint to destination. Twist the dial until "N" on the dial matches up with the north end of the compass needle. Finally, read off the dial of the compass the bearing of your destination (the number of degrees away from north).

Stash the map. Put the compass in your hand with the needle still aligned with "N" on the dial. Start walking along the compass bearing toward your destination. Once you get the hang of it, don't bother with constantly referring to the compass. Just pick out a landmark such as a big tree that lies along your line of travel and shoot for it. When you get there, make a new sighting on a new landmark and put away the compass again.

If you get lost, or it gets late, the quickest way out is usually along your backtrail: turn the compass dial 180° to get the opposite bearing from the line you followed in.

Tree Climbing

Tree climbing has always been great fun for kids. It can be just as much fun for adults—it gives you a great feeling of exhilaration, and it's pretty good exercise, too. Pushups and pull-ups and touching toes can't loosen up those muscles any better.

Rule One in tree-climbing: pick your tree with care. Unless you want to undertake an extensive study of trees, a quick judgment of the size, spacing and strength of a tree's branches will have to suffice. By grabbing the first branch within reach and swinging from it, you should be able to determine immediately whether you've picked a winner. If the branch snaps, you haven't.

The American elm is an excellent climbing tree—it has a trunk of gray bark furrowed with broad, scaly ridges that almost form a staircase. And the American sycamore, with its many thick, sturdy branches, is always a good choice.

Other rules for successful tree climbing: never place full body weight on a single branch. Always have a hand firmly grasping a branch above. If you hear a cracking sound, move immediately to another branch, preferably one lower down. And *climb* back down the tree, don't jump—I've suffered three broken ankles in overly quick descents.

Finally, take someone with you when you go out to challenge a tree. That way, if you get stuck once you reach the upper branches, your companion can go for a ladder.

—Gail E. Barnet

Orienteering Is Running Like Hell With a Map and Compass in Your Hand

For those of you who used to love summer camp and games of capture-the-flag and steal-the-bacon, not to mention week-long treasure hunts—now there is orienteering. This relatively new sport, combining cross-country running, map reading and compass calculation, was devised in Scandinavia in 1918 and has become immensely popular there—a recent Swedish meet drew more than 10,000 participants.

Orienteering involves using a map and compass to determine the fastest path through the woods to a goal. Participants must hit specific checkpoints along the way and punch their scorecards with plastic perforators hanging at the checkpoints to prove they were there. The winner is the person who completes the course in the fastest time, having visited all the checkpoints in order.

Orienteering can be practiced as a challenging competitive sport or enjoyed as a family outing in the woods. Learning the basics of orienteering is a good way to develop the skills (and the confidence) that can be invaluable if you become lost on a hike or backpacking trip.

In competition, the orienteering course—usually set up in wooded, hilly terrain so that there is a minimum of visibility—is kept secret until the beginning of the event. At one-minute intervals, participants visit a master-map area and copy the positions of the checkpoints onto their own maps.

The paths each competitor takes to the points are left up to him—this is the point of the contest. Competitors must make spontaneous navigational analyses—and quick decisions. Will it be more efficient to run along a long, good trail or to take a shorter, more rugged path? Is that hill indicated by the contours on the map such a steep one that you'll spend more time going over it than around? Can you make better time by avoiding the swamp or just slogging straight through it?

And there is always the problem of winding up just *at* the checkpoint. Brightly-colored control markers hang at each checkpoint, but they are placed so as to be visible only from a very short distance. You could be off by only a few degrees and still miss the hidden marker.

You must become skilled in navigating in unfamiliar territory to enjoy orienteering, and to succeed at it. (Enjoyment, and the sense of personal accomplishment on reaching each checkpoint, are stressed in orienteering as much as winning.)

Conversely, *while* you're enjoying orienteering, you're developing your navigational skills. Boy Scouts have been orienteering ever since the sport was introduced here in the 1940s, and prior to 1900 map and compass games like this were practiced all over the world, particularly as military "training games."

Orienteering as such was introduced in the United States by a Swede named Bjorn Kjellstrom who, with a brother, founded Silva, Inc. Their compass-manufacturing company now makes and markets a special orienteering compass.

There are several different levels of orienteering competition—beginners run a one-mile course with easy-to-find checkpoints; the advanced or "elite" course is about five miles long, includes as many as eight to 16 checkpoints, and may involve wading knee-deep through swamps, crossing swift-moving streams and sliding down cliffs.

Orienteering has now been expanded to include cross-country ski orienteering, bike orienteering and night orienteering. In 1971 a group of orienteers formed the U.S. Orienteering Federation, which now numbers 3,000 members. Enthusiasts are hoping to make orienteering a recognized Olympic sport by 1980.

For more information on orienteering, write:

The American Orienteering Service
Highway 39 North
LaPorte, Ind. 46350

Jack Dyess, President
U.S. Orienteering Federation
c/o University of Ohio
Athens, Ohio 45701

Bjorn G.A. Kjellstrom
RR 2, Box 192
Honey Hollow Road
Pound Ridge, N.Y. 10576

–Lynn Young

Hiking the Klondike Gold Rush Trail

One of America's and Canada's most historic trails is the 1898 Gold Rush stampeder's route from Skagway, Alaska to the Canadian Klondike. Maintained by Alaska and Yukon Territory agencies, it's open to anyone who wants to hike it, from mid-June through early September. The 30-mile trail over the Chilkoot Pass is frequently steep but never really dangerous. Along the way there are glaciers, waterfalls and remnants of the Gold Rush: rusting machinery, horseshoes, old sleds.

If you're lacking in gear or companionship, an energetic guide service called Klondike Safaris (Box 1898, Skagway, Alaska 99840) will furnish guides, food, super-light packs and other camping equipment for treks over the trail—and for float trips from the end of the trail on down the Yukon River.

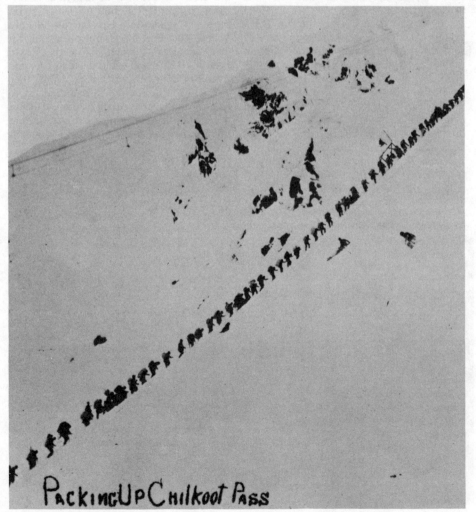

PACKING UP CHILKOOT PASS

All That Glitters Is Not Gold
It's Also Backpacking and Camping

By Peter Janssen

Modern gold prospecting has changed. Many folks are panning and digging as much for the outdoor adventure as for the hopes of finding a good-sized nugget.

For some reason, gold has not lost its charm. If large-scale commercial mining has declined, the old-timer still tries his luck with a pan. If washing gold no longer supports a man and his family, it has not stopped him from going out on weekends and vacations to pan the rivers and streams of the West.

Today, too, gold prospecting has taken on some changes. Many prospectors are panning and digging as much for the outdoor adventure of backpacking and camping as because they hope to find a good-sized nugget or a pan full of gold dust. The modern gold digger can seek the thrills of the 49er without the hardship.

He has more options as to where he can go: from the San Gabriel placers of Los Angeles to the Big Ben and Fraser River deposits of Vancouver, from the creeks and mines of central Colorado to the once-rich terrain and creeks of the Black Hills of South Dakota, from the Salmon River placers of Idaho to Northern California's Mother Lode, where Jim Marshall found "some kind of mettle" on the south fork of the American River in 1848.

One word of caution. Although half of the placer (the *a* sounds like plaster, not racer) mines of yesteryear were squatting on someone's property and the owners cared little whether an old-timer panned for gold, there is less tolerance today for trespassers. The modern prospector will encounter "no trespassing" signs. These should be respected. This doesn't mean you can't ask whether you can work a stream. You might be making some new friends. You could be invited to lunch or dinner.

Remember too that Indian reservations are not open to the public without permission.

When we write about where to go to look for gold, we're only saying that those locations are where gold has been found. Many locations have been marked by mining operations and some have been worked over a number of times. The critical point is really the prospector's own ingenuity. After all, gold is where you find it and no book can claim credit for your own discoveries.

One of the best places to look for gold is along the rivers draining California's Mother Lode country—the Feather,

Yuba and American—and in the Klamath mountains farther north. Start in towns like Rough and Ready, Angels Camp, Poker Flat—and Poverty Hill—and head into the hills.

Colorado's rivers and streams also are good bets, particularly in the Cripple Creek area west of Colorado Springs, where the mines produced $15 million worth of gold a year at the turn of the century; there is still some left. In Colorado, however, be careful to prospect along streams that rise in the mountains rather than those on the plains, unless they have some gold-bearing tributaries.

Start by placer mining, or panning for gold that has washed away from its parent vein onto the rocks and crevices of a stream bed or into the running stream itself. Gold usually is found in quartz veins in lighter colored igneous rock. The forces of nature—heat from the sun, frost, grinding ice, chemical change, even the roots of growing plants—separate it from the vein, and rain water washes it away.

Once gold is in a stream it gradually drops through the water, sinking toward the lowest point. It flows downstream in a mass of slowly moving sand and gravel; the heavier nuggets fall close to the original vein, perhaps dropping into the crevice of a submerged rock. Where it stops depends on the water current, turbulence and the nature of the stream bed.

If you find a rough nugget keep looking; you probably are close to the parent vein. (Nuggets are the real pay dirt. The largest nugget ever found in California weighed 161 pounds—worth $283,360 at the current price of $110 an ounce.) As the flow continues, smaller particles are pounded smooth into gold dust until eventually minute specks of gold flour are washed into the ocean.

Streams flow fastest in their center, so most of the gold is carried there. As the power of the stream lessens, gold drops along the way—on the inside of bars, at bends, in still water, on flood plains.

Not all gold is in running water, however. In the Sierra Nevadas, streams change course and cut deeper every year. Bars and floodplains of a former stream bed may be perched hundreds of feet above the present level. In early Gold Rush days, most miners panned running streams; some, however, looked higher, tracing earlier beds to grandfather bars half a mile up the slope.

Today, it probably would be most productive to look along the stream bed itself. The heaviest gold falls to the bottom, so look where the bottom is ragged, rough or uneven. The natural action of the stream also may concentrate gold on the sheltered sides of submerged rocks, old trees and other obstructions which form riffles. If the bottom is soft, gold particles may sink, so burrow deeply. Where the bottom is uneven, gold can drop as far as 50 feet below the stream bottom. (During the Gold Rush prospectors diverted entire rivers from their course to mine the dry stream bed; today huge commercial dredges can suck up great quantities of river bottoms, spitting out rocks and debris and occasionally even some gold.)

Along the stream bed, sample the bedrock, digging into it if it's soft. Dig through "false bedrock," dig around boul-

It's not exactly the days of '49 or the long trek up the rivers of the Klondike but it is fresh water, clean air and a few nights under the stars.

HOW TO DO IT

Panning is the basic way to find gold. The gold pan itself is your most important tool. It must be clean, smooth and free of rust.

Start by filling the pan three-fourths full of gravel. Immerse the pan in the stream, breaking apart fragments of dirt and clay with your fingers. Then rock the pan in a circular motion so the heavier gold will work its way to the bottom while the lighter—and worthless—pebbles and sand spill over the side. Panning is complete when a mixture of black sand and gold remain in the bottom of the pan. This is the mixture of "concentrate" that you keep until the end of the day when you amalgamate the gold with mercury.

If you find any "colors"—specks of gold—in the pan, there is the promise of more gold in the stream bed. Walk along the water's edge until you find rocks with cracks or crevices made under water during the winter. Pry them open with a crowbar and sweep out the dust with a whiskbroom. Look on the upstream side of large rocks and tree snags, along eddies and whirlpools. If you find any black sand or clay, pan it. Probe the stream itself by panning here and there. A prospector's rule of thumb is that if there are seven flecks of gold in the first panful, stick around and pan for more.

Panning sometimes gets tedious and offers meager rewards. Even the most experienced prospector can pan only about a yard of sand and gravel in a 10-hour day. During the Gold Rush, miners sifted 50 pans a day—and most were lucky to average $2 to $5 from them. But two partners became famous when they panned $17,000 worth of gold out of a 100-foot-long stream trench in one week.

Most serious miners now use sluice boxes to let flowing water do much of the panning for them. One of the first sluice boxes was the "Indian log," a set of notches cut into a log. Indians anchored it in the stream in the fall and pulled it out in the late spring to recover the winter's flow of gold. (If you have a favorite camp site near a placer, leave some Indian logs in the stream and return a few weeks or a season later.)

For a more sophisticated sluice, rig some baffles in a lightweight box and stagger them so water will run both around and over them. Put a napped cloth over the baffles to catch the gold. Place the head of the box so water runs in under its own power, and then set it so the "tailings" (waste material) will wash away without covering any of the gravel, sand and gold to be saved. The angle of the box is important. Too steep an angle will require too much water and could wash away the gold; too low an angle could form a sludge and generally slow things down.

Whatever method, the pan or the sluice box, the end result will be black sand containing—hopefully—gold and other heavy minerals—titanium compounds, magnetite, chromite, garnet, hematite and platinum—in a black mass. The next step is to separate the gold from the mass. Some prospectors with particularly dexterous thumbs perform this operation by hand; others rely on mercury to amalgamate the gold.

Do the amalgamation in a pan, but not the same pan you use for prospecting; it's almost impossible not to leave a thin film of mercury on the metal surface which could hide gold flecks in the future. Place a few drops of mercury in the pan and roll them around. They will race among the gold particles, gathering them into a body of mercury drops.

The next step is to separate the mercury from the gold. The easiest way is to cook the mixture on a pan over a low fire. Make sure you do this outdoors, since mercury and its fumes are *poisonous*. If the mercury is still wet, place it in a cloth sack (such as a sugar or salt sack) and squeeze it. The mercury, free from gold, will pour out.

Another method is to cut a white potato in half and carve a scoop out of one half. Place the gold and mercury mixture in this space and wire the potato back together again. Wrap the potato in aluminum foil and bake it in hot ashes for an hour. The potato will absorb the mercury and leave the gold by itself in the middle of the potato. Throw the potato away—it's poisonous.

---

ders, brush out the crevices at the edge of the stream. Clean out cracks and natural riffles, search through stumps and snags, around bridge pilings and any natural dams. Pan the inside of all bends and check the junctions of creeks that flow into the stream—if the results are good, definitely try the creek itself. Search around whirlpools rather than in their centers, since heavy gold will be thrown to the outside.

Look along the lower reaches of the river delta where tiny polished fragments may be lifted from the water to form a pay streak along the ocean shore; the current can push gold in thin black bands of sand along the shore. Several of these bands have been found along the California, Oregon and Alaska coasts. One beach near Nome, Alaska—only 200 feet wide—has produced more than $2 million in gold.

In most places you probably won't be hassled unless you pan on posted, private land. You can prospect along navigable rivers, open public land, all National Forest land—but not in National Parks and Monuments, except Death Valley. Staking a claim is a different matter; for that, consult the state bureau of mines. □

WHAT TO TAKE

Pan

Tweezers

Prospector's pick

Plastic sacks or bottles with firm lids for nuggets

Crevicing tools (spoons, prybars, icepicks)

Knife

Broom

Dustpan

Shovel

Sluicing equipment

Lightweight bucket

Magnet

Food

Matches in waterproof case

Maps

Compass

Waterproof flashlight

First aid kit with snakebite kit

Gloves

Notebook and pencil

Fire permit, if required

In addition, most prospectors need lightweight camping equipment and transportation; a four-wheel drive vehicle is ideal. Whatever the vehicle, make sure it has extra gas, water, oil and flares.

SOMETIMES YES & SOMETIMES NO

Rinaldo Daneri left Italy in 1924 to live with some relatives who were mining for gold in Downieville in the Mother Lode country. He went prospecting almost every day.

"I always picked up some here and there. It might take a week to find some. Then in 1937 I heard about a dump from an old mine that had slid into a creek. It was on Hungry Mouth Creek half a mile north of Downieville. If you knew anything about mining you knew enough to be there and dig it out. I was panning along the creek on bedrock, picking up a nugget about the size of half a walnut. It was worth more than $50 at the old price. I was kind of expecting to find something. I was happy, but not too surprised. I kept on prospecting for two more days but didn't get much. There were lots of other prospectors there so the creek got pretty well cleared out. I heard that someone took out a piece twice the size of mine, but I didn't see it. I've been prospecting ever since then, but I haven't found a nugget like that. Sometimes now I find something, sometimes I don't."

FOOL'S GOLD

It is easy to confuse iron and copper pyrites ("fool's gold") with the real thing. They glitter, but they have flat faces instead of the lumpy appearance of gold nuggets. They also are not quite as heavy as gold. Mica also glitters underwater, but small flakes will float away during panning.

REAL GOLD

WHERE TO FIND IT

California

Northern California: Klamath River between Humbug Creek and Clear Creek (also work the creeks leading in); Smith River, including the north and south forks; Trinity River between the towns of Lewiston and Willow Creek; Cottonwood Creek and Dry Creek below the city of Redding; Butte Creek and the west branch of the Feather River near Chico; Yuba River, including north and south forks between Smartville and Sierra City on the north fork and Washington on the south fork; American River, between Folsom and Emigrant Gap on the north fork and between Folsom and Placerville on the south fork; the Consumnes River tributaries near El Dorado; in the Mother Lode; the Calaveras River, Mokelumne River, Stanislaus River, Tuolumne River and numerous creeks and forks; northeast of Yosemite National Park are the Dogtown and Monoville placers and the Bodie and Aurora mines. Various gold-prospecting maps and atlases are available in the area.

Southern California: most of the workable sites are dry placers. Of these, gold has been found in beds and tributaries leading to the Colorado River, from just north of Blythe south to Yuma. Just across the border in Arizona, findings have been made in the Kofa and Tank mountains. Near Los Angeles, sites include San Gabriel Canyon, Tugunga Canyon and Placerita State Park, located north and east of Pasadena, and Holcomb Valley north of Big Bear Lake (which produced the "Gold Frenzy of 1860"). Northeast of San Diego, near Ramona, is the Ballena placer. North of the San Fernando Valley are placer sites at Piru Creek and four canyons: the Santa Felicia, San Francisquito, Bouquet and Texas.

Arizona

In the southwestern corner of Arizona, there are sites along the Gila River above and below the town of Dome. Laguna Dam, where construction revealed nuggets and a small vein, is another. There were richer diggings and pannings on the Hassayampa River and its tributaries between Prescott and Buckeye. Northeast of Phoenix: Camp Creek, Cave Creek and Sunflower Creek. North of Tucson: Canada del Oro and Alder Canyon. Southeast of Tucson: the Madera Placer and the Greaterville Placers, rich gravels that have been worked for 100 years and are still being worked. Southeastern Arizona, near Clifton: the Gold Gulch and Gila River placers. South of Prescott: placer locations called Humbug, Black Canyon, Big Bug and Hassayampa. Southeast of Hoover Dam: Eldorado Canyon, the Colorado River bars, Gold Basin and King Tut Placer.

New Mexico

Southeast of Santa Fe: between the towns of Madrid and Golden where placers caused the "Gold Rush of 1828." Southeast of Albuquerque, in Hell's Canyon, between Isleta and Chilili. North of Carrizozo, between Ancho and White Oaks at the Jicarilla and Baxter Gulch placers. The best bets seem to be near Taos. Southwest and northwest of Taos: the Rio Grande Canyon and Rio Grande Valley. Northeast of Taos: the Red River Placer and Lode, Rio Hondo placer, the Aztec Lode, Ute Creek placer and the Moreno Valley, which has been worked extensively since 1866 with results.

Nevada

Most of Nevada's gold deposits are in mines. However, there are placers southeast of Virginia City and Carson City, the Big Canyon and Artesia placers and the placer near Rawhide, which caused the "Gold Rush of 1908." In northwestern Nevada, other areas include the tributaries leading to the Humboldt

River between Lovelock and Winnemucca: Rosebud Canyon, Placeritas, Dun Glen, Barber Canyon, Rockhill, Spring Valley and Rochester. Southeast of Elko, deposits have been found near Battle Mountain at Copper Basin, in Copper Canyon, and at the Mud Springs and Tenabo Dry placers. West of Elko, people have been working four creeks: Rodeo, Lynn, Sheep and Maggie. In the northernmost part of the state, between Mountain City and Charleston, placers are at Gold Creek, Deep Creek and Tennessee Gulch.

Utah

There are a few placers but not many: Horseshoe Bend on the Green River southwest of Dinosaur National Monument; Browns Park downriver from the Flaming Gorge Dam; Bullion Canyon near Marysvale; and near Bingham Canyon southwest of Salt Lake City.

Colorado

Most of the placers are located west of an imaginary line drawn through Boulder, Denver and Colorado Springs. The entire length of the Arkansas River between Leadville and Salida, including all tributaries, have yielded gold. Farther north, on the Blue River from Dillon to Climax to Fairplay, plus tributary creeks. From Boulder to Denver west to the Rockies: between Golden and Central City, the Clear Creek and Chicago Creek placers, Russel Gulch, Empire, Gamble Gulch and Gold Hill.

Oregon

In Oregon, the best places to seek gold are either in the southwest or northeast corners of the state. Near the California border, placers are located southwest of a line from Medford to Coos Bay: many

portions of the Rogue River beginning as far upstream as Gold Hill, plus tributaries like Grave Creek, Wolf Creek; the Illinois River, particularly upstream near the California state line and creeks like Briggs and Silver. On the Pacific Ocean, there are also beach placers located near creek and river mouths between Gold Beach and Coos Bay. In the northwest, along the Burnt River and Willow Creek between Huntington and the Unity Dam; along the Snake River between Huntington and the Brownlee Dam; along the Powder River between Baker and Bourne.

Washington

Placer deposits are few but there are some located near Seattle and northeast sections of the state. North of Seattle, on the Stillaguamish River above Granite Falls, on the Skykomish River between Gold Bar and Sultan. Farther east, placer locations are on Icicle Creek and the Wenatchee River just up and downstream from Leavenworth. In the northeast, placers are found on the Similkameen River above Oroville and on the Columbia River above Northport.

British Columbia

The Fraser River discoveries started a gold rush in 1858, and placers are located from Hope (just east of Vancouver) all the way up to Prince George and beyond, a distance of more than 300 miles. The best worked tributaries to the Fraser (beginning in the south) are: Thompson River, Cayoosh Creek, Bridge

River, Quesnel River and Swift Creek, Lightning Creek, Antler Creek and Hixon Creek. To the east, on the big bend of the Columbia River, the Big Bend Placers are on the Columbia and on Goldstream and Carnes Creeks. Scattered placers are also found in the southeast corner of the province.

Idaho

Placers are scattered throughout the state. In the north, in Prichard Creek, between Prichard and Murray; at the headwaters of the St. Joe River, particularly Heller Creek (and a few miles away in Montana at Cedar Creek, Trout Creek and Oregon Gulch). Toward the central part of the state, the Salmon River Placers run for about 25 miles between White Bird and Riggins. Nearby are placers on the south fork of the Clearwater River, from upstream of Elk City (the "Rush of 1861") to Golden and Grangeville. More to the south, in the Boise Basin, placers have yielded gold in Pioneerville, Placerville, Centerville and Idaho City. There are also placers along the entire length of the Snake River as it winds its way through the state: just above Idaho Falls, below Blackfoot, between American Falls and the Minidoka Dam, below the Minidoka Dam to Burley, downstream of Twin Falls, from King Hill to Hammett, up and downstream of Grandview; and the Snake River Placers between Huntington, Ore. and the Brownlee Dam.

Montana

Most of the gold deposits in Montana are found in an imaginary triangle bounded by Great Falls, Missoula and Virginia City; within this triangle are Helena and Butte. Between Great Falls and Helena are the creeks and gulches leading to the Missoula River along the Big Belt Mountains: Trout Creek, Magpie Creek, Avalanche Creek, Whites Gulch and Confederate Gulch (a $12 million placer). Between Helena and Missoula are many more: near Lincoln, the Jay Gould mine, Lincoln Gulch and McClellan Gulch; near Marysville, Silver Creek; between Helmville and Finn, Nevada Creek and gulches Buffalo, Jefferson and Washington; southeast of Missoula, creeks Elk, Deep, Eight-Mile, Three-Mile and Henderson; between Butte and Virginia City, Fish Creek, Moose Creek and Meadow Creek and Norwegian Gulch; between Virginia City and Alder along the Ruby River, the Alder Gulch Placers and the Ruby Dredging Ground. One other area of the state should be mentioned: southwest of Butte are the Argenta Placers of Argenta and the dredgings along Grasshopper Creek between Bannack and the Beaverhead River.

Wyoming

We recommend one area south of Granite Peak in the Wind River Range: the creeks leading to the Sweetwater River near South Pass City and Atlantic City, areas called Miner's Delight, Gold Creek and Cariso Lode.

South Dakota

Most of the deposits are located between Mt. Rushmore and Deadwood in the southwestern part of the state known tragically in American history as the Black Hills. Northwest of the Homestake Mine —the largest gold mine in the United States—are the placers of Whitewood Creek and Bear Creek. West of Lead, placers are found at the headwaters of Beaver Creek and Little Spearfish Creek, located between Tinton and Cheyenne Crossing. Farther south, deposits have been found in Castle Creek and Rapid Creek upstream from Mystic and downstream to Silver City. Another location is up and downstream of Big Bend in Rapid Creek. Other locations are Spring Creek near Hill City and Rockerville, Battle Creek downstream from Keystone (the closest to Mt. Rushmore) and French Creek near Custer.

BASIC READING

Summer Gold, by John N. Dwyer. North Star Press 1971. $1.95. 72 pp.

Gold Fever and the Art of Panning and Sluicing, by Lois De Lorenze. ATR Enterprises 1970. $1.95. 70 pp.

Gold Diggers Atlas, by Robert Neil Johnson. Naturegraph 1972. $2.50. 64 pp.

Gold Finding Secrets, by Edwin P. Morgan. 1966. $2. 77 pp.

Diving and Digging for Go 1, by Mary Hill. Naturegraph 1973. $1.50. 24 pp.

Spend a Day in an Agate Pit

Mecca for pilgrimaging lapidarians is Souris, a small town in Manitoba that sits on one of the best agate fields in North America. Rockhounds come from across the United States and Canada to uncover gemstones at Souris. Many of them pitch tents in overnight campsites near the gravel pits for an early-morning start on their diggings.

The agate pits, located less than a mile east of Souris, yield some specimens found only in that area.

Agate is a broad term applied to a group of minerals of the striated chalcedony variety. At the Souris site, they come in shades of brown, gold, grey, green and black. Also found are: moss agate, which bears a dendritic imprint resembling plant life; jaspers in hues of pink, wine, yellow and brown; and agatized wood and petrified wood.

Rockhounds at the site pay an entrance fee of $1.50 per family, which limits them to 10 pounds of rocks. Larger amounts of agate are assessed at 20 cents per pound.

—Mike Michaelson

ON THE ROAD

Gold Prospecting in the Superstition Mountains

A bit more than an hour's drive east of Phoenix, Ariz., you hit the town of Apache Junction. Beyond that lie the Superstition Mountains. And there, legend has it, a lost gold mine waits for the man who will find it. On The Road again: Charles Kuralt.

Kuralt: There may be gold hidden somewhere along this rocky trail. Many a man thinks there is. Of all the legends of buried treasure in the West, the most enduring is that when old Jake Waltzer died in 1891 he carried to his grave the secret of a fabulous treasure here in the Superstition Mountains. Hundreds of prospectors are still searching for the Lost Dutchman.

As for us, we are risking sunstroke and saddle sores to get to the heart of the legend. Here's Weaver's Needle, whose shadow is supposed to fall across the opening of the Dutchman's cave. But we are in the company of nonbelievers, a genial cowboy guide named Bill Crader, and three horseloads of Forest Service experts who say there is no gold up here and never was, and who are growing weary of all these treasure hunters digging holes and starting fires and otherwise messing up the Superstition wilderness. They are waiting eagerly for Dec. 31, 1983, when, by law, all prospecting in wilderness areas will come to an end, and the search for the Lost Dutchman will be over.

Would you go searching for the Lost Dutchman?

Dennis Lund: I wouldn't now. When I first arrived here five and a half or six years ago, I was curious about it. The longer I'm here and the more I learn about the country and the geology of this area, I really don't believe that—that the Lost Dutchman Gold Mine is here. There may be a Lost Dutchman Gold Mine, but it's not in the west end of the Superstitions. I think there has been more gold packed out of people's teeth out here than they've taken out of the ground.

Kuralt: These mountains are full of holes, all right, and with only nine more years to find the Lost Dutchman, if it's ever going to

be found, frantic prospectors are abandoning one camp after another, moving on, staking new claims, trying again. Almost all of them feel they are very close, that with just a little more effort the Dutchman can be theirs. One such is Ted De Grazia, who wanders the Superstitions with his sidekick, Luke Short, grandson of the Western badman. Ted De Grazia is an artist, a dreamer and a devout prospector.

Do you think there's gold in those mountains?

Ted De Grazia: You betcha, I know there is. I've heard a lot of stories about it, and I have seen gold come out of there, too. They tell you that there isn't gold out there, but maybe they haven't gone deep enough.

Kuralt: When are you going to go back in looking for it?

De Grazia: Well, I'm going back in in a couple of weeks, and I'm going to stay there a week. And of course I'm interested in everything, Indians, legends, gold, stuff that they buried. I look for almost everything. I've found a little here and there, different things that make me want to go back and look some more, and I think that is what's good about it. There's always interest, you know. You want to go back, and back again. And I'll keep on going back till I can't go anymore, and as I look at them, I will still dream. That's the dream that I'm looking for.

Kuralt: So the dream persists. Joseph Conrad wrote: "There is something in a treasure that fastens upon a man's mind. He will pray and blaspheme and still persevere, and will curse the day he heard of it, and will let his last hour come upon him unawares, still believing that he missed it by only a foot."

Well, prospecting ends here in nine short years, and we found ourselves thinking: wonder if anybody ever looked behind that rock. But after two days on the trail behind Bill Crader, the only gold we found was in the desert flowers. Those who have searched a lifetime have found no more.

—Charles Kuralt, CBS News, On The Road in the Superstition Mountains

Digging the Past

By Barbara Sleeper

Archaeological artifacts are but random threads of man's history and prehistory, bits of a tapestry of abandoned caves, forgotten huts, ancient cities and vanished civilizations. You can find some too.

We know now that seafarers from the Mediterranean came to America long before Christopher Columbus made his journey in 1492. We also know that explorers from Greenland reached these shores and established settlements more than half a century before Columbus. Traits that could only be of African origin have been found in artifacts in eastern South America. And classical Chinese texts tell us that Hui Shen visited the west coast of the American continent in 458 A.D.

On other shores, archaeologists have found and restored parts of the walls of Babylon, x-rayed the pyramids of Gizeh, probed the depths for Atlantis, walked the streets of Pompeii, decoded the Rosetta Stone, found the Code of Hammurabi and raised the walls of Troy. These—the exquisite but random threads of man's history and prehistory—are part of a tapestry of antiquity that archaeologists have been painstakingly reweaving for the past few centuries. It is a tapestry of ancient cities and vanished civilizations, richly woven of walls, huts, stones, buildings, bones, cloth, shells, potsherds, animals and man himself. And you can become part of the reweaving of that fine fabric. No matter how great or small your discoveries, your contribution to archaeological knowledge will be important.

You need not spend years and years in college classrooms to become an archaeologist. True, the discipline of archaeology has become highly organized and refined in the past few years. But all you really need to go out and dig up clues to man's past is a sincere interest, a love of the outdoors, and the willingness to work and to learn the necessary skills. As you gain experience, you'll want to learn more about archaeology, maybe even concentrate on some particular age or location or on some special aspect, like carbon dating. You'll dig into study courses, visit sites, wander around museums.

And there's no need to sail to Byzantium. Throughout the United States there are so many different kinds of sites that you can begin almost anywhere—if you know where to look and dig. Prehistoric American Indian sites, for example, may be found in or near one of the following: caves, rock shelters, mines, quarries, mounds, shell heaps, middens, drinking water, navigable streams, swamps and fishing spots, dead or down wood areas,

workable stone locations. Just start reading local history and scanning local terrain with a critical eye.

A good place to begin your education in archaeology is with a book. *The Amateur Archaeologist's Handbook*, by Maurice Robbins and Mary B. Irving, is considered standard for the beginner. Published by the Thomas Y. Crowell Co., it costs $7.95. It tells you how to know where to look and how to excavate a site; it gives you an idea of what you'll find; it explains how to date your artifacts

and restore them. It also lists archaeological sites open to the public, archaeological societies, archaeological museums and places where you can take study courses.

However, if you'd rather begin by simply joining an expedition for a week or a month, then find a local college or university field team, or an organization like the Smithsonian Institution or Educational Expeditions International (EEI). With such groups, enthusiastic beginners and amateurs can make significant physical— and nominal financial—contributions to scientific research. (You pay your own way, plus some.)

EEI teams work with distinguished scientists and make field investigations in astronomy, ecology, marine biology and geology as well as in land and marine archaeology and anthropology. The expeditions are open to men and women of all ages, and for most, no professional qualifications are required. We've listed some on the following pages.

(Above) *The Gatecliff Shelter in Nevada's Monitor Valley produced artifacts documenting an uninterrupted sequence of occupation from 1500 B.C. to recent times, when it was occupied by Shoshone peoples. The site has yielded a 600-year-old bone bed containing remains of at least six butchered antelopes. Such bones, and pollen remains, are ecological indicators that provide an insight into ways of life that are over 2,000 years old.*

(Right) *On the western reef flats of Bermuda, in an area with white sand bottom and water clear enough to allow visibility of up to 200 feet, lies a 16th-century wreck, as yet unidentified. Expedition teams have been exploring, measuring and excavating the wreck and preparing scientific drawings of artifacts and hull structures. Simultaneously, a series of lectures are conducted ashore, covering aspects of underwater archaeology, including search operations, measuring, excavation, drawing-field preservation of artifacts and other methodology. The results of the field work will add to what is already known about trade and warfare at sea in the late 16th century.*

(Right) *North of Lake Kivu in the Virunga volcanic range in the Congo (Zaire) are two particularly active volcanoes, Nyamlagira and Nyragongo. Dr. Haroun Tazieff, who was the first to climb into the Nyragongo crater, in 1948 (and is seen here climbing Nyragongo in a black and white watch cap), has continued to lead research teams into the crater and down to a lake of molten lava 425 yards below the rim. The Nyragongo teams were part of a National Geographic Society television special in 1973 and in previous years were joined by volcanologists from France and the U.S.S.R.*

(Below) *The Okavango region of Botswana is one of the most inaccessible parts of southern Africa and is still largely unexplored. Here team members are seen crossing the Okavango River by dugout canoe. The river itself is full of crocodiles and hippopotami. The team proceeds to Kxaugwe, a community of 35 widely-scattered villages under the leadership of Nduna Shuka. There, members study the relationship of the Okavango River peoples to their environment—their ecological adaptation, their use of natural resources, their cosmology.*

(Below) *In eastern Zambia at Mbangombe is a rockshelter containing artifacts from the Iron Age and the Late and Middle Stone Ages. For some years, teams have been excavating the Kalemba rockshelter, a mountain cave which has served as a refuge for various peoples during the past 30,000 years. The cave is situated about three miles northeast of Mbangombe village, a Chewa settlement near the spot where the expedition sets up its base camp. Since 1971 excavating teams have been recovering artifacts from the site; the oldest are from the Middle Stone Age. The archaeological deposits continue to an unknown depth. Team members fly to Chipata, a small town in eastern Zambia, via Lusaka, and proceed by truck to the base camp 60 miles away. Field work is conducted within a radius of five miles from the camp. The expeditions are led by Dr. David Phillipson, who is director of the Zambia National Monuments Commission.*

Photography courtesy of Educational Expeditions International

(continued on next page)

JOIN AN EXPEDITION

Gatecliff Rockshelter, Nevada, U.S.A.	Archaeology	This is an excavation of an American Indian rockshelter with a history of occupation since 1500 B.C. Evidence of the uninterrupted sequence of occupation is supported by 15 radiocarbon dates. The shelter is a shallow cave located in the sagebrush foothills of Nevada's Monitor Valley. At an elevation of 7,000 feet, the site most recently had been occupied by the Shoshoni people. During the 1974 season workers will attempt to reach the bottom strata of the site. Preference will be given to applicants under the age of 35.	July 7-26	$590
Bison Kill, Nebraska, U.S.A.	Archaeology, paleoecology	The Bison Kill site is one where Plano-Tradition peoples once slaughtered animals for butchering. Dating back 9,000 years, the site is unique because it contains remains of species representative of four regions of the country: the Rocky Mountains, the Great Plains, the Southeast and the Southwest. Since such dated Paleo-Indian sites are quite rare, large yields at this location have made it important. Temperatures will run as high as 110°F.	July 7-24; July 27- Aug. 12	$590
Natural Trap, Wyoming, U.S.A.	Paleoecology	Team members will recover and investigate remains of recent and Pleistocene animals caught in a geological natural trap. Since Pleistocene times, an inconspicuous cave in the western foothills of the Big Horn Mountains has acted as both trap and tomb for a variety of unsuspecting vertebrates that have slipped down its 65-foot vertical shaft. Team will live in three abandoned miners' cabins near the cave. After rope instruction, members will rappel to the cave floor. Anyone not able to do 10 push-ups, deep squats or jog half a mile should not apply.	Aug. 4-24	$490
Dying Reefs, Key West to Key Largo, Fla., U.S.A.	Marine biology	The only coral reefs of the North American continent are now reported to be in jeopardy and in danger of extinction. This is a four-stage survey to determine which species are most threatened and to identify the major causes of the deterioration. Teams will use scuba techniques and wet submersibles. All participants must be scuba certified, preferably with ocean diving experience.	I & II: March, April; III: Sept. 14-28 IV: Oct. 5-19	$690
Mott Farm, Rhode Island, U.S.A.	Historical archaeology	A field school and excavation of one of the best preserved 17th-century farm sites. Adam Mott, one of the founders of Portsmouth, came to America from Cambridge, England in 1635. His 1640 farm has survived essentially intact to date. Team will excavate and identify earlier farm buildings, wells, walls, pits and privies. Though not required, experience in fields ranging from drawing and drafting to zoology, sociology and history would be helpful.	Team I: June 23- July 10 Team II: July 14-30	$490
Cinteopa, Amatlan, Mexico	Archaeology, geology, botany, history	This is an excavation of Cinteopa, the Temple of the Corn God, a center of Teotihuacan culture and the birthplace of the great Toltec king Quetzalcoatl. Previous work has led to reconstruction of the pre-Columbian agricultural calendar and its synchronology with the European calendar. An important site from Mexico's Classic Period. Spanish helpful but not required.	Sept. 1-17	$690
Carrie Bow Key, British Honduras	Marine biology	Studying and investigating the ecosystem of a barrier reef system, second in size only to the Great Barrier Reef of Australia. Wedged between the Caribbean and the Gulf of Honduras, this island is virtually untouched by pollution and lies in crystal clear waters 12 miles from the mainland. Team members who plan to scuba dive should have certification but there will be shallower, non-scuba work. Second year of study.	May 25- June 9	$925
Uaxactun, Tikal, Guatemala	Archaeology, art	Clearing and cleaning what was once the beautiful white-stuccoed exterior of a Mayan pyramid. This pre-classical pyramid once gleamed through the surrounding Peten forest, but the jungle and the rain forest have reclaimed it. Reconstruction of a permanent national monument for Guatemala.	I: June 2-15 II: June 16-29 III: June 30-July 13 IV: July 14-27	$690
Longrigg, Cumberland, England	Astro-archaeology, archaeology	Once the focal point of commerce for Neolithic and Bronze Age Man, Longrigg is an unplundered cairn complex located in a spectacular region of lakes and high peaks in the English Lake District. The team will excavate three cairns to gain more insight into the ritual and agricultural practices of groups who lived there from 1500 B.C. to 500 B.C.	Aug. 25- Sept. 14	$990
Garigliano River, Minturnae, Italy	Archaeology	This is an investigation of the ancient Roman port of Minturnae. As a waterfront trading city, Minturnae was a strategic point on the military route between Rome and southern Italy. Many important artifacts and coins have been found here, but this is the third and final season for this underwater archaeological expedition. Members must be scuba certified.	July 7-27; July 28- Aug. 17	$890
Ayios Stephanos, Skala, Greece	Archaeology	A small team of distinguished British archaeologists will continue excavating this provincial Bronze Age site located above the fertile plain of southern Laconia. Such settlements, dating from 220 B.C. to 1200 B.C., were primarily farming communities. In Mycenaean times, this site was thought to have been a promontory in the Gulf of Laconia. The team is trying to establish connections between this community and Menelaion, near Sparta. It's also theorized that this settlement had cultural relations with Crete.	I: July 10-29 II: Aug. 4-23	$890

Dates are for 1974. To learn of new expeditions in subsequent years, contact Educational Expeditions International, 68 Leonard St., Belmont, Mass., 02178.

AND SEE THE WORLD

Location	Field	Description	Dates	Fee
Deya, Majorca, Balearic Islands, Spain	Archaeology	Recent evidence found in the Cave of Son Marge indicates that man lived there with domesticated animals as early as the eighth millennium B.C., 6,000 years earlier than previously supposed. In fact, cave and rock shelters there contain one of the richest sources of new information on a prehistoric species of antelope-gazelle that until recently was thought to have died out more than 40,000 years ago. Majorca has also provided data that suggest that Stone Age man may have not only set up trade routes between the Balearic Islands and other European communities, but may also have begun what is now called the Balearic Megalithic Bronze Age Taloyotic culture, between 1900 and 1500 B.C. This is a new theory in archaeological circles and has only recently been accepted by various authorities.	I: March-April II: July 21-Aug. 9 III: Aug. 11-30 IV: Sept. 22-Oct. 5	$790
Carthage, Tunis, Tunisia	Classical art, archaeology	At the invitation of the Tunisian Government and UNESCO, this project is part of a five-year plan to excavate and preserve the ancient Punic capital of Carthage before modern civilization encroaches further. The American team is part of an international effort, including British, French and Italian expeditions. Site excavations will include the Phoenician cultural center, the ancient Punic burial ground (necropolis) and the Roman water supply system. Live in a villa on the Mediterranean.	Aug. 25-Sept. 14	$790
Ein Gev, Tiberias, Israel	Archaeology	Near Tiberias, on the east side of the Sea of Galilee, archaeologists recently uncovered a late Paleolithic hunting site with five Stone Age huts and evidence of a female burial. The expedition team this year will uncover the remains of three floors within this tiny site, plotting the distribution of artifacts and bones and assessing whether the hunters who lived in Ein Gev used the site as a major base camp or whether it served them as a brief seasonal camping spot.	I: May 19-June 1 II: June 2-15 III: June 16-29	$690
'Ubeidiya, Tiberias, Israel	Archaeology	Located on the shores of the Sea of Galilee, 'Ubeidiya was on one of the routes that early man took as he moved from Africa to Asia and Europe. This excavation will attempt to obtain samples of important microfauna and human remains. Close similarities between this site and famous East African sites like Olduvai have already been noted. Because this season is the final expedition to 'Ubeidiya, team members will participate in discussions on a final report for world archaeological review, to be published by the Israel Academy of Sciences and Humanities.	Aug. 4-24	$790
Tell Fara, Beer Sheba, Israel	Archaeology, ecology	The Negev is a majestically stark, isolated, semi-arid section of Biblical country, bisected by deep dry river beds and stately geological formations. For centuries, man has labored to maintain life in this area and his economy has fluctuated between mere subsistence and near-starvation. While the archaeological sites range from Byzantine farmsteads to living floors of the Middle Paleolithic period, this expedition will try to substantiate the presence of Neanderthal man at Tell Fara, near Beer Sheba.	July 13-27	$790
Meroë, Sudan	Archaeology	The isle of Meroë, between the Nile and Atbara rivers, was the capital of Meroitic Kings from 300 B.C. to 300 A.D. Then their culture essentially disappeared. Excavations will focus on this civilization, its dispersal, relations with Lower Egypt and its influence on contemporary African culture. Team members will camp at the site and live in mud huts.	Dec. 9-29, 1974; Dec. 10-30, 1975	$990
Pokot, Nginyang and Weiwei River, Kenya	Anthropology	The Pokot, one of the most interesting and colorful of the Kenya tribes, occupy a remote area of exceptional beauty. They are one of the few Kenya tribes still following the old traditional way of life, and anthropologists feel it is essential that a study of their culture be made before rapid development forces them to adopt cultural changes. After a short induction course in Nairobi, the team will travel to the Nginyang area north of Lake Baringo to study the pastoral Pokot. Later, the team moves to the Weiwei River to study the agricultural Pokot.	Aug. 1-17	$990
Ol Doinyo L'Engai, Kenya and Tanzania	Volcanology	Ol Doinyo L'Engai, the only active volcano in East Africa, last erupted in 1966-67. Since this eruption entirely changed the interior of the crater, mapping the new face is one of the major goals of this expedition. Participants will have a chance to collect lava from various bubbling pools in the active crater. This expedition program is subject to change in the event of a new eruption of the volcano. Experience in hiking, rock climbing, chemistry and photography would be helpful.	Sept. 13-29	$890
Total Solar Eclipse, Point d'Entre-casteaux peninsula, Australia	Astronomy	On June 20, 1974, a path of darkness will cut across the Indian Ocean from Madagascar to Tasmania, touching land only on the southwest corner of Australia. An EEI solar eclipse team will set up camp on this tip of land, with laboratories, darkroom, intra-Mercurial object search systems and polarization studies. Total eclipse at the site on the Point d'Entrecasteaux peninsula will last four minutes and 41 seconds. Team members will be able to view the full scope of the eclipse, from the partial phases about an hour beforehand, through the phenomena of Baily's Beads, totality, diamond ring and the final partial stages. Area climate is Mediterranean, with mean winter temperatures between 50° and 55°.	June 11-22	$725

Chart by Barbara Sleeper and Min S. Yee

The fee does *not* include air fare.

Taking Refuge in America

By Joel M. Vance

There are hundreds of refuges set aside for animals but also open to just plain folks — hikers, backpackers, bicyclists, campers, anyone who likes country more favored by beasts and birds than people.

The idea first hit me when I was crouched thigh-deep in marsh grass, slowly sinking out of sight in Missouri River bottom mud. "Wouldn't this be a terrific place to ride a bicycle?" I said aloud to nearly 20,000 geese.

"Oh, not here in the muck, but up there on the dike road," I amended, gesturing. You tend to get a little flaky after spending a few hours trying to look like a muskrat so you can photograph wild blue and snow geese.

At any rate, a week later, my entire family and I were on bicycles riding through the crisp splendor of an autumn day on the backroads of Squaw Creek National Waterfowl Refuge in northwest Missouri.

There were thousands of blue and snow geese overhead and gossiping in the refuge pools. Eagles circled in the bright blue sky, joined by a variety of hawks cruising on pulsing rivers of air. A covey of quail thundered out of the roadside ditch, launching my heart into a nifty fandango. Mallards sprang quacking indignantly from the rustling marsh grasses.

Bicycling is one of the virtually undiscovered activities possible in the nation's 330 federal wildlife refuges. I polled a dozen or so refuges at random across the country and found that almost no one cycles in refuges, even though most of them have roads open to bicycles. Other activities, such as hiking, nature photography and fishing are more prevalent, but still are not overused.

Refuge activities generally are daytime only. Few refuges have camping areas and few permit backpacking, but most are within a few miles of state or federal camping areas and many western refuges are near national forest or national park land where backpacking is permitted. Best bet on camping is to ask at refuge headquarters where the nearest good campground is.

The nation's cartographers have overlooked our wildlife refuges and you will not find them on many road maps. I can't imagine why — something that covers thousands of acres is, you would think, substantial enough to be mentioned by some sort of mapmaker's symbol. But Rand McNally has not discovered the sign of the flying goose — the symbol of the National Refuge System.

Only in the last few years has the NRS come to realize that wildlife and sightseers can be compatible. More and more refuges are developing hiking or auto trails. There still must be large chunks of the areas that remain off-limits to people — areas where birds nest or where especially shy wildlife can find peace and quiet. But most wildlife species have developed a tolerance for man — something that man has not accomplished with himself. Geese feed quietly beside the roads, one eye casually trained on the sightseers, the other exploring the ground for succulent grass shoots.

Most of the nation's refuges are for birds, especially waterfowl, but there are special refuges for bison, for elk and even for the Texas longhorn. There are refuges where vestiges remain of the once great prairie dog colonies. In addition to areas in the federal refuge system, there are many state-operated refuges, state and national parks, and other special sanctuaries such as national grasslands and national monuments.

The wildlife refuges are the most undiscovered. Many have been operated

over the years as closed corporations and people just are not oriented to visiting them. The lure is in the rich variety of the wildlife found there. The areas are created and managed to attract and concentrate wildlife, and the results usually are spectacular. Of the 330 national wildlife refuges, some 69 are for other than waterfowl — Port Aransas in Texas, for example, is the wintering home of the rare whooping crane. But I think the waterfowl areas are the nicest for bicycling. They are flat, making for easy pedaling. The resident wildlife is far more visible than in wooded or hilly refuges and there are generally high concentrations of waterfowl. And, though it appears to be a minor problem in refuges, I'd sooner try to outrun an irate goose than I would an irate bull bison. (Animals of uneven disposition generally are shipped to the Back Forty of the refuges, leaving only the nicest elk or buffalo you'd ever want to meet.)

A good pair of binoculars is almost a must for bird-watching in the refuges. And a book to help you identify what you're seeing is a good thing to carry in your pocket. (See the list on page 132 for recommended reference and guide books.) Refuges, since they are for the most part ecologically balanced, have a much richer tapestry of natural life than most privately-owned lands do. Not only will you see "big" things, like bison or geese, you'll see many birds, insects and other life forms that you don't normally run into.

Anyone planning a refuge tour should first pick the spot and then write ahead to find out about special regulations or restrictions. (*The Sign of the Flying Goose* contains the most complete list of refuge names and addresses.) Every area has leaflets that give a good picture of what to expect. Every refuge I polled had roads open to bicycles, but some may not. Most had hiking trails. Some refuges close during hunting season; some do not. Others close, but may issue special permission for bicycling or allow you to camp in a normally closed area if you ask or smile sweetly enough.

Always check in at area headquarters. It is common courtesy, it gains you on-the-spot, valuable information, and it could save your neck. In some cases, refuges are many thousands of acres large and it would be relatively easy to get lost in them. Malheur in southeastern Oregon, for example, has 181,000 acres. The Charles M. Russell area in Montana has a million. On Malheur, there are about 60 miles of riding road and the refuge even has bicycles for rent. But the roads are rough and rocky, and tough on narrow-tired bikes — and, it is a minimum of 30 miles between camping spots.

Most refuge roads are graveled. Some, surfaced with chat or small gravel, are quite smooth, but others are scary to ride a bike on. Some turn into bogs in wet weather. If you're traveling to the refuge by auto but plan to get out and bike around when you get there, take a quick trip over the proposed bike route in the car unless you're the adventuresome type who thrives on unpleasant surprises.

Of all the times of day, dawn is the best to be about in a refuge. Ducks whisper overhead on hurried wings. Hen mallards, talkers all, gossip in the marsh grasses. Deer stand in the open fields. Then come the geese, their wavering lines forming and reforming.

In the northern tier of states, waterfowl will be in refuges during September and, unless severe cold sets in, during October. The central part of the country can look for the peak waterfowl influx during September, October and November. Some big flocks will still be present in early December. Southern refuges will be filled with migrating birds October through January. □

AMERICA'S WILDERNESS PARKS

Refuge	Size in Acres	Nearest Town	Best time to Visit	Primary Attractions	Other Attractions	Hiking	Biking	Fishing	Camping	Nearest Good Campground
Tule Lake, Calif.	37,300	Tule-lake	Oct.	Waterfowl	Hunting	Yes	Yes	No	No	Modoc Nat. Forest, Lava Beds Nat. Monument
Lower Klamath, Calif.	21,500	Klamath Falls	Oct.	Waterfowl	Hunting	Yes	Yes	No	No	Winema Falls Nat. Forest, private at Klamath Falls
Malheur, Ore.	180,650	Burns, French-glen	May-Oct.	Swans, cranes, waterfowl	Steens Mtn. Scenic Area	Yes	Yes	Yes	Yes	On refuge, or at Frenchglen
Bear River, Utah	64,895	Brigham City	Nov.-Dec.	Whistling swans, ducks	Waterfowl hunting	Yes	Yes	No	No	Cache Nat. Forest, private at Brigham City
Red Rock Lakes, Mont.	40,300	West Yellowstone	Summer	Trumpeter swans	Hunting	Yes	Yes	Yes	Yes	On refuge, nearby resorts
Charles M. Russell, Mont.	1,000,000	Lewistown	Sept.	Prairie dogs	Boating, hunting	Yes	Yes	Yes	No	Nearby state parks
Bosque del Apache, N.M.	51,191	Socorro	Jan.-Feb.	Sand hill cranes	—	Yes	Yes	Yes	No	Socorro, Truth or Consequences
Sand Lake, S.D.	21,459	Colombia	April-Sept.	Geese, ducks	—	Yes	Yes	No	No	Aberdeen
Fort Niobrara, Neb.	19,122	Valentine	June-Oct.	Longhorns, prairie dogs	Canoeing on Niobrara River	Yes	Ask at HQ	Yes (river)	No	Big Alkali Area
Valentine, Neb.	71,516	Valentine	Oct.	Waterfowl	Spring prairie chicken booming	Yes	Yes	Yes	No	Big Alkali Area
Aransas, Tex.	54,829	Rock-port	Oct.-April	Whooping cranes	Gulf beaches	Yes	Yes	Yes	No	Goose Island State Park, Port Lavaca Park
Agassiz, Minn.	60,744	Thief River Falls	May-Nov.	Moose, waterfowl	Auto ecology tour	Yes	Yes	No	No	City park in town
Squaw Creek, Mo.	6,800	Mound City	Oct.	Snow geese	Eagles, deer	Yes	Yes	No	No	Big Lake State Park
Wichita Mountains, Okla.	59,020	Lawton	Oct.-Dec.	Elk, buffalo, longhorn	—	Yes	Yes	Yes	Yes	On refuge
Salt Plains, Okla.	32,400	Jet	Oct.-Nov.	Franklin gulls	Dig selenite crystals	Yes	Yes	Yes	No	Nearby state park
Moosehorn, Maine	22,565	Calais	May-Oct.	Birds	Seacoast, clam digging	Yes	Yes	Yes	Yes	On refuge, private at Calais
Parker River, Mass.	4,650	Newbury-port	Aug.-Oct.	Waterfowl	Swimming, ocean beach	Yes	Yes	Yes	No	Salisbury Beach Reservation
Mattamuskeet, N.C.	50,177	New Holland	Sept.-Nov.	Geese, swans, ducks	Waterfowl hunting	Yes	Yes	Yes	No	Near refuge Headquarters
Chincoteague, Va.	9,000	Chinco-teague	April-Aug.	Shore birds, free roaming ponies	—	Yes	Yes	No	Yes	On refuge, several private at Chincoteague
Carolina Sandhills, S.C.	45,000	McBee	Oct.-Jan.	Waterfowl, turkey, deer	Deer, dove hunting	Yes	Yes	Yes	No	Private at Camden
St. Marks, Fla.	65,000 plus 31,300 water	Talla-hassee	Oct.-March	Canada geese, eagles, ducks, alligators	Many historic sites	Yes	Yes	Yes	No	Newport Park Nat. Forest

BOOKS FOR REFUGE REFUGEES

Most of the available information about the nation's wildlife refuges is gathered in a pair of excellent books that should be required reading for anyone planning a tour.

The Sign of the Flying Goose, by George Laycock, discusses over a dozen refuges in detail, and also contains a list, by state, of the names and addresses of more than 200 refuges. This is the most complete listing of refuges in print. (First published in 1965 by the Natural History Press, this book was out of print for awhile and has just been reissued as a Doubleday Anchor paperback. At your bookstore for $2.95.)

Waterfowl Tomorrow, published by the Department of the Interior, gives an overall picture of the ways of waterfowl, including their breeding habits and flyways. A general work, this is a basic reference book on all species of waterfowl (published in 1964; available at U.S. Government Printing Offices for $4).

Field Guide to the Birds, by Roger Tory Peterson. *The* bird identification guide, it even lists the musical range of the call of each species. Includes 1,000 illustrations with 500 in full color. Invaluable for both beginning and highly advanced bird-watchers. (Published by Houghton-Mifflin. The 2nd revised edition in a sturdy waterproof soft cover sells for $3.95.) The *Field Guide* is sponsored by the National Audubon Society and is available from their office—950 Third Ave., New York, N.Y. 10022—as well as in most bookstores.

Ducks at a Distance, published by the Department of the Interior. This 24-page pamphlet contains color illustrations of the male and female of every duck species, with descriptive text that calls attention to the main characteristics of each (available at Government Printing Offices for 35 cents or free if you write to the Bureau of Sport Fisheries and Wildlife, Washington, D.C. 20240).

The Golden Nature Guide series. The series includes several little pocket books that will help you identify everything from moths to rocks. With simple titles like **Flowers, Mammals** and **Rocks & Minerals,** these books are available in supermarkets and on magazine racks (Western Publishing Co.; $1.25 a title).

L caught this morning morning's
    minion, kingdom of daylight's
    dauphin, dapple-dawn-drawn
    Falcon, in his riding
Of the rolling level underneath
    him steady air, and striding
High there, how he rung upon the rein
    of a wimpling swing
    swing,
In his ecstasy! then off, off forth on
    As a skate's heel sweeps smooth
    on a bow-bend:
    the hurl and gliding
    Rebuffed the big wind.
    My heart in hiding
Stirred for a bird—the achieve of,
    the mastery of the thing!

—GERARD MANLEY HOPKINS

Condor Watching

From the Condor Lookout atop 8,831-foot Mt. Pinos, near Gorman, Calif., you often see what looks like a small, black glider. It isn't. It's a bird, the largest bird in North America. The giant California Condor averages nine feet from wing tip to wing tip, and some are even larger.

Once numerous, these huge birds have dwindled to a band of a few dozen fighting for existence in the Sespe Condor Sanctuary deep in the rugged mountains of Los Padres National Forest. There they nest in caves high up in the cliffs and lay only one egg every two years.

Tales of these great birds carrying off lambs are ridiculous. They are giant vultures, eating only carrion. That's why the Condor Lookout is effective. After deer hunting season opens in August, hunters often leave the carcasses of illegally killed deer in the valleys around Mt. Pinos and the condors feed on them.

The lookout is high up in the Tehachapi Mountains but handy to Interstate 5. A sign there informs you: "The California Condor, a rare and endangered species fully protected by state law, can be seen from this point.

"Adult birds can be identified by their large size, black color with red heads and by the triangular white patches on the underside of each wing. Riding favorable air currents, the condor can soar and glide for more than an hour in steady flight."

To reach the lookout, take Interstate 5 up over the Tehachapi Mountains and just north of Gorman, head west on Frazier Mountain Road. At Lake of the Woods, detour left on Lockwood Valley Road to the Chuchupate ranger station to inquire about the state of the lookout road. The last two miles are unpaved; the road is graded once a year, but this stretch can be bad after winter storms. After you've made sure the road is passable, go back to Lake of the Woods and left on Cuddy Valley Road for an easy climb up Mt. Pinos. The views over the valleys are magnificent.

—Alan R. McElwain

Creepy Crawly Reptile Gardens

About six miles out of Rapid City, South Dakota on the road to Mt. Rushmore, you come upon a complex of buildings whose highway sign says "Reptile Gardens." If you are like most people, the thought of visiting a place of creeping, crawling creatures is enough to make your skin do some crawling of its own. Still, to miss the Gardens is to miss one of the most fascinating private collections of such critters in the world. Among the hundreds of live exhibits (obviously well fed, incidentally, and very comfortable and contented) are monster-sized Galapagos tortoises which are so tame you can pet and even ride them, alligators with which trained wrestlers grapple daily, deadly Nile crocodiles whose environs no one can invade, lizards and iguanas, dozens of venomous and harmless snakes plus exotic, brilliantly colored birds from all over the world. Many of these reptiles (the non-dangerous ones) live uncaged and untethered beneath a giant dome in which a jungle environment has been created. Visitors can walk among them and many do—some for the first time in their lives losing their fear of snakes and other reptiles.

Be Ferocious! Join a Birding Team

Bird watchers can add the excitement of ferocious competition to their otherwise placid hobby by joining one of the birding teams most likely to win the annual Christmas bird count. The winning team is the one that reports spotting the most different species within a given 175-square-mile area during a given 24 hours. More than 1,000 teams all over North America compete for the title, but birders are most likely to wind up on winning teams if they join the groups at Freeport, Tex., Cocoa, Fla. or Santa Barbara, Calif.

To get the address of the leader of the Christmas count team nearest you, or of one of the champion teams, write:

    Robert Arbib
    c/o American Birds
    National Audubon Society
    950 Third Ave.
    New York, N.Y. 10022.

Kenya's Treetops: See Rhino by Floodlight

About 100 miles from Nairobi, Kenya is Treetops, a unique experience in animal watching guaranteed to provide you with enough conversational gambits to last a lifetime.

Don't associate Kenya, on Africa's east coast, with the steaming jungles of the Congo and old Tarzan movies. Nairobi is 5,700 feet above sea level and Treetops is 6,100 feet up, so even though it's only seven degrees south of the Equator, the climate is great.

Treetops derives its name from the fact that the original, burned during the Mau Mau uprisings, actually was built in a tree. It could accommodate less than a dozen persons; Queen Elizabeth was a guest there when word came of her father's death and her ascendancy to the throne of England.

The replacement is located across the water hole. There are accommodations for 40 persons, two to each tiny room. Guests sleep on army cots; there are lavatories and wash basins at the end of each hall in the two-story building. (Bar and dining room on the second floor.)

Animal watching is done either from the roof or from the comfort of airplane seats on the veranda of each floor. The water hole that attracts the animals is about 100 yards in diameter. In the background is the majestic beauty of Mount Kenya. Salt is spread liberally around the water hole as an added inducement for game.

Tour operators make this offer: no charge if you fail to see one of the Big Three —elephant, rhino or water buffalo. At night, floodlights facing east, south and west are turned on, the better to see the game by. (The animals think it's moonlight.)

Because of the limited accommodations, visits are limited to one night. However, you always can go back to Nairobi again and start over.

(Travel agents and airlines will be glad to make arrangements for you to stay at Treetops. It is wise to make reservations well in advance.)

—Frank J. Gillespie

Cage the People, Let the Animals Run Free

The automobile has recently been recognized as a safe and mobile cage for men in zoos. Wild animals such as lions are left to roam free in large compounds and the caged humans go among them in cars. This appears to be the best situation for everyone involved: the lions can have several acres to roam and the people can see the lions as a pride in a setting approximating the natural African one. Sometimes the humans can see the lions at close range while driving past.

Two such wild animal zoos on the West Coast are Lion Country Safari on Highway 405 at Moulton Parkway, eight miles inland from Laguna Beach in southern California, and World Wildlife Safari in Winston, Ore., four miles west of the Winston-Coos Bay

Falconry Survives—with Help from Its Friends

Falconry, the sport of kings that has survived from the Middle Ages, is alive and well and flying in various parts of the United States. According to a recent survey, there are an estimated 1,225 raptors—or birds of prey—in use for falconry in this country. They are mostly short-winged hawks and the longer-winged members of the falcon family. The latter generally hunt game birds such as pheasant and water fowl, and make their dramatic strike in midair. Hawks, on the other hand, are predators of mice and other rodents. Great horned owls also are used by some falconers.

Practicing the old traditions, falconers make their own equipment, mostly from leather: the gauntlet that protects arm and forearm, the bird's swivel perch and leash, the hood that is slipped over the bird's head, and the bag which, filled with a lure of meat, is used to recall a bird to the falconer's arm. Falconers, who raise and care for their own birds, also cultivate a knowledge of veterinary medicine.

Though falconry is surviving, practitioners of the ancient sport are concerned about the decimation of predator populations that has resulted from use of DDT and widespread hunting of the birds. To help preserve predatory birds, the North American Falconers' Association has created the North American Peregrine Foundation. Designed to protect the species from extinction, the Foundation's primary goal is the establishment of a gene bank.

—Mike Michaelson

(Highway 42) exit off Interstate 5.

Though the zoos are similar in many respects, the southern California venture has many more lions, elephants and rhinoceroses on the auto pathway. However, the Oregon zoo contains Asian as well as African fauna, so go there to see a Tibetan yak.

Both zoos charge $3.25 admission for adults and $1.50-$1.75 for children. Interpretive tapes on a portable cassette recorder are given to you at the entrance. You turn the tape on and off as you pass designated animal areas. Petting parks outside the zoo enable children to touch small animals. This kind of zoo happens to provide a favorable breeding environment for animals that would otherwise not procreate in captivity. Both zoos pride themselves on breeding their own cheetah populations.

—Lee Foster

Texas Zoo for Endangered Species

The Gladys Porter Zoo in Brownsville, Tex. has the largest collection in America of animals on the endangered species list—it has 24 groups of rare animals, including a magnificent pride of cheetahs.

Importing of endangered species is, in general, rigidly prohibited by federal law; the Gladys Porter Zoo is the only one for hundreds of miles around with a license permitting it to bring in wild specimens and sell the progeny to zoos not armed with the license.

The endangered species you can see at the zoo are:

Red Uakari	Gorilla
Orangutan	Douc Langur
Cheetah	Ring-tailed Lemur
Hooded Crane	Ruffed Lemur
Leopard	Spider Monkey
Tiger	Great Indian Rhinoceros
Jaguar	Brazilian Tapir
Ocelot	Mountain Tapir
Darwin's Rhea	Parma Wallaby
Swinhoe's Pheasant	Cuban Crocodile
Barasingha Deer	Morelet's Crocodile
Pileated Gibbon	Galapagos Tortoise

—Bern Keating

Make a Dinosaur Footprint for Your Living Room

Dinosaur State Park, about five miles south of Hartford, Conn. on Highway 91, offers an unusual opportunity for you to make an authentic, historic replica—you can cast your own dinosaur footprint there! Thousands of dinosaur footprints were discovered at the site in 1966, and thanks to an inspired individual in the Connecticut State Park and Forest Commission, several of the footprints have been made available to the public for making plaster casts. (You can also see a large slab of bedrock with more than 500 dinosaur footprints in it at the park.)

Two kinds of footprints were found in the Triassic rock (180 to 225 million years old)—a few are small, six-inch-long prints made by the dinosaur Coelophysis, but most are about 12 inches long, made by an as-yet-unidentified dinosaur. On the basis of the footprints, the dinosaur probably was about 10 feet tall and up to 25 feet long. It may have been an ancestor of the giant carnivorous dinosaur Tyrannosaurus that lived nearly 100 million years later.

Scientists use the name Eubrontes for the large three-toed prints found at the park. Dinosaur tracks are relatively abundant in the red sandstones and shales of the Connecticut River Valley, but the prints at the Dinosaur State Park site are perhaps the most spectacular and best preserved. The footprints available for casting are raised prints and the cast you make looks like a real footprint. The procedure is simple: brush some oil on a clean footprint, put an iron casting hoop (supplied by an attendant) around the print and pour in your plaster mix. A 10-pound bag of plaster of Paris is required for each cast. You can buy plaster at the site. When the plaster sets, you tap it gently and then lift it off the footprint.

At home, brush on a coat of slate gray paint and set up your link to the past in a suitable place of honor. But watch out for the ignoramus who will try to use your precious pseudo-fossil as an ashtray.

–David Popoff

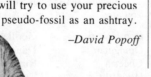

America's Ugliest Town

If you need an antidote to Disneyland cuteness and trim-lawned suburbanness, make a visit to Eckley, Pa., which prides itself on being America's Ugliest Town. Five years ago, when it was nearly as ugly as it is today, Eckley was not aware that it looked much worse than hundreds of other grim mining towns. But then fortune struck in the form of a Hollywood scout looking for a depressing background for a movie about mining life.

Paramount spent $500,000 removing television antennas, making the paved main street into a muddy dirt road, prying off aluminum porches and generally making Eckley look as it might have a century ago, the period in which the film *The Molly Maguires* is set. The residents of Eckley were mostly retired anthracite miners and their families; since the mines had been shut down for years, the town already had a natural gloominess before the movie folks turned up.

After the movie was filmed, a banker from Hazleton, 10 miles away, got the idea of making a living museum of the dreary town. Visitors could see real live coal miners living in actual coal miners' houses. Paramount agreed to leave all its stage-set "improvements" so the place could keep its aged look. A coal operator still owned the whole town and all the houses in it, and he was happy to have the banker take it off his hands for $100,000. The banker then got the state interested in taking over Eckley as a state-run exhibition, and there is now a visitors' center, with a mining museum planned. The state man on duty says: "We believe Eckley offers a rare opportunity for people to learn about a little-touched and seldom understood chapter in our history."

The visitors' center is open daily except holidays, 9 a.m. to 5 p.m., and the old miners don't protest very much about being looked at through the windows of their houses.

–Roy Bongartz

Killing Animals in Comfort and Style

An area into which good solid American efficiency has never really been incorporated is hunting, the sport involving chilled, silent men who stand rigid and bored for many hours, even for days, without getting so much as a shot at a crow or a groundhog. The "no-kill-no-pay" policy of the Y.O. Ranch, a 125-square-mile expanse of Texas cactus and sagebrush near the crossroads hamlet of Mountain Home, has put an end to such wastes of time. All the many thousands of animals who live here are separated by species into 75 fenced-off pastures, and all you have to do is choose the kind you want and have a guide drive you out to shoot it. If you don't own a gun they'll lend you one.

Most of the animals are exotic breeds from foreign lands and thus do not come under hunting laws, so there are no seasons or licenses to worry about. The guide will take you right up to a herd of, say, Indian Axis deer, and you can knock off any one of them you like. The price for the Axis is $1,000. Other beasts come cheaper: an Indian blackbuck antelope is $750, a Corsican ram is $300, a European fallow deer is $400, a North African aoudad sheep is $750.

The hunting is so efficient that many visitors order a second, a third or a fourth target before lunch, and run up their bills into the thousands of dollars. When they have killed enough animals they can retire to a rustic bunkhouse (rooms cost $20 a night, including meals), or to a restored early post office or stagecoach stop (more luxurious, at $30 a night). Women and children are welcome to kill as long as they're big or strong enough to hold a hunting rifle. For reservations write Mrs. Anne Snow, Y.O. Ranch, P.O. Box 222, Mountain Home, Tex. 78050; phone (512) 640-3222.

–Roy Bongartz

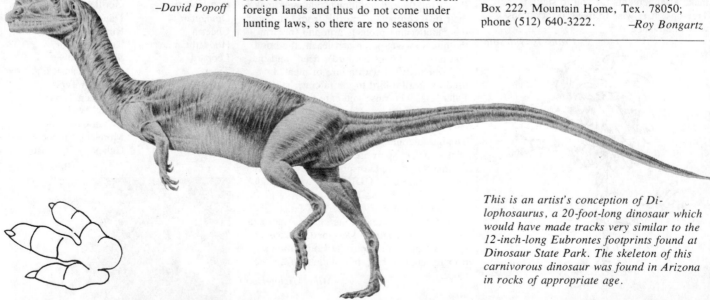

This is an artist's conception of Dilophosaurus, a 20-foot-long dinosaur which would have made tracks very similar to the 12-inch-long Eubrontes footprints found at Dinosaur State Park. The skeleton of this carnivorous dinosaur was found in Arizona in rocks of appropriate age.

How to Become a Blacksmith

Smithing is for innovative, experimental, sensible, moderately coordinated people who don't mind a few minor burns now and then, and who are willing, at first, to tolerate the blisters that eventually turn into calluses. Just a couple of hours of forging will be enough to convince you that you love smithing—or that you hate it. The iron is right there, red hot (or, better, light yellow), and it will only remain in that malleable condition for a few seconds—you have to throw your whole body into motion immediately and develop the strong, sensitive rhythm that will shape that hunk of metal into an object.

Most professional blacksmiths still around today are older men; often they're semi-retired and wary of people who claim they want to become smiths. But if you can find a blacksmith and convince him you really want to learn, you can get valuable instruction on how to forge weld, how to handle fires, how to select an anvil and tools. Watching a professional smith in action and asking questions is the best way to learn the art.

Forges may be made, or bought from old smiths' shops. (Note: most portable ones are insufficient for doing anything much more complicated than horseshoes.) If you really want to be an antiquarian you can build yourself an 1840s-style forge with bellows. Professional smiths can provide you with plans for building your own forge.

Besides a forge, the beginning blacksmith needs:

An anvil. Most old ones are either hopelessly mangled or made of cheap cast iron—save your money and get a new one from Sweden or Germany. A beat-up anvil's scars show up on the other side of whatever you're forging.

Cross pein hammers in several sizes. Rasp yourself a grip in the handle of each one,

making sure to get all the varnish off so your hand won't slip.

An electric welder, electric grinder and electric drill press.

Centerpunch, ruler, tape measure, square, level, dividers, calipers, leather gloves, and soapstone for making lines on iron (this last is available from gas welding supply stores).

You'll also need to locate some pieces of stump or some old bridge or dock timbers to make yourself an anvil block with. Your anvil, on the block, is the correct height if your knuckles are level with the anvil face when you're standing relaxed.

There are a number of professional and amateur artsmiths in the country who belong to the Artist Blacksmith Association of North America. Through their organization you can meet other smiths; they hold an annual convention and also publish a newsletter. For information, write:

ABANA
873 Spring St.
Atlanta, Ga. 30308.

You might also want to get a copy of *The Art of Blacksmithing*, by Alex W. Bealer (Funk & Wagnalls, $10.95)—this book can teach you a lot.
–Ivan Bailey

Ghost Towns: the Past Recaptured

After the Gold Rush of 1849, countless new settlements sprang up in the western United States; they began as rude camps, turned into towns and then grew into cities. One newcomer to Bovard, Nev. in the late 19th century claims that he saw nothing but four or five tents the morning he arrived; when he returned in the afternoon, there was a thriving Main Street a full mile long.

The mining towns lasted only as long as the ore did. In some places—Butte, Mont., for example—they still mine ore; other towns survived by turning to industry or agriculture. But the slopes and foothills of the

Sierra Nevada (where two of the greatest ore deposits were discovered) are littered with ghost towns.

The first great strike was made at Sutter's Mill on the American River in the foothills of the Sierras. This was the heart of the Mother Lode country—a deposit of gold nearly 200 miles long was discovered. Colombia, now a California state park, is a good restoration of a deserted mining camp; it's 3½ miles down a paved road from Sonora, Calif. Volcano, which was among the very first camps in the Mother Lode country, is a ghost town now too. It's just southeast of Sacramento, Calif., about two miles down a road off Route 88 at Pine Grove.

The second major strike in the West was made in west-central Nevada—the Comstock Lode yielded mainly silver, but also some gold. The largest settlement in the area was Virginia City; it once had a population of 30,000 and supported no fewer than 110 saloons. Today, barely 700 people live in Virginia City, and it retains the look of a century-old mining town with its old wooden mansions, saloons, opera house and mines. It lies off Nevada Route 17, northeast of Carson City, the state capital.

Many ghost towns are situated in uninviting no-man's lands. Bodie, Calif., another state park, lies on the eastern ridge of the Sierras 2½ miles from the Nevada border and north of Mono Lake; to get there you must drive 13 miles down a dusty, unpaved road off Interstate 395. Bodie mushroomed into a mini-metropolis of 13,000 people after gold was discovered there in 1859. More than $100 million in top-grade ore was taken from 25 mines, and in its heyday the town had 47 saloons, 15 brothels and even 13 law firms. Bodie claimed it had the wickedest men, the widest streets and the worst climate in the West. (The weather is truly merciless; winter snows literally bury the site in 20-foot drifts.) Today the 5 percent of the town that escaped fire and decay is carefully preserved in a state of "arrested deterioration" by California's Division of Beaches and Parks.

Some of the towns may prove to be disappointments—you may see nothing more than a plaque, a crumbling mine shaft that is too dangerous to explore, some rotting pine planks where houses and shops once stood. Still, even these sites are as rich in history as they once were in ore, and their dusty ruins haunt us with reminders of an America that will never return.

Before setting out for a ghost town, check local tourist information centers or state historical societies. Detailed information on ghost towns can be obtained from:

Nevada Department of Economic Development
c/o State Capitol
Carson City, Nev. 89701

California Office of Tourism
and Visitor Services
1400 10th St.
Sacramento, Calif. 95814
–Evan Kriss

Skiing in the South

By Charles Kuralt

Yes, they do ski on grits and plastic in the South, but they also ski on real snow, even in Alabama.

The Blue Ridge mountains are not exactly the Austrian Alps, but you wouldn't know it at a glance these days. A-frames and Swiss chalets outnumber mountaineers' log cabins in the North Carolina mountains, MGs with ski racks are replacing pickup trucks on the roads, and fashions are shifting rapidly from overalls and clodhoppers to stretch pants and ski boots. The ski boom is on, and while this is a source of some regret to those of us who remember the Blue Ridge mountains and the Smokies as they were, we may as well sigh and get on to detailing things as they are.

In North Carolina

Beech Mountain, off N.C. 194 near Banner Elk, N.C. Three triple chairlifts, two double chairlifts, a gondola, assorted J-bars and rope tows, and 10 slopes and trails, all of which end up at a pleasant village at the bottom of the mountain. Beech Mountain even had a bar until the sheriff raided the joint last spring. (Bring Your Own Liquor everywhere in North Carolina, in a flask if you must, but local etiquette calls for a brown paper bag.) Beech looks like Bavaria and, to repeat, is not, but its slopes are nothing to sneer at. Its parking lot is higher than the top of most New England mountains.

Sugar Mountain, on N.C. 184, about three miles east of Banner Elk, N.C. The second best place to ski in the South, with the greatest vertical drop, 1,200 feet, 11 slopes, indoor tennis, heated pool, pretty good restaurant.

Cataloochee, off U.S. 19 at Maggie Valley, N.C. You'll have to stay down in the valley, because there is no lodging on the mountain. Nice slopes.

Seven Devils, on N.C. 105, 10 miles west of Boone, N.C. Five slopes, two double chairlifts, still more of those alpine chalets to rent.

Applachian Mountain, between Boone and Blowing Rock, N.C. Appalachian has a 2,700-foot-long ski trail about 25 feet wide for hot-doggers. What it lacks in vertical drop it makes up for in pine trees whizzing past.

High Meadows, at Roaring Gap, N.C. Has a pleasant inn with a good restaurant. A good place to learn.

Hound Ears, west of Boone, N.C. on N.C. 105. An even better place to learn. A wonderful lodge and still *more* Austrian scenery, of which the most scenic is Kitty Falger, Innsbruck-born instructor.

Mill Ridge, near Hound Ears on N.C. 105. Beginner's and intermediate slopes and the inevitable chalets.

Illustration by Karl Nicholason

Wolf Laurel, just north of Asheville, N.C. on U.S. 23. Five slopes, and ice skating and tobogganing to boot.

In Virginia

Bryce Mountain, on Va. 263 near the village of Basye, Va. Four slopes, bar, heated pool.

Cascade, at Fancy Gap, Va. Three slopes.

Homestead, at Hot Springs, Va. Oldest ski resort in the region, opened in 1958. A fancy place with seven slopes and a *750-room* hotel; ice skating, indoor pool and all that.

Massanutten, east of Harrisonburg, Va. on U.S. 33. Eight slopes, and they're building more. Easy to get to from Interstate 81.

Mountain Run, on Route 730 north of New Market, Va. Four slopes, and they're also building.

In West Virginia

Snowshoe, at Mace, W. Va. This is going to be the biggest deal in the South someday, if the gasoline shortage doesn't curtail skiing. Ten slopes already, with a 1,500-foot vertical drop planned, not to mention a *1,200-room* hotel, also as yet unbuilt. With a 150-inch annual snowfall, Snowshoe is one of the few Southern resorts beckoning cross-country skiiers.

Canaan Valley, at Davis, W. Va. Rela-

tively uncrowded, with 11 slopes and trails. Offers a nursery for skiing mamas and papas.

In Tennessee

Gatlinburg. This is a little unusual. You reach the ski area via aerial tramway from the middle of Gatlinburg, Tenn., which has become a pretty big city. After that, you take the chairlifts to one of four slopes.

Deerhead, at Dunlap, Tenn., about 30 miles north of Chattanooga. Two winter slopes and a plastic one for skinning yourself up in the summer.

Renegade, at Crossville, Tenn. Five slopes, 500-foot drop.

In Georgia

Sky Valley, on Route 406 north of Dillard, Ga. Two slopes, for beginners.

In (believe it or not) Alabama

Cloudmont, three miles south of Mentone, Ala. There's a 1,000-foot slope with a rope tow for when it's cold enough to make snow, and a poly-snow slope for when it's not.

Plastic mountains are springing up all over the South, but at none of the slopes above do they ski primarily on plastic, or on grits—it's all snow. Many Southern resorts offer night-time skiing, and most have good instructors who use short-ski teaching methods. □

Simplify, Simplify! on Cross-Country Skis

There are those who quite flatly label cross-country skiing as *the only* winter sport worth pursuing. They have a point. It is difficult indeed to imagine another activity involving snow and ice that is so satisfactory in so many ways—it is economically sound, ecologically pure, a magnificently strenuous physical undertaking and a soul-soothing aesthetic experience. There is nothing quite like it and, though it hasn't yet overtaken the glamour-game of downhill skiing with its tight sexy pants on the slopes and its warm sexy après-ski drinks in the lodge, it has attracted thousands of new advocates in the past several years. In fact, G. H. Bass & Co., of Maine, imported a couple of hundred pairs of the lovely, light wooden touring skis in the winter of 1969-70 for distribution all over the United States. One year later, they were swamped with orders for tens of thousands of pairs.

The contrast between cross-country and downhill skiing is extreme. Start with the costs: it is difficult to appear fashionably (or efficiently) on the slopes of even your average sort of downhill ski resort without first spending about $400 for equipment, clothes and sundries. (It has been said that an African safari and alpine skiing are not so far apart in high cost.) But a beginner in cross-country skiing can fix himself up with skis, boots and poles—all he really needs—for less than $80. Since socializing is not an important part of cross-country skiing, any old clothes will do—Levi's, army jackets, whatever.

Cross-country skiing is not only cheap, it is easy—anyone who can walk can ski tour; there is none of the exasperating, ego-bludgeoning, $15-an-hour instructional stuff that is so necessary in learning to ski alpine style. The average semi-coordinated, middle-aged, overweight American person who has never been on skis before can learn to ski tour in a matter of a few hours. And anyone who likes to walk will love ski touring, because the emphasis is on the touring, rather than the skiing, even though there is a great sense of grace and speed in the splendid, gliding strides.

The touring technique is the oldest in skiing (Norwegians were doing it 4,000 years ago)—it is a sort of sliding walk on those long light skis. You plant the pole into the snow, shift your weight to the opposite foot and push ahead (this is on level land). To climb hills, a simple herringbone walk—ski tips pointed outward, edges dug in—or a sidestep will suffice nicely. In going downhill, a novice must learn—first!—how to stop. The classic, ancient and honorable snow plow—ski-points pigeon-toed inward—is the most common way of stopping. But John Caldwell, former U.S. Olympic skier and lately American team coach, points out that the most foolproof way to halt a downhill plunge is to fall down. "It never fails," he says, "and the chances are you won't get hurt even a little bit if you do it *soon* enough!"

Other instructors also advise beginners to slow themselves down by reaching out and grabbing brush or branches—a blatantly graceless technique, but very effective.

You can ski tour anywhere—even in city parks or suburban back yards. Golf courses are perfect, and the unmanicured countryside always beckons. And, consider this—in almost every case, the agitated farmer who habitually refuses access to snarling, air-fouling cavalcades of snowmobiles will smile and welcome the gentle cross-country skier to his woods and pastures.

In cross-country skiing there is none of the maddening standing in line, shifting from ski to ski, waiting for the next lift to the top. Cross-country skiing is *safer* than downhill skiing because the boot is a pliable thing. And cross-country skiing is *friendly*. There is almost instant equality, and thus togetherness, because it is almost impossible *not* to master the art immediately. There is no pecking order in ski touring, either. At the typical alpine ski resort, no one is more derided than the "brown baggers," people who bring their own lunches—they often wind up miserably munching their sandwiches in some corner or cellar of the lodge, humiliated by their lack of big-spender wherewithal. But the cross-country skier finds it both natural and comfortable to carry his own lunch in a bag and his own wine in a bottle and to grab his nourishment somewhere sitting on a log.

State recreation departments in all skiing states, including those in the Midwest, have brochures on, or at least lists of, cross-country ski groups or resorts that are particularly good. Another good source of information on the sport is:

Ski Touring Council, Inc.
342 Madison Ave., Room 727
New York, N.Y. 10017

The Council has a guide to trails in the United States and Canada for $1, and can give you information on where to get lessons and on good places to go cross-country skiing.

–William Johnson

Barrel Staving in Vermont

Don't head for Niagara Falls with that old barrel. Knock it apart and use a pair of the staves to slide down a hill of snow on. That's exactly the use to which some of our pioneer forebears put old cider keg slats —with a couple of jar rubbers to hold them in place. Now, barrel staving has been resurrected as a "new" snow sport, particularly around Killington, Vt.

It started as a joke when, in 1961, the founder of Killington Ski Area appeared in a costume parade with cider barrel slats strapped to his feet. Somehow, the novelty caught on and within four years a small local company was producing barrel stave skis and Killington was sponsoring the first World Barrel Staves Championship Race. Fifty-eight stavers entered—the winner was a young girl. Although the company has stopped manufacturing stave skis, they are still available in Killington for sale or rent, and each spring, when the snow is right and spirits are high and carefree, the sport comes alive.

Commercially-made stave skis are the solid oak slats used for making whiskey barrels, with the bottoms painted with plastic and steel edges and cable bindings added. You could visit your local cooper, get some staves and make your own skis, using straps and buckles from a surplus or auto supply store and one-inch bands cut from a car tire inner tube. Sand and finish with varnish or oil.

Up Killington way, they say the stave is easier to use on pre-season or late-season corn snow than a conventional ski and is especially effective in deep powder snow, generally considered tricky even by expert skiers. Less than three feet long, the stave is convex—it is rounded both lengthwise and crosswise. Only the center section, or less than 20 percent of the ski, comes in contact with the snow. If you can twist, you can turn on barrel staves—and this quick-turning feature makes them ideal for wooded areas. Novice stavers quickly acquire basic skills and brimming confidence.

–Mike Michaelson

A Guide to Hard-Core Skiing in British Columbia

By Patrick W. Lowe

If fast, hard, mindbusting skiing is more important to you than fashion and fireside chats — go to western Canada.

Skiing used to be a genuine kick. It started early, with bummed doughnut halves and watery hot chocolate; and it ended late, with cold fingers and hot wine. It was sex, only better.

It was a good — kind of austere — feeling, being "hard-core." We didn't care if the Nitty Gritty Dirt Band was playing at the foot of Ajax, or if the San Moritz Tavern had the best pepper steak in Vail. We just came down off the hill, fried up a couple of eggs, got wasted and went to bed.

It's different now: GLM, and *No Jumping* signs, a legion of pink-cheeked little turkeys traversing or "swishing" the baby slope, and color-coordinated flatland darlings who keep coming out of their "binders." Most of what used to be skiing time seems now to be spent lurching along behind an endless army of LTD wagons, or waiting in hour-long lift lines once you get to the slopes. The question is, are we to be forever stuck with this kind of bullshit?

Not necessarily. Just across the Canadian border is British Columbia. A place where conditions are consistently good, and hassles consistently absent.

Vancouver, British Columbia is the city that's everything San Francisco wishes it was. And there, 10 minutes from the center of the city, is Grouse Mountain. Drizzly and not particularly cold, from the base it hardly looks like a ski area. But 2,700 vertical feet up via huge aerial tram, Grouse comes alive. Four double chairs and two T-bars (and a four-rope-tow beginners' corral) service this unique mountain day and night, from early December into May. It's *plenty* cold up top, with optimum visibility of maybe an arm's length. But the snow is deep, squeaky and easy to turn in; and there are a few pretty challenging runs — runs hairy enough for the Canadian Olympic Team, which holds workouts there.

All in all, though, Grouse's good skiing has to take a back seat to its atmosphere of fair-haired English charm, hot brandied cider, and city lights through the fog. Why, it's enough to make your poles stand straight up just thinking about it!

Seventy-five miles north of Vancouver is Whistler Mountain. Boasting a 4,280-foot vertical rise, Whistler is the giant among North American ski areas. The stats speak for themselves: a gondola, five double chairs, two T-bars and aerial transportation to the peak of Whistler Bowl, Fitzsimmons Glacier or any of several other nearby permanent snowfields in Garibaldi Park.

Here, sport skiers as well as wildmen can find their own kind of euphoria, from hip-deep powder bowls to winding, cat-groomed trails up to seven miles long. Whistler's season runs from early November through July. Winter is a monumental exercise in frostbite resistance (when I was there, it was just under zero on top, with a 30 m.p.h. wind), and summer (when you can comfortably ski in a work shirt and jeans) offers super moguls and corn snow.

In fact, the International Acrobatic, Aerial and Hot Dog Ski Championships are to be held at Whistler, with Toni Sailer, Nancy Greene and Wayne Wong coming in to supervise three 10-day junior racing camps during June and July.

Get down with this: imagine yourself cruising up 7,000 feet in a jet-powered helicopter. You point yourself almost a straight mile down, and then you start tracking through the deep powder above the timberline. You jet through the moguls; you do your Robert Redford tuck in the flats. And, if you still have anything left, you save your ass on the "tourist trap" drop-offs — all in a single run. Imagine.

Even less known than Whistler are the areas of the Okanagan Valley: Apex Alpine, Big White and Silver Star. Okanagan powder is dry, fluffy and fast — think of it as Colorado powder, without Texans.

Apex Alpine is a small area that has earned its reputation as a mountain for experts. Two runs here are guaranteed to eat your lunch: "The Chute" and "Gunbarrel." Several others might take a good bite.

A 6,000-foot chairlift and three T-bars (one of which is 5,500 feet long) run day and night at the second of the Okanagan areas, Big White. Powder freaks will get off on "Panorama Ridge" or "West Ridge." The big horror shows are "The Cliff" and, west of the chair, "Speculation," "Perfection," "Roller Coaster" and "Exhibition." Because of its elevation, Big White's base snow is very deep, and its powder is probably the best in the valley.

As long as you're in the area, hit Silver Star for a day, and ski "Suicide Face."

Without a doubt the most utterly mindblowing skiing in Canada — probably in the entire world — lies in three British Columbian icefields: The Bugaboos, The Cariboos and The Monashees. Helicopters and ski planes carry 20 to 40 skiers (maximum) per week to runs up to 10 miles in length.

Bugaboos: 300 square miles of orgasm for your feet. Nearly 600 in the Cariboos; and skiable peaks to 10,300 feet in the Monashees.

Should you attempt one of these mind-boggling adventures, the best way to go is with an outfit called Canadian Mountain Holidays (CMH). It provides a guide for every group of nine to 11 skiers. Physical conditioning and experience are basic requirements for acceptance into the program. So, although each group skis at its own speed, the pace can usually be expected to be fast and grueling. Naturally, winter weather is bitter, with the deepest powder falling between Christmas and the end of February; corn snow does not arrive till April or early May.

Heliskiing, any way you cut it, is an expensive proposition (it averages $725 per week). But the mileage one can accumulate in that time is incredible. Last season's average was something over 17,000 vertical — that's *straight-down* — feet per week. No other area can begin to compare to that.

Canadian skiing isn't a fetish. It's a way of life. There are 13 other ski areas in British Columbia; nearly 50, in all, throughout Canada. For information, write:

Department of Travel Industry
Government of British Columbia
1019 Wharf St.
Victoria, B.C., Canada

Canadian Mountain Holidays
P.O. Box 1660
Banff, Alberta, Canada

The Canadian Government Tourist Bureau
Ottawa, Ont., Canada □

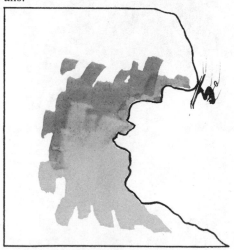

CIVIC PRIDE

Georgian Bavaria

Travelers going north from Atlanta toward the recreation areas of Chattahoochee National Forest find their eyes going out on stems as they come into the whistlestop hamlet of Helen, Ga. It's instant culture shock when you lay your eyes on the wide main street lined with houses that have Bavarian peaked roofs with overhanging eaves, gingerbread balconies, rococo towers, dormers with tiny window panes, scalloped fascia boards and wooden signs swinging from wrought iron standards. Many stop their cars, get out and stand dazed in what is clearly an Alpine village.

It's hard to believe, but behind all this is a little old Georgia town that just wanted to stop tourists from racing through, to catch their interest so they'd do a little business in the town. Six years ago Helen was a street of concrete-block buildings with tin roofs. Then Jim Wilkins, a clothing factory owner, and two of his employees decided to put the town on the map. They got an Atlanta artist who had actually been to Germany to sketch new facades on pictures of every building in town. Working from these, local carpenters put pretty arched windows into a new version of the Ice Burg Drive-in, a clock tower and steeple on Charlie Maloof's law office, rich wood panels on the Exxon station (and a deer's head over the gas pumps) and another steeple on the telephone booth.

Every merchant paid for his own renovation, at costs that ran from $1,500 to $20,000, and there were no holdouts. A town ordinance now requires all new construction to be in the Bavarian style, and so the new home of the Brown Bag liquor store, the new town hall and a new laundromat are all "Bavarian."

A newspaper in nearby Statesboro said of Helen: "Its people glow with confidence in what they are doing. They are pleased as Punch with themselves." If it stops tourists, it has to be good.

—Roy Bongartz

Hot Dog Skiing— Not for the Timid

It is a combination of aerial acrobatics, ballet grace and slapstick pratfalls. The serious-minded call it freestyle skiing. But to its more flamboyant practitioners it is a new subculture known as hot dog.

It has become more of a lifestyle than a mere craze, with an ostentatious mode of dress (hot colors and bright bandanas) and its own lucid vernacular. Every skier, for example, can execute a Butt Crusher, but it takes a practiced hot dogger to perform a 360° airborne maneuver known as a Helicopter or cross skis sickeningly to describe the Iron Cross. And the sport has been exported to Europe, with touring American hot dog exponents putting on exhibitions for eager Europeans in search of freedom of spirit and wider skiing horizons.

Shunning the discipline of slalom, the rigid rules and critical split-second timing of the downhill race, hot doggers are turning to somersaults and forward and backward flips. With each flight an ego trip, they attempt triple flips, aerial cartwheels and other stunts in space.

The first national hot dog championships were held three years ago at Waterville Valley, N.H., but latter-day competitive hot doggers will find contests—such as the Super Hot Dog Open—at many ski areas. They'll also find instruction—many ski schools now offer special courses in basic hot dog.

Hot dogging, as actor Robert Redford (who also operates a ski area in Utah) noted in *Ski* magazine, "blows the mind and screws up the hill." It also may be a definite hazard to health, but apparently many skiers love it.

—Mike Michaelson

*A*nd all woke earlier
    for the unaccustomed brightness
Of the winter dawning,
    the strange unheavenly glare:
The eye marveled—
    marveled at the dazzling whiteness;
The ear hearkened to the stillness
    of the solemn air;
No sound of wheel rumbling nor of foot falling,
And the busy morning cries
    came thin and spare.

          —ROBERT BRIDGES

The Mountains of Maine by Summer Ski Lift

The first mountains of the United States to be seen by arriving European colonists were those of Maine: the forlorn hump of Schoodic, the winding roller-coaster Camden Hills, the smoothly sculptured domes of Mt. Desert, which has carried its French pronunciation since Samuel de Champlain named it in 1604.

There are ways to see a little more of Maine at one glance than you can at sea level, and even people who wouldn't dream of climbing a mountain themselves can enjoy them. One of the best ways to get to Maine's mountain tops is to take a ski lift in the summer.

In the western part of the state, near the Canadian border, the White Mountains spill over into Maine. Among their peaks are many of Maine's highest. Saddleback, standing at the eastern edge of the Rangeley Lakes, rises 4,116 feet, and you can reach the summit by summer ski lifts. Up top, you get long views to New Hampshire, Quebec and Vermont with the broad, deep Rangeley Lakes spread out in the foreground.

Big Squaw is wild and lonely and the farthest north of Maine's ascendable peaks. It stands where the communities and farms of central Maine come to an end and the northland wilderness begins. Just off Route 15 outside of Greenville, get on the ski lift and go 6,000 feet up for a breathtaking view of Moosehead Lake and the bays that extend into the misty northland. (Big Squaw shouldered the first forest fire lookout tower in the United States. It was built in 1905.)

From the ski lift on Pleasant Mountain, in southern Maine, you can view both the coast and inland summits. If you look towards the west you'll see the soaring peaks of the Presidential Range in New Hampshire.

A Brief Guide to Summer Skiing

If you're a dedicated skier, all you need for skiing out of season is a little altitude and determination. There's skiing all summer, for instance, at Austria's Rudolfshutte on the Weisee; at Switzerland's Piz Gorvatsch above St. Moritz; at Italy's Stelvio Pass, Cervinia, or at the Col du Géant near Courmayeur; at France's Val d'Isère or Tignes. (The bikinis are spectacular at Tignes.)

Ski and boot rentals are generally available at the resorts, so you needn't lug your gear along. The super switch for the serious skier, of course, is Chile's Portillo in the Andes or New Zealand's Toneariro National Park, where our summer is their winter. For detailed information, contact national tourist offices.

—James Egan

Hike, You Huskies!

What with snowmobiles and daring bush pilots, you don't hear much about sled dog teams in the Yukon and other parts of the frozen North anymore. But there are still plenty of them around, and if they aren't frequently racing out into blizzards to save people in distress the way they used to in "Sergeant Preston of the Yukon," they *are* frequently racing. Sled dog racing has become a popular sport in the coldest parts of this country and in Canada.

The International Sled Dog Races, held annually at Kalkaska, Mich., are a very big event, second only, perhaps, to the World Championships held in Anchorage, Alaska. Smaller events are held all across the country—at Laconia, Vt.; Grand Valley, Mich.; Ely and St. Paul, Minn.; Park City, Utah; Williams, Ariz.; Mount Hood, Ore.; Dorrington and Big Bear Lake, Calif.; Fairbanks, Alaska; and in Canada at Montreal, Quebec and Winnipeg. (You can write to the Chamber of Commerce in any of these cities for full details on the event held there.)

Contrary to what you see in the movies, almost no one who races yells "Mush!" at his sled team—racers cry "Hi!" or "Hike!" or just whistle instead. There are four classes of competition: Class A (11 to 13 dogs to a team), Class B (five to seven dogs to a team), junior class (three to five dogs to a team) and children's class. In the children's class, boys and girls—some barely school age—compete for fame and glory with one-dog "teams." This event may lack the excitement of the 18-mile Class A race, but it's always a real crowd-pleaser.

Sled dog racing is a tricky sport to learn, and it's not inexpensive—a good lead dog for your team can cost as much as $500. If you're interested in taking up the sport—or just learning more about it—you should get a copy of the beginner's handbook put out by the Sierra Nevada Dog Drivers, Inc. club. The handbook and other information on sled dog racing is available from the International Sled Dog Racing Association, P.O. Box 55, Watertown, N.Y. 13601.

—Bill Thomas

Skibobbing

Take a bicycle frame complete with seat and handlebars, mount it on a pair of skis, strap to your feet a small pair of ski runners, and you are ready for skibobbing.

With four points of gravity, the skibob offers an extra measure of security to the reluctant downhill skier. It can give the not-so-supple winter sportsman or novice skier a manageable sample of downhill thrills. On gentle slopes, the *sitz ski*, as Europeans descriptively call this contraption, probably is easier than Alpine skis for the tyro to master. Experts negotiate slalom courses and compete in downhill races; converts say the skibob is as easy to maneuver as a bicycle. Nonetheless, the machine should be approached with a healthy degree of caution—the existing world skibobbing record is a breathtaking 102 m.p.h.

The modern, lightweight skibob actually is a revival of a 19th-century invention called an ice-velocipede that didn't catch on. It has been popular in Europe since the late 1940s. You can buy skibobs for about $50, rent them at some ski resorts or build them at home from kits.

—Mike Michaelson

Skiing + Surfing = Snurfing

Snurfing is a snow-skimming sport that is a cross between skiing and surfing, with a touch of pure skateboard thrown in for good measure. Using a laminated wooden board four feet long by seven inches wide (it resembles a water ski), the snurfer rides downhill in the upright position—for as long and as far as he can. (Wipe-outs occur as often as in the ocean version of the sport.) Holding onto a tether the rider shifts foot pressure to achieve balance and direction. A keel helps provide maneuverability; wax applied to the bottom adds speed.

The snurfboard first saw the light of snow when it emerged from the home workshop of one Sherman Poppen, a father looking for something new to occupy the playtime of two snowbound daughters. This was in Muskegon, Mich., a town which, as a result, now holds the Annual National Snurfing Championships.

Within five years the sport has grown to the point where more than a million snurfboards are sold each year. Cost of a snurfboard—which is adaptable to sand dunes in warmer climes—is about $10.

—Mike Michaelson

Every little wile you hear people talking about a man they don't nobody seem to have much use for him on acct. of him not paying his debts or beating his wife or something, and everybody takes a rap at him about this and that until finely one of the party speaks up and says theys must be some good in him because he likes animals. . . .

Well, friends, when you come right down to cases they's about as much sence to this as a good many other delusions that we get here in this country, like for inst. the one about nobody wanting to win the first pot and the one about the whole lot of authors not being able to do their best work unless they are ½ pickled.

But if liking animals ain't a virtue in itself I don't see how it proves that a man has got any virtues, and personly, if I had a daughter and she wanted to get married and I asked her what kind of a bird the guy was and she said she don't know nothing about him except that one day she seen him kiss a leopard, why I would hold up my blessing till a few of the missing precincts was heard from.

—RING LARDNER

Trekking to Mt. Everest in Rubber Thongs

Mt. Everest! The very name sounds forbidding. Lucky is he who will ever see, let alone walk to, the foot of that lofty mountain. But as strange as it might sound, that's not such a fantastic idea. And it isn't that difficult as long as you don't mind walking through some of the most beautiful scenery you will ever see in your whole life.

I went to Mt. Everest in October 1970. Everybody told me to get a good pair of shoes, but I had been walking in rubber thongs for several years and could not have gotten used to shoes in time to leave. So I just bought a spare pair of thongs and left, carrying a back pack with a sleeping bag, blanket, some food and a few clothes.

To get on the trail, you have to take a bus from Kathmandu and travel north about 100 miles. In a Nepali bus that means about three and a half hours of bumpiness. At a place called Lamu Shangu you start walking. You cross a bridge and ask your way. Someone shows you the trail to Everest and there you go. . . .

As you climb, the scenery opens up; the river down at the bottom of the trail gets smaller. All the hills are terraced and little farms are spread all over. There is always somebody going down the path carrying a load. Along the way there are special places to rest: small walls of stones have been built exactly high enough so you can rest your pack on them without taking it off.

The first night I slept under someone's porch. In these mountains every house provides a place for travelers to sleep. In exchange they sell you firewood, fish, eggs or vegetables. Quite unexpectedly, I was awakened at five the next morning by someone who said, "Let's go, sir." I figured that these folks know what they're doing, so I got up and followed them. I was to travel with them for many days. One was a Sherpa man with his son and daughter returning to their village, and one was a young Tibetan Lama with two porters.

After five days' walk through gorgeous valleys and 10,000-foot passes, the trail begins to climb a new mountain. It is an eight-hour climb, and you begin to feel that you are really going somewhere special.

The pass is at 11,000 feet. It is amazing. You stand on top of the mountain and look back to see all the innumerable valleys you have already crossed. When you turn around and look forward, everything is 5,000 feet higher. This is Jumbesi, the first big Sherpa town.

From then on, you are in Sherpa-land. Every day now you are walking at elevations between 9,000 and 13,000 feet. The valleys turn into precipitous gorges. The trails are steeper and the air is light and brisk. The last town before the high mountains is Namche Bazar.

From Namche, set off on the main trail towards Tyangboche. This is a beautiful Tibetan monastery, perched on the side of a sheer cliff overlooking a tremendous gorge. (I had a good night's sleep there.) A few miles farther on, I passed the last houses, where I bought some milk and eggs. Then I was alone, going full speed towards the lofty valley of Khumbu Glacier. It took me till evening to reach the top of the moraine. There I found a few abandoned sheds, and there I spent the night. The only other trace of civilization I could find was a bunch of empty cans and boxes left by previous expeditions: California peaches, Mother's Instant Cake.

At 15,000 feet, in terrible cold, the best I could do was to cook some soup and hole up in my sleeping bag. (I thought there couldn't be another living creature in this solitary place, but in the middle of the night I heard some scratching close to my head. Switching on my flashlight, I discovered a tiny mouse trying to nibble at the food in my pack. It was a charming creature, but nonetheless I chased it away and closed my bag tightly.) It was so cold I could hardly sleep, so at five in the morning I got up and started to walk again.

I was now following the rim of the glacier. Ghostly boulders of ice the size of apartment houses were lined up in rows. Sometimes I could hear a huge crack in the ice. At about ten in the morning I arrived at the foot of the mountain I was going to: Kala Patar ("Black Rock").

Two hours later, I was sitting on the top at 18,000 feet, looking at the spectacular scenery: Everest was directly across the valley, enormous and forbidding, and all around I could see the most amazing landscape stretching all the way into Tibet. I was tired, happy, high from the air, and I didn't know what to do. It was so hard to conceive that in a mere two weeks' walk I would be back to the civilized world—if my thongs held up!

—Jacques Bessin

50 m.p.h. Downhill— in a Canoe

Canoeists up in Maine and thereabouts are prepared to acknowledge the existence of winter but are quite unwilling to yield to it. When the streams turn to ice and the air turns frigid, they simply tote their aluminum and fiberglass canoes to the top of a ski slope and enjoy a hair-raising dash down. Many a skier at Big Squaw Mountain in Moosehead, Maine has been astonished to find a canoe hurtling toward him down the slope, its begoggled, helmeted occupants yelling for right-of-way as they steer with paddles, ski poles, brooms or feet—and prodigious amounts of body English.

Canogganists career down the slopes at speeds which may range from 35 m.p.h. to as high as 50 m.p.h., depending upon the quality of the snow and the angle of the incline. For this reason it is sound practice to scout an intended run for trees, rocks and other hazards before uttering the traditional blood-curdling yell that signals the start of another canogganing run. It also is prudent to make some trial runs with your canoe on lesser slopes before tackling the big one. And a hard hat is an essential part of your canogganing outfit.

On sunny weekends entire families take to the slopes with their canoes or—in some cases—kayaks. The more reckless exponents of canoeski, as it also is known, hold downhill races, while at Sugarloaf Mountain in Carrabassett, Maine, ski-slope sailors hold slalom races, sliding between poles and ending up in a pond of ice water.

—Mike Michaelson

Downhill Biking

You say you like the fresh air, sunshine, the sound of birds singing and the clickety-clack of your 10-speed on quiet country lanes—but you *hate* changing all those gears to huff and puff *up* hills so you can glide down dales, eh?

Then how about a 12-mile *downhill* ride through California's gold country? Nirvana is right there waiting for lazy bike riders about an hour east of Sacramento near the old gold town of Placerville, Calif. The bike route runs from "Daffodil Hill" to Fid-dletown, which got its name from the neighborhood saloon musician in the bawdy old days.

To fully enjoy the outing you must, alas, rely on the automobile, actually two of 'em. The way it works, dear lazy riders, is that you drive *up* the hills from Fiddletown (in two cars), leave off the bikes and most of your gang at Daffodil Hill, then drive back down to Fiddletown (in two cars) and leave one car there. It takes about half an hour to make the round trip run, but at the end of your ride and your reverie in the local saloon, you'll be glad to piggyback the bikes on that nice handy car.

While the chauffeurs are taking care of the ferry service operation, the rest of the group can hunt wildflowers, talk to the range cattle or hunt for gold. There are actually two spots on the hill from which to begin your biking: the first is for the truly lazy biker, the other for the guilt-ridden rider who wouldn't enjoy the downhill ride without *some* huffing and puffing. The masochists should not stop at the crossroads at the summit of Daffodil Hill, but should park their car and begin one mile south (just across the road from the ranch with the typ-ical barnyard creatures like peacocks). Even the most dedicated masochist can get his jollies out of pedaling back up the steady mile grade to the crossroads, which is where the fun begins.

The old Fiddletown Road, needless to say, is not a major highway, so once you point your bike downhill you're pretty much a free spirit. It's not a ride for the timid at heart —some of the curves approximate respect-able hairpins—and it's not strictly 12 miles downhill—there are some flat stretches and some short climbs, but daredevils can pick up enough speed on the downhills to coast over those parts. The countryside is fan-tastic—big pine and oak trees, babbling-brook-lined pastureland; there is even an old Elks Club cemetery, the final resting place of the town's early-day Babbits. (It makes a pleasant picnic spot for necrophiliacs and gravestone rubbers.) From the graveyard, it's only a short distance into town for a cold beer and a game of pool with the locals at the old saloon.

—Lynne Joiner

Smile once more; turn thy wheel!

—WILLIAM SHAKESPEARE

Books About Bicycling

One of the most pleasant things about being introduced to any sport is getting acquainted with the best books about it. Bicycling is fashionable these days, and there are easily 10 times the books about bikes there used to be. There are two that stand out from the rest, however, both for the quality of the information they give you and for the quality of the writing.

The first is the standard work on bicycling: anyone interested in the sport should have it. Eugene A. Sloane's *The Complete Book of Bicycling* (Trident Press, 1970; $9.95) is a thorough, clearly written introduction to bicycling, with chapters on health and safety, buying and fitting a bike, how to ride. There's an excellent chapter on the murky subject of gears (for those buying 10-speeds), and chapters on touring, bike racing, the history of bicycling, tires and accessories—and finally, as good a preventive maintenance guide as you'll find anywhere except in the second book I'm recommending. If there's an essential book on bicycling, this is it.

If you want a book on bicycle repair, your choice is equally simple: get *Anybody's Bike Book,* by Tom Cuthbertson (Ten Speed Press, 1971; $3). Amazing to say, it's a how-to book that is good reading even if you don't give a damn about repairing bicycles. ("When tightening an 8 or 9mm nut, don't try to demonstrate your virility; show some sensitivity. Threads are delicate.") Cuthbert-son makes you want to buy a bike just so you can really be serious about reading his book. There are also excellent drawings by Rick Morrall of what Cuthbertson is talking about.

—The Editors

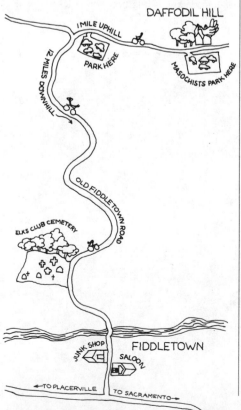

Teton Bike Trip

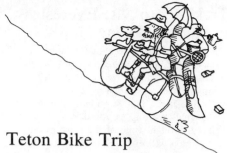

Most vacationers, when they visit Grand Teton National Park in Wyoming, do their sightseeing the typical American way—by car or by tour bus. Especially during the current gas shortage, there's a better way to see and explore this relatively small but ex-traordinarily beautiful national park. The bet-ter way is by bike.

For only 80 cents an hour the Grand Teton Lodge Co. will rent you an easy-to-use, fairly lightweight, three-speed bicycle. The advantages of biking in the Tetons are many, but perhaps most noteworthy is the fact that from the saddle of a bike you're likely to see considerably more wildlife than from behind the wheel of a gas-drinker. Why? For one thing your vision is totally unrestricted. For another, a bicycle is quiet.

Two recent visitors to the park deserted their bus-bound tour group and, on bikes, saw two coyotes, several moose, a fleeing round critter that may have been a black bear, elk, a beaver and various species of birdlife (in-cluding a rare trumpeter swan, of which there are only 1,500 in the world). This on one day's journey along the highways, bike-ways and some back byways of the park. That same day the couple's motorcoach counterparts saw only the elk.

The scenery of the Tetons, too, is much more impressive if you see the mountains, lakes, streams and waterfalls from a slow-moving bike. Nor do you need to miss big chunks of the park by touring it on a bike —since the whole place is only about 20 by 35 miles long, you can cycle over all of it in just two or three days.

How tough is the pedaling? Not bad at all, if you do any biking to speak of at home. If you haven't bicycled for several years, how-ever, it would be best to limit your first ex-cursions to an hour or so of pedaling close to the lodge complexes at Jackson Lake, Colter Bay and Jenny Lake. Even on such "shorty" trips you can have great fun and the scenery is rewarding.

—Mike Miller

Wanted: More Downhill Bike Rides

Do *you* have a favorite downhill bike ride? Make it famous—tell TGE about it. Send a description of the route, the ride and the scenic attractions, plus a map (aw, go ahead—draw one yourself) to:

The Great Escape
150 Shoreline Highway
Mill Valley, Calif. 94941.

The Century Rider: 100 Miles by Bike

There's something magical about the figure 100—whether it's being employed to record home runs, touchdowns or longevity. And so it is with miles of road and the bicyclist.

The so-called "century run" is a 100-miles-in-one-day test of pedaling endurance that definitely is *not* a race. In fact, these pedaling marathons frequently are completed by a sprinkling of retirees and pre-teens.

Dozens of these 100-milers are held in various parts of the country each year, usually sponsored by a local bicycling club, frequently by an affiliate of the League of American Wheelmen (for information write to National LAW Headquarters, P.O. Box 3928, Torrance, Calif. 90510). Most sponsors provide a jacket patch to those who complete the 100 miles.

Usually, centuries take the bicyclist through scenic terrain and rejoice in such colorful appellations as the Hilly Hundred (Bloomington, Ind., each fall), the Flamingo Run (a late-winter jaunt through the Everglades) or the Wheeling 100 (a scenic run through northwestern suburban Chicago).

And then there's the Indy 500 of bike touring, the famous Tour of the Scioto River Valley (called "TOSRV" by bike cognoscenti). Actually a 200-mile, two-day event, the TOSRV is a round-trip pedal through south-central Ohio from Columbus to Portsmouth and return. It attracts more than 2,000 bicyclists, including singles, family groups and some overseas entrants. It is held each spring. However, it's become so popular that participants should enter early. Write: TOSRV Communications, P.O. Box 2311, Columbus, Ohio. —*Mike Michaelson*

See Medieval York on a Yellow Daisy Bicycle

York, England is a delightful old town, and a local girl has come up with an ideal way to see this small, slow-paced town with its narrow, medieval streets. Rosalind Pearcy has opened a bike shop called Daisy Daisy, where she rents bicycles built for one or two, all painted bright yellow with daisies.

Sights to see in York include the 500-year-old Minster, the largest cathedral in Northern Europe, with its famous Three Sisters stained-glass window. This summer the cathedral will offer a sound and light show telling the dramatic story of the Minster from the time it was built through the present. (You'll hear, for example, how during World War II the stained glass was removed and buried for safety.) The production will feature Sir John Gielgud among other stars.

Suit Yourself With a Custom Bike

Your custom-built cycle can be easily the finest you will own. These suggestions will help you buy the bike that is right for *you*.

You can have a bicycle built for you, a machine, designed by you and the builder for your type of riding and your body. In Great Britain, Europe and the United States there are bicycle makers who produce not thousands of bikes per year, but dozens. These craftsmen build each machine to the customer's specification—and yet they often cost no more than a good mass-produced bike.

You'll know when you're ready for a tailor-made bike. You'll notice that the machines on the dealers' shelves, even those sporting $500 price tags, have a certain sameness about them. You'll wonder why they don't make bikes for people as tall or short as you, why luggage carriers and lights aren't built in rather than precariously clipped on. You will be looking for a bike the color of your fiancée's eyes, when the "in" color this year is red. That's when you should seek out one of the custom bike craftsmen.

Your tailor-made bike can be a unique and wonderful machine, but as many have discovered, it can be a costly disappointment. You need not be an engineer to order a custom bike, but you should know something about bicycle design. You must understand your own cycling needs and be able to communicate them to the builder.

You have two alternatives: tell your builder your measurements and the sort of riding you will do and let him handle design, or design the bike yourself and have him build it. Bicycle design is no arcanum, but it can be complex, and few cyclists know enough to juggle tube angles, clearances, tubing wall thicknesses and alignments into a bike that works. Your builder handles the tubes and torches daily, so he can spot problems most of us wouldn't think of.

Custom-made bikes often bear the maker's name: Cinelli, Hetchins, Ken Ryall. They are built with the care a man takes when his name is his trademark. Workmanship, however, is only one virtue of the tailor-made bike.

Your tailor-made bike will do what you want it to do—it's designed that way. Take the poor cycle tourist, for instance. Most high quality mass-produced bicycles are designed for racing. The tourist will find them uncomfortably stiff and ill-equipped for touring. I know: I toured 800 miles on one, and I felt every speck of gravel between Yorkshire and Gloucestershire. The tourist needs a stable, smooth ride, rigid, brazed-on pannier carriers and accessory brackets and a lower range of gears. Most custom builders will do a touring bike with these features, and make it light and responsive at the same time.

For the racer, too, the custom builder has a lot to offer. He can create a special-purpose machine for each event from track pursuit to cyclo-cross (a lighthearted event in which the cyclist rides and carries his bike around a usually muddy cross-country circuit). A stable of special-purpose bikes costs plenty, but such bikes offer an advantage to the serious competitor.

Of course, the tailor-made bike is built to fit your body, almost regardless of size. The custom builder is virtually the only hope for the person who is very short or extra tall. Handicapped persons will find the custom builder can meet their needs as well.

Finally, the very finish of your tailor-made bike will be done to your specification, including paint, chrome and lugwork. Lugs are the steel sleeves that join the frame tubes together. Some builders are known for their fancy lugwork, cutting blank lugs into lacy scrollwork fantasies. Condor's Monte Young says it takes a man one whole day just to cut a set of Condor's fanciest lugs.

It's a real thrill to ride a machine you designed yourself, to feel it almost lift you up a steep slope, then bank off the fast downhill bends without a hint of wobble—but before you can do it, some preparation is necessary. First, study a copy of *Cycling*, the exhaustively complete bike racing guide published in Rome by the Federation International Amateur d'Cyclisme. (About $12—the price may go up anytime—from Velo-Sport, Inc., 1650 Grove St., Berkeley, Calif. 94709.) This invaluable book includes a fine chapter on racing bike design, and will enable you to create the basic shape of a bicycle that will fit your body and handle safely and responsively. If you are really serious about designing your own bike, your second step should be to measure and study as many fine bicycles as you can find in your frame size.

Your custom-built bike need not cost more than a similarly equipped bike off the production line. A basic British frame built of finest Reynolds 531 double-butted tubing will cost $80-$100. Continental builders are competitive. Chrome plating, fancy lugwork and brazed-on fittings will cost extra.

Air freight charges plus customs duty will bring the total cost of your custom frame to near $200, delivered. (Surface shipment of a single bike is not worth the effort or risk involved.) The added parts needed to complete the bike—the wheels, handlebars, brakes and gear mechanisms—will cost from $200 to more than $400 in this country. It adds up rapidly, but the total is reasonable when complete mass-produced machines are selling in the United States for up to $600, frames for up to $250.

There are other ways to save. Try fitting your bike with good, but less costly, components, or have your builder complete the bike with parts at (sometimes) lower prices.

Or, take delivery of your bike while you're abroad on vacation. You can bring your bike back on most airlines as luggage for a small

(continued on next page)

(continued from previous page)
fee or free; and as accompanied luggage your bike will qualify as part of your $100 duty-free allowance. In any case, order well in advance. Many builders have waiting lists, some longer than a year. With time you can make sure both you and your builder know just what sort of bike you want.

—Walt Greenwood

Where to Buy Them

Choosing a builder is the most difficult step in ordering a custom-made bicycle. Many builders enjoy excellent international reputations—among them Hetchins, Bob Jackson and Cinelli. Others are less well known and sell mainly to local buyers. If you can't find a bike by your prospective builder for inspection, and can't find someone who knows his work, you'll either have to take a chance or decide to buy from a better-known firm.

Some of the larger firms may require that you order through an American distributor. Plan to pay for this.

Here are the names and addresses of several builders, with some comments. As the custom builder is largely an English institution, most are English.

Ellis Briggs, Ltd.
18 Otley Road
Shipley, Yorkshire, England

One of the most beautiful bikes I have seen is a gold and black one by Ellis Briggs. In England I was told that an American importer offered to buy Ellis Briggs' entire output. He was turned down.

Cinelli & Co.
45 Via Edigio Folli
Milan, Italy 20134

Cinelli has been a leader in establishing modern racing bike design, and the quality of Cinelli craftsmanship is justly famous. The design chapter in *Cycling* follows Cinelli's ideas. Cinelli used to do some custom work, but may not now due to demand for standard designs. Prepare for a long wait.

Condor Cycles
90 Gray's Inn Road
London WC 1, England

Building frames that range from the light, lugless Barrachi to the ornate Superbe, Condor's Frank Westell and Monte Young work in a tiny, jammed London shop. Among their bikes is a rococo number they made for rock guitarist Eric Clapton.

Brian Decker
P.O. Box 95
Tenmile, Ore. 97481

Decker built bikes in California before moving to Tenmile, a little town near Roseburg, Ore. Among his bikes is a clever dual-purpose machine for both track sprints and short road races. It is basically a compact, stiff sprint bike with brakes and a derailleur for the road—a truly unique machine.

Hetchins Lightweight Cycles
798-800 Seven Sisters Road
Tottenham, London N 15, England

Hetchins is best known for ornate lugwork, some of which extends six inches down the fork blades. The unique Hellenic stay design, with the seat stays crossing the seat tube to join the top tube ahead of the seat, is another Hetchins trademark.

Schwinn Bicycle Co.
1856 N. Kostner Ave.
Chicago, Ill. 60639

For $40 more than the standard price, Schwinn will build its Paramount bicycle to custom dimensions. Custom lugwork and brazed-on accessories are probably not available, but quality is first-rate.

—W. G.

Off the Road!

Off the main roads, life is once again full of luster and perfume. People know this now, and they're demanding a technology to let them enter their dreams.

"Off-the-road vehicles" —ORVs—began with the World War II jeep. The jeep begat the dune buggy which begat the trail bike which begat the snowmobile which has done an amazing job of begatting. More than 500,000 ORVs were sold last year for escaping into woods, hills, swamps, beaches and the other assorted wilds of America.

The newest type of ORV is the All-Terrain Vehicle, a chunky fiberglass tub with a lightweight engine and six huge cross-treaded balloon tires.

The ATV is efficient: it gets more than 35 miles to the gallon and is reportedly a "minimal polluter." The bozo tires contain only one pound of air pressure; they're so squishy they can grip almost anything—rocks, sand, gravel, snow, even the placid water of a swimming pool.

Those peculiar wheels on an ATV don't turn, but run in a straight line like a tank. You steer by braking all the wheels on one side while the wheels on the other churn you around.

There are 16 major makers of ATVs in the United States, but ATV Manufacturing Co. of Pittsburgh controls about half the market. It builds the Attex (pronounced "Addex") and offers the widest range of vehicles, starting with Crazy Colt, which sells for $995. Like a passenger car, the machine comes with scores of options, including a 110-volt generator and a four-man trailer tent that can be towed anywhere the Colt itself will go.

The Coot, made by Cummins Engine Co. of Dallas, is another popular ATV. It steers by wheel and not by braking levers. The Coot offers a four-wheel steering option that works like a hook-and-ladder truck; in a left turn the front wheels point to the left, the rear wheels to the right. The Coot also has a two-part steel body, hinged in the middle so the front and rear sections track independently for tight turns. With a top speed of 20 m.p.h., the Coot is slower than most ATVs. But its 1-to-164 gear ratio will slog it up almost anything. The Coot can carry a 1,000-pound load, and comes in three models starting at $1,895.

If you only want three wheels on the ground, try the new ATC (All-Terrain Cycle), a balloon-tired spinoff of the trail bike. The ATC is basically a trike with a motorcycle engine mounted on a fiberglass body an ATC can go anywhere the standard ATV can go except over deep water.

The most popular ATC is the Tricart made by the New Holland Division of Sperry Rand in Lebanon, Ohio. It has a rear-mounted engine, can hit 45 m.p.h., climb a hill with a 45° slope and stay upright on a 30° slope. It comes in four models ranging in price from $375 to $695.

The Honda ATC 90 is also popular and can roll and bounce over almost any surface. The Honda's two rear wheels are on a solid axle, however, so it can be tricky to handle. All ATCs are illegal for road use, but the Honda's components can be dismantled with a wrench and stuffed into the average car trunk for carrying to and from the wilds.

To get yourself off the ground entirely, try a hovercraft. Commercial 130-foot-long hovercraft have been ferrying passengers and cars across the English Channel since 1968. New smaller one-person versions are being built to float a few inches above suburban devilstrips.

Most hovercraft use two fans, one to blow the vehicle off the ground and another to drive it forward. The popular Air Cycle, made by Air Cushion Vehicles of Troy, N.Y., has a 33-hp engine coupled to a sole fan. The Air Cycle, with airfoil trim control and thrust spoilers, handles better than most hovercraft, even at its top speed of 40 m.p.h. It also can climb a 20° slope. The Air Cycle costs $1,500.

—Peter Janssen

Uphill Racers

Travelers suffering from dashboard daze or steering wheel slump may find a quick cure by paying their $2 to join the 19th annual Pike's Peak Marathon Run this August. This one is on foot—not to be confused with the famous auto race—but you can either make it or bust this way, too. The race, sponsored by the Chamber of Commerce of Manitou Springs, Colo., was first run in 1936 by 38 men and two women. It starts off from the cog railroad station 10,000 feet below the 14,110-foot summit. Contestants have to run 13 miles up Barr Trail. "No short cuts allowed," reads one rule.

The official entry folder says: "The objective is to get the legs and hearts of everyone in condition by climbing the Barr Trail where the air is pure and invigorating." The record for going up is held by Chuck Smead, who ran all the way to Pike's Peak in two hours, nine minutes and 30 seconds. He then ran back down in another hour and a half, and was named King of the Mountain.

There are divisions for girls, boys, juniors, teenagers 16 to 18 years old, women, veterans and masters. You can watch them arrive at the finish line at Buxton Avenue from noon on, if all goes well. But you may well prefer to try racing yourself; the Colorado air does wonders for people.

–Roy Bongartz

Los Angeles Fights the Fuel Crisis
Candy Broffman demonstrates a typically Los Angeles way to beat the high cost of gas. She tools around on this motorized pogo stick, which is still not forbidden on freeways. The stick runs on a single-cylinder, two-cycle engine and gets 30,000 hops per gallon.

Sand Sailing in the Mojave Desert

Back in the days when the mines of the Mojave Desert in Southern California were pouring out millions in gold, the miners used to unship the heavy iron wheels of their wheelbarrows, rig them onto rude wooden frames, hoist sails and take their girls for Sunday spins over the bed of the nearest dry lake. Reputedly they did 60 m.p.h.

Today the "sand sailer" has been modernized and whole fleets of them compete in regattas, just as yachts do on water.

Probably the best place to watch them or perhaps even get a ride is El Mirage dry lake in the southern Mojave. El Mirage is an expanse of dried chemical mud, whitish gray, flat as a billiard table and about 10 miles long. The shores are studded with islets green with desert growths, and all around are pastel red and yellowish hills.

On weekdays sailplanes from nearby El Mirage gliderport may be towed into the air behind automobiles speeding over the lake bed. But on weekends the lake is overrun with scooting motorcycles, sports cars and sand sailers.

People make their own sand sailers. They still use wheelbarrow wheels, but today these are rubber-tired and roll easily on ball bearings. Three wheels are mounted on a T-shaped frame of welded metal tubing, in much the same way that the runners on ice boats in the cold country are mounted. The wheel that steers is up in front, connected by cables to an auto steering wheel in the cockpit. A single striped sail completes the rig.

The sand sailers are brought to El Mirage, either knocked down or folded up, in trailers and pickup trucks. On weekends you'll see them by the dozen skimming over the dry lake bed. While they're waiting for a good wind, the sand skippers are happy to talk about their rigs. Most belong to sand sailer clubs that stage organized regattas.

To reach El Mirage, head north on U.S. 395 out of San Bernardino, Calif. and ask directions at the little community of Adelanto.

–Alan R. McElwain

Pedal Cars: Do It with Your Feet

You're bored with your 10-speed. You'd really like to get behind the wheel of a car again, and you think wistfully of those little Fiats that get 34 miles to the gallon. But with the environment in the state it's in, and with the fuel shortage haunting you, it makes you feel guilty to think of burning even that much gas.

Maybe what you need is a PPV. A PPV is a People Powered Vehicle. It's a three-wheeled pedal car for one or two adults, it costs no more than a really good 10-speed bike (around $500) and best of all it has wire wheels, a three-speed transmission and is guaranteed to be non-polluting. It runs on *your* energy, and just think what you can do for this country by *not* drinking two gallons of gas a day!

PPV dealerships have sprung up all over the country. For the name of the one nearest you, write:

EVI
6345 Product Drive
Sterling Heights, Mich. 48077.

–Richard John Pietschmann

Come live with me, and be my love,
And we will some new pleasures prove
Of golden sands, and crystal brooks,
With silken lines, and silver hooks.

—JOHN DONNE

different strokes for different folks

By John R. Fuchs

I don't know why but riding motorcycles just makes me grin inside.

–Robert E. Lee,
Class "C" motorcycle racer

At a time when urban congestion is growing and gasoline costs are soaring, the world of motorcycling offers fantastic yet economical opportunities for both the commuter and the leisure-time rider. On a motorcycle you can make an unhurried jaunt to the grocery store or a bracing run to the office. You can travel at a snail-like 2 m.p.h. if you're cow-trailing or at 160 m.p.h. on an aerodynamically-styled road racer or a fuel-injected drag bike.

Motocross One of the simplest, most popular—and roughest—forms of motorcycle competition is called motocross. It's a race between any number of motorcycles (from five to 50) over a natural terrain course that can be anywhere from ¼ mile to 1½ miles long. Bikes are divided into classes according to engine size—100cc, 125cc, 175cc, 250cc and open class, for example—and the rider's experience level—beginner, novice, amateur, junior, expert; in each class there are two or three heats a day. Points are awarded based on finishing position in each heat, or moto, so the winner is the guy who accumulates the most points in the day's motos. The courses are always very rough, with uphill and downhill sections, tight turns, spectacular jumps, maybe a mudhole or stream to cross, and plenty of closely-spaced, deep, washboard-type bumps known as whoop-de-doos.

Motocross is considered the second most physically demanding sport in the world (after soccer) and all you have to do is ride one moto to find out why.

All you need to race is a small entry fee and your motorcycle. Helmets are required and other safety equipment like heavy boots, padded pants, gloves and padded jerseys are strongly recommended. The best motocross bikes are the lightest ones, without lights, horns, mirrors, instruments or other street-type equipment.

Information on motocross tracks and events in your area can be obtained from your local motorcycle shop or by writing:

American Motorcycle Association
P.O. Box 141
Westerville, Ohio 43081.

Desert Racing In vast areas of desolate and arid land in the southwestern states, thousands of avid motorcyclists engage in their favorite pastime: desert racing. Like motocross, this sport pits men and machines against each other and against nature; here nature includes rocks, dirt, gullies, washes, uphills, downhills, unending whoop-de-doos and immense stretches of soft sand and fine, powdery silt. Races are held almost every Sunday throughout the year and are sponsored by motorcycle clubs belonging to the American Motorcycle Association or by organizations like the Desert Racing Association (DRA) or the Sportsman Racing Association (SRA). There are two major types of desert races—they're called Hare Scrambles and Hare-and-Hound.

In the Hare Scrambles the course consists of two or three 30- to 45-mile loops through the desert marked off with lime and colored ribbons; the loops start and finish in the same place. Hare-and-Hound races, on the other hand, run from one starting point to a different finishing point over a distance of 100 miles or more. The longest Hare-and-Hound race held annually is the Check Chase, a 250-mile contest through the desert from Lucrene Valley, Calif. to Parker, Ariz.; it's run every October. The *largest* Hare-and-Hound race held annually is the Barstow-to-Vegas classic, a 170-mile event that attracts upwards of 3,700 riders. (The average number of entrants in an ordinary Southern California desert race is between 800 and 1,000.)

Further information on desert racing can be obtained from your local bike shop, from the American Motorcycle Association or from *Cycle News*, an excellent weekly newspaper on motorcycling that's sold in most bike shops.

Desert Riding If you'd love to ride the desert but don't want to enter an organized race, there are still hundreds of challenging areas where groups of people can go to play-ride. Lately the Federal Bureau of Land Management has sought to close specific sections of the desert to off-road vehicle traffic, but there are still many areas open to motorcyclists. Since desert riding has been going on for quite some time most of the areas offer hundreds of miles of exhilarating trails and fireroads—you can pick the type of riding you like best and go just as fast or slow as your heart desires.

Photography by Leslie Lovett

There are also many areas of private property that have been set up as "motorcycle parks" where you pay a fee for the privilege of riding all day or all weekend on the land. These are much like conventional ski resorts, except they're not quite so crowded, they operate year-round and there's no chair-lift to get you up the hills. Precise information on the location of public and private riding areas in your locale can be obtained at your local motorcycle shop. There are also a number of well-researched paperback pamphlets and books on the market specifically designed as guides to the best off-road riding areas in particular regions.

Cow-Trailing Cow-trailing is the Midwestern and Eastern counterpart of desert riding; the rocks, sand and parched wilderness of the Southwest are replaced by trees, mud, streams, narrow logging roads and mountainous trails. The motocross and desert model bikes can be used for cow-trailing, but most play-riders prefer the "enduro" models that have instruments, lights and universal tires with a semi-knobby tread pattern.

Observed Trials Motocross and desert racing are distinguished by their speed and fury; trials riding is just the opposite. Trials is a contest of skill, maneuverability and balance—riders try to take their motorcycles at very slow speeds over exceptionally treacherous sections of terrain. The sections may be anywhere from 10 yards to 100 yards in length; riders must traverse the section without falling off their bikes and without putting a foot down for balance. Each time the foot is put down (this is called a dab), the rider receives points and the winner, of course, is the rider with the fewest dabs and the fewest points. Trials bikes must have certain operating characteristics: the engines must be capable of running without stalling at ridiculously low speeds yet they must have sufficient torque (pulling power) to climb a 60° banking or hurdle a log or rock 15 inches in diameter. Trials bikes are very narrow (so they fit between closely-spaced trees), very light, usually have no lights or instruments and have only token seats—most trials riding is done while standing on the pegs.

Watching a good trials rider at work is like watching a skilled artist or musician; these sportsmen can do things with a motorcycle that most people consider impossible. (On a flat road a good trials rider can pick up the front wheel and balance the bike on its back wheel and then ride it down the road for miles if he so desires.) The courses selected for trials competition are chosen for their degree of difficulty and will include rocks, fallen logs, gullies, sheer uphill and downhill embankments, water crossings and soft sand. About the only thing a trials rider doesn't have to do is climb up the side of a tree, but many of them could probably do it anyway.

Side-Hacks Three-wheeled motorcycle and sidecar combinations, commonly referred to as "side-hacks," are generally used for leisurely touring, but they also participate in motorcycle races. In races, the sidecar is replaced by a simple but effective platform arrangement which holds another rider. The platform rider spends most of his time moving around to transfer his weight to the place where it will do the most good and hanging on for dear life to the myriad of tubes that support the platform and provide handholds. Because of his wild motions and weird hanging-over-the-edge positions the platform rider is called the "monkey."

Information on hacks is hard to come by, except from hack racers themselves. Some people think you have to be crazy to drive a hack . . . and even crazier to be a monkey.

Mini-Bikes Mini-bikes are for kids. They can be anything from crude steel-tube frames with seats, handlebars and lawn-mower engines to exact duplicates of the larger bikes in 4/5 scale.

Most parents find that a kid who's interested in motorcycles will spend all his free time astride his bike—at least as long as there's some daylight. Favorite motorcycle competitions for youngsters may be anything from simple oval-track races to all-out scale-model motocross on smaller versions of actual motocross tracks.

Café Racing "Café racing" is for those who like to stay loose. Motorcycle enthusiasts convert their street bikes into highly-modified machines much like the road racing cycles and then race or just ride for the fun of it along twisty, challenging backroads—and they get the thrills of road racing with none of its rules or constraints.

The sport originated in England where it was called pub racing or TT (tavern-to-

(continued on next page)

(continued from previous page)

tavern) racing, and in Europe where it was called café racing. Riders emulating road racing heroes would race each other from café to café or from pub to pub, and then relax at each watering hole behind a tall cool one. Admittedly, the racing got a little ragged by the end of the day, but it was still fun for those who wished to compete. Though the name is still used in this country, the actual café-to-café jaunts are much rarer—the phrase is simply used to describe enthusiasts who have personalized their machines and enjoy riding them fast over difficult, out-of-the-way sections.

Café racing bikes usually feature fairings, clip-on handlebars, racing seats and gas tanks, modified engines, top-dollar paint jobs and even racing tires and lightweight magnesium wheels. Café racing is a form of personal expression first and a high-speed sport second.

Speedway Racing Speedway racing can best be described as motorcycle pandemonium. A night of speedway racing consists of several short heats in each division or class that qualify the riders for the longer Main and Consolation events at the end of the evening. Speedway tracks are small dirt ovals averaging anywhere from 200 to 300 yards around. Rules require that the bikes be single-cylinder machines no larger than 500cc. Because of these limitations, almost all speedway bikes are either the Czechoslovakian Jawa or the English JAP—these are manufactured specifically for the sport.

Speedway is a sport that has to be seen to be believed. It's a symphony of colorful racing attire, the sound of big-bore motorcycles and the smell of all sorts of exotic fuels. The bikes have no brakes—riders stop by straightening up the bike and turning off the throttle or by falling off, whichever is easier.

The race consists of a combination of short bursts of speed down the straightaways followed by full-bore sideways slides through the corners. From the standing start the racers charge for the first turn with the throttle full-on; then suddenly they fling the rear end of the bike around sideways and plant the steel-plated left boot onto the track for balance and stability while pointing the front wheel in the direction of travel—the

result is that they slide wildly through the corner with the spinning rear tire flinging dirt everywhere.

All you need to race is a bike, an entry fee and the proper safety equipment. Information on this growing sport can be obtained at your local Jawa or JAP motorcycle dealer.

Motorcycle Enduros In motorcycling the enduro is the equivalent of an automotive rally—it's a contest of time, speed and distance. The object of the event is to stay on the course, stay on time and "zero" the checkpoints.

Unlike the stripped-down motocross and desert bikes, enduro models have lights and instruments, and enduro riders also carry watches for calculating time and speed. The best enduro riders are the ones who can maintain a set speed and stay on schedule. Most enduros are anywhere from 100 to 200 miles long and cover areas such as the rough desert sections in California or the muddy backwoods trails of Michigan. One of the best known enduros is the Greenhorn, a 500-mile, two-day event that is held every May in California. Another great enduro is the annual event called the International Six Days Trial, where teams of riders from many countries compete against each other in six straight days of enduro-type riding against the clock.

Enduro events all across the country are open to anyone with a motorcycle, an entry fee and the safety equipment required. Information on enduros can be obtained from your local motorcycle shop, from *Cycle News* or from the American Motorcycle Association.

Street Touring Street touring enthusiasts are people with no desire to race or challenge the elements of nature—they simply enjoy the sense of freedom and relaxation that only riding a motorcycle can instill. If you've never felt the wind in your face at 65 m.p.h. or even looked out at the world through goggles or a face shield, then you have no idea of the immensely pleasurable sensation that you get from simply finding a quiet backcountry or mountain road and going for a ride on your bike. The grass is greener, the air smells cleaner and the troubles of the urban world seem to disappear—whether you're just going to the grocery store on a 250cc street bike or you're going cross-country on a 750cc tourer fitted with fairings, saddlebags and floorboards. Street touring is a sport for everyone, the young and old, rich and poor, male and female.

Different strokes for different folks, even in the world of motorcycling! □

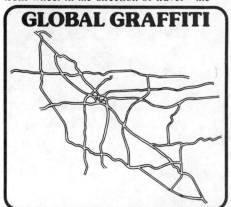

GLOBAL GRAFFITI

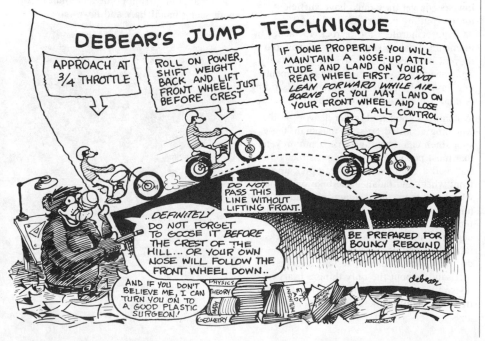

DEBEAR'S JUMP TECHNIQUE

APPROACH AT 3/4 THROTTLE

ROLL ON POWER, SHIFT WEIGHT BACK AND LIFT FRONT WHEEL JUST BEFORE CREST

IF DONE PROPERLY, YOU WILL MAINTAIN A NOSE-UP ATTITUDE AND LAND ON YOUR REAR WHEEL FIRST. DO *NOT* LEAN FORWARD WHILE AIRBORNE OR YOU MAY LAND ON YOUR FRONT WHEEL AND LOSE ALL CONTROL.

DO NOT PASS THIS LINE WITHOUT LIFTING FRONT.

..DEFINITELY DO NOT FORGET TO GOOSE IT *BEFORE* THE CREST OF THE HILL.. OR YOUR OWN NOSE WILL FOLLOW THE FRONT WHEEL DOWN..

AND IF YOU DON'T BELIEVE ME, I CAN TURN YOU ON TO A GOOD PLASTIC SURGEON!

BE PREPARED FOR BOUNCY REBOUND

Going to the Opera in Style

There are bugs and compacts and family cars and station wagons and luxury cars. There's also the Mohs Opera Sedan. It's different, really it is, and if you have $19,000 to $26,000 to spend, the Mohs Corporation will get you to the opera in style. They even call it the Mohs Ostentatienne Opera Sedan.

Bruce Baldwin Mohs, who is an inventor, designs and builds cars. And he builds them with, as he puts it, "the greatest degree of safety and comfort [and] convenience and luxury."

He builds them one at a time. Although options are for the buyer-owner to decide, his standard equipment may be enough: refrigerator, two-way all-transistor radio (with two base stations for home and office), 17-gallon gasoline tank, 50-pound butane supply, 24-carat gold inlay walnut-grained instrument panel, ¾-inch Ming Dynasty carpet with ⅜-inch velvet upholstery, stereo, AM-FM radio, air compressor air horns, power steering, power brakes, power aerial, water-cooled automatic transmission, full floating rear axles, twin spotlights, dual hot water heater of 12,000 b.t.u. capacity, air conditioning, 7.50x20 Denman custom-built whitewall tires filled with pure nitrogen (good for 100,000 miles plus), 74-inch wheelbase, and rear center entrance-exit door (an added safety feature during stops in traffic). All this with option to convert the standard multi-fuel International V-8 engine into a butane operation.

Mohs is proudest of his safety seat designs. As a precaution against head-on collisions, the Mohs seat is designed to swing centrifugally and pivot into the horizontal. Full-length arm rests conceal chassis rails at elbow height for protection against side collisions. Concealed roll bars and cantilever roof beams are also standard safety features.

According to Mohs, the options are limited only by state and federal regulations, "and the purchasers' and manufacturers' imagination, practicality or whimsical value." No automatic transmission is available for the 549-cubic inch V-8, but the 549 does come with manual synchromesh five-speed, and Mohs notes that it will "tow the largest trailer home through the Rocky Mountains with ease." He adds that it is offered for "those owners who demand the impossible and expect the improbable."

If you're unsure, ask the person who owns one—viz., Tom Jones, Johnny Carson, Glenn Campbell, Doc Severensen, Agnes Moorhead, David Jansen.

You can reach the Mohs people by writing 2355 University Ave., Madison, Wis. 53705 or telephoning (608) 233-9717.

Ever wanted to be a butterfly? Or race in the Lepidoptera Le Mans? Me neither. But the guy in this picture wants both, and he doesn't just sit on his thorax, either. This car goes by flapping its wings, and steers by a long lever attached to the abdomen.

Wanted: Paying Guests to Work as Racing Mechanics

First, there were driving schools. Then, there were racing schools. Now comes the school for racing mechanics. The first one we heard of is in Rockville, Md., where the Quicksilver Racing Team revs up. Quicksilver is the team of Chuck and Jim Sarich, the brothers who have recently been dominating the Formula B racing competition.

During the school, student mechanics are allowed to work under real racing conditions for five days at the team's shop. The entire Quicksilver organization pitches in, teaching the finer points of a mechanic's life on the big circuit. Somehow, this includes surviving the week on Big Macs, Cokes and two hours of sleep while driving 1,500 miles to repair three broken engines on successive mornings beginning at dawn and finishing at three in the morning.

To duplicate real life conditions, the student racing mechanics receive no salaries, but have the privilege of paying $500 for the rather masochistic program. Presumably, the Big Macs and Cokes come as part of the tuition. Interested people should make their reservations with Quicksilver at 1101 Gude Drive, Rockville, Md.

The sports-car owner thinks chrome trim interferes with the "classic" look of his car. In other words, he wants to simplify the thing. The customizer thinks chrome interferes with something else—the luxurious baroque Streamline. The sports-car people snigger at tailfins. The customizers love them and, looked at from a baroque standard of beauty, they are really not so trashy at all. They are an inspiration, if you will, a wonderful fantasy extension of the curved line, and since the car in America is half fantasy anyway, a kind of baroque extension of the ego, you can build up a good argument for them.

—TOM WOLFE

There's Only One Right Way Around the Track: The Fastest

By R. C. Smith

A visit to a driving school where the instructors begin where your high school driver's training left off, and introduce you to the heel-and-toe downshift, taking a late apex through a turn, and skidding without fear.

If you're beginning to get the feeling, in the face of pollution and now fuel shortages, that owning a car is little more than an expensive way to commit mayhem against the public good, you may be right. But if you're determined to drive anyway, and if you're determined moreover to drive a sports car, you owe it to yourself to become the best driver you can be, and to learn what your car will do.

Maybe the best place in the country to accomplish both these goals is the Bob Bondurant School of High Performance Driving in California. Bondurant has raced most kinds of cars worth racing, and he believes that most people never learn how to drive well—they drive just well enough to get a license, and let experience and the gods take it from there. They have very little notion of what their cars are capable of, and no inkling at all of the fine points of braking, steering and shifting. But this kind of knowledge not only makes driving more enjoyable and helps your car work better and last longer—it might some day save your life.

And this knowledge is just *part* of what you can pick up in a course at Bondurant's school at the Sears Point International Raceway in the wine country north of San Francisco.

On a cold and foggy morning last winter five students were beginning a road racing course. They sat shivering in the tower of the Sears Point Raceway taking ground school from Steve Cook, Bondurant's chief instructor and an experienced race driver, who was trying to talk and smoke himself into full humanity early on a nasty Monday morning. On the foggy green hills behind the track a herd of dairy cows was grazing. But the students in the tower had each paid $950 for the five-day course, and they weren't looking at the cows.

One student was a United Airlines stewardess from New York whose ambition was to buy a Formula Ford and race it. Another was an engineer, with the eyes of a character in a Dostoevsky novel and an engineer's single-minded curiosity about things mechanical. He was in the course, he said, not necessarily to learn to race, but to plumb the mysteries of whatever the hell it was that drivers, who were vague and subjective romantics,

wanted from engineers and mechanics, who were precise and objective technicians.

The third, already a racing driver, was going through the ground school before taking an advanced race-driving course from Bondurant himself. The fourth was a heavy equipment driver and part-time student who wanted to experience more sprightly kinds of machinery. The last was the 18-year-old son of an Ohio Datsun dealer who wanted to race Datsuns for his father.

Steve Cook was projecting slides on the wall behind him. He talked about the mental qualities necessary for good driving. He said that concentration was the most important. There was a model of a Formula Ford on the table in front of him. It had four-wheel independent suspension so that he could demonstrate the principles of weight transfer to his students. He had a steering wheel to demonstrate how to grip the wheel and how to handle the wheel in turns. (Very few people do it the best way, which is to *avoid* the hand-over-hand wheel-slapping.) He explained the principles of oversteer and understeer, and of rear-wheel drift to the right and left.

He explained the best way to corner, saying that most amateur and many professional drivers did not corner the most efficient way. Most people roar into a turn as fast as they can, trying to make the apex of the turn happen roughly in the

middle of the corner. Cook pointed out that races are won on the straightaways, and the sooner a car can accelerate onto the straightaway, the better that car's lap time will be. Therefore, it's best to brake down fairly strongly and then use trailing brake while entering the turn, "take a late apex," and then gun out onto the straightaway as early as possible.

He talked about receiving information from the car, pointing out that the seat of the pants was often the driver's most productive source of information. He emphasized the importance of a tightly cinched seat belt in giving the driver a consistent feel from the car. (The inertia-reel belts standard in most production cars are useless except in accidents, he said. They let your body roll and sway too much in turns.)

As if to tantalize the students, a Formula Ford taking some practice laps appeared on the Sears Point track. It came roaring down the straightaway like The Wasp That Ate Pittsburgh, geared down smoothly for the 180° turn around the tower, screamed up a short straightaway and vanished into a left curve like a car in a silent movie. Everybody looked reluctantly back at Cook and his slides.

After lunch the students got their first chance to drive. They took turns driving three orange Datsun 610s equipped with Interpart racing suspensions around a practice oval. The idea, demonstrated first by Cook, was to try out the techniques and principles learned in ground school: steering properly, finding the best line through the turns, feeling what the car was doing—taking the first steps, in other words, towards real high-performance driving. Cook told them to drive consistently: it was almost impossible, he said, to help someone who never does the same thing twice. And driving is not a creative, spontaneous activity. There's only one right way to take a car around a track: the fastest and the smoothest way.

A few times around and each student is driving differently. The engineer is careful. He pays more attention to establishing the right line through the turns than in going flat out. The heavy equipment driver, on the other hand, is a heavy driver. He is attracted to speed, and tends to fight the car through the corners because it pains him to slow down. Cook rides with each student and tells them what they're doing right or wrong, while the other one or two students in the car listen, and hopefully learn by comparing themselves with the others. (Cook thinks students learn more when there's a group than when it's one-to-one: in a group comparisons are possible and students are stimulated to do as well as they possibly can.)

Later in the afternoon the students learned the heel-and-toe downshift, which is simply a way of raising the engine speed to meet the rear-wheel r.p.m.s without loss of speed and wasteful drag on the transmission. First the toe brakes, then the heel accelerates for the downshift. Heel-and-toe downshifting, Bondurant says, can double the life of a gearbox.

Over the next four days the students went on to work on the skid pad and accident simulator. Both of these improve a driver's response to emergencies: he learns to do the right thing to regain control quickly in a skid or to head for the open spaces in an accident, instead of freezing, locking the brakes and addressing the Deity in a loud voice. Finally, the students practice intensely on the Sears Point track itself, in Datsun 240Zs and Formula Fords. By Friday afternoon they had joined the list of more than a thousand students who have completed a Bondurant course.

Taking a Bondurant course is a far cry from learning to drive the way most of us did, with teachers who emphasized coming to a full stop at stop signs, and parallel parking.

The Bondurant school, incidentally, is not only for would-be race drivers; it offers courses for drivers of nearly any level of competence and ambition. There is a half-day skid-control course ($75), a one-day course in advanced highway driving ($137.50), a two-day course in high-performance driving ($275) and the five-day racing course. None of the courses except the five-day includes cars, but they are available for an extra $25 a day.

What if you can't afford a course? Bondurant himself has some advice: go to gymkhanas or rallies and find someone who will teach you. It's pretty hard to pick it up out of the air.

The Bob Bondurant School of High Performance Driving is at Highways 37 & 121, Sonoma, Calif. 95476; phone (707) 938-4741. □

TURN ON, TUNE UP AND BURN OUT

A Guide to Auto Racing

By John R. Fuchs

Down in Flippin, Ark. or up in Coeur d'Alene, Idaho, they might as well never have heard of baseball. First there's horse racing and then there's auto racing. As a matter of fact, with some 40 million people attending them, auto races are the second most popular spectator sport in the whole country! Horse racing is forever first, and football, basketball and the alleged "national pastime" get left back in the burn-out lanes.

For you 60 million adults left over who've never been to an auto race, or for those who'd like a little of the inside track, here's what's going on:

Drag Racing

Perhaps the simplest form of auto racing is drag racing, also called "the drags." Two competitors race each other over a measured distance of ¼ mile from a standing start, and the first one to the finish line is the winner.

The great thing about this sport is that there's a place for everybody in it. The races are so short that hundreds of participants can race their cars several times in the course of an afternoon, and there are so many classes that almost anything and anybody with wheels can compete.

(Drag racing tracks usually sell special tickets called "pit passes" for a dollar or two more than the regular admission price. The pit pass allows the spectator to roam the pit areas where drivers and crews will be working on their cars. You can see the machinery close up and watch the expert mechanics work on it, and you can talk to your favorite drivers.)

To give you an idea of the range of cars at drag races, here is a brief description of seven different classes of dragsters:

Top fuel dragsters are known as the kings of the sport. They're the long spindly-looking creations with narrow spoked wheels at the front and gigantic treadless racing slicks at the rear. The engines are supercharged and fuel-injected, with displacements of 425 to 500 cubic inches, and they develop anywhere from 1,500 to 2,000 hp. A good top fuel dragster can cover the ¼ mile in slightly less than six seconds, with a top speed of 235 m.p.h.!

(continued on next page)

The Aquarium is gone. Everywhere, giant finned cars nose forward like fish; a savage servility slides by on grease.

—ROBERT TRAILL SPENCE LOWELL

Modified is sometimes considered the true hot rodder's class because it includes a lot of back-yard specials and shade-tree muscle-cars that would be illegal elsewhere. Moderate customizing, use of Plexiglas windows and moving the engine towards the rear of the car are several of the modifications allowed.

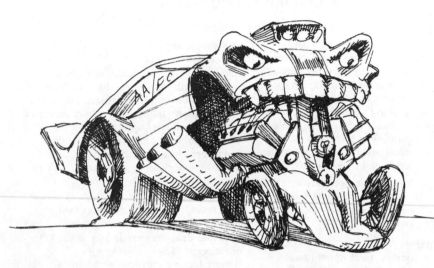

(continued from previous page)

Funny cars are close behind the top fuelers; they're special plastic-bodied creations, a shortened version of a top fuel car covered by a fiberglass replica of a recent model American car like a Vega, Mustang or Barracuda. Funny cars are usually the crowd favorites, since they're capable of tremendous, thundering, smoky burn-outs that sometimes last almost ⅛ mile.

The **Pro Stock** class is the highest class available for an American stock car; it's called Pro Stock because almost everyone competing is a professional drag racer. The cars must start life as Detroit cars and, although they're highly modified, must use an engine built by the same manufacturer that built the car. They must use automotive-type carburetors, burn pump gasoline, have full tube-frame roll cages, and use basically the original body.

Competition is the first of the classes actually designated for amateur drag racers. It's a conglomeration of what drag racers call the "hot cars." Here you'll find a host of non-supercharged fuel dragsters, sometimes called Junior Fuelers: supercharged gasoline dragsters, non-supercharged Funny Cars, altereds, and supercharged gas coupes and sedans. They are the fastest of the drag cars outside the Top Fuel and Funny Car ranks.

Super Stock is a class for people who want to race Detroit's passenger cars but would like to modify them slightly. Certain specific modifications like a change of camshaft or intake manifold are allowed, as are steel-tube exhaust headers and fat slicks —but otherwise these machines must remain the way they came off the showroom floor.

Stock cars are the least expensive and usually the slowest of dragsters. Stockers (or "showroom stockers") are the closest thing in drag racing to real drive-'em-on-the-street cars; only a few minor modifications are allowed. Some racetracks even require that stock cars be driven to the event and driven home afterward, rather than trailered in like the other cars.

For further information on any aspect of drag racing—from the rules to the location of the closest drag strip—I suggest that you contact one of the following drag racing sanctioning bodies:

National Hot Rod Association
10639 Riverside Drive
North Hollywood, Calif. 91607

American Hot Rod Association
11080 Granada Lane
Overland Park, Kan. 66204

International Hot Rod Association
Bluff City Highway
Bristol, Tenn. 37620

Sports Car Racing

In organized sports car racing, each class or group of cars simply races around a twisty uphill and downhill closed road-racing course for a certain number of·laps and the driver who's leading at the end is the winner. The rules allow different modifications for different types of cars, but all must meet rigid safety requirements and all drivers must wear approved fireproof clothing.

Racing sports cars may be production sports cars and sedans, formula cars with only one seat in which the driver sits in front of the engine, real race cars with special aerodynamic bodies or Group 7 cars. The Can-Am cars—so called because they compete in the annual series called the Canadian-American Challenge Cup Series—are Group 7 cars; they are the ultimate cars in sports car racing.

Special licenses are required for sports car racing; they can be obtained only by attending a private driving school or a driver's school sponsored by one of the sanctioning bodies.

For further information on sports car racing, write one of these organizations:

Sports Car Club of America
P.O. Box 22476
Denver, Colo. 80222

International Motor Sport Association
P.O. Box 805
Fairfield, Conn. 06420

NASCAR Racing

The National Association for Stock Car Auto Racing is one of the oldest auto racing sanctioning bodies in the country and is responsible for several different types of racing. Most NASCAR racing takes place on dirt or asphalt oval tracks, anywhere from 0.4 mile to 2¼ miles long. Just as in sports car racing, the drivers in each class race each other around the track for a certain number of laps and the driver who's leading at the end is the winner.

Grand National cars look like the medium-sized sedans and hardtops produced by Detroit, but except for the sheet metal the cars aren't the least bit "stock." A race car starts with the front suspension; every other piece is added at exactly the right point in accordance with the rules, and the sheet metal pieces and the floor pan are usually the last parts to go on the car. The Detroit-built engines are highly modified for racing, though they must still use carburetors and they must burn gasoline. A competitive Grand National car costs about $35,000 and can run about 220 m.p.h. down the straightaway of one of the major race tracks like Daytona or Talledega.

Late Model Sportsman is a junior version of Grand National, using similar cars and similar tracks—but everything is on a much smaller scale. Late Model Sportsman cars need not be nearly as strong and fast as Grand National cars, so it's possible to put a good one together for $5,000. Neither the tracks nor the races are as long as in Grand National racing.

Further information on NASCAR racing can be obtained from:

NASCAR
P.O. Box K
Daytona Beach, Fla. 32015.

Rallying

The automotive rally is very much like the motorcycle "enduro" in that it is a contest of time and navigation as well as speed. Each car is occupied by a two-man team—one driver and one navigator—and they must follow a prescribed course, travel at a prescribed speed and arrive at randomly-placed checkpoints at exactly the right time (usually to the second).

Rallying is very popular as an international sport and there is an international rally series that features events all over the world—they include the East African Safari Rally, the Monte Carlo Rally and the Press-On-Regardless Rally in upstate Michigan.

A rallyist can use any sort of car he wants and can modify it in any way. But since almost all rallies take place upon the public roads, cars must be entirely street legal. For further information, write:

Sports Car Club of America
P.O. Box 22476
Denver, Colo. 80222

Gymkhana

This type of event is basically a road racing event that has been scaled down in size and in scope. Gymkhanas take place in large parking lots every Sunday all across the country, and they are an excellent training ground for anyone who wants to have fun with his car and perhaps learn how to be a race driver.

After selecting an appropriately large parking lot the organizers lay out a challenging course with pylons. The course is much like a real road racing course except the distance is shorter and the speeds slower. There are classes for almost every imaginable type of car, but competitors race the clock rather than each other. All you need to race is a car and a helmet, so your drive-to-work car can be used as your racer. For more information, check with your local car club.

Concours d'Elegance

This is the gentleman's automotive competition; it is a contest of aesthetics. It's a "sport" for people who restore antique cars—it gives them a chance to compete against one another. Cars are judged on the basis of beauty, cleanliness, attention to detail and the accuracy of the restoration work that has been done. The owner will lose points for any non-original part that has been substituted for the original, for any part that is not immaculately clean, for any work that is poorly done.

A Concours d'Elegance is usually sponsored by a car club specializing in a certain type of auto, and the best way to find one is to keep an eye on the newspapers. □

NOMADICS

Photography by George Gerster (Rapho Guillumette)

We shall not cease from exploration
    And the end of all our exploring
Will be to arrive where we started
    And know the place for the first time.

—THOMAS STEARNS ELIOT

All that wander are not lost.

—J. R. R. TOLKIEN

Passage, immediate passage!
    The blood burns in my veins!
. . . Have we not stood here like trees
    in the ground long enough?

—WALT WHITMAN

"Whooee!" yelled Dean. "Here we go!"
 And he hunched over the wheel and
gunned her; he was back in his element,
everybody could see that. We were all delighted, we all realized we were leaving
confusion and nonsense behind and performing our one and noble function of the
time, move. And we moved!

—JACK KEROUAC

I would cross the Yellow River,
But ice chokes the ferry;
I would climb the T'ai-hang Mountains,
But the sky is blind with snow. . .
I would sit and poise a fishing-pole,
Lazy by a brook
But I suddenly dream of riding a boat,
Sailing for the sun. . .
Journeying is hard.
Journeying is hard.
There are many turnings.
Which am I to follow?
. . . I will mount a long wind some day
And break the heavy waves
And set my cloudy sail straight
And bridge the deep, deep sea.

—LI T'AI PO

LONDON TO SINGAPORE WITHOUT A BACKWARD GLANCE

By David Saltman

Let's face it: there's a dearth of snake charmers. We might have the greatest standard of living in the world, but for some reason we can't attract those snake charmers. They seem to prefer it somewhere where they can squat, where someone's playing a little buzzflute and someone's wearing an orange turban. If you want to see them there's no alternative: you have to make that fabled trip to the Orient.

The trip itself is as much a phenomenon as the ports of call. "Overland to Singapore"—it has a magical ring, one of those rings you rub and a genie comes out.

Get comfortable with us on our flying armchair, because we're going to make the journey through Asia in the next three pages and dish up some tantalizing tastes of the whole voyage, from Khaizarian *bastourma* to the *chapatis* of Bombay.

We'll start in London; it's easiest to get to from the United States, and the connections are excellent. We'll get through Europe at a pretty good clip, just stopping to gamble in one or two legendary casinos, and we'll be in Turkey before you know it. These flying armchairs are amazing.

Turkey is the home of sacred music and whirling dervishes and Mount Ararat; this is where they wear the fez and the *yashmak*. This is the legendary home of the legendary Mulla Nasrudin, the wise fool of Asia, who has a pithy saying for every ticklish situation.

Here and hereafter, you have to realize that the Orient is different. To most Americans, Asia is a largish, vague continent full of strange and savage tribes. Its size is usually compared with that of Europe or America, but the truth is that you could fit several of Europe into Asia and still have a whole continent left over. Asia is so vast that there are whole nations and whole peoples that are virtually unknown: Feraghan, Baluchistan, Kurdistan, Sabah, Mustang, Rub al-Khali, Jammu . . . these are just a few. Even Asians themselves have never heard of many of them. Mapmakers wish *they* hadn't.

When you consider that Russia alone has 198 separate and independent nationalities, speaking hundreds of languages and dialects, you get an inkling of how vast Asia really is. In India there are over 600 political parties. Indonesia, a remote and little-known place, is the eighth-largest country in the world, with more than 100 million people. Yet how many of us know what language they speak there?

Asia is full of mysteries, full of *Arabian Nights* tales and enchanted palaces and trance dancers and, of course, snake charmers. There are fakirs and emirs and mullahs and prophets; there are wazirs and bandits and nomads and incredibly elevated philosophies. There are wise men and lowlife, gurus and craftsmen in mother-of-pearl.

Essentially, in Asia there is life lived from right to left, the mirror image of our own.

Well, the flying armchair is pretty well cranked up now (it was made by a one-armed Turkish carpenter named Mustapha) and we're ready to fly. Snake charmers—look out!

Monte Carlo *"Neuf. Rouge. Impair et manque."* Two million golden *louis* change hands. A South American *latifundista*, in his whites and mustachios, is ruined. A Prussian officer with a monocle hands the chit to his aide-de-camp. Life goes on in Monte Carlo.

The soft whirr of the double-eagle wheel, the slap of the cards out of the baccarat shoe, the melodious French *croupier* calls, the elegant players, the gin palace glory—this is the permanent thrill-ground of Europe, the casino. The gambler always gets a tingle in what the Hindus call the *muladhara chakra*: a spot halfway between the genitals and the asshole. That's a clinical fact, and if you want personal proof, just stop off at Monte Carlo on your way to the Orient.

Campione There's a little square of Italian territory right in the middle of eastern Switzerland. You don't need a passport if you come on the direct train from Milan. But you can walk right into Swiss territory through an open gate. It's the embezzler's dream, and the only barrier between the train station and the Swiss border is . . . the casino. It's probably the richest in Europe, and the least known. It's understood among gentleman-thieves that what you drop in the casino is the price of your "exit visa." (You accept your losses with a philosophical Italian shrug.)

The name of this sticky-fingered hamlet is Campione, and it's definitely worth a look.

Trieste A nice town for polyglots and word carvers. James Joyce taught at the Berlitz School in Trieste, and Italo Svevo (who?) grew up here. It's not exactly clear whether it belongs to Italy or Yugoslavia or Ireland, but in any case it's an interesting and picturesque international city.

Don't do anything with dinars; it'll always be wrong and they'll confiscate them—just spend lira instead.

(Okay, okay. Italo Svevo was an Italian novelist.)

Dubrovnik A lovely town for photographers, fishermen and lazybones. There's a 10th-century *(continued on next page)*

Illustration by Larry Duke

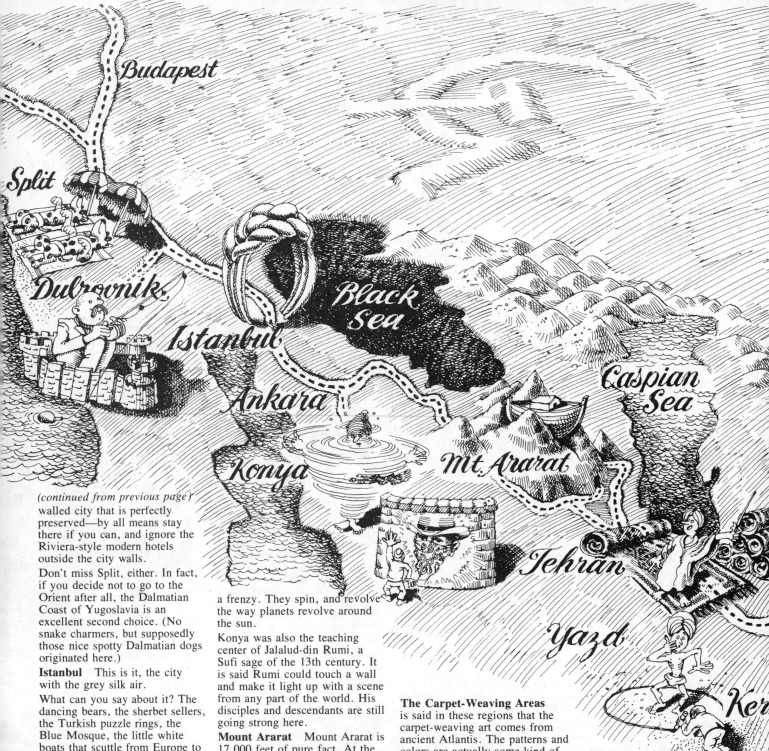

Budapest

Split

Dubrovnik

Istanbul

Ankara

Konya

Black Sea

Mt. Ararat

Caspian Sea

Tehran

Yazd

Kerm

(continued from previous page) walled city that is perfectly preserved—by all means stay there if you can, and ignore the Riviera-style modern hotels outside the city walls.

Don't miss Split, either. In fact, if you decide not to go to the Orient after all, the Dalmatian Coast of Yugoslavia is an excellent second choice. (No snake charmers, but supposedly those nice spotty Dalmatian dogs originated here.)

Istanbul This is it, the city with the grey silk air.

What can you say about it? The dancing bears, the sherbet sellers, the Turkish puzzle rings, the Blue Mosque, the little white boats that scuttle from Europe to Asia and back again. . . .

The food is sensational, probably the best in the world. Constantinople is cheap, fascinating, a dream. See for yourself the Golden Horn, the Stamboul Nights, the Orient Express, the jade backscratchers, the Grand Bazaar. Mustapha the Carpenter learned to whittle magic wands here, and drank a little *raki* on his time off.

Konya A day trip out of Ankara. This beautiful and exotic city is the ancestral home of the whirling dervishes. They hold a two-week whirl in December, and it's a truly marvelous thing to behold. The dervishes do not dance, and they're not whirling in a frenzy. They spin, and revolve the way planets revolve around the sun.

Konya was also the teaching center of Jalalud-din Rumi, a Sufi sage of the 13th century. It is said Rumi could touch a wall and make it light up with a scene from any part of the world. His disciples and descendants are still going strong here.

Mount Ararat Mount Ararat is 17,000 feet of pure fact. At the foot of the mountain is the world headquarters for the Armenian Church. At the summit are the remains of Noah's Ark.

Ararat is in the Van region, a bleak area with a thrilling history. The people are Kurds, rebels who refuse to speak Turkish—instead, they speak an ancient Persian dialect. They wander freely in their own century, preferring to live in ancient Asia Minor rather than in Turkey, Russia, Persia or Afghanistan.

This part of Turkey used to be Armenia, and is full of archimandrites, Caucasian rugs and snake- and peacock-worshippers.

The Carpet-Weaving Areas is said in these regions that the carpet-weaving art comes from ancient Atlantis. The patterns and colors are actually some kind of secret code to hidden knowledge—well, find out for yourself.

The main rug-weaving areas run from eastern Turkey through the Caucasus and Trans-Caspian khanates across a wide arc through Baghdad, Isfahan, Kerman, Meshed and into Afghanistan. If you plan to buy, it would be wise to learn the Armenian, Persian, Arabic and Farsi equivalents for: "Akh, Mohammed . . . you would rob a blind man!" and "Bah! I wouldn't sell that piece of dreck to a Karabakh jackass!" A properly bought Persian rug should take you at least three days to negotiate.

Kerman looks like the oasis on a pack of Camel cigarettes.

The Persian Dawn Persia. It is the birthplace of kings and devil-worshippers. Northwest of Tehran is the valley of the Assassins, who were the original hashish army. Southeast lies Isfahan, famous for flowered carpets and blue eggshell mosques. (You can get in if you dare to say you're a Moslem.)

Further on lies Yazd, ancestral home of the Yazidis. It is said if you draw a circle around a Yazidi, he cannot get out of it. If you manage to forcibly drag him out, he falls into a faint and cannot be revived except by certain incantations.

The Persian dawn is not just daylight—it is a fairy tale.

The Water Train   Eastern Persia and Baluchistan are fierce desert, and full of bandits. The governments desperately want to stop the smuggling between Persia and Pakistan, but they also feel a responsibility to care for the people who choose to live in such a bleak region.

So they send the water train through the desert, to keep the villagers from dying of thirst. But the train is armed, and if anyone of those selfsame villagers should even show his face—he'll be shot on sight! Everyone knows that all the people out there are smugglers!

It's possible for foreigners to ride this curious train, and it's undoubtedly the safest way through the desert. It costs about $5 for a three-day ride, in the back, with the cops. (The train has been known, however, to run out of gas about 60 miles from the teahouses and caravansaries of Pakistan.)

The Hindu Kush   Better start skulking—you're in Kafiristan. The Kafirs are a mysterious and dangerous people who have baffled all the anthropologists who have made it out of here alive. The area between Chitral, Pakistan and Gilgit, India is full of bandits, and it would be foolhardy to even venture there, if it weren't for that incredible black hash.

They say Padma Sumbhava was born in the Hindu Kush—he was the saint who brought Buddhism to Tibet. There's a sacred lake in these cold mountains and every full moon a large hand emerges from the middle of it and points in the direction of the Potala Lamasery of Lhasa.

The Khyber Pass   It's between Waziristan and the Kingdom of Swat. (Yes, there really is a Sultan of Swat.) Between Kurram and Nangarhar, between Jalalabad and Islamabad, lies the stronghold of the Pushtus, the scourge of the British, the shadow of poets, the Valley of Power—the Khyber Pass. It is fully spectacular, a blazing exit from Afghanistan into the heresies of the Sind.

Amritsar   A temple made of solid gold. Free food, all you can eat, at any time. Free hospitality for five days. This is the unbelievable capital of the Punjab, the land of the Sikhs. Their code impels them give hospitality to anyone who wants it—even a mortal enemy.

The Sikh people are unique in India. They eat meat, they drink wine and they are very militant. Every Sikh man is bound to carry a dagger at all times. Their code obliges them to defend anyone in trouble, and they do.

You'll wish they were around when you run into the dacoits of Jaipur, the original thugs of thuggee.

Kathmandu   This trip gets more and more incredible. The Kathmandu valley was supposedly formed when Krishna drained a lake with one cut of his saber. The city is like a village in Heaven, like a Hobbit-town where Buddha preached. The

buildings have eyes, there are sheep in the temples and mountains almost six miles high. If you want to climb Mt. Everest, there it is. You have to walk to Namche Bazar (that'll take you two weeks) and buy a pair of Chinese sneakers. They'll last you up to 18,000 feet.

There are virtually no roads in the whole of Nepal. If you want to visit the extreme west, you have to walk for a month.

Calcutta and Benares   Take New York City and multiply it by 10. Give up? It's Calcutta. There's a street here where all the poor men and all the poor women who have no one to sleep with gather every night and sleep with each other.

Take Mohammed and multiply by wiseacres. Add Krishna and a little-bit-of-something. Give up? It's Benares, where Buddha began to preach, where they burn holy human flesh by the Ganges, where they play sitar by the sex carvings, where everything shimmers and gleams like a silver dream.

Mandalay   Kipling got a little looped out by this place, and invented flying fishes for it, but it's the *emotional* truth that counts, and the rhyme. The city was built on the orders of Buddha himself, so all poets are forgiven.

Southeast Asia begins in Mandalay, and you trade your mountain walls for your creeping tiger forests. People keep pet elephants here, and in Nagole there is even a *school* for snake charmers!

(continued on next page)

Khyber Pass

Amritsar

Kathmandu

Calcutta

(continued from previous page)

Angkor Wat This was once the largest city in the world—it had a glorious civilization long before America was even discovered. Angkor Wat is now a tomb—for some mysterious reason, its two million citizens left and never returned—but the city is perfectly preserved. Just imagine a town five times bigger than Washington, D.C. with *every square inch* covered by incredibly intricate carvings! The most delicate amber cameo is not more carefully whittled out than the stones of Angkor Wat. It sits there today, 300 miles up the Mekong River from Saigon, a gorgeous pawn in the ugly Asian wars.

Kota Bharu Moon kites and skin puppets. Sorcerers and shadow plays. Curved rooftops, houses on stilts, tiger shamans, mouse deer, butterflies the size of dogs. This is the utterly unknown state of Kelantan, on the east coast of Malaya.

The most beautiful batik in the world is made here, by hand. Kite-flying is the national sport and shadow puppet plays are much better than any television. Snake charmers are a dime a dozen, and the snakes are cobras.

Singapore Singa Pura: City of the Lion. A unique mixture of the stock exchange, the shadow play and the Chinese screen. The opium merchants declare proudly, "This is the cleanest city in Asia!"

Singapore is building madly these days. The heavy construction force is mainly Chinese women, who wear special blue robes and red headcloths.

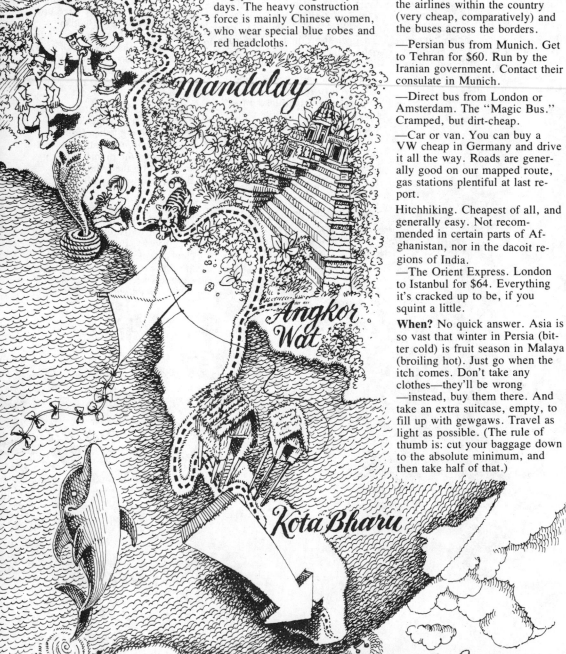

This is a good place to stop and consider. You could spend your life here, easily. Westerners find it very congenial. But then, there's Hong Kong just up north, and you haven't seen Bali yet, and land is just 10 cents an acre in Australia. . . .

Practical Dope

How?
—Local buses. Cheap and interesting. Easy to meet the local people this way.

—Direct air passage. Fast and good, if you want to visit only a few places. Not so cheap, but local airlines are cheaper than the big ones (e.g., Turkish Airlines to Istanbul).

—Domestic airlines and local buses. A good compromise. Take the airlines within the country (very cheap, comparatively) and the buses across the borders.

—Persian bus from Munich. Get to Tehran for $60. Run by the Iranian government. Contact their consulate in Munich.

—Direct bus from London or Amsterdam. The "Magic Bus." Cramped, but dirt-cheap.

—Car or van. You can buy a VW cheap in Germany and drive it all the way. Roads are generally good on our mapped route, gas stations plentiful at last report.

Hitchhiking. Cheapest of all, and generally easy. Not recommended in certain parts of Afghanistan, nor in the dacoit regions of India.

—The Orient Express. London to Istanbul for $64. Everything it's cracked up to be, if you squint a little.

When? No quick answer. Asia is so vast that winter in Persia (bitter cold) is fruit season in Malaya (broiling hot). Just go when the itch comes. Don't take any clothes—they'll be wrong —instead, buy them there. And take an extra suitcase, empty, to fill up with gewgaws. Travel as light as possible. (The rule of thumb is: cut your baggage down to the absolute minimum, and then take half of that.)

Health? This is debatable. My personal experience is that if you're fated for dysentery, you'll get it no matter what you eat. Be careful, consult your doctor before you go, make sure your teeth are in good shape. Asian doctors are usually first-rate, especially the Indian and Chinese ones. Many countries have American, English and French hospitals, and a great number of Asian doctors speak English. Get all the shots, including cholera, typhoid and gamma globulin (for measles and hepatitis). Malaria pills don't work.

Food? You never know. Probably best not to worry about it, and use your intuition. Taste is great. Drink tea instead of water, especially in tropical zones.

Language? In West Asia, Arabic is the most useful. In Central Asia, it's Turkish. In East Asia, English. It always pays to learn the basic words of the local tongue—at least "hello" and "thank you." Language records are pretty good to get you used to the sound. Phrase books are not bad either. But there's no substitute for learning the real thing.

Culture? Varies incredibly and there's no way to second-guess. You eat with your fingers in India and wipe your ass with your left hand. In Japan, this would be an outrage. Women take their lives into their hands in Turkey, but they are totally ignored in Afghanistan and Nepal. A good rule is: "When in Afghanistan, do as the Afghans do, unless you're in the Hindu Kush regions, when you have to do as the Kafirs do, with the exception of certain areas of the High Pamirs, when you will probably run into Kirghiz tribesmen." In general, Moslems do not like to have their pictures taken.

Dope? Jeez, I nearly forgot. They do have large quantities of dope in Asia. You can buy ingots of hash, cones of Chitrali *charis*, bushels of *ganja*, gallons of *teryaak*, spoonfuls of *majoom* (and that's all you'll want!). In some places, like Nepal and India, some of these drugs are legal. In some places, like Holland and Morocco, they're tolerated. In other places, like Turkey, they're pretty much underground. In general, it seems that the more educated and wealthier people of Asia regard dope as a drag, an evil and a drain. The common people either don't think much about it at all, or they dig it. Just don't get busted in Turkey, because if you do you may never make Singapore. □

How She Stowed Away

It all started the night before my ship sailed from New York to Southampton.

A friend gave me a farewell party. It wasn't much, a few smiling people . . . and Samantha. She was a petite red-haired lady dressed in a wool pants suit. She weighed about 90 pounds.

She asked me if I had my visitor's pass, and yes—she *did* want it, because she wanted to come to the ship to wish me good luck. She said she loved ship departures.

I gave her the card. Quite honestly, I never expected to see her again.

The next morning, the ship was about two hours out to sea when I saw Samantha again. There she was talking to a passenger, and it hit me: Samantha was a stowaway!

Several days passed. I would see Sandra occasionally. (Samantha, I mean Marlena, had changed her name again. This time to Sandra Laney.)

She was no longer hiding out. Indeed, she'd become the center of attraction. She'd had to surface, and her only hope was to blend in with the other passengers. She needed all the goodwill available.

After nine days, we arrived at Southampton. I was happy. All the poor seasick wretches were happy. But Sandra Laney was not happy. It was the time of reckoning.

She nervously paced back and forth. Her victories on the voyage lay now like garbage on the sea.

I was her oldest friend. She came to me for counsel. "What am I to do?" she asked mournfully.

I didn't know. But I said, "Go to the captain, explain your story, show him your passport and offer to pay him for the passage."

She looked startled. "Completely unacceptable!" she said. "I don't have money for a phone call, much less for the passage. And furthermore, I don't have a passport!"

I was amazed. She was in a totally different world. I had no more advice, so in desperation I said, "Hope for a miracle."

And a miracle happened. Disembarkation was handled in this way: each passenger presented himself to one of four Customs officials. The officer would then check the ship's manifest, find the appropriate landing card, stamp your passport and impatiently gesture to the next in line.

Possession of a blue landing card was the key. Sandra had to have one. With a blue card in her nervous little hand she could leave the ship and enter England.

She gathered her bag and strode over to the gangplank. I followed her.

She was stopped at the gangplank.

"Blue card, please," the official said, his mustache quivering.

"But my husband has already given it to

you," Sandra said, peering down onto the docks and the hundreds of disappearing passengers.

She seemed so frail, and terribly alone. The official sympathetically turned and looked onto the dock with her.

They listened to her story with concern. "While I went to my cabin for my bag, my husband must have given this man my blue card." She held up her plastic bag, for everyone to see.

"Your name?"

Sandra used the name of the wife of a couple she had met on board.

"Your passport, please."

"I haven't my passport," Sandra said. "My husband has it with him."

The Captain seemed impressed. He conferred with the first mate, and finally said: "Madame, if you are who you say, then you must go to Customs."

The four officials were sitting at their table. Sandra was told she must pick out the official who had processed her passport.

This was the moment of truth. Sandra looked at each one of them, searchingly, beseechingly. After some deliberation, she pointed to the one on the far right.

He searched his stack of cards. Miraculously, he came up with the right one. He looked at Sandra for a minute.

"Ah, yes. I remember you," he said, shaking her hand.

The Captain apologized for the inconvenience. We walked across the deserted dock, and I offered to pay her train fare into London.

"Thank you," she said. We stopped at the curb and a new Jaguar pulled up. A voice inside said, "Vanessa?"

"Good-bye, Robert," she said to me, and stepped into the car.

—Robert Cummings

Stowing Away at a Glance

Stowing away is freeloading, and therefore illegal and nerve-wracking.

A stowaway travels light.

A stowaway is tremendously clever.

A stowaway uses camouflage, either blending in like a chameleon or being so outrageous that no one believes it.

The stowaway can be detected by an astute observer, and must know in advance what to do if cover is blown.

A stowaway shouldn't demand too much.

A stowaway must be courageous, and lucky.

Before disembarking, the prospective stowaway should read Thomas Mann's *Confessions of Felix Krull, Confidence Man.*

How to Pick a Travel Agent

When travel agents are good, they're excellent. When they're lousy, you end up stranded in the Gobi Desert. Here are a few ways to tell what you're getting in for:

● See if he books freighters. Only a travel agent who's willing to make a little extra effort will handle them. The others will tell you they're unavailable, expensive or inelegant.

● See if he knows the freebies. Does he tell you you can visit Mexico City free if you're flying from Los Angeles to New York? Or that you can stop in the Bahamas free on your way to Europe?

● See if he knows the cheapies, like Icelandic Airlines or International Air Bahamas to Luxembourg. Turkish Airlines to Istanbul. Night flights, mail runs, etc.

● Make sure he doesn't get away with laziness. If he tells you *you* have to find that elusive ferry connection once you get to Labrador, you can bet you'll soon be spending a cold, furious and unscheduled night in Goose Bay.

● If he gives you the cheapest fares first, rather than the "normal" ones, he's probably OK. If he tells you about "economy" flights (without meals), he's not bad. (You save $7 to $12 on them, not to mention your stomach.)

● Ask about "Ile Clipperton." If he actually calls up the French Consulate to find out about it, he's a gem.

● Make sure he's traveled himself.

–David Saltman

. . . from a New York Subway

One of our editors tells this story about a friend of hers who's one of those tall striking beauties known as "a former actress." She loves flamboyance, and so is a natural target for the feel-up men who work the subways in New York City.

But she gets away from them like a pro. She's got an actress's voice, see, and she knows how to use it. For her, shame is far more powerful than Mace.

In the crowded subway, when one of the flesh artists gets his hands on her scrantz (and continues reading his *Wall Street Journal* like nothing's happening), this beauty simply removes the offending hand and holds it high aloft like a piece of rotten liver.

And then she exclaims, in her most piercing and lordly tone, "And whose hand is this?!"

For Women Alone: Rules for Hitchhiking

As surely as a rose is a rose is a rose, a woman is a woman is a woman—not a person—when she's hitchhiking. I've hitched through 10 countries, and I've come up with a few rules for the road for women hitchhiking alone.

Hitching alone can be one of the best travel experiences a woman will ever have. For sure, hitchhiking is a good way to meet the people and get some first-hand information about a country. I also found it was a good way to get to know myself better, to learn about my strengths and weaknesses.

There are the guidelines I set for myself—do whatever is good for you. Happy trails.

1. Never get into a car with more than one man. (In the vast majority of cases, my rides were with men driving alone; occasionally I got rides with couples, but what follows applies to rides with one man.)

2. Have a sign of destination, and before getting into the car ask the driver where he's going. I always carried a map so he could point if there was a language problem. If he doesn't have a definite destination and seems nervous, say, "No, thank you" and shut the door.

3. If you do accept the ride, the first few minutes will establish the rapport you'll have for the rest of the trip. If the man starts out with questions like "Why aren't you wearing a bra?" or "How is it that a sexy little lady like you is traveling alone?" you have to come on strong—immediately. Be offended, ask why he can't treat you as he would a male hitchhiker, etc.

4. Only in a few cases did I ask a driver to stop to let me out. You must be furious and definite when you tell him to stop; sometimes I knew the language, often I did not, but I was always able to get my point across.

5. I never let myself fall asleep. You can be mellow, but you always have to be a little on the defensive. If my energy was down, I would stop for a while or jump on a train in order to take a nap and rest up.

Don't let all this scare you; with a few precautions, hitching alone is quite safe and a lot of fun. Just be happy, rested, inquisitive—and keep believing in the basic good of humanity.

–Sondi Field

The Cheapest—and Most Nerve-Wracking—Way to Fly Across an Ocean

One of the least conventional and least expensive ways to get across the ocean is to arrange to ride in a light plane being flown abroad to a new owner. Of course, you do have to travel light, be prepared to leave on very short notice, and put up with a certain lack of luxuries (like toilet facilities) aboard the plane.

Apparently it's more economical to hire a pilot at $100 a day to deliver a plane abroad than to dismantle it, ship it and reassemble it at the other end. There are a dozen firms specializing in such transoceanic aircraft deliveries; the best places to find them are near aircraft manufacturing plants. In Wichita, Kan., for example, right handy to the Beechcraft and Cessna plants, are Ferry Services, Inc. and Flo Air; Aviation Services International is in the Poconos, not far from Piper's headquarters in Lock Haven, Pa. Anywhere there's a light plane assembly line there's likely to be an air ferry firm.

Louise Sacchi of Sacchi Air Ferry Enterprises in Massachusetts has made over 200 transoceanic trips, many in planes smaller than Lindbergh's *Spirit of St. Louis*. She points out that pilots who fly small planes across large oceans often must travel alone—"With all the additional fuel you have to carry to make the distance in small planes, the seats may have to be removed to make room for extra gas tanks," she says.

Even when there is room for a passenger, his seat may be none too comfortable. When I rode to London in a Piper Aztec that was being ferried from Teterboro, N.J. my seat and the pilot's were jammed nearly to the instrument panel to make room for two huge fuel tanks in back. We had about as much space as we might have had in a small sports car, and when you're above the Atlantic you can't stop to get out and stretch your legs.

You need strong nerves for this kind of travel: I flew to London with a pilot who smoked heavily most of the way even though there was all that high-octane gas right behind him; an oil leak dripped persistently on my right leg; our heater alternately roasted and froze us; one of our radios conked out. But the sense of accomplishment when we landed in Britain was something you can't get on a BOAC jet—and the saving on air fare isn't something BOAC gives you, either.

–Hilary Ostlere

Traveling With Heroes

When I was a child, my favorite books were *Alice in Wonderland* and the Oz stories —and most of all, *The Once and Future King* by T. H. White. So, last spring, I decided to take a fairy tale tour of England. I packed my watercolors and took off to follow the glorious path of King Arthur.

Tintagel Castle, where Arthur was born, is a wild and craggy ruin on the northern coast of Cornwall, England. It was my first stop (you have to take this tour in chronological order for full impact). When Geoffry of Monmouth, the 12th-century chronicler of the Arthurian legends, first saw Tintagel it was the ruin of a Celtic monastery. I stood where he had stood—I saw what Geoffry of Monmouth must have seen: when the skies grew dark and menacing and waves lashed the ramparts, I could nearly see the shadow of King Uther Pendragon, faint in the light of the campfires by which his men awaited dawn, when it would be time to lay siege to the castle again.

Merlin the Enchanter has disguised Uther Pendragon to look like King Borlois, the lord of the castle—the real Borlois is away. Uther enters Tintagel to share the bed of the beautiful Queen Ygerne, and Arthur is conceived.

Arthur's famous Round Table, which was a wedding present from Guinevere's father, is now hung in the old Winchester courthouse. It is not on public display, but I pleaded with a friendly guard to open the doors for me, and finally he did. The Table was discovered in Henry VIII's time, and Henry

painted it white, green and red with the names of all the Knights and the Tudor rose in the center.

The site of Camelot is believed to be a spot near the Devon-Somerset border. For centuries the townsfolk of nearby Camel have been plowing up skeletons, Roman coins and artifacts; Cadbury Hill is rumored to be a great secret cavern. Legend has it that somewhere there is a golden gate which, if the moment is right, stands open so that you can see King Arthur sleeping inside. And near this "Camelot" flows the Somerset Cam; by this river Arthur fought his last battle, at Camlann.

Twelve miles from Cadbury Hill is the town of Glastonbury, where the first Christian church in England was founded by Joseph of Arimathea in 60 A.D. Joseph brought with

Air Travel Tips: Know Your Plane

The trick is to Know Your Plane. Take a look at the seating chart they keep up at the airline ticket counter. Everyone wants a comfortable seat, but not everyone knows that in a 727 the most comfortable seat (in tourist class) is seat Number 11. It's also the safest, because it's right at the emergency exit (and that's what gives it the extra legroom to make it comfortable).

The worst seat is the one at the rear bulkhead. You can't tip backwards, you get the bumpiest ride and it tends to be noisy and claustrophobic.

In general, you get the smoothest ride (not to mention the best views) if you sit ahead of the wings.

Of course, it also depends what state you're in. If you're hungry, it pays to sit as close as possible to the stewardesses' area. If you're nervous, go first class—you feel more contact with the pilot that way.

There's not much you can do for your dignity up in the air, but here's one tip. It appeared in Ann Landers once, I believe. A woman wrote and said she'd never told her husband her correct age. But now they were going to Europe and she had to get a passport, and of course the cat would be out of the old bag. What to do?

Ann answered that if you get a *joint* passport, only the husband's age appears! Have a nice trip.

him to England the chalice used during the Last Supper—the Holy Grail. He buried it at Chalice Hill, near the wonderful Glastonbury Tor, an odd cone-shaped hill surrounded by plains.

Sir Lancelot searched all his life for the Holy Grail; it eluded him until his life was nearly over. Then, as he stood on the summit of the Tor, the chalice magically, briefly, appeared to him—only to disappear forever.

I climbed the Tor at sunrise. On the top is an old church tower, and from there it is easy to see how beautiful Glastonbury must have been when the long plains around it were covered with water. Glastonbury was then the fabled Isle of Avalon. Arthur is buried here and, like Lancelot, I had a brief vision of an ancient beloved treasure.

—Sandra Forrest Wright

Air Hitchhiking Advice From a Pilot

Malcolm Doak, Time Inc.'s assistant director of flight operations, has been ferrying *Time*'s important persons around since 1964. For the record, he would discourage air hitchhikers (he refused, quite courteously, to give me a lift out of Westchester County Airport), but he also drops some clues for those who would try: "There were more kids trying to air hitchhike a year or two ago. They seem to be straighter these days. Also, because of hijackings, security at the airports is tighter. You have to come through the operations terminal looking like a responsible citizen. The largest corporate bases are Westchester in New York, Hobby Aviation in Houston and Allegheny County in Pittsburgh. Other cities with heavy activity are Denver, St. Louis and Wichita, Kansas.

"Then there is a real sleeper—the transcontinental fueling stop in Grand Island, Nebraska. It's an outfit that specializes in fast fueling—thirty minutes from touch-down to take-off—that has long runways and good approach facilities. It's midway between the two coasts and is almost solely populated by corporate planes. I would say that at least twelve a day run through there. I have no idea how they would treat a hitchhiker—but the people in Nebraska are mighty friendly."

—Marion Knox

Some Other Motif Tours

How about a Sherlock Holmes tour of Europe? You'd visit all sorts of out-of-the-way corners of London, from Baker Street to the East End Docks, as well as obscure pieces of England from John O'Groats to Stoke Moran. For your trip to the Continent you'd follow the route in *The Final Problem*, changing trains in Southend to foil Moriarty. You'd visit Bohemia and of course the Reichenbach Falls in Switzerland. (If you really wanted to do it up you could go to Tibet, where Holmes once "looked in on the head lama," and Khartoum where the Great Man paid a mysterious call on the Khalifa.)

You could follow the route of Odysseus, in Homer's *Odyssey*: from Troy to Ithaca, in the Land of the Lotus Eaters.

You could follow the conquering hordes of Alexander the Great: from Macedon to the Balkans, from Egypt through Persia to the Punjab.

You could follow the Arabian Nights: from the Maghreb to the Baghdad caliphate.

You could take a literary tour: Hemingway's Europe, Joyce's Ireland, Fitzgerald's France, Twain's America.

It's another way to organize your vacation, to get a different slant on history or fable, and a different kind of perspective on what the world looks like, how your heroes must have lived.

Flying by Thumb

By Marion Knox

If you know what you're doing, you can fly anyplace on earth for free — just save 45 cents for a sawdust sandwich.

An energy crisis, eh? TWA on strike? A three-block-long line to get out of Buffalo? The 10:30 a.m. Monday flight from New York to Boston canceled? Wait! You can always air hitchhike.

There is a world of air travel that exists completely apart from the commercial. It belongs to the nation's corporations and businesses, whose executives fly joyfully, easily, without pain to their various appointments across the land. IBM has planes. So do Seagram's and General Motors, ITT, the Chase Manhattan Bank and a hundred other smaller firms with affairs to settle in Chicago, Denver, Atlanta or Detroit. They use executive or private airfields that are often close to commercial airports. You can enter this world, and while you won't necessarily get where you're going precisely when you want to, hitching a ride on a corporate plane is free. A dedicated hitchhiker can fly anyplace on earth with no outlay of cash except for the 45 cents he'll pay for a sawdust sandwich from the airport concession machine.

Because businessmen are valuable cargo, the executives' pilots are good — they're usually commercially licensed, well-paid and cheerful. When they are deadheading — flying without passengers — they are often happy to say yes to a polite request for a lift. If you want to go just anywhere, it's particularly easy. It becomes more of a gamble when you have a specific destination in mind — then you have to choose the flight that takes you in approximately the right direction while keeping you within the mainstream of corporate energy flow.

I did this a while back — I went from the East Coast to the West Coast. My trip, which took eight days, cost me a whopping $37.50 (because of a bad choice), but I saw some country that I had never planned to visit.

I started my trip with a bit of trial and error at New York's Westchester County airport, where amateur pilots earn their ratings. They were all lovingly hosing down their Cessnas and Pipers when I arrived at the flight school. I might have stayed even when I found out that they navigate in the air by eyeballing highways and smaller roads. But when one big guy with his shirt open on his hairy chest wheezed a promise to "take me to Cinncy the next day, sweetie," I realized that I was in the wrong place. I discovered something important at that airport, though. If you're in a plane and something happens, say, the pilot dies or faints, you should reach into the cockpit, put the communications dial on 121.5 (an internationally monitored frequency), explain your position and listen carefully while the nearest control tower gives you instructions for landing a plane. How did I find this out? I asked.

Butler Aviation, adjacent to New York's La Guardia Airport, was a better choice. It's an easier place to wait — it has big lounge chairs, air-conditioning, lunch counters and black coffee. It is also busy, with many more planes coming in and taking off. I had changed from jeans to a skirt (at the suggestion of one of the "ramp rats," or members of the ground crew) and had taped a sign saying "Ride wanted, going west" to the chair I was sitting in. By two that afternoon, I had spied an efficient-looking man with a butch cut who was apparently waiting for someone — a pilot, and yes, he was going west to Chicago, and yes, I could go along.

Five minutes later I was boarding a small, six-person Mitsubishi with five Chicago businessmen, one of whom was called "God" by his companions. He was the boss; the others were subordinates. They played gin rummy and drank scotch until Chicago. By seven the next morning, I was at Chicago's Midway airport whispering to pilots and finding out from ground crews where the empty planes were bound.

A Mormon businessman in a Saberliner interior decorated with paintings of huskies and Eskimos took me all the way from Chicago to Cody, Wyo. — where I got stuck. I enjoyed drinking tea and eating cookies en route, and I liked Cody, a town framed by mountains and hazy brown in color like the Remington paintings displayed in its Buffalo Bill Historical Center. But the Saberliner was the only executive plane that ever came into Cody, or left, and I had to hop a commercial plane to Denver to get back into circulation.

The authorities at Denver frown on hitchhiking, but the real people are friendly. I spent the night in the pilots' lounge under a borrowed, ragged pink blanket, and the next morning while I was sipping coffee in the mechanics' shed I was told by a pilot that he was heading further west and would take me with him. Not only did we take off in his majestic Gulfstream to trip over the Rockies and irrigated valleys of the Colorado and Gunnison Rivers for 300 miles to Grand Junction, Colo., but when we arrived, he met friends going on to Los Angeles who promised to give me a ride.

Two days later I found myself squeezed into the back seat of a plane no larger than a Volkswagen — I was finding out what a Cessna 310 was. As we circled Las Vegas for a fuel stop, the hot desert winds began bouncing the plane around as if it were no more than Kleenex in the air. There were dark clouds and lightning, and I weakly promised the pilot that I wouldn't consider him a coward if, if we ever landed, he decided to spend the night in Vegas. He got us down successfully. We played the slot machines waiting for the weather to behave and finally, after another hour and 20 minutes in the air, the endless, hungry lights of Los Angeles came into view.

Mission accomplished. For those who want to try, don't forget the 121.5 on the dial, exercise the smile muscles, wear a skirt or some other straight attire (if you're a man, be sure to look earnest, too), bring some books — *War and Peace* is a good length — and avoid Cody, Wyo. □

A Primer on Air Fares

On the New York City subway, you pays your money and you takes your choice. You drop a 35 cent token into the turnstile, and you can ride any train to any station. But before you board an international flight at New York's JFK Airport, you'll need a computer, an abacus and an astrolabe to figure out what choices you get for your money.

Fares are set by an organization called the International Air Transport Association (IATA), which is simply a cartel of the world's airlines. The only block is the Civil Aeronautics Board. (Actually, the fares must be approved by the governments of each country affected, but since most foreign lines are government-owned, it's usually simply a question of the right hand's approving the actions of the left.)

Complex as it is to the layman, to the airlines the rate structure operates with a simple logic. It's designed to spread the passenger load, to avoid having to add extra planes in the peak summer season or fly half-empty in the lean winter months. A $15 surcharge is tacked on for those who leave on the busy weekends and cut rates are offered to induce those who normally don't fly to fly, and to induce those who *do* fly to fly at other times.

At the top of the price ladder is the first-class ticket—nobody except millionaires, movie stars and those on expense accounts should pay this fare. A rung down is the economy fare. On both first-class and economy tickets, you can make the return trip at any time within a year.

Next come the most popular rates for vacationers—the excursion fares. The gim-mick here is that the traveler is required to spend a certain minimum amount of time abroad—22 to 45 days on the cheaper ticket, 14 to 21 days on the more expensive.

Finally, there are the group-inclusive tours. You have to be a member of a group of at least 15 persons traveling together to get this rate, and a minimum stay of 10 days in winter and 15 days in summer is also required. On the group-inclusive tour, the traveler must purchase at least $70 in non-transferable ground accommodations, but the savings on the flights are so great that many executives who have to take business trips abroad find it cheaper to book a group-inclusive tour and simply tear up the vouchers for ground accommodations. Group-inclusive tours are put together either by travel agents or the airlines themselves—among the most popular are BOAC's London Show Tours and Lufthansa's alpine ski outings.

For those seeking still greater bargains, there are two other alternatives—charters, and flights on the non-IATA lines. For example, International Air Bahamas, a non-IATA line, flies from the Bahamas (a $15 hop from Miami) to Europe at about half the fare charged by other lines. Icelandic makes a similar flight from New York. But these lines have been censured by virtually every country in Europe and have transatlantic landing rights only in Luxembourg.

Finally, for those with an unconquerable wanderlust, there is a round-the-world air ticket you can buy for $2,500. It's good for one year with unlimited stops, as long as you keep going in the same direction.

—Paul Hoffman

How the Air Fares Stack Up

The following air fares are listed for purposes of comparison only.

New York to:	First Class	Economy			14-21 Day Excursion			21-45 Day Excursion		
		Winter	Spring and Fall	Summer	Winter, Spring and Fall	Summer		Winter	Spring and Fall	Summer
Amsterdam	$888	$452	$504	$636	$382	$445		$229	$255	$324
Athens	1,244	704	756	872	505	578		355	381	439
Copenhagen	930	494	536	678	412	475		240	261	334
Frankfurt	930	494	536	678	412	475		240	261	334
London	888	430	484	590	349	412		219	240	313
Madrid	888	452	504	636	382	445		229	255	324
Paris	888	452	504	636	382	445		229	255	324
Rome	1,036	588	640	746	462	525		292	324	387
Shannon	780	388	430	536	312	375		211	230	278
Tel Aviv	1,474	882	924	1,030	661	724		544	570	628

These are the fares as set by the IATA. Because of the dollar devaluation, the actual prices are about 5 percent higher; because of differences in rounding amounts into native currencies, prices may differ by $1 or so from airline to airline.

The IATA has agreed upon a fare hike of 2 to 12 percent because of inflationary pressures. The exact amount will be determined by the CAB.

The IATA has also asked for a 6 percent fare hike, effective Jan. 1, 1974, to meet increased fuel costs. Again, the rise is subject to CAB approval.

These rates are not given here to show current rates; they are given to show relative prices. They are liable to change at any time, and the rates are only for IATA members.

Icelandic Airlines, a non-IATA member, is charging $374 round trip to Luxembourg during the off seasons. In the peak season, it's $494.

—P.H.

Breaking the Air Fare Monopoly

For those of us who aren't millionaires, there's still only one cheap way to fly to Europe: on Icelandic Airlines. It's the only international airline flying out of New York that's not a member of IATA, the airline price-fixing cartel. They run flights every day from New York to Luxembourg, via Iceland, for a base price of $374 round trip. Been doing it for years.

The airline offers a one-day stop in Iceland—hotels, transport, sightseeing and meals included—for $29. Two days costs $55 and three days costs $71.

Destination Luxembourg might seem a little strange to some people, but it turns out to be one of the loveliest and most interesting places in Europe, and it's about a six-hour train ride to Paris.

Icelandic also offers excursion fares on the following basis: $239 round trip for 22 to 45 days in the low season, $266 round trip May to June, and $343 round trip in June, July and August. Icelandic can be contacted, toll-free, at (800) 223-5500.

Finagle With Triangles

One of the best travel bargains in Alaska is a free trip to Hawaii.

Sounds too good to be true? It isn't, really. Western Airlines operates daily flights from California to Anchorage, Alaska. The carrier also flies daily from California to Hawaii, and twice weekly from Anchorage to Hawaii. When you travel to Anchorage from San Diego or Los Angeles you can—by taking advantage of Western's "triangle" offering—route yourself to Hawaii and lay over there for as long as you want on your way to or from Alaska. From Los Angeles or San Diego this tropical stop-over is available at *absolutely no additional charge*—you pay only the regular California-Alaska round trip fare. From San Francisco, San Jose and Oakland there is an additional charge of $18.37.

In fact, you can get extra stopovers on nearly any long air trip. For instance, if you fly Eastern Air Lines from Los Angeles to New York round-trip, you can stop off in Mexico City for free.

Or, if you take a 14-day excursion from New York to Rome, you can stop off in London and Paris for free. On the way back, if you want, you can stop in Madrid and Lisbon. (On the 22-to-45 day excursions, no stopovers are allowed.) If you take an excursion to Australia, you can visit Tahiti, Samoa and New Zealand for no extra charge.

Flying from Los Angeles to Bombay, you can stop in Hong Kong, Tokyo and practically any other city that is more or less en route.

Note: with the current wild confusion in air fares, make sure you check with the airline for current prices and stopover plans.

BEAUTIFUL BUS RIDES

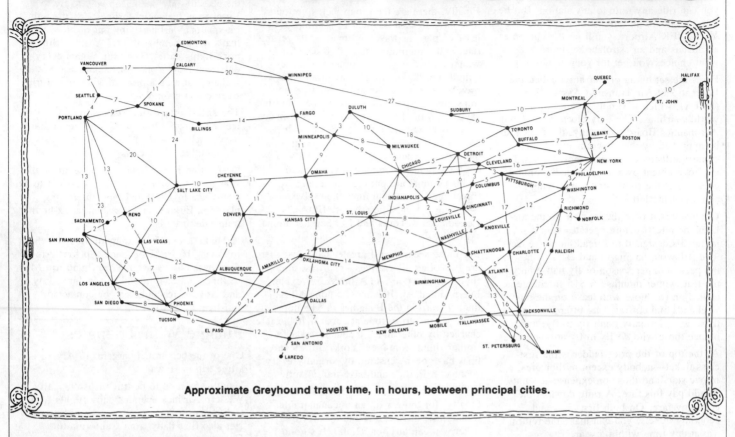

Approximate Greyhound travel time, in hours, between principal cities.

Most people think the only advantage to taking a bus is that it's the cheapest method of travel. Although that's still true, consider this: if you're into just picking up and going and like the idea of free-wheeling sightseeing, you can take some of the most beautiful and exciting rides *anywhere* in the country on a regular old bus. The following trips are highly recommended, and I advise you to consult a bus tour travel agent in only two cases (both involving national parks). These rides are guaranteed to take you far away from the straight and narrow.

San Luis Obispo, Calif. to Monterey, Calif. (via Route 1)

The drive up the California coastline through Big Sur is absolutely breathtaking.

Takes half a day. Fare is $6.80 one way.
Buses leave approximately once a day.

Portland, Ore. to San Francisco, Calif. (via Route 101)

Another spectacular ride; this one goes down the Oregon coastline through Eureka and the Redwood Forest.

Takes two to three days. Fare is $27.25 one way.

Buses leave approximately four times daily.

Vancouver, B.C. to Banff, Alberta, Canada

Taking the new Trans-Canada Highway, this bus goes through the Canadian Rockies, which some people consider the most

exquisite sight in the northern hemisphere.

Takes two days. Fare is $19.60 one way.
Buses leave approximately once a day.

Livingston, Mont. to Flagstaff, Ariz. (via Route 89)

Starting at the top, the ride winds down through Wyoming's Yellowstone National Park and Grand Teton National Park to Utah's Lake Powell to the Grand Canyon area in Arizona. This is a summer seasonal special, and it's best to have a bus tour agent map it out for you. Takes about four to five days. (Your agent will tell you about the fare.)

Mt. Vernon-Burlington, Wash. to Spokane, Wash. (via state Route 20, Route 155 and U.S. 2)

A gorgeous trip over the Cascade mountain range, around the Coulee Dam and into Spokane, the site of Expo '74. Again consult a bus tour agent for this one. Takes two days (fare information from your agent).

Front Royal, Va. to Cherokee, N.C.

Front Royal is a small town between Washington, D.C. and Charlottesville, Va. Starting from Front Royal the bus goes along the Blue Ridge Parkway following the ridge of the Blue Ridge Mountains. It's a very scenic glimpse of some of the southlands.

Takes two days. Fare is $24.15 one way.
Buses leave once a day.

Hartford, Conn. to Montreal, Quebec, Canada (via Route 90)

Especially lovely in the fall, this one winds through unspoiled old colonial New England towns—Leigh, Lenox, Great Barrington, Bennington. A particularly good trip for antique buffs.

Takes one to two days. Fare is $18.60 one way.

Buses leave four times daily.

Miami to Key West, Fla. (via Route 1)

This ride through the Florida Keys is like an island hop from sand bar to sand bar. It goes over the 11-mile bridge; the marine and bird life are feature attractions.

Takes one day. Fare is $7 one way.
Buses leave twice daily.

Pensacola, Fla. to New Orleans, La. (via Route 90)

Skimming the edge of the Southeast, this one is interesting because you pass through major southern cities like Mobile, Ala. and Biloxi, Miss.

Takes one day. Fare is $10.80 one way.
Buses leave three times daily.

All these are Greyhound bus trips except the one from Front Royal, Va. to Cherokee, N.C., which is a Continental Trailways trip. You should keep in mind that you can save about 5 percent on a round-trip ticket, and that all fares (and schedules) are subject to change.

—Rachel Gallagher

TERRIFIC TRAIN RIDES

There are rock freaks, tennis buffs and chess crazies, and then there are railroad nuts. After talking to a bunch of them, you'd think there was only *one* way to travel—by rail.

Taking the train may not be as fast as flying, but it can be lots of fun (not to mention cheap), especially if you take one of the 10 great trains listed below. Anyway, who ever said getting there *fast* is all there is to travel?

Probably one of the greatest travel bargains on the North American continent is the Canadian train trip from Montreal and Toronto to Vancouver, British Columbia:

Canadian National Railways, Montreal/Toronto to Vancouver

You can travel clear across the country for as little as $67, and a lot of people are taking advantage of it—you just pay rail fare and order a coach seat. There's a snack bar and diner, or you can wait till you get to a station to eat. (There are about 10 station stops on the three-day trip.) Another plus is that the trip goes through the Canadian Rockies from Edmonton, Alberta to Vancouver, British Columbia.

Fares June 1 to Sept. 30:
  Montreal (M,T,W), $76 one way; $85 other days
  Toronto (M,T,W), $74 one way; $82 other days
Fares Oct. 1 to May 31
  Montreal (M,T,W,Th), $69 one way; $76 other days
  Toronto (M,T,W), $67 one way; $74 other days

Accommodations regardless of season:
  Upper berth with meals, $55 additional
  Roomette with meals, $89 additional

The following nine are all Amtrak trains; fares shown are one-way—round-trip fares are simply double. Pick up an Amtrak National Schedules brochure for detailed information on just about every train ride in the country. (Remember that all fares and schedules are subject to change.)

The Coast Starlight/Daylight, Seattle to Los Angeles

The Starlight, out of Seattle, is an all-reserved night train featuring all of the first-class luxuries available: lounge car (recreation), dining car, sleeping cars, coaches and checked baggage. Everything is streamlined. Halfway between Oakland, Calif. and Los Angeles, the route follows the Pacific coastline and the train becomes the Coast Daylight. Night or day there's something for everyone.

  First class (including charge for a roomette that sleeps one), $102.70
  Coach (normally guarantees a reclining coach seat), $55
  Daily departures

San Francisco Zephyr, Chicago to Oakland, Calif.

Train has a dome lounge car—free to all passengers—from which you can view the scenery from Denver, Colo. onward (where the real beauty of the trip begins). You pass through Cheyenne, Wyo. on the way to Ogden, Utah (where Mt. Ogden is both a summer and winter recreational spot) and also go through Reno, Nev. and the famous Donner Pass area, considered by some to be *the* scenic spot in the country.

  First class, $148.80
  Coach, $90
  Daily departures

Superchief, Chicago to Los Angeles

Kansas City, Dodge City, the Santa Fe Trail, Flagstaff, Cimarron, Taos, Albuquerque, Gallup, the Mojave Desert— these sound like names of places in a Hollywood western, or possibly lyrics for a John Denver song. If you like cowboys and Indians, desert and sagebrush, you'll love this ride. Also, the Superchief is considered the number one train in the country for luxury service, accommodations and comfort.

  First class, $148.80
  Coach, $90
  Daily departures

Sunset Limited, New Orleans to Los Angeles

The train passes through five states, with stops at Houston, San Antonio, El Paso (from which it's just a short bus trip to Carlsbad Caverns National Park), Tucson, Phoenix and Indio, Calif. (the station for jetset Palm Springs). You make stopovers without paying extra if you make your arrangements in advance.

  First class, $125.05
  Coach, $74
  Departs Monday, Wednesday, Friday

(continued on next page)

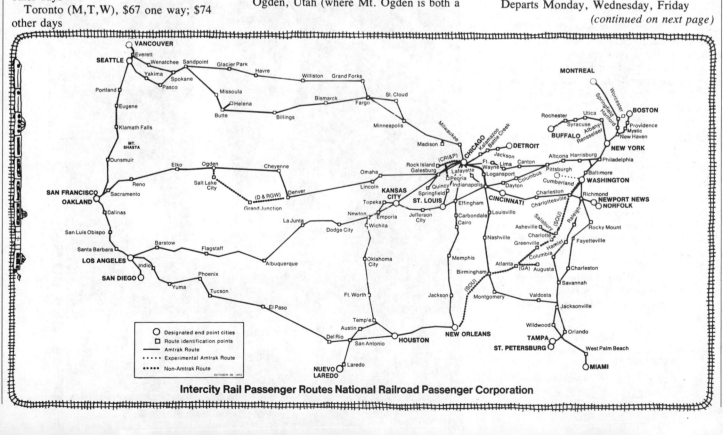

Intercity Rail Passenger Routes National Railroad Passenger Corporation

(continued from previous page)

Silver Meteor, New York to Miami

You can get off at Charleston, S.C. and Savannah, Ga. to do a Rhett Butler-Scarlett O'Hara fantasy tour. Or you can get off at Orlando, Fla., gateway to Walt Disney World, whose fantasies need no explanation. There is also a full entertainment schedule on this train: bingo, fashion shows and movies are ongoing. All-reserved train.

First class, $112.70
Coach, $62
Daily departures

The Washingtonian/The Montrealer, Washington, D.C. to Montreal

The action really starts with the 9 p.m. ride out of New York City. The specialty is a bar car called Le Pub, which features a piano and a pianist. A young ski crowd flocks to this train, which is usually standing room only. That, however, is half the singles-bar-atmosphere fun. All-reserved train.

First class, $63
Coach, $30
Departures depend on daily quotas

Empire Service, New York to Syracuse

Although the trip along the Mohawk Valley is scenically worthwhile, the star attraction on this ride is a conductor who gives impromptu lectures on the history of the valley. A conductor for 25 years, he quietly studied on his own for 15 years, then one day began to expound. Among the lore on things historic is some juicy stuff about the love life of the Indians.

All fares, $13.50
Daily departures

TurboTrain, Chicago to St. Louis

This is an experimental, brand-new turbo-train. In terms of speed and smooth riding, it is incomparable. On its opening run, a journalist sat on the floor holding a glass of water for the entire trip. Not one drop was spilled. Add a little scotch to the water and that's an accomplishment. This is considered to be the train of the future.

All fares, $14.50
Daily departures

Metroliner, New York to Washington, D.C.

This is a ride for non-train buffs who want to get there in a hurry—as comfortably as possible. Advantages of taking it over a shuttle plane, aside from any flying phobias you have, are: swivel seats, meals served at the seat, small side desks for paperwork (and longer time to do it in) plus first-rate club car service. Anyway, this was the train ride that began to give train-riding a good name again.

First class, $30.90 (Metroclub)
Coach, $19
Daily departures

—Rachel Gallagher

Narrow-Gauge Landmark

The coal-burning, diamond-stacked engine of the Denver & Rio Grande Railroad puffs along laboriously in front of its vintage yellow wooden cars. But it is in no hurry. It's been riding these same narrow-gauge tracks since 1882 and, after all, how many other trains that still operate are genuine registered historic landmarks? As it crawls around a curve, clinging like a caterpillar to the rough-hewn face of a sheer cliff, the passenger cars groan their protest, and lean alarmingly toward the edge. Some 300 feet below are the churning green waters of the Animas River, named Rio de Las Animas Perdidas—River of Lost Souls—by Spanish explorers who visited the area in 1776.

The old train makes a nine-hour round trip into the mountainous, unspoiled wilderness of the San Juan National Forest, a journey that takes you from elevations of 6,520 feet at Durango to 9,288 feet at Silverton, Colo. There's a stop at Tank Creek for boilers to take on water and another to view the 13,000-foot peaks of the Needle Mountains. There are elk on the slopes, waterfalls, snowfields, meandering creeks with wild names like Crazy Woman Creek, and there's the "community" of Tacoma—"Population 17, more or less" reads the sign.

Since the Denver & Rio Grande line first opened in the wild and woolly days of gold strikes and gun-toting outlaws, the little train has hauled out some $300 million in gold and silver ore, has carried vittles to hungry miners and has become a movie star. Appearing in such western epics as *Night Passage*, *Colorado Territory* and *Ticket to Tomahawk*, the train has been pursued by many a band of "outlaw" Hollywood extras, while its passenger cars have echoed to the footsteps of such actors as David Niven (in *Around the World in 80 Days*). There's a two-hour stopover at Silverton, which, with its "Old West" saloons, gambling places and ornate Grand Imperial Hotel, has also been featured in movies.

Round-trip fare on the train is $8 for adults, $5 for children five to 11. Open Memorial Day through Labor Day. Even though an extra train is put on to handle peak tourist demand, summer mornings find tourists hanging around the ticket office waiting hopefully for cancellations. Avoid this with reservations—write Agent, Rio Grande Depot, Durango, Colo. 81301—or phone (303) 247-2733.

—Mike Michaelson

The All Curves and High Bumps Railway

Originally called the All Curves and High Bumps Railway, the Algoma Central offers day-long excursions into the rugged Algoma wilderness country north of Sault Ste. Marie, Ontario. Bound for Agawa Canyon some 120 miles distant, the train chugs past sheer cliffs and tumbling waterfalls, through narrow gorges and broad, tree-lined valleys.

Living up to its nickname, the track starts curving almost as soon as it leaves the Sault Ste. Marie terminal and continues its tortuous course for most of the journey, creating for its sightseeing passengers a series of ever-changing vistas. The Curves and Bumps loco never tops 40 m.p.h., and sometimes throttles down to a leisurely crawl to give passengers a chance to soak up the scenery and to take photographs. A running commentary is supplemented by information on a mile-by-mile fact sheet.

At Mile 90, the train crosses the Montreal River on a long, curving, 130-foot-high trestle, at the base of which is a huge power dam. One hundred feet below the trestle, a foaming torrent cascades over massive boulders and pours through a tree-lined gorge into Lake Superior. After a relaxing, four-hour journey, the train reaches Agawa Canyon at about noon and makes a two-hour stop to give passengers time for picnics on the banks of the river and a chance to wet fishing lines.

This train ride was once strictly a spring-through-fall excursion, but last year service on winter weekends (January through March) was established. In winter, waterfalls and rocky cliffs are masses of ice and the branches of spruce and pine are laden with snow. The train skirts the frozen shores of Algoma's many lakes, carrying its passengers in a warm, picture-window coach with comfortable reclining seats—but outside temperatures may dip as low as 40° below zero.

Fares are $10 for adults, $5 for students and children (kids under five ride free). A full breakfast costs about $1.50, hot and cold lunches about $2.

–Mike Michaelson

Amtrak *au naturel*

Amtrak tells us that on one of their runs, the Coast Daylight train between Los Angeles and San Francisco-Oakland, the scenery recently has been more spectacular than ever. Just south of Santa Barbara, the train runs along a ridge overlooking a nudist beach. Those in the know sit on the left side northbound and the right side going south (it's a reserved-seat train). Amtrak employees call it "the only X-rated railroad ride in the world." On a clear day you can see everything.

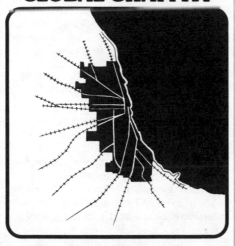

GLOBAL GRAFFITI

Chihuahua Choo-choo

Only recently completed and hailed as a triumph of modern engineering, the Chihuahua & Pacific Railroad runs through the Sierra Madre Occidental of western Mexico from the Rio Grande to the Pacific coast. The train is equipped with sightseeing cars especially designed by Fiat and with flat cars to carry automobiles and recreational vehicles for passengers who want to continue through Mexico on their own wheels.

The scenery along the train's route includes the Copper Canyon, a spectacular hole in the ground bigger even than the Grand Canyon. Along the railroad right-of-way live the Tarahumara Indians, still frozen in an almost-Stone-Age culture. (They get their kicks by running—whole villages, people of all ages and both sexes, trot across the rugged country for prodigious distances just for the sake of running.)

The town of Los Mochis at the Pacific terminal doesn't offer much, but the colonial ghost town of Alamas with its abandoned churches and *portales* is only a short drive away. And Baja California with its great fishing is a comfortable ferry ride from nearby Topolobampo. Most passengers turn right around, however, and ride back through Copper Canyon for a second look.

Travelers can drive from El Paso, Tex. to Chihuahua, Mexico and catch the train there, or they can board the train at Ojinaga, just across the Rio Grande from Presidio, Tex. If you drive from El Paso and get the train at Chihuahua, you'll see most of the best scenery, but if you drive to Ojinaga from San Antonio, Abilene or Lubbock, Tex. you can make a short detour to the little-visited but magnificent Big Bend National Park. It's definitely worth the trip.

For more information and/or reservations on the Chihuahua & Pacific Railroad, write:
Herb Ruiz
Pan American Travel Agency
410 Alameda Ave.
El Paso, Tex. 79993.

–Bern Keating

Key West Conch Train

It has to be one of the best tourist bargains around: a ride on the Conch Train at Key West, Fla. For $1.25 (children 75 cents) you get a 14-mile, hour-and-a-half ride through the quaint, narrow streets and wide, palm-lined boulevards of the southernmost city in the United States. A ticket on the train, with its jaunty open cars and miniature locomotive, also buys an entertaining and amusing commentary. "Here we have three refugee ladies from Cuba," booms the amplified voice of the driver-guide, incurring the haughty displeasure of a trio of chic matrons who have pulled up alongside in their convertible.

Trundling merrily around town, the train is a great thing for newcomers to the historic city, since it offers a capsule preview of major points of interest. Riders view the naval base, the Little White House (the one popularized by former President Harry Truman), the picturesque shrimp fleet and turtle *kraals* (holding pens for giant turtles, some weighing upwards of 300 pounds), the conch-shell vendors, Sloppy Joe's bar—favorite tippling hangout of Ernest Hemingway—and the novelist's Spanish-Colonial house with its luxuriant tropical gardens and dozens of lounging cats. Another much-photographed home, for which the driver alerts riders to ready their cameras, is the "house with seven kitchens." Shutters click dutifully as they record for posterity "the residence of Mr. and Mrs. Kitchen and their five children."

The architecture in the houses you'll see from the train is a *mélange* of Spanish-Cuban and New Orleans French, with a liberal sprinkling of New England and Bahamian—the latter, adorned with ornate gingerbread, having been sturdily built by ships' carpenters who used wooden pegs instead of nails. Today, you notice a predominantly Cuban influence in Key West. Take advantage of it—when you disembark at the depot, buy a bag of hot *bollos*—spicy, meal-covered black-eye peas—from a Cuban vendor.

–Mike Michaelson

The only authentic, working, logging line in the country, the Cass Railroad in Cass, W. Va. attracts steam train lovers to the Appalachian community. Engine No. 5, the 80-ton Shay shown here, was built in 1905.

Cog Railways

There are quicker ways to go places, and neater ways as well. Yet there is a charm about a cog railway, with its straining puffer-bellies and showers of soot, that makes it impossible to worry about wasted time and soiled shirts.

The world's first mountain-climbing cog railway was completed in 1869 at Mt. Washington in the heart of New Hampshire's Presidential Range. When it was first proposed by an inventor named Sylvester Marsh, one state legislator snidely compared the idea to "building a railroad to the moon." Nevertheless, the 3½-mile track to the peak of the highest mountain in the northeastern United States (6,288 feet tall) was completed in just a little more than three years. Its average grade is 25 percent, its steepest 37.4 percent—and that's quite an incline.

During its vertical rise of 3,719 feet to the summit, the train chugs from a base station at Marsh-Field, where the countryside is studded with great stands of spruce, past the timberline to rocky slopes where only scrub grass and alpine flowers grow. The train uses a ratchet wheel to grip pinions set in a center track to keep it from slipping. The

LI *ailway termini . . . are our gates to the glorious and the unknown. Through them we pass out into adventure and sunshine, to them, alas! we return.*

—EDWARD MORGAN FORSTER

coal-burning locomotives take nearly an hour to push a single 56-passenger car to the top, and dense, acrid smoke billows wildly in the strong winds that whistle across the mountain's barren, rocky shoulders. At the summit, there are a cafeteria with a roaring fire, a museum and a U.S. Weather Station. On a clear day, you can see for 100 miles—as far as the Atlantic Ocean to the east and Canada to the north.

For the hardy or the broke, it can be fun to climb to the summit and take the cog railway down for $3.50 instead of making the usual round trip for $6.95. A dozen trails have been laid out by the Appalachian Mountain Club; one of the easiest is the 4½-mile Ammonoosuc Trail, which begins at the Marsh-Field station. About two-thirds of the way up, at a spot poetically called Lake of the Clouds, is a large mountain cabin with sleeping and eating facilities.

Just beyond the cabin the timberline ends, and from that point on the trail is all rock and completely exposed to the perpetually howling winds. A sign warns hikers: "DANGER! Beyond this point is found some of the worst weather in the world." Whoever posted the sign wasn't kidding. It frequently hails and snows in August, and the Weather Station has clocked winds of up to 243 m.p.h. and temperatures as low as −46° F. Understandably, the cog railway operates only from Memorial Day to Columbus Day; at other times, nobody visits the mountain except the weathermen and suicidal skiers bent on conquering Tuckerman's Ravine.

Some other cog railways worth noting:

The world's steepest line rises from the Swiss village of Alpnachstad, 1,437 feet above sea level on Lake Lucerne, to the 7,000-foot peak of Mt. Pilatus. Completed in 1889, the railway has a breathtaking maximum grade of 48 percent. En route to the summit, the Pilatus Railway chugs past meadows with nearly 500 species of flowers. Even more spectacular is the view from the top—a broad expanse of the snow-covered Bernese Oberland, including the massive Jungfrau, and below, the glittering lake and the city of Lucerne. The Swiss Federal Railroads and the Swiss National Tourist Office handle ticket reservations.

The world's highest cog railway rises from Manitou Springs, Colo. up the south side of Pike's Peak to the 14,110-foot summit. The coach is glass-topped for a better view of the Continental Divide. Trips generally start around Memorial Day and go through mid-October. Contact the Manitou & Pike's Peak Railway in Manitou Springs.

The world's most scenic cog railroad may be any one of the above, but some people hold out for the Drachenfels line in West Germany. Rising from the shore of the Rhine River near Bonn, it climbs 1,050 feet in a one-mile route to the top of Drachenfels, or Dragon's Rock. At the summit are the ruins of a 12th-century fortress.

–Ronald P. Kriss

The Last New Orleans Trolley

No longer is it possible to ride along New Orleans' Bourbon Street on a streetcar named Desire. The trolley line has long since been discontinued and the world's most famous streetcar, retired from active duty, has been restored to its former glory and is on permanent display at the French Market. But there is one streetcar line still operating in New Orleans—it probably survives in the cause of nostalgia and tourism. Complete with clanging bell and motorman, the St. Charles Street trolley provides a pleasurable, relaxing ride out to the Garden District, where century-old antebellum houses are shaded by giant live oaks and towering palms. Many are still occupied by descendants of the original owners, and among these homes are fine specimens of classic, unadorned, Greek revival architecture.

You board the trolley at the edge of the French Quarter, and the ride takes you along a broad, tree-fringed thoroughfare and into a fashionable area settled by wealthy Anglo-Americans who couldn't bring themselves to live in the French Quarter. You'll pass the Sheraton-Charles Hotel, which (libbers please note) still has a special entrance for ladies, a holdover from the 19th century. At Lee Circle—once the home of visiting circuses—is an immense statue of General Robert E. Lee.

Then comes Gallier Hall, once New Orleans' city hall, where the mayor reviews Mardi Gras parades; the beautiful house where Confederate president Jefferson Davis died and Christ Church Cathedral, which was built in 1886 and was the first non-Catholic congregation in the Louisiana Purchase Territory. You'll also see the broad campuses of Tulane and Loyola universities, a long park that extends to the levee on the banks of the Mississippi River and a zoo that claims the distinction of housing the only whooping crane in captivity. Near Maple Street you can take advantage of opportunities for some fine boutiquing, antiquing and snacking. Allow at least two hours for the round trip—longer if you plan to get off to browse.

–Mike Michaelson

The Underground Kingdom of IRT and IND

It's sunrise on 72nd Street. A hundred humans shuffle reluctantly down the avenue. The earth growls, gapes and gulps. The hundred humans vanish. They fidget for a moment in an underground maze. Suddenly the metal minotaur bears down upon them. They are startled, swallowed, forgotten.

Most subway passengers don't notice the drama, much less the mythology. In fact, a recent study by the *New York Times* reported that few ever understand their subway as anything more than a locomotive necessity. Such distressing ignorance about the underworld and its attractions indicates that both natives and newcomers would benefit from a tour of the subterranean.

A Guide to the Underworld

Like all good guides, this one begins with a bit of history. The Western kingdom of transit is divided into two countries—IRT which undermines the Broad Way and IND which skirts the jungle. Because IRT was accepted into the kingdom in 1904, its tunnels are narrower than those of IND, which achieved statehood in 1932. As a result, IRT cannot accommodate RH44 cars—the latest accomplishment of transit technology. True subway aficionados will want to treat themselves to a ride on one of these sleek futurized vehicles. Wait for the IND express at the 59th Street station. Step into the orange and beige compartment. Listen for the delicate little bells that signal your departure. You'll need the warning, for the train glides swiftly and noiselessly all the way to 125th Street.

Climate in the underworld parallels that of the upper though the authorities do try to keep their cars at an even 60 degrees whatever the weather.

Population fluctuates wildly. Fifty percent of the subway citizens pass through their state between 7 a.m. and 9 a.m. and 4 p.m. and 6 p.m. The government tries to regulate its services to match the needs of the populace. Trains run with the following frequencies:

Every 2-4 minutes—Rush hour
Every 8-12 minutes—Daytime, evenings
Every 15-20 minutes—After midnight
Every 8-15 minutes—Weekends

Tourists determined to see a concentration of natives should lash themselves to a post during rush hours.

Commerce The economy of the country is dependent upon the sale of metal discs called tokens. These admit citizens to the rights and privileges of ridership. They are available to aliens who apply at the appropriate booths.

Armed forces include 3,300 men, a sizeable army. You'll find a representative on parade in every train and station between 4 p.m. and 8 a.m. Soldiers from the adjacent upperworld kingdoms are occasionally enlisted as reinforcements in the battle against guerilla troops. The most frequent

skirmishes occur at 72nd Street on the IRT and tourists are advised to have their papers in order before venturing into that zone.

Culture The most highly developed art is graffiti—a form consisting of bright and often contrasting lines of paint applied with spray cans. The authorities, who regard the art as primitive and perhaps subversive, have made frequent efforts to wipe it out. In many stations they have been successful, but as one official states, "We are always looking for new solvents."

Facilities Although both states have the musty air of a decaying amusement park, travelers can expect basic amenities—

working phone, trash cans and pay scales—in all stations. Seating is scarce. Usual distribution is eight places on the uptown platform and 12 on the downtown, and the wise will make reservations during peak seasons. Pay toilets are available in most stations, though in many IRT stations the uptown women's room has been preempted by workers, and in IND stations, one or the other room is likely to be locked. At five cents use of these restrooms is often a bargain and tourists are advised to take advantage of them before inflation doubles the fee. Price hikes are already rumored.

—Carolyn Jabs

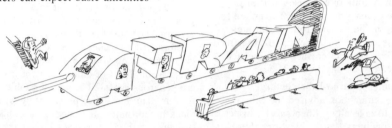

STATION RATINGS

IRT		Upkeep	Security	Art
125	★	swept clean by a river wind	station in danger of collapse; passengers in danger of mugging	an overwhelming collection, but without a masterpiece
116	★★★★	pistachio shells on the platform and sand in the corners	the exit at the southern end of the station is an unprotected pocket	traditional mosaics and bas reliefs in honor of learning
110	★★★	lots of leaflets crumpled in the entranceways	unpredictable	definitely a Renaissance station
103	★★★	overall dinginess but the restrooms are new	topside can be trouble, but the station is all right for stopovers	works by Tyce, Sly and Snap
96	★	lots of trash on the tracks	guerilla forces have headquarters upstairs and often spill into the tunnels	don't miss the miniatures on the vending machines
86	★★★★	an occasional scatter of confetti-sized paper bits	don't worry about it	look at the ceiling
79	★★★	beer cans on the track with their crumpled cups pining on the platform	entrance includes a metal maze in which you can see the track but can't get at it	rare signature of "ghost writer" on the 33rd silver post from the south (uptown side)
72	★	congestion in the passages and unpleasantness on the platforms	not so good	the entrance here is one of two remaining kiosks in the entire universe of transit
66	★★★★	an occasional gum wrapper and a random tissue	the Muse protects this place when she's not busy at Lincoln Center	ceiling mural in the best manner near the stairs at the downtown end of the uptown platform
59	★★★	much used and looks it	safety in numbers, use the Gulf Western entrance	no room for it
IND				
72	★★★	the platform is litterless but paint is peeling from the ceiling	snug and safe in the winter, especially the 72nd Street entrance	works from the Blue Period
81	★★★	spotless except for dinosaur dust from the Museum of Natural History	neighbors say that Gus, the flower peddler, keeps away the muggers	lots of social commentary including Capone's famous quote, "I like what I like"
86	★★★	platform showed one cigarette butt and a speck of spit	a little lonely, but no guerilla garrisons	scattered drawings except for the 85th Street exit where Shark has his own showing
96	★★★	unpleasant wet places	lots of corners in the entrance ways—98th Street is well-lighted	don't miss the anonymous laughing portrait, center of the downtown platform
103	★★	a diverting assortment of trash on the platform and peculiar paint formations on the ceiling	stay centered in this station—the ends of the platforms are dead	"102 can't stop"
110	★	sawdust and stagnant water grace the tunnel	the customs area between the upper and lower worlds may prove treacherous	a small collection of autographs with some unusual post etchings

Russia's Trans-Siberian Railroad: 5,900 Miles of Tea and Camaraderie

Imagine taking a train from the Equator to the North Pole. Or from New York to Honolulu. The Trans-Siberian Railroad, the world's longest, travels a distance comparable to either of those journeys as it winds across the vast Siberian continent from Vladivostok on the Sea of Japan to Moscow, 5,889 miles and eight time zones away. It rumbles within eyesight of Russia's disputed border with China, chugs past countless sleepy villages undisturbed by the roar of the automobile, pauses at Irkutsk where the czars' prisoners once marched to the mines in chains and rolls on through Sverdlovsk, where an American flyer named Francis Gary Powers crashed into the rich Siberian earth one day in 1960.

Back around the turn of the century, Baedeker's guidebook advised the Siberian journeyer to take along linen sheets, insect powder ("bedbugs, the cruelest enemy of all," lamented Chekhov) and a revolver to stave off thieves. Train No. 1, the *Rossija*, is still not exactly a triumph of sybaritic splendor, but the sheets are furnished and there is no evidence of bedbugs or thieves. The journey should be approached, however, with a spirit of gung-ho (it makes the discomforts more tolerable), and you should take a supply of gum and ballpoint or felt-tip pens (they will be greatly appreciated by your new Russian friends). In return, you'll get a surprising assortment of lapel pins, and a sense of who the real Russians are.

The train runs daily, and the eight-day trip can be made in either direction. There are three classes, just as in the days of the czars. Tourists are permitted a choice of two. Soft, or first, class ($229 one way including meals) is a two-berth compartment in an old, ornate car whose varnished wood trim, blue faille walls and linen seat-covers exude an air of faded elegance. A small table and lamp complete the furnishings. Hard, or second, class accommodations ($179) are in sleek, modern cars imported from East Germany. The catch is that there are four in a compartment, which can be too cozy for comfort, particularly since the Russians think nothing of indiscriminately putting men and women up together. One toilet spewing scalding water and a relentlessly icy tap suffice for each car.

The lack of facilities is somewhat offset by the ministrations of a uniformed hostess who keeps a samovar bubbling and delivers hot tea to your seat first thing in the morning and at frequent intervals thereafter. As elsewhere in Russia, tea is served in glass and silver containers, lending a distinct touch of class to the journey. During the winter, the hostess picks up buckets of coal at each station and shovels it into burners to keep everyone warm.

The easy informality of the train has a way of causing everyone to let their hair down a bit. One portly army general, a permanent fixture in the corridor, would hastily don his lavishly embroidered greatcoat and enormous fur hat whenever the train rolled into a station. Strutting about the platform, he looked fit to lead the Red Army. But no sooner had the signalwoman dropped her flag than he would strip down to his usual riding costume, a pair of black pajamas, which he wore every day for the duration of the trip.

For much the same reason, the train is an ideal place to meet a cross section of Soviet society. Neighbors stop in to say hello and compare wages, rents and apartments. Language is no problem, for in almost every group there is someone who knows English and translates for the others. The "comraderie" reaches its peak in the dining car. There is no vodka but plenty of local cheer in the form of cider and wines, which are generously passed around the table. The food is plain but good: plenty of eggs, fresh black bread, butter and cheese for breakfast (because of the slow service breakfast usually becomes brunch); dinner is usually beefsteak or chicken. Prices are remarkably low.

In other parts of Siberia, the Russians are mounting a superhuman effort to exploit some of the largest gas and oil reserves in the world. Whole new cities, dams, roads and railroads are being carved out of the wilderness at a cost of $20 billion a year. But the traveler sees little of that. Along the Trans-Siberian life is humble and, it seems, hard. The villages are unrelievedly drab except for the occasional house that has been pridefully decorated with fretwork shutters. Peasant women in babushkas sell berries and canned fruits at station kiosks, scrape ice from the sidewalks or work side by side with men to repair the railroad tracks.

A couple of words of caution. Many Russians are loath to have their pictures taken, and some still subscribe to the notion that an American with a camera is a spy, so it is best to use caution in picture-taking. Secondly, do not sell any belongings or exchange money on the flourishing black market that exists in some places. Both are illegal and can result in expulsion from the country.

Stopovers at such points as Khabarovsk, Irkutsk and Novosibirsk are possible if arranged beforehand. Flagships of the Soviet-owned Far East Steamship Line connect with the Trans-Siberian Railroad at Nakhodka, a port about 50 miles from Vladivostok, which is off-limits to foreigners. The two-day trip between Yokohama, Japan and Nakhodka costs from $73 to $176, depending on accommodations.

Information on the Trans-Siberian can be obtained from Intourist, the Soviet travel agency; write them at 45 E. 49th St., New York, N.Y. 10017. Bookings, however, must be made through a travel agency accredited by Intourist and paid for in advance. Travel agencies will also arrange for visas. Allow at least three weeks for bookings and visa applications to be processed.

—Marguerite Johnson

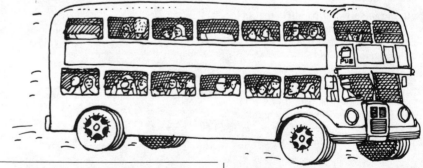

Paris History on Foot

The most relaxed (and cheapest) way to see Paris is on foot. The Historic Monuments Center, located in the 17th-century Hotel Sully in the rue Saint Antoine a few blocks from the Bastille, offers evening walking tours in the handsomely lit, historic Marais Quarter from June through September. English-speaking guides lead the tours, which cost only 5 francs (about $1.15) and begin at Number 1 Place de Vosges at 9:15 p.m. each night.

Other walking tours on various days through the week: Les Halles District Wednesdays; Ile St. Louis Fridays; the Latin Quarter Sundays. Free maps and information are available from the Historic Monuments Center in the Hotel Sully, 62 rue Saint Antoine, Paris.

—James Egan

London's Redrover Bus Pass

Travelers eager to see as much of London in a day as cheaply as they possibly can should check into the all-day bus passes available at any ticket office. Known as the Redrover Pass, this inexpensive ticket allows a passenger unlimited travel on any of the city buses for one whole day. Just choose a bus, flash the pass, and hop on for a ride anywhere within London. If you have the time, it's a fun way to explore the city in a double-decker bus.

—Barbara Sleeper

Hemingway's Michigan

For Hemingway aficionados, the names of many of the places around Petoskey, Mich. have a magical ring. It is in this north country of breeze-swept bays and green, rolling hills that Ernest Hemingway the boy and young man spent 21 of his first 22 summers. And Hemingway the author described this setting in many of his famous Nick Adams stories.

Horton Bay on Lake Charlevoix, about which Hemingway wrote in "The End of Something" and other short stories, has changed very little since the first decades of this century. The general store with the "high false front" is still as he described it in "Up in Michigan"; Horton Creek is still just as rustic as when he fished it as a boy; the bay itself—"blue and bright and usually whitecaps on the lake out beyond the point"—is quite the same. Still there is the cottage of his friends the Dilworths, where the young writer spent much time and where, on his wedding day, he enjoyed a favorite dinner of chicken and dumplings (the like of which you now can order across the street at the charming Red Fox Inn). The Red Fox also serves, in season, corn from the farm of John Kotesky, who 50 years ago drove newlyweds Ernest and Hadley to their honeymoon retreat at Windemere, the Hemingway family's summer home on Walloon Lake. Today, that house is occupied by Hemingway's sister, "Sunny" Miller.

On the approach to Walloon Lake is a tiny country schoolhouse which likely is the one mentioned in "Ten Indians." Near Windemere is the overgrown site of what was once a primitive Ojibwa Indian camp; it is described in the violent short story "Indian Camp," in which young Nick Adams sees his physician father perform a Caesarean section with a jackknife.

The Petoskey Chamber of Commerce has set up a 10-stop, self-guided tour of Hemingway-associated landmarks in the city. These include the Potter home, where Hemingway rented a room in the winter of 1919-20 and drafted many of the early Nick Adams stories; the library, where Hemingway as a wounded young soldier just back from Italy told a meeting of the Ladies' Aid Society about his experiences at the front; the barber shop where young Ernest came to get his hair cut and to gossip; the building that once housed Braun's Restaurant, disguised by Hemingway in *Torrents of Spring* as Brown's Beanery ("The Best by Test").

Petoskey is full of Hemingway places and people who either knew the writer or knew someone who did. And beyond the town is picturesque Little Traverse Bay. Hemingway was reminded of the bay shortly after he left Michigan for good and was on his way to Paris. His ship docked briefly at Vigo, Spain, and Hemingway was taken by the many sailboats gliding across the bay—just as they do on Little Traverse Bay.

—Mike Michaelson

New Student Travel Center in London

Tours and food tailored to student purses, not to mention help in finding accommodations, are offered at the recently opened British Student Travel Center. Located in the Grosvenor Hotel next to Victoria Station, and near Victoria Coach Station (buses) and the BOAC and Pan Am air terminals, the British Student Travel Center gives advice on sightseeing, airports, transfers and all kinds of student travel. Also available there are guidebooks, maps, tours of London and inexpensive food, and the center lists a wide assortment of accommodations at all prices. Telephone in London: 574-4401.

—James Egan

The English Have an American Museum

The *Manchester Guardian* called it "the most entertaining museum in England." The American Museum in Britain—the only comprehensive museum of Americana outside the United States—occupies Claverton Manor, a Regency mansion two miles from the Georgian city of Bath, where Winston Churchill made his first political speech. The manor now houses a remarkable display of American decorative arts and crafts from the late 17th to late 19th centuries, in 18 completely furnished period rooms and several galleries. Outdoor exhibits include an authentic Conestoga wagon and a replica of George Washington's garden.

The museum draws more than 70,000 visitors a year, mostly British (Princess Margaret has been there twice). A corps of proper British ladies from Bath serve as guides. They supply an informed and refreshingly British commentary on 200 years of our country's history. One guide, who was conducting a group of Bristol schoolchildren around, pointed to an Indian war club and said, "Here's a jolly useful thing for donging your enemy with." (On Indian Day, by the way, American Indian buffs from all over Britain gather around the museum's teepee and perform dances in full war paint and feathers.)

Perhaps the most popular exhibit is Conkey's Tavern, a precise reproduction of a Massachusetts tavern with "June ye 21st 1776" carved over the original fireplace. Adding to its popularity is a hostess in period costume who bakes gingerbread in a beehive oven and dispenses it to visitors free.

The museum is open from Easter to the end of October, daily (except Monday) 2 p.m. to 5 p.m. Admission: adults 30 pence (about 75 cents); children 20 pence (about 50 cents).

—James Egan

They say when good Americans die they go to Paris.
—OSCAR WILDE

Hightailing It Around the World in Two Days

Why would you want to go around the world in two days, you might ask. The only answer we can give is, "Because it's there." Not only is it there, but there are two ways you can do it: Pan Am Flight One, or Pan Am Flight Two. They both go around the world every day. The fare is approximately $1,600, and if you go first class you get a meal from each port-of-call.

Here's the complete itinerary for both flights:

FLIGHT ONE
Lv. L.A. 8:45 a.m. Arr. Honolulu 12:20 p.m.
Lv. Honolulu 1:50 p.m. Arr. Tokyo 5:35 p.m. (Crossing International Date Line)
Lv. Tokyo 6:55 p.m. Arr. Hong Kong 10:25 p.m.
Lv. Hong Kong 11:30 p.m. Arr. Bangkok 1:05 a.m.
Lv. Bangkok 2 a.m. Arr. Delhi 4:30 a.m.
Lv. Delhi 5:30 a.m. Arr. Tehran 7:25 a.m.
Lv. Tehran 8:35 a.m. Arr. Beirut 9:25 a.m.
Lv. Beirut 10:40 a.m. Arr. Istanbul 12:20 p.m.
Lv. Istanbul 1:20 p.m. Arr. Frankfurt 3:05 p.m.
Lv. Frankfurt 4:20 p.m. Arr. London 4:50 p.m.
Lv. London 6 p.m. Arr. New York 8:35 p.m.

Of course, you will have spotted the flaw in Flight One. By crossing the International Date Line the wrong way, you lose a day. Flight Two takes care of that by going the opposite direction, and you make the whole thing in two days flat:

FLIGHT TWO
Lv. New York 7 p.m. Arr. London 6:40 a.m.
Lv. London 8 a.m. Arr. Frankfurt 10:25 a.m.
Lv. Frankfurt 11:35 a.m. Arr. Istanbul 3:20 p.m.
Lv. Istanbul 4:20 p.m. Arr. Beirut 5:50 p.m.
Lv. Beirut 6:50 p.m. Arr. Tehran 10:30 p.m.
Lv. Tehran 11:50 p.m. Arr. Karachi 1:40 a.m.
Lv. Karachi 2:55 a.m. Arr. Delhi 5 a.m.
Lv. Delhi 5:50 a.m. Arr. Bangkok 10:50 a.m.
Lv. Bangkok 11:45 a.m. Arr. Hong Kong 3:15 p.m.
Lv. Hong Kong 4:35 p.m. Arr. Tokyo 9:05 p.m.
Lv. Tokyo 10:30 p.m. Arr. Honolulu 10:05 a.m. (The same day!—by crossing the International Date Line)
Lv. Honolulu 12:20 p.m. Arr. L.A. 7:25 p.m.

So it's something to think about, the next time you want to get from New York to Los Angeles: go via Karachi!

Pan Am says the only person they know of who has taken the flight all the way around is . . . well, you guessed it . . . the wife of the president of the company!

—The Editors

Travel Through the Jungle on Horseback

It's quite easy—and fairly inexpensive—to arrange a horseback journey through the jungles of Mexico. Chiapas—the southernmost state of Mexico—is still a very primitive area and the home of several Indian tribes of the Tzotzil race. Here you can rent a horse, with or without a guide, and ride through beautiful region.

The local people all seem to have horses and are quite ready to rent them out. The going price is $2 a day for the horse, and if you want a guide, it will cost another $4 to hire him and his horse.

It's best to carry as little baggage as possible—you can leave your extra things with the people you rent your horse from, as collateral.

Wherever you intend to rent your horse, have a good look around first to make sure you'll get a good, healthy horse. And your guide should *not* be the owner of the horses—if he is, he'll be more concerned about the horses than about you.

A good place to begin your journey into the jungle is San Cristóbal Las Casas—the old Spanish capital of Chiapas. Take a bus to Ocosingo and rent a horse and guide. You'll ride for two days through forest-covered mountains before arriving in the jungle. On this ride you should try to get to Bonampak, where Mayan ruins have just recently been found by archaeologists.

You can go at your own speed; when I made this trip, I averaged about six hours a day actual riding time—you get up before sunrise and ride during the cool of the morning. I had a sleeping bag, but for the most part did not use it; I stayed in Indian villages every night, where I got a dinner and a straw mat in a hut to sleep on. This cost me about $1 a night plus a little extra for corn for my horse.

You'll have no problem drinking the good, fresh water from the many streams. Take some alcohol along to treat insect bites.

You can rent horses and guides in nearly every town in Chiapas; just get yourself a map of the state and figure out where you want to go. Traveling through the jungle on horseback—seeing the vivid parrots and butterflies, the monkeys, the endless lush green vegetation—is one of most impressive experiences Mexico has to offer.

—Jean-Louis Etienne with Sondi Field

The Buzzards of Hinckley

William Faulkner once said if he were reincarnated he'd like to come back as a buzzard. "Everyone lets you be, and you can eat anywhere," he said.

But this hasn't sunk in for the residents of Hinckley, Ohio nor for the 30,000 tourists who go out there in droves each year to scan the skies for signs of the great and lonely birds.

For the last 150 years the buzzards have come back to Hinckley Ridge on exactly the same date: March 15. (It's a little bit uncanny that March 15 is the same day the swallows return to San Juan Capistrano, too.)

The buzzards have never failed to return to Hinckley on that particular day. No one knows why.

Even though it was something they could count on, the people of Hinckley despised those buzzards for years. Faulkner was happy. But in 1957, a handful of Hinckley citizens, along with a few park officials and a Cleveland newspaper, decided to turn carrion into cash-on-hand.

The publicity was devastating, but of course the buzzards knew nothing about it at all.

So now the citizens of Hinckley grudgingly tolerate these unlovable birds. The shoulder patch of the police uniform has three soaring buzzards set against a rising sun. School kids paint buzzard pictures for Parent's Day. The Chamber of Commerce's welcome sign depicts an Al Capp cartoon of "Buzzy Buzzard." And every year, thousands of tourists come out to watch them gather in the dead and gnarled pines of Hinckley Ridge.

Faulkner would vomit.

(If you want more information on the Hinckley Buzzard Festival, contact the Chamber of Commerce, Hinckley, Ohio 44233 or the Metropolitan Park District, Cleveland.)

—David Saltman

Swallow, Swallow, flying, flying South,
  Fly to her, and fall upon her gilded eaves,
And tell her, tell her, what I tell to thee. . . .

O tell her, Swallow, that thy brood is flown:
    Say to her, I do but wanton in the South,
  But in the North long since my nest is made.

O tell her, brief is life but love is long,
    And brief the sun of summer in the North,
  And brief the moon of beauty in the South. . . .

—ALFRED, LORD TENNYSON

Trail Riding in the Badlands

Shades of Teddy Roosevelt! Your quarter horse picks a trail through a carpet of sagebrush and circles to the top of a tall, craggy butte, typical of Dakota badland country. You've seen a golden eagle soar overhead and spotted a small herd of the 200 buffalo that roam the Theodore Roosevelt National Memorial Park near Medora in southwest North Dakota. You've been intrigued by a prairie dog "town," the fat little rodents sitting boldly beside their burrows as you pass. You've ridden through cottonwoods along the snaking Little Missouri River and crossed a dried-up creek. You've seen a sampling of the park's wild bounty of plums and sweet honeysuckle, wild asparagus and pungent onions, buffalo berries and choke berries. And you've enjoyed a trail breakfast—eggs, bacon and doughboys (fried bread dough) sizzling in a black skillet.

Saddle horses are available Memorial Day through Labor Day from the Tescher Ranch, the only livery in the park, for about $2.50 an hour, $10 a day or longer by arrangement (prices include guides). Young children are welcome, and "tenderfoot" riders are their business. Cost for a trail-cooked breakfast is about $1.50 per person (but phone or write in advance). Chuck wagon meals are available by arrangement for groups of 10 or more. Contact: Tescher's Trail Rides, Medora, N.D. 58645.

After a ride, take a scenic drive through the park and absorb the rugged badland scenery—the graceful oxbow of the river, the spectacular Painted Canyon. See a perpetually-burning coal vein (ignited by lightning in 1951) and visit a museum dedicated to the wild and woolly history of cattle ranching in the region. —*Mike Michaelson*

Horsing Around in France

Consider the leisurely pleasures of a horseback tour through France, now offered by Cheval Voyage in Paris. Equestrian excursions through the delectable French countryside are designed for both the seasoned and the inexperienced rider—instruction in all riding disciplines is part of the package.

You often lodge in chateaux and riding clubs, and you frequently have the chance to swim or play tennis. Rates range from 700 to 880 francs (about $160 to $200) a week; this includes room, board and horses.

Riding vacations may be arranged in Brittany and Normandy, in the Garrone and in Perigord, in southwest France. The season is usually Easter through October.

If you like the idea of seeing France at a leisurely pace but you don't want to actually

De Camptown Races in Ashland, Va.

A happy mixture of horse race, fancy dress show, Woodstock lie-in, bourbon drinking tournament, and country picnic is the annual running of the Camptown Races on the second Saturday of every May—it's a "mile of people" sprawled along a grassy slope outside Ashland, Va. This year again some 20,000 spectators will set out their blankets and their coolers full of canned beer and containers of purple Jesus (grape juice and drugstore alcohol); college students will arrive in rented moving vans, which offer room for love-making inside and for viewing the races on top.

Seven races attract some 70 entries; there are registered quarter horses, thoroughbreds and Arabians. Most of them race professionally elsewhere, but there's no open betting done at the Camptown Races. (There *are* plenty of private bets, though.) Although the real Camptown Races took place a century ago up in Pennsylvania, the Ashland boosters figured that since nobody was using the title these days they might as well borrow it for their happy occasion, which was dreamed up in 1951 to raise money for a war memorial in Ashland.

The Stephen Foster song mentions "De Camptown race track nine miles long''; the Ashland track is somewhat shorter, but no one minds.

—*Roy Bongartz*

We have a phrase in English, "straight from the horse's mouth." I never knew why the particular animal chosen was a horse, especially as most horses are generally not very communicative.

—JOSEPH CLARK GREW

---

ride a horse, consider renting a comfortable, horse-drawn caravan equipped with four berths and bedding, lighting, two-burner gas stove, sink, gas refrigerator (or ice box), table and kitchen implements. You get a horse chosen for his quiet disposition, and you follow an itinerary through Normandy or Brittany that takes in splendid scenery and points of interest.

You can rent caravans by the week from late March to late October. Rates per four-person caravan (including the horse's feed, but not your own) are 600 to 980 francs (about $136 to $222) a week, depending on the season.

For more information on both riding and caravan tours through France, see your travel agent or write Cheval Voyage, 8 rue de Milan, 75509 Paris.

—*James Egan*

GLOBAL GRAFFITI

The Smithsonian Has Everything

If you hanker to explore the curious anthropoid called Man, not to mention assorted other beasts, no place is more beguiling than Washington, D.C.'s Smithsonian Institution. The Smithsonian occupies seven huge museums on the Mall between the Washington Monument and the Capitol building. It also runs a zoo, has a display of portraits and American art at the old Patent Building, and operates the recently opened Renwick Gallery devoted to design and crafts, and the National Observatory.

The Smithsonian has culled clutter from the world's attic that is as personal as the contents of the steamer trunk in Grandma's back room. You can't help yourself—you get involved. I pressed a button to turn on a nickelodeon-size sound-and-light spectacular and spent 20 minutes learning about the workings of an electric toothbrush. At another exhibit, I got squeamish when I saw how an Eskimo hunts—by inserting a bent whale bone into frozen blubber to impale the wolf that eats the blubber. I sat in a moon module with a dummy astronaut, probed the universe at the Observatory and learned from a curator at the zoo that there was a brief bamboo crisis after the Chinese pandas, Ling-Ling and Hsing-Hsing, arrived. (The playful pandas chomp bamboo like candy—it's their favorite food, and Washington, alas, was short on bamboo.)

We're indebted to English scientist James Smithson for the Smithsonian. Although he'd never been to the United States, he bequeathed half a million dollars to the American people in the mid-1800s "for the increase and diffusion of knowledge." His money has been spent well.

You can usually visit the Smithsonian between 10 a.m. and 5:30 p.m. daily, and the museum buildings are often open as late as 9 p.m. during the summer. Shops on the premises sell artifacts, books and post cards at sensible prices, and cafeterias at several buildings serve good food. Admission is free.

—*Ralph H. Peck*

Eating the Wind in Malaysia

By Orlando Flane

When the British were there they called it Malaya and it was the remotest place on earth. Now Malaysia is independent, and it's a fat, luxuriant land where the people still think all orang puteh—*white folks—speak the same language.*

So you're out on the hashish trail, let's say, and you're a little tired of running into people from Philadelphia in the streets of Kabul. You'd like to go somewhere where your stomach can recuperate, and maybe even soak up a little native culture.

Or maybe you're like me, an incurable nomad and wanderer, and you feel like having acupuncture or hunting tigers or learning magic from The Source and not some fourth-string translation.

My friend, it's time to *makan anging*—to "eat the wind." In Malaysia, that's what they call taking a holiday.

When the British owned it they called it Malaya, and it was the remotest place on earth. Now it's independent, and the headhunters of Borneo are trading on the Singapore Stock Exchange. It's a fat, luxuriant land with a paltry trickle of tourists, and in the countryside they still think all white people speak the same language. They don't differentiate between Americans and Yugoslavians—they're all *orang puteh*, white folks, and that's fine with them.

You fly into Kuala Lumpur, the capital, over hundreds and hundreds of miles of unadulterated virgin jungle. All you see from the air is a strong latticework of dense, feathered, green palm tops. But you know that beneath that impenetrable roof tigers are prowling and Negrito pygmies are worshipping the stars.

Every now and then a skinny brown ribbon of roadway snakes through the voluptuous green mat, connecting a tin mine with a rubber plantation. The rubber plantation is probably owned by a ruddy Britisher (doubtless married to a beautiful Eurasian woman) who came out here to make his fortune before retiring in Tunbridge Wells. But the dirt road is empty.

On your approach to K.L. (they always call Kuala Lumpur K.L.) you fly over the state of Kedah, the rice bowl. From Kedah you may fly along the seacoast, past Penang (where the hippies hang out), and if your pilot is a proud Malay he may take a short excursion to pass over Malacca.

Malacca is the home of the "rain bird," what the English call the "blue-billed gaper." It's magnificent; it's the size of a starling, colored black and deep claret with white stripes on its shoulder, and it has a broad bill that is cobalt blue on top and bright orange underneath.

Its eyes are sea green, and it was a prize ornament when Malacca was the thriving and mysterious capital of the Vijayat kingdom of the eighth century.

Malacca is now a sleepy but elegant Malay town with Portuguese, Chinese, Indian and Parsi influences; it is the home of the Malacca walking-stick and blocks and blocks of ancient Chinese mansions; and, it is the place to keep your ears tuned for echoes of the remote glory of the archipelago.

Your plane will now fly over Kuala Lumpur itself, on the way to the airport. You'll pass over the enormous Templer Park (with the world's only 10-story waterfall), go by the Batu Caves (inside which is a yoga ashram, a Hindu temple and a real five-legged cow), over the Pasar Minggu—the Sunday Market (where you can buy anything from handmade batik to Chinese medicine) and past Weld Supermarket (where you can buy anything from Hewlett-Packard calculators to Kellogg's corn flakes).

Just on your right you'll see the brown and white Tudor houses of the Selangor Club. That's the English gentlemen's sporting club, of course, and somehow it seems to fit right in between the red-and-white striped mosque and the Chinese Dragon Temple.

When the British cricket team was on its Asian tour two years ago, the Malays spent days trimming and clipping the Club's cricket pitch. They got it just right. But they were extremely worried about rain.

It was right in the monsoon season,

and you can't play cricket in the rain. If it rained that day, the Malaysian team would lose face. It was a grave problem, and it was finally presented to the King.

They call him the *Yang di-Pertuan Agong*, the Big Ace Wheels, and believe it or not he gets *elected* every five years! The present King comes from the state of Kelantan, on the east coast, the state best known for its powerful *bomohs* and fighting kites.

When the King heard the cricket problem he immediately made a decision. He ordered his viziers to get in contact with the famous Pawang Mustapha, the Tiger Shaman of Kelantan, and bring him under royal escort to Kuala Lumpur.

This was done. The Pawang is a younger man, in his forties, clean-shaven with longish hair slicked back, tremendously powerful arms and a commanding presence. Even a King must be circumspect with a genuine *bomoh*—the magician is a law unto himself.

The King explained the problem to Pawang Mustapha and asked for help.

On the day of the match—you can look it up—the monsoon rains slashed the entire country of Malaysia, from Singapore in the south right up to the Siamese border. But there were 11,000 witnesses to the fact that one spot stayed perfectly dry—the cricket pitch of the Selangor Club in Kuala Lumpur.

You finally land at Subang Airport, a small and quite elegant field hacked out of the bush by the rubber barons. You step off the plane, take a breath of the tropical air . . . and *wham*! You're drenched in sweat. It feels like you're in a sauna bath and the air is heavy with steaming moisture and the scent of frangipani. It's clearly a place where magic *works*.

A lovely Chinese girl in a miniskirt gives you a big smile and pins an orchid on your breast.

"Welcome to Malaysia," she smiles, speaking flawless English. "Customs is that way." □

Kuala Lumpur / Malaysia

REALLY CHEAP THRILLS!

IN

CHICAGO

By Carol White

Chicago: the Windy City, City of the Big Shoulders. It's home for some of the most corrupt politicians in the country, the world's busiest airport (O'Hare International) and *Playboy* magazine. It's the city where those bloody riots took place during the Democratic National Convention in 1968, where Al Capone and associates thrived in the Thirties (there's a story, probably untrue, that a Russian visitor's first request in Chicago was, "Pliz, I vould like to zee a gungster"), and where Enrico Fermi began the Atomic Age in 1942. In a city like *this* you're supposed to find cheap thrills?

Well, believe a Chicagoan: most of us who live here not only survive it, but—strange to say—we learn to love the place. And that's at least partly because we know where to find the good things—cheap.

Baseball   Even if the Chicago Cubs aren't your favorite team, you can hardly help but enjoy a summer afternoon at Wrigley Field if you sit in the outfield with the "bleacher bums." The most loyal, most rabid—and most broke—fans sit in the bleachers; seats there cost $1 on a first-come, first-served basis, and for important games bleacher bums may line up hours in advance for seats. Standard equipment in the bleachers: a T-shirt, a tattoo and a paper cup of Schlitz. Wrigley Field (owned, like the Cubs, by P. K. Wrigley, the chewing-gum king) is one of the oldest and prettiest ball parks in the country; no night games here, and no Astroturf—there's real honest-to-God grass—and the brick walls are covered with ivy.

Crêpes   Some of the finest crêpes you can find outside of Paris are made at La Crêperie, 2845 N. Clark St. The large, light, lovingly folded and lavishly buttered French pancakes served here are filled with delicious combinations of ham, eggs, cheese, tomato, spinach, chicken and seafood. A complete meal, including salad and dinner and dessert crêpes, runs about $3. (Try the banana crêpe for dessert!) Bring your own wine. This is a very small, very popular spot, so come early or be prepared to wait.

Movies   Not far from La Crêperie, at 2433 N. Lincoln Ave., is the Biograph, the movie theater where John Dillinger was shot. The little lobby contains a musty display of Dillinger memorabilia and a huge counterful of penny candy where you can buy enough jawbreakers, licorice whips and baby Tootsie Rolls to keep you going through the entire double feature for under 25 cents. (They have things like popcorn, too, if you really want to blow your wad.) Admission is $1.25; the Biograph shows second-, third- and fourth-run movies as well as a respectable smattering of genuine old classics. Since the management is averse to advertising in the papers the easiest way to find out what's showing is to call 348-4123.

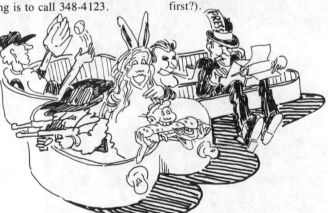

Royko   In a city where political corruption is more or less a way of life, the most outspoken and tenacious crusader for reform is Mike Royko, a newspaper columnist. For a mere 10 cents you can buy the evening *Chicago Daily News* on any corner and enjoy Royko's column (on page three at the far left). Even if you didn't even know that Mayor Daley is Irish, you can get a kick out of the column, for Royko exposes the egos and the subterfuges of Chicago's politicians with a witty combination of intelligence, humor and plain factual reporting. Royko is one of the main reasons that people can not only stand to live in Chicago, but enjoy it.

Second City   The satirical revues at Second City, 1616 N. Wells St., are among Chicago's finest entertainment offerings—they're topical, a little crazy and usually hilarious. Admission and drinks can run pretty high, especially on weekends, but you can drop by weeknights (Monday through Thursday) at 11 p.m. and Saturdays at 1 a.m. and for free watch the troupe do improvisations and work out skits for their next show. Note: if you do go to one of the regular shows, all you really need to spend is the price of admission; you're not required to buy any drinks.

Transportation   Chicago's public transportation is about the most expensive anywhere—a ride on a CTA bus, subway or elevated train will cost you 45 cents, an extra 10 cents if you want to transfer. If you're with two or three other people and you're not going too far, a cab can actually be cheaper. But some rides are worth it for what they show you of the city.

For example, take the Halsted Street bus (number 8) and get a good look at non-Lake Shore Drive Chicago. Beginning at 3900 North, the bus follows Halsted straight south for 16 miles of Chicago without makeup: it's often ugly, but never boring. You see, in reasonably quick succession, most of the ethnic neighborhoods (Jewish, black, Lithuanian-Latvian, Irish, more black) that make Chicago the grubby, fascinating, vital mess that it is. And just southwest of the Loop, you go by the Chicago Circle Campus of the University of Illinois, the only campus named after an expressway interchange (why didn't L.A. think of that first?).

At 79th Street, walk six blocks east and get on the Dan Ryan Rapid Transit Train, which will carry you back north to the Loop much faster than the Halsted bus brought you south. The train runs down the median strip of the Dan Ryan Expressway, so you can observe—smugly—one of the biggest permanent floating traffic jams in the world, up to 18 lanes of it.

(If you want a good cheap guidebook, Chicago has one of those, too: it bears the fundamental title *The Chicago GuideBook*, and it's published by Henry Regnery Co.; $1.95 in nearly every bookstore in town.)

Exploring the Silent Places, with Mountain Travel

Mountain Travel is a kind of travel agency that specializes in wilderness trekking. You can go on their tours anywhere from the High Pamirs to the Sahara Desert. You'll get a good workout, but you won't get bitten by wild camels.

Here's what they say about their trips:

"Our clients come from a wide variety of backgrounds; they range in age from late teens to mid-sixties. They have in common a love of adventure, excitement with safety, and the new and unusual. They would rather travel to places where the unexpected is the rule than follow the well-traveled route.

"There won't be too many or too few in a group—perhaps a dozen and never more than 18. You can get to know them individually and not consider them as 'the rest of the tour group.'

"You will be accompanied by a professionally-trained leader who has been in the area before and knows it well. He will not march at the front of the column with a flag in his hand, though—his job is to make things easier and more enjoyable for you and your group.

"To us, such places as Buenos Aires, Nairobi, New Delhi and Rawalpindi are way stations on the route to the places we most enjoy—Tierra del Fuego, the Masai Mara, Namche Bazaar and the Karakoram."

The Copts of Ethiopia

As this Coptic priest slowly makes his way down the lush path, the Ethiopians fall on their faces and kiss his feet. The Copts are direct descendants of the ancient Egyptians, and they still speak a language close to the language of the Pharaohs. Priests still rule.

Yet, they are Christians. The staff he is carrying is called the Coptic Cross. His power derives from the Alexandria Patriarchate and the Council of Chalcedon in 451 A.D. The Copts of Ethiopia are the last link with ancient Christianity and dynastic Egypt.

The Omo River

The awesome Omo River in southwestern Ethiopa winds through the most remote part of all Africa. Snaking its way through 4,000-foot basalt gorges and grassy, rolling hills, the Omo passes from colorful desert terrain to lush, dense jungles. Zoologically it is a wonderland; the river is the life source for hundreds of exotic species of African animals and birds. Colorful and unstudied peoples inhabit the lower shores of the Omo.

Mountain Travel offers two trips to the Omo River region for people who are in excellent physical and mental health and who have the experience to cope with the variables of a demanding and often unpredictable trip. The group travels in specially-designed whitewater rafts manned by professional river boatmen, veterans of Colorado River runs. The group is also accompanied by Ethiopian guides and a physician who is a specialist in tropical medicine.

Popocatepetl Volcano

Entry into Middle Earth. The Popocatepetl volcano spewed out the Valley of Mexico, which waited in silence for centuries until an eagle caught a serpent. The Aztecs built their great city Teuochtitlan on that spot, and mightily feared the smoke and rumblings that came out of the volcanic pit.

Popo is more than 17,000 feet high—one of the highest volcanoes in the world. It is perpetually covered in snow, cloud and firesmoke.

Hoggar Mountains, Sahara Desert

The Hoggar Mountains are in a region of the Sahara that is seldom explored and offers a wealth of discovery. There are sleepy oases where Touaregs have lived in the same way for centuries. There are magnificent rock carvings and paintings, unclimbed granite domes, distant rocky plateaus and awesome volcanic spires.

Touareg guides, nomads of the desert, accompany the Mountain Travel party touring this area, giving the group an opportunity to sample the Touaregs' way of life intimately.

Photography courtesy of Mountain Travel (U.S.A.)

Nepal, Rooftop of the World

The greatest concentration of high mountains in the world is within the Nepalese frontiers. Beyond the cities the country is essentially roadless, and access to the hill country is by way of ancient trade routes and trails that are heavily used to this day. The majority of the population of Nepal (nearly 11 million people) lives in the remote countryside, in scattered small villages and hamlets that have stood basically unchanged for hundreds of years.

Shown here is a Gurung village in central Nepal, surrounded by rice terraces.

Mountain Travel Trips: What They're Like and What They Cost

Bhutan-Sikkim-Darjeeling (Asia)
Total days: 28 Grade: moderate
Cost including air fare:
$1,700 from New York

Britain
Total days: 23 Grade: easy
Cost including air fare:
$1,153 from New York

Caroni River, Venezuela
Total days: 21 Grade: moderate
Cost including air fare:
$1,813 from Miami

Caucasus (U.S.S.R.)
Total days: 23 Grade: strenuous to extremely difficult
Cost including air fare:
$1,589 from New York

Colorado River
Total days: 13 Grade: easy
Cost: $515 plus 3 percent Arizona state tax

East Africa Climbing
Total days: 23 Grade: strenuous to difficult
Cost including air fare:
$2,242 from New York

Mt. Everest
Total days: trips one and two, 35; trip three, 41
Grade: strenuous
Cost including air fare: trips one and two, $1,773 from New York; trip three, $1,873 from New York

Galapagos Islands
Total days: 26 Grade: easy
Cost including air fare:
$1,327 from Miami

Guatemala
Total days: 22 Grade: moderate
Cost including air fare:
$1,015 from Miami

Sahara Desert
Total days: 21 Grade: moderate
Cost including air fare:
$1,998 from New York

Humla (Nepal)
Total days: 59 Grade: strenuous
Cost including air fare:
$2,821 from New York

Japan
Total days: 21 Grade: moderate
Cost including air fare:
$1,759 from West Coast

Kanchenjunga (Nepal)
Total days: 37 Grade: strenuous
Cost including air fare:
$1,746 from New York

Kathmandu Valley (Nepal)
Total days: 24 Grade: easy
Cost including air fare:
$1,661 from New York

Kenya-Tanzania
Total days: 27 Grade: easy
Cost including air fare:
$2,342 from New York

Khumbu-Himal (Nepal)
Total days: 35 Grade: strenuous to difficult
Cost including air fare:
$1,868 from New York

Manaslu (Nepal)
Total days: 33 Grade: moderate
Cost including air fare:
$1,673 from New York

Springtime in Nepal
Total days: 32 Grade: moderate
Cost including air fare:
$1,705 from New York

Omo River (Ethiopia)
Total days: 34 Grade: strenuous
Cost including air fare:
$2,827 from New York

Patagonia-Tierra Del Fuego (Argentina)
Total days: 30 Grade: easy to hard
Cost including air fare:
$1,862 from Miami

Peru Cultural Trek
Total days: 30 Grade: moderate to strenuous
Cost including air fare:
$1,651 from Miami.

Tassili (Sahara Desert)
Total days: 21 Grade: moderate
Cost including air fare:
$1,890 from New York

Turkey
Total days: 28 Grade: moderate
Cost including air fare:
$1,603 from New York

Climbing Mt. Kilimanjaro

From Mt. Kenya the Mountain Travel tour group drives to Amboseli Game Refuge to make camp in a game-rich area for several days. The group then climbs Mt. Kilimanjaro (19,340 feet) via its northern slopes, away from the usual tourist routes. There is a night of camping in Kilimanjaro's crater, a most unusual experience.

The Mountain Travel outing ends with a trek to the rarely-visited coastal area near the Tanzania-Kenya border.

To Find Out More . . .

Mountain Travel will be happy to supply you with all the details on their trips. Write:
Mountain Travel
1398 Solano Ave.
Albany, Calif. 94706.

Mt. FitzRoy, Remotest Patagonia

Expeditions to Patagonia have found this far-away land to be extremely beautiful. Vast glaciers push their icy snouts into huge lakes. There are guanacos, ostriches, armadillos, parrots, flamingos; there is outstanding fishing; there are views of the stupendous peaks of the Mt. FitzRoy area, where massive towers of pink and white granite thrust 6,000 feet into the sky from crevassed glaciers. There is the solitary guard at Parque Nacional Los Glaciares—he's the only person who lives in Patagonia. In April, the leaves on the Magellan beech trees are red and yellow, reminding you that April means autumn in lands south of the equator.

Mountain Travel's expedition to Patagonia is a rugged journey for hardy people who want to encounter a wild land before tourists get to it.

Running into a Gig When You're Abroad

By David Saltman

The material question raises its ugly head, right in the middle of the casbah.

It's been known to happen that occasionally one runs out of money.

I was in Tangier once, low and grimy (I hadn't found the public baths), and I discovered there must have been a hole in my pocket or something. Somehow I was in dire need of that famous Moroccan *flus* — in a word, *cash*. I sat in the Café Central with a mint tea, pursed my lips and considered the situation.

I got out my map of Tangier and idly traced with my finger the intorted labyrinth of the streets of the Casbah, the Ancient City. As I sat in this café in the center of the maze, it occurred to me that the easiest way out led directly through the jail! This was not a comforting thought.

Then I noticed, on the other side of the map, one of those intriguing large white areas. A little voice inside hinted this was worth investigating. I finished the tea and started hiking up towards the Grand Bazaar.

You can hardly find an Arab (or one who'll admit it) in the French Quarter. You'd think you were in Paris, except when the electricity goes off to save the government money. This is the land of the Colonial Powers, who have graciously departed, according to the history books, and left their brainchildren to live in the house that Jacques built.

I walked up rue San Francisco, passed the Spanish School, the Spanish Institute, the Spanish Consulate and the Spanish Hospital and turned left onto rue Christophe-Colomb. Christoper Columbus Street. According to the map this led directly into that mysterious white area, and my little voice had been right. Up on a pleasant hill, far from the guts of the Casbah, perched a modern building with a basketball court, and a sign out front said "The American School in Tangier." Suddenly, the pungent smell of dollars was in the air.

As I reconnoitred I noticed a bushy-haired young man walking out. I went up and introduced myself, and soon learned he was the supervisor of the dormitory. I asked if there were any jobs available, and he said it just so happened he was quitting the very next day. He wanted to start a poetry magazine instead.

We seemed to hit it off, so we went over to his apartment to discuss strategy. The dollar smell grew stronger. He lived in this beautiful flat, with views and rugs and records and innumerable bottles of wine. Cost him $40 a month, and his salary as dorm supervisor was . . . $250. We arranged it that he would introduce me, just as he was leaving, and I would take it from there.

I had no previous experience. In fact, I had always shied from schools like they were impetigo.

But they needed someone and I got the job. Even a professional dorm supervisor, if he had written in advance with references from the Imam Mahdi, wouldn't have done. They needed someone immediately. There were dozens of other Americans working there, and most of them had come under the same circumstances. There were also quite a few Moroccans, Spaniards, Gibraltarians and Frenchmen. The headmaster was American. The kids were about half American and European and half Moroccan, of all ages. They were all charter members of the fast international set. Inside, the place practically stank of dollars, dirhams and Swiss francs.

My job was simply to live in this large, well-furnished room with a shower (rare as emeralds in Morocco). That was it. For just living there I would get $250 a month, free room and three exquisite meals a day cooked by the former chef at the Minzah Hotel. They'd bribed him by giving his kid the well-known "American education" for free. They provided me with a typewriter, a tape recorder, an excellent library and a fabulous inlaid mother-of-pearl Moroccan desk. I had a view of the setting sun over Souani hill, and by walking out back I could see snake charmers in the little Berber village a few hundred yards to the south.

At night I had to make sure all the kids went to bed on time. But there were about 40 of them, and they were sneaky, and the school officials realized you couldn't do much about someone climbing out of a window at night.

They also had a rule about smoking dope. But, as you can imagine, in a country like Morocco that's just about impossible to enforce. So as long as they didn't smoke on school grounds — well, whaddya gonna do?

It was a pretty amazing scene, this little fancy Dan school in North Africa, where the kids all spoke five languages but never knew where their parents were. Nobody lasted too long there — students,

faculty or dorm supervisors — and jobs were always cropping up. I understand that the reason the area is white on the map is that it all belongs to the U.S. government and is being made ready for the University of North Africa.

As for life in Tangier, well. . . . It is mellow. There are camels grazing just outside the town gates and spectacular empty beaches at Ras Spartel, 12 miles west. There are hills with villas, and there is the Casbah. There are infinite layers of history. You peel off the inedible skin of the French and you get a succulent onion. The thickest layer is Arab (with remnants of English, Spanish and Portuguese), followed by Roman and Phoenician and stripping right down to an irreducible kernel of Berber. The Berbers are still a mystery. They've been here since the Ages of the Arcane, and no one really knows where their languages come from. Plato says Tangier was the tip of the continent of Atlantis, if that figures in somehow. □

HOW TO GET STARTED

If you want to work abroad and stick to it for awhile and you have a skill of any kind, you might want to look into the Peace Corps or one of the other volunteer agencies. It's a free ride both ways, good benefits and high pay (compared to what the natives make) and an entree into the highest government circles. It's usually a two-year commitment, but you can quit at any time with no hassle if you really want to. Write to:

Peace Corps
c/o ACTION
Washington, D.C.

or to:

Russell Tuttle
American Friends Service
    Committee
160 N. 15th St.
Philadelphia, Pa.

If you are a professional and would like to try it somewhere new, you might be interested in working for the United Nations. They are selective, but the more languages you know and the more skilled you are the better chance you have. You can apply at whichever agency interests you, or write to:

Miss Jean Landreth-Smith
Administrative Officer for the
    Assistant Secretary-General
Personnel Services
United Nations
New York, N.Y.

At present, the UN employs several hundred Americans.

Other than these, the best way to find a job is to go where you want to be and take a risk.

Teaching Gigs Around the World

Africa

Ethiopia
Addis Ababa
Kenya
Kijabe
Nairobi
Nigeria
Ibadan
Libya
Benghazi
Tripoli
Morocco
Rabat
Tangier
Zambia
Lusaka

The South Pacific & Asia

Afghanistan
Kabul
Ceylon
Colombo
Guam
Agana
Hong Kong
India
Calcutta
New Delhi
Punjab
Indonesia
Djakarta
Japan
Hiroshima
Hokkaido
Kobe
Kyoto
Sendai
Tokyo
Yokohama
Laos
Vientiane
Malaysia
Kuala Lumpur
Nepal
Kathmandu

Okinawa
Ginowan
Pakistan
Lahore
Rawalpindi
Singapore
South Korea
Seoul
Taiwan
Taipei
Thailand
Bangkok
Chiang Mai

Central America, Mexico, Caribbean

Costa Rica
San Jose
Dominican Republic
Santo Domingo
El Salvador
San Salvador
Guatemala
Guatemala City
Haiti
Port-au-Prince
Honduras
Tegucigalpa
Mexico
Coahuila
Durango
Mexico City
Monterrey
Puebla
Queretaro
Torreon
Netherlands Antilles
Aruba
Virgin Islands
St. Croix
St. Thomas

Europe

Austria
Vienna
Belgium
Antwerp
Brussels

Denmark
Copenhagen
England
London
France
Paris
Greece
Athens
Thessaloniki
Holland
Rotterdam
Terneuzen
The Hague
Werkhoven
Iceland
Reykjavik
Italy
Bologna
Florence
Genoa
Milan
Naples
Rome
Turin
Norway
Stavanger
Rumania
Bucharest
Spain
Barcelona
Switzerland
Bern
Lausanne
Leysin
Montreux
West Germany
Berlin
Dusseldorf
Frankfurt
Hamburg
Munich
U.S.S.R.
Moscow
Yugoslavia
Belgrade

Near East

Egypt
Alexandria
Cairo
Iran
Abadan
Tehran
Jordan
Amman
Lebanon
Beirut
Sidon
Saudi Arabia
Jedda
Turkey
Istanbul

South America

Argentina
Buenos Aires
Bolivia
La Paz
Brazil
Recife
Rio de Janeiro
Salvador (Bahia)
Santos
São Paulo
Chile
Santiago
Colombia
Bogota
Cartagena
Medellin
Paraguay
Asuncion
Peru
Arequipa
Uruguay
Montevideo
Venezuela
Caracas
Maracaibo
Valencia

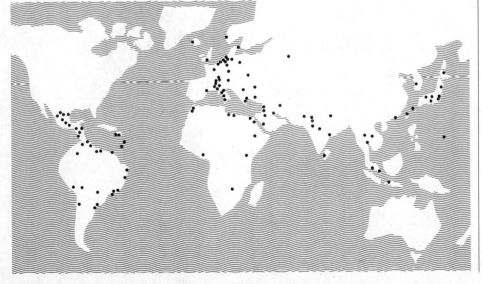

Becoming an Interpreter

Anyone with ears who goes abroad for the first time notices something strange: languages exist. At first it is a shock, then it becomes quite annoying and finally it becomes either an insurmountable obstacle or a fascinating challenge.

People who find languages challenging go on to learn them. It is not unusual to find someone nowadays who speaks five or six languages fluently, and is confident he could learn six more. Anyone who learns to speak, say, French becomes intrigued by the possibility of working with languages in some way. Sir Richard Burton, the explorer, used to say he could learn any language whatsoever in two months.

What is it like to be an interpreter? What are the requirements and how does one learn?

First off, you must know both languages fluently. Now, this doesn't necessarily mean you must speak them without an accent —although that's desirable, of course. But you must understand them perfectly and be able to speak them both flawlessly. An interpreter is far more than a translator, and has no recourse to dictionaries.

The United Nations requires its interpreters to have lived in the second-language country for at least two years, and to be completely familiar with slang and customs. A good interpreter often becomes a semi-expert on the subject he's working in.

The hard thing, naturally, is listening to one language and simultaneously speaking in another. (For me, it is not a question of "thinking" in French or English. It is far beyond that—more a matter of *not* thinking, and just speaking.) It is head-breaking work, which is why the UN simultaneous interpreters work only 15 minutes at a time, make $40,000 a year and take long vacations.

There's a great deal of interesting work available for interpreters (and translators too—for translators the requirements are much less rigorous)—everything from international conferences to courtrooms to travel agencies to teaching to scientific documents and foreign service. Just about every language school has a special course for conference interpreters, and issues a certificate recognized by all international organizations.

If your language is French, the Alliance Française offers excellent training on all levels at a very low cost. It has schools in many cities in France and in major cities throughout the world.

If you are interested in working for the UN, write to:

Interpretation and Translation Section,
UN Secretariat
United Nations
New York, N.Y. 10017.

The official languages are English, French, Spanish, Russian and Chinese. A simultaneous interpreter must usually be qualified in three of them.   *—Ivan Abdul Cserdamst*

How to Be Stranded

The scene takes place several times a day at the rich, imposing U.S. Embassy on the Champs Elysées in Paris. The French receptionist looks up and sees—without astonishment—an American teenager. He (she) is badly dressed. A worried face, with tired eyes. "I don't know what to do! I haven't a franc left. Completely broke. Stranded!" Often they're in tears.

Our embassies in foreign lands don't prove terribly helpful. They're prepared to make a (collect) long-distance call to the United States to summon help from family or friends. Pride prevents hundreds of young people from letting their parents know. So they stick it out somehow in Europe. Americans sleep like *clochards* (bums) under Seine bridges. Others have to beg for food in London. Others borrow enough for a plate of soup a day.

If those worn shoes fit someone you know, here are some suggestions for survival:

A first-rate American secretary who speaks a foreign language can always get a temporary job. She should search for American scientists, professors, writers, editors and businessmen and offer her services. Similarly, good translators should have no trouble finding an occasional day's work.

French households are in dire need of maids, cooks and governesses who receive room and board, plus a salary. Women aged 18 to 30 can apply at L'Acceuil Familiale, 23 Rue du Cherche Midi, in Paris.

The Swiss and German restaurant industry is hungry for waiters, busboys, waitresses, barmaids, dishwashers. So it's worth hitch-hiking to Munich, Frankfurt, Zurich and other places, including resorts. Languages useful, but not essential.

In Copenhagen, young clean-cut types may manage to get summer jobs as guides in Tivoli Gardens. Other part-time offers appear on university bulletin boards. European universities are often clearing houses for temporary jobs.

Americans who know the Alps have wangled occasional employment as mountain guides for American or British hikers and alpinists. In winter, a few certified skiing instructors are sought by French, Austrian and Swiss ski schools.

Those who are down to just enough money for their last meal ought to find the nearest U.S. Army base. Officers' Messes often take on help for short periods. "K.P.s" (Kitchen Patrols) earn as little as 75 cents a day, but that's better than nothing.

Good drivers (male) should seek out American car rental agencies. Automobiles are constantly being rented all over Europe, and cars must be picked up and returned from airports.

Artists have managed to put up easels almost everywhere to draw portraits for a few francs. Hippies play their guitars for hand-outs in many picturesque spots, including the

Landing a Job Abroad

The speediest route to employment and adventure in a foreign land these days is by way of the little-known organization. If you want to get a job abroad, you can't do better than to track down the new or small company—and this goes for women as well as men. A young lady executive, for instance, should concentrate on the thousands of small U.S. businesses that plan to go into foreign trade within the next few years. A secretary may have better luck with a letter to an almost-unknown U.S. firm operating in Australia than with a letter to General Foods. Stewardesses can often get jobs faster with small foreign air carriers than with international super airlines. And American teachers will reach a U.S. missionary outpost in Africa or Asia quicker than the fancy American school in a European capital.

New, undiscovered organizations also often have heavy personnel turnover—and therefore lots of job openings. This is especially true in the most primitive countries—there are plenty of civilian jobs in Asia right now, for example.

Women with experience as computer programmers are in great demand in Greenland. (The demand is *so* great, as a matter of fact, that just one year of experience will do.) You usually have to sign up for at least 18 months, and if that seems like a long time to spend in Greenland—well, there are compensations. One technician saved enough money in six years in Greenland to buy herself a villa in Spain.

Depending on your skills (or your zeal), the following organizations may be able to place you in jobs abroad:

Commission on World Mission
475 Riverside Drive
New York, N.Y. 10027

This is a free referral service for more than 40 American Protestant Mission boards and agencies. There are currently openings for teachers, technicians, administrators, agriculturists, stenographers, social workers—for almost anyone, as a matter of fact. You name it, and CMW needs it, especially in

Africa, Asia, Latin America and the Middle East. Salaries are modest.

American Friends Service Committee
160 N. 15th St.
Philadelphia, Pa. 19102

Many Americans have never heard of this organization, in spite of the fact that it has devoted almost 50 years to helping victims of disasters, famines and wars. You'll find AFSC volunteers aiding refugees in Hong Kong, helping peasants raise rabbits in Mexico, teaching women to sew in war-torn Vietnam. Volunteers need not be Quakers. The committee pays your fare to and from your post and gives you a maintenance allowance, but no volunteer has ever gotten rich.

American Red Cross
National Headquarters
Washington, D.C. 20006

The Red Cross has always been connected with the U.S. military. Right now, the Red Cross is recruiting some 500 secretaries and social and recreational workers for posts in Okinawa, Korea and Vietnam, among other places. Salaries go up to $7,600 a year, and the chosen women get free housing and a fine chance to travel.

International Voluntary Services
1555 Connecticut Ave. NW
Washington, D.C. 20036

This will remind you of the Peace Corps —total commitment, long hours, hardship posts, lots of satisfaction and very little money. For volunteers, skills and attitude are more important than age; jobs go to stable, hardy, outgoing people.

American Nurses Association
10 Columbus Circle
New York, N.Y. 10019

Thanks to an "International Council of Nurses Exchange Visitor" program, nurses with two or more years of experience can spend six months or longer abroad. Some ANA public health nurses, nursing educators and administrators have found niches in the World Health Organization (WHO) and in American company hospitals abroad.

—*Curtis W. Casewit*

Ponte Vecchio in Florence. While the guy makes music, his girl passes the hat. Later, they can stroll through the green, cool, stately Boboli Gardens—one of Italy's great free sights.

These prosperous days, no one should go hungry, least of all the young. One day last summer, three American students stood before our Paris Embassy receptionist. Suddenly the phone rang. Another American out of luck. She told him, "I'll talk to you in just a moment! *Ne quittez pas!* Hang on!"

That's good advice for any foreign job seeker.

—*Curtis W. Casewit*

Observatory Hopping: Touring by Telescope

Part of the American heritage is scientific, and one science that received a lot of attention in this country in the 19th century (and still does today) is—astronomy. There are scores of observatories sprinkled across the nation—some modest college installations, some major research facilities—and you have but to visit one or two to be hooked on astronomy. Just seeing the incredible telescopes in observatories is fascinating—imagine, that piece of metal and glass six stories tall functions as precisely as a fine Swiss watch!

Many observatories have visiting hours during which you can look *at* the telescopes, and some are open several nights each month so you can look *through* a telescope at the stars or planets. Admission is generally free. Some big ones with regular visiting hours:

The Lick Observatory at Mt. Hamilton, Calif., east of San Jose, is 4,200 feet up. Allow yourself a good hour to make the trip from the base of the mountain up the 19 miles of winding mountain road to the observatory. Also, be sure to take your own water and fill your gas tank—it's a long way to the nearest service station or Coke machine. The visitors' gallery in the main building, where you can see the 120-inch reflecting mirror telescope (third largest in the United States) is open every afternoon, and tours are given inside the dome of the 36-inch refracting lens telescope every half hour. During the summer there are sometimes observing nights for tourists. Write for details to Lick Observatory, University of California, Santa Cruz, Calif. 95064.

The Hale Observatories of the California Institute of Technology are two separate installations. One is at Mt. Wilson, Calif., northeast of Los Angeles; the other is at Palomar Mountain, Calif., between Los Angeles and San Diego. Both are about 5,000 feet high. Mt. Wilson has a visitors' gallery where you can see the 100-inch reflector (which looks like it was built from old locomotive parts), and at Palomar you can see the 200-inch reflector, the largest in the United States. Both observatories have museums and they are open during the day, but there are no observing nights.

Kitt Peak National Observatory on Kitt Peak, west of Tucson, Ariz., has an array of some two dozen unusual instruments. In addition to the 158-inch reflector (second largest in the United States), there are a number of smaller telescopes, and the McMath solar telescope that looks like a giant white upside-down check mark. The museum here is particularly nice—it has a do-it-yourself solar telescope.

The McDonald Observatory, near Fort Davis, Tex., has the fourth largest reflector in the country—it's 107 inches in diameter.

(This is the one that was shot at by a deranged optician in 1970.) There is also an 82-inch reflector and several other telescopes, including one used to observe at millimeter radio wavelengths.

When you visit these observatories, don't be put off by the glassed-in visitors' galleries—the telescopes must be maintained at nighttime temperatures 24 hours a day, so having hundreds of tourists' warm bodies trooping under the optics is *verboten*.

Most major observatories are in the Southwest because the atmosphere is clearest and steadiest there. Washington, D.C. does have the U.S. Naval Observatory which offers public observing programs once a month (call for exact dates and to make reservations). You will get to see standard clocks too, because the observatory provides standard time to correct atomic clocks.

If you can't make it out west and you yearn to visit a big observatory, don't despair. About 70 miles northwest of Chicago you can visit the largest refracting telescope in the world at **Yerkes Observatory** in Lake Geneva, Wis. This lens, built in the 1890s (just about five years after Lick's), is 40 inches across.

These are only a few of the largest observatories. Don't neglect the smaller ones: you'll have a better chance to look *through* the telescopes, and you'll probably have more fun, too, because the people at smaller observatories tend to be less preoccupied with research and are more willing to show you around. You might go to visit:

Chabot Observatory in Oakland, Calif. (has a 16-inch refractor).

The Griffith Observatory at Griffith Park in Los Angeles, Calif. (there's also a planetarium here).

Harvard College Observatory in Cambridge, Mass. (has a 15-inch refractor 130 years old).

Sperry Observatory at Union College in Cranford, N.J. (an active amateur astronomy group meets here regularly and looks through the 10-inch refractor and 12-inch reflector).

The serious amateur astronomer might want to write to the observatory he intends to visit to see if it's possible to have a behind-the-scenes look-see. If you make an appointment, you'll get to spend a marvelous few hours hearing all the wonderful stories behind the telescopes and the people who built them and the current work being done at the observatory. But note: this behind-the-scenes stuff is *not* recommended for the casual tourist, because it can get pretty heavy with jargon and detail—and besides, it's not too cool to take up the time of a busy scientist if you're not truly interested.

—Trudy E. Bell

The Sad Saga of Christine Jorgensen—Chronology of an Escape From One's Sex

Late 1952 George Jorgensen, Jr., 26 years old, born in the Bronx, ex-U.S. Army clerk, is changed into a woman by Danish doctors. Takes the name "Christine." The process is a series of operations and hormone treatments. As the story breaks (on Dec. 1), it is revealed that there are 10 similar cases under treatment at Presbyterian Hospital in New York.

Dec. 15, 1952 Christine Jorgensen gives the first public showing of her travel film, *Denmark*, in Copenhagen.

April 6, 1953 The *New York Post* reports that Christine Jorgensen is not "really" a woman after all. The *Post* interviewed the three Danish doctors who performed the operations, and declared the surgery did not actually give Christine female organs.

May 28, 1953 The Three Danish doctors report on their work in the *Journal of the American Medical Association*. They claim they didn't "really" make Christine Jorgensen a woman, but just gave "him" the appearance of a woman, to help him "fit into society."

May 29, 1953 The Hotel Sahara in Las Vegas cancels Christine's two-week nightclub contract for $12,500 a week on the grounds that the ex-GI misrepresented "himself" as a woman.

April 3, 1959 Christine Jorgensen, now 32 years old, is refused a marriage license in New York because her birth certificate lists her as male. Her fiancé, Howard J. Knox, 38, of Waukegan, Ill., loses his job as a statistician when his boss finds out who he's betrothed to.

Oct. 8, 1971 Vice-President Agnew refers to Senator Charles Goodell as the "Christine Jorgensen of the Republican Party." Miss Jorgensen protests, but Agnew describes her as nothing but a publicity seeker.

Since Christine Jorgensen, there have been scores of sex-change operations in several countries. They don't all turn out so sad: around the time Miss Jorgensen was causing a stir in Denmark, Dr. Elizabeth Forbes Sempill, a 40-year-old Scottish doctor, was changed into a male. She took the name Ewan, and became heir-presumptive to the baronetcy of Sempill.

The Underground Crash Pad Directory

By Ben Fungo

The directory will list you along with thousands of others but there is a catch, Catch-1: you also must be listed and willing to let others crash at your place.

When I was in need of overnight lodgings on my way to the Adirondacks recently, I took out my copy of the *Travelers' Directory* and called Larry—a total stranger—at his health food store in a college town in upstate New York. He said, "Come on over," and when I arrived he and his wife, Ronnie, greeted me with a tall glass of guava juice. We spent the afternoon and evening discussing everything from Buddhist chants to the quick buck while their four-month-old daughter gurgled in her crib. When night fell, they dragged a mattress into the store, locked the street door, pulled the curtain and bade me good night in a room full of organic delights. I slept between the papaya jelly and buckwheat groats—for free.

Early next morning I awoke, mindful that I had to vacate the store before the first customers came. I ate a little almond butter, joined Larry and Ronnie in some tea, and went on my way.

As I said, I had never met Larry or Ronnie before, yet they welcomed me and gave me a free night's lodging. What is more, I can repeat this experience—be almost assured of free lodgings and hospitality—just about anywhere in the world, from Antarctica to Yap.

How is this possible? Who ever heard of free hospitality for strangers—except perhaps in Bedouin country where the law of the desert decrees that if a stranger appears at your tent, you have to put him up for three days?

I was able to get in touch with Larry and Ronnie through my copy of the *Travelers' Directory*, a twice-a-year, 130-page publication that lists some 500 people who will put you up—without charge—all over the United States and throughout the world. You cannot get a copy of the Directory, however, unless you agree to list yourself in it, thus offering your own hospitality to strangers.

To list yourself is easy—you simply submit a short biography (up to 100 words) to the Directory's publisher, along with a donation of $5 (more, if you wish) to help him with his printing costs. And the rule seems to be that the funnier, the more intriguing your self-description, the more visitors you are likely to get. Fame has little to do with it, and the groupies don't seem to materialize, even for the better-known listees. The publisher until late last year was a 37-year-old hip printer named Peter Kacalanos, known to the listees as "Supergreek." Married and the father of an infant daughter, he operated out of Woodside, N.Y. Late last year he turned over the directory to David Miller of Lancaster, Pa.

The listings in the Directory are supposed to give you some idea of whom you want to stay with when you are traveling, and I'll give you some examples of them before I tell you how the Directory got started and how it seems to be working out.

Jefferson Poland, founder of the Sexual Freedom League, lists himself this way: "Writer and agitator for sexual freedom, bohemianism, LSD and anarchy. An ordained minister of the Neo-American Church, can perform legal weddings. Offers a guided tour of a Sexual Freedom League nude party."

A 24-year-old girl named Patt, living in Oakland, Calif., is listed thus: "University of California graduate criminology student. Formerly button manufacturer and seller, carny (wrote thesis on carnivals), bowling scorekeeper and dominoes hustler. Interests include social deviance, bohemianism, gypsies, religious existentialism, mysticism, astrology, surrealism, happenings, writing, poetry, Dylan, bluegrass, jazz, Russian gypsy music, the *Catholic Worker*, the IWW, Venice West, slang, camping, fog and Zpodism. Offers listees tours of coffee houses, Skid Row, Berkeley, San Francisco and Oakland, plus conversation, wine, food and floor space."

Listings can be short and simple, like Al and Kate's: "Have wide interests. Enjoy conversation and happy people. Camping and overnight bedding on a relaxed farm are offered to one or two listees."

Or they might be long and complex, like 23-year-old Mary's: "Gemini poet and student, interested in selling, buying and exchanging poetry booklets with other listees, and looking for another publisher. Especially likes the outdoors, adventure of all sorts, hiking, camping, skiing, photography, art, music, science, the occult, correspondence, paradox, solitude and simplicity, people and complexity. 'Have a pet monkey looking for a cheap way to Europe.' Offers in the Syracuse area: sightseeing advice, conversation, companionship and perhaps a place to crash, depending on circumstances, finances and vibrations."

Evie, from the Bronx, sort of sums it all up: "Teaches modern, creative and folk dancing to children and adults. Interested in people with un-set minds, and travelers who get more than just a visual experience and sore eyeballs from their travels. Can offer a bed for a few days, and will help listees find their way around New York City."

So you begin to get the idea. There are listees not only in the United States but all the way from London and Paris to Bombay, Sydney and Hong Kong.

Don, 24, and Carol, 23, are stationed in Liberia and their listing reads: "Peace Corps volunteer teachers in a transitional urban tribal community outside Monrovia. Interested in people, photography, the outdoors, motorcycles, children and other peaceful things. Don and Carol were surprised that so few listees visited Liberia last year, but once again offer a place to stay. African food, a beautiful beach (and borrowed surfboard) and an honest look at what's happening."

Ex-publisher Kacalanos says that "one listee recently toured Africa, staying with other listees in Uganda, Ghana, Liberia, Sierra Leone and Spanish Morocco." Still, as might be expected, the United States is the best represented country in the Directory, "with hundreds of listings in major cities or rustic areas in every state," according to Kacalanos. New York City alone has over 80 listings.

To keep all addresses and listings current, each listee must resubmit his name every year and make the $5 donation. (It used to be $3.) No listing is carried over to the next edition automatically. "Despite this policy," says Kacalanos proudly, "many current listees have managed to be listed in every edition since the first one in 1960. We must have been doing something right."

The Directory grew out of an offhand remark in the late 1950s by John Wilcock, then a columnist for the *Village Voice*.

"I was going to Mexico," Wilcock remembers, "and I mentioned it in the column. Several people wrote and offered to put me up along the way. I followed some of the offers up, and met half a dozen or so very nice people.

"When I got back," he continues, "I recorded my experiences in the column, telling how I'd met so many good people, and suggested starting some kind of club, where the only dues are that you offer hospitality to the other members. Names came in, you know, and we listed them and ran off about 100 copies. I kept it going for a few years, but the pressure of other work was too much and I had to give it up. It was such a good idea, though, that we hated to see it die. So a couple of other people took it over and then Peter, who's really expanded it tremendously."

What did people think of it in the early days?

"Well, you know," says Wilcock, "that was back in those innocent naive days. I mean, it was the kind of thing where if someone said he needed a place to stay, you know, we figured he really needed it. Now everyone thinks that any listing of people is some kind of sex society!"

Well, yeah, what about the sex angle?

"Well, I don't know," Wilcock laughs, but suggests that the listing simply mirrors "real life," whatever that is.

The Directory tries to protect itself from misuse by its policy of requiring all subscribers to be listees. I can't swear that if you list your name in it, you'll never have an unwanted visitor, but I couldn't find anyone who reported a bad experience either as host or guest. No rapes, no robberies, not even bad manners. (Incidentally, all listees are expected to call or write in advance to make sure it's OK to stay when they want to. No listee is really *obligated* to put anyone up, either.) I guess there's no *guarantee* that you'll be safe from crime if you list yourself — except that if you feel funny about someone who calls to crash, you can simply refuse.

Kacalanos says that notwithstanding reports that communes try to discourage visitors, more and more communes are listing themselves in the Directory, interested in meeting new people.

A number of underground folk heros have been listed in the Directory at one time or another, including Dave Dellinger (Chicago Seven and *Liberation* magazine), Alan Katzman (*East Village Other*), Paul Krassner (*The Realist*), Tuli Kupferberg (The Fugs), Lawrence Ferlinghetti (the West Coast poet), Marvin Kitman (the humorist and put-on Presidential candidate), Louis Abolafia (another Presidential candidate), Jaf (*Village Voice* cartoonist) and a number of editors of underground newspapers. Some of these are still listed; others have dropped out for fear of being mobbed by groupies.

This fear, as I said earlier, seems groundless. One underground folk hero, for example, says: "I've been listed every year since 1960 and really had very few people call me up. But I'm going to Europe soon, to nomad around, and I expect I'll be calling on Directory listees and meeting them and so on." On the other hand, some less famous listees report having "people stacked four or five on top of each other, all the time." Perhaps they're better Bedouins, with deliberately intriguing listings.

(Those interested in becoming one of the intriguing listees should send $5 to Traveler's Directory, 535 Church St. #4, Lancaster, Pa. 17602.) □

A Spot of English Tea

Robin and Pat Evans, a couple who live in Warwickshire, England, have rounded up about 30 English homeowners who will take in paying guests for short stays, with all the amenities. The Evanses traveled more than 5,000 miles to select gracious homes in England's historic countryside. Their object was to find not only attractive houses, but hosts who like people and offer a hospitable welcome as well. If you stay in one of these English homes, you'll be entertained as if you were a friend of the family.

Homes range from sizable country estates to modernized Elizabethan cottages in picturesque villages. They are scattered through the English counties and Wales, and are set in some of Britain's loveliest countryside. Hosts range from "a publishing executive with literary interests" to "the widow of a Viscount, has many sporting interests, including fishing and racing."

My wife and I stayed with Mrs. Sylvia Silley in a charming stone Cotswold converted schoolhouse in Wyck Rissington, Gloucestershire. Our hostess, a writer for the racing press and a wizard gardener, provided a well-appointed guest room with private bath, and gourmet cooking and good conversation.

Fees are paid directly to English Private Homes on confirmation of booking, so no money changes hands between guest and host. Current fees depend on the dollar-exchange rate, but last year they ran from about $16 to $20 per person per night, depending on number of persons and length of stay. Children under 12 with adults are charged about $12 per night. Transportation can be provided. Fees include accommodations, English breakfast and evening meal with cocktails and wine.

For a list describing homes, locations, accommodations and hosts' interests, write Robin and Pat Evans, English Private Homes, The Old Orchard, Long Compton, Shipston-on-Stour, Warwickshire, England. Telephone: Long Compton 256.

—James Egan

How to Run Away and Join the Circus

God bless them, they still hire almost anybody who's over 18 and can tell a joke. Every year, the Ringling Brothers Barnum and Bailey Circus takes on some 300 new people to train as grooms, elephant handlers, stagehands, clowns, showgirls and what-have-you.

Whenever the circus plays a major city, one guy acts as employment manager. There are always hundreds of jobs open to unskilled people. The takers are those who still have their sense of adventure, their nomadic spirit and their honorable American desire to get away from everything and sneak under the Big Top.

This hiring policy holds true for everyone except clowns and showgirls. "Clowns," says the circus, "well—that's serious business."

—David Saltman

Meet the Danes

Copenhagen is a lovely city, but if you really want to understand the character of Denmark, you must take to the country. Denmark is a nation of farms (they cover almost 75 percent of its land) and a week or two on a Danish farm offers you a change of pace, a chance to relax and, best of all, a chance to really get to know some Danish people. You won't get wall-to-wall carpeting, maid service or private bathrooms on a farm, but you will get pleasant rooms and hearty meals at minimal cost, and friendship, and the nice, warm feeling that you're a special guest rather than just another tourist.

The Danes offer a variety of exciting programs and tours to better acquaint visitors with their country—the farm vacation program is one of them. Because there are vacation farms near all the larger towns and cities, it is relatively easy to use the farm as a central base from which to explore all of Denmark.

The farm vacation program is supervised by local tourist associations, and their standards for host farms are high. Rooms are clean and comfortable, bathrooms modern, food generally very good and rates reasonable. For approximately $35 a day our family of four had adjoining rooms and three enormous meals. We shared the bathrooms, living rooms and garden with the farm family and four other guests, and usually we all ate our meals together. The "garden," incidentally, was nothing less than a large green lawn fenced in by century-old trees, and in it there was a small pond for fishing.

To encourage a personal atmosphere, farms rarely take more than eight paying guests at one time. The minimum stay is seven days. Since English is a second language to most Danes, at least one person on the farm will speak it.

You can eat lunch on the farm or you can take it with you—your hostess will pack a picnic basket for you in the morning at your request. If you want to combine meals at a Danish inn with your farm vacation, you can request only two meals a day on the farm. You'll get breakfast and lunch or dinner and pay a bit less per day.

Denmark consists of the peninsula of Jutland and some 500 islands, of which 100 are inhabited. We chose farms on the two largest and most notable islands—Sealand, on which Copenhagen stands, and Fyn, called the fairytale island because it inspired the stories of Hans Christian Andersen.

For a wealth of information that will be valuable in helping you plan your trip to Denmark, write to:

The Danish National Tourist Office
505 Fifth Ave.
New York, N.Y. 10017

or to:

The Scandinavian National Tourist
Office
3600 Wilshire Blvd.
Los Angeles, Calif. 90010

Once you get the feeling of the many different things Denmark has to offer you'll be in a better position to decide whether you want to combine your farm holiday with stays in hotels or hostels, or whether you want to just stay at farms in different parts of the country.

Since there are participating farms throughout Denmark, write directly to the local tourist association in the area you most want to visit. Let them know which sights interest you most and if you want to be able to fish, ride, swim, boat or play golf or tennis, and they will keep all this in mind when they place you. Be specific about how many of you there are, the ages of your children, how many rooms you'll need, the exact dates of your stay and whether you'll want full board or just breakfast and one other meal.

During the main season (June 18 to Sept. 30), full board, which includes room and three meals daily, is about $9.60 per person per day; half board, which includes room, breakfast and lunch or dinner is about $8 per person. Off season rates (Oct. 1 to June 17) are about $7.60 for full board and $6.20 for half board. Children four to 12 years old pay 75 percent of these rates and children under four pay 50 percent.

Although it is most convenient to travel by car, Denmark's low rolling landscape makes bicycling possible. Many of the tourist associations can also help you arrange a combination bicycle-train farm holiday.

–Shelly Seltzer

Meet the Japanese

"It's the best way to learn about Japan —people are more important than monuments," said a recent American participant in Japan's Home Visit System. The Home Visit System, provided in Tokyo and six other Japanese cities, arranges for foreign visitors to pay a call on a Japanese family.

Some 70 families in the Tokyo area have opened their doors for "Drop-in-and-have-a-chat-after-dinner" visits, usually lasting for one or two hours. All are typical middle-class Japanese families who have been screened and selected by the Tourist Information Center. At least one member of the family speaks English, and most homes will receive from one to five persons for a visit.

The visits, arranged free of charge, offer a unique opportunity to enter a Japanese home—unique because, traditionally, the Japanese have been reluctant to receive visitors in the home, preferring to entertain elsewhere. Judging from my personal experience—a visit to the home of Senkei Kuwabara, Master of the Kuwabara School of Flower Arranging in Kyoto—the guest will be awash in green tea, stuffed with rice cakes and aglow with international good will before the evening is over.

To arrange for a home visit in Tokyo, apply in person between 10 a.m. to 4 p.m. at the Tourist Information Center on the ground floor of the Kotani Building. In Kyoto, Osaka, Kobe, Otsu, Nagoya or Yokohama, apply at the local tourist office or through your hotel.

–James Egan

Gloomy and gray is
my land's native heather,
Thick, though, beneath it
the wee flowers throng;
And o'er the graves
in the mild April weather
Larks thrill the waste
with a rapture of song.

—STEEN STEENSEN BLICHER

When I have gone away
and said farewell to home
and left my house empty,
O plum-tree beside my roof,
do not forget
to blossom each spring!

—SUGAWARA MICHIZANE

A tent with rustling breezes cool
Delights me more than palace high,
And more the cloak of simple wool
Than robes in which I learned to sigh. . .
And more than purr of friendly cat
I love the watch-dog's bark to hear;
And more than any lubbard fat
I love a Bedouin cavalier!

–THE LADY MAISUN

Home Swapping

There's a new way to vacation for those who have had it with hotels—you can avoid the cost and hassle of a hotel by swapping or renting digs in the spot where you want to vacation. You eliminate some of the sorrier aspects of travel and also save on meals, since most of the swaps or rentals have kitchens.

Home swapping is firmly established—at least four major firms offer a swap-or-rent service. All operate alike, charging a yearly fee to list your home, cottage, apartment, cabin, houseboat or trailer in their directory. You receive the directory, pick a few swaps in which you're interested and negotiate the deal—either directly or through the service. Some swaps include cars, maids and other services. You work out the details, including length of time and time of year.

Directories list swaps all over the world—*casas* in Mexico and Spain, villas in France, apartments in Sydney. An eager swappee had best be warned, however, that a swap sometimes takes months to finalize—so start early. Here are the four firms I know of:

Adventures-in-Living, Winnetka, Ill. 60093. Costs $10 per year to list; one main directory plus three supplements yearly.

Holiday Exchange Bureau, Grants, N.M. 87020. Costs $15 yearly to list ($10 if you're retired); monthly bulletins.

Home Exchange Club of California, San Leandro, Calif. 94577. Costs $15 to list for the first year, $8.50 thereafter; directory issued four times each year.

Vacation Exchange Club, 119 Fifth Ave., New York, N.Y. 10003. Costs $9.50 to list, plus $3.50 for a photo (optional); annual directory plus two supplements in the spring.

Condominium rentals are something fairly new in the hotel-avoidance line. One major advantage of condominium renting is that you can book a place in the normal way through a travel agent and thus avoid the messy negotiation period involved in successful swapping. But condominium rentals aren't exactly cheap. Figure on $30 a day absolute minimum (though often several people can split the cost).

Condominiums are usually nearly new and are located in the most popular areas—Hawaii, Spain's Costa del Sol, Morocco's Algarve, Acapulco, the Caribbean. Condomart and Creative Leisure are two active firms in the condominium rental field.

Condomart, 655 Madison Ave., New York, N.Y. 10021.

Creative Leisure, 1280 Columbus Ave., San Francisco, Calif. 94133.

—Richard John Pietschmann

Cheap Places to Spend the Night

Traveling on a shoestring doesn't need to be a drag. For example, you can turn finding a cheap place to spend the night into quite a game (if you don't cheat by planning to camp or crash with relatives or friends in town).

You can make the same moves in most larger cities. Usually you can ride a hotel bus from the airport to get to the local Y, because YMCAs and YWCAs are usually located in the center of town.

The Salvation Army has residences in many cities; rooms at these and at the Y run about $5 a night. You get the usual amenities of a regular hotel or motel on an only-slightly more modest scale, and you can generally get a hearty breakfast in the morning for around 75 cents.

In the western part of the country (as far east as Pittsburgh, actually) there is a chain of motels called Motel 6 that rent rooms for anywhere from $6 for one person to $9 for four people per night. Most of these motels have swimming pools, and the accommodations are quite nice—definitely a super bargain for the price.

University towns have always been full of cheap places to spend the night, and this summer things will be better than ever. Several big companies (notably Eastern Airlines) are sponsoring a service called the Campus Hostel Plan. You pay $6 for a bed-check, which entitles you to one night in a dorm at one of over 40 colleges across the United States and in Canada, Mexico and the Caribbean. If you don't use your bedcheck you can get your $6 back, and accommodations are guaranteed. For information, write:

Eastern Airlines
10 Rockefeller Plaza
New York, N.Y. 10020

Finally, there's that old stand-by—the youth hostel. For more information on these, write:

American Youth Hostels, Inc.
National Campus
Delaplane, Va. 22025.

—Trudy E. Bell

Meet the Moroccans

The Arabs live in the only group of nations in the world that is united by a common language and a common religion. Their culture may be foreign, but it's definitely worth studying; it can give you new ideas for alternative lifestyles. And if you play your cards right, you could get invited home to live for awhile with an Arab family in Morocco.

I was traveling alone and ended up at the Youth Hostel in Casablanca—a real hole, but it's located in one of the few parts of Casablanca that retains the color and the flavor of the past. A Moroccan student who was working at the hostel invited me to his uncle's house for dinner.

"Dinner" was a feast for the month-long Ramadan, a religious holiday. (The dates change each year, but Ramadan is usually celebrated during late September and early October.) During Ramadan, Moslems fast from about 6 a.m. to 6 p.m. every day—they take no food or water, and don't smoke anything. All the food is prepared in advance, and when the speakers on the mosques announce the end of the fast, the first meal of several that go on throughout the night begins. Between the meals, you smoke the good home-grown variety, sing and dance and catch quick naps. It is a wonderful, crazy time—people work only part of the day, emotions are explosive, and there is a very special Ramadan humor.

The Moroccan student and his cousin also took me south to their native village of Safi. I met countless of my student friend's relatives and ended up living for several days in his aunt's house; for those few days, I lived as a part of the household, among seven children. We spoke a little French, but for the most part our communication was through gestures and facial expressions.

Many Moroccan men have worked in foreign countries and had a taste of other cultures, but the women have stayed in their homes in the villages and have had little contact with the outside world. They are very eager to learn and to be exposed to new things, and as a woman I was in the unique position of being able to communicate many things they wanted to know. In turn, they dressed me in a robe and veil so I could see the village through their eyes. We went as a family unit to the public baths and spent a lovely evening together.

To meet the Moroccans, stay away from the big cities—people in the small villages are much more eager to meet foreigners. Becoming friendly with students is definitely the best way to get to meet other people. When you visit Morocco take as few personal belongings as necessary, and be ready to share whatever you have with the people.

–Sondi Field

Pleasantest of all ties is the tie of host and guest.

—AESCHYLUS

Caretaking

Free Lunch at Frazzle Top Farm

By David Saltman

How a poor Joe can live like Rockefeller— for free!

At a certain point, I decided I knew all I cared to know about cities. The sameness had gotten to me, and the artificial light. I began longing for open spaces and healing winds.

Just then, as if by magnetism, a friend appeared who said: "Hey—how would you like to live in the woods . . . for free!"

He had heard about this farm—"Four hundred acres of pine trees," he called it —up in the Adirondacks. It needed a caretaker; the old gent who'd looked after it for years was going blind or something. The house needed someone to run the water, to keep the pipes from freezing. Also to make sure the furnace didn't blow up. The owners lived in England, in the house of a former Prime Minister. They hadn't been back in 20 years.

"There's five thousand books in the house," my friend said, "and the best trout stream in New York State runs through the front yard!" It didn't take much more convincing. I turned the wheels, flew directly to Burlington, Vt. and took the ferry across Lake Champlain into the 13-million-acre wilderness called the Adirondack Forest Preserve.

The house belonged to Donald Ogden Stewart, a famous American humorist and screenwriter of the Thirties. He'd bought it in 1935 for $12,000, lived in it for a year and then only used it in the summers. In 1950 he'd left the country in disgust with McCarthyism and never returned. The place was filled with antiques and memories: Harry Bridges had hid out here, there were letters from Picasso in the attic, and renegade Russian princesses had danced on the balcony.

It was a big yellow house on a wooded hill, surrounded by nothing but trees, mountains and rivers and the atmosphere of the Academy Awards and the Hollywood Ten. People would visit and exclaim in awe: "This place is . . . magic!"

It was in the style called "Country Georgian"—big quaint woody rooms in each corner with a corridor straight through from front to back. They had hung a huge caribou head on the wall halfway up the stairs, and there were fireplaces in every room.

In 1826, an artist and a writer had built it because they wanted to escape the crime and pollution of New York City. They had named it "Frazzle Top Farm." It still had the original floors.

It was like existing in a Victorian novel, where the house itself is a living and major character.

What's immediately useful to everyone is this: Frazzle Top is located in a region full of magnificent farms, and most of them are empty 11 months of the year. Most of them need caretakers.

As a direct result of living at Frazzle Top, I was offered another caretaking job in the Catskills, and later was offered a fantastic deal on a mountaintop 15 miles from Denver. The thing snowballs, and you can live in luxury, for nothing, all over the world.

We really grew attached to that house. I learned all its lore from previous tenants and the old ex-caretaker. I got to be like a slave in the old days, glorying in the status and accomplishments of my master. It was almost like *I* had won the Oscar in 1935—like *I* had hung out with Robert Benchley and could drop in on Picasso at any time. I became a measured and crusty old gentleman farmer, lord of the manor, rich and famous writer living in seclusion among the pines and first editions.

One year passed in perfect harmony. And then the knell came, the death bong for caretakers: the house was up for sale.

The dream broke. Free lunch was over. I actually tried to buy it myself, but I couldn't match the bids of the Italian restaurant and dragstrip developers.

But somehow, by Arab telephone I guess, word got around. I got a call from a man in New York who owned a farm in the Catskills. He needed a caretaker.

For various personal reasons I turned that job down. But later on, in California, I happened to see an ad in the *Los Angeles Times*—for a caretaker. It was a Spanish rancho on a mountain near Denver. I went for an interview—same deal. This guy was a rich oilman who made movies in his spare time. They offered $800 a month, a free car, two weeks vacation and the entire bottom floor of their mansion!

I began to get the idea that these outrageously rich people kind of *like* to have artists and writers hanging around. (And, of course, it's an organic fact that we writers and artists *love* to have oil millionaires around!)

What happened in this case is instructive, and shows the hidden cost of free lunch: uncertainty. I accepted the job, and it was arranged that I'd call them that afternoon. When I called, though, the deal had queered somewhere. They really liked me, they said. But they had found a Nicaraguan couple who would work for half the wages and had hired them on the spot. Sorry, but keep in touch.

OK, I figured, so easy come easy go. I devoted myself to other enterprises and was just starting to take off. Two weeks later the oilman called me again—the Nicaraguan was an alcoholic. Would I come?

I turned it down. But the door is still open. I occasionally check the papers, and have seen a number of similarly juicy offers.

I guess it's like cleaning ladies. The word gets out about a good caretaker and you build a clientele. Invariably you end up living in astounding luxury, something only the super-rich can afford, and only their servants can enjoy.

Like I said, though, there are hidden payments. I wouldn't call them drawbacks—just facts. For instance, after they sold Frazzle Top (". . . out from under me!") I took off for the West Coast. The farm was a golden memory, 13 months of priceless wonder. I had promised all my Adirondack friends I'd come back some day. I still silently longed for the mountains and the silver river. But I knew it would be hard to drive by the old place.

Just recently, I went back. It had been almost two years since I left and I thought I finally felt strong enough to revisit a dream.

I rented a car in Montreal and drove like an automaton down into New York State. All the old places greeted me. I marveled how they had survived the years, in this country where grist mills change overnight into parking lots. Everything was the same: the winding river, the old geezers in the American House, the hunting lodges, the town bridge. I streaked out onto the old highway, into the bosom of the mountains, through 13 million acres of Scottish plaid autumn in the northeast. I was so borne up by the momentum of past times that I nearly overshot the northern boundary of the farm.

I realized where I was and slowed down. The river was just to my left, mountains to my right and in the distance on all sides. No sign of civilization except this black roadway. I round the familiar curve and see the bridge over the river, *our* bridge—I had stood on it one night and bellowed, "A man *needs* a piece of bridge!"

"They" had painted the bridge yellow. It looked nice, I had to admit, and it seemed significant. I slowed down and crept past the inshoot, which gives onto a long carriageway. I stopped.

It looked inhabited. I backed up. I crept past again. I backed up again. Finally, I couldn't stand it; I said, "I've got to go up there."

So I dealt myself the former caretaker's blues. New owners. No more antiques. Books gone. Pop art electric clocks, Detroit modern furniture. It hit me seven different ways at once, so I mumbled a lot. They were very nice.

I asked permission to take a hike along the old trails. Of course, they said. I went into the forest, my forest, my pine grove, my thinking rock—*my* trail. I was devastated.

They had logged the trees. What had been a secret and lush wild forest had been turned into a prim and civilized wood. Debris was everywhere, and the trail was wide enough for a car. I came to a certain turning, by some tall cedars, and broke down crying.

That was the epilogue to an era, for me. A little solace came when I found out they'd changed the name of the place. Apparently they never knew it was called Frazzle Top, so they are calling it "Yellow Bridge." □

Tips on Caretaking

Check the newspapers. Sometimes the ads are under "Domestic Help," sometimes under "Help Wanted—Couples," sometimes in the regular Help Wanted sections.

The handier you are the more luck you'll have. Some caretaking jobs are only for someone who can handle maintenance, repair, gardening and errand-running. But don't let this throw you—plumbing, electricity and carpentry are all simple. They only require steady hands and logical thinking.

Get the best references you can. This counts heavily with rich people who are going to put you in charge of their houses and grounds. Previous experience in a related field (e.g., apartment managing) is very valuable.

Don't get too attached to the place.

Fetish Cities for Extremists

Minor travel pitfalls can usually be planned around by heeding sound advice from an airline or travel agent, or by reading a few travel guides. What *is* hard to find is travel information for the travel fetishist. Maybe you want to visit the oldest cities in the world, or the largest, or the highest. Maybe you want to avoid warm cities, or wet ones. Depending on your quirk, this list of places that are *the most* in seven categories could be invaluable in helping you plan your trip.

Big Shanghai is the largest city in the world, with a population of 10.7 million. Peking is second (10 million), so China has the top two. Tokyo cops third with 8.8 million, while our own New York is fourth at 7.9 million. London, Moscow, Bombay, Seoul, São Paulo (in Brazil) and Cairo round out the top 10.

High Tibet is right up there—Lhasa at 12,002 feet has the highest elevation of any city in the world. You drop a few feet to La Paz, Bolivia's 11,910 feet, and it's all downhill from there. Cuzco in Peru at 11,152 feet nails down third, and Sucre in Bolivia is up there at 9,331 feet, for fourth. The rest of the high top 10 are Quito, Ecuador; Toluca, Mexico; Bogotá, Colombia; Cochabamba, Bolivia; Addis Ababa, Ethiopia; and Asmara, Ethiopia, which has a very respectable elevation of 7,789 feet. Denver Chamber of Commerce publicity aside, the highest U.S. city is Santa Fe, N.M.—19th in the world at 6,950 feet.

Old Gaziantep in Turkey is probably the oldest city in the world, settled *before* 3650 B.C. Jerusalem and Kirkuk, Iraq tie for second, having appeared around 3000 B.C. Zurich was founded right around 3000 B.C.; we'll award it a fourth for being European. The rest of the top 10 oldest are Konya in Turkey, El Giza in Egypt, Sian in China, Asyût and Luxor in Egypt, and Lisbon and Porto in Portugal and Shao-hsing in China (all three settled in 2000 B.C.).

Hot It's a tie for warmest city in the world between Timbuktu in Mali and Tirunelveli in India—they both have an average annual temperature of a steamy 84.7°. But the drop isn't much for third-place Khartoum and

Omdurman in Sudan, both at 84.6°. Then there are Madurai, India; Niamey, Niger; Aden, Southern Yemen; Tiruchirappalli and Madras, India; and Ouagadougou, Upper Volta.

Cold Ulan Bator in Mongolia is the coolest city in the world, with an average annual temperature of 24.8°. Russia takes over from there, copping the next *24* places. After Ulan Bator, the top nine coldest cities are Chita, Bratsk, Ulan-Ude, Angarsk, Irkutsk, Komsomolsk-na-Amure, Tomsk, Kemerovo and Novosibirsk—household names all. Probably the best-known cold city is our own Anchorage—it's 28th coldest, with an average temperature of 35.2°.

Wet The city with the most precipitation is Monrovia, Liberia, in West Africa, racking up an easy first place with 202.01 inches of moisture every year. Second goes to Padang in Indonesia (187.56 inches) and a third to Conakry in Guinea (170.91 inches). The competition falls off fast in the rest of the top 10, which are Bogor, Indonesia; Douala, Cameroun; Freetown, Sierra Leone; Hilo, Hawaii; Mangalore, India; Manado, Indonesia; and Makasar, Indonesia, which has a mere 126 inches of rainfall each year. Rangoon in Burma, Singapore, Hong Kong and Manila are up there for big *and* sodden cities.

Dry Egypt has the least-precipitation crown locked up—the top seven driest cities are in Egypt. Luxor is first, with all of .02 inch of precipitation each year—it's twice as dry as second place Aswân, which gets a hefty .04 inch each year. Things get considerably wetter from there in Asyût, Suez, El Giza, Cairo and Zagazig—which gets a big 1.18 inches each year. Lima, Peru; Aden, Southern Yemen and Tanta, back in Egypt, complete the dry top 10. Back home, Las Vegas is the driest we can do—a worldwide 19th with 3.90 inches of rainfall every year.

Final fetishist note: if you've got just one chance to gratify your travel fetish, Egypt could well be the answer. It's got cities in the top 10 for bigness, hotness and oldness, so you can be crowded and parched and soak up some history, all at the same time. Happy travels!

–Richard John Pietschmann

PLACES

Illustration by Sandra Forrest

I should like to rise and go
Where the golden apples grow;
Where below another sky
Parrot islands anchored lie,
And, watched by cockatoos and goats,
Lonely Crusoes building boats;
Where in sunshine reaching out
Eastern cities, miles about,
Are with mosque and minaret
Among sandy gardens set,
And the rich goods from near and far
Hang for sale in the bazaar. . . .

—ROBERT LOUIS STEVENSON

You're out of the woods,
You're out of the dark,
You're out of the night,
Step into the sun,
Step into the light.
Keep straight ahead
For the most glorious place
On the face of the earth
Or the sky.
Hold onto your breath,
Hold onto your heart,
Hold onto your hope.
March up to that gate
And bid it open.

—E. Y. HARBURG,
HAROLD ARLEN,
HERBERT STOTHART

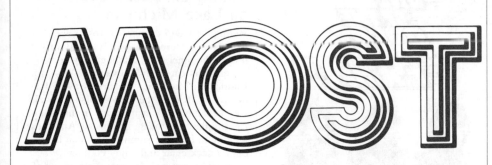

Wonders of the Natural World

Wonder	Place	Why
Tallest Geyser	Yellowstone National Park, Wyoming	World's tallest active geyser, the "Giant," erupts at intervals varying from a week to 3 months, throwing 200 feet of spray at a rate of 700,000 gallons an hour.
Oldest Rock	Godthaab, Greenland	Reliably dated at 3,800 million years old, the Amitsoq Gneiss of West Greenland is considered to be the world's oldest rock. The Morton Gneiss of Minnesota, at 3,550 million years old, is a distant second.
Deepest Ocean Trench	Marianas, Pacific Ocean	The Marianas Trench is the deepest measured part of the ocean; it's between 35,760 and 36,198 feet deep.
Highest Unclimbed Mountain	Karakoram, Kashmir	Ranked as the 15th highest peak in the world, Gasherbrum III rises to 26,090 feet.
Tallest Mountain	Hawaii	Measured from its underwater base in the Hawaiian Trough to its peak, Mauna Kea (Mountain White) has an overall height of 33,476 feet, surpassing Mt. Everest by more than ¾ mile.
Longest River	Nile, East Africa	Some claim the Amazon is longest, but hydrologically speaking the Nile wins hands down at 4,145 miles.
Fastest Rapids	Lava Falls, Colorado River	Has been navigated, but rapids run as fast as 30 m.p.h. with waves churning up to 12 feet.
Highest Waterfall	Angel Falls, Venezuela	Has a total drop of 3,212 feet, and the longest single drop—2,684 feet. Angel Falls was discovered by an American pilot, Jimmy Angel, in 1935. Highest waterfall in the United States is Yosemite, California, at 2,425 feet.
Longest Natural Bridge	Arches and Canyonlands National Park, Moab, Utah	Set about 100 feet above the canyon floor, Landscape Arch spans 291 feet. It narrows to six feet at one place. Larger, and nearby, is Rainbow Bridge, which spans 278 feet and is more than 22 feet wide.
Deepest Cave	Gouffre de la Pierre Saint-Martin, Pyrenees, France and Spain	It is measured at 3,850 feet below the entrance. Deepest in the United States is Neffs Cave, Utah, at 1,184 feet.
Longest Cave	Mammoth-Flint Ridge Cave System, Kentucky	It was last measured at 122 miles and it could still be growing.
Deepest Gorge	Hell's Canyon, Oregon and Idaho	Plunging 7,900 feet from the Devil Mountain to the Snake River, Hell's Canyon is part of the dividing line between Oregon and Idaho.
Largest Gorge	Grand Canyon, Arizona	Extending a distance of 217 miles, from Marble Gorge to the Grand Wash Cliffs, the Grand Canyon is up to 7,000 feet deep. It is 13 miles wide at its widest points.

Some Unusual Museums

When you find that you're bored stiff by the stuffed platypus in your local natural history museum, refresh yourself. Take in a new museum, an unusual museum. We can recommend these:

The Branford Trolley Museum, East Haven, Conn. Trolleys from all parts of the country and all eras. Trolleys available for charter by writing to the Branford Electric Railway Association, P.O. Box 457, Short Beach, Conn. 06405.

The Museum of Navaho Ceremonial Art, Santa Fe, N.M. A really incredible museum of Navaho sand paintings and assorted Indian lore. Fascinating and friendly.

The Musical Museum, Deansboro, N.Y. Hurdy-gurdies, antique pipe organs, pianolas, music boxes—even a mechanical bird that flies from branch to branch and chirps!

The Houdini Museum, Niagara Falls, N.Y. Collected magicalia, posters, displays and some of Houdini's most incredible stunts recreated.

The Museum of the American Circus, Sarasota, Fla. Run by Ringling Brothers Barnum and Bailey.

Dard Hunter Paper Museum, Appleton, Wis. (at the Institute of Paper Chemistry). The exhibits tell you everything you ever wanted to know about making paper. There is even a display of the earliest oriental paper molds, circa 600 A.D.

Sod Town Prairie Pioneer Museum, Colby, Kan. Completely furnished reproductions of the sod buildings that settlers in the treeless prairie regions lived in between the 1840s and the 1930s. There are also displays of Indian artifacts and live prairie animals and plants. This museum is the headquarters of the Sons and Daughters of the Soddies (with 25,000 members)—if you or any of your ancestors were sod house dwellers, you can become a life member of this organization for $2.

The Great Stone Fortress and Military Museum, Ticonderoga, N.Y. This is Fort Ticonderoga, where Ethan Allen and the Green Mountain Boys touched off the American Revolution. The Fort is restored. The Museum has more artifacts from Revolutionary soldiers than any other museum.

The Valley Railroad, Essex, Conn. A railroading museum that operates a steam train in the old style, one sporting gleaming brass and polished woodwork. The train connects with a boat ride along the Deep River.

The Whaling Museum, New Bedford, Mass. Pie crimpers, scrimshaw, spanker booms, stern carvings, a half-size replica of a whaleboat. On Johnny Cake Hill in New Bedford. *Moby Dick*'s opening scenes take place in New Bedford.

The Baseball Hall of Fame, Cooperstown, N.Y. Famous mitts on display. The Brook-

(continued on next page)

(continued from previous page)

lyn Dodgers, Judge Landis, Ty Cobb and
The Babe. Also, they make the best sharp
cheese in the world in Cooperstown.

Edison Home Museum, Fort Myers, Fla. A
vast collection of original Edison inventions,
including no fewer than 160 Edison phono-
graphs and, of course, plenty of light bulbs.
The museum is housed in the nation's first
pre-fabricated house—it was built in Maine
in 1884 and brought to Florida by boat.

Henry Ford Museum, Dearborn, Mich.
Right near the first Henry Ford's home
town, this museum has acres of displays—
here you can see virtually every Ford vehicle ever manufactured, including the Edsel
and Ford-built aircraft.

McKee's Museum of Sunken Treasure, on
Plantation Key, Fla. Just what the name im-
plies, and gold doubloons and pieces of
eight are only two of the fascinating treasures you can see here.

—The Editors

ONE OF THE GREAT ESCAPES

. . . to a Photo Machine
Well, sure, a photo machine is a place.
And you need photos to get from place to
place—photos for your passport, your in-
ternational driver's license, your ID, etc.
Sure. Besides, there's the fun factor.

—The Editors

Taking an Ocean Cruise—on Lake Michigan

Riding the C&O car ferry across Lake
Michigan is more than merely a way of getting to the other side, although if you're
traveling by car from Milwaukee, Wis. to
Ludington, Mich., it will surely save a lot
of driving. Riding the ferry is also a novel
way to sample an ocean cruise in miniature,
right in the heart of the Midwest. And those
seeking to beat the summer heat can latch
onto a deck chair and enjoy cooling
breezes—or splurge and rent a stateroom (for
less than $5 in the daytime, less than $10 at
night).

It's a six-hour trip across the lake on the
Spartan and her sister ships, and a round-trip
voyage affords a relaxing day "at sea." For
weekenders, Milwaukee offers many
charms—a fine conservatory, a lakeshore art
gallery, the best German food outside of
Germany and lots of beer—while Ludington
is gateway to the scenic charms of the vacation country in the upper half of Michigan's
mitt.

Aboard ship, visit with bicycle tourists
headed for Michigan's country lanes, or
backpackers off to sample the many fine
trails of the Badger State. Maybe you'll run
into the gray-haired couple who make the
voyage every year to celebrate the anniversary of their honeymoon cruise. Or you can
talk to the crew, many of them veteran
sailors of this inland sea with tales to tell of
fierce storms involving gale-force winds and
waves crashing over the bow of the ship.
(Children find these stories especially edify-
ing.)

In season—Memorial Day to Labor Day—
there are two crossings a day each way,
with irregular service during fall and winter.
You must make a reservation if you plan to
take your car across, but it isn't necessary if
you're not. Bicyclists can walk aboard with
their bikes. Fares are: adults $6.50 or $8.95
round trip; children $3.50 or $4.50 round
trip; cars $11.50 or $13.50 round trip. Information from General Agent, C&O Dock,
Ludington, Mich. 49431. Phone (616)
843-2521.

—Mike Michaelson

Uruguayan Minnesota

It may seem strange to encounter an 11-foot
bronze statue of José Artigas, hero of
Uruguayan independence, dominating the
main thoroughfare of a small town in Minnesota; but you have to consider that that
town is named Montevideo. It acquired this
unlikely appellation around the turn of the
century, when a wanderer named Cornelius
J. Nelson decided that the name of the
Uruguayan capital—which translates roughly
to "I see a mountain"—also was appropriate
for his north country home town located
amid steep bluffs at the confluence of the
Minnesota and Chippewa Rivers.

Montevideo, Minn. maintains many ties
with its South American sister city. The
liveliest and most spectacular event held in
Montevideo, Minn. is Fiesta Days, started
back in 1946 and held every summer since.

This celebration attempts to capture the lifestyle of the Uruguayan capital and usually
there are visits by officials from the U.S.
State Department and the Uruguayan Embassy, as well as such festive goings-on as
costume pageants, concerts, dancing, cook-
outs, water fights, the inevitable beauty
queen contest and one of the largest parades
held in the state—some 200 units make up
the parade. There also is an art fair featuring
many art objects from the town's South
American namesake. A permanent cultural
display at the town library includes
Uruguayan paintings, sculpture and a miscel-
lany of gifts that have been presented over
the years by the Uruguayan city to the Minnesota community.

Not to neglect good old Americana, the
town has also reconstructed a pioneer village, moving in from their original locations
19 authentic buildings—schoolhouse, log
cabin, blacksmith's shop, general store, fur
trading post, millinery shop, etc. To get a
taste of South American and early North
American culture all at once, visit Montevideo, Minn.

—Mike Michaelson

Cheap Thrills in Ludington, Mich.

Ludington, Mich. used to be a one-horse
town. Now it's a one-zip-code town and it
hasn't changed much, but that doesn't mean
it's dull. When you get off the C&O ferry
from Milwaukee, check out these local attractions:

Orgie's Cafe On Ludington Avenue right
in the heart of town (ask anyone). "Orgie's"
is pronounced with a hard "g," as in
"organ"—which is natural, because the
place is owned by the Organ family. Waffles
and pancakes are the specialty here—they're
cheap (around $2 for a big plateful with
bacon, sausage or ham), they're exquisitely
light, and you get a choice of at least four

kinds of syrup. During the summer,
blueberry pancakes are made with fresh fruit
straight from the blueberry farms in the area.
This is a family restaurant and kids will
most likely be given a free balloon when
they leave. If the huge, "hand-tinted" photos
of car ferries and beach scenes on the walls
at Orgie's get you down, the waitresses will
cheer you up again—they're all nubile young
high-school girls and jolly as can be.

Pere Marquette shrine South of town
(drive or hike out U.S. 31) on a bluff overlooking the lake. Ludington's greatest claim
to fame is that Father Marquette (who, with
Louis Joliet, was the first to travel all the
way down the Mississippi River from Lake
Michigan to the Gulf of Mexico) died here,
with only a few Indian friends attending

him. From time to time, one or another
town on Michigan's west coast has claimed
that Marquette actually died near *it*, but so
far Ludington is the only town with a shrine.
It's a pleasant little monument with a nice
view.

Ludington has over a dozen good motels (for
brochures, write to the Chamber of Commerce), and you can also camp out in the
state park if you go for the kind of "camping" that involves parking your car and
pitching your tent 10 feet from the next
guy's. If you do plan to camp, make reservations for a spot—the campgrounds are
packed from Memorial Day to Labor Day.
Write State Park Headquarters, Ludington,
Mich. 49431.

—Suzan Smith

A Cabin in the Wilderness—Alaska's Most Fabulous Vacation Bargain

If your vacation dreams are of wild and untamed country, of wild and hard-fighting fish, of wildlife and birdlife in nature's true domain, picture this: the place is Alaska; a warm and weather-tight Panabode log cabin, rugged but not unattractive, sits amidst an otherwise undisturbed virgin forest of giant spruce and hemlock trees. Mountain country, this, as well as forest wilderness; through the trees and over their tops you see snowcapped peaks all around.

A few steps from the cabin is a cold, clear lake known to contain abundant populations of big, voracious, fast-striking rainbow and cutthroat trout and Dolly Varden char. You can cast for these beauties from shore or you can use a small skiff beached nearby for your convenience.

The cabin itself contains bunks for six or eight persons. Furnishings include table, chairs and a cookstove. Toilet facilities are down a path out back. You provide your own grub, cooking gear and sleeping bag.

Here's the best part. "Civilization" is 25 to 50 miles away, maybe even farther. It wouldn't matter if it were only half that distance. Your cabin, your Shangri-la in the wilderness, can be reached only by float-equipped charter "bush" aircraft. That's how you go in; that's how you'll get out. In the meantime the biggest disturbance you'll hear is the soulful howl of a wolf in the night or the honk of geese in the day—or the cry of delight from one of your companions when he brings a particularly big rainbow to creel.

And if that's the best part, here's the most incredible part: this cabin (and 150 others like it) rents to the public for the ridiculously low price of $5 per party per night. And *per party* doesn't mean *"per person"*—it means *per group*!

The cabins are spread throughout Tongass National Forest in the southeast Alaska panhandle and throughout Chugach National Forest in the state's south-central region. Most of the units are located on freshwater lakes and streams; some are located on saltwater bays; a very few are located along hiking trails.

One exotic unit, situated adjacent to a natural hot springs (which itself is fully enclosed for luxurious bathing), fronts upon the open Pacific Ocean.

Reservations are required for all the cabins in the system. If you're interested in receiving a map showing each cabin's location plus information about how and when to book the unit of your choice, write to the U.S. Forest Service, Regional Forester's Office, Juneau, Alaska 99801.

—Mike Miller

Natural Bridge

Ever had the urge to walk out on a natural bridge? Blanding, Utah, a tiny town tucked away in the deep southeastern corner of the state, is the starting point for a 45-mile drive to Natural Bridges National Monument to the west.

There are several natural bridges in the area but this, carved by eons of erosion, is the most accessible and is almost 300 feet long.

It's quite a climb down from the parking area, then up to the bridge itself, but the path is clearly marked and, as the photo shows, it can be done.

ON THE ROAD

The Livermore Light Bulb

Charles Kuralt has seen a lot in his years On The Road. This is a report from Livermore, Calif. on one of his most incredible discoveries—a light bulb that doesn't burn out.

Kuralt: In 1897, Thomas Alva Edison invented the electric light bulb. Twenty-two years later, in the year 1901, they hung one of the new-fangled gadgets in the Livermore, Calif. Fire Department, and turned it on. It's still here, and still on.

The old bulb has almost never been turned off in 71 years. By today's standards it should have burned out 852 times by now, but clearly we are not dealing with today's standards. We are dealing with somebody who made light bulbs to last. The bulb, hand-blown, with a thick carbon filament, was made, apparently, by the Shelby Electric Co., which did not become one of the giants of the nation, for an obvious reason. They made light bulbs to last, and nobody ever re-ordered. One burns on, a memorial to Shelby Electric.

Needless to say, the bulb is accorded a kind of awesome respect by Fire Captain Kirby Slate and his men.

Capt. Kirby Slate: We started out with this light bulb over at Second and Elm—that's the old fire station, that's where it was first

put. Then it was taken from there and moved to here, and since that time the only knowledge that I have of it not working was when the WPA was here in 1937; it was out for about a week.

Kuralt: And you never turn it off?

Slate: Never turn it off. Now, we have a switch on it. But to my knowledge no man has ever turned that switch.

Kuralt: And better not?

Slate: And better not, that's right. That's right.

Kuralt: Do you sometimes have the fear that as you glance up at it it's going to go out?

Slate: Well, let me put it this way: I just hope that I am not on duty when it goes out.

Kuralt: As the Livermore firemen went about their work, we stood around for the afternoon, just watching the old bulb burn and thinking long thoughts about the planned and unplanned obsolescence that rules our lives. In a time when gadgets are forever falling apart or burning out or breaking up, it was kind of nice to spend a day watching a dusty 71-year-old light bulb just go on and on. If you're ever in Livermore and need reassurance, we recommend it.

—Charles Kuralt, CBS News, On The Road, Livermore, Calif.

Country Auctions

By Brian Vachon

When you watch one, you're watching a show that spans the entire breadth of a region's age and character. And the show is free.

Country auctions saved my marriage. Or at least they headed off some potentially destructive eruptions. It's this way: I once spent 15 minutes in a showroom trying to decide what kind of car to buy, and that's the longest—the absolute outside longest—time I ever spent trying to decide on any purchase. The nasty word for that is compulsive, but you could also call it decisive, firm, deliberate.

My wife can—and often does—spend 15 minutes deciding what kind of margarine to buy. Prudent, exact and agonizing. We recently purchased a home in Vermont (I was sure we should buy in eight minutes and my wife concurred a week and a half later), and we were faced with some usual questions about furnishing it. Only in our case, the questions weren't at all usual. A cornucopia of impatience, accusations, threats and retaliations loomed. The questions were hitting at the essence of our incompatibility. Country auctions were our help and our redeemer.

Country auctions go on in probably any place where there's country, but the ones I know about are in New England. They occur on Saturdays, beginning in early summer and continuing into late fall. You can read about them in the preceding Thursday's newspaper, where the ad says something like: "AUCTION at the Old Pierce House, Randolph Center, Vermont, starting at 10 a.m. Saturday, to settle the estate of Mrs. Emma Pierce. Consisting of antiques and furnishings, a partial list of which is as follows. . . ." The partial list parades out a few items to kindle the interest of bargain hunters or antique dealers. There always seems to be a Victorian sideboard or two, some Windsor bow-back chairs, a mahogony Sheraton canopy bed, and invariably "other items too numerous to mention." It's those "other items" that attracted us—those little things with which to furnish a house.

Country auctions are a kind of ultimate entertainment. When you watch one, you're watching a show—there's no question about that—and it's free, requires no equipment, and you can arrive and leave any time you want. They are amiable affairs, almost invariably light-hearted (as the big city rare book or Western cattle auctions are not) and without making so much as a single bid on a single item, you're almost bound to enjoy yourself.

Ah, but the bidding is the essence of what the country auctions are all about. As a participant, you face not only pleasure but also excitement and quite possibly reward. For just as they symbolize a kind of ultimate in entertainment, country auctions, and especially those that are being held to finalize a private estate, are actually the presentation of the ultimate supermarket. All accumulations and trappings of a country home—from bath tubs and lawn mowers to magazine racks and teacups—are to be sold to the highest bidder. And rather than being morbid, they create an infusion of life, a rush of vitality is injected into the objects offered for sale. When was the last time you saw a set of breakfast plates get that much admiration and attention? Or generate that much enthusiasm?

"Here, I got a beautiful set of antique breakfast dishes, whaddaya gonna give for 'em?" the auctioneer intones. Country auctioneers have little in common. They span the entire breadth of New England age and character (which is a wider breadth than normally credited), but if they're going to be any good at their trade, folks are going to have to like them. Very simply, they have to generate a quality of likability when they're on the block. That's the key—that, and maleness, which seems to be an auctioneer requirement in New England.

"Hey, whaddaya gonna give. We got six, seven, eight beautiful antique breakfast dishes. Near perfect condition. Couple have a few age lines, and we got a chip here on this one. Whaddo I hear?"

Country auctioneers also have to be honest.

"Let's start the bidding at five dollars for these beautiful dishes."

"One dollar," someone shouts from the crowd.

"Sold for one dollar!" the auctioneer shouts back, and the show is rolling. The first item for sale at a country auction usually goes on the first bid to get things moving, and it's generally the last item of the day to do so. For the rest of the sale, the auctioneer will coax a dozen or more bids out of a cooperative audience but the pace seldom slackens. When he's rolling nicely, he can usually sell two or three items a minute and still exact a reasonable price for them. They say there are no bargains left to be found at a country auction, but they said that 20 years ago and they'll say it 20 years from now. And they're wrong. There are bargains at every auction. Maybe there are fewer "finds." It's certainly true that the auctioneer pretty carefully combs through an estate before listing its contents for sale. Any prize items are extracted to be sold to a more discriminating audience. But for people who have furnishing a house in mind, or for people who are open to buying a couple of things to round out a home—an electric can opener, maybe, or a set of TV trays—a country auction is the only place to buy.

"Hey, we got a real nice, antique, hand-painted teapot here, whaddaya gonna give for it?" the auctioneer says, and that reminds me that I started out talking about my wife and the potential problem in our marriage. I, the immediate shopper; she, the ultra-fastidious one. Let me go back to the beginning of this particular auction on this particular day. We had followed the red arrows posted on telephone poles and barns that morning until we arrived at the site of the auction. A gentleman farmer had passed away some months earlier, leaving a somewhat imprecise will. As is very often the case, his estate was being decided by public sale. The auctioneer set up the block right on the front porch of the farm house. It was one of those chilly, early summer mornings and a tent-like covering had been stretched out over most of the front lawn to accommodate the customers. It was the usual mixed lot. City people stuck out here and there, but there weren't so many as to be threatening. (Too many city people can ruin a country auction by overbidding on every item.) There were also a few antique dealers who had backed their trucks into the lawn, and we were glad to see them. Dealers are good for an auction. They generally never pay more than half what they think they can sell again for, and to bid right after a dealer has quit bidding and to win the item is a way to ensure getting a bargain.

We've brought along folding chairs, and as I am pulling them out of the car trunk and setting them up on the lawn, my wife has wandered to the front of the house where she will spend a considerable amount of time for the rest of the day inspecting the merchandise. When I'm set up, I go over to the bookkeeper and get myself a number, written big on a slip of white paper. To keep auctions moving briskly, cash payment on a single item is discouraged. Bidders flash their numbers when they win an item and the transaction is recorded in a ledger. When the bidders are ready to go home, they visit the bookkeeper again and settle up. Checks are always accepted.

I return to my folding chair and get comfortable. It's beginning to drizzle and there is an added dash of comfort and fellowship under the tent. We're all there to be entertained, to make a few purchases maybe, to have a good time.

Okay, now we're back where the auctioneer was offering the hand-painted teapot. I look at it from where I am sitting on the lawn, and I like it. I decide I'm going to make a bid or two but I also decide that two bucks will be my limit. Meanwhile my wife returns to our chairs. She has also looked at the teapot. She has, in fact, scrutinized the teapot, turned it upside down, held it up against the light and rubbed her finger around the inside of the rim. She also has come to like it.

"I'm going to bid for it," I say.

"How much?" she asks, trying to show disapproval.

"Up to two dollars," I say.

"One dollar!"

"Ah come on, it looks like a nice teapot."

"The handle has a crack in it."

"How about a dollar fifty?"

With hesitation and some pain, she agrees.

"All right, who's gonna give me five dollars to start the bidding on this really beautiful, antique, hand-painted teapot?" the auctioneer asks. If he asks for five dollars to start, I figure he'll accept three but no less. Enough city people could drive the price up to $20.

"One dollar," I offer, trying to look bored.

"Hey we got a dolla, dolladolladolladolla, who'll give me two dollars on this beautiful Victorian piece?" I am mentally writing off the teapot. It's going out of my range. I look up to the porch to see what other items are being moved toward the block. Half the pleasure for me is not knowing what will be offered next.

"A dollar and a half," a girl behind me shouts out.

"Hey we got a dollaranhalf, who'll give me two? Two? Two?" The auctioneer is looking at me, nodding his head with aggressive affirmation. I nod slightly back.

"Hey, we got two dollas, who'll give me three?"

My wife punches me. "You said you'd stop at a dollar fifty," she says, but she's not looking very angry.

"Three? Three anyone? It's a beautiful antique item. No price on this Victorian piece. Three anyone? . . . Sold then, for two dollars, to number . . ." — I triumphantly hold up my card — ". . . number forty-eight!"

"You don't even drink tea!" my wife says, but she's grinning.

"It's a nice piece," I say. And it is. I'm pleased with my purchase — my trophy — and pleased that it took about 30 seconds to buy. My wife is also pleased. She considers the teapot hers, and it took her more than an hour to make the transaction.

Go enjoy a country auction. Save your marriage. □

The Randolph Auctions: The Real Maine

For a real slice of life in rural Maine, there's nothing that beats the Randolph Auctions —every Monday, rain or shine, at 1 p.m.— whether you're buying, selling or gawking.

There's a good crowd that gathers, too. It all comes together in a barnyard just off Route 126 in Randolph, at the Central Maine Livestock Auction. It's the weekly sale of farm animals that draws small farmers and cattle dealers, but once all the critters have been disposed of, auctioneer Sherm English invites bids on anything from old tools to old shoes, from a set of horse hames with shiny brass knobs to a bag of new-grown Maine potatoes.

Folks bid by raising their hands, and a visitor, says Sherm English, better dang well remember to "keep those hands down unless you mean business. Around here you don't so much as scratch an ear 'less you mean to buy."

—Min S. Yee

London's Eccentric Shops

A curious new bargain center has recently joined London's list of eccentric shops. The Reject Shop on Brompton Road is owned by a London couple, Anthony and Anna Hawser, who spent a year writing and visiting manufacturers to ask for slightly damaged or imperfect goods. The results astounded even them. They opened up with a vast stock of everything from glassware and cutlery to Continental pots and pans, wearing apparel and lighting equipment—all at bargain prices.

The Reject Shop joins such odd and fascinating London shops as "Anything Left-Handed" at 65 Beak St. in Soho; Weinthorp on Berwick Street, which sells off-size shoes (starting at size 1); and John Lewis on Oxford Street, which carries probably the world's largest selection of paper dress patterns, all sizes.

If you happen to know any left-handed bargain hunters who wear size 1 shoes and sew, you should point out to them that London is their town. Even if you're right-handed, wear size 9 shoes and can't thread a needle, you can't help but enjoy these eccentric shops.

—James Egan

CIVIC PRIDE

How Much Is That Doggie on the Auction Block?

What the people of Fredericksburg, Va., which calls itself "America's Most Historic City," are most proud of is the fact that their town has the world's oldest dog auction (it had its 275th annual running last Oct. 7). The famous Fredericksburg Dog Mart began in 1698 when the English colonists signed a treaty with the local Pamunkey Indians that included trading agreements by which the English would supply manufactured goods to the Indians in exchange for furs and dogs. Apparently there have always been a lot of dogs around Fredericksburg, even before the town itself was built.

In any case, dog trading soon became a way of life in Fredericksburg, and it goes on in force to this very day. A few Pamunkey Indians have survived to take part in the annual festivities, the high point of which is the auctioning of dogs at 12:30 p.m. on the

big day. There is no registration, and it costs nothing to take part either as seller or buyer. The only strict regulation is: "Dogs may be placed on block only one time."

After the auction there is a dog show (what else?) followed by speeches of welcome by town dignitaries and an Indian. Then there is a dog parade. Other activities that fill out the occasion include Indian dances, a turkey-calling contest, a fox-horn blowing contest, an old fiddlers' contest, a hog-calling contest, a harmonica contest and a folk guitar contest.

The police from Richmond show off their K-9 Corps, and prizes go to show winners, including ones for best miscellaneous dog and ugliest dog. Many persons dissatisfied with their dogs take them to Fredericksburg, trade them in and leave happy. For information, write Information Center, Fredericksburg, Va. 22401; phone (703) 373-9391.

—Roy Bongartz

Garbage Cans Can Be Department Stores

You can find wonderful things in garbage cans. And you can have a lot of fun finding them. All you need is a pair of gloves, a healthy lack of inhibitions and a desire to get something for nothing. If the desire is strong enough, you can skip the gloves.

In order to get into garbage cans, it is important to realize that one man's garbage is not necessarily another's trash. In the past year I have turned "garbage" into my living-room couch, a toaster, clothing and several hundred dollars in cash (in a roundabout garage-sale sort of way).

People throw away the damnedest things. I've found everything from 15 pairs of panty hose to an expensive watch. I don't know why they were thrown away, but they were.

A few basic tips are in order for the beginning scavenger. Limit your rummaging to the tops of the cans (this does not apply to debris bins, which I'll cover in a moment). I learned this very early in my career, after pawing through several feet of week-old lasagne and finding nothing.

Pay particular attention to brown paper bags that are neatly folded. Again, I don't know why, but the majority of treasures I've uncovered have been neatly packaged, as if the previous owner vaguely realized the worth of the object before it was thrown out.

Limit your search to garbage cans on public streets. You'd be amazed at how protective people become of their garbage if it's on private property.

Invest in a small tool repair kit. So many valuable things are tossed out because they're thought to be broken, especially things electrical. I have a friend who found an air conditioner once which needed nothing more than a new plug. He sold it for $75.

About debris bins. These are the department stores of scavenging, measuring about five feet by five feet by seven feet. They can be found in large metropolitan areas where they are rented by people who have a large amount of trash to dispose of. About 80 percent of them are used when a house is being vacated and the owner is cleaning it out.

Debris bins contain a plethora of unwanted goodies: furniture, books, toys, clothes, rugs, jewelry, china—you name it. The only way to properly "shop" a debris bin is to climb inside it and start digging. This is not at all unpleasant, as debris bins rarely (if ever) hold "true" garbage like the aforementioned lasagne.

You will soon find that garbage cans are like stores: quality merchandise is more often displayed in better neighborhoods. I once found a table in the ritzy Pacific Heights section of San Francisco that I later sold for $150 at a garage sale. There was absolutely nothing wrong with it when I found it.

After your first few "finds" you'll begin to realize the true beauty of this pastime, which I'll illustrate with one of my favorite garbage stories. We had been needing a vacuum cleaner for some time, and had finally saved enough to buy one. We now have a beautiful Hoover upright. It cost me 50 cents for a new drive strap. I found it in a debris bin one block from the store.

–Robert A. Lacey

The World's 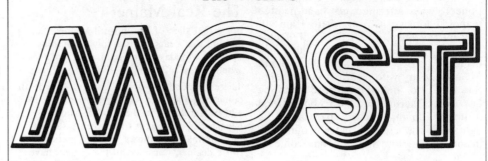 Markets

Name	Place	Atmosphere
The Arab Market	Jerusalem	Ancient spice merchants, camel caravans, storytellers and sages
Ranch Market	Hollywood	Steve Allen, poodles with sunglasses, everyone beautiful, strange and a movie star
Portobello Road	London	Antique lace, mauve fingernails, assorted junk and someone videotaping it
Benteng	Kuala Lumpur	Sunset by the Red Mosque, a market on the riverbanks, squid sellers and fresh banana juice
Les Halles	Paris	Still a 3 a.m. tradition—onion soup and red wine
Fulton Fish Market	New York	The Ultimate Fish Market
Grand Central Market	Los Angeles	A great, raucous, delicious funky Mexican-American bazaar
Djemaa el-F'na	Marrakech	A daily nine-ring opium circus with Gnaoui dancers
Mercado de la Libertad	Guadalajara	Roast kid, Don Juan, mariachis and endless artistic piles of beautiful stuff
Northridge Shopping Center	Los Angeles	A dazzling zircon lost in a sea of gangrene
Haggle Alley	Taipei	Haggle, haggle, haggle. Over jade, ivory, paintings, rice cookers and toilet paper

Light Up Paris at Night

You're in Paris, you've got a few extra francs in your pocket, and you'd really like to impress a certain someone—that exquisite boy who goes to the Sorbonne, your future mother-in-law, the guy who found backers for your underground newspaper in Peoria. You could send a jeroboam or two of champagne and a couple of dozen roses, but, hell, anyone can think of that. Why not have the Eiffel Tower lit up in especial honor of the party in question, instead? You can do it —all it takes is $70 (that's about 350 francs) and a phone call to the Lighting Department of the Paris City Hall (phone in Paris, 277-15-40).

If you're not 350 francs rich, don't despair, and don't fall back on the champagne and roses. Because, for $35 you can light up the Arc de Triomphe; for $12, Notre Dame or the Pont Neuf; and, for those with big ideas but small purses, there's the obelisk in the middle of the Place de la Concorde—*that* you can have lit for a mere $9.50 (about 48 francs).

The Lighting Department will arrange to light up any of these any time, at your request; in fact, they have a list of no fewer than 149 landmarks, monuments, gardens and fountains that they'll light up for you. The list is supposed to be more or less secret, but if you're persistent they'll show it to you. Then you can pick just the right thing to light up for your future mother-in-law—the statue of Liberté, Egalité and Fraternité in the Place de la Bastille, maybe? You can have it lit for only $11.50!

To Market, to Market, to Buy a *Feng Shui!*

Every self-respecting market hound has to have a slew of curios for his den. A caribou head bagged in the Alaskan highlands, a painted wooden statue of the Garuda of Indonesia, a Taoist spirit house, a Siamese shadow puppet—that kind of thing.

On my last trip to the Far East I got such a bee in my woolly bonnet over a certain gewgaw that I have literally searched half the world for it. This particular cherished item the Chinese call *feng shui*, and it's a kind of astrological compass.

It's a circular disc about nine inches in diameter made of wood or baked clay and lacquered bright yellow. It has a small magnetic compass in the center, surrounded by 16 movable concentric rings with Chinese characters etched on them.

For some reason, I wanted one of these peculiar things, and I looked everywhere. In Singapore they said you can get them in Kuala Lumpur. In Kuala Lumpur they said you have to go to Hong Kong. In Hong Kong they say you can only find them on the Chinese mainland. Obviously, as happens in Chinese communities, someone wasn't talking.

A mildly disreputable source assured me you only see them during the "Festival of the Hungry Ghosts."

This festival fell in August last year, when I happened to be in Hong Kong. The festival marks the time when the spirits of the ancestors return to Earth. The Chinese say that what with their trials in the nether world, the ancestors are *ravenous*. If you don't give them food, they'll eat your spleen.

"Hungry Ghosts" starts on a nearly full moon, a shadowlit night. The music of a Chinese opera is wafting in from some supernatural realm. There is smoke everywhere, and incense burning. The crowd parts for an instant, and I see—food!

It is all beautifully laid out, everywhere, on wooden platforms. The first one I pass groans under the weight of five whole roast suckling pigs. The second one supports an incredibly lavish pyramid of at least 30 kinds of brilliantly colored tropical fruits, from nut-brown lychees to hairy red rambutans to orange-and-green ripe papayas. The third table—! Well, let me tell you, there is literally *half a mile of food*!

There are statues made from sweet rice balls. There are intricate Chinese historical tableaus sculpted out of spinach and fruit. There are artful little temples built of red and white sweetmeats. Between each drooling table, incense is burning, actual *trees* of fuming frankincense 10 feet tall, ornately carved and colorfully painted with the terrifying likeness of Yen Lo, the Ruler of the Underworld.

Directly in the center of all the action a traditional Chinese opera is wailing nonstop, the performers in winged helmets, dragon robes and fiercely painted faces. Accompanied by the twangy two-stringed lyre *ching hu*, they are performing a play called "Disturbance in Heaven," featuring our rascally hero The White Monkey, who steals the sacred peaches of Paradise and decides to chuck the uneventful life of Heaven to live with his friends in a country cave. This infuriates the Gods of Thunder and Lightning, and especially the Dragon King. They declare war on the Monkey, but our hero's magic wand—not to mention his somersaults and his utter effrontery to all authorities—is too much for them.

And in the midst of this I'm supposed to find a *feng shui*? I don't even know where to begin. Besides, all this food is making me hungry. I go into an eating shop to get my bearings and have a bowl of *mee* soup. (The food outside is just for show right now. Afterwards, the families that made it will eat it, on the principle that hungry spirits, after all, can only eat the *spirit* of the food.)

After catching my breath and filling my stomach, I go back into the tumult. I look on every table, I search every booth, I watch every kung fu expert, medicine man and shrouded Taoist priest. I ask fortune tellers, Ping-Pong players and kite fliers. I lurk in opium dens and spice markets, and silently canvass eerie Buddhist temples.

There is mystery. There is life. There is the stuff of movies and picaroons' plots. But, damn it, there's no *feng shui* anywhere!

The upshot of this story is that months later, as I am walking down the street in Berkeley, Calif., I happen to wander into the Lowie Museum of Anthropology.

And would you believe that all of a sudden I am face to face with a genuine Chinese geomantic compass, the famous *feng shui*? But it's behind a thick wall of glass, and it might as well be 10,000 miles away.

—Orlando Flane

This little pig went to market;
This little pig stayed home;
This little pig had roast beef;
This little pig had none;
And this little pig cried, "Wee, wee, wee!"
All the way home.

—CHARLES PERRAULT

The Longest Escape

The Guinness Book of World Records tells us that the greatest escape from prison that anybody knows about was pulled off by one Leonard T. Fristoe, who killed two sheriff's deputies in 1920. In 1923 he escaped and began a stretch of illegal freedom that lasted for 46 years.

Why, after all that time, was the law able to find its inexorable way back to Leonard Fristoe? For the unhappy reason that his own son turned him in.

(By definition, of course, the greatest prison escapes are those that never end in recapture, and thus never come to the attention of the Guinness people.)

Big Money

Dominating the skyline as you approach Sudbury, Ontario from the west on the Trans-Canada Highway is a nickel 30 feet in diameter, a giant replica of the Canadian 1951 commemorative five-cent piece. This is not altogether inappropriate, since Sudbury—which calls itself "the Nickel Capital of the World"—does, in fact, produce something approaching 80 percent of the world's supply of the metal. (Local mines also are the world's top producers of platinum and rank fifth in copper production.)

The big nickel is part of Sudbury's unique Numismatic Park. It's a park without grass, a lake or even picnic tables. And the view from its high vantage point of smokestacks and mountains of charred slag. But both the park and its location are appropriate to this rugged, hard-working city that is a gateway to the Canadian North.

Other giant coins on display include a 20-foot replica of the 1964 U.S. Kennedy half dollar flanked by an eternal flame, a Sir Winston Churchill five-shilling coin and, amid this grandeur, a 1965 Canadian penny. Souvenir medallions of these coins are available at the park along with a selection of ore and rock samples and, for dyed-in-the-wool numismatists, a "coin corner."

Visitors also may don a hard hat and ride a cage down a 60-foot vertical shaft into a model mine. The model simulates conditions found in an operational mine, with exposed ore bodies adding to its authenticity. At night, the high-lying park offers a fine vantage point for viewing a colorful, and eminently photographable, sight—the fiery display created by rail cars dumping cargoes of molten iron silicate onto mounds of accumulating slag.

—Mike Michaelson

Great Walls Make Good Neighbors

The only man-made thing the astronauts could see from space was the Great Wall of China.

When this piece of intelligence came down the wires it led to deep discussions of walls. Is there something that doesn't love a wall? Do walls have ears? Would you bet your money on a walleyed pike? Should you speak to the wall so the door may hear?

It is a profound subject. Here are some other walls, great (though not quite so great as the Great Wall of China), and still standing:

—The Walls of Babylon

—The Berlin Wall

—The Wailing Wall in Jerusalem

—Hadrian's Wall on the Solway Firth

—The Walls of Carcassonne

—The Walls of Jericho

—The Walls of Troy

—The Graffiti Wall in Stockholm

–June Thum

In France, a Medieval Walled City

Probably the largest remaining walled city in the world is Carcassonne in southern France. Part of the walls were built by Visigoths in the sixth century as defense against the Franks in the north, the rest in the 12th and 13th centuries. Restored in the last century, the city is ringed by two concentric stone walls studded every few feet with towers, *barbacanes*, drawbridges, *mâchicoulis*—all the rigging of medieval fortification. Seen from a distance, the conical roofs of defensive towers and the rambling stone ramparts crowning a hilltop have an almost overwhelming romantic charm.

A so-called "new" city sprawls at the foot of the hill, but visitors will get more out of their stay by putting up at the Hotel du Donjon or Hotel de la Cité within the old walls. Reserve well in advance, especially in mid-season. The city is an easy drive southeast from Toulouse—rent a car, or hire a car and driver, through any European travel agent.

–Bern Keating

Turkey's City of Heroes

At Ephesus, on Turkey's Aegean Coast, antiquity comes alive in weathered, sun-drenched white marble ages removed from commercial pander. Ephesus is an excavated city that appears to have been abandoned only hours ago, and clover in the empty countryside fills the streets with perfume. In Ephesus, you feel compelled to whisper, so as not to disturb the sleep of heroes.

Ephesus was a Greek city visited by Alexander the Great in 334 B.C. Later it became the capital of the Roman Province of Asia. St. Paul preached his gospel to the Ephesians in 53 A.D., and assertions made at the stormy Ecumenical Council in Ephesus in 431 A.D. held that the Virgin Mary lived and died in the city. Her house in a sweet-smelling eucalyptus and olive grove on the cool nearby mountain is now a chapel; numerous miraculous cures there have been documented.

Ephesus has been only 20 percent reclaimed from the layers of silt deposited by the Cayster River. Silt preserved the mile-long marble Arcadiane, the main street repaved by the Romans in 400 A.D. The Arcadiane is bordered by the Temple of Hadrian and the Library, which contains the still-unopened sarcophagus and lead coffin of Celsus, the immensely rich man who endowed the edifice. At one end of the Arcadiane is the great ampitheater, which is among the finest Greco-Roman antiquities still intact. And in Ephesus there is what may be the world's first advertisement—it touts the whorehouse, the provocative mosaics of which may still be seen.

Mark Antony may have roistered at the whorehouse—Plutarch, the historian, wrote that Antony "caroused as Bacchus" in front of adoring crowds in Ephesus. It's also known that Antony shopped for trinkets with Cleopatra in the city's goldsmith shops and that he commanded the people to revere Cleopatra as his queen. The heady air of Ephesus apparently made him forget his legal wife, who was scheming and knitting away back in Rome.

–Ralph H. Peck

CIVIC PRIDE

"Who Has the Gall to Bypass Wall?"

It is not exactly a surprise to come upon the world's largest drugstore when you arrive in the small town of Wall, S.D., because of the highway signs you'll have seen for hundreds of miles along the road: "U Wall Come to Wall Drug," "Wall I'll Be Drugged!" "Who Has the Gall to Bypass Wall?" "Wall to Wall Hospitality" and "Have You Dug Wall Drug?" among them. There's a sign in a Paris Métro station reading "5,961 miles to Wall Drug Store" and one in Lahore, Pakistan, "Wall Drug Store 10,728 miles." More signs advise, "All's Well in Wall" and "Get the Wall Drug Bug."

Most of the main drag in Wall, S.D. is taken up by storefronts housing Wall Drug—in fact practically the whole town is a drug store, starting with the 30-foot-high concrete dinosaur in front of the Wall Drug Auto Livery. Life-sized animated stuffed cowboys in the store's show windows play Western music as tourists consume thousands of 35-cent breakfasts and buy

hundreds of thousands of dollars' worth of pottery, Western clothing, hunting knives, mounted longhorns, Western art, wood shingles burned with ranch brands, grab bags, lariats, Indian headdresses, stuffed jackalopes, cuspidors, plastic rattlesnakes, live burros and electric toilet tissue (that's a corncob with cord and plug attached).

Bill Hustead, who runs the store his father started in 1936, recalls his pre-store childhood: "There wasn't a damned thing to do in Wall. We played rubber guns. We made shields out of orange crates and threw spears at each other." Then his father put up a sign reading "Free Ice Water—Wall Drug," and it made the place famous, until today the store employs 150 clerks in the peak summer season. The store's birthday, on July 10, is always a lot bigger occasion than the Fourth of July, Hustead says.

Signs reading "Wall Drug, South Dakota" are free to anybody who agrees to put one up in his home town. Hours are 6 a.m. to 10 p.m. every day of the year.

–Roy Bongartz

GLOBAL GRAFFITI

Building with Bottles— Oregon's Bottle Ranch

The most fantastic example of bottle architecture and sculpture in Oregon—maybe the world—is The Bottle Ranch, a mile west of Dallas, Ore. on the Ellendale Road. The artist, designer and builder was a retired carpenter, H. F. Dirksen, who died in July 1972.

Visitors have come from all parts of the United States and Canada and from Norway, Italy, Mexico and half a dozen other countries to see The Bottle Ranch. What you see at first glance is enough to take your breath away, and further investigation keeps you busy mumbling "incredible" and "beautiful." A friend of mine, who has been to The Bottle Ranch three times, calls Dirksen the "Leonardo da Vinci of bottle artistry."

Besides the gate, built of wine and pop bottles, you will see a wishing well, a replica of a space needle, a garden arch, a globe-shaped contraption that Dirksen's widow Helen calls a "moonglow," a great star, a totem pole, a cactus, a windmill, a Christmas tree and a chapel—all built of bottles; and a lawn fence made of jars.

The bottles are colored in shades of blues, greens and reds, and a lot of them were milk of magnesia containers.

Dirksen's son, Leonard, who lives in a trailer back of The Bottle Ranch, says: "Most of the bottles Dad got by picking them up alongside the road. He had a big box on his pickup and he and Mother would drive along the roads looking for bottles."

Dirksen made only one change in The Bottle Ranch before he passed away, says Leonard. "The totem pole was next to the road and kids in cars would stop late at night and throw things at it and break some bottles, so Dad moved the totem pole near the house."

(There is no admission charge to The Bottle Ranch, but visitors may leave contributions in the chapel, which took Dirksen three months to build and was finished Aug. 31, 1970, on his golden wedding anniversary.)

–Ralph Friedman

Ohio's "Chinatown" Without Chinese

The fact that Archbold, Ohio, a neat, squared-off town of 3,000, proudly calls itself Chinatown U.S.A. causes the occasional traveler who strays off the interstate to study the local gas station attendants, supermarket shoppers and barflies for telltale signs of Oriental features. But they see only the Germanic blond ruddiness of northern Ohio, and they soon learn that the town's fame rests on its being the home of the world's largest Chinese food producer, La Choy Food Products.

A visitor on the lookout for the Chinese chefs behind the great enterprise is detoured to the world's largest mung-bean sproutery, where they turn out 700,000 pounds of bean sprouts a week. Jeep-like vehicles with plows shove the stuff out of bins into canning rooms. "Nobody in the United States knows how to grow sprouts like us," John J. McRobbie, general manager, says proudly.

Insisting on meeting the elusive Chinese who must have founded the place, who must be hidden back in there somewhere, will get you nowhere; you are finally informed that La Choy was founded by a couple of University of Michigan graduates and that as far as anyone knows no actual Chinese has ever set foot in Archbold. At the Carriage House, a restaurant next door to the La Choy plant, no Chinese food is served. "Got a nice steak, though," the waitress will say, if you ask.

–Roy Bongartz

Block Island: A Delightful Place for Doing Nothing

This is a place where there's nothing whatever to do.

It's got an atmosphere: early New England. It's got beaches: good clean sand. It's got air (you remember that stuff). It's got green hills, white birds and two nice little harbors.

There are a few hotels, a few rooming houses, a few charming restaurants and some seasonal cottages.

But basically, and we stress this, there is nothing to do. Not a worry, not a care, no Presidents, Watergates or telegrams.

You get there on a trim little ferry. It leaves from Point Judith, R.I. once a day during the winter and several times a day during the summer. There's another one that goes from Providence and Newport, R.I. once a day all year around. And another from New London, Conn.

All the ferries take cars, bicycles and motorcycles. The fare is around $4 for adults and $14 for a car.

If you'd like information, you can write to the Block Island Chamber of Commerce, Block Island, R.I. 02807.

Reservations for both ferries and lodgings should be made in advance.

–Waldo Grade

VISIT THE SOVIET BLOC

By Brooke Shearer

For Americans, there is always something vaguely mysterious about visiting the "Communist bloc" countries. The ancient cobbled streets seem to have a black border around them; peoples' windows are ringed with garlic, which repels werewolves. The light and easy languages of The-Europe-Which-Points-To-Paris are forgotten; here, the best you'll get is broken German.

Eastern Europe is an unsung gold mine. Whether you go camping in the High Tatras or beer-drinking in the bistros of Prague, you'll find hardy and friendly people and a vigorous, unique way of life. You'll also find that your money goes very far: in Czechoslovakia, for instance, foreign exchange gets an automatic "bonification" of 125 percent over the official rate.

Furthermore, the countryside is truly beautiful, you won't be segregated from the natives as you would be inside the U.S.S.R., and only in Eastern Europe can you find tourist attractions like Dracula's castle and the oldest salt mines in the world.

To get the most out of a visit to the Soviet bloc countries and independent Yugoslavia, you need a sturdy sense of humor and deep reserves of patience. Traveling in the socialist world means doing business with infuriatingly bureaucratic, often incompetent state-run tourist "services," which at times are moved to justify their existence by concocting hassles that seem like the result of a diabolical collaboration between Franz Kafka and Joseph Heller.

But the hassles are worth it if you know what to look for in Eastern Europe. Here are some suggestions.

Yugoslavia   The Yugoslav coastal resorts of Split, Dubrovnik and Sveti Stefan have already established themselves as tourist meccas. Smaller towns tend to be more interesting, less crowded and cheaper.

But just because it's overrun by tourists in the summer is no reason to avoid Dubrovnik altogether. If you want to mix with the locals—who are more Latin in temperament than Slavic and therefore are fun to mix with—go to the Restauran Sarajevo on Ulice Marojice Kaboge in the evening.

The newest and most ambitious tourist facility in Yugoslavia is the nudist camp on the Montenegrin island of Ada, a bird sanctuary and wilderness preserve midstream in a river that marks the Yugoslav-Albanian border. Guests—mostly "naturalists" from West Germany and Scandinavia—live in bungalows modeled on Thai huts, explore the island in donkey-drawn carts, dine in what the brochure advertises as "the world's largest nudist vegetarian restaurant," and disport themselves at volleyball, tennis and lawn bowling. Many of these goings-on take place within binocular range of stern-faced Albanian frontier guards, whose thankless job it is to defend the borders of one of *the most* unswinging societies on earth.

Sarajevo is a half-day's drive from Dubrovnik; it's a Moslem city and its skyline is dominated by the minarets of eight mosques. Here you can see the bridge where Bosnian nationalists assassinated the Austro-Hungarian Archduke Ferdinand and touched off World War I.

Yugoslavia's only Chinese restaurant is in Sarajevo; it was opened last year on the occasion of—what else?—an international Ping-Pong tournament. The Peking serves Szechuan food and imported Chinese beer and wine. (The Chinese Embassy in Belgrade obligingly sent down two of its chefs to teach their hot-and-spicy recipes. But now the Chinese have gone back to Belgrade, leaving behind a uniquely hybrid experience in good eating—a Sino-Bosnian cuisine.)

In Belgrade, Yugoslavia's capital, you can go to one of the best movie theaters in Europe, the Musée Kinotheque. It's a small run-down establishment and it shows at least two, sometimes three selections a day from its immense library of film classics. For about 25 cents you can see a John Huston or Sergei Eisenstein feature, or sit in on one of the theater's frequent Humphrey Bogart, Bette Davis or Edward G. Robinson festivals.

Hungary   Despite the air pollution, Budapest is probably the loveliest and liveliest city in Eastern Europe. Here you can see for yourself Clara Szalon, Eastern Europe's leading *haute couture* establishment—the shop's owner, Klara Rotschild, dresses the wives of the Communist elite. And don't miss the Viennese-style coffee house called Vorosmarty at the end of Vaci Street. In the afternoon it's usually crammed with elegant and defiant old ladies, eating mountainous pastries and radiating the conviction that the Austro-Hungarian Empire never ended. (Perhaps it is in the same spirit that Budapest still maintains in working order the city's antique, turn-of-the-century subway.)

Czechoslovakia   Before the Soviet invasion of Czechoslovakia in 1968, Prague rivaled Budapest as the Paris of Central Europe. Now this former capital of the Holy Roman Empire seems grim. While the shops have been stocked with imported consumer goods in hopes of buying popular support for Party Chief Gustav Husak's regime, the people seem much more frightened of foreigners and more cynical about their own country's fate than elsewhere in Eastern Europe.

If you do go to Prague, though, be sure to visit one of the city's most popular and handsomely decorated restaurants, the Chinska Restaurace. Czechs come here from all over the country to celebrate anniversaries and birthdays with a Chinese meal. The Chinska is furnished with dark wood furniture inlaid with mother-of-pearl, and the waiters are courteous and prompt to every customer, whether he's a Western diplomat or a worker from a provincial Skoda auto factory. (Dinner runs about $4 a person.)

The High Tatra Mountains in Slovakia afford hiking in the summer and skiing in the winter. There are no Matterhorns in the Tatra range, but near Tatranska Lomnica the peaks reach to almost 9,000 feet—high enough for anyone except a jaded Nepalese. To reach the mountains, you can take a plane or train to Poprad; the 10-hour rail journey from Prague costs $12 for a first-class sleeping compartment.

Poland   Poland is an incredibly cheap country to visit. You can get a good meal for under $1, and a single room in a first-class hotel, such as the Bristol in Warsaw, costs only $6 a night. If you want to stay with a family in Warsaw (for about $2 a night), check in with the booking office at the Hotel Polonia and the clerks there will find you a room. (Most likely your host will have at least one relative in Chicago, Pittsburgh or Cleveland and, with his smattering of English, will proudly display a working knowledge of American football and baseball.) You will find Poles openly making fun of the Communist system—in

refreshing contrast to their Czechoslovak comrades.

Warsaw, too, has a Chinese restaurant, a popular and lively student hangout called the Szanghaj. Unlike its counterparts in Sarajevo and Prague, the Szanghaj has an honest-to-God Chinese cook—he's named Chiao Hua-lin; he has lived in Warsaw for 13 years and is married to a Polish woman. Mr. Chiao speaks Polish with a thick Chinese accent, a fact that makes his speech one of the seven linguistic wonders of the world. His specialty is Peking duck.

If you prefer Warsaw duck, there's a restaurant in the Old Town section of the capital called The Duck, which serves half a dozen duck dishes—and nothing else.

Two hundred miles south of Warsaw is the cultural center and university town of Cracow. Polish tourist officials are very proud that only eight miles from Cracow, in the town of Wieliczka, visitors can see the oldest salt mines in the world. Perhaps because they are mindful that salt mining is traditionally not a very glamorous profession in the Communist world, Polish officials hasten to explain that the Wieliczka mines are now used for salt baths to cure various ailments. Just for good measure, visitors to the mines are invited to inspect an underground chapel and tennis court carved in the salt.

Hitchhiking in Poland is marvelously reliable. In an attempt to encourage and regulate what the Poles call "thumbing," the state sells numbered booklets that contain maps and lottery coupons. The kit, called Autostop, sells for about $1.50 at offices of the PTTK (the domestic travel bureau) and at the University of Warsaw on Nowy Swiat. The hitchhiker gives the driver who picks him up a certain number of lottery tickets, depending on the distance of the ride. The driver thus gets a free chance to win a washing machine, radio or TV. If any mishap should occur on the road, the state can trace the parties involved through the numbered Autostop booklets.

Rumania   The government of Rumania is more independent of the Kremlin than the government of any other Warsaw Pact country, and the country is fascinating. The capital, Bucharest, is a city with an inferiority complex—it wants to be Paris, and has even built its own Arc de Triomphe. The people are quick to remind you that their language is closer to French than Russian.

Particularly worth seeing in Rumania are the colorfully painted monasteries of Moldavia. Depicting the heavenly visions of the saints and battles between Moldavian warriors and Turkish invaders, these extraordinary paintings have withstood 400 years of weather.

Perhaps the best-known Rumanian of all time was a 15th-century Prince of Wallachia, known as Vlad the Impaler because of his penchant for impaling his enemies—and subjects—on stakes. (According to some historical estimates, Vlad may have

skewered 20 percent of the entire population of Wallachia, as well as tens of thousands of neighboring peoples and Ottoman raiders, in his brief lifetime.) Vlad is immortalized in literature as Count Dracula.

Vlad is regarded as something of a national hero in Rumania—he did, after all, strike fear into the hearts of the Turks. Therefore, while the Rumanians are flattered by all the attention Dracula has gotten thanks to Bram Stoker's book and to Hollywood, they would rather he not be known as a vampire. So the state tourist agents are all too happy to arrange a tour of sites connected with "the historical Dracula," including Vlad's castle near Targoviste and his grave at Snagov (where he was buried, ominously enough, *without* a wooden stake in his heart).

Bulgaria   If Bulgaria is known at all in the West, it is as a land of yogurt, tomatoes and octogenarian peasants. This Lower Slobovian image is unfair—and getting more unfair all the time. Bulgaria has made more economic progress than any other East European nation since World War II. The people are proud, friendly and outgoing, and, for a small country, Bulgaria has more than its share of beautiful scenery.

The Bulgarians have recently launched a campaign to attract Western skiers. The drawing card is the price. The cost per day at any of the country's three major winter sports resorts—Vitosha, Borovets and Pamporovo—is about $10, with accommodations, lift fees and equipment rental included. And you can combine a visit to the Bulgarian capital of Sofia with a skiing holiday. Just 40 minutes from downtown Sofia are the lifts and chalets of Mount Vitosha. The area has two chair lifts, one T-bar and two drag lifts.

If you should be visiting Bulgaria on a package tour, prepare yourself for the $10-a-day Grand Hotel Sofia in Sofia, for Balkantourist, the state agency, will probably book you into it. This "deluxe class" modern monstrosity is known affectionately among the diplomatic corps as "The Comrade Hilton." □

A Confident Escape

Airey Neave was an RAF officer captured at Calais in 1940. He escaped from his first prison camp in Poland, but got caught and sent to rot behind the thick walls of Colditz Castle, the "escape-proof" camp near Leipzig.

Neave's escape was very cleverly executed, and it proves you can beat the system no matter what. It occurred to Neave and the other prisoners that an old castle was probably honeycombed with secret passages. And sure enough, one lay under the floor of the castle's theater, underneath the stage.

Using lockpicks made of stolen wire, the prisoners made their way through the secret passage. It led to an attic above the guardhouse, directly over the German Officers' Mess.

There were a number of Dutch officers at Colditz who had elected to remain captives rather than capitulate to Hitler. They all spoke excellent German, with accents that could pass for Westphalian. What was equally important, they had cloaks that could pass for the German field-grey.

Neave and a Dutch lieutenant named Toni Luteyn became escape partners. They took Dutch Home Army greatcoats and converted them to look German. They cut epaulettes out of lineoleum from the bathroom floor and painted them silver with paint stolen from the theater. Their officers' stars were whittled from wood and painted.

The moment came during a light snowfall. The *Appell* rang for exercise, and the men slipped into the secret passage.

Outside, on the moat bridge, a German soldier came towards them. Neave remembers: "He reached us, stopped and stared deliberately. I hesitated for a moment, ready to run, but Luteyn turned on him quickly and in faultless German said crossly, 'Why do you not salute?'

"The soldier gaped. He saluted, still looking doubtful. . . ."

They hastened across the bridge, saluting the sentries, and headed for the railway station at Leisnig, six miles away. Four days later they rushed the border and were safe in Switzerland.

–The Editors

Ile St. Pierre

Really and Truly France

By Mose Ritter

You can actually get to France without leaving North America. And that includes wine and a full belly, too!

The first thing I thought was: what a great place to make a movie!

Imagine a little Basque fishing village on a little island off the coast of Newfoundland. It seems to be 1910. There is rum and wine everywhere, and the food makes you kiss your fingers with pleasure.

In fact, it still exists—in a little, forgotten corner of the French Empire, the last French possessions in North America: the islands of St. Pierre, Miquelon and Langlade. They sit like wee magnets off the Grand Banks of Newfoundland, just an airline ticket from Montreal. The French here is so pure it hurts your lips, and the wine is always on the table. The women buy their *baguettes* early in the morning and cross themselves when they pass the church. *Gauloises* are dangling from every chiseled grin. *Cravates* are muffling every grizzled chin. Yes, this is it, La France in person, *berets, gendarmes* and *pu, pu, pu.*

These rocky islands are in the middle of the trickiest waters in the world, which accounts for the amazing fact that more than 600 ships have gotten wrecked here since 1850. They're also in the middle of the richest fishing waters in the world, which accounts for why the 600 ships came in the first place. In any case, there are innumerable tales of sunken treasure, piracy and innate French brilliance when it comes to the dangerous *sauce morue.*

There is also the cold sober fact that booze here costs less than half what it costs in Canada and the United States. Add the sailing and trading skill of even your rawest St. Pierrais and you see why one man in the know says: "There are more millionaires per capita on St. Pierre than anywhere else in the world." According to him, this is where the Kennedy money was made.

This is the atmosphere that fills your head here. Equally important is what fills your stomach. My impartial and detailed investigations have conclusively proven that they eat more and better here on this two-bit island than anywhere, with the possible exception of Les Troisgros in the Motherland herself. Every hotel has a French chef who wears a high white toque and personally whomps up two six-course meals a day. This is still an official part of France, and the wine is authentic. It is against the law to leave the table before folding your hands on the summit of your belly, inhaling a bushel of air and cogitating on the state of modern times.

This place gives you this kind of perspective. It is Old France—not modern at all. Oh, yes, they have electricity and radio, and TV is piped in from Newfoundland. But the life is the life of 65 years ago. It is as if you had wandered into an isolated sea village before World War I, where the inbreeding and character stare a stranger down. The pace is too incredibly slow, even compared to a place like Mexico. Everything is vague. Time is reckoned by winds and seasons and no one understands our desire for exact information. The slightest incident becomes a screaming headline. The same man has sat on the same bench since 1906.

The atmosphere here is like the waters: calm on the surface, but deceptively dangerous and jagged underneath. The small islet of Grand Colombier, a little north of St. Pierre, is made entirely of lodestone. Any ship coming within its radiations goes haywire—you can't get a

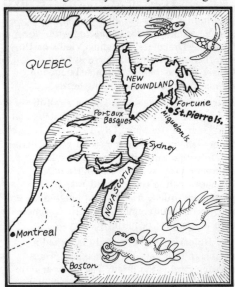

true compass reading. When the heavy ocean fog is in, well . . . you can see for yourself, there are at least a dozen wrecks, rusted and jutting, within safe spittle distance of a warm hotel.

The faces and the ambience are the attraction for foreigners, plus the old-fashioned French fireworks on Bastille Day. It's a little bit of a rugged place, a northern place, grey skies and fresh bright paint and hardy green gardens. There are tales of highbinding and native ruses: during Prohibition, when the Canadian Customs cutter would spot a contraband skiff from St. Pierre, the natives would quickly chuck the booze into a kind of carton made out of salt and cork. As the cutter pulled alongside they'd toss the crate overboard and pretend to be innocently fishing. The Customs men would find them clean. But as the salt dissolved underwater, the cork gradually floated the hooch back to the top. The wily St. Pierrais would come out a couple of hours later and pick up their swag. They say in the time of "la fraude" they ran 25,000 cases of scotch into the United States *every day!*

Most of the respectable and undoubtedly wealthy merchants in St. Pierre will tell you freely that they were—and still are—rumrunners.

Of course, it's always the same with these interesting and remote places: it's not that easy to get to. If you ask a travel agent, he'll probably say he's never heard of it. And then he'll tell you you can't get there from here. And then that there's no scheduled service, that you have to go to Port aux Basques, Newfoundland and inquire about buses or horses to Fortune, where you catch some ferry or other and why not just take the eight-day tour of Amsterdam?

Well, the fact is that if you are careful you can get here with no hassle. First, you get to Montreal. Then you fly to Sydney, Nova Scotia. From there you can take Air St. Pierre direct to the island.

You can also take the Canadian National Railroad from Montreal to North Sydney, Nova Scotia. Then you take the CN ferry to Port aux Basques. From there, it's a bus or a taxi to Fortune, where you get another ferry to St. Pierre. The advantage of this route is that you get to see all of Nova Scotia and Newfoundland, and the cost is about the same as flying.

In truth, if there's any problem at all here, it's not getting in. It's getting *out.* Sometimes, in the summer, the fog socks in the plane for a week. You can go a little stir-crazy, cooped up in someone else's century. But it's not so bad at all—as someone in Nova Scotia told us: "Ah, you're going to St. Pierre! It's very nice—they're very friendly there. They dance all night!" □

New Caledonia, New Hebrides: the Islands of Maugham and Michener

The islands of Maugham and Michener, long secluded and sleepy, are making up for lost time. New Caledonia and the New Hebrides, island groups at the edge of the Coral Sea north and east of Australia, are beginning to emerge from their famous isolation. This far corner of the South Seas has discovered the fiscal wonder of tourism.

The world seemed to forget these islands when World War II ended and the Americans abandoned their bases and airfields and went home. The French resumed their rule of New Caledonia, and the unique joint French-English government again became responsible for the New Hebrides.

Then it was discovered that 250-mile-long Grand Terre (part of New Caledonia) contained an astonishing amount of nickel. Fortune-hunters by the thousands rushed to New Caledonia from France; in a few years nickel had created 20 billionaires, and hundreds of mere millionaires. Then in 1972 the boom abruptly died, a victim of greed, speculation and worldwide stockpiling of nickel.

New Caledonia found in tourism a nice, non-polluting replacement for the nickel industry. Island fathers stood back and discovered they had an ideal set-up for tourists —turquoise lagoons, coral reefs and swaying palms combined with a subtropical climate that is not too hot, too humid or too rainy. And they had Noumea, a cosmopolitan city from the South of France splashed down in the South Pacific.

New Caledonia is only now beginning to build for tourism. Noumea has most of the total of 750 hotel rooms; the deluxe Chateau Royal outside Noumea has 330 rooms (at a flat rate of $43 a night for a double). Two tiny islands with excellent thatched-roof style hotels are a short hop from Noumea on Air Caledonie. Relais de Kanumera on Ile des Pins costs $53 a night for a double with all meals, and rates at the Turtle Club, on Ile Ouen, are about the same.

Noumea's Chateau Royal, scheduled to open this spring, ought to give tourism in New Caledonia a boost—it will be the first casino in the South Pacific.

Many call the 80 islands of the New Hebrides chain the last unspoiled spots in the South Pacific, and they didn't have to discover tourism—it discovered them. These are the islands Michener wrote of in *South Pacific* (Bali H'ai is Aoba), so it's easy to imagine what they're like—lush and beautiful and slow. Port-Vila, the capital (population 12,000) on Vate Island, is a true South Seas trading port, complete with island wanderers and an infamous waterfront bar. (The bar, Bar des Sportifs, usually has a brisk business going by 10 in the morning. After listening to a few hours' worth of stories from a collection of South Seas characters you begin to think that Maugham and Michener were reporters, and not novelists.)

The New Hebrides have only 250 hotel rooms; Port-Vila's Le Lagon remains the only "classy" hotel (rates are about $55 a night for a double with meals), although the city also has the Rossi and Vate hotels.

Since Michener was right about the New Hebrides, it can't be long before everyone else finds out. You might like to try to go there before they do.

–Richard John Pietschmann

GLOBAL GRAFFITI

Canada's Icelandic Island

For better or for worse, Hecla, an Icelandic fishing settlement on one of the islands in the inland sea that is Lake Winnipeg, recently joined the rest of the world. At the same time, the island is gaining a 213,274-acre provincial park, to open this year, which will contain a replica of an Icelandic village. Using the island's existing buildings, the village will honor the memory of settlers who landed there 100 years ago.

Until the opening of a two-mile causeway, a ferry that moved a few vehicles back and forth each day was all that kept Hecla's handful of islanders from total isolation from the mainland. In fact, the boat will still be the only way to reach several smaller islands in the Hecla archipelago.

Hecla, the settlement, is named after an Icelandic volcano that erupted in 1873, forcing those who lived nearby to move away. Those who emigrated to Canada began transforming a lakeside tract of Lake Winnipeg into what has become the largest settlement of Icelandic people outside Iceland. Those who settled on the island encountered mixed fortunes: the original 26 families were first reduced by one-third by a smallpox epidemic, but then (once the emigrants learned to adapt fishing techniques to Lake Winnipeg's ruthless temperament) the population blossomed to 200 in 1879 and 500 by the 1920s. With the decline of fishing and the lure of urban life the population has dwindled—today, there are only a few families still living on the island.

Hecla is as rich in natural beauty as it is in cultural history. Western grebes inhabit the marshland at the southern end and blue heron rookeries are scattered throughout. The lonely, haunting call of the common loon often drifts through the morning mists when the lake is calm and the breezes are still. Mallards, canvasbacks and Canada geese inhabit the marshes, arriving in spring via the Central Flyway of North America to mate and nest. Hecla is thickly studded with spruce, balsam and stands of birch and poplar. Moose never have been hunted, with the result that this is one area where these animals can often be seen. Coral root, one of Manitoba's orchids, grows alongside the four-mile footpath from the village to the harbor.

–Mike Michaelson

South Carolina's Gullah Blacks

By Mose Ritter

The Gullah blacks gave us some of our most cherished legends, tax-free imports from West Africa like Brer Rabbit and Brer Fox. And while the Civil War is long over, the Gullahs still have their "laughing place." It's Charleston, South Carolina, and it's a way of sliding right back into the last three centuries, back to plantations, back to African crafts and culture.

If you want to slide right into the last three centuries without hardly leaving your armchair—go on down to Charleston. It's the loveliest, most atmospheric, best preserved city in this whole country. There's not a whit of "planned quaint," and for a Northerner like me it's full of surprises and clues.

For instance, they still have plantations. Now, I didn't know that. The Middleton Plantation is still in the hands of Middletons, is still a working farm, and still employs blacks who wear African bandannas and white Mammy aprons. You can even buy a plantation yourself.

Charleston proper is still basking in its silver-bangle days as Queen City of the South. Many of the streets are the original cobblestone, and they're lined with tastefully grandiose examples of English architecture that struck it rich. But I mean, the *whole city* is like this! They still light gas lamps at night, and the streets are so quiet you can hear the whisper of live oaks hung with Spanish moss.

There's a place called the Old Slave Mart that's been turned into a little museum. It gives all our racial questions a different slant—at least it did for me. I never realized that slaves were *expensive* —an ordinary slave would cost over a thousand dollars. Skilled ones were more than five thousand. Slaves were never sold around ladies; they were auctioned in a building called the "Barracoon."

It also never really hit me that slaves, and American blacks, are really and truly *Africans.* You don't get much of Africa in the Oakland ghetto, I guess. But in the South, especially in the Carolina Low Country, African crafts and culture are flourishing pretty much intact.

I saw baskets in the City Market that could have been made in Kenya. I asked the lovely old black woman where she learned to make them: "Sittin' on the floor and watching my mother. And she sat 'pon it and watched my grandmother. Sweet grass." The granddaughter of a slave. She still speaks the local black dialect, the Gullah-talk, a melodious combination of Elizabethan English and African.

The Gullah blacks gave us some of our most cherished legends. Brer Rabbit and Brer Fox are tax-free imports from West African folklore. (In the African version, Brer Rabbit is actually a certain kind of clever furry spider.)

If you drive out of Charleston a ways, in the direction of the Sea Islands, you see scenes that are straight out of Africa. Little villages along sand roads on Edisto Island, a dozen families and a hundred children living communally and gathering around a small white church in times of need. The women wear the kerchief and loose robes, the men always a hat and their dignity. They still communicate by "the drum"—if someone dies, a wail goes out: "Mossy, she muddah e gone! Tell Mossy she muddah e gone!" The wail is boosted from house to house, clear across the island, in the fields, in the bypaths, on the road, news on the wind until it reaches its sad destination.

The houses on Edisto are still painted with bright blue window-jambs, in order to keep off the "sparits." No photographs —don't you know our white man's box eats a piece of your soul? Two fine ladies on a fence, palavering in ageless "she-she talk."

This is America, 1974, and it could be Togo or the jungles of Malaya. Here the particular spirit-of-place has the vibration of a bamboo fishing pole held between the toes, a lazy yellow butterfly, and rolled-up pants legs. Sweet grass and Huck Finn. Honest and quietly and no wiseacrin': it really is this way. Half a day from Washington and never heard of Watergate.

Their traditions say the Gullah blacks are descendants of an African king who was shanghaied over here in the early days of slave trading. They have always been the backbone of the South, from the Sea Island cotton days to Resurrection City. Even today they keep the South alive, and it is because of them, I think, that old times here are not forgotten.

And Don't Forget the Belly

The food in Charleston is simply sensational.

They make this specialty, "She Crab Soup"—female crabmeat, heavy cream, sherry, Worcestershire sauce, white wine and an army of spices—woo woo!

Most eating places have lunch and dinner buffets which are stupefying. All the restaurants use fresh vegetables exclusively, grown on that black low country soil that made such fine silky cotton.

I can't even carry on about it. I could talk about Low Country Okra Gumbo or Palmetto Heart Pickle or Brown Oyster Stew or Kedgeree. But try it for yourself. □

An African woman weaves sweetgrass baskets, outside of Charleston

Photography by Barbara Saltman

Land of the Amish

In northeastern Ohio, about halfway between the rubber mills of Akron and the glass factories of Steubenville, 17th-century Bavaria is still biding its days.

It's all there—the whitewashed churches, the black horse buggies, the immaculate rolling green hillocks, the trim white wooden houses. The women all wear white prayer bonnets and the men wear chin beards and suspenders and widebrimmed hats. Cars are virtually unknown.

This is Amish country. The Amish first came to the United States from Bavaria and Switzerland almost four centuries ago, and their life has hardly changed since then. They were religious mavericks, following the teachings of a man named Menno Simon, and the religious glue has held even through the *Sturm und Drang* of modern civilization.

Today, in the county seat of Millersburg, Renaissance German is still spoken. At the county courthouse there's a hitching post, with parking meters, that says "Horses Only." The town is full of shoe shops and pumpkin-bread bakeries and blacksmiths—but there are no garages in sight.

To outsiders, the Amish are incredibly friendly. Somehow, they got a reputation for shunning "civilians," but that just isn't true (although they don't like to have their pictures taken).

And the Amish are industrious. Until the recent juggernaut of California agribusiness surpassed them, they were the most prosperous farmers in the world—using their 17th-century hand tools and absolutely no machinery!

Their most outstanding feature is that they refuse to drive cars. As you enter Holmes County, the scenery suddenly clicks into old-fashioned sharp focus, and a sign says "Entering Horse Drawn Vehicle Area."

The Amish are settled throughout the rural regions of Pennsylvania, Ohio, Iowa and parts of Ontario. A visit to an Amish market makes a great weekday outing: at the Amish market near Streetsboro, Ohio, for instance, I met a man who was born into slavery during the Civil War; I bought an old wagon wheel, dirt cheap (and it had the original dirt still on it); I tasted Amish honey and *schwarzbrot* and bargained in the old-fashioned way, via innumerable cups of tea and immeasurable amounts of banter, for a set of fancy old dueling pistols. Living as they do, in the country and close to their God, the Amish have a very acute sense of value. Visiting them is another excellent example of that joyful experience called "Jeez, and just 40 minutes away from Akron, too!"

—Mose Ritter

Living Historical Farms

During the 1930s, a group of Swedes in the United States established living-history villages to bring to life historical experiences and cultures. Today, the National Park Service runs three living-history farms in the Washington, D.C. area modeled after the Swedish villages.

Wakefield, Va., the birthplace of George Washington, is a 30-acre colonial working farm. It is far less grand and prosperous than Washington's own plantation at Mt. Vernon, but at Wakefield, visitors can watch costumed women in the colonial kitchen cook pumpkin cookies and cherry pies from period recipes. The food on the farm comes from the colonial garden, which is worked by oxen and horses and Park Service "farmhands" in colonial costumes, and there are blacksmith and carpentry shops where workmen not only give demonstrations but actually construct the gate hinges, candles, sawhorses and other items used daily on the farm.

Oxon Hill Children's Farm in Oxon Hill, Md., uses the actual tools and methods employed by farmers at the turn of the century. The 375-acre farm, half of which is wooded trails, includes corn, wheat and sorghum fields, a silo, a windmill and three barns for cows, horses, pigs, ducks, goats and sheep. When the horses are not drawing plows, they are sometimes available for hay rides for the children, and there are continuous demonstrations of spinning, carding and dying wool with natural dyes, carving apple-faced dolls and making cider with an old-fashioned cider press.

Turkey Run Farm, in McLean, Va., is the first living farm to re-create what rural life was like for the common man *before* the Revolutionary War—and to do it as authentically as possible. Two Park Service employees, who work the farm during the day as the "farmer" and his "wife" (they are not actually married), have cleared 11 acres of land, planted the crops and constructed the one-room log cabin using colonial methods and tools. Their quarter horse and two Red Devon cattle are animals that were familiar throughout the colonies during the period. A special breed of "colonial" chickens has been achieved through back breeding; the large, dented-kernel "she-corn" that is being raised is also the result of back breeding. The farmer and a "hired hand" tend the fields, build corn cribs and split logs; the wife sees to the house and garden, and does the laundry and cooking. Twentieth-century visitors can help pick vegetables, build fences, feed the animals or work on a two-man saw.

—Lynn Young

In his hands are the deep places of the earth:
the strength of the hills is his also.
The sea is his, and he made it: and his hands
formed the dry land. . . .
We are the people of his pasture, and the sheep of his hand. . . .
Let the heavens rejoice, and let the earth be glad;
let the sea roar, and the fulness thereof.
Let the field be joyful, and all that is therein:
then shall all the trees of the wood rejoice before the Lord.

—THE PSALMS

The Big Sur Inn Is an Authentic European Roadside Inn

The Big Sur Inn is more than an authentic European roadside inn. South of Carmel and Monterey on California's fabled coastal route, U.S. 1, its ramshackle and rough-hewn structures reflect the mood and free spirit of this wild and surf-tossed region—and of the people who have chosen to live here.

There is little doubt that the Big Sur Inn is an inn apart, at least in this country. The music is Bach and Beethoven. The air is crisp and clean, even in August. The water is without chemicals, the food is without guile, the rooms are without plastic (and without some basic conveniences). But there *are* cats—usually as many as you want to each room.

It was all made possible by "Grandpa" Deetjen who, until his death in 1972, presided over his unique domain. The old gentleman was something of a traveler in the stormy literary world of the Thirties and a confidant of Henry Miller and Lawrence Durrell. He had his special table near the dining room, and always had a glass of wine handy.

Deetjen is gone now, but his special inn continues much as before. There are rumors of new plumbing and wiring now that a Monterey bank is trustee. Maybe now the telephone will be answered with increased regularity when calls are made for reservations. But still the rooms go for $9 to $20 a night and meals are hearty and simple—*if* you arrive during dining hours. (Breakfast and dinner only; wine is available with dinner.) It may be many things, but the Big Sur Inn is absolutely not a hotel. One of the things it *is* is just about the only hostelry on a craggy and forested and beautiful coast. There are 17 rooms, three with fireplaces, all with hot and cold running cats.

Reservations should be made by mail four to six weeks ahead, especially for weekend stays. Write Deetjen's Big Sur Inn, RR 1, Big Sur, Calif. 93920. Their phone number is (403) 667-2377.

—*Richard John Pietschmann*

"Having Wonderful Time—On $2,100 a Week"

Want to live like a millionaire and have anything you want anytime you want it? Want to do it at the world's most expensive and exclusive hotel hideaway? Then hie thee to Frenchman's Cove in Port Antonio, Jamaica. There, you can be outrageously indulged for a paltry $2,100 a week per couple.

Millionaires from all over the world, anxious to escape cold, snow or pollution, are always hopping into Air Jamaica planes to fly to this luxury resort. (Ten international airlines will also take you there.)

At this richnik retreat built with a Canadian cookie fortune, you can bask in sun, service, seclusion, splendor and status. You'll have a private butler for yourself, and personal maid for your spouse or soulmate. "Your butler is working only for you," will be your greeting. "You are his sole responsibility." Your quarters will be a hidden, air-conditioned, stone-and-glass one- to three-bedroom "cottage" overlooking the sea, with a $1,500 stereo and a Swedish phone that warbles like a dove.

You can eat and drink all and what you want at no extra charge and have all your meals served when and where you wish—if you like, order Beluga caviar for breakfast, Dom Perignon champagne for lunch, Scotland grouse and French pâté de fois gras for dinner. (Menus? They're for commoners! One of the four European chefs will discreetly visit you early in the day and inquire what

your palate would relish for dinner that evening. You can eat in your sunken tub or while lazing on a waterfloat on the sparkling Caribbean Sea, watching a bamboo beach fire or rafting down the Rio Grande on a starry night with a calypso band and a generous supply of 150-proof Jamaica rum. An army of attendants will do everything except stuff the food and booze down your throat.

On this hardship holiday, you can, of course, do *what* you want *when* you want. You can daily enjoy diving, deep sea fishing, snorkeling, glass-bottom boating, golf, tennis, massages and steam baths—and in between be serviced by your barber or hairdresser. You can make free telephone calls to any part of the world.

You won't exactly be elbowed to death at Frenchman's Cove, either. A maximum of 72 guests at a time are looked after in the 18 cottages and Great House by a year-round staff of 120 meticulously trained Jamaicans. Children under 14 are simply not accepted during the busy winter season.

The cost for all this? A paltry $300 a day per couple during the winter season (from Dec. 15 to April 15). But you must book for at least two weeks then, which ups the tab to $4,200. Should you be a bargain hunter, though, you can stay in a Great House suite for a trifling $89 to $109 a day per person. At Frenchman's, you never have to prove how rich you are. When you leave, one check will do for everything—a very large one, of course.

Las Brisas: Pink and Private

Richard Joseph, the travel writer who has tried every major hotel in the world, rightly called Las Brisas in Acapulco, Mexico one of the three best hotels in the world. Although it's not a good hotel for meeting people (the cabins are very secluded), if you go there with someone you love, you'll love Las Brisas. Every guest is given his own tiny little house, and half of them have their own small swimming pools. Every pool has flowers floating in it, and if you're wondering how that could keep happening accidentally so perfectly, it turns out that there's a man who puts those flowers in the pool each morning. Every cabin has a magnificent view of Acapulco Bay, and there's enough privacy that if you forget your bathing suit it may be more of a blessing than a disaster.

The special gimmick at Las Brisas, though, is that *everything* is pink. The Jeeps they give you to ride around in are pink, the cabins themselves are pink, and so are the walls, bedspreads, sheets, refrigerators, bath-towels, toilet paper, flowers and writing paper in each room. Some sophisticated travelers find it to be a bit much, but most people who go there are, well, just tickled pink over it.

—*Paulette Cooper*

A Resort in Alaska's Mt. McKinley Wilderness

In the interior of Alaska, on the border of the sub-Arctic wilderness of Mt. McKinley National Park, a relatively small and very special resort offers a relatively small and very special clientele one of the greatest environment-conservation-nature experiences you can get in North America. The place is Camp Denali, a resort of rustic but comfortable cabins and lodge buildings within view of the continent's tallest mountain (McKinley is 20,320 feet tall).

Comfortable as it may be, the prime function of the camp is to serve as a jumping-off place for day-long or overnight treks into the tundra to study the flora and fauna of a wilderness largely untouched by the hand of man. Visitors frequently see herds of caribou, moose, grizzly bears, wolves, foxes and Dall mountain sheep.

Recently the Society of American Travel Writers awarded Camp Denali its "Connie" award in recognition of the contribution the camp has made to the "conservation, preservation and beautification of man's environment."

Inquiries may be directed to Camp Denali, c/o McKinley Park, Alaska 99755 in the summertime, and c/o Box D, College, Alaska 99701 during the balance of the year.

—*Mike Miller*

The Celestial Suite Is to Hotels What Astroturf Is to Crabgrass

It's as American as the thousand-dollar bill, and as comfortable as Disneyland.

Actually, it'll set you back two and a half of those G-notes to stay overnight, and there's nothing Mickey Mouse about that. It's the Celestial Suite, on top of the Astroworld Hotel in Houston.

The 13-room suite is the brainchild of Judge Roy Hofheinz, the man who brought you indoor baseball. He's also the board chairman of Ringling Brothers Barnum and Bailey Circus.

The Mini-Dome parlor and bar, modeled after the Astrodome itself, is the suite's *pièce de résistance*. The Mini-Dome has a genuine Astroturf carpet, a mini-baseball diamond with an electrical scoreboard, and a huge pink chandelier at the top of the dome.

At the opposite end of the suite, through the Foyer of Fountains and the Lane of Lanterns (lined with plastic trees on Astroturf plots), lie the Adventurers' Suite, the Fu Manchu Room, the Mandarin Bath and the Tarzan Room. The interior decoration of these is pretty splendid—the Tarzan Room, just for example, is lined with leopard hides and some rare orange-and-gold zebra skins.

A Marble Library features stained glass windows and plush velvet chairs. It's a little weak on books, unfortunately—bring your own, if you want to read. The library is given over to such titles as *Homicide Blonde* and *Doctors Also Die*—and to 200 *Reader's Digest* condensations.

The Crusader Room has suits of armor, ashtrays made from swords and a color TV under the velvet canopy of the knight-sized bed. The room opens onto a Roman Bath with a 100-gallon tub and a shower that holds six.

The Celestial Suite also has seven bedrooms, each named after a famous lady. The Lillian Russell Room has a brass bed and a Bouquet Bath, where tiny hand-painted blossoms decorate the antique toilet (inside and outside). The Sadie Thompson Room is designed like a South Pacific bamboo hut; it even has mosquito netting and a ceiling fan. It also has a large mirror hung on sloping walls so guests can see themselves in bed.

The entire suite actually does get rented (at $2,500 a day), 150 to 200 days a year, mostly by corporations for promotions and conferences. Individuals do stay there, however; the suite even housed a family reunion once. There are few complaints. Spiro Agnew once spent the night in the Crusader Room and liked it so much he stayed four hours past checkout time.

—Peter Janssen

The World's Most Hotels

(In no special order)

Name	Place	Who?	Why?
The Mills House	Charleston, S.C.	Clark Gable	Most Old South; gaslight, carriages and ballrooms
The Mamouniya Palace	Marrakech, Morocco	Winston Churchill	Most Arabian Nights; archways, harems, perfumed gardens
Del Coronado	San Diego	U.S. Grant, JFK	Turn-of-the-centuriest; spectacular architecture, splendid appointments
Algonquin	New York	Robert Benchley	A country inn in New York City; strong literary heritage
Georges V	Paris	International jewel thieves	Most toffeenosed; out-Parises the Parisians
Raffles	Singapore	Somerset Maugham	Most Maugham; ceiling fans and intrigue
Claridge's	London	Queen Victoria	Most *elegante*; the only hotel Her Majesty ever set foot in
Chelsea	New York	Andy Warhol	Greatest fleabag
Las Brisas	Acapulco	Rich Texans	Most private; every room a seaside villa
Eden Roc	Cap d'Antibes, France	Rothschild, et al.	Most Fitzgerald; backdrop for *Tender Is the Night*
The Ritz	Paris	Charles of the	Most . . . Ritzy!
Meurice	Paris	Dickens, kings	Most uppa crust; the only place for royalty
Beverly Hills	Los Angeles	The Stars	Most True Hollywood; every room a movie set
Parizh	Prague	Kafka	Most Old European; true faded elegance
Chateau Gutsch	Luzern, Switzerland	Prince of Prussia	A 13th-century castle-hotel with spectacular views
Gritti Palace	Venice	Maugham again	Most gracious; a grand mansion

The World's Most Private Hotel Room

A mysterious locked door on a private neck of forest-like land is part of the elegant Jamaica Inn in secluded Ocho Rios, Jamaica. The help can't even get to this door directly. It leads to a hush-hush "White Suite" where everything is white—from the lavish fur rug to the silk gauze mosquito netting.

Because he was an enthusiastic repeat guest, this suite is known as the "Winston Churchill Suite." Ex-British Prime Minister Harold Macmillan, Richard Burton, Ginger Rogers and mystery writer Alistair McLean have stayed there too. The late King Peter of Rumania, who also did, tried to beat the hotel out of his $5,500 bill—but didn't succeed.

In winter months, the suite is always occupied. Grateful guests generally have made reservations from year to year. In fact, reservations are now taken during the winter only to establish priorities.

Actually, the "White Suite" isn't a suite at all, but a super-large room that was created by knocking down partitions in two suites. It opens on three sides to verandas—the Caribbean wavelets softly break below. Moreover, it has a private terrace and its own swimming pool (where you can bathe nude in unquestioned solitude). Trees and shrubbery screen it from the rubbernecking public; not even the gawker with a telescopic lens can see you.

The cost? A modest $175 a day per couple from Dec. 15 to April 15, and a paltry $75 a day during the rest of the year.

For reservations, contact your travel agent or Ray Morrow, 51 E. 42nd St., New York, N.Y. 10017; telephone (212) 697-2340.

–The Editors

The Museum of Baseball Bats

A tip for a rainy day in Louisville, Ky.— make a visit to the world's only baseball-bat museum, which, fittingly, occupies space in the world's largest baseball-bat factory. The Hillerich & Bradsby Co. turns out bats at the astounding rate of 4.5 million a year. The bat turners make bats to order for professionals by matching the bat being turned on the lathe with a bat model out of a collection of 50,000 in the bat museum. Every professional in both major and minor league has his particular bat represented here, and there are old bats going back to the turn of the century.

Back in 1884 a teenager named Bud Hillerich saw his favorite player on the Louisville Eclipses, Pete "The Old Gladiator" Browning, break his bat when he went for a fast pitch. Bud, whose father was a cabinet maker, took the opportunity to offer to make a new bat for his hero. He made it out of

Escape to Alcatraz

The legendary Alcatraz—for 30 years the home of criminals too "mean" to be contained by any other pen and, more recently, a generator of American Indian energy— opened to the public last fall for the first time in 125 years.

Now you can catch ferries every half hour from San Francisco's Fisherman's Wharf to this new National Park to inspect the cells, mess halls, library, showers and playing fields where Al Capone, Machine Gun Kelly, Alvin Arpus and the Birdman did time. ("We're trying to downplay the romantic aspect of the gangsters," says a Park Service guide. Fat chance.)

But your experience at the "Rock"—if it's anything like mine—won't be very romantic anyway. Yes, the ferry ride and the view of San Francisco are lovely—but the cells, the horrifying cells! If the regular cells don't make you wonder about a society that does *that* to its criminals, the solitary confinement cells, or "holes "—where the "worst" prisoners were kept in total darkness—definitely will.

The island was discovered by the Spanish in 1775 and named Isla de los Alcatraces ("Island of the Pelicans"). It was ceded to the United States in 1848 along with the rest of California. In 1853, the U.S. military started building a fort there, a fort which became a federal prison from 1934 to 1963. American Indians occupied it for 19 months in 1970-71. The graffiti the Indians left behind them has not been painted over, for, as a Park Service guide said, "We feel the Indian remains are also a part of the island's history."

–Susan Sands

ash, a resilient wood that doesn't break easily, and Browning's new bat went down in history as the world's first custom-made bat. (In spite of tests with many other woods and with metals, rubber and plastics, almost all bats made today are still made of ash.)

Honus Wagner, "The Flying Dutchman," was the first player to let his signature be used on Louisville bats—that was in 1905. In the Louisville museum, you can ask to see any famous bat you like, including the one Babe Ruth notched 21 times, one for each homer he hit with it. Honus Wagner used to boil his bat in creosote, and Ted Williams gave his a daily alcohol bath. Babe Ruth's was the heaviest—54 ounces (today's heaviest are only 40 ounces). Frankie Frisch cured his bats by hanging them in a barn.

The museum, at the Hillerich & Bradsby Co., Jackson and Finzer streets, Louisville, Ky., is open Monday through Friday except holidays; tours begin at 10:30 a.m. and at 2:30 p.m.

–Roy Bongartz

CAVING

Cave exploring is an old pastime— archaeological evidence from central Kentucky indicates that people were exploring caves there at least 3,000 years ago. Today, cavers all over the United States say that spelunking attracts them because it offers them physically demanding activity, aesthetic satisfaction and the joy of discovery all in one package. Some cavers are curious about where the cave passages go; others love discovering new caves or passages (to think *no one* ever knew they were there before!); some get high on the beautiful flowstone formations and gleaming crystals that abound in limestone caves.

Limestone caves are by far the commonest type; other kinds of caves are **lava tubes** (formed during volcanic eruptions), **ice caves** in glaciers, **rock shelters** in sandstone, **sea caves** along the shores of oceans (formed by wind and waves) and **talus caves** under rock falls in the mountains.

Cave passages range from those just big enough to walk through to huge twisting and sloping corridors the size of subway tunnels. Passages often cross each other and interconnect so that they resemble the streets of a city. Rooms of all sizes are found in caves;

What You Need to Go Caving

Exploring wild caves is strenuous in the same way that rock climbing is, and requires many of the same skills. Top physical condition is essential. A caving outfit (which can be assembled for under $60) should include the following:

    Coveralls or other old, grubby clothes
    Sturdy hiking boots or work shoes
    Hard hat with lamp bracket
    Carbide lamp with carbide, and two baby bottles with nipple seals for carbide
    OR,
    Battery cap lamp with batteries
    One-pint canteen
    Plumber's candle, matches
    Flashlight
    Army-surplus gas mask bag with shoulder strap

Also highly desirable, though not essential, are:
    Cement finishers' rubber knee pads
    Waterproof matchbox with compass in cap
    Spoon and can opener
    Small pliers, six inches of wire for repairs, lamp parts kit

Keep in mind that most experienced cavers won't take the neophyte with them unless he has the equipment. And it's bad manners to borrow—that's on a par with asking an athlete if you can borrow his mouthpiece and jock strap.

–Roger W. Brucker

they may be up to hundreds of feet in height and diameter. Many caves have several levels connected by sloping passages, and underground rivers and lakes are very common in caves.

There are about 15,000 known caves in the United States. Fortunately for us, many hundreds of the most beautiful and unusual ones have been developed and are open to visitors. These are generally called commercial or **public caves** to distinguish them from wild or undeveloped ones.

A few caves offer self-guided tours on a developed and lighted trail. Guides are often stationed at points along the route in this kind of cave to explain the features and to keep you from going astray. It's next to impossible to get lost in a commercial cave, but don't tempt fate by poking into unknown holes, pits or passages off the marked and lighted route.

If you want to see an undeveloped or wild cave, be sure to do so only in the company of experienced cavers. Caving alone, especially if you're a neophyte, is just another name for suicide. (You'd be as safe sky-diving without a parachute or rock climbing with cotton clothesline.) If you're at all interested, I suggest you get in touch with an organized caving group in your area.

To find one, write the following organization, which may have a local chapter in your area. As a courtesy, enclose a stamped, self-addressed return envelope:

The National Speleological Society
Cave Avenue
Huntsville, Ala. 35810.

This national organization is devoted to the study and preservation of caves.

Or write:

The Sierra Club
1050 Mills Tower
San Francisco, Calif. 94104.

Ask for information on Rock Climbing Sections that also go caving. And, you might check the outing or recreational associations at local colleges and universities. They often have caving clubs or sections. If you can't find a caving group any other way, try asking at a nearby commercial cave. Owners and guides often know about local groups that have visited the cave.

Nearly every state has at least a few caves open to the public. The following list is only the briefest survey of the most famous ones. In almost all areas, there are several more caves near the ones listed. For a more complete list, consult the book *Visiting American Caves*, by Howard N. Sloane and Russell H. Gurnee (published in 1966 by Crown; $4.95). You might also want to read my own beginner's guide to cave exploration, *Amateur's Guide to Caves and Caving* (published in 1973 by Stackpole; $2.95 in paperback).

Another way to find out about caves you can visit is to inquire at local auto clubs, state parks departments and chambers of commerce.

Alabama
Cathedral Cavern (Grant). Large and spacious. Beautiful formations. Huge entrance.

Arizona
Colossal Cave (Vail). A desert cave known for its use by Indians, train robbers and animals. Many attractive formations.

California
California's commercial caves are modest in size but have beautiful formations. Well worth a visit: *Boyden Cave* (Kings Canyon National Park), *Crystal Cave* (Sequoia National Park)—both these are closed in winter—*Lake Shasta Caverns* (Redding), *Mercer Caverns* (Murphys), *Mitchell Caverns State Park* (Essex) and *Moaning Cave* (Vallecito).
Lava Beds National Monument (Tulelake). One of the world's best examples of lava tubes. Over 300 of them, the longest more than 1½ miles long.

Idaho
Craters of the Moon National Monument (Arco). Lava tubes, self-guided tours. One cave has year-around ice floor.

Indiana
Wyandotte Caverns (Wyandotte). Impressive stone mountains, large corridors and rooms. Indian artifacts.

Kentucky
Mammoth Cave (Mammoth Cave National Park). World famous cave, and justifiably so. Recently linked by exploration to Flint Ridge Caves System, this is far and away the world's largest cave system, with a combined length of 144 miles (more than twice that of Hollock in Switzerland). Mammoth offers a wide range of tours, anywhere from 1½ hours long to day-long; there are also boat rides. Worth a special trip all by itself. Also plan to visit many other fascinating caves nearby.

Missouri
Fantastic Caverns (Springfield). Entire one-mile tour made in a trailer towed by a jeep.
Mark Twain Cave (Hannibal). The impressive cave made famous in *The Adventures of Tom Sawyer*.
Marvel Cave (Branson). Huge 20-story-high room where a manned balloon once rose to the ceiling. Impressive waterfall. Three-car electric railroad brings visitors back to reception area.

Nevada
Lehman Caves National Monument (Baker). A highly decorated cave recently extended into some newly discovered areas.

New Mexico
Carlsbad Caverns (Carlsbad). World famous for its huge rooms, passages and formations; contains the largest room in any cave, 14 acres in area and 285 feet high. Elevators whisk visitors to the 800-foot level where most tours begin. Spectacular flight of 500,000 bats spirals out of the entrance at dusk every day April through October.

New York
Howe Caverns (Cobleskill). Largest cave in the Northeast. Underground river with ¼-mile boat ride. Elevator to cave level. Other nearby caves: Secret Caverns (Cobleskill) and Knox Caverns (Altamont).

Oregon
Oregon Caves National Monument (Crater Lake). An attractive cave with many large stalagmites.

Pennsylvania
Penn's Cave (Centre Hall). Entire one-mile cave trip made by boat. Other interesting caves in Pennsylvania: *Crystal Cave* (Kurztown), *Indian Echo Caverns* (Hummelstown) and *Woodward Cave* (Woodward).

South Dakota
Wind Cave National Park (Hot Springs). Opened in 1892, this cave is noted for its unique minerals and unusual formations.

Tennessee
Cumberland Caverns (McMinnville) A large cave system (16 miles long). Many leaching vats, tools and wooden pipes, relics of extensive saltpeter mining.
The Lost Sea (Sweetwater). Contains a 4½-acre lake, believed to be the world's largest underground lake. Glass-bottomed boat tours.

Texas
Natural Bridge Caverns (San Antonio). Beautiful cave with impressive 60-foot-wide entrance. Tastefully developed and lighted. Indian artifacts.
Caverns of Sonora (Sonora). Possibly the most beautiful cave in the United States. Spectacular and varied helictites and many other unusual formations.

Utah
Timpanogos Cave National Monument (American Fork). Three caves connected by tunnels with colorful formations; cave walls encrusted with pink and blue crystals.

Virginia
Endless Caverns (New Market). One of the largest Virginia caves. Variety of beautiful formations. Stone Age Room with murals patterned after prehistoric paintings of Spain and France.
Luray Caverns (Luray). Large, beautiful formations, plus Great Stalactite Organ, an actual instrument using stalactites to produce musical tones.

West Virginia
Organ Cave (Ronceverte). Visited by Thomas Jefferson in 1778. Century-old saltpeter mining equipment.

–David R. McClurg

Winchester House: A Maze for Dumb Ghosts

In San Jose, Calif., there is a house of mystery, a house created by spirits. The atmosphere is enough to give you the creeps: a Victorian mansion with 160 rooms!

Even as you go through the creaking oak door there are more in your party than you can see. You feel a clamminess at your elbow; someone seems to be looking at you from the corner, the closet, the musty ceiling.

You see a stairway that leads nowhere, a window that opens to a wall, a doorway that leads to nothing. It is baffling. Mrs. Sarah Winchester meant it that way—she wanted to baffle the ghosts. A crew of 50 carpenters spent 38 years working full-time on this house.

"It's the ghosts," a medium confided to Mrs. Winchester in 1880. "They are angry because the rifles made by the Winchester family have killed so many. Many of them are Indians." Distraught, Mrs. W. wanted to know how she could ward them off.

"Build a house with endless rooms," was the reply. "But I warn you—if your house is ever completed, then you, too, will vanish into the world beyond."

So, in 1884, Mrs. Winchester purchased an 18-room house near San Jose. An observation tower shot up, only to be choked by other structures, until nothing could be seen from it. Cupolas and bell towers were constructed and then sealed off. Stairways inside led to the ceiling—with no opening. Hallways came to dead ends, with no way to turn but back.

On the heels of the carpenters came landscape gardeners who planted a towering thick hedge, cutting off all view of the premises from the Los Gatos Road. Seven Japanese gardeners were employed by Mrs. Winchester until the day she died, keeping the hedges so no one could see through them. None of the employees saw Mrs. Winchester themselves, except on rare occasions when she appeared as a veiled little figure, flitting through the halls like a ghost herself. Only one servant—the Chinese butler—was permitted to see her face as he served the meals on her $30,000 gold dinner set.

But today the monstrosity covers most of a six-acre estate and is considered San Jose's major tourist attraction. (For more information, contact the Chamber of Commerce, San Jose, Calif.) —Bill Thomas

---

He thought he saw a banker's clerk
    Descending from the bus.
He looked again and found it was
    A hippopotamus.
"If this should stay to dine," he said,
    "There won't be much for us."

—LEWIS CARROLL

Tunisian Troglodytes

Fatima is perhaps the richest lady in Matmata. She is a troglodyte—a cave-dweller. Her house looks like nothing but a big hole in the ground.

Surrounding the courtyard of her house at the bottom of the hole are six rooms, dug into the surrounding rock. And there is one upper room, reached by a palm tree trunk that serves as a ladder. This room is the attic; it's used for storage. A narrow shaft from the surface down into this room permits easy dropping in of dates, olives and grain.

Fatima herself is a henna-dyed hag of 40 or so, burned by the desert sun, tatooed on chin and cheeks—but when she smiles there's joy all around, and her few snaggly teeth add to it. She's gracious, entertaining, a good hostess in the best Berber tradition. Her ancient cave is a favorite with tourists.

You could eat off the floor in any of Fatima's rooms (except the one where she keeps her two goats). The floors are smooth and polished like the floors in a floor-wax commercial.

There are about 5,000 troglodytes in Matmata. The Tunisian government wants to bring all the troglodytes into the 20th century and has offered to build modern masonry houses for them. The village of New Matmata, several miles from old Matmata, has a population of about 3,000

former troglodytes who accepted houses, but the other 5,000 decided that underground is better, and they're staying.

Matmata has two underground hotels, the Marhala and the Sidi Driss. You get dinner, bed and breakfast in either for about $3.50 a night. You might have up to five roommates, though, and the upstairs rooms are a little tricky—you have to shinny up a rope, placing your feet carefully in holes in the rock, to get to them.

The Marhala has 43 rooms and about 150 beds. The "wings" of the hotel are actually different sunken courtyards, connected by tunnels. (No private baths, but there are common bathrooms in caves with running water, showers and flush toilets.)

One of the caves serves as a sort of cocktail lounge; behind the bar, instead of shelves, there are small hollows in the cave wall to hold the bottles of booze. The courtyard outside the bar has stools all around it so you can sit with your drink and watch jugglers, belly dancers and snake charmers.

The quickest way to get to Matmata is to fly via Tunis to Gabès and rent a car there to make the 50-mile trip. Or take a bus tour —tours out of Tunis, 270 miles from Matmata, include the village in five- and six-day sightseeing trips. Contact Saharatours, or Transtours-Tunisie.

—Robert Scott Milne

If you would keep your soul
    From spotted sight or sound,
Live like the velvet mole;
    Go burrow underground.

—ELINOR WYLIE

Baldasare Forestiere's Underground Mansion

Most people build a house. Baldasare Forestiere *dug* his.

Forestiere, a Sicilian immigrant, bought a seven-acre farm at Fresno, Calif. only to find that it was underlain by a tough hardpan, making farming it impossible. The summer was hot and Forestiere was used to digging—he had worked on the Boston subway. So he dug himself an underground room beneath the hardpan.

The room was a comfortable 20 degrees cooler. So Forestiere dug another room. Then another and another. By the time Forestiere died in 1946 at the age of 67, he was living in a catacombs of 100 rooms, courts, patios and passageways, all roofed over by the indestructible hardpan.

On a hot summer day you can take the ramp down into this "house" and enjoy the cool that he liked so much. There's an underground kitchen, Forestiere's bedroom (he slept on a shelf cut into the wall), the guest

room—which a prospective wife tried but didn't like, a library and even a chapel with a hardpan pulpit.

Forestiere liked to fish, and often brought his catch home alive and kept it fresh in an underground pond room. He grew a citrus orchard in a big chamber open at the top for the trees to stick through. Another room was a vegetable garden, still another a vineyard. When he died, Forestiere was working on an underground ballroom.

Forestiere did all the digging in his spare time (he worked as a horticulturist), using only a pick and shovel, a wheelbarrow and a mule-drawn scraper.

The weird home, known as the Forestiere Underground Gardens, is open daily, 9:30 a.m. to 4:30 p.m., from April through October and 10 a.m. to 4 p.m. weekends and holidays in winter. Admission is adults $2, juniors $1.50, children 75 cents for the guided tour. The underground mansion is seven miles north of downtown Fresno, Calif., two blocks east of U.S. 99, on Shaw Avenue.

—Alan R. McElwain

The Magic Castle

Life these days can be dull as rusty nails, or glorious as a flight of wild geese. It depends on what you choose to ignore.

In Los Angeles, the sexpot of America, there's an establishment devoted to making life fascinating, marvelous and strange. It's called The Magic Castle, of course, and it's inside an old turreted mansion in the Hollywood Hills. Inside the castle everything normal is ignored, and all things magical, mysterious and unexplainable run wild.

You walk into what seems to be a book-lined study—something out of an English manor house, maybe. There's a girl there to take your money or membership card, but she is completely uncommunicative. There's nothing else except the books, the empty leather chairs and a stuffed owl.

The magic starts right here. You'll be locked out all night unless you march right up to that owl and say in a loud, clear voice: "Open Sesame!"

By . . . well, by *magic*, the owl's section of the bookcase will silently swing open, like in the late movies, and you'll find yourself inside a dark and comfortable bar. There's a tinkly piano off in the distance and a vague feeling that things are seldom what they seem.

But after all, it's nothing but a bar. You sit at the rail and nurse along that Margarita. You get to talking with that lovely woman next to you, looking straight into her left eye, when all of a sudden you notice she seems awfully *tall*. Hm. Probably would never have worked out. My God, she must be six-foot-six if she's an inch! She's towering over you, and you can barely get your elbow on the bartop. She must think you're a school kid, or something. Funny, she didn't seem so tall when you first sat down.

Slowly it dawns on you that something's not quite right here. You're practically sitting on the floor, and the woman is positively statuesque. You pull yourself out of the conversation and notice that somehow your stool has found its way, ever so slowly, down to the ground.

The bartender chuckles. The woman turns out to be a little over five feet tall.

In the spirit of the thing, I won't give all the secrets away. But there's a piano without a pianist that plays all requests. There's an invisible bird in a cage. There's a little magic museum. And there are the feature attractions: the magicians themselves.

The Magic Castle is nonstop magic, all night. There are three little tables outside the bar where a procession of conjurors perform all manner of astonishing feats.

There are three galleries, specially built for the performance of close-up, nightclub and stage shows. The shows change all the time. You can watch Senator Crandall manipulate the cards and the ladies, and then catch the fabulous Shimada producing his live doves and flaming torches from thin air.

It's an incredible place, and I don't think there's anything like it anywhere else in the world. It's the Mecca for magicians, and everything serious and somber is strictly forgotten.

(Note: The Castle is a private club. To get in, you have to become a member, or go with someone who knows someone whose brother-in-law is a member.)

—*"The Great Saltini"*

Going Underground in Seattle

The ancient ruins of Pompeii it isn't, but the ruins of the Seattle Underground are fascinating, and now you can tour through them.

You didn't know Seattle had an Underground? Well, it wasn't always underground. In the 19th century, the shops in the Pioneer District of Seattle were built on such low ground that tides from Puget Sound threatened them daily. When the city was rebuilt after the devastating fire of 1889, the streets were raised, but the shops stayed below for years, brightened a little by light coming through thick glass windows set in the sidewalks above.

The Seattle Underground was forgotten for years, but in the mid-1960s an enterprising newspaperman named Bill Speidel publicized the ruined old shops and organized tours through them. The two-hour tour costs $1 a person, and for that price you not only get to see a little bit of Seattle's history—you get to hear about a lot more of it. Tour guides are all well versed in the lurid history of the era when the Underground was thriving, and their many anecdotes will take you back to the days when 87 percent of the city's revenues came from wine, women and vice.

The ruins of the Underground have not been restored, and you should be prepared to see a fair amount of dirt everywhere. Beneath the corner of First and James Streets for example, in the cellar of a deserted bank, the vault's gilded doors hang open to reveal cobwebs and mounds of dust.

In the rear of Moses Korn's department store you can still see the step-up bathroom with its fixtures crazily propped three feet off the floor to gain enough water pressure for operation. You'll also visit the ruins of a Chinese laundry, the Bijou Theater, a gospel mission and a Chinese opium-and-lottery den.

Since the tour takes you up and down many flights of stairs (it also covers some above-ground historical sights) and along cobblestone sidewalks slightly tilted from years of sinking, it's a good idea to wear tennis shoes or other sensible flat walking shoes. Dress in something warm and grubby—even in the summer it's usually a little chilly in underground Seattle, and it's always dirty. It's a good idea to carry a flashlight, too, for peering into nooks and crannies.

For reservations for a tour, write or call the Underground Ticket Office—108 S. Jackson St., Seattle, Wash. 98104; phone (206) 682-4646.

—*Bill Thomas*

The Last of Ancient America

By Orlando Flane

The Mayans are still alive. They were not conquered. They merely retreated to their wilderness. They still speak the ancient language and tell how things were before these strange white invaders drove them mad.

A jaguar screeches in the jungle, and flushes up a flight of brilliant turquoise birds with tails like Indian arrows.

A Mayan Indian shaman, loaded on *pulque* at night, spins wild legends of ancient times for a silent group of big-eyed children.

Out of the blistering heat of the main road and the living steam of the jungle suddenly juts a huge gray pyramid, silent, cool and powerful over the vast kingdom of Chichen Itza.

This is Yucatan, a forbidding and mysterious region that cuts like a saber into the Caribbean Sea. Officially it is just another state of Mexico. But it is as different from Mexico as jade is different from green glass.

This is a place where they remember ancient kings, a place where the blood of conquest is still salty and stinging on brown Mayan lips and where the rituals of ancient priests are still half-performed.

From the Usumascinta River in the mountains of Chiapas to the swamplands of Quintana Roo, the jaguar jungle rests like a fetid carpet on the floor of this peculiar peninsula. There is a certain psychic state about a jungle. Anything can happen; it is not like the cool abstraction of high mountains or the hyper-rational chaos of a city. In the tropics—the jungle —there are fevers in the air. In Jamaica they call it "the pressure." In Malaya it is "running amok." There's no name for it in Spanish, but the Mayans say "*balam x-pulyaa*"—"to be taken by the tiger-witch."

Just a dozen generations ago this land was the center of a thriving and learned empire. Only a confusion of dreams permitted the Spaniards to take over. Even now, the worst thing you can call someone publicly is a *malinchista*—it means a turncoat, a traitor, a person who wants to let in foreign diseases. The word comes from *La Malinche*, the Indian woman who became Cortes's mistress. As I say, for the Mayans the Spanish conquest is still within recent memory.

Before the Conquest, according to the legends, life was settled and the causes of things were known. The panoply of gods was well-cared for, each by those he protected. Thus Ich-K'in, a little wizened old man who always sits in a fetal position, was worshipped by the priests and initiates. Chac, the rain god, was venerated by the people.

When the Spanish came, with their famous horses and *mustachios*, the Mayans let them in. It is a well-known and grisly story. The Europeans took over, and their first move was to kill the priests and initiates. The harmless rain god was elevated to the first place, because the common people couldn't communicate with Ich-K'in themselves. Their power line had been cut.

For millions of Indians now living throughout the Americas, Yucatan is the reminder that something great and essential was lost. It has a different taste from other Mexican states; it is somehow still the seat of a wild, arcane empire.

The foreign traveler in Yucatan must basically stick to the single Spanish highway, Number 180, which connects Campeche with Merida and points east.

But you don't really go to Yucatan for the towns.

The great attraction of the region is that you can become—without any of that tiresome education—an instant archaeologist. You can rest assured that your own personal speculations, no matter how off-the-wall, are just precisely as good as those of the most eminent German scholars who've ever been here. The fact is that no one knows nuttin'!

On the Yucatan Peninsula (including the states of Yucatan, Campeche and Quintana Roo) there are literally hundreds of ancient cities and temples. Most of them are still unexcavated. Even in Chichen Itza, the most famous of them all, only one little area has been fully cleared and unearthed. The jungle still claims the rest. The secrets of ancient America are still overgrown by jealous ferns and guarded by jaguars. They await their discoverer.

For me, the main feature of the region is simply this: the Mayan Indians are still alive. They were not conquered. They merely retreated to their wilderness. In a census taken by a French anthropologist in 1940, nearly two million Mayans were found still living in their ancient homelands. One tribe, called the Lakandon, are even now living in the ancestral temples of Bonampak. (It's a six-day horseback ride through the mountain jungles of Chiapas, if you're interested in making a visit.) Mayans still live in Chichen Itza, in Palenque, in Peten and in most of the other ruined sites. They still speak the ancient Mayan language, and endlessly relate how things were before these strange white invaders drove them mad.

We talk to a young Mayan mother, who lives two kilometers from the ruins of Chichen Itza.

"So, uh, what do you think—living down the road from the ruins and all?" we ask.

She smiles. "For us, it is always the same. Nothing changes. We live here at Chichen. Our children do not play in the ruins."

Walking down the road toward the mighty ruins. It is a thin black swath cut into the jungle. The tip of a gray pyramid can be glimpsed over the trees. Elliptical

Looking up the steps of the Temple of the Jaguars at Tikal, Guatemala

mud and straw huts alongside the road; inside one, a magnificent woven hammock stretched from the beams, a grandmother and two children gently swinging, nodding off in the heat of the day, a little Mayan song on the grandmother's lips.

A beaten red dog sleeps in a patch of shade. Here is a regal Mayan woman, white dress embroidered with brilliant red and blue flowers. She wears gold jewelry in the morning and silver in the afternoon. The color, and the heat, and the distant wail of jaguars. The clouds move and the sun blasts in like a thousand sauna baths.

At the ruins. A few halfhearted Mexican guides, imitating American accents, swigging beer under a canopy while tourists from Michigan or New York walk among the curiously placed giant monuments. The Mayan who spends his days building ever-finer cages for his songbirds. The inscrutable jungle path we follow, hoping to uncover some important treasure still overlooked (it leads to an airport). And always the heat, and the jungle.

In a way I've always felt I couldn't understand the United States without understanding Mexico. The histories and blemishes are interconnected, like alcoholism and cirrhosis. And, I think Yucatan is the key to all of Mexico. Here you can still find unmurdered the ancient tribes and rituals, and you can get a taste of life before the Burger Barns.

In one sense Yucatan is a fragile region. It is only too easy to go down and return with a load of Mayan bric-a-brac, for sale in front of the Cooper Union. But in another sense, the jungle takes care of its own. It is a hard region. There is the fever, and the heat, and the sense of impending stupefaction. Anything can happen in the jungle, especially when one has the reflexes of urban man. This protects the natives, who have long ago made their peace with the Feathered Serpent.

The food in Yucatan is superb. They specialize in venison and turkey—how could you go wrong? It is totally unlike the rest of Mexican cooking, and of course it is very cheap.

For serious traveling through the region, the only practical base of operations is the provincial capital of Merida. It's a lovely town, interesting in its own right. Has some first-rate hotels, in an old and elegant tradition—charming and inexpensive. Many hotels provide free transportation to the major archaeological zones. (The hotels near the zones are generally expensive and scuzzy.)

There's recently been an outbreak of typhoid fever in certain parts of Mexico. Shots are not absolutely required at this time, but they might not be a bad idea. Also, make sure any water you drink is purified—it usually is, but it doesn't hurt to make sure. □

Egypt: The Stampeding Camel Scam

The camel drivers around the pyramids have got their act down cold, which is only right since they've had some 4,000 years or so to work on it. They have taken everyone from Julius Caesar and Napoleon on down, conquering the conquerors with the professional élan of real hustlers.

Tim Leary, the joyous traveler you see above, was making a tour through the Middle East when he had an urge to see the pyramids and fell into one of the world's oldest tourist traps.

You see, close by the pyramids sit an undistinguished and somewhat ragtag group of camel drivers. Lolling nearby are a pack of camels. The drivers steadfastly refuse to understand any languages you speak, save monetary units as expressed in seventeen Indo-European tongues.

After you've refused the price of the ride, they pull out the bargain basement sit-on-the-camel-and-we'll-take-your-picture-with-the-pyramids souvenir special. It's a bargain, especially after the quoted price of a camel ride.

So, like Tim Leary, you sit on the camel and smile. The camel, however, stampedes, causing great mental anguish to its driver, who chases after the beast, cracking his whips and all. By the time you, the camel and the driver return from a bouncy jaunt across the sands, you dig into your pockets to placate the drivers for frothing the poor beast—and you have been had.

Create a Pyramid, Mummify a Slug

Here's how to build your own pyramid: cut four pieces of heavy cardboard into isosceles triangles (i.e., triangles with two equal sides). The proportion of base to sides should be 15.7 to 14.94. Tape them together, so the pyramid stands exactly 10 units high. Using a compass, orient the base lines to face north-south and east-west. Make a stand 3.33 units high and put it inside with its center point directly underneath the apex of the pyramid.

If you put a dull razor blade on this stand, with its cutting edges facing east and west, it will get sharp—all by itself!

If you put a dead slug on it, it will mummify!

—The Editors

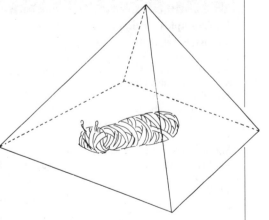

The Minnesota Runestone: a Message from the Vikings?

It's been around, the Kensington Runestone. With its Viking inscription, the stone is claimed by folks in Alexandria, Minn. to be proof positive that the site of their town is the "Birthplace of America," that it was discovered in 1362. Found on the farm of Olof Ohman in 1898, the stone for a time reposed in the Smithsonian (although it has never been authenticated by that august body) and was exhibited in the 1965 New York World's Fair. Now it is on permanent display in Alexandria, with a museum built around it. And there is a 28-foot statue of a Viking at the foot of Main Street to commemorate the town's claim to fame. To Alexandrians, Christopher Columbus most definitely was a Johnny-come-lately.

When pioneer farmer Ohman found the stone at Kensington (about two miles from Alexandria), he consulted the editor of a Swedish-language newspaper in Minneapolis who, in turn, referred it to the University of Minnesota. Soon there was excitement over discovery of a 14th-century Norse expedition into Minnesota.

Later, Norwegian experts discounted the inscription on the stone as an amateurish forgery. Then came one Hjalmar R. Holand, a historian of the Minneapolis Norwegian

A. Triumph's Triumph: Amazing!

Mr. Arch Triumph, the well-known court jester of Henry VIII, was once imprisoned by the king for making a bad pun. Rather than throwing him into a dungeon, however, King Henry threw him into an elaborate maze—he was determined to either drive the jester out of his mind or make him funny.

But jesters must be clever, and Arch quickly found his way out—even though the maze was pitch dark. How did he do it?

Send answers to:

The Great Escape (Maze)
150 Shoreline Highway
Mill Valley, Calif. 94941

Society and a graduate student of the University of Wisconsin. He believed in the authenticity of the stone and dedicated more than 50 years to searching down evidence to support his faith. Along the alleged route of these Norse explorers he found Viking implements and mooring holes drilled in rocks Viking-fashion, and he assembled extensive documentation. Many runic scholars and historians have credited Holand's findings. Others dispute them bitterly (claiming, for example, that the drillings were made by latter-day surveyors). And so the debate goes on. But not as far as citizens of Alexandria are concerned. They stand by the inscription, which translates to read:

"Eight Goths and 22 Norwegians on exploration journey from Vinland over the West. We had camp by two skerries one day's journey north from this stone. We were and fished one day. After we came home (found) 10 red with blood and dead. Ave Maria, save from evil." And on the edge of the stone: "Have 10 of our party by the sea to look after our ships 14 days' journey from this island. Year 1362."

–Mike Michaelson

Desert Museum

The Arizona-Sonora Desert Museum west of Tucson is a unique "living" display of the animals and plants of the desert region. The desert, stretching through the American Southwest and northern Mexico, supports a startling range of fauna and flora. Everything from the scorpion to the mountain lion, from the boojum tree to the saguaro cactus inhabit this vast range. You could spend a lifetime in the wilds acquainting yourself with these plants and animals.

Or you could spend a day at the Arizona-Sonora Desert Museum.

Located 14 miles west of Tucson, the "museum" is inappropriately named if the word conjures up visions of musty stuffed bobcats. The animals in the museum are living specimens, and they all live in simulated natural settings. For example, the small cats of the region, the jagarundi, ocelot, margay and bobcat, are housed in canyon-style compounds that enable them to climb and romp freely, give them access to the open sky, and yet give people a chance to look at them close up. Particularly interesting is the display of desert snakes. The museum has an example of virtually every creature that lives in the desert.

Plants of the desert have not been neglected in the museum's collection. Of particular interest to people concerned with the conservation of water is the display called the "desert garden," which instructs the viewer on aesthetic combinations of desert plants suitable for home landscaping. (A proper understanding of attractive desert plants can persuade the newcomer to Arizona to plant his yard with cactus, rather than green grass, which has a destructive thirst for water that must be satisfied if its greenness is to be maintained!)

–Lee Foster

Taos Pueblo

If I remember my third grade learning right, one out of eight Americans has Indian blood. The Indians used to be all over the country, from New York City to Georgia, and everywhere in the West. They invested the land with a certain spirit-of-place that, on the East Coast, has gotten absorbed into the freeway system. But in the Southwest, and particularly New Mexico, the Indians still live the ancient life.

In the Taos Pueblo, 70 miles north of Santa Fe, there is a thriving and beautiful Indian village that hasn't changed in 800 years. There are two huge, five-story communal homes facing each other, walled like medieval casbahs. They form two semicircles with openings to the east and west. Between them lies a large open field. A sparkling creek runs through the center, spanned by small log bridges. The pueblos are undulating salmon-brown and brick, with brightly painted windows and doorways, usually blue. Dark brown wooden beams jut out from the walls. Overshadowing everything is the enormous hump of Mt. Wheeler, the highest mountain in New Mexico, directly behind the village.

As I am gawking in awe, a medium-sized man walks slowly and consciously across the field. He nods and says hello. We get to talking.

"I am a doctor," he says, "and I'm going to see a little girl who has broken her leg in a fall from her horse."

I ask how he learned to be a doctor, and he smiles.

"From the animals. I have killed many animals. And also from people. *Indian* medicine. Our Indian medicine is very good."

Suddenly another Indian in a truck pulls up, and they begin speaking in the Taos dialect. The man in the truck turns to me and says in English, "Can you leave in ten minutes?"

I am shocked. His voice is an abrupt mixture of great authority and meek pleading, commanding and questioning. I say of course. He drives off.

The doctor turns to me and smiles. His eyes are clear. "In ten minutes," he says to me, "the Indian people must make their religion. Other people must go. Perhaps I will see you tomorrow."

There are some 19 Indian pueblos within easy distance of Santa Fe, not to mention hundreds of other Indian settlements throughout the country. Visiting in an Indian pueblo is a bit of a ticklish encounter for me, the grandson of immigrants, and I imagine it would be the same for most white Americans. But the true and ancient spirit of our country is in the pueblos. Taos Pueblo was civilized and flourishing at the time of the Battle of Hastings, and when the Crusades were just futuristic dreams.

–David Saltman

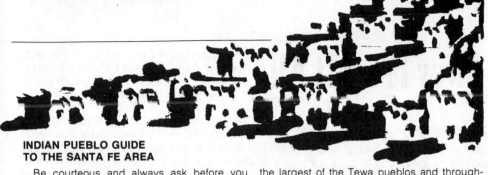

INDIAN PUEBLO GUIDE TO THE SANTA FE AREA

Be courteous and always ask before you take anyone's photograph. Some may charge a fee. A pueblo is similar to an apartment house complex, so never enter any doors without permission. Remember, you are entering homes.

Tesuque Pueblo (*Tey-soo-kay*)—North of Santa Fe eight miles on U.S. 285-64 is the small pueblo of Tesuque. This pueblo of about 240 inhabitants is near the Rio Tesuque and for years the principal occupation of the people has been farming. Recent archaeological excavations have indicated that structures were being built on the pueblo site as early as the year 1250 A.D. Religious ceremonies are celebrated at Tesuque and most of the ceremonial dances (as in all pueblos) are open to the public. Picture-taking and sketching may be prohibited if the dance is part of a sacred rite.

Pojoaque (*Poh-whah-kay*)—This reservation, 16 miles north of Santa Fe, is between Tesuque and Nambé, and although it is small there are still 75 persons living there. The pueblo itself is only a memory.

Nambé (*Nahm-bay*)—Twenty miles north of Santa Fe on N.M. 4 is Nambé Pueblo. Festivities are held annually on the 4th of July at Nambé Creek just above the pueblo. The dances and other festivities attract many visitors, as do the October feast day observances.

Picuris (*Pick-u-reese*)—As you proceed along U.S. 64 through Dixon, 55 miles north of Santa Fe, you will arrive at one of the ancient pueblos. Picuris is nestled in the valley of the Rio Pueblo some 7,360 feet above sea level. Archaeologists estimate that Picuris was founded between 1250 and 1300 A.D. A modern community building adds a flavor of the present era to contrast with the ancient ruins through which the Indians guide visitors. Pottery may be purchased at homes indicated in the readily available guidebook.

Taos Pueblo (*Tah-os*, as in *house*)—Slightly over an hour's drive and just 67 scenic miles north of Santa Fe is Taos. Immediately north of the city of Taos is one of the largest, most impressive and most exquisitely preserved Indian pueblos—San Geronimo de Taos.

Of all the pueblos in New Mexico only Taos has kept its fortress-like appearance. The two great communal houses are of adobe construction, and reach four and five stories into the sky. Sparkling Taos Creek, which irrigates the Indians' farms, flows through the pueblo and is spanned by log bridges. The high walls of Taos present an incomparable view of native architecture unique in this area, while the highest mountain of New Mexico, Mt. Wheeler, 13,151 feet high, serves as the backdrop to the pueblo.

San Juan—Twenty-eight miles north of Santa Fe on U.S. 285 is the site of the first capital of New Mexico. On July 11, 1598, at San Juan de los Caballeros, the Spaniards established their first capital. A new and permanent capital was later built in Santa Fe. San Juan is the largest of the Tewa pueblos and throughout the year it presents colorful dance ceremonies. Worthy of note is the craftsmanship in skillfully decorated pottery and wood carvings.

Santa Clara—The second largest pueblo in the Tewa group is Santa Clara on the west side of the Rio Grande, on N.M. 30, 27 miles north of Santa Fe. This is a well-preserved and typical example of old pueblo architecture.

San Ildefonso (*Sahn-Eel-day-fohn-so*)—Twenty-two miles north of Santa Fe on the route to Los Alamos is the pueblo of San Ildefonso, long noted for the production of outstanding pottery.

Maria the Potter is as famous as the pueblo itself for the black matte and burnished ware that she developed. Many other ceramists also fashion outstanding decorative pottery.

The economy of San Ildefonso was based on farming until the Indian men and women began commuting to Los Alamos to work as the nuclear age developed. Although most pueblos celebrate feasts in the summer, the feast of San Ildefonso is not celebrated until Jan. 1. It features unusual and spectacular animal dramatizations.

Cochiti (*Coh-chee-tee*)—Thirty miles south of Santa Fe is the home of the northernmost of the eastern Keres Indian groups. The pueblo, located on the west side of the Rio Grande between Santa Fe and Albuquerque, is reached by taking N.M. 22, which turns northwest from U.S. 85.

The Cochitis, who originally lived in Frijoles Canyon (now part of Bandelier National Monument), are outstanding artists, craftsmen and potters. They are well known for their double-headed drums fashioned from hollowed-out aspen or cottonwood tree sections and covered with leather tightly laced with rawhide thongs. At the Cochiti Corn Dance (an annual feast day held on July 14) you can hear the resonant beat of the drums as it reverberates through the air.

Santo Domingo—Thirty-two miles south of Santa Fe is Santo Domingo Pueblo, largest of the eastern Keres pueblos. Among the Santo Domingos religion continues as the core of their social life. One of the most dramatic pueblo ceremonies is the important Corn Dance, which takes place on Aug. 4. Other interesting events of special significance are held throughout the year.

While visiting Santo Domingo it is worth your while to stop at the trading center to see the interesting art, jewelry, rugs and handicrafts you may purchase.

You will note that much farming is still done by the Santo Domingos, who enjoy the serenity and sunshine of the Southwest in the Rio Grande Valley. No photography is allowed.

For current information on Indian dances, contact the Santa Fe Chamber of Commerce—the phone number is (505) 983-7317.
—The Editors

Aztec Ruins in a Subway Station

Just 20 miles north of Mexico City are the immense ruins of San Juan Teotihuacan, which rank with Egyptian pyramids in size and splendor. The entire Mexico City area was once the site of a flourishing Indian civilization founded about the time of Christ. (There are even temple ruins in the middle of a subway station!)

The buildings were burned by invaders, but the ruins still awed tribes like the Aztecs, who thought that only the gods could have created so vast a city. The original builders of San Juan Teotihuacan are unknown, lost in the deep well of time.

The ruins are an easy drive from Mexico City. Start at Cuauhtemoc's statue in front of the Chateau Riviera Hotel (formerly the Hilton) and drive out Insurgentes Norte. From the city limits follow the signs. Or negotiate with the English-speaking guides who have their cars in front of all major hotels. (Negotiate tough, because prices are flexible.) Or, sign up for a guided tour at any travel agency or with your hotel *concierge*. You can also take city buses. There are sound and light shows at the ruins during the dry season. Be sure to take a sweater because the evening breezes are chilly at that altitude.
—Bern Keating

A Museum of Firefighting

If old fire engines are lucky in their declining years, they end up in the careful hands of George Getz of Scottsdale, Ariz. Getz's passion for firefighting equipment and paraphernalia began in the 1950s and has blossomed into an elaborate museum called the "Hall of Flame" at 3626 Civic Center Plaza, Scottsdale.

The collection includes such varied pieces as a horse-drawn pumper that saved part of Chicago in the disastrous inferno of 1871, a Japanese hand pumper built about 1800 for a wealthy rice planter and several ornamental parade pieces from the days when fire companies were part of a "high society" that included the most prominent citizens.

Elaborate collections of badges, hats and insurance insignia dazzle the visitor at Getz's museum. Much energy goes into interpreting the pieces effectively. The fire insurance insignia, for example, date from the time when insurance companies in Europe felt they could cut losses by organizing fire companies that would save burning houses. If fire swept your neighborhood and you happened to sport an insignia on your doorway, you were in luck. Otherwise the firemen passed by and you sought new quarters.

Getz also has several Currier and Ives prints showing scenes of early American firefighters in action. And, of course, there is a fire bell that children delight in ringing until deafened adults restrain them.
—Lee Foster

Getting Your Kids Away From It All

By David Saltman

A visit to Story Town or Santa's Workshop or one of the many other "theme parks" in northeastern New York State can be a thrill of a young lifetime for a little kid, and it's not so bad for adults either—quaff a flagon of Coca-Cola at the King's Arms in the Land of Make-Believe and just see if you don't feel a little mellower.

Yes, friends, step right up. The roadside attraction racket is still hanging in there.

Drive up the Adirondack Northway—the most scenic freeway in America—sometime, and you'll be surrounded by rodeos, Robin Hoods and fairy godmothers. They inhabit the North Country's "theme parks"—miniature fantasy kingdoms that continue to enchant millions of visitors each season.

The season is short up here in northeastern New York, running from about Memorial Day to Columbus Day. Nevertheless, theme park operators did a land-office business this year, as usual. (And the land office did a pretty good business, too!)

Story Town, in Lake George, N.Y. It is the leviathan of the Adirondack Attractions Association, a group of 11 tourist spots that includes most of the theme parks in the North Country. Story Town has all the bangles and finery: a stunning lakeside setting in the lower Adirondacks, graceful swan boats, a dense jungle with authentic swaying bridges and mechanical headhunters who pop out of the bush wearing bloodthirsty leers, a green fire-breathing dragon train, a gunslingin' ghost town and even a one-ring circus.

Yes, you better load up the Kodak, parents! You're going to thaw quick when you see that funky circus. We come in just as three chimps dressed like Turks are riding unicycles to music, ending with a mobile chimp pyramid on top of a glittering two-wheeler.

Here's what your theme parks are all about. See the giant gila monster! See the rare reindeer! Take off your Florsheims, America, and let the gypsy woman tickle your toes! Frontier Town, Gaslight Village, Adventure Town—mobile America's gypsy stations.

One of the nicest of these, just a short drive from the lovely Au Sable Chasm on Route 9N, is Santa's Workshop, in Wilmington, N.Y. Or, rather, in North Pole, N.Y. This lovely little park is entirely devoted to Santa and his helpers. It happens to be the oldest theme park in the whole country, and one of the places Walt Disney had in mind when designing

Disneyland. It takes in a lot of territory, and features, among other things, a magician, a potter, a glass-blower, workers with plastic, amusement park rides, a church and a nativity pageant.

The workers at Santa's Workshop take time out to jaw with you; they aren't so worn out as those at Story Town, who've had to contend with Brooklyn accents all day long. This isn't a stuff-'em and send-'em-home park at all. Loitering is encouraged. There's even an actual North *Pole*, a seven-foot column of ice in the park's center. I don't know how they keep it from melting—that's part of the magic, I guess.

Speaking of magic, Santa's Workshop has a fine old Wizard who amazes and delights every three hours. It's standard magical fare, I suppose, but the stuff never fails to thrill me. He does some beautiful flower productions, a version of the old die box trick involving a lovely princess and her three suitors, some flourishes with brightly colored silks and a really elegant item where he somehow makes an umbrella change into a pompon.

For my money the real attraction of Santa's Workshop is the live (not plastic or mechanical) craftsmen. Kids may indeed like to go dizzy on merry-go-rounds or death-daring roller coasters, but they surely just as well love to watch a skilled potter conjure up a cup right in front of their eyes. Or to have a blacksmith hammer them a ring out of the nail from a reindeer's shoe. Santa's place is loaded with slightly over-age elves who come here from all over the country to ply their crafts.

On a holy, flowered hillock separating the old-time church from the blacksmith's shop you find the North Pole's Bethlehem. Every couple of hours they re-enact the nativity scene, complete with Adirondack wise men, real shepherds and a Christ child who winds up dangled by one ankle when the Virgin Mary becomes just plain Sally Jean Johnson with her rubber doll again. It's the thought that counts, of course, and the wise men *do* wear truly magnificent robes.

By now we are really getting into

theme parks. We can discuss eloquently the use of wood versus Celastic, the varying atmospheres and ambiences. We note that many of the exhibits in various parks seem to be built in the same style—a kind of gingerbready "cute" style that falls just short of being too much. Sure enough, it turns out that the author of most of the scenery in Story Town and Santa's Workshop (and in dozens of other parks around the country) is a man not unlike an elf himself, Mr. Arto Monaco. Arto runs the Land of Make-Believe in Upper Jay, N.Y., just a few miles from Wilmington on Route 9N. During the summer, his Land is the epitome of theme parks; in the winter he is busy designing and building new Cinderella pumpkin carriages, swan boats and stagecoaches for use in New York, New Hampshire, Kansas and anywhere else that theme parks flourish.

In my opinion, the Land of Make-Believe slips over that intuitive boundary between just another roadside attraction and a real work of art. The Western town ("Cactus Flats") isn't just your store fronts and board sidewalks, but a *real* (kid-sized!) Western town, filled with authentic period paraphernalia. You get the feeling that everyone just stepped out for a minute — they'll be right back to serve you in the style of the 1870s.

You can stoke the fire in the blacksmith's shop, play the nickelodeon in the hotel ("No Drummers Or Actors"), sniff decoctions of henbane or mandragore in the herbalist's or count horses' teeth in the livery stable. Anyone who hankers for the old days—as Arto Monaco surely does—can get his fill here.

There's more to the Land of Make-Believe than just Western lore. You can climb through a semi-authentic King Arthur castle, quaff a flagon of Coca-Cola in the King's Arms, or float from one fairy tale to another embodied in little houses belonging to The Three Bears, Mary Quite Contrary (whose garden is beautifully tended) and your own favorites. Beyond the fairyland is River Rat Pete's boat landing, an Indian village and an African safari. You can catch all these in panorama on the stage coach ride, or sailing on an authentic Mississippi sidewheeler slowly up and down the little lily lake that forms the eastern border of the park. Watch out for the three-card monte man!

Even more remarkable than the land itself, to my mind, is the guts and guiding light of the whole operation: Arto Monaco himself. He is a medium-sized, mustachioed, grey-haired little kid, who spends his days puffing away on a smelly old pipe and always tinkering with some new contraption or other.

Back in 1937, Arto was one of Walt

Disney's cartoonists and he also worked for MGM and Warner Brothers in Hollywood. But he longed for the mountains where he was born, he says, so he chucked a lucrative Hollywood career and came back to the Au Sable Valley.

"Why should I kill myself out there for someone else? I'd rather have it small, and be my own boss and have some time for fun," he says emphatically, with a puff and a twinkle. He has little cause to regret his move, now that his park draws over 100,000 visitors each summer and he has more work in the winter than he can possibly handle.

I'm convinced Monaco and his coworkers could build *anything*. I've watched them take a bunch of old wood scraps, tinker around for a while and emerge with a perfect replica of a giraffe, nine feet tall. The men at the shop built—from scratch—an entire double-decker English bus that now transports the tourists around Lake George's Gaslight Village. They've built stage coaches, dioramas and revolving 3-D logos. They've put African natives onto a raft floating in a pond brimming with Monaco's ferocious crocodiles. They've built fountains, bridges—entire cities!

"Where are the great artists of today?" wail the New York intellectuals. Well, some of them are here, upstate, building Disneylands and shopping centers and designing cigarette packages. In the old days the king would patronize the arts and thinkers of all kinds flourished at court; nowadays, only Madison Avenue makes it worthwhile. In any case, more people have been able to enjoy (for instance) Arto Monaco's art than will ever see Peter Paul Rubens.

As we were leaving Arto's shop, I heard a customer ask one of his artists:

"Say, how would you build a structure shaped like an egg shell?"

Aha! I thought. That's a stumper for sure!

The artist thought a moment, and smiled.

"That's easy," she finally replied. "We'd make it out of chicken wire!" □

Other Theme Parks

Here's a sampling of some other theme parks in northeastern New York State.

Gaslight Village At the southern edge of the village of Lake George, N.Y. Ride in a shaving mug or other accoutrements of the 1890s.

Thousand Animals Farms at Lake Placid and at Au Sable Chasm, N.Y. Live Arctic and desert animals—everything from Himalayan bears to Barbary goats. You can buy excellent furs here, too.

Time Town Six miles north of Lake George. Travels into the past and future, not to mention to other planets. Also an observatory.

—*The Editors*

Stuffed Guinea Pigs, Anyone?

Perhaps Britain's most fascinating museum—if your taste runs to oddities, that is—lurks under the Palace Pier in Brighton, the popular seaside resort about 50 miles south of London. It is Potter's Museum of Taxidermy, and the displays include such whimsical animal tableaus as "The Death and Burial of Cock Robin," "The Guinea Pigs' Cricket Match," "The Kittens' Wedding," "The Rabbits' Village School." Mark you, these are all real birds and beasts—stuffed, mounted, encased in glass and equipped with miniature props down to the last relentless detail.

Potter's Museum was founded in 1861 by Walter Potter (a dedicated young taxidermist) in the small Sussex village of Bramber, where it flourished until 1973. Recently moved to more accessible Brighton, Potter's life work continues to amaze and amuse visitors. If you ever had the urge, for example, to study 34 stuffed guinea pigs up on their hind legs portraying a village cricket match—complete with two teams, a brass band and beer-guzzling spectators—you can satisfy it here. "The Death and Burial of Cock Robin" displays 98 specimens of British bird life acting out the gruesome nursery rhyme.

Since Potter was also an obsessive collector of nature's freaks and assorted curios, you can gaze, if you wish, on a lamb with two heads or a duck with four legs, not to mention a Siamese war saddle, a mummy's hand and a piece of the Great Wall of China. And there's more. In all, Potter assembled some 5,000 works of taxidermy and uncounted curios before he died. His successors have carried on nobly.

Potter's Museum of Taxidermy is open from March to November, 10 a.m. to 10 p.m. Admission is adults, 15 pence (about 38 cents); children under 14, 10 pence (about 25 cents).

—*James Egan*

REALLY CHEAP THRILLS!

IN

LOS ANGELES

By Richard John Pietschmann

Thrills aren't as cheap as they once were in Los Angeles. In the halcyon mid-Sixties days of the Strip, teenyboppers lifted their Mexican peasant tops to sell 25-cent "peeks" to prowling out-of-town businessmen. But that was before the street people departed and Sunset Strip sold out to the record company glitter freaks. Now it's tough to find a peek at any price.

The counterculture was a good free show in Los Angeles while it lasted. Picking up hitchhikers (or hitching around on your own) was a decent diversion—until a few nuts started making it too dangerous for anyone to play. Swap meets were the last stand of free freak entertainment, but now most of these have moved outside city limits.

Indeed, the state of cheap thrills is depressing in Los Angeles. Hollywood has turned the corner from odd to degenerate. Pacific Ocean Park is closed and crumbling. Even Muscle Beach is gone.

For the most part, the vacuum created when the flame of "the revolution" went out has been filled in Los Angeles with traditional things to do. But not entirely. After all, it still is Los Angeles, and we all know how they are out there.

Art Yes, Penelope, there *is* art in Los Angeles. A whole lot of it, no matter *what* Johnny Carson may lead you to believe. The Los Angeles County Museum (it's at 5905 Wilshire Blvd.) possesses an excellent standing collection that is helped along by loans from Norton Simon's private store of treasures. New shows every month, too (1973's big art event was the visiting Russian collection). Standing collection is free, special exhibitions usually cost a buck. Open Tuesday through Friday, 10 a.m. to 5 p.m.; Saturday and Sunday, 10 a.m. to 6 p.m.; closed Monday.

Auctions Usually free, but you might want to buy a program just to catch the flavor of the action, and the action can get heavy indeed when famous works of art or estates go on the block at Sotheby Parke Bernet (7660 Beverly Blvd.; phone in L.A., 937-5130). This upper-crust house holds auctions September through June once a week (usually on Monday or Tuesday evening). They'll put you on the mailing list if you write or call. There are lots of other fine auction houses in the same area of West Hollywood, and there are the La Cienega Boulevard art galleries, which are open for browsing every Monday evening.

Beach Here, at the beach, is where most stories about Los Angeles *are* true. It's the best remaining free show in Los Angeles. The L.A. beach mystique stretches all the way from Malibu in the north to Laguna in the south. There must be 100 miles of beaches, but the finest close-in spots for heavy-duty vicarious brain damage are the Will Rogers (foot of Sunset), Santa Monica and Venice beaches. On the right day you can see all the elements of the California Dream. And more, too—like some of the finest world-class volleyball (on the sand at Manhattan Beach), championship Frisbee (everywhere, but especially Laguna), surfing (best is when there's a good storm at sea) and hang gliding (one of several good spots are the cliffs over Redondo Beach). And, there's what is possibly the only surviving five-cent merry-go-round ride in the country (Santa Monica Pier). Just head west until you hit the Pacific, but be warned that the natives are there in any numbers *only* in the summer.

Bus Public transportation was once the laugh of Los Angeles, but no longer. What better way to get from place to place? Why, even the people who *live* in Los Angeles are beginning to use them. The best bus deal around Los Angeles is the dime-a-ride Mini-Bus in downtown Los Angeles. Your dime takes you all over downtown; you can stop at such big-name attractions as Olvera Street, Chinatown, the Music Center, the Civic Center and the new Arco Plaza. One place to catch it is at the corner of 5th and Hill across from Pershing Square. It runs 9 a.m. to 4 p.m. daily; keep in mind that you'll see few natives if you ride on the weekend. The Southern California Rapid Transit District (RTD) also has a free map and a free tour brochure ("20 Guide-Yourself Trips by Public Transportation") —write RTD, Public Information Department, 1060 S. Broadway, Los Angeles, Calif. 90015.

Coffee (and Cheesecake) L.A. has a few really fine outdoor spots to sip good coffee, eat good cheesecake and watch the decadence mince past. Strong black coffee, nothing like that insipid New York stuff, as many refills as you want, is usually 25 cents. Unusual cheesecakes (tried chocolate? carob? date-nut?), but they *do* cost a buck or so. Four top spots with a view of the sidewalk and at least a half-dozen certified L.A. freaks every 15 minutes: Chopping Block (Beverly Hills on Wilshire), Melting Pot (West Hollywood at the corner of La Cienega and Melrose), Old World (West Hollywood on Sunset Strip) and Source (weird, robed people on the Strip in West Hollywood).

Concerts Good music sometimes comes cheap in Los Angeles. The Los Angeles Philharmonic plays its summer season (July-September) at the huge outdoor Hollywood Bowl. Then it moves indoors to the Dorothy Chandler Pavilion at the downtown Music Center for the winter season (October-April). This is genuine classical music (there are some semi-classical and show tune concerts) with high-powered conductors from all over the world. Concert times at the Music Center are usually Thursday and Friday evenings and there's a Sunday matinee ($2.50 Sunday matinee is the lowest priced ticket). At the Bowl it's Tuesday, Thursday and Saturday evenings (minimum is usually $2). Biggest music buys in L.A. are the three "marathon" nights at the Bowl—6 p.m. to midnight concerts (usually on Wednesdays) for something like $2.

Female Personwatching (Formerly Girlwatching) In a city famed for its native daughters, Century City in West Los Angeles (just west of Beverly Hills) is generally conceded to be the best turf on which to sort fact from fiction. Pick a convenient bench in this shopping-office building complex and watch the traffic flow. The shopping area of Beverly Hills isn't bad, but it's tough to look inconspicuous. Perched right next to UCLA, Westwood Village isn't bad either. But the right beach on the right summer day can't be beat (a coed volleyball game can provide considerable entertainment). There—I said it and I'm glad, Gloria, Kate et al.

Observatory Griffith Park is supposed to be the largest park in any city. Much of it is actually wild and inaccessible mountainside. But plunked atop one of its many mini-peaks is Griffith Observatory, an honest-to-pete telescope place and planetarium. It costs $1 (50 cents for those under 18) for the planetarium show—at least twice daily except Monday; call 664-1191 to ask hours the day you want to go. The astronomical display, open daily 2 p.m. to 10 p.m., is free. But the big draw for fans of heavenly bodies is the telescope itself, and you may look through it every clear evening except Monday between 7 p.m. and 10 p.m.

Swap Meet and Flea Market The biggest around is the one in Pasadena, near the Rose Bowl. Lots of nifty old stuff, recycled clothing and a few genuine antiques. Just about everything for sale you ever remember seeing in your grandparents' attic. Only once a month on the second Sunday, from 9 a.m. to 3 p.m.

Troubadour Good folk and rock music clubs (are they called nightclubs?) are dying everywhere, but this one is doing fine, thank you. Owner Doug Weston gave a lot of top stars their first exposure here (Elton John played his first U.S. date here), and most of them return from time to time to the tiny club as a thank-you. Top rock and folk acts almost always, partly because this is the record industry's sounding board. That makes the audience interesting, too. The prevailing style is high superfunk and admission hovers around $3 plus a modest requirement that you buy two drinks (make it tea or coffee and you get off for under $5). Could be the best spot in the country for top and comer stars in an intimate relation with the audience. West Hollywood right next to Beverly Hills at 9018 Santa Monica Blvd. (phone 276-6168). □

Try Mackinac Island— No Cars Allowed

You may not believe it, but there's at least one place in the United States where motor vehicles are not only banned—they were never permitted in the first place. It's Mackinac Island, in Lake Huron just off the tip of Michigan's mitt. You get there by ferry from Mackinaw City, Mich. It is quiet, it is peaceful—you'll swear you've been transported back to the 1890s. There *are* a couple of olive green trucks around—maintenance vehicles—and there is one lone movie house that seems to specialize in showing motorcycle flicks, but otherwise Mackinac Island looks just as it did in the days when it was *the* watering spot for the very rich in the Midwest.

There are still scores of elegant summer mansions on the island—you can rent a horse or bike and take a leisurely tour past them. The rich folks who didn't have mansions stayed at the sumptuous Grand Hotel (which boasts the world's longest veranda), and you can, too, but the Windsor is considerably cheaper (about $13 a night) and has its own kind of charm. It's a three-story white frame hotel that's clean, quiet and old-fashioned in a way that's reminiscent of visits to Grandma's house. (For reservations, write Windsor Hotel, Mackinac Island, Mich. 49757.)

The whole island is actually a Michigan state park, and there are lovely wooded hills for rambling and picnicking in. (The Mackinac Island grocery store will sell you provisions for picnics.) There are several inexpensive restaurants and the fudge, sold all over, is an island specialty—be sure to try it.

When you go to Mackinac Island, take along a good book, a deck of cards or a Monopoly game, because nightlife there is nonexistent. You go to Mackinac Island not to live it up but to retreat, collect your thoughts, gather your resources, breathe clean air and listen to the quiet.

Shepler's Mackinac Island Ferry runs from Mackinaw City several times a day May 15-Oct. 15, and will occasionally make the run in other seasons if the weather is fine —but don't count on it. Round trip fares are $2.75 for adults, $1.50 for children five to 11 years old; children under five ride free. No reservations required. Tip: leave as little gas as possible in your car when you park it in the lot in Mackinaw City—if you leave much, the local kids will siphon it off.

—Carol White

Midwest Hiking Guidebook

Everyone knows about the great hiking in the East and West, but the Midwest is usually assumed to be a wasteland for backpackers. A book due out in the spring of 1974 should help put this misconception to rest. It's *Hiking Trails in the Midwest*, by Jerry Sullivan and Glenda Daniel ($5.95, from your bookstore or from the GreatLakes Living Press, P.O. Box 11311, Chicago, Ill. 60611).

One of the most beautiful and exhilarating storms I ever enjoyed in the Sierra occurred in December, 1874. . . . The day was intensely pure, one of those incomparable bits of California winter, warm and balmy and full of white sparkling sunshine, redolent of all the purest influences of the spring, and at the same time enlivened with one of the most bracing wind-storms conceivable. . . . When the storm began to sound, I lost no time in pushing out into the woods to enjoy it. For on such occasions Nature has always something rare to show us, and the danger to life and limb is hardly greater than one would experience crouching deprecatingly beneath a roof.

. . . The air was mottled with pine-tassels and bright green plumes, that went flashing past in the sunlight like birds pursued. But there was not the slightest dustiness, nothing less pure than leaves, and ripe pollen, and flecks of withered bracken and moss. I heard trees falling for hours at the rate of one every two or three minutes; some uprooted, partly on account of the loose, water-soaked condition of the ground; others broken straight across, where some weakness caused by fire had determined the spot. . . .

The force of the gale was such that the most steadfast monarch of them all rocked down to its roots with a motion plainly perceptible when one leaned against it. Nature was holding high festival, and every fiber of the most rigid giants thrilled with glad excitement.

I drifted on through the midst of this passionate music and motion, across many a glen, from ridge to ridge; often halting in the lee of a rock for shelter, or to gaze and listen. Even when the grand anthem had swelled to its highest pitch, I could distinctly hear the varying tones of individual trees—spruce, and fir, and pine and leafless oak—and even the infinitely gentle rustle of the withered grasses at my feet. Each was expressing itself in its own way—singing its own song, and making its own peculiar gestures—manifesting a richness of variety to be found in no other forest I have yet seen.

—JOHN MUIR

The Sphinx is still the greatest riddle of all time: the body of a lion, the head of a pharaoh and eyes that pierce into Eternity.

In ancient times, the Sphinx was said to have a human voice. She inhabited the region of Thebes, in Egypt, and gave riddles to all travelers who passed by. Whoever could not answer was instantly devoured.

The Egyptian oracles told the Thebans that the Sphinx would kill herself if they could answer this riddle:

"What goes on four feet, then on two feet and three,
But the more feet it goes on the weaker it be?"

At length, the riddle was solved by Oedipus, who gave the answer, "Man."

The Sphinx that remains on the outskirts of Cairo is said to have been built around 3000 B.C.

Giza Pyramids   The Pyramids at Giza are said to be the remains of an intricate network of astrological observatories. There are long, slender pipes built into the brickwork, which make it possible to stand inside the pitch-dark chambers and see the stars during the daytime.

According to the person who x-rayed the pyramids in 1967, there are still probably chambers that have not yet been discovered. All we know now, since the Middle East war has cut off exploration, is that the x-rays turned up some mysterious blobs on the film.

It is said that people have been known to descend into the King's Chamber, in the center of the pyramid, and disappear forever.

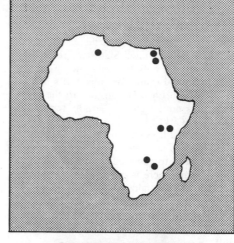

SEVEN WONDERS OF AFRICA

Mt. Kilimanjaro, the Roof of Africa
Legendary Mt. Kilimanjaro is the highest point in Africa. For the first three days on the ascent, you wind through flower-dotted alpine meadows, game reserves abounding with gazelles, leopard and monkeys, forest belts and boulder-strewn lava plains; finally you reach Kibo Hut at 16,000 feet.

Early on the fourth day, braced by a pot of brisk tea and some crackers, you scramble up the last 3,000 feet for your reward —sunrise streaking the snows of Kilimanjaro. The view sweeps away dramatically to lesser volcanic peaks, expansive plains and the fertile farmlands of the Chagga tribesmen. Looking into the volcanic cone of Kilimanjaro you see spectacular ice walls and bluish glaciers scraping the crater floor.

Ngorongoro Crater   Imagine a crater that would hold the city of San Francisco—and is filled with thousands of wild animals! That's Ngorongoro Crater in Tanzania, where patterns of black and white zebras make optical illusions and impalas hold early morning high-jump contests. Pink flamingos study their reflections in the alkaline lakes and the roars of lion, elephant, buffalo, rhino and leopard shatter the evening calm. Skitterish wildebeests scatter as you approach. You'll be astounded by the sheer bulk of the eland; at 2,000 pounds, this doe-skinned antelope somehow still manages to look elegant and graceful. You might see wild hunting dogs or black-backed jackals trotting through acacia forests in search of their favorite prey—gazelles.

Nearby is Olduvai Gorge, where the bones of earliest man were discovered, and 40 miles to the northwest is the great savannah of the Serengeti.

Great Zimbabwe, Early Bantu Ruins
The ruins of Great Zimbabwe are thought to have been the sanctuary, temple and fortress of the mysterious King of the Bantus. No white man ever looked upon these carved fish-eagles and strange elliptical temples while the great Bantu Kingdom flourished.

On top of a hill stands the acropolis, a complex of walls and platforms built to enclose a gold works. On the plain below is the mysterious double-focus tower, the function of which is unknown (though it is believed to have been a magic temple for fertility and rain-making ceremonies). The famous carved soapstone birds resembling African eagles were found here.

The Bantu ruins are near Fort Victoria, about 200 miles south of Salisbury, Rhodesia.

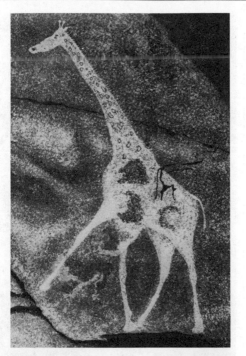

Tassili n'Ajjer People who live on the outskirts of the Sahara can tell you exactly where to find whole ancient cities, buried under centuries of sand and wind. At one time, they say, the desert was a fertile and lush land, the center of the earth.

This would sound less credible than a fairy tale if it weren't for the cave paintings at Tassili n'Ajjer. Protected from the wind by the strange mountains of the Hoggar, the paintings are clear evidence of a brilliant and rugged civilization some 10,000 years old.

Mad sorcerers singing lovely tunes;
Ancient pigments rhyming
More fluently than runes.

Victoria Falls The Zambesi River rips through the rain forest and suddenly, like a panther striking, ruptures and steams into a thundering cascade, a million gallons a second crashing over huge cliffs on the way to the Indian Ocean.

This is Victoria, the largest waterfall in the world. It makes Niagara look like a fast faucet. The first white man to see it was David Livingstone ("Dr. Livingstone, I presume!") and even in the heart of Zambia he thought to honor his queen.

—Christine Hoover and the Editors

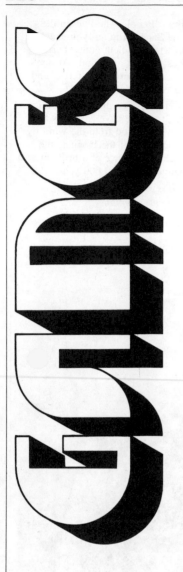

There are few things that are so unpardonably neglected in our country as poker. The upper class knows very little about it. Now and then you find ambassadors who have a sort of general knowledge of the game, but the ignorance of the people is fearful. Why, I have known clergymen, good men, kind-hearted, liberal, sincere, and all that, who did not know the meaning of a "flush." It is enough to make one ashamed of one's species.

—MARK TWAIN

Tennis, anyone?

—HUMPHREY BOGART

I'd break my bozzonga to beat that guy.

—BILLIE JEAN KING

Capablanca's [chess] play was like clear water; Alekhine's was like clear water with a drop of poison in it.

—G. KOLTANOWSKI

How to Keep Young

1. *Avoid fried meats which angry up the blood.*

2. *If your stomach disputes you, lie down and pacify it with cool thoughts.*

3. *Keep the juices flowing by jangling around gently as you move.*

4. *Go very light on the vices, such as carrying on in society. The social ramble ain't restful.*

5. *Avoid running at all times.*

6. *Don't look back. Something might be gaining on you.*

—LEROY "SATCHEL" PAIGE

Five Spontaneous Games

Spontaneous games require no game board, no complicated instruction booklet and no special apparatus. All you have to do to play them is decide to play them.

"The Dictionary Game" Best played with a group of four or more. The only apparatus needed is a dictionary, pencils and many small pieces of paper.

Someone leafs through the dictionary and finds an obscure word he thinks no one will know the meaning of. He asks, for example, if anyone knows the word *favus*, and spells it aloud. If someone does, he selects another word, but if no one knows, then *favus* is the chosen word.

Everyone writes a definition for *favus* on a piece of paper. The dictionary-holder writes the true definition ("A contagious skin disease caused by a fungus"); everyone else makes up a definition that sounds like it *might* be true (e.g., "Of high birth or exalted rank or station; aristocratic;" "Any of numerous flowering herbs of the genus *Favonia*;" or "The Roman god of safe travel").

The dictionary-holder collects all definitions, mixes the true one with them, then reads them all through once or twice. (He should read them through silently, first, in order not to stumble over strange words or bad handwriting.) Each player then votes for the definition he or she believes to be the true one. A player collects two points for guessing the correct definition, plus one point for every vote that is cast for his own, bogus definition. The dictionary-holder doesn't vote or collect points, of course, so after each round the dictionary passes to someone else.

Some people are good at writing plausible, fake definitions that suck everyone into voting for them. Other people rack up points by being able to pick out the real definition from the phony ones. Other people don't really care who wins and make up some of the worst puns and the most disgusting, corny definitions you ever heard.

"The Adverb Game" No apparatus required. Can be played with three or four persons, but the more the merrier.

One player leaves the room. The others then decide on an adverb (e.g., confidently, seductively, awkwardly, slowly, left-handedly, reluctantly, suspiciously, etc.).

The chosen player then comes back into the room and starts giving orders: "Bill, light a cigarette that way," "Sue, walk around the table that way," "Don, straighten your tie that way," "Sandy, go sit on Bill's lap that way," etc. Everyone gets to be a ham actor,

and the person who is "it" keeps giving directions and guessing adverbs until he gets the right one. Then someone else leaves the room.

Forget about keeping score—it just slows the game down. It's more fun to keep the action moving and not worry about it.

"Pushover" or, **"The Female Chauvinist Sow Game"** Only apparatus required is a matchbox. Kneel on the floor and set the matchbox on end one forearm's length in front of your knees. Hold your hands behind your back and lean forward slowly: try to knock the matchbox over with your nose without losing your balance.

Men usually find this difficult, whereas most women can do it easily, because of their lower center of gravity; hence, the game's subtitle. "Pushover" should be played in mixed groups, where it may reveal hidden insecurities in men who are threatened by the fact that they can be beaten by women in a physical task.

"Four-Letter Words" A game for two players. Each person writes down a four-letter word in which all letters are different. The object is to guess your opponent's word before he or she guesses yours.

The best way to explain the play is by example. Suppose the word you have chosen is *bear*, and your opponent's first guess is *blue* (all guesses must be four-letter words). There are two letters in *blue* that are also in *bear*, and one of them, the B, is in the same position in both words. So, in response to this guess, you would say "Two letters, one hit." If your opponent had guessed *rape*, your response would be, "Three letters, no hits." If the guess was *slim*, the answer would be "No letters." By eliminating and rearranging letters in subsequent guesses, one proceeds to narrow down the possibilities until the opponent's word is known. Keep a record of guesses, both yours and your opponent's, and the responses given to each.

One may guess words in which a letter appears twice, but this is generally a poor strategy, since the double letter counts as

only one in deciding on the response. For example, if *baby* were guessed when the true word was *bear*, the response would be "Two letters, one hit."

Once you master this game, try the more advanced version—"Five-Letter Words."

Killer Only apparatus required is a deck of cards. Select as many playing cards as there are persons in the room, and include the ace of spades among them. Deal out one card to each person—the one who gets the ace of spades is the "killer." His object is to "kill" the other players by winking at them, eye-to-eye, before anyone can guess that he is the culprit.

For those who don't draw the ace, the object is to guess who the killer is without getting killed themselves. That is, they must try to avoid direct eye-contact with any suspected killers, but at the same time keep an eye out for all suspicious behavior.

If a player is winked at, he's dead and can no longer guess. He lets everyone know he's been killed, either by simply saying so or, if he's dramatically inclined, by going into his big Hollywood death scene. He should do

this discreetly—not immediately after being winked at, but after a few seconds' pause, in order not to reveal who just killed him. At any time, anyone can ask, "How many people are dead so far?" and those who are dead must identify themselves.

If a player can catch the killer in the act of winking at someone else, or can deduce who the killer is from the pattern of deaths around the room, he announces his guess. If he's right, he wins the round; if not, he is killed. A person who is incorrectly guessed must reveal that he is not the killer, of course, but he is still in the game and can still guess. The game proceeds until the identity of the killer becomes known to everyone.

"Killer" isn't much of a game all by itself—it leads to a room full of people afraid to look at each other for fear of getting winked at. To eliminate such inhibition, "Killer" is never played by itself but is superimposed on another game or activity. You play it while playing "Adverbs" or "The Dictionary Game" or just while eating dinner.

—Scot Morris

Invent Your Own Games

I used to be good at chess, but it got too mechanical. I was always skulking around the corners of the board waiting for an opening, or calculating long and involved combinations where a bishop comes streaking in from nowhere to pin the rook, or generally working myself into a warlike dither when it seemed to be going a little rough. This last especially when I played with my wife.

So I invented myself a new game. Still chess, still the same rules. But with a different philosophy.

This was Peoples' Chess, Marxist Chess, Revolutionary Chess. In this game, based on my definite political ideas, a pawn was worth as much as the king, at least emotionally. I couldn't just go around sacrificing them willy-nilly. I had to consider their families.

I got into it even more. There's a certain kind of generalship that goes with revolutionary armies. For this reason, I always wanted to play Black—so I wouldn't fire the first shot. From that point on, I would try to conform as much as possible to the tenets of guerrilla warfare. I would establish friendly bases, pawns covering pieces, and nip out from there under cover of dark power: the queen, sitting proud and fiery, at Rook Four. I would never exchange a piece if I could help it—a guerrilla army doesn't have much ammunition, except what it can capture from its opponents. I tried to remember that everything the other side did was nothing but a sneaky fascist maneuver that had to be smashed.

This game went along fine, but my political ideas began to change. I got so I didn't really care that much about Marxist philosophy, and all armies seemed equally deadly. But I still liked chess, so I invented another version called Intuitive Chess.

In this game, winning or losing doesn't really count. What matters is that you make the move that *feels* right, without thinking about it too much. If your gut tells you the knight should go into mortal danger to redress the balance somehow, then that's where he goes. What counts is an artistically satisfying game, one where all the energies come out aesthetically balanced. Sometimes you lose and sometimes you win.

It's when you're a kid and games are super-important that you invent some of the best new games. I remember one rainy night, with my brother and sister, and we were bored stiff. All we had was a deck of cards, but the normal card games left a flat, cloying taste in our mouths. So I said:

"OK. Let's play Blaps!"

They looked a little puzzled. "How do you play?" my sister asked.

"Just play. You'll get the hang of it."

So I dealt. She got the Queen of Diamonds and two black fours. My brother got a nine, a six and a three. I got both one-eyed Jacks and the seven of diamonds.

"Regal clear. Two, seven," I said authoritatively, and swept their cards into a pile by me.

They looked at me a little funny, but didn't say anything. I dealt another round, this time one face down and two face up.

I had two eights up, and a ten down. My brother had a deuce and a three up, and my sister had a Queen and a five.

I looked things over, and turned up my ten. "Overscore," I said, and took all their cards except my brother's three.

"What do you call this game again?" my brother asked.

"Blaps," I said.

I dealt the third round, this time four cards face up. I looked at them and called, "Ten four finesse," and started to sweep up the cards again. But my sister held out her hand.

"Wait a minute! I've got the red queen on this one. That's a cull!" She started to sweep the table, but I stopped her.

"No, you can't cull on the third round. Blaps."

My brother chimed in. "Hold it. Both of you lose. I've got the weener!" He turned down his ten of hearts and took my sister's cards. I reached for his pile, but he took mine instead. I turned up the first card on the top of the deck and shouted:

"Oho, that's it! I've got picaroons, and that beats any weener!"

"Not on the third round, it doesn't!" my brother yelled.

"You've just started playing," I said cunningly. "You don't know all the rules yet!"

He picked up the deck and threw the first ten cards at me. My sister grabbed his pile and called "Blaps!" at the top of her lungs. I grabbed my brother by the arm and gave him a "visitor" in the pit. He picked up a pillow and threw it at me.

Just then, my father walked in.

"No pillows!" he boomed.

"Aw, Dad . . . we're just playing," we whined, and all burst out laughing.

—David Saltman

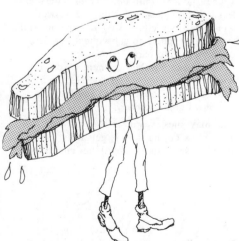

Descriptions Game

"Paul? Well, he's tall, kinda thin, not as loose as he could be, a little cool sometimes—he's nice, but not very exciting."

Do you ever get tired of describing people—or for that matter, looking at people—in the same old way? Try this on:

"Paul? I see him as a peanut butter and grape-jelly sandwich on plain white bread. He's a black 1960 Lincoln Continental with air conditioning and the windows are rolled up. He's an Eisenhower jacket, buttoned almost to the top, no medals on the front and it's starched."

You get the idea. You start looking at people differently, you start describing them in terms different from the ones you're used to. It stretches your imagination, gives you insights into others and yourself and, if you choose to share your descriptions, can get you into some damned interesting conversations.

I've used this idea as a structured exercise in creative writing and human relations classes and every once in awhile it pops up in conversation with good friends. You might try it like this, as a game with friends: sit across the room from the person you are about to describe. Sit close enough to feel his or her presence, but far enough away so you can see all of his or her body easily.

Think of the person as, say, a sea creature. Appearance is an easy start, but you may want to go deeper than that and try to describe something about that person's personality or way of relating to people.

Write down your description. Be as uninhibited as you can be in describing the person and add as many details as you can. If you're using an article of clothing, for instance, don't just say a sweater. Say something like: "You're a bright red, V-neck, loose fitting sweater with the sleeves rolled up a bit."

It works best for members of a group to circulate, describing—in writing—different people, until everyone has been described by everyone else at least once. (It's most interesting if you decide to describe one person as, say, a bird, the next as a plant, the next as a color, etc.) Then group members may volunteer, one at a time, to hear all of their descriptions read to them.

The people describing really have to look at and see the person they're trying to describe. The people described end up with some valuable feedback about themselves and how other members of the group see them relating.

I've described people as land animals, fish or sea creatures, birds, cars, articles of clothing, foods, plants, states of the union and countries, colors, famous personalities and publications. And *you* can think up your own unique people-slots.

—John Wood

Combative Games for Backyard Gladiators

If you're getting a little bored with the vicarious thrill of television fist fights, and arm-wrestling just doesn't seem to give ample expression to your pent-up and smoldering lust for violence, here are a few variations on the one-on-one combative contest that are guaranteed to work off a lot of excess energy, satisfy those basic killer instincts and prove once and for all which of you is the better man (or woman).

As with the old Roman gladiator fights, these are enjoyable spectator events, so invite your friends. After all, everyone likes to watch somebody else get beaten.

The Leg Pull Contestants stand on one foot, facing away from each other, three feet apart. They are tied together by a rope that is attached to the ankles of their uplifted feet. Ten feet in front of each of them is an object (say, a ball). At the signal, each tries to hop on one foot to the object and pick it up without touching the tied foot to the ground. The one who gets his object first is the winner. While a good sense of balance is helpful here, the greatest asset, as with so many things in this world, is brute strength.

Torso Wrestling Opponents sit on the ground, back to back, with their legs spread wide and their arms interlocked at the elbows. The object is to lean to the left far enough to pull the opponent over so that his right arm or hand touches the ground. Add incentive by putting a sprig of poison ivy on the ground on each side.

Snail Tug-O-War Draw a line on the ground. Opponents stand on opposite sides, back to back. Each bends down and puts his right hand back between his legs and grasps the other's right hand. The one who is pulled completely across the line loses. All manner of grunts and groans acceptable, but no blasphemy, please.

Cumberland Wrestling Contestants stand face to face with chests touching. Each puts his right arm over the opponent's left shoulder and clasps his hands behind the opponent's back. At the signal, the object is to lift the opponent off the ground. This one is a cinch for those who are used to pulling themselves up by their bootstraps. Variation: instead of trying to lift the opponent, try to get around behind him with your arms still circling him.

Leg Lift The contestants sit on chairs facing each other with their arms folded. Each contestant places one leg over and the other leg under the legs of his opponent. Each tries to lift the opponent's leg that is over his own, without letting the opponent do the same to him. With a little imagination, this one could put both of you in the hospital with hernias.

Handicapped Pillow Fight Contestants stand inside automobile tires, three feet apart. They are blindfolded and each has a pillow. At the signal, each tries to knock the other out of the tire. This one is an espe-

cially fine spectator amusement.

Stick Fight Each contestant holds the opposite end of a four-foot broomstick. On the ground between them is a handkerchief. At the signal, each tries to pick up the handkerchief without releasing the end of the stick. Whoever gets it, wins.

Back-to-Back Lift Contestants stand back to back with arms interlocked at the elbows. At the signal, each tries to lift the other off the ground.

Butting Match Contestants stand about five feet apart facing each other with their ankles tied together and their arms folded over their chests. At the signal, each attempts to knock his opponent to the ground. For greater spectator interest, this one should be done in a cow pasture.

Palm Push Contestants stand facing each other toe to toe and chest to chest. Each raises his hands and places them against the palms of the opponent at shoulder level. At the signal, each pushes and attempts to make the other step back. If opponents are not equally matched, this one may be done on the edge of a swimming pool, sulfur pit or tall building to even the betting odds.

Toe Wrestling Contestants sit on the ground facing each other with both arms wrapped around their own knees and their toes touching the opponent's toes. At the signal, each attempts to get his toes underneath his opponent's toes and roll him over backwards. Tennis shoes are better than street shoes for this, but for best results do it barefoot, as the toenails are good for gouging and causing the opponent to scream as he goes over. This gives a more pleasing sense of victory.

Hog Tying Contestants face each other at a distance of about six feet. Each has a piece of rope four feet long. At the signal, each tries to tie the other's feet together. Winner is disqualified if opponent sustains any broken bones or loses either of his feet due to lack of circulation when the rope is too tight. Variation: tie the rope to any other part of the opponent's body.

Abbreviated Donnybrook Opponents, having failed to dispose of each other in all previous contests, now get *mad*. Each picks up whatever he can find that might serve as a weapon—preferably something heavy with sharp edges. All spectators are obliged here to join in the action or run for cover. At the signal, everybody begins to punch, kick, bite, scratch, pummel, pinch, gouge, mash, stomp and so forth, until one or all opponents are dead or say "uncle." Anyone remaining after this goes inside and turns on "Mission Impossible."

–Dirk Kortz

Macramé a Playground for Your Kids

You can't *buy* a macramé playground for your kids yet—but you can make one by following the example of artist Alexandra Jacopetti. She and her friends built one for the town of Bolinas, Calif., an artist's community an hour's drive north of San Francisco.

The playground, 12,500 feet of Dacron sailmaker's rope ($670 worth) tied in square knots and double half-hitches, is kept tight by turnbuckles and strung from a 12-foot-square eucalyptus wood frame. The supports are sunk into cement pits; a sand pit lies beneath the "trampoline" section.

Not only is the macramé structure safer than the usual steel playground equipment, it is a fluid medium to which the *children* can give form. A swing, a trampoline, a cave, a house, a gigantic spider—it can be anything kids want it to be.

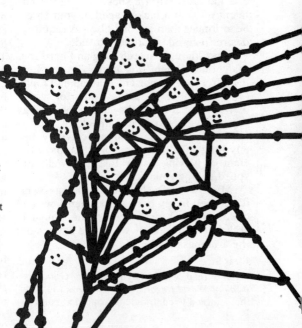

How to Set a World Record

By William Allen

You haven't really lived until you've set a world record. Here's how to do it, from the man who set the world's record for domestic broom balancing.

Absolutely anyone can set a world record. The key to doing something better, longer, faster or in larger quantity than anyone else is *desire*. Desire fostered by proper attitude.

Before I set my world record, I was a great fan of *The Guinness Book of World Records* and read each new edition from cover to cover. I liked knowing and being able to tell others that the world's chug-a-lug champ consumed 2.58 pints of beer in 10 seconds, that the world's lightest adult person weighed only 13 pounds, that the largest vocabulary for a talking bird was 531 words, spoken by a brown-beaked budgerigar named Sparky. There is, of course, only a fine line between admiration and envy, and for awhile I had been secretly desiring to be in that book myself —to astonish others just as I had been astonished. But it seemed hopeless. How could a nervous college sophomore, an anonymous bookworm, perform any of those wonderful feats? The open-throat technique necessary for chug-a-lugging was incomprehensible to my trachea— and I thought my head alone must weigh close to 13 pounds.

One day I realized what was wrong. Why should I want to *break* a record at all? Why not blaze a trail of my own? Now, as you can see, I definitely had desire, but more than that I discovered I had talent. This is where we may differ. You may have no talent at all. If not, you can still go on to set a world record that will be well worth setting. It requires no talent to wear a sock longer than anyone else has ever worn a sock. It requires no talent to wear a nickel taped to your forehead longer than anyone else—it requires desire fostered by proper attitude.

First, though, search long and hard for that hidden talent you may possess. Let me offer one important guideline. Don't follow the beaten path. Look for your own personal gift, the little something that you've always had a knack for, a certain way with. It could conceivably be anything at all—sewing on buttons efficiently, waxing a car fast yet well, or speed-rolling your hair.

My own gift—broom-balancing—was developed in my back yard when I was a child. When I remembered the unusual ability, I immediately wrote the editors of the Guinness book in London.

Dear Sirs:

I have read with enjoyment *The Guinness Book of World Records* and want you to know that I intend to contribute to your next edition.

Thinking back today, I recalled that as a child I had an uncanny talent for balancing a common house broom on the end of my forefinger. Rushing to the kitchen, I found that I have retained this gift over the years. Since almost everyone must have at some time attempted this feat, I think it would be an appropriate addition to your book.

I would like to know exactly what must be done to establish a world record—how many witnesses, what sort of timing device, etc. If you will provide me with this information, I will provide you with a broom-balancing record that should astonish your readers and last for years to come.

Sincerely,
William Allen

The reply came the next week.

Dear Mr. Allen:

In order to establish a world record of broom-balancing, we would like to have the confirmation of a newspaper report and an affidavit from one or more witnesses. With regard to the timing device, I think that a good wrist watch with a second hand would prove sufficient for this purpose.

Please let us know the duration of your best effort.

Sincerely,
Andrew Thomas
Assistant Editor

It sounds simple, but a lot of preparation must go into setting a world record. You can't just set it. You must advertise, generate public interest. The purpose of this is to lure in the news media. It's absolutely necessary to have a write-up if your record is going to stick. And, of course, you will want the article for your scrapbook later on. Imagine what would happen if you just went into the bathroom and brushed your teeth for eight hours and then called the newspapers. They would think you were crazy. But if you generated interest beforehand— involved a local drugstore chain, got a name-brand toothpaste to sponsor you— then you wouldn't be crazy at all. You might even come to be something of an authority and make a career out of promoting things to do with teeth.

I took a slightly different tack. I ran an ad in the college newspaper which read, in part: "FREE BEER! FREE BEER! Come one, come all, to Bill Allen's Broom-Balancing Beer Bust! Yes, friends, Bill will attempt to balance a common house broom on his forefinger for at least one hour to establish a world record. The editors of *The Guinness Book of World Records* in London are anxiously awaiting the outcome. The

evening will be covered by the press. Ties will not be necessary. Come one, come all, to this historic event!"

May I suggest you find yourself a good manager before you try to set your record. My roommate, Charlie, was mine and he proved to be invaluable. On the big night, he drew with chalk a small circle on the living room floor so I would have a place to stand. He cunningly scattered copies of the Guinness book on the coffee table. He had the good sense to make me wear a coat and tie: "You don't want to go down in history looking like a bum, do you? Of course not. You want to make a good impression."

The ad in the paper paid off, naturally. Over 50 people showed up, filling our apartment and spilling out onto the lawn. Some left after their two-beer limit, but most remained to see the outcome. There

was some problem, though, in holding the group's interest. For the first 10 minutes or so, they were fine, placing bets, commenting on my technique. After that, their minds tended to stray. They began to talk of other matters. One couple had the nerve to ask if they could put music on and dance in the kitchen.

Charlie handled the situation like a professional. He began to narrate the event, serving as a combination sportscaster and master of ceremonies. "Ladies and gentlemen, give me your attention please. We are at mark 15 minutes. At this time, I would like you to look at Bill's feet. You will notice that they are not moving. This is an indication of his skill. If you've ever tried broom-balancing yourself, you know that the tendency is to run around the room in an effort to maintain stability."

Someone said, "He's right. I tried it today and that's exactly what you do."

At the 20-minute mark, Charlie said, "Ladies and gentlemen, I have an announcement. Bill's previous top practice time was 20 minutes. He has just beaten his own record! Anything can happen from here on in, folks. Pay attention."

You might be wondering about my emotions at this point. I hadn't slept well the night before, and all day I had been a nervous wreck. I hadn't been able to eat. I had a horrible sinking feeling every time I thought about what was coming up. But once I started, I found I wasn't nervous at all. Not a trace of stage fright. In fact, I blossomed under the attention. I realized this was where I had belonged all along — in the center. Someone began to strum a guitar and I foolishly began to bob my broom in time to the music. "Don't get cocky," my manager warned. "You've got a long way to go yet."

At mark 30 minutes, Charlie held up his hands for silence. "Listen to this, folks! The halfway point has been passed! We're halfway to history! And I want you people to know that Bill is feeling good! He's not even sweating! I swear I don't understand how he does it. How many people can even stand in one place that long?"

I had no clear idea who was in the room, or what they were doing. In order to balance a broom, you have to stare right at the straw. I'm not sure why this is, but it's certainly the case. You can't look away for even a second. By using peripheral vision, I was able to see a vague sea of heads but it wasn't worth the effort and I gave up. While in this awkward position, I heard the low, sinister voice of a stranger address me: "You know everybody here thinks you're crazy, don't you? I think I'll just step on your feet and see how you like that. You couldn't do anything about it. You wouldn't even know who did it because you can't look down."

"Charlie!" I called. "Come here!"

My manager had the situation under control in seconds. After he had hustled the character out the door, he said, "Don't worry, folks. Just a heckler. One in every crowd, I guess."

I must say that Charlie's earlier remark that I was in good shape was a lie — and I was feeling worse by the second. At mark 45 minutes, my neck seemed to have become locked in its upward arch. My legs were trembling and the smaller toes on each foot were without feeling. My forefinger felt like it was supporting a length of lead pipe. But more startling, I think, was the strain on my mind. I felt giddy. Strange that I have this gift, I reflected. I can't even walk around the block without occasionally wobbling off to one side. It suddenly seemed as though all the balance normally spread throughout the human body had somehow converged in my forefinger. Wouldn't it be ironic, I thought dizzily, if I just toppled over? I sniggered, seeing myself flat on my back with the broom still perfectly poised on my finger. Then I began to observe the broomstraw in incredible detail. Each stick seemed huge, like trees . . . logs . . . telephone poles. . . .

"Are you okay?" Charlie asked. I snapped out of it and reported my condition. He turned to the crowd. "Folks! With only ten minutes to go, I would like us to reflect on the enormous physical and mental strain Bill is suffering right before our eyes. It's the price all champions pay, of course, when they go the distance, when they stretch the fibers of their being to the breaking point." His voice became lower, gruffer. "You may as well know. Bill has been hallucinating for some time now. But think of it, folks. While all over this country of ours, people are destroying their minds with dangerous drugs, Bill here is achieving the ends they seek —" his voice rose; he cried, "— with *no chance* of dangerous after-effects!"

Even in my condition, I knew he was going too far. I called him over to loosen my shoelaces and whispered, "Cut the speeches, okay? Just let them watch for awhile."

The hour mark came amazingly fast after that. There was a loud 10-second countdown, then the press's flashbulbs and strobes began going off like starbursts. Everybody began clapping and cheering. Using my peripherial vision, I saw that the crowd was on its feet, jumping around. I saw the happy, grinning faces.

I kept balancing. Charlie conferred with me, then yelled, "Folks! Bill is not going to stop! He says he will balance till he drops! Isn't he something? Take your seats, ladies and gentlemen. You're witnessing history tonight. Relax and enjoy it." The group was for seeing me drop, all right, but they didn't want to wait around all night for it. They became louder and harder to handle. They wanted more beer. At mark one hour, 15 minutes, I was on the verge of collapse anyway, so I gave in and tossed the broom in the air. With a feeble flourish, I caught it with the other hand and the record was set.

But no world record is *truly* set until someone has tried and failed to break it. After the congratulations, the interviews, the signing up of witnesses, it was time for everybody else to try. They didn't have a chance, of course. Most lasted only a pitiful few seconds, and the two best times were seven and 10 minutes. These two had talent but lacked the rest of the magic combination.

My record never appeared in *The Guinness Book of World Records*. I'm not sure why. Maybe they thought I should have gone longer. Maybe the plane carrying the news went down in the Atlantic. At any rate, they never wrote back and I never bothered to check on it. I knew by then that it didn't matter. The record had still been set. I had the write-up — and this alone brought me all the acclaim I could handle.

You, too, can enjoy the same success. And don't worry if you don't have a talent such as mine. There is a man in Iowa who collects dirty oil rags. He has over a thousand so far — more than anyone else in the world. He's not in the Guinness book, either, but people still stop by almost daily to see his collection and ask his opinion about this or that. His picture often appears in the local papers.

All it takes is desire fostered by proper attitude. □

10 World Records Waiting to Be Set

1. How many pennies can you fit in your mouth?
2. How far can you throw an ostrich feather, standing at ground level with zero wind velocity?
3. How much weight can you gain in one week?
4. How many beers can you pour in before they begin to pour out?
5. How long can you look at yourself in the mirror, with eyelids taped open to avoid blinking?
6. How many pairs of black and navy blue socks can you mate in one hour under an artificial light?
7. How many milkweed seeds can you pile up on a plate 10 inches in diameter?
8. How long can you carry a brick?
9. How many *New York Times*es can you eat at one sitting?
10. How many world record possibilities can you think of in 10 minutes?

The "Crawdaddy 300"

Some people—like the gourmets of Louisiana—enjoy eating crawfish about as much as other folks enjoy eating truffles or snails. The crawfish, varying in length from two to six inches, are pureed into an exquisite bisque.

But the folks over in South Carolina, down Greenville County way, are making sport with crawfish. Come each June, there's the annual running of the "Crawdad 300."

Now if you want to race your favorite crawdaddy in the "300," you ought to be aware of the three classes. The "Runt" class is for crustaceans two to three inches long, while the "Jumbo" class racers are three to four inches in length. Of course, there's also the "Colossal" class, in which entrants tape in at five inches and above, and can actually be considered baby lobsters.

The crusty little things race in dry heats of four. (They call it a "dry" heat because that's what makes the crawfish run: they're whipping their claws to get back into the water.)

The annual race has drawn entries from the governors of South Carolina, Louisiana, Virginia and Delaware, and if you want to compete, 'long about June, drop a note to the Greenville branch of the Amateur Athletic Union, Greenville, S.C.

Six of the Most Dangerous Things You Can Do

1. Disguise yourself as a Moslem and try to go to Mecca. It has been done two or three times successfully. But the penalty for discovery is death. Consult Sir Richard Burton's *Travels in Medina and Mecca.*

2. Cheat in a card game with The Godfather.

3. Tell the chief of the Ibans his daughter is pretty (or, on the other hand, tell him she's *not* pretty). This has been done by two or three who have lived to tell about it. The Ibans are in Borneo, and they are still headhunters—though usually friendly.

4. Walk a tightrope over Niagara Falls. The Great Blondin did this and maybe you can, too.

5. Travel alone in Rub al-Khali. That's "The Empty Quarter" of the Saudi Arabian desert, where no infidel and few Moslems are permitted.

6. Hunt Turkestan tigers. There are guides who will take you out there, but no guarantees they'll stick around when *tigris altaica* catches your scent.

A Trivialist's Bookshelf

If the purpose of the trivialist's bookshelf is not only to settle any argument, however obscure, but also to one-up opponents with your dazzling knowledge of the arcane, an absolutely indispensible study is Gertrude Jobes's huge *Dictionary of Mythology Folklore and Symbols* (Scarecrow Press). Scouring the literature and folk histories of virtually all of the world's cultures, past and present, Jobes has packed some 20,000 fact-filled entries into more than 1,800 pages. Norse, Greek and Roman deities are exhaustively covered, each with a genealogy that would do credit to *Genesis*; there is also plenty of information on the gods of the American Indians, the Celts, the Slavs, the Finn-Ugrics, the Mayans, the Ceylonese, the Sea Dayaks of Borneo and many, many others.

Every page is studded with gems. Practically everybody knows, for instance, that Nepenthe is the river of forgetfulness; how many are aware that the river of remembering is Anamnesis? Or that *kaffir*, an epithet used by some South African whites for Bantus, was originally an Arabic term of contempt for those who reject Islam? Or that the Finnish name for Cinderella (who, incidentally, appears in many folk histories) is the rather unmelodious Tuna? Or that Min is the Egyptian god of procreation, a sort of Nilotic Pan who is often portrayed with a ram's head? Or that the exotically named Vukub-Gakix is a Kiche Indian giant who causes day to dawn by stealing the moon and hiding it in his underground cave, then brings on nightfall by yielding up the moon and stealing the sun? Jobes also provides the origin and meaning of virtually every given name. Richard, for example, was a Germanic name later adopted by the Norman French and means, among other things, "stern ruler."

For straight Greek mythology, probably the best work from both a scholarly and artistic viewpoint is Robert Graves's two-volume study, *The Greek Myths* (published by George Braziller). Graves, a poet, writes with gusto, erudition and obvious relish about the wayward ways of Cronos, Rhea, Zeus and the rest of that unruly crowd.

If your preoccupation is the obscure origins of words, a difficult but useful addition to the bookshelf is the *Concise Etymological Dictionary of the English Language* by the Rev. Walter W. Skeat (Oxford University Press). Skeat tells us, for example, that "great" comes from the Anglo Saxon and appears in Middle English as *gret* or *greet* before assuming its modern form. "Escape" comes from French via the Latin *ex cappa*, meaning "out of one's cape." And "trivia" also comes from French via the Latin *trivia*, meaning "a place where three roads meet," hence common, something that can be picked up anywhere.

For foreign words, there's C. O. Sylvester Mawson's *Dictionary of Foreign Terms* (Bantam Books), which offers more than 15,000 key phrases, proverbs, mottos, menu terms and the like in 50 languages, including Eskimo, Icelandic and Sanskrit. It begins with the French *à bas!* or "down with . . ." and ends, fittingly, with a phrase from Goethe, *zwischen uns sei Wahrheit*, or "let truth be between us."

The political buff will find William Safire's *The New Dictionary of Politics* (Collier Books) useful in tracing the origin and development of terms old and new. It begins with "abominable no-man," the sobriquet pinned on Sherman Adams, who was Dwight Eisenhower's H. R. Haldeman, and ends with "zinger," a barb or telling punch line in a speech.

Of course, no true trivialist would be without the *Guinness Book of World Records* by Norris and Ross McWhirter (Sterling Publishing Co.), which is chock full of totally nonessential information. Such as: most children born to one woman is 69; they were produced by one Mme. Fyodor Vassilet, who turned out 16 pairs of twins, seven sets of triplets and four sets of quadruplets in 19th-century Russia; largest crossword, 3,185 clues across and 3,149 down, published in 1949 but as far as is known never completely worked out by anybody; greatest welfare swindle, perpetrated in France by Anthony Moreno who, by forging birth certificates and school registration forms for 3,000 nonexistent children, collected an estimated $6,440,000 in eight years before fleeing in 1968 to Spain, where he now is reputed to be living quite comfortably, thank you.

–Ronald P. Kriss

Playing "Fox and Geese"

Out there where the sweet grass grows steep as a horse's face they like to play this little game while they're waiting for the mill to grind up their corn.

It's called "Fox and Geese," and traditionally you use 22 kernels of white corn and two pieces of red. The whites represent the Geese, and the reds are the Foxes. You play on a patterned board or piece of paper, and the set-up is like this:

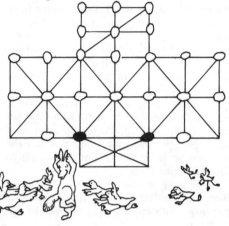

The foxes can capture geese by jumping them, as in checkers. The geese can't capture a fox, but they can try to surround him so he can't move anywhere. A fox always moves first.

One fox can go onto an intersection or corner that the other fox is occupying; the geese can't do this, and they can't jump either. The object of the game is to try to corner the foxes so they can't go anywhere. It's challenging.

Riddles

Riddles are little dramas that prove that the laws of grammar are not the laws of the universe. From premise to premise to more-than-obvious conclusion, they are invaluable in developing insight, intuition and insanity. Riddles form the basis for children's games, jokes, detective stories and medieval epics. By logically testing the resources of the mind, they force you into another dimension, another plane of thinking.

The answers to the following riddles appear below, upside down.

1. What's the difference between a jeweler and a jailer?

2. Why does a mirror reverse left-to-right instead of top-to-bottom? (A riddle of science.)

2. Simply because of bad syntax.
1. One sells watches, the other watches cells.
Answers

"Pong" Without a Ping

"Pong" is one of those games that can tear you off your daily track, make you forget that job interview and get you scrabbling in your jeans for a quarter before you know what's happened.

It sits there in bus stations, bars and hangouts like a proper sophisticate, definitely a cut above those sleazy space lasers and rhino hunts. "Pong" is a computer screen inside a gunmetal grey box with knobs on either side and a yawning hole begging for a quarter in return for 10 minutes of nirvana. No mind.

Just whirl that knob. A computer-generated light paddle follows your instructions, and bats a little square blip that's as ornery as a universe back and forth.

The rules are essentially the rules of tennis and Ping-Pong. (But some models only go up to 15 points, instead of 21.) The strategy is essentially the same, too, except that you have to take the computer into account along with your opponent's weaknesses.

For instance, the serves. They are done for you—you can't do much about them except control where they go. And you have to figure out the vagaries of each machine you play on. In general, the nature of the serve depends on where you put your paddle during the delay between the last point and the new service. (Incidentally, in "Pong" the service goes to the winner of each point, rather than changing every five points as in Ping-Pong.)

The corners of the "court" are crucial—most amateurs (well, of course, I don't consider myself a *professional*, but . . .) can't return a good hard shot to the corner.

If you get it just right, you can also put considerable spin on that blasted "Pong" blip, enough to cause your opponent to actually "hit it into the net."

"Pong" was invented by Nolen K. Bushnell, a man who had it in his cards to become a millionaire. His company, Atari, Inc. of Los Gatos, Calif., can't turn the machines out fast enough. Competitors have sprung up all over.

The point is, you see, that a good "Pong" machine can make more than $250 a week.

—David Saltman

CIVIC PRIDE

The World Capital of Rope Jumping

When Wally Mohrman came to teach physical education in the schools of Bloomer, Wis. back in 1960, he found a pleasant town of 3,000 that nobody had ever heard of. He set about to put it and his pupils on the map by making Bloomer the Rope Jumping Capital of the World. Now on the last Saturday of every January nearly 2,000 spectators crowd the junior high school gym to watch Bloomer contestants, who are the fastest jumpers in the world, twirl their ropes at speeds reaching 70 m.p.h. and skip 40 to 50 skips in 10 seconds.

World's record holder is LuAnn Stolt, 13, who made 57 jumps in 10 seconds in 1972. The sight of her rope spinning is a blur. Two boys have set a male record of 50 jumps in 10 seconds; Mohrman's assistant, Phyllis Hawkins, explains diplomatically: "It's probably because girls mature earlier." Only plain hemp ropes, knotted at each end and about nine feet in length, qualify for the finals. Says Mohrman: "We don't want some kid whose father might have money coming around with one of those twenty-dollar ropes with ball-bearing swivels that boxers use."

An aura of show biz has begun to color the contest in recent years, so that, besides the speed tests, spectators are treated to a sort of floor show put on by the Swinging Safari Girls, 60 girls in pretty costumes dancing to music and moving in skipping drills, jumping madly away the while, their ropes whizzing. A select platoon called the Black-Lites also appears, their hands and ropes glowing in ultraviolet light while the rest of their bodies remain invisible.

Mohrman believes ultimate jumping speeds have yet to be reached. "There has to be a physical limit," he says, "but it's kind of like the four-minute mile or the fourteen-foot pole vault. Once those barriers are broken, the record keeps getting better. We do know that, as of now, nobody can beat our kids. We'll just keep jumping." Mohrman's ambition is to make rope jumping an Olympic event.

—Roy Bongartz

REALLY CHEAP THRILLS!
AT HOME

By Scot Morris

The Zilch

A zilch is the world's cheapest light and sound show. All you need is one of those plastic dry-cleaning bags that come back with your shirts.

Twist the bag along its full length into a tight rope. While holding both ends, run the rope slowly back and forth over a candle flame. The plastic will stick to itself and will not come undone.

Now tie a short length of string to one end of the zilch, and tape the string to the ceiling in the center of the room.

Next get a frying pan, fill it with water, and put it on the floor directly under the zilch.

Light the bottom of the zilch with a match. The plastic will burn slowly, with a low flame and surprisingly little smoke. Flaming drops of plastic will bombard the water below.

The zilch (I've also heard it called a flaming groovy) is a light and sound show, so get the room as dark and quiet as possible. Listen to the eerie noise of flaming plastic as it whistles through the air, and dig the string-of-pearls effect as the dripping plastic passes your eyes. Look at the pulsating shadow the zilch casts on the ceiling.

Variation: instead of running the twisted laundry bag through a candle flame, form the zilch by tying knots in the bag every two or three inches. The knotted zilch is easier to construct, but it often goes out and must be relit after a flaming knot splashes spectacularly into the water.

The show will last five to 10 minutes. Be sure to cut the string (or snuff the zilch with a wet cloth) before the flame gets high enough to burn the ceiling.

A Homemade Strobe Light

Unscrew the protective frame and the blades from an electric fan.

Cut a circle, one to two feet in diameter, from a large sheet of stiff cardboard.

Make a hole in the disc three to five inches in diameter, somewhere near the outer rim.

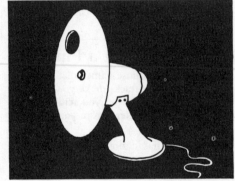

Poke a hole in the exact center of the cardboard circle and attach it with nuts and washers to the center spindle of the fan.

Stand the construction in a corner of the room, and place a bright table lamp close behind it, so that the light shines into the room only when the hole is directly in front of it.

When you turn on the fan and the light, the room will become a pulsating, vibrating experience, and your staccato movements will look like scenes from an old-time movie.

Variation: add a rheostat to the fan's wire, and you will be able to control the rate of the strobe pulse.

Kinetophonic Sound

Find two hi-fi speakers small enough to be held comfortably, one in each hand. The speakers inside portable stereos are ideal.

Have a friend lie down while you put on some quiet, rhythmic music. Turn off the lights and say, "Close your eyes."

Holding one speaker in each hand, kneel close to your friend and move the speakers in time to the music. Wave them, swing them, roll them, bring them close to your friend's ears and then far away. Your friend will probably smile and say, "Oh, wow!"

It is possible to use one monaural speaker. This reduces the experienced depth of the music, but with just one hand you can concentrate on more elaborate, intricate movements.

You will want to have someone wave the speakers while *you* listen, but half the fun of the experience is being the tour director for someone else's trip.

The Toilet Paper Torch
(or: Don't Touch the Charmin)

Save the cardboard center from a roll of toilet paper.

Light one end all around the rim, and stand the roll on a table.

When you turn out the rest of the lights in the room, you can watch a lovely blue flame that burns all around the cylinder for several minutes.

If the roll rests on a flat table there will be very little smoke—it will all stay in the cylinder. Use a piece of paper to protect your table from contact with the smoke.

If you stand the roll in a curved ashtray or dish, a little air will be sucked into the bottom of the roll, producing a column of smoke which, when the ventilation is right, may come in rhythmic puffs or perfectly formed smoke-rings.

With some brands of toilet rolls you can blow out the flame and watch the circle of glowing cardboard slowly consume the rest of the roll.

Put it out before it burns your table.

Chinese Hanger

Cut a piece of strong thread about five feet long, and tie the ends to the two corners of a metal coat hanger.

Stand up, lean over and loop the string over your head so that the hanger is suspended upside-down in front of you and the thread hangs near your ears on each side.

With the tips of your index fingers, push the thread into your ears.

Get someone to tap the hanger with a fork.

Gonnnnnnnnggggggg. Gonnnnnnnnggggggg.

It sounds like Big Ben.

Variations: try to shorten or lengthen the amount of string between your ears and the hanger. Try waxing the string. Try using a grill from the charcoal stove or broiler instead of a hanger.

Then let your friend listen while *you* bang the fork.

The Light Box

Get a deep box or wastebasket with a top opening seven to 10 inches across, and a string of eight multi-colored Christmas tree lights. Use the bulbs that blink on and off independently of each other.

Cut a small hole in the bottom of the box. Place the lights in the box and feed the plug out the small hole.

Now salvage a shirt cardboard large enough to cover the top of the box. Cut a small star, a circle and a triangle in it. Plug the lights into an extension cord and place the box in the center of the room.

When you turn off the room lights, your ceiling will be a kaleidoscopic canvas with eight stars, eight circles and eight triangles—all in different colors and all blinking on and off at different times.

You can make a more advanced light box if you find boxes just the right size. Mount the lights through eight holes in the bottom of a shallow box which is just small enough to fit inside a large, deep box. This keeps the lights pointed up and equally spaced. And since the little box can be moved up and down in the big box, you can adjust the distance between the lights and the holes in the shirt cardboard.

With the shirt cardboard over the shallow box alone, the whole ceiling will be covered with images, but they will be fuzzy and indistinct. When you place the lights at the bottom of the deep box, the images on the ceiling will be small, but they will be sharp and clear.

By poking a hole in the side of the small box, and several holes up the side of the large box, you can hold the small box and the lights at any height by sticking a pencil through both boxes.

Variation: fill the shirt cardboard with pin-holes or unusual shapes. Put loose-knit fabric over the box or use a "Pie in the Sky," described below. Or take the cardboard away and make multicolored hand-shadows.

Burning a Ping-Pong Ball

Try it. Just try it.

Cornstarch

Grandmother used cornstarch to make puddings and pies and to thicken gravy. Perhaps that was because she dug playing with the cornstarch itself. You can still buy it at groceries for about 25 cents a box.

Dissolve ½ cup of cornstarch in about ¼ cup of water. Pour a puddle out onto a waterproof table or kitchen counter.

Stick your fingers in it. Play with it. Roll up your sleeves and get into it. The concoction has a curious consistency somewhere between water and silly putty.

Sometimes the puddle acts like a liquid —if you move your fingers slowly through it, it will act like thick cream. But if you sweep your fingers quickly across the cornstarch, it acts more like a solid—your fingers skip across the top surface of the puddle, leaving it apparently undisturbed.

Put your hand on top of the puddle and move it around as if you were rolling a ball of clay. You will feel a very solid ball forming under your fingers. But as soon as you lift your hand, the ball is gone.

Try to pick up a handful of the stuff and roll it between your hands. A nice, solid ball of cornstarch will take shape between your palms—you can feel it and see it. But as soon as you stop rolling the stuff it turns back into liquid and drips through your fingers.

The correct proportion of cornstarch and water is critical. If you have too much cornstarch, it will become dry and flaky—just add more water. If you have too much water the mixture will be insufficiently viscous and will act like ordinary liquid. Either add more cornstarch or just play with the guck for a while until some of the water evaporates.

Pie in the Sky

Get a glass pie plate big enough to fit over the shade on a table lamp. Set the lamp on the floor in the center of the room. Put the pie plate on top, and pour in enough water to fill the pan ¼ inch deep.

Turn out all the lights, plug the lamp in, and enjoy the liquid patterns on the ceiling.

Tap the plate or lamp with your finger.

Try tapping the lamp with your foot in time to music.

Try adding food coloring to the water. Or color some salad oil and add that to the water.

Add a goldfish to the water.

Or, put the pie plate on top of the "Light Box" described earlier.

When you decide to quit, unplug the lamp before you take the plate off.

Sky Pictures

A friend has suggested a variation on the usual slide show. Set a flat shaving mirror in front of the projector so that the images are reflected up to the ceiling. Your friends can lie down to watch the show.

And if you have a remote-control slide-changer, you might even enjoy the show yourself.

Foilavision

Get a piece of aluminum foil (or tape two pieces together) about the size of your TV screen. Poke a couple of dozen holes in the foil with a pencil.

Tape the foil lightly over the TV screen. Turn off the TV sound and all other lights in the room.

Now sit back and watch the designs that appear in the little holes. Try to figure out what the full picture on the screen would look like.

Foilavision works best on a color set, and is especially fun with commercials, news programs and shows with lots of action.

Unidentified Flying Laundry Bag

Save one of those plastic dry-cleaning bags, the kind that you used for making a zilch. With about 20 cents worth of supplies you can make it fly.

Get two very narrow strips of balsa wood, about 17 inches long. Their cross sections should be about ⅛ inch by ⅜ inch. You can buy them for a nickel at the model airplane department in a hobby store.

Glue the strips together at their midpoints into the form of a plus sign.

Mount two dozen birthday candles on the balsa, toward the center of the plus, with six candles on each strut. Birthday candles are cheap—about 15 cents for a box of 36. An easy way to mount them is to drip hot wax

(continued on next page)

(continued from previous page)

from a candle onto the balsa, then hold the base of a birthday candle in the wax until it hardens into place.

This is the propulsion unit.

Now to prepare the nose cone.

Put cellophane tape over the top edges of the polyethylene bag so that the top end is *completely air tight.* If there are any holes in the bag, put tape over them.

Stretch the open, bottom edge of the bag over the four struts of the propulsion unit, and tape it securely to the balsa.

You now have a wonderful flying machine, a hot-air balloon that will fly for 10 minutes or more—until the candles burn out. By that time it should be hundreds of feet in the air, so that all fire will be out when it falls back to the ground.

The hard part is getting a lot of those candles lit quickly. It helps to have a launch crew, with two people lighting candles simultaneously while someone else holds out the bag, to keep the plastic from getting too close to the flames. Once a few candles are lit it won't be necessary to hold out the bag—the hot air will do that.

Soon the whole structure will start to rise, sometimes before the last candles are lit. It will fly with the wind for about 10 minutes. By that time it may have traveled a mile away or more, and be so high in the sky that it looks like just another flickering star.

Laundry bags can be flown only on calm windless nights. If there's a crosswind the thing is very hard to light, and once it's started it may fly laterally so fast that it hits a tree or a house or sets your best friend on fire before it can pick up enough altitude.

If you hold a UFLB over a hot toaster or some charcoal embers it will fill immediately with hot air, making it easier to light the candles.

Try launching two or three laundry bags, one after the other. They will fly in formation as they ride the same airstream.

Laundry bags are fun to fly near revivals ("Look! A flaming cross in the sky!") and Flying Saucer Club meetings. Taping strips of aluminum foil to the bag has an especially amusing effect near Air Force bases that have radar. I knew one freak who started a full scale Red Alert. □

Puzzling Through Your Problems with Jigsaws

A good part of a jigsaw puzzle's psychological value lies in self-deception. You may think that you are concentrating on one problem (the puzzle), but in reality you are ruminating over another. While your eyes search out a place to put that segment of deep blue sky, your mind, at a lower level of awareness—where it doesn't hurt—may be tossing around the possibilities of where to look for your next job, who to invite to Saturday night's dinner party or what to buy your mother for her birthday. Ernest Hemingway would defrost his refrigerator when he had difficulty writing; but in this advanced era of frostless freezers, a jigsaw puzzle around the house makes a good (and a far less messy) substitute.

Jigsaw puzzles also provide instantaneous reward for concentrated effort—you get a thrill each time you put a piece in the proper place. There's that all-out search for the white-and-red splotch (you know you've seen it, but where?), that solid click of interlocking pieces when you've found it, that surge of triumph, that glow of achievement, that feeling that you have just beaten someone (it doesn't matter who) at his own game.

A jigsaw puzzle is a lot like a good book; you feverishly race to complete it, then find yourself terribly disappointed when it's done. At this point, with the reluctance of Lee surrendering to Grant, most people take their puzzles apart. But there are a number of ways you can get more mileage from your creation.

Leave the puzzle around a few days to impress your friends. If the puzzle is new, pick it up by the corners and tack it to the wall, or slide it under a glass table- or dresser-top until you've got another to replace it. For more permanent and practical uses, bind the puzzle together by coating the surface with a few layers of clear varnish. Then mount the puzzle on a piece of poster board, or glue it to a table top, to the top of a cardboard or wooden box or to a notebook cover.

To use the puzzle as a place mat, cover the bottom with cloth or vinyl. For a tray, paste the puzzle to a piece of balsa wood, or apply a few coats of papier-mâché to the back. You might attach hardware items (like small brass doorknobs) to make legs.

—Ellen J. Weber

A GUIDE TO SELECTING A JIGSAW PUZZLE

● You *can* tell a puzzle by its cover. In general, the more intricate the pattern—that is, the more colors, shading or recognizable objects in the picture itself—the easier the puzzle will be to put together. Scenery and still life paintings are the easiest to complete, but you can make them more challenging by choosing a puzzle that has at least 750 pieces.

● The simpler picture—one with, say, three colors, no shading or repeated geometric designs—is more difficult. Abstract paintings, op art, pictures of Mickey Mouse all fall into this category. Here, 500 pieces is more than enough.

● Know the market. Springbok puzzles are certainly the most challenging and unique sold today, but they are also the most expensive, at $4 for the standard size no matter where you buy it. Among less expensive puzzles, Big Ben is the best brand.

● While you can't usually tell this from the box cover, a good puzzle has pieces that are cut in a variety of shapes, rather than into just three or four configurations; if you can distinguish your pieces according to shape as well as color, the puzzle immediately becomes more interesting.

● For the less serious jigsaw puzzler, *Playboy* puts out canned puzzles of its centerfolds ($3) and Playmate of the Year ($5). Along the same (but wider) lines is "Bridget in the Buff," a blubbery nude pictured in various erotic poses or with a fat daddy. And finally, for the true puzzle devotees, the *New York Times* publishes a crossword puzzle puzzle; it comes in several weekday editions but at the moment there are, unfortunately, no jigsaws of the Sunday behemoth.

● Know thyself. Always remember to do your puzzle on top of a piece of poster board, so you can move it quickly and easily if necessary. Place the puzzle in a room in your house that you frequently pass through but do not work in—or you'll find yourself finishing lots of puzzles but no work. (If you're concerned about your self-control, put the puzzle in an area where you can't possibly make yourself comfortable for any length of time.)

In the exclusive set (no diphtheria cases allowed) in which I travel,
I am known as a heel in the matter of parlor games.
I will drink with them, wrassle with them . . . but when they bring out the bundles of pencils and the pads of paper
and start putting down all the things they can think of beginning with "W,"
or enumerating each other's bad qualities on a scale of 100
(no hard-feeling results, mind you—just life-long enmity),
I tiptoe noisily out of the room and say: "The hell with you."
. . . For, I forgot to tell you, not only am I a non-participant in parlor games, but I am a militant non-participant.
I heckle from the sidelines. I throw stones and spit at the players.

—ROBERT BENCHLEY

Slither

The rules are simple. You and your opponent take turns drawing one-unit segments (no diagonals) connecting the dots of a five-by-six-dot matrix. The segments have to form a continuous line, but you can add new ones to either end. The player who is forced to close the path is the loser.

The illustration shows a typical game, where the next move must be a losing one.

So far, no one has discovered a winning strategy for "Slither," which makes it a good replacement for tic-tac-toe. It seems that wins are about equally divided between the player who moves first and the one whc moves second. (In tic-tac-toe, you can always force a tie.)

–The Editors

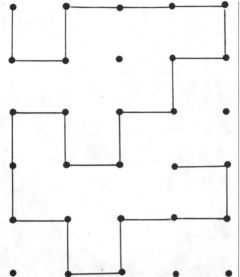

"What did you say?" I say
tonight. It's early yet.
I'm standing at the window
with a flashlight and a pocket mirror
contriving to become the evening star
for someone who lives across the bay.
"I said that nothing happens here."
Upstairs the man who knows one hundred
one
different ways of playing solitaire
shuffles all the cards and lays them out
again.
Here, I raise my star
By standing on a kitchen chair.

—BELLE RANDALL,
"A GAME FOR ONE PERSON"

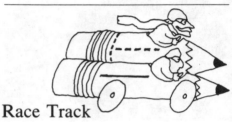

Race Track

This game is widely played in Europe, where a stockbroker will tell you, "I am a racing driver" when you ask him what he does.

You play on graph paper, with colored pencils or pens. Draw a racetrack on any length or shape—the curvier the better. Make sure it's wide enough for the number of players you've got.

The game is very simple: you just move your car from one point to another on the track. There are only three rules:

1. The new grid point and the straight line joining it to the old one must lie entirely within the track (no crashing through the sidewalls).

2. No two cars may simultaneously occupy the same grid point (no collisions).

3. For accelerations and decelerations you can only change your speed by one unit distance per move. For instance, if your previous move was three units vertically and four units horizontally, your next move could be two, three or four units vertically, and three, four or five units horizontally. In other words, you accelerate and decelerate gradually, just as on a real race track.

The first car to cross the finish line wins. If you collide or leave the track, you're out of the race.

If you get into it, there are all sorts of possible embellishments: you can put "oil slicks" on the track, and force the cars to move at a constant speed and direction through the slick. You can add upgrades and downgrades and pretty girls, all of which force the cars to speed up or slow down. You can even run a steeplechase, where the cars run in and out of numbered posts.

In any case, have fun.

–The Editors

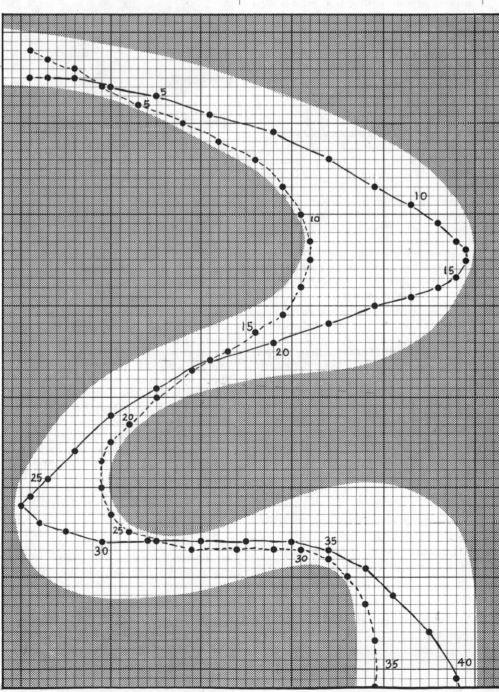

Shuffleboard on Ice

A kind of shuffleboard on ice, with a fillip of golf, the ancient Scottish sport of curling has become one of the hottest things on ice without ice skates. Since 1959, the number of Americans playing this game (with brooms and stones) has grown from a sprinkling of 5,000 to close to 30,000.

Enthusiasts are even predicting that curling will one day become as popular in the United States as it is in Canada, where an estimated 750,000 players have made it a leading participant sport. In fact, Canadian curling leagues are rather like bowling leagues in this country. Here the sport has spread to Florida and California, where ice and rocks are more commonly associated with a popular mind-altering liquid from curling's homeland.

Undoubtedly contributing to the game's growing popularity is the fact that it is ideal as a family sport. Curling can be enjoyed by people of both sexes and most ages—between about 12 and 90. Games can be as vigorous or as subdued as you desire.

Curling is a team game, with four players to a team, or "rink." It is a game of high strategy, with a "skip" directing moves and plotting the game plan.

The object is to slide the rock—a 42½-pound granite stone with a gooseneck handle—down a "sheet" (of ice) toward a target of concentric circles 12 feet in diameter (called the "house"). The idea is to get as close as possible to the center of this target and at the same time knock away opponents' rocks. When a rock is released, other members of the team move down the ice ahead of it under the skip's direction, sweeping vigorously with their brooms to slicken the surface and thus control the rock's speed and trajectory.

A game consists of 10 innings, called "ends" because they are played alternately from opposite ends of the ice (there is a house at each end). Sixteen stones, two per player, are directed at the target during an end. Scoring is simple and similar to that in horseshoes—only those rocks within the house and closer to the bull's-eye than the closest stone of the opposing team count. Thus, the maximum possible score for an end is eight points. Achieving this score often is more difficult than making a hole-in-one in golf or pitching a no-hitter in baseball.

—Mike Michaelson

*And through the drifts the snowy clifts
Did send a dismal sheen:
Nor shapes of men nor beasts we ken—
The ice was all between.*

*The ice was here, the ice was there,
The ice was all around:
It cracked and growled, and roared and howled,
Like noises in a swound!*

—SAMUEL TAYLOR COLERIDGE

The Polar Icecap Open Is a Golf Match on Ice

Golfers have long been recognized as some of the most avid and devoted sportsmen around. So, naturally, it had to happen sometime—golfers in northern climes took to playing on snow-covered "greens." (Well, if you can't get away to Florida, whatcha gonna do?)

It was only to be expected that golf tournaments on ice and snow would begin popping up next, and two of these chilly contests are now held annually. Both were started in February 1970 as nine-hole par-three tournaments. At the Lake George Polar Icecap Open in Lake George, N.Y., contestants still play just nine holes. But the tourney held on Spring Lake (near Grand Haven, Mich.) was expanded in 1971 to include both nine- and 18-hole contests.

While winter golfing definitely has its disadvantages, it has its good features too. There are no pesky insects buzzing around, no leaves to obscure your view, no chance of getting sunburnt or suffering a heat stroke. No sudden rain showers leave you soaked to the skin. Your ball certainly can't sink to the bottom of a water hazard, and sand traps are nonexistent.

U.S. Golf Association winter rules apply in snow-and-ice golf tournaments—with a few special rules thrown in. Two minutes look time is allowed for a lost ball (needless to say, players do *not* use white balls), with a one-stroke penalty. Any ball off the fairway may be put back on the fairway, no nearer the hole, with a one-stroke penalty. A ball over the green may be put back on the fairway the same number of paces from the green, with a one-stroke penalty.

Winter golfers need to have constitutions like polar bears, for temperatures tend to hover around zero at tournament time. Devotion to their sport apparently takes golfers a long way—163 players turned out for the first Polar Icecap Open in Lake George, even though the wind-chill factor that day made it around 33° below zero. No wonder that sometimes towards the end of a game it becomes increasingly difficult to distinguish the sounds of swishing irons from the sound of chattering teeth!

For further information on the Polar Icecap Open write to the Chamber of Commerce, Lake George, N.Y.; the Chamber of Commerce in Grand Haven, Mich. will send you details on the Spring Lake tournament.

—Bill Thomas

Afghani Stick Ball

The idea in this game is to hit a ball past a group of fielders, run to a goal and return without being tagged or hit by a thrown ball. We suggest using a soft sponge, plastic, rubber or tennis ball and any suitable bat. Once up at bat, the batter continues as long as he can. The fielder who puts him out becomes the batter, or players can move up in positions according to some agreed-upon order. One of the fielders serves as pitcher and, as in baseball, the batter gets three strikes. Sometimes the game is played as a team sport with one side batting until all have been tagged out or an agreed-upon number of outs are made.

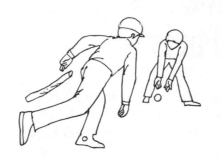

Canadian Balloon Ball

Eight to 10 players on a side sit facing each other so that the soles of each player's feet touch the soles of the player opposite him, and a balloon is tossed into the middle of the line by a referee. The object is to bat the balloon over the heads of the opposite team. A point is scored each time the balloon lands behind one of the teams. Players are only allowed to use one hand and if anyone loses contact with his opponent's feet, the team forfeits a point. The referee decides the awarding of points.

Catch the Dragon's Tail

This game is played in many Asian countries. Six or more players form a line, each person holding the belt of the player just in front of him. The front player, who is the head of the dragon, tries to swing around and catch the last player, and the last player, who is the tail, tries to elude the head without breaking the line. If the line breaks, the head becomes the tail. If the head catches the tail, a new tail—the player who was next to the end—takes his place.

. . . from Weight Watchers

This is one of the great escapes, but we can't tell you what it's an escape from. That's part of what you have to figure out for yourself.

Here's the situation:

Let's say that one day you wake up. You happen to live on the Equator, and you're in the habit of weighing yourself every morning. You get onto the scale, which is guaranteed accurate, and are astounded to find out that your weight is . . . zero!

The question is, very simply, how long would the day be?

That's right. How long would the day be?

There's a real answer to this question, and it can be figured out from the information given, plus, oh, maybe one or two facts that are more or less common knowledge.

If you get the answer, send it on a card to:

The Great Escape
150 Shoreline Highway
Mill Valley, Calif. 94941

The first person with the right answer wins a handmade Möbius strip.

—The Editors

Organize a New Games Tournament

You should try new games—even if you have to make them up yourself. That was the idea behind the first New Games Tournament held last October just across the Golden Gate Bridge from San Francisco. The new games favored there were those in which winning or losing either didn't exist (as in Earthball), or where the winning was a gentle pleasure.

The tournament was held in a meadow close to the Pacific, and included music, food, a tentful of new board games, hang gliding, martial arts demonstrations and people boffing the bejesus out of one another with styrofoam swords.

It was all the idea of Stewart Brand, of *Whole Earth Catalog* fame, so for information, or to exchange ideas, please write Stewart Brand, New Games Tournament, Box 428, Sausalito, Calif. 94965.

—The Editors

Great Moments in the Pinball History of Paris

By Harry Stein

The first mass-marketed pinball machine, D. Gottlieb's "Baffle Ball," paid the rent for a generation of Depression-Era barkeeps. In 1947, the late Harry Mabs invented the solenoid-activated flipper, les flippers, *as they say in Paris. The French took it from there.*

The guy that everyone calls "Pompidou" walks into Le Gymnasme, a classy Parisian café on the Boulevard Bonne Nouvelle, a little after 4 p.m. and heads directly for "Jungle," the pinball machine in the corner. The regulars at the café, who have been expecting him, surround the machine and wait for action. "Jungle" is a tough machine, a Gottlieb to be taken seriously, but Pompidou, who thinks of himself as a pinball wizard, is the picture of nonchalance.

He reaches into the coat pocket of his grey pinstriped suit, fishes out a franc and drops it into the machine, which comes to life and purges itself of the last game with a burst of machine gun clatter. Pompidou studies the board before him. On both the left and right sides are a series of triggers, each of which registers 1,000 points when hit. In the center, surrounded by a rubber cushion, is paydirt—a bumper that reads "1,000 When Lit, 100 When Unlit."

Pompidou slams the plunger with his palm, French style, shooting the first ball into play. It barely misses the center bumper and, despite his vigorous shaking of the machine, nudges but one of the triggers before dropping between his outstretched flippers and out of play. Pompidou takes a Gauloise from his vest pocket, lights it, and inhales deeply. It takes 50,000 points to beat "Jungle." His score reads 1,420.

His second ball begins badly. After a single ricochet off the center bumper, it heads downward, apparently lost forever. Only a masterful combination shot, a quick left followed by a lightning right, catches it and sends it back upwards, over all five triggers on the left, into a perfect arc and down over the triggers on the right. "*Belle*," murmurs one of the spectators. But Pompidou isn't finished yet. At the base of its arc, he traps the ball with his right flipper, holds it for a moment, and then shoots it up into the domain of the center bumper. It careens madly between the bumper and the rubber cushion like a frantic molecule trapped in a test tube, racking up thousand after thousand. When it finally falls down the center and into oblivion, the scoreboard reads 47,360.

His third ball is almost anticlimactic. Pompidou aims for the triggers, again picks up all of them and ends up with a score of close to 70,000, good for a pair of free games. "*Bien joué, Monsieur le Président*," shouts a friend in the crowd, "*C'était magnifique!*" Only then does his composure break and he allows himself a small smile.

Of course pinballs are by no means an exclusively French preoccupation. Indeed, virtually all the 20,000 machines in Paris are manufactured by the American firms of Gottlieb, Williams and Bally, which also do an enormous business domestically. And the machines have impressive numbers of devotees elsewhere on the Continent, as well as in Britain, where they provided the basis for a rock opera. In Germany, models of local manufacture compete with the American brands.

But in a real sense, Paris is the pinball capital of the world. Since their introduction to France in the postwar period, the machines have become as fixed a part of the Parisian routine as croissants in the morning and love in the afternoon. Where in other countries pinballs are the almost exclusive preserve of the young, *les flippers* cut across France's often rigid generational, class and ethnic lines. As an integral part of café culture, they are played—often obsessively—by all the kinds of Frenchmen who hang around cafés; workers in blue coveralls play in workers' cafés, students play in cafés near their classrooms, businessmen in tailored suits work the machines in bourgeois districts.

At Le Tournon, the café off the Place Odeon where Jean-Luc Godard sometimes plays, a young fulltime organizer for the leftist P.S.U. (Parti Socialiste Unifié) plays "Jungle" with the kind of intensity that makes revolutions. Eyes ablaze behind cracked tortoise-shell glasses, he shakes the machine like a maniac. "*Putain!*" he shouts when a ball falls between his outstretched flippers. "*Merde!*" The card players behind him usually just look up and smile. They've heard it all before.

At Le Ballon d'Alsace, below Montmartre on the Rue des Martyrs, a trio of high school students play "Jungle" every afternoon after school. Genuine virtuosos, they can sometimes win an hour's worth of free games with a franc or two.

Robert van Wilder, who has a memory for pinballs like a lot of other Frenchmen have for women, spends a great deal of time thinking about the magnificent machines of the past. As the largest importer-distributor of machines in Paris, his principal pleasure is also his business and he drops the names of classic machines with the nonchalance of a gossip columnist ticking off the names of her celebrity pals.

For some of the French, particularly on the outskirts of Paris where there's really nothing to do, the machines play a vital role in the mating game. On Saturday nights teenagers put on their best clothes and, pocketsful of francs at the ready, head for the local cafés.

Pinballs play a more obvious sexual role in the lives of some Frenchmen a few years older, those in their mid-twenties. Resplendent in skin-tight denims with zippers everywhere, *these* café cowboys swagger around the student haunts looking for action. Their whole routine, down to caressing the flipper buttons with their index fingers, is designed to kill.

It is clear that M. van Wilder, whose outfit imports the six or so new models that go into general circulation in Paris every year, has a good deal to do with the emotional well-being of his neighbors. It is a responsibility he does not take lightly. In the back of his offices on the Rue de Navarin is a workshop where samples of all new models from Chicago are assembled and tested. Though no longer a café player himself, he makes a point of subjecting each new machine to rigorous personal scrutiny.

"Look here," he says, pointing to a machine called "High Hand," "this just came in. Believe me, it's going to be a real winner."

He switches a lever and, lights blinking and innards churning, the machine comes to life. He stations himself before it. "I know about these things," he says. "I've been doing this for twenty-three years. In six months there'll be more Parisians standing in front of these than all the pissoirs in town." □

For Americans, a Way to Make Friends

A great many Americans in Paris—particularly those who stick to the Right Bank tourist areas around the Opera and the Champs Elysées—manage to remain completely unaware of the French preoccupation with pinballs. And of those Americans who do notice it, not many have the gumption to walk into a Parisian café, walk up to a "Jungle" or an "Orbit," and begin feeding it francs. They're afraid they'll look ridiculous or, worse, inept.

The important thing to remember here is that in France almost everyone plays the machines from time to time and if aficionados bothered to pay attention to every schmo who played a few games, they'd have no time to spend their own money. Anyway, it's *fun* to play pinballs, especially in Paris. American tourists are eternally concerned with meeting the natives, but waiters, shop clerks and hotel deskmen are about the only examples of the French species that any of them actually get to meet. In cafés, though, everyone in the vicinity of the machines is part of the club, united in the struggle against glass and metal. Americans are welcomed as readily as allies in that war as they were in 1917 and 1944.

There's a place even for those who don't speak a syllable of French. Chances are that if they wait long enough, some Frenchman—flushed out by a particularly fine game or a couple of glasses of *vin rouge*—will walk over, smile and try out his rotten English on them.

For Americans who play pinballs, there are a couple of things to keep in mind: first, games go two for a franc in Paris, a miserable rate, but then, café owners have to eat too. Those who expect to play more than a few games are thus well advised to keep a sizeable cache of francs at the ready. Also, one is expected to buy a drink or two while hanging about the machines; café owners like to eat well.

Pinball machines are all over Paris, but some areas provide better sport than others. The student cafés (5th and 6th arrondissements) are often crowded and smoke-filled, but the machines are probably played with more gusto there than anywhere else in town. The 9th arrondissement, below Montmartre, and the 4th and 2nd, below that, are likewise hotbeds of pinball activity, though the large, impersonal arcades and game rooms that flourish in these areas should be avoided. Great pinballs require the intimacy of good cafés.

How to Win at Pinball

Pinballmania isn't restricted to France. In the United States, pinball machines can be found in amusement centers, bowling alleys, pool halls and occasionally in the homes of well-to-do pinball addicts. The following tips are intended to help the novice select an acceptable machine so he can get a slight edge (maybe) over typically poor odds.

Pinball machines differ in quality, price per game and age. Generally, the newer the machine the more noise it will make and the more flashing lights it will have. The older machines tend to be slower and less exciting—though some classics like "Magic City" and "Lady Luck" offer more adrenaline-producing moments than many of the newer, more expensive models.

On most pins there are at least three separate ways to win a free game: making a *higher final score* than the "top" score on the machine (top scores differ from machine to machine; check the information card, usually under glass in the bottom left-hand corner of the playing field); *matching* the last digit in your score with a randomly selected number appearing on the backboard at the end of the game; and maneuvering a ball through a lighted "Special" lane or alley (Specials usually light up in red and offer repeated chances for an extra game).

Compare. Observe another player at the pins for awhile to determine what's good or bad about that particular machine. Of course, success often depends upon the player's idiosyncrasies and the right combination of lucky bounces. But some machines offer some built-in advantages too. Look for a machine:

● that provides at least three different opportunities for winning a free game (high score, matching, Specials).

● that offers the most balls for the lowest price. Prices vary from five games for a quarter to two games for a quarter. Usually there are five balls per game, but lately some of the East Coast machines have been getting away with three balls per game.

● where the ball does not run abnormally fast down through the field.

● that has a relatively small gap between the flippers.

● where a tilt does not end the game but only disqualifies the ball in play.

● where the previous player's final score comes close to the top score for that machine (you may not be as good or as lucky as the player before you, but at least there is some assurance that it will be possible to win).

Because the pins are so exciting, they can also be extremely frustrating, disappointing and expensive. Picking a winning pinball machine is the first step in cutting back on the expense, avoiding the disappointment and becoming a first-class pinball wizard.

—Michael C. Lester

Have Magic With Your Lunch

There's a place in New York where magic prevails.

It prevails so much you can hardly eat lunch without finding an ace of spades (which you've previously chosen) inside your fresh grapefruit.

What seems to be nothing but a rather good restaurant is in reality the home port for the world's greatest specialists in the bizarre, the arcane and the sensational.

It's called The Magic Table, and it happens every day of the year in Rosoff's, on West 43rd Street just off Broadway. Anyone who loves magic is welcome.

Kuda Bux is there—he's the "Sightless Vision Man," who can fly jet planes blindfolded.

Jim Steele drops in occasionally. He'll produce live doves from thin air, and he can pick your pocket while your hand is in it.

Tony Spina might be there. He levitates his own children. Jose De La Torre does magic with penknives.

Any given day, you will find mind readers, card manipulators, stage illusionists, sword swallowers . . . every imaginable variety of expert in the fine and secret art of deception.

Luncheon talk will be illustrated profusely with card fans, dove productions and cups-and-balls routines. There will be men there who remember Houdini, reminiscing about the time the Great Master made a full-grown elephant disappear in the New York Hippodrome.

"Let me show you a miracle with the six of clubs. . . ."

"Now, I take this black knife and push it into my hand like this. . . ."

"Choose a card from the running pack. . ." These men have made a detailed and practical study of human nature and human weakness. They know the flaws of the eye and the fallacies of the brain. They are shrewd psychologists and clever actors.

At Rosoff's they claim all those marvelous psychic feats are nothing but third-rate night club sleight-of-hand. The truth is that any decent magician could duplicate any spiritualist's act—and in fact could do things much *more* incredible.

Magicians as a rule are tongue-in-cheek; it's a rare one who steadfastly claims he's got real magical powers. Somehow, the *seriousness* of a person like that just doesn't sit right with the regulars of The Magic Table.

—"The Great Saltini"

Abbott's Get-Together: A Michigan Festival of Magic

For 361 days of the year, the little town of Colon, Mich. has a population of about 1,200 absolutely normal people and is in every way a typical small Midwestern town. But for four days in the 3rd week of August, Colon is the site of something called Abbott's Get-Together. Its name is innocuous enough, but this is no innocuous event—it is a colossal convention of magicians both professional and amateur from around the globe.

For four days, there are almost nonstop sessions of trick-swapping, lectures on all phases of magic art, and afternoon and evening shows in the local school gyms to which the public is invited. And for four days, the sidewalks of Colon are crowded with men and women enthusiastically showing each other their magic. There are card tricks, bouquets of flowers that appear from nowhere, a skimpily-dressed young woman floating in midair, a runaway flying carpet racing down the street with its owner in pursuit.

For more than 35 years, magicians have been gathering here annually for Abbott's Get-Together. Why in Colon? Why, because Colon is the home of the Abbott Magic Co., world's largest manufacturer of magicians' props. Harry Blackstone, the great illusionist, came to Colon in 1925 and bought a piece of property at the edge of town. His magic brought other magicians to town, including Percy Abbott, an Australian, who settled in the town and started manufacturing magicians' props. Abbott's Magic Co. is still the chief sponsor of the annual festival.

More than 250 magicians attended Abbott's Get-Together last year and delighted thousands of spectators with their performances, both formal and impromptu. For full particulars on this year's event, write the Abbott Magic Co., Colon, Mich. 49040, or phone (616) 432-3504.

–Bill Thomas

How to Cheat at Cards —and How Not to Be Cheated

This isn't for everyone. Just those who like big danger and big bucks.

A certain kind of man (and maybe woman, though I never knew one) is fascinated by the prospect of knowing how to cheat at cards. I don't mean nickel and dime stuff like peeking at the bottom card during a gin rummy game. But the real item: dealing off the bottom, dealing seconds, stacking the deck, switching decks, palming, jumping the cut, false shuffling and how to go undetected.

I personally am a professional card manipulator. I'm more or less retired now from my grueling and high-tension profession. But I had my days of sitting in on suspicious card games and spotting the cheaters—for a

The Mechanic's Grip

Dealing Seconds

Dealing Off The Bottom

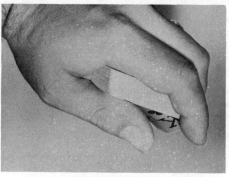
The Peek

fee. For a higher fee, I would out-cheat them.

I learned this esoteric art in all sorts of places. It really started when I got into big-money poker games to break the monotony. I knew the odds in poker well enough, and I knew how to judge players. But there were just some times when the odds seemed to go blooey, and psychological judgments had to give way to four aces.

I didn't get it, until I thought about cheating.

The fact is, as a long and impartial investigation showed me, that in at least half the card games in this country, serious and casual, someone cheats. If you play cards it behooves you to learn something about it.

The first thing to look for is what we call the "Mechanic's Grip." A "mechanic" is a card mechanic, a finger flinger, someone who knows a little more than you. Invariably, the professional card mechanic will hold the deck in a certain way—with his forefinger curled over the front corner, while dealing. This is the only way to deal seconds and bottoms without getting caught. My advice is that if you ever sit in a game where someone holds the deck like that, *get out*. You won't catch him and you'll lose your shirt.

The second defense against cheaters is to *insist on the cut*. Many casual players forget about the cut, thinking it's a kind of insult to the dealer. This is ridiculous. Insist on it, and watch the dealer from the time he completes the cut to when he begins dealing. If he reaches for a cigar or a drink in that little interim—he may be cheating. He may be nullifying the cut, using a fairly simple one-handed maneuver.

For those who want to *become* cheaters, that maneuver is easy, and many people who don't know the first thing about cheating can do it. It's nothing but a one-handed cut itself—dropping half the pack into the palm (holding the rest in the fingertips) and pushing it up with the forefinger. The top half drops underneath almost automatically. The mechanic will crimp the original bottom card, and can cut the deck right back to it.

A third defense is to *insist on a riffle shuffle*. None of these overhand shuffles—you might as well just give the dealer your money. The false riffle shuffle is one of the most difficult maneuvers to do right, and unless the man is a real master, insisting on a riffle shuffle will prevent a lot of grief. But, if he's a master, the sign of a false riffle is a fast cut immediately after the shuffle. Watch for this, and walk out if you see it.

Stacking the deck is talked about a lot in card circles. Unfortunately, it's so easy to do that I might scare you off if I told how. So just insist on those riffle shuffles and cuts—that'll take care of it.

As for dealing seconds and bottoms: listen to the deal. Even the best second dealer can't avoid making a slight "swish" sound, as the second card slides past the top one on its way down to the table. You won't be able to see it. Hearing it is hard enough.

Dealing off the bottom is almost undetectable if the dealer is good enough, but it looks a little bit funny. You can't put your finger on it, exactly. My advice again: *walk out.*

For potential cheaters: it took me about two years to learn to deal a perfect second. I still can't get bottoms just right, and I've been practicing that one for about 15 years. False shuffles and cuts are second nature to me now—it's hard for me to do a legitimate one!

The first and last word on cheating at cards is in a little and fairly hard-to-find book called *The Expert at the Card Table.* It's written by a man named S. W. Erdnase. If you can't get that, there is a good one on how to detect cheaters, called *Scarne's Complete Guide to Gambling*, by John Scarne.

—Anonymous

The Erdnase System of Palming Cards

The art of card palming can be brought to a degree of perfection that borders on the wonderful. It is very simple to place one or several cards in the palm and conceal them by partly closing and turning the palm downward, or inward; but it is entirely another matter to palm them from the deck in such a manner that the most critical observer would not even suspect, let alone detect, the action. I originated the following method, and I believe it to be the most rapid and subtle ever devised.

Top Palm Method.—Hold the deck in the left hand so that the first joints of the second and third fingers will be against the middle of one side, the thumb against middle of opposite side, the first joint of little finger against middle of end and first finger curled up against bottom. Bring the right hand over top of deck, the third, second and little fingers close together, first joint of the little finger being against the end corner, the first finger curled up on top and the tip of thumb resting idly at end, above left little finger. To palm, press the right little finger, exactly at the first joint, firmly against the top cards, pull them up about half an inch at corner, freeing them from the left second and third fingers, keeping the three right fingers (little, second and third) perfectly straight. The cards to be palmed are now held firmly between the right little finger, and the left little finger. (See Fig. 1.) Straighten out right first finger, swing left little finger with the cards to be palmed free of the end of the deck, press the cards into the right palm

How to Become a Magician

Every magician is a specialist. Personally, I specialize in elegant sleight-of-hand: the classical white-gloved magic, manipulating endless fans of cards, bright yellow billiard balls, lit cigarettes, flashing crimson silks, soft sponges, big red thimbles and silver coins.

If you want to participate in this lovely little art you'll have to decide what kind of tricks you want to do—will it be cards, billiard balls, silks, coins, ropes, rings, thimbles or cups-and-balls? Or would you like to try illusions, mentalism, mathematical tricks, closeup, stage or memory work? Maybe you want to work with doves, rabbits, canes, torches, candles or confederates. Do you want a feke, a pull, a load, a shell or a set of Twentieth Century Silks?

Magic has one of the largest literatures in the world, and there's a book dealing with each of these specialties, and there are books dealing with all their possible permutations.

Just for a starter, if you are interested in card magic, the best book is *Closeup Card*

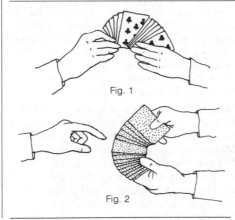

Fig. 1

Fig. 2

with the end of the left third finger. (See Fig. 2.) Draw the deck out about half way from under the right hand, and release the left hand entirely. (See Fig. 3.) Then the right drops the deck on the table to be cut. After the hands are in the first position the whole process does not occupy half a second.

The deck should be kept in view as much as possible, and the right first finger is curled up on top for that purpose until the instant the palm is performed. The action of drawing the deck into view when the cards are palmed is made a part of the whole movement.

—S. W. Erdnase

Magic by Harry Lorayne. Billiards balls vanish, reappear and are beautifully multiplied in *Expert Billiard Ball Manipulation* by Burling Hull. A smattering of all kinds of tricks are explained in Jean Hugard's *Encyclopedia of Magic.*

Once you've picked up some rudiments from the books, the best way to become a magician is to watch magic. The best places to watch magic are these:

Lou Tannen's, a magic shop, at 1540 Broadway, New York City. Saturday afternoon is the big time here, when all the best magicians in New York gather informally to hype themselves and show their latest wrinkles.

Al Flosso's, a magic shop on 34th Street in New York. Same deal as Tannen's, but darker and eerier.

Joe Berg's, a magic shop, on Hollywood Boulevard in Los Angeles. The West Coast version.

The Magic Castle, a private club in the Hollywood Hills. Continuous magic shows every night by top professionals. You have to know someone, or buy a membership.

—"The Great Saltini"

The Force

The sleight with this title consists of compelling a spectator to select a certain card, and is indispensable in certain tricks.

It is next to impossible in writing to teach the novice to force a card; but the idea will very soon become apparent after the learner has made a few experiments. The card which you desire selected is, in the first place, in the middle of the pack. The pack is spread out fanwise, the second finger of the right hand meanwhile pressing on the bottom of the necessary card, as in Fig. 1. A spectator is now asked to select a card from the pack, the performer meantime running the cards quickly from hand to hand, and, as the drawer's fingers approach the pack, the second finger of the right hand literally pushes the desired card into his hand, as in Fig. 2. The card to be forced should be a little more exposed than the rest. This, however, is only the A B C of the "force," the successful operation of which can only be accomplished after innumerable trials. Above all, don't be in a great hurry to get it over. Endeavor to appear to be absolutely indifferent as to where the card is taken, even going so far as to say: "Have your choice, sir; take any card you wish."

If by any chance the force fails, and another card is chosen, the performer need not fear a *contretemps*, but with a "Thank you, sir; kindly replace your card anywhere you like in the pack," put the little finger on it and make the "pass" bringing it to the top, from which position it can be palmed off, or the trick finished as fancy dictates. The first card is now "forced" on some more accommodating person.

—Howard Thurston

Fig. 1

Fig. 2

Fig. 3

Casinos Around the World
Where to Drop Your Bundle Legally

By Ronald P. Kriss

There's penny-ante, back-of-the-garage gambling, and there's casino gambling. The first is fine for Damon Runyon groupies but there's nothing like the thrill of losing it all elegantly.

To the true gambler, action is action, and it makes little difference where it happens. Since there are 86 million Americans who gamble at least occasionally, according to games expert John Scarne, that makes for quite a bit of action, and not always in the most elegant surroundings. Somebody's dining room table, a seedy hotel room, the back of a local saloon—anyplace at all will do. In many cities, a bellhop or a cab driver can direct you to a game of poker or blackjack, to the nearest numbers runner or to a handy bookmaker.

Of course, all of this sport is strictly illegal. Within the limits of the law, a considerable amount of action is available. Nearly two-thirds of the 50 states permit some form of gambling—usually parimutuel betting on horses and dogs, and state-operated lotteries.

For those who want to play at other games within the law, and with a touch of class and comfort, few things can surpass casino gambling. In the United States, that means Nevada, the only state where casinos are legal. Practically any town in Nevada big enough to have a name also has what *it* calls a casino—though this may often mean three one-armed bandits and a single blackjack table covered with moth-eaten green baize. The Big Three in terms of size and elegance are Lake Tahoe, Reno and Las Vegas. All have casinos offering the standard craps, blackjack, roulette, row upon jangling row of slot machines and a numbers game called keno; in the larger casinos there are baccarat tables surrounded by velvet draperies and wall-to-wall pit bosses to make sure everything is on the up and up.

Each of the Big Three gambling towns has a distinctive style. As a sports center (offering skiing, skating, tobogganing, water-skiing, sailing and swimming) and a place of surpassing natural beauty, Lake Tahoe lures a mixed crowd. There are youngish, bronzed, informal people who go to the lake primarily to enjoy its ski slopes or its waters, who consider the gambling a strictly peripheral dividend if they pay it any heed at all. And then there are tourists who drive to Lake Tahoe in unwieldy campers or are bused in from San Francisco and Sacramento; these are distinctly unathletic types whose sole objective is a few hours of gambling, who are usually unaware that nearby are some of the best ski slopes in the United States.

Reno, which bills itself as "The Biggest Little City in the World," has the feel of a place that isn't quite certain whether it should aspire to be a senior Tahoe or a junior Vegas—a big little city or a little big city. Nevada's big-time gambling, launched in the early 1930s, focused first on Reno, so there exists a certain sentimental devotion to the place. But there are many who prefer Tahoe for its outdoorsy ambience or Vegas for its unabashed devotion to the gaming tables (and its sheer size).

Vegas, of course, is the gamer's Mecca. If the Strip doesn't enchant you, with its overdone aura of hotel luxury, there's always Casino Center downtown, which is in the midst of a building and refurbishing boom. Somewhere in Vegas, there's somebody who will place a bet for you on anything—the next Super Bowl, the Indy 500, the Soapbox Derby, when Richard Nixon will a) be impeached, b) resign or c) become a grandfather—you name it.

The pace of play can get frenetic, so beware if you're a nervous novice. If you dawdle too long over hitting that 14, smoke will begin curling from the dealer's ears and your fellow players will start muttering nasty things under their breath. Since it's *your* money, such reactions shouldn't bother you, but if they do, head for Tahoe.

Outside the United States, the opportunities for casino gambling are almost too numerous to catalog. South of the Rio Grande, skip Mexico and head for Panama for real action. In Latin America proper, you can find thriving casinos in Argentina (in Bariloche, Mar del Plata and Rio Hondo, among other places), Ecuador (in Quito and Playas), Paraguay (in Asuncion) and Uruguay (in Montevideo and Punta del Este). Asia?

Everybody knows about the wide-open scene in Macao, 40 miles off Hong Kong, but there are also major operations in Jakarta, Indonesia, and in Seoul, Korea the government runs a huge casino complex called Walker Hill.

Africa? There's casino gambling at the Nile Hilton and the Sheraton in Cairo, and in Alexandria. And there's action in Tangier and Marrakech and just outside Casablanca in Morocco; in Accra, Ghana; in Nairobi, Kenya; and in a sprawling operation just over the border of South Africa at Mbabane, Swaziland, where high-rolling whites and blacks mix without anybody ever mentioning *apartheid*. In the Middle East, there's the Casino du Liban 12 miles north of Beirut, Lebanon; and while Istanbul's hotels don't have their own operations, they *will* summon taxis to take you to a spot on the outskirts of the city where blackjack, craps and roulette are available.

In Europe, you're never too far from a casino. First, there's the principality of Monaco, home to what may be the world's best known casino—Monte Carlo.

Germany had 13 casinos at last count, the most famous being the 200-year-old operation at Baden-Baden. Casino gambling is prohibited in most places in Italy, but the government licenses houses in Venice, San Remo, St. Vincent and Campione. The Swiss have casinos for *boule* (a low-stakes form of roulette in which the maximum bet is roughly $1.20) in at least eight cities, and there are casinos in cities in Austria, Belgium, Portugal, Yugoslavia and at Black Sea resorts in Bulgaria. There's even a casino next door to the Rock Hotel on Gibraltar and, on Malta, there's the Dragonard Palace Casino.

For the bulk of U.S. gamblers, three areas outside the country are most accessible—and most inviting:

France has roughly 150 casinos; the best are at the coastal resorts, where you can avail

yourself of superb food and rejuvenating sunshine when the action goes sour: try Deauville, Biarritz, Le Touquet, Nice or Cannes. Monte Carlo, of course, is handy to any of these French resorts.

England had some 1,200 casinos in the early 1960s, when a too-liberal gaming law made it possible to open a house for as little as a few shillings. There are only about a score of casinos in London today, but the British capital is still a fine place to gamble. When the British tightened the gambling rules in 1970, most of the benefits went to the player, rather than the casino owner. Examples: in roulette, the 00 has been eliminated, and the payoff for a single number is 35 chips rather than the 34 given almost everywhere else. In blackjack, players are prohibited from making fools of themselves by splitting tens, fives and fours, which sober novices and inebriated initiates have been known to do—to their sorrow—in casinos elsewhere. In craps, the new rules outlaw "Big 6" and "Big 8" bets, which are sucker wagers.

All of London's casinos have 48-hour waiting periods for tourists, who must give notice of their intention to gamble and then wait two full days before actually doing so. The fees for joining the casinos (more properly "clubs") are modest, tipping is forbidden, and the tables close at 4 a.m., which gives you a chance to revive before re-entering the fray at noon.

The Caribbean has a plenitude of places to play, if you steer clear of the U.S. Virgins and Jamaica. In the Bahamas, both the Paradise Island Casino just off Nassau and the Lucaya-Freeport complex 30 air minutes from Miami offer lavish, Vegas-style operations. Both are a trifle impatient with the bumbling low-roller, though, so you might occasionally have to deal with a coldly condescending *croupier* or dealer. As I advised before, try to ignore him—it's your $50 or $100.

Puerto Rico has clamped down on its once loosely-run casinos. Low maximum limits help keep the real high-rollers—and the mob influence—away: the limits are $100 at craps and blackjack, and $180 for even-money roulette bets. Puerto Rico also helps to keep things civilized by limiting operations to the hours from 8 p.m. to 4 a.m., which leaves the addict with 16 hours to sleep, eat, swim and indulge in similar time-killing activities.

Antigua has a modest operation at the local Holiday Inn. Aruba and Curaçao are into casino gambling in a big way, as are Haiti and the Dominican Republic. South of Miami, in short, you can hardly go wrong unless you stumble onto Cuba, which, ironically, was once *the* place for the casino gambler from the eastern United States.

Plainly, action is available almost anywhere you wander on the globe. Just remember to set yourself a limit and count on buying a few hours of enjoyment, not a pension fund. □

Nova Scotia Casino Ferry

If you're headed for Nova Scotia and you're steeling yourself for a loooooong drive, consider this: you can save yourself time and energy by taking one of the luxury ferries that shuttle between Portland, Maine and Yarmouth, Nova Scotia. Overland, it's an 858-mile trip through Maine, New Brunswick and western Nova Scotia, along the Bay of Fundy—a good 18 to 20 hours of hard driving. Aboard the boats of the Lion Ferry Co., it's an extremely pleasant, totally relaxed 10-hour voyage spiced with snappy breezes and a whiff of salt water. And you can take your car along with you.

Lion Ferry operates two new, well-appointed vessels on the Portland-Yarmouth route (a Bar Harbor-to-Yarmouth ferry ended operations in 1973.) One is the 488-foot MS *Bolero*, launched in February 1973; she has room for 230 cars and 885 passengers in overnight cabins. The *Bolero* features moonlight dancing, a swimming pool, three bars, two lounges and a casino for the gambler who doesn't mind a blackjack table that occasionally sways with the waves.

The second ferry is the 389-foot MS *Prince of Fundy*, launched in the spring of 1970 and offering room for 200 cars (or campers, motor bikes and mini-buses) and cabins for 525. The *Prince* lacks a pool, but like the *Bolero* has a large sun deck, casino, rooms for formal dining as well as cafeteria-style meals, and a duty-free shop amply stocked with liquor, perfume and jewelry.

In June and July, the *Bolero* leaves Portland Harbor every evening and reaches Yarmouth just after sun-up, in time for a splendid view of the picturesque fishing port; after a brief stop it heads back to Portland, arriving in time for a late dinner on shore. The *Prince* leaves Portland every morning for Yarmouth, stops there briefly in the evening, then makes the overnight journey back. In August and September, the sailing schedules are reversed, with *Bolero* departing from Portland in the morning and the *Prince* at night. From October through May, the *Prince* sails from Portland at 10 p.m. daily (except Sundays) and from Yarmouth at 11 a.m. daily (except Mondays).

One-way fares are $14.50 for adults, $7.25 for children five to 11; children under five ride free. Cabins range from $18 for two berths and no private facilities to $36 for a deluxe two-berth cabin with showers and private toilets. The charge for autos is $35, for motorcycles $12, for bicycles $5.

For reservations call the *Prince of Fundy* line in Portland at (207) 775-5616, or in Yarmouth at (902) 742-3513. In the spring and summer, you can call toll-free if you're in the eastern United States—the number is (800) 341-7540.

—Ronald P. Kriss

Be the First on Your Block to Own a Pocket TV Camera—Only $6,000

First came the pocket snapshot camera; then everyone was buying the pocket calculator that could do the job of an old-fashioned desk-top adding machine. Now, three companies have introduced the forerunner of the pocket TV camera. The prototype is about the size of a package of cigarettes, and the expectation is that some cameras will be as small as wristwatches. The amazing thing is that these pocket TV cameras can shoot pictures in anything from sunlight to dim indoor light without any auxiliary light sources.

Fairchild Camera, RCA and General Electric are the pioneers in the pocket TV camera field. They have developed a new kind of solid state electronic device that converts light directly into electrical charges, which then are read off in sequence, amplified and transmitted without further modification to the television set. These photosensors are called "charge-coupled devices" (CCD) and are the newest class of semiconductors to be developed. Much of the basic research was done under U.S. Navy contracts for low light reconnaissance devices.

Fairchild is already marketing a package, Model MV-100, with a camera, a wide range of lenses, a remote battery package that permits wireless transmission up to 100 feet, and a television monitor—all for about $6,000. Improved models of the camera are likely to come quickly, along with significant price decreases. With mass production, the price of the camera could drop tenfold in a year and another tenfold a year or two later, just as the price of the pocket calculators did between 1970 and 1973.

Picture definition on the prototype camera is only adequate, but future models should produce picture quality comparable to present vidicon tubes. It will probably take some time for *color* mini-cameras to be developed.

If you can't wait for the price to drop and want to buy a camera immediately, write:

Joseph Keller
Electro Optical Systems
Fairchild Space and Defense Systems
300 Robbins Lane
Syosset, N.Y. 11791.

—David Popoff

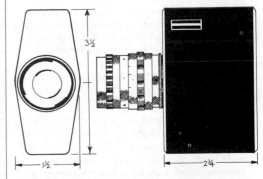

Playing Number Games —for Money

OK, look sharp now! A guy with a mustache comes up to see you, see. He's got this new game, "Tiger Toss," and you look like a good sport.

You take an American flag (nothing unpatriotic about this game!) and drop wooden matches on it. Friend mustache is willing to bet you your match will *never* land wholly inside one of the stripes. If it lands parallel to a stripe, or a little bit crosswise at an angle—you win. But if it touches two stripes in any way—he wins. Since you have 360 degrees of the circle going for you, and he only wins if it lands in one or two special ways, it seems like the fool is just throwing money away.

Well, don't forget about that mustache.

This kind of game is called "proposition betting." There is nothing better for expert "gaffers"—that is, people who rig games. In most of these bets, the trick is so subtle that you have to be pretty nifty on the draw to get it.

For instance. Let's say we take two decks of cards. You shuffle them both. I'm willing to bet you that if I turn over the top cards of each deck, simultaneously, that by the time I get all the way through all 52 cards, I will turn up *two identical cards* at least once!

Sounds hard to believe, doesn't it? But I tell you what—you look like a sport!—I'll even make it more worth your while. I'll bet you *two to one* that I turn up the two identical cards, and I'll bet you fifty-fifty on a second hit, too!

It's lucky this is just an article. Better get the decks and try it yourself, first.

Here's another one, of the cocktail party variety. Let's say you're at a party with, oh, about 30 people. I'm willing to bet you, friend, that at least two of these people have *exactly the same birthday*! (Day and month, not necessarily year.) How about it? Want to try ten bucks? After all, there are 365 days and only 30 people. . . .

Well, you'd probably lose. The fact is that in any group of more than 23 people, the chances are that two of them have identical birthdays. It can be proved mathematically. With 30 people you might as well just hand over your money.

In a true proposition bet, the "gaff" is inherent in the terms of the bet itself; there's no sleight-of-hand involved—just sleight-of-mind. This implicit understanding has won (and cost) a lot of people money.

Here's one to chew on. You have three poker chips—all identical. One of them has an X on one side. The second has both sides blank. And the third has Xs on both sides. In other words, there are six faces in all, and three of them are blank and three of them have Xs.

Now if I put these chips into a hat and we draw one out at random . . . and just slap it down on the table . . . I'll bet I can tell you what's on the underside!

Want to bet?

—David Saltman

Games Computers Play

Because the memory banks of computers are so easy to program, they offer an ideal format for developing "live" games. For those who have access to a computer, a variety of entertaining possibilities are available, ranging from the trivial—tic-tac-toe—to the profound—computer chess, for example. Some games that have caught the fancy of computer programmers have eaten up thousands of hours of computer time. One game buff, intrigued with the game of "Life," used up more than 70 hours of time on his company's Honeywell computer; "Spacewar" freaks all over the country have used up hundreds of hours more.

The most serious computer games research is taking place in the intellectual field of chess. Why chess? Well, it's fun; but more important, when the pattern-recognition problems involved in chess are solved, the solutions will lead to helping computer robots to see and perhaps even *think* for themselves.

MIT has a computer chess program, MacHack, that reportedly can be played by long-distance telephone. Other universities with good computer chess programs are Northwestern, Columbia and the University of Southern California. But anyone who has a yen to become involved in computer chess should contact the public relations department or computer center at any large university in his area. Many have informal groups working on chess programs.

An annual computer chess tournament is sponsored by the Association for Computing Machinery; it pits computer against computer. For details, write:

Association for Computing Machinery
P.O. Box 4566
Atlanta, Ga. 30302.

Are computers good chess players? If you try playing one and you're only average at the game, you may well lose. The better computer chess programs have won more than half of the games they've played with humans.

There are a host of other computer games: business and management simulations, city government simulations, "Save the Environment," "Futurology," and so on. On the fun level are the games that you play against the computer or with it. Almost any game that has a winning strategy can be (and probably has been) programmed into a computer.

—David Popoff

Here's a coded message of great interest to gamers: BEBMSPWKMDASNTJ.
If you decode it, send the answer to us and you will win an authentic Vigenère tableau.

What Do You Do When a Superior Being Wants to Make You Rich?

Suppose that you are informed that someone has deposited a large amount of cash in a bank vault for you. When you arrive, you are told that Vault A contains $10,000. You can see the money through a window. Then you are told that Vault B, which has no window, contains either $100,000 or nothing. You are given a choice: you may either open only Vault B, which may contain $100,000, or open both vaults. You are also told that the money was deposited by a Superior Being after he predicted what you will do. If the prediction is that you will open only Vault B, the $100,000 will be there. If the prediction is that you will open both vaults, then Vault B will be empty. This Being can be regarded as the equivalent of God or perhaps a Super Computer. At any rate, you must assume that his prediction ability is very good.

Clearly, it is not to your advantage to open only Vault B—after all, if by some fluke the Being made the wrong prediction, you would get nothing. On the other hand, if you choose to open both vaults and the Being has predicted your action, you will end up with only a portion of the potential money available. But you must also keep in mind that the money in Vault B is either already there or it isn't, and your present action will not change this. How do you maximize your gain? Take one? Take both?

William A. Newcomb, a California physicist, created this paradox. When it was published (in a slightly different form) in July 1973 in Martin Gardner's "Mathematical Games" in *Scientific American*, it aroused a tremendous response, and few of the respondents agreed with each other.

Try the paradox on your friends—it's bound to start interesting arguments. And send us a note on *your* choice and why you made it. Who knows? We might find out what it takes to be a free soul. The address:

The Great Escape
150 Shoreline Highway
Mill Valley, Calif. 94941.   *—David Popoff*

A Handicapper Tells How to Bet the Horses

As millions of Americans know, going to the racetrack and betting on the horses is *fun*—even if you don't win a cent. If you've never done it before, you should, and here are some pointers on what to do when you go to the races for the first time.

The first rule in betting on the horses is the hardest to learn, for it is the easiest to forget. It says that betting on thoroughbreds is an entertainment and not a way to get rich quick. If you approach your day at the races with this in mind, you should have a fine time at the track.

Betting on horse races is simple. The track brings together a field of horses to race a set distance; the horses in each race are the same age and of similar ability. All you have to do is decide which horse is going to prove best. You then back your opinion at the pari-mutuel windows, which are plainly marked as to cost and classification—win, place and show (that is, first, second or third). You wager with the aid of the official program, which lists the horses by number—you will mention your horse's number when betting. The program also has explanations of other forms of betting, but simplicity should be the keynote, so stick with the easiest approach—bet on your horse to win, place or show.

In addition to the official program, racing fans use the *Daily Racing Form*, which tells about the past performances of the horses. The information in this publication is the most complete available to racing fans anywhere in the world. There are graded handicaps, selections and instructions on how to read the past performances. (There are also graded handicaps and selections in most local newspapers.) All this is yours for the buying. Included in these publications and the program are lists of the top trainers and jockeys, which will help you frame your estimate of the probability of a particular horse's winning.

In addition to the program and the racing form, a pair of binoculars is a piece of equipment that is indispensable at the race track. Buy or rent them.

Your serious handicapping begins when the horses come on the track. (Going to the paddock is for the advanced bettor only.) One thing to look for in the post parade is a horse that is "broken out"—sweating profusely. This is a sign that the horse may be too upset to run his best. And look for bandages on the legs—not the small ones, but the ones that run up the shins of the front legs. These could be a sign of problems.

When the horses gallop off, bring your glasses into play. Watch for a horse with his neck bowed under the restraint of his jockey. Watch the horses' strides—a smooth, seemingly effortless stride is good and a choppy gait is bad. A smooth strider who acts as if he were "crying to run" could be a good bet. Remember to allow yourself enough time to get to the betting windows. Sometimes the lines are quite long.

A few other hints: race track design being what it is—something like Ming Dynasty—the embryo racing fan should put some effort into seeking out a good vantage point from which to watch the races. Don't even think of watching them on TV—too much is lost, for the camera, of necessity, must concentrate on the front runners. To watch a race develop, you must watch *all* the horses—here, again, use your glasses. Do not indulge in just staring at your horse to the exclusion of the others. Scan the field. You know your horse by the colors his jockey is wearing (it's in the program).

If you've combined your own observations with the expert opinions in the program and racing form, your horse should give a good account of himself, even if you don't win any money. (After all, even the favorite wins only 33 percent of the time.) The great sport at the track is in picking your horse yourself—reveling in your own cleverness if you do win is just part of the fun.

–Nick Sanabria

How to Become a Movie

 STAR

Although the famed Schwab's soda fountain, where a Hollywood High School sweater girl named Lana Turner was "discovered," is now gone, with a little wiliness it's easier than ever to become a movie star. For one thing, stardom no longer requires smashing looks. Ordinary is in. Think of Michael J. Pollard, Dustin Hoffman or even bony Helena Kalleniotis (who makes a neat living in roles like that of the Lesbian cleanliness freak in *Five Easy Pieces*). Timothy Bottoms looks like any studious kid in the college library, and almost any black guy can now keep telling himself, "If somebody named Thalmus Rasulala [the previously obscure star of *Cool Breeze*] can make it, so can I."

Talent? It's always helpful, but can be developed later, after your first smash hits have provided enough money for those method-acting classes in which you scratch your armpits a lot. Much more important in the beginning is making yourself the right face in the right place at the right time. And that mainly means keeping a sharp eye out for Cinemobiles.

Painted in cream, blue and gold stripes, a Cinemobile is a bus containing a studio on wheels. Nearly all films are now done on location in such unlikely locales as Abiquiu, N. M., Nashville and Oklahoma's Macalester State Penitentiary. The next time you spot a Cinemobile—odds are there's one working within 100 miles of you right now—come to a screeching halt, make discreet inquiries about the kind of picture being made, and then try to become a part of the "local color" that the film maker has journeyed so far to find. Edge over to the script girl and ask what kinds of parts are being cast from among natives. Duck into a phone booth, make the necessary adjustments and, after a tug at an assistant director's sleeve, you might win raves, as did the slack-jawed mountain kid who played "Dueling Banjos" in *Deliverance*, or the drooling Louisiana pickup driver and his buddy who gleefully shotgunned Peter Fonda and Dennis Hopper in *Easy Rider*.

Chances are that the film is in the hands of struggling independents who can't pay you very much. But there is nothing more harmful than offering to work for free. Instead, make the producer's mouth work helplessly in awe-struck respect as you rattle off the phrase, "I'll take a deferment." This means you'll receive no money now but will get a payoff out of future profits. It sounds terribly professional.

Subscribe to *Variety*, and when you read that your first film is about to be released, move to Hollywood. There you can use your experience to land an agent, maybe even a press agent who will make up gags in your name and supply them to gossip columnists. The agent will place ads in the trade papers trumpeting you as the star of that film you were in. Likely as not, the ads will feature photos of you with few or no clothes on.

If stardom is a bit slow in coming, pay your dues at little-theater groups and acting workshops. Paul Winfield did it that way, and when last seen he was co-starring in *Sounder*.

Movie stardom prospects are also very bright in New York right now. The only trick is to look Italian and mention street names like Mott, Elizabeth and Cherry. Then, join the police force. The next big trend is cop pictures, and if your exploits are newsworthy enough Paramount will sign you as a "technical consultant," pay you hundreds of thousands of dollars to dictate your life story to a screenwriter and, if you look particularly fanatical, pop-eyed or unshaven, plant you in the title role. Of course, your movie career could be sidetracked if you are shot by a burglary suspect. But if you live through the incident, it will be worth a fortune when you re-enact it on the street, as the generator whirrs silently in the Cinemobile.

–Martin Kasindorf

Wargaming

Sure, the Duke of Wellington smashed Napoleon's dream of a European empire at Waterloo in 1815. And sure enough the Russian tank offensive in the summer of 1944 destroyed Germany's Army Group Center. That's something weird called history. But what would happen, say, if *you* were Napoleon and you were fighting the same battle with the same forces on the same terrain? Or what if *you* were the German commander of the Russian front in the summer of '44? It could be interesting. That's what wargaming is all about.

There are two kinds of wargames. One kind is played by professional soldiers or policy makers for training and predicting possible real-war futures. The other is played by a growing number of civilian aficionados for entertainment and historical interpretations. What we're talking about here is the latter.

The first simulation wargame that went far beyond chess was invented in 1780 by Helwig, a Prussian (naturally) and then Master of the Pages for the Duke of Brunswick. Helwig devised a game which was played on a board with 1666 squares. Each square bore a color that represented a certain kind of terrain. Each army defended a fortress and the game was won by capturing the enemy fortress; each side had 120 fighting units, including infantry, cavalry and artillery, some pontoons, and about 200 entrenchment counters.

According to Helwig's rules, infantrymen could move eight spaces, heavy cavalry could move 12 spaces and light cavalry could scamper across 16. The pieces themselves were miniatures, superbly carved.

As years passed and wars became more complicated, so did wargaming. One innovator dispensed with the square grid pattern and replaced it with military maps scaled at 1:8,000. Later, the squares gave way to hexagons, because hexes provided equidistant movement in more directions. Time scales, such as "each move equals two minutes of real time," were developed. Whenever the units of two sides clashed in combat, an umpire or the players would throw dice and consult an odds table, which had been devised to represent the attack and defense capability of various kinds of units.

Almost all of the changes in the past 100 years in wargaming have come from the Germans, whose wargames—called *kriegsspiel*—were adopted by most armies all over the world. (The Germans had impressed the entire military world in 1870 when they beat the French, who had previously been considered the best soldiers in the world. The Russians thought wargaming was not worth the bother until they were beaten by the Japanese in 1904; the Japanese gave much of the credit for their victory to their wargaming exercises, and the Russians went back to the gaming boards. The English played avidly and so did the Italians—but the Italians kept losing real wars.)

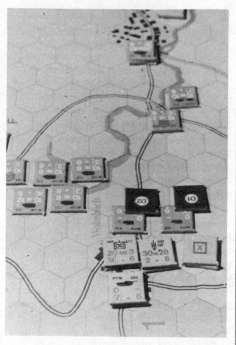

Since the turn of the century, there has been as rapid a change in wargaming technology as in military hardware. Since World War II, the United States has become the center of serious wargaming and the U.S. defense complex has witnessed the playing of games on every possible defense subject. One of the more traditional Marine Corps games is called the Landing Force Game—it can apply anywhere from between the halls of Montezuma and the shores of Tripoli to the beaches of the Dominican Republic and the sands of Cam Ran Bay, it can be played with any number of situations or scenarios, and it is a game with a set of rules that fills two thick volumes. It uses an electronic random-number generator instead of dice and it takes about four months of real time to equal 30 hours of game time. The Marines play for real and almost for keeps.

Fortunately, we, as gamey civilians, don't have such problems. As pure fun, modern wargaming on boards can be credited to one man and one game. Charles S. Roberts invented a game called "Tactics" in 1953. The game was a battle between two hypothetical countries, each of which had an army with post-World War II technology.

The real heartbeat of board wargaming as a hobby and entertainment pastime, however, came a few years later, from the logistic and graphic genius of two men, James F. Dunnigan and Redmond A. Simonsen. The meshing of the talent came at Simulations Publications, Inc., which publishes a conflict simulation magazine called *Strategy & Tactics*. Published six times a year, each issue is both a magazine about wargaming and a game. That's right, they package the game right in the periodical. You can buy their games separately, of course, in real boxes with the plastic covering and all, but you don't need to. Our other favorite game designers are the guys at Guidon Games and Avalon Hill. Here are the addresses of all three and a list of who makes what:

–Min S. Yee

Ancient
Alexander the Great (GG)
Armageddon (SPI)

Medieval
Dark Ages (SPI)
Musket and Pike (SPI)

Napoleonic
Waterloo (AH)
Borodino (SPI)
Napoleon at Waterloo (SPI)
Grenadier (SPI)
The American Revolution (SPI)

19th Century
Gettysburg (AH)
Wilderness Campaign (SPI)
Franco-Prussian War (SPI)

World War I
1914 (AH)
Flying Circus (SPI)

World War II
France 1940 (AH)
Panzerblitz (AH)

D-Day (AH)
Battle of the Bulge (AH)
Destruction of Army Group Center (SPI)
Barbarossa (SPI)
Sniper (SPI)

Recent Wars
Korea (SPI)
Year of the Rat [Vietnam] (SPI)
Sinai (SPI)

Future Wars
NATO (SPI)
Red Star, White Star (SPI)

Where to Write:
Avalon Hill Company
4517 Hartford Road
Baltimore, Md. 21214

Guidon Games
P.O. Box 1123
Evansville, Ind. 47713

Simulations Publications, Inc.
44 E. 23rd St.
New York, N.Y. 10010

Games You Can Play on Your TV

The beginnings of what might be called the electronic game era can be found in "Odyssey," a black box by Magnavox that hooks up to a television set (the screen has to be 19 inches or larger) and turns it into a live game board. The basic game is table tennis: a small square light (the ball) bounces back and forth between two large squares of light (the players) on the TV screen. Two persons play the game; each has a control unit that enables him to maneuver his square to hit the ball. A knob on the control lets a player impart "English" to the ball, making it travel at a slant.

The TV game is an outgrowth of the same technology that brought us the pocket electronic calculator. A miniaturized circuit on a silicon chip less than ¼ inch square can now do the job of thousands of transistors. With "Odyssey," each game is programmed by a card that contains a circuit chip. While the first games are relatively simple (mostly variations on batting a ball back and forth or finding a way through a maze) the future potential is almost unlimited. Eventually, chips that are mini-computers containing the entire "logic" of a game will be designed and the action of the game will unfold (perhaps even in color) on your TV screen as you play.

The basic "Odyssey" package consists of 12 games: table tennis, tennis, hockey, "Cat and Mouse," football, "Ski," "States," roulette, "Haunted House," "Analogic," "Submarine" and "Simon Says." Each game has a plastic overlay that goes on the TV screen. Additional games are available. "Shooting Gallery" gives you an electronic rifle and moving targets to shoot at. Other ball games are baseball, handball and volleyball. The most sophisticated is basketball. Players can shoot, dribble, steal and block the ball.

"W.I.N." is a game of words, images and numbers, a sort of TV "Scrabble." "Brain Wave" involves trying to establish telepathic communication with an opponent or trying to break his train of thought.

You can pick up "Odyssey" for about $100 at most Magnavox dealers. —*David Popoff*

The Induction Game

Here's a card game to sharpen your powers of induction. You use a regular deck. One player deals all the cards until everyone has an equal number. Any extra cards are put aside.

The dealer then secretly makes up a rule for the game. The object of the game is for the players to get rid of their cards—which is easy once the rule is figured out.

The dealer tells each player in turn if his play is right or wrong. The complete rules for this game can be obtained from the Association of American Playing Card Manufacturers, 420 Lexington Ave., New York, N.Y. 10017.

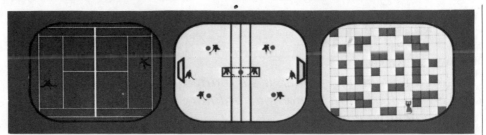

TENNIS. All the excitement of Wimbledon as you serve, volley and score.

HOCKEY. Face-off, dig for the net, maneuver the puck . . . goal!

CAT AND MOUSE. Electronic hide and seek as the clever mouse tries to elude the cantankerous cat.

Fooling Around With Computers

As far as we know, there's only one place in the country where an ordinary person can walk in and fiddle around with a computer, no questions asked, for only 75 cents an hour.

It's the Lawrence Hall of Science, in Berkeley, Calif. Terminals are available to everyone on a first-come first-served basis. You can play all kinds of strategy and number games, draw comic characters and figure your bio-rhythms. There's someone to help you get started, if you want, but basically you're on your own.

The world's most powerful computer is the Control Data Corporation CDC 7600 first delivered in January, 1969. It can perform 36 million operations in one second and has an access time of 27.5 nano-seconds. It has two internal memory cores of 655,360 and 5,242,880 characters (6 bits per character) supplemented by a Model 817 disc file of 800,000,000 characters. . . . The most capacious storage device is the Ampex Terabit Memory which can store 2.88×10^{12} bits.

—GUINNESS BOOK OF WORLD RECORDS, 1974

SPACEWAR!

By Stewart Brand

Among the computer bums, it's a matter of Fanatic Life and Symbolic Death. Among us ordinary folks, it's one helluva new game.

Ready or not, computers are coming to the people.

That's good news, maybe the best since psychedelics. It's way off the track of the "Computer—Threat or Menace?" school of liberal criticism but surprisingly in line with the romantic fantasies of the forefathers of the science such as Norbert Wiener, Warren McCulloch, J. C. R. Licklider, John von Neumann and Vannevar Bush.

The trend owes its health to an odd array of influences: the youthful fervor and firm dis-Establishmentarianism of the freaks who design computer science, an astonishingly enlightened research program from the very top of the Defense Department, an unexpected market-flanking movement by the manufacturers of small calculating machines and an irrepressible midnight phenomenon known as "Spacewar."

Reliably, at any nighttime moment in North America hundreds of computer technicians are locked in life-or-death space combat computer-projected onto cathode ray tube display screens. They spend hours at a time ruining their eyes, numbing their fingers in frenzied mashing of control buttons, joyously slaying their friends and wasting their employers' valuable computer time. Something basic is going on.

Rudimentary "Spacewar" consists of two humans, two sets of control buttons or joysticks, one TV-like display and one computer. Two spaceships are displayed in motion on the screen, controllable for thrust, yaw, pitch and the firing of torpedoes. Whenever a spaceship and torpedo meet, they disappear in an attractive explosion. That's the original version invented in 1962 at MIT by Steve Russell. (More on him in a moment.)

October 1972, 8 p.m., at Stanford's Artificial Intelligence (AI) Laboratory, moonlit and remote in the foothills above Palo Alto, Calif. Two dozen of us are jammed into a semidark console room just off the main hall containing AI's PDP-10 computer. AI's Head System Programmer and most avid "Spacewar" nut, Ralph Goring, faces a display screen that says only:

THIS CONSOLE AVAILABLE.

He logs in on the keyboard with his initials: click clickclickclick click.

L1, REG
CSD FALL PICNIC. SATURDAY 11
AM IN FLOOD PARK . . .

He interrupts further announcements, including one about the "First Intergalactic 'Spacewar' Olympics" at 8 p.m., with: click ("run") clickclickclick ("Space War Ralph") click ("do it").

R SWR.
WELCOME TO SPACEWAR.
HOW MANY SHIPS? MAXIMUM IS 5.

Click: 5 (five players). This is for the first familiarization battles in the Spacewar Olympics, initiated by me and sponsored—beer and prizes—by *Rolling Stone*. Friends, I won't be able to explain every computer-technical term that comes by. Fortunately you don't need them to get the gist of what's happening.

KEYBOARD   BUTTONS?   (ELSE REGULAR.) TYPE Y OR N.

"Yes." Click: Y

THE STANDARD GAME IS:
1 CONSOLE, 2 TORPEDO TUBES, (NORMAL) SCORING, NO PARTIAL DAMAGE, NO HYPERSPACE, KILLER SUN. SHIPS START IN STANDARD POSITIONS. TYPE Y TO GET A STANDARD GAME.

Ralph wants other features. "No." Click: N

HOW MANY SPACE MINES DO YOU WANT?
CHOOSE FROM ZERO TO 4.

Click: 4

PARTIAL DAMAGE?

Click: N

DISPLAY SCORES?

Click: Y

TWO TORPEDO TUBES?

Click: Y

HYPERSPACE?

Click: N

RANDOM STARTING POSITIONS?

Click: Y

Immediately the screen goes dark and then displays five different spaceships, each with a dot indicating torpedo tubes are loaded, five scores, each at zero, a convincing starfield, and four space mines orbiting around a central sun, toward which the spaceships are starting to fall at a correctly accelerating rate.

Players seize the five sets of control buttons, find their spaceship persona on the screen, and simultaneously turn and fire toward any nearby still-helpless spaceships, hit the thrust button to initiate orbit before being slurped by the killer sun, and evade or shoot down any incoming enemy torpedoes or orbiting mines. After two torpedoes are fired, each ship has a three-second unarmed "reloading" time. Fired torpedoes last nine seconds and then disappear.

As kills are made the scores start to change. It's 1 for a successful kill, -1 for being killed, 1 for being lone survivor of a battle. Personalities begin to establish themselves in the maneuvering spaceships: the pilot of the ship called *Pointy Fins* is a dead shot but panics easily in cross fire. *Roundback* tries to avoid early dueling and routinely fires two torpedoes "around the universe" (off the screen, so they reappear lethally unexpected from the opposite side). *Birdie* drives for the sun and a fast orbit, has excellent agility in sensing and facing toward hazard.

In the "First Intergalactic 'Spacewar' Olympics," Pointy Fins and Funny Fins are maneuvering to fire torpedoes at Roundback and Birdie.

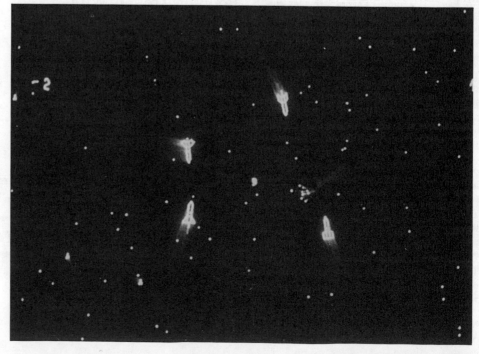

Funny Fins shoots a lot, singling out individual opponents. *Flatback* is silent and maintains an uncanny field-sense of the whole battlesky, impervious to surprise attack.

A game is over when only one or no survivors are displayed. The screen then blanks out, counts down 5-4-3-2-1, and redisplays a new battle with ships at new random positions equidistant from the sun and showing scores accumulated from previous games. A spaceship that is killed early in a battle will reincarnate after 16 seconds and rejoin the fray, so that a single battle may last up to five minutes with a weak player perishing several times in it.

The 20 or so raucous competitors in the Spacewar Olympics quickly organize three events: Five-Player Free-For-All, Team Competition (two against two) and Singles Competition. The executive officer of the AI Project, Les Earnest, who kindly okayed these Olympics and their visibility, is found to have no immediate function and is sent out for beer.

The games progress. A tape recorder kibitzes on the first round of Team Competition, four ships twisting, converging, evading, exploding.

For four intense hours, there is much frenzy and skilled concerted action, a 15-ring circus in 10 different directions . . . and really it's just a normal night at the AI Project, at any suitably hairy computer research project.

The "hackers" are the technicians of this science — it's a term of derision and also the ultimate compliment. They are the ones who translate human demands into code that the machines can understand and act on. They are legion.

A distinction exists between low-rent and high-rent computer research, between preoccupations of support group (hackers) and of research group. "Spacewar" players are more from the support groups than the research groups.

The first opportunity was at the Massachusetts Institute of Technology (MIT) Electrical Engineering Department back in 1961-1962. The earliest mini-computer, Digital Equipment Corporation's PDP-1, was installed in the kludge room with a cathode ray tube display hooked on. ("Kludge" — any lash-up, often involving chewing gum, paper clips, Scotch tape; it works if no one trips over a wire; unadaptable; a working mess.) There it was that Steve Russell and his fellow hackers Alan Kotok, Peter Samson and Dan Edwards introduced "Spacewar" to the world.

Back in 1962 Steve Russell was a hacker, 23 or so, a math major two years out of Dartmouth working in the brand new field of computer science for John McCarthy at MIT.

His account of the invention of "Spacewar" is not only intriguing history, it's the most sophisticated analysis of good game design I've ever run across — elegant work. But that's in retrospect; back then it was just kids staying up all night.

"We had this brand new PDP-1," Steve Russell recalls. "It was the first mini-computer, ridiculously inexpensive for its time. And it was just sitting there. It had a console typewriter that worked right, which was rare, and a paper tape reader and a cathode ray tube display. (There had been CRT displays before, but primarily in the Air Defense System.) Somebody had built some little pattern-generating programs which made interesting patterns like a kaleidoscope. Not a very good demonstration. Here was this display that could do all sorts of good things! So we started talking about it, figuring what would be interesting displays. We decided that probably you could make a two-dimensional maneuvering sort of thing, and decided that naturally the obvious thing to do was spaceships."

Naturally?

"I had just finished reading 'Doc' Smith's *Lensman* series. He was some sort of scientist but he wrote this really dashing brand of science fiction. The details were very good and it had an excellent pace. His heroes had a strong tendency to get pursued by the villain across the galaxy and have to invent their way out of their problem while they were being pursued. That sort of action was the thing that suggested 'Spacewar.' He had some very glowing descriptions of spaceship encounters and space fleet maneuvers."

The pride of any hacker with a new program is its "features." Fresh forms of "Spacewar" with exotic new features proliferated. As Russell tells it, everything at MIT had priority over "Spacewar," but it was an educational computer after all, and developing new programs (of "Spacewar") was educational, and then those programs needed testing. The initial game of simply two spaceships and their torpedoes didn't last long.

Gravity was introduced. Then Peter Samson wrote in the starfield.

Within weeks of its invention "Spacewar" was spreading across the country to other computer research centers, where new wrinkles were added.

There was a variation called Minnesota Hyperspace in which you kept your position but became invisible; however, if you applied thrust, your rocket flame could be seen. . . . Score-keeping. Space mines. Partial damage — if hit in a fin you could not turn in that direction.

Then "2½-D Spacewar," played on two consoles. Instead of being God viewing the whole battle, you're a mere pilot with a view out the front of your spaceship and the difficult task of *finding* your enemy. (Perspective could be compressed so that even though far away the other ship would be large enough to see.)

Adding incentive, MIT introduced an electric shock to go with the explosion of your ship. A promising future is seen for sound effects. And now a few commercial versions of "Spacewar" — 25 cents a game — are appearing in university coffee shops.

John Lilly (of dolphin, acid and bio-computer fame) tells a story that IBM once forbade the playing of "Spacewar" by researchers. After a few suddenly uncreative months of joyless research the ban was rescinded. Apparently, frivolous "Spacewar" had been the medium of important experiments. □

Discover the Crossbow

The bow and arrow were very big in the days of Robin Hood and his Merry Men, and they're coming in again. But for some reason the trusty crossbow hasn't been included in the revival. This seems strange, since the crossbow is, in its usual form, much more powerful than conventional bows. It is also more accurate, because you don't have to exert any muscular effort while aiming the arrow and you can therefore concentrate on aiming.

Crossbows with steel bows cut from automobile leaf springs may be made to pull at several hundred pounds—the conventional hunting bows seldom pull at much over 50 or 60 pounds. This means that if you're good enough, you can use a crossbow to pot at that deer standing 200 yards away.

Light crossbows may be comfortably set by hand and are sufficient for small to medium game. They are silent and can be nearly as accurate as a hunting rifle within their range, which, in many kinds of terrain, is nearly as great as that of a gun.

If you want to make your own crossbow, you might try to locate the "C" volume of the old *Popular Mechanics Do-It-Yourself Encyclopedia*. It has an excellent article under "Crossbows," explaining how to make one—but it is a fairly complicated construction job. So unless you're a skilled craftsman, you might as well buy your crossbow. Wham-O Manufacturing sells one through sporting goods stores that costs $40 to $50. Custom crossbows are made by Dave Benedict (P.O. Box 343, Chatsworth, Calif. 91311) and George Stevens of Huntsville, Ark. Prices, however, run about $150 and up.

The crossbow can be legally used to hunt game animals in around 20 states. (Laws are always changing; check on the current laws in states where you want to hunt.) Our guess is that varmit hunting is legal in all areas but you should check with your local Fish and Game Commission beforehand.

You should also note that the crossbow is one "primitive" weapon efficient enough to be subject to a certain number of legal firearm restrictions, so you might check out the laws in locales where you plan to use it.

—*Min S. Yee*

The "Game of Life"

It is rare for a new game concept to gain rapid success. But in the late 1960s, an English mathematician named John Horton Conway perfected a simple game involving birth, growth, movement, destruction and death. He called it the "Game of Life." When it was published for the first time, in Martin Gardner's column, "Mathematical Games," in *Scientific American's* October 1970 issue, it evoked an instant and massive response. It could be said that the game took on a life of its own.

Basically, "Life" is a pattern-generating game that mimics the dynamics of population growth and decline. You begin by creating simple life forms. By applying two simple rules, you cause the life forms to grow and change. The game can be played on graph paper or on a checkerboard but, as computer buffs throughout the country quickly realized, it is also a beautiful game to play with a computer.

The game is played on a large grid of squares. Each square is considered to have eight neighboring squares: the four cells at its top, bottom and sides, and the four cells that touch it diagonally.

Begin by creating a life form—to do this, put three Os or three black counters in a row. You are free to choose any pattern you desire. The two rules that govern the action of the game are:

Each empty cell that has *exactly* three occupied neighbors becomes a **birth cell**. It becomes occupied with an O or counter on the next move.

Each occupied cell that has *four or more* occupied neighbors **dies** (from overpopulation); and each occupied cell that has *one or no* occupied neighbors **dies** (from isolation). Only occupied cells with two or three occupied neighbors survive to the next move.

All births and deaths occur simultaneously.

The next step is crucial. A good procedure to follow is this: scan the life form pattern and mark all birth cells with a small dot or put colored counters on them. Next, check each occupied cell and determine if that cell lives or dies (remember, newborns do not affect the generation from which they spring). Draw an X through each dying cell. After you have double- and triple-checked, copy out the pattern—minus the dead cells and with the newborns—on a new area of your grid. This pattern is called the **first generation** of your life form (the starting form is called generation zero). If you are playing with counters, place a second counter on top of the counters that will die. After all births and deaths have been checked, simply remove all the double counters from the board and replace the colored (newborn) counters with black counters.

Unusual and fantastic patterns emerge unexpectedly from simple beginning life forms. Following Conway's lead, people have given names to the more interesting life forms that

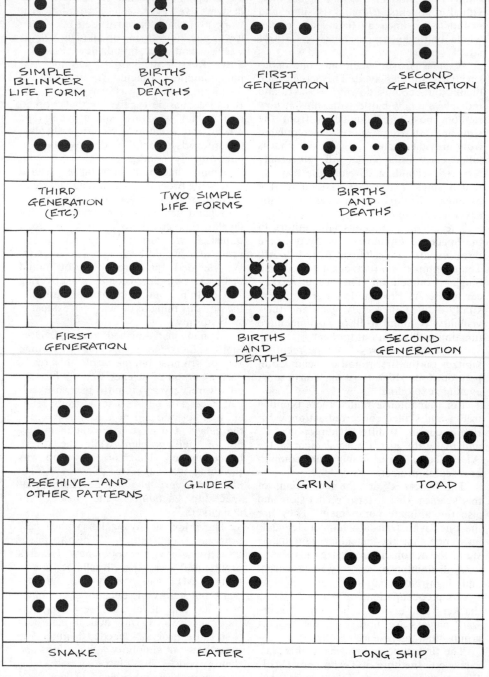

SIMPLE BLINKER LIFE FORM · BIRTHS AND DEATHS · FIRST GENERATION · SECOND GENERATION

THIRD GENERATION (ETC.) · TWO SIMPLE LIFE FORMS · BIRTHS AND DEATHS

FIRST GENERATION · BIRTHS AND DEATHS · SECOND GENERATION

BEEHIVE—AND OTHER PATTERNS · GLIDER · GRIN · TOAD

SNAKE · EATER · LONG SHIP

they've discovered—names like blinker (the form shown here), pinwheel, tumbler, queen bee, glider, spaceship and eater. Some life forms are stable; others oscillate from one form to another and back again; yet others appear to grow indefinitely. The glider moves across the field diagonally; an eater that is capable of ingesting most other life forms and then returning to its original shape has been discovered; and it's interesting to see what happens when one eater meets another.

Lifeline, a quarterly newsletter for enthusiasts of John Horton Conway's game, is published by Robert T. Wainwright, a young man who became one of the first "Life" aficionados and who has made a number of intriguing observations about the mechanics of the game.

Wainwright has also created a small, transistorized device that hooks up to an ordinary black-and-white television set. The device, which he calls "Genesis," automatically computes and displays successive generations—either in slow motion or at a rate of 30 generations per second. The life forms are displayed as spots of light on the screen. Watching a spontaneous population explosion followed by a rapid extinction of most life forms is enough to make you suspect that the name given to the game has an eerie element of truth behind it.

For information about the newsletter, write:

Lifeline
c/o Robert T. Wainwright, Editor and Publisher
56 Old Highway
Wilton, Conn. 06897.   *—David Popoff*

Cryonics: Preserving Your Bod for Posterity

If you happen to have a thing for this planet and want to take a gamble on doing a return engagement with that neat body of yours, there's someone out there with a smile and a cylinder full of liquid nitrogen. His name is Robert Nelson, he's from the Cryonics Society of Southern California, and he would like to keep your body "fresh" after you die. If you sign with him, he'll make all the arrangements for your lengthy stay at one of his three places.

You'll need $5,000 for your cylinder and initial supply of liquid nitrogen. And, at current rates, it will cost you $30 a month for maintenance. (If you have a little savings account you can make arrangements for someone to send the guy who is changing your nitrogen some cheese or something at Christmas. It may help.) If you're lucky, you'll be re-animated in a few hundred years and possibly you'll even have the chance to reverse the aging process and pick an age to be "forever."

Anyone who decides to participate in this adventure is notified that participants will meet at Disneyland, near the Pirate's Cove, on July 1, 2150, at noon. If Disneyland isn't around, we'll meet at Mt. Rushmore, same time, under the head of President Guzik. It's gonna be great.

—Don Novello

Zyrardow, Pol. *Zyrardow* (both: zhirar´dooi), city (pop. c.30,000), Warsaw prov., E central Poland. A textile center, it also manufactures leather products. The city is named after F. Girard, who moved his weaving mill here in 1833.
Zyrians: See KOMI.

—The Columbia Encyclopedia

. . . of a Tea Master

[*Rikiu, the tea master, has been condemned to death by his lord, and has elected to die by his own hand. He gives one final tea ceremony for his closest friends.*]

Each in turn is served with tea, and each in turn silently drains his cup. The chief guest now asks permission to examine the tea-equipage. Rikiu places the various articles before them. After all have expressed admiration of their beauty, Rikiu presents one of them to each . . . as a souvenir. The bowl alone he keeps. "Never again shall this cup, polluted by the lips of misfortune, be used by man." He speaks, and breaks the vessel into fragments.

The ceremony is over; the guests with difficulty restraining their tears, take their last farewell and leave the room. One only, the nearest and dearest, is requested to remain and witness the end. Rikiu then removes his tea-gown and carefully folds it upon the mat, thereby disclosing the immaculate white death robe which it had hitherto concealed. Tenderly he gazes on the fatal dagger, and thus addresses it:

> "Welcome to thee,
> O sword of eternity!
> Through Buddha
> And through Dharuma alike
> Thou hast cleft thy way."

With a smile upon his face Rikiu passed forth into the unknown.

—Okakura Kakuzo, The Book of Tea

Great Endings

Au revoir,
pleasant dreams.
Think of us
when requesting yo' themes.
Until the next time, when
possibly you all may tune in again,
keep the old maestro
always in yo' schemes.
Yowza, yowza, yowza.

Au revoir.
This is Ben Bernie,
ladies and gentlemen,
and all the lads
wishing you a bit of
pleasant dreams.
May good luck and happiness,
success and good health
attend your schemes.
And don't forget,
should you eva, eva
send in your requesta,
why we'll sure try
to do our besta.
Yowza.

Au revoir.
A fond cheerio,
a bit of tweet-tweet,
God bless you
and pleasant dreams.

—Ben Bernie

This that was a being has become the dust of the street. It has several times been annihilated; but in the meanwhile it has been able to learn a hundred secrets of which previously it had not been aware, and in the end it receives immortality, and is given honour in place of dishonour. Do you know what you possess? Enter into yourself and reflect on this. So long as you do not realize your nothingness and so long as you do not renounce your self-pride, your vanity and your self-love, you will never reach the heights of immortality. On the Way you are cast down in dishonour and raised in honour.

And now my story is finished, I have nothing more to say.
*—Faridudin Attar,
The Parliament of the Birds*

"And they lived happily ever after."

"Abba-dee . . . abba-dee . . . abba-dee . . . abba—that's . . . abba—that's all, folks!"
—P. Pig

"Say goodnight, Gracie."
"Good night, Gracie!"
—Burns and Allen

"Well, what're we gonna do next?"
—The Editors

"And so this is Bob Elliot reminding you to write if you get work . . ."
"And Ray Goulding reminding you to hang by your thumbs."
—Bob and Ray

In the Midst of the Labyrinth of Life,
One Searches for Escape

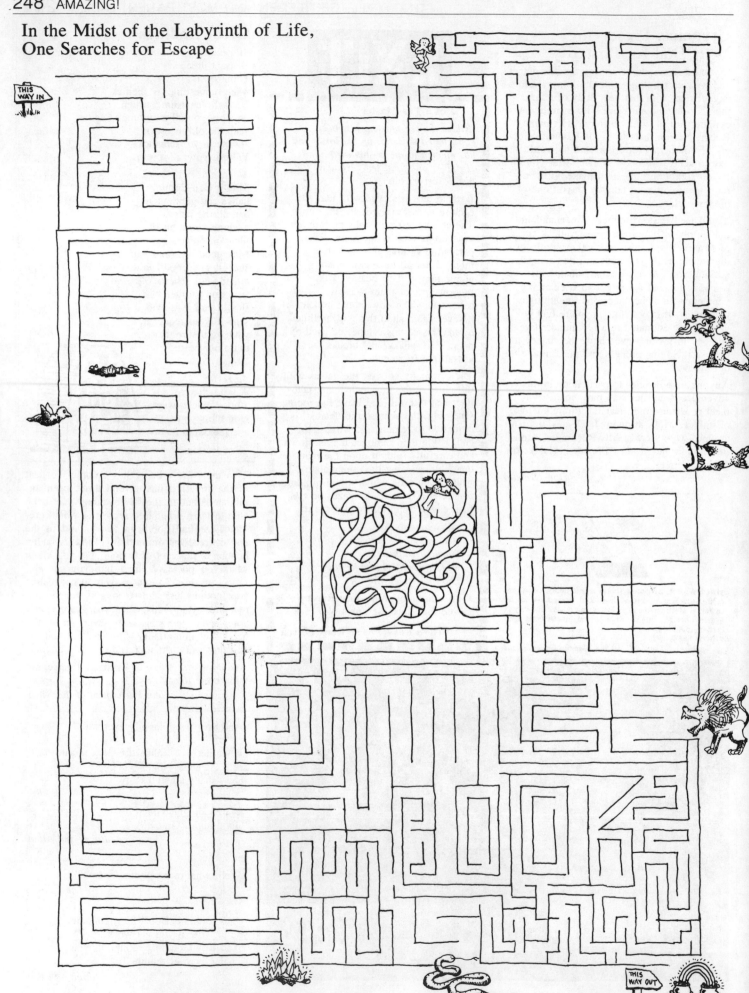

From Abbreviated donnybrook to Zoos without cages

Answers to Global Graffiti

P. 23: Mediterranean, Black Sea
P. 37: The Greek Isles
P. 84: Mississippi and Tributaries
P. 93: J.F.K. International Airport
P. 148: Los Angeles freeway system
P. 167: Chicago
P. 173: Louisiana
P. 196: The Vatican
P. 201: Paris

to Print

our greatest responsibility
readers, we would like to hear from
What it all boils down to is a simple,
direct question with a few embellishments.
What do you think of *The Great Escape?*
What's missing? What would you like to
read more about? What are your greatest
escapes? Many of the folks who wrote
articles for us have never been published,
but they had wonderful ideas about how they
enjoyed spending their time. We would like
you to become part of the book. We'll be
doing it again, and we'd like your help. We
will pay as generously as we can, and
promptly, for any ideas or articles we use.
Don't worry about writing. Just write it like
you'd tell it to a friend.

Please write us at:
The Great Escape
150 Shoreline Highway
Mill Valley, Calif. 94941.

–The Editors

Our Gang

Nobody knew anybody. I thought of it
and went to Don Wright with a title and two
years' worth of newspaper and magazine
clippings. Don, you should know, designed
this book. The heart and soul of it began as
his and mine. Now, hundreds of pages and
photographs and illustrations later, it is and
belongs to all of us.

When I began talking with Don about it,
he was art directing the still-gurgling
Saturday Review. (I knew before I met him
that he had designed *Psychology Today* and
Intellectual Digest.) I outlined the
idea to him and he said he'd think it over.
The next day, he invited me to his house
and when I walked in I saw something like
36 different sample logos spread all over
tables and hanging on the walls. We formed
a partnership. And then we went to work,
me on the writing end and Don on the
designing end. We blocked out the rest of
the idea and raised some money.

We didn't have to go far to find an
illustrator because Sandy Forrest (Don's
wife) had been part of the "team" at all
three magazines. As you can see, there is
the most charming whimsy in what they do
together. Not only that, but Sandy and Don
generate article and art ideas faster than we
can catch up with them. Not to mention that
they're very agreeable and fun, too.

David Saltman used to write a travel
column for *Rolling Stone*; I read and liked
one of his pieces. I called, we dickered, and
now David is our writing wheels. He sits at
a high desk with a conical cap and uses a
goose quill which comes from a certain
remote part of the goose. The man is a
writing genius, the only guy I've ever met
who can write about *anything* and hand it in
faster than you expected it. Between naps
(while the rest of us are editing) and
gourmand repasts, David wrote a book, *The
Marrakech Express*. He used to write long,
fun pieces for the *New York Times* Sunday
travel section, but we hope to keep him too
busy for that from now on. David lives quite
a ways from the office, so he commutes to
work by helicopter across San Francisco
Bay.

R.C. Smith (he allows his friends to call
him Bob) was shanghaied out West from
Chicago to work for *Saturday Review*—he
arrived on our wild shores just as that
magazine went under. He went to work for
awhile as managing editor of *Two Wheel
Trip*, a bicycling magazine that conveniently
folded just when I was looking for a
managing editor. Before he turned ever so
slightly California mellow, Bob taught
literature and writing at Northwestern
University, worked (reluctantly) as a
Chicago cab driver and was an editor at
Today's Health.

Our toughest editor is Suzan Smith; she
gets her jollies out of ruthlessly expunging
weak paragraphs and dangling modifiers
from pieces of writing. Her sarcastic notes
about copy have always delighted me.
Before coming to the West Coast she was an
associate editor at *Advertising Age* in
Chicago. She won't admit to liking many
people, but we do know she's crazy about
dogs and cats. She grew up in Ludington,
Mich., which is why we're heavy on
Ludington stories.

Lynn Johnson could be the only sane
person around here. She likes to have a good
time and she knows how to fly a plane—at
least after it gets up in the air. And she's
meticulous and careful about everything she
does and everyone she talks with. She also
checks her horoscope every day.

Me, well—I'm kinda the dreamer around
here. I worked a few years in Asia as a
stringer (that's when an outfit keeps you
dangling on a string) writing for the *New
York Times* and *Time* and *Life*. But Vietnam
got to me and I escaped to a real job with
the *Boston Globe*. Then, *Newsweek* hired
me and moved me west to California. I
vowed never to leave the mellow and the
warm of California and left *Newsweek* to
write a very depressing book called *The
Melancholy History of Soledad Prison*. In
the midst of my own melancholia over the
book, Pat Bell (who is godfather to one of
my sons) said, "Why don't you do a book or
a magazine about unique vacations?" After
six months as managing editor of *Ramparts*,
why not? So I escaped to this.

Well, it was one of those things.
Somewhere, some Big Cheese of the
Universe decided on a new balance for our
small world in Mill Valley. He called on
one of his cosmic *croupiers* to reshuffle the
deck. A fluke, a coincidence, a chain gang
of monkeys and typewriters, a moonbeam
with handles—somehow, we all came
together with fun in our hearts, and we put
together *our* Great Escape.

–Min S. Yee

David Saltman

R. C. Smith

Suzan Smith

Donald K. Wright

Lynn Johnson Min S. Yee

Sandra Forrest Wright